Acclaim for Carole Seymour-Jones's

Painted Shadow

"Superbly well-researched. . . . A moving, powerful, and sympathetic biography of a talented, frail woman who deserves to be rescued from the obscurity to which she was condemned."
—*The Spectator*

"If you want to know how 'The Love Song of J. Alfred Prufrock' came to be penned, this homey little volume provides as good an interpretation of sexual dynamics as any. Highly recommended to all literature lovers."
—*The Tampa Tribune*

"Brilliant, deeply researched, utterly compelling. . . . [A] magnificent study."
—*The Guardian* (London)

"Knowledgeable. . . . Fair and subtle."
—*The Daily Telegraph*

"A nuanced portrait of an independent spirit coming unhinged. . . . A chronicle of a fine mind—highly unstable but not necessarily insane."
—*Publishers Weekly*

"Unsettling. . . . Gives us some intriguing ways of looking at Eliot and his work."
—*San Jose Mercury News*

"[Seymour-Jones's] portrait of Vivienne is fair, sympathetic, and well-supported, making her a far more real and vivid figure than in most studies of Eliot."
—*Chicago Tribune*

"Gripping . . . immaculately researched. . . . Sensational."
—*The Observer* (London)

Carole Seymour-Jones

Painted Shadow

Carole Seymour-Jones was born in Wales and educated at Oxford University. She is the author of several books, including *Beatrice Webb: A Life*. She spent five years researching the life of Vivienne Eliot both in England and in the United States, where she was awarded a Paul Mellon Visiting Fellowship at the Harry Ransom Center, University of Texas, Austin. She divides her time between Surrey and London.

Also by Carole Seymour-Jones

Beatrice Webb: A Life

*Journey of Faith: The History of
the World YWCA, 1945–1994*

Painted Shadow

PAINTED
SHADOW

The life of

Vivienne Eliot, first wife of

T. S. Eliot

Carole Seymour-Jones

Anchor Books

A DIVISION OF RANDOM HOUSE, INC.

NEW YORK

FIRST ANCHOR BOOKS EDITION, NOVEMBER 2003

Copyright © 2001 by Carole Seymour-Jones

All rights reserved under International and Pan-American Copyright Conventions.
Published in the United States by Anchor Books, a division of Random House, Inc.,
New York, and simultaneously in Canada by Random House of Canada Limited,
Toronto. First published in the United Kingdom by Constable Robinson Publishers in
2001. Subsequently published in hardcover in the United States by Nan A. Talese,
an imprint of Doubleday, a division of Random House, Inc., New York, in 2002.

Anchor Books and colophon are registered trademarks of Random House, Inc.

Title page photo of Vivienne Eliot (detail) courtesy of Houghton Library, Harvard
University (*AC9. E1464.Zxx II, env.13)

The Library of Congress has cataloged the Doubleday edition as follows:
Seymour-Jones, Carole.
Painted shadow : the life of Vivienne Eliot, first wife of T.S. Eliot, and the long-
suppressed truth about her influence on his genius / Carole Seymour-Jones.—
1st ed. in the United States of America
p.   cm.
ISBN 0-385-49992-2
1. Eliot, Vivienne, 1888–1947.   2. Eliot, T.S. (Thomas Stearns), 1888–1965—Marriage.
3. Authors' spouses—Great Britain—Biography.   4. Poets, American—20th century—
Biography.   5. Hysteria—Patients—Biography.
I. Title.
PS3509.L43 Z93 2002
821'.912—dc21
[B]   2001055694

Anchor ISBN: 0-385-49993-0

Author photograph © Lisa Bowerman
Book design by Ellen Cipriano

www.anchorbooks.com

Printed in the United States of America
10   9   8   7   6   5   4   3   2   1

In memory of my brother,
Nick Seymour-Jones, 1947-2000

Contents

Illustrations

Painted Shadow

A restless shivering painted shadow
In life, she is less than a shadow in death.

—T. S. ELIOT, *THE FAMILY REUNION*, 1938

"Dearest Ottoline . . . The truth will all come out,
if not in *our* life—*then after it.*"

—VIVIENNE HAIGH ELIOT TO
LADY OTTOLINE MORRELL, 31 DECEMBER 1933

Preface

Posterity will probably judge Vivienne harshly,"[1] wrote Herbert Read in 1967, and so it has proved. Committed to an asylum in 1938, Vivienne has been all but obliterated from literary history; stigmatised as insane, it is she who has been the scapegoat for the failure of her marriage to T. S. Eliot. No verdict upon Vivienne is more memorable than that of her contemporary, Virginia Woolf: "She was as wild as Ophelia—alas no Hamlet would love her, with her powdered spots."[2] Woolf's often-quoted description, "this bag of ferrets is what Tom wears round his neck,"[3] has damned Vivienne in literary history as the madwoman in the attic, T. S. Eliot's own Mrs. Rochester, as surely as the poet's own portrait of a wife in *The Family Reunion* who is "a restless shivering painted shadow."

Later memoirs and biographies have continued to be largely hostile towards Vivienne. "Poor Tom Eliot married the landlady's daughter,"[4] a remark quoted by Ronald Kirk, typifies the widespread sympathy for "poor Tom," as his friends invariably described him, and the contempt for his allegedly vulgar and intellectually inferior wife. "Eliot met," wrote T. S. Matthews, author of *Great Tom* (1974), "the girl who was to plow up, harrow and strip his life to the bone,"[5] losing no time in comparing Vivienne to Zelda Fitzgerald, another literary lion's wife who ended her days in an asylum. Aldous Huxley considered Vivienne a *femme fatale*, who trapped the shy New Englander by means of her sexuality. Even modern biographers have tended to paint Eliot as the victim in the marriage, a man who bore the burden of an intolerable wife with patience and devotion: "I believe he went towards her with a kind of child-like trust,"[6] writes Peter Ackroyd. The myth of Eliot the martyr, a latter-day St. Thomas, had been born.

Such a version of history seemed to justify Vivienne's committal in 1938. And on Eliot's death in 1965, his status as the greatest poet of the twentieth century was confirmed by a plethora of tributes. Condolences came from the White House. A memorial service was held at Westminster Abbey. Over the years his reputation remained impregnable, his privacy impenetrable. Criticism of Eliot's work was policed by the New Critics who directed readers to the poetry not the poet, and acted as guardians of the poet's mysterious personal life. As scholars followed his impersonal theory of poetry into a literary cul-de-sac, Vivienne sank into deeper obscurity.

A few dissenting voices were raised. In 1963 Randall Jarrell had written prophetically in *Fifty Years of American Poetry:*

> Won't the future say to us in helpless astonishment: "But did you actually believe that all those things about objective correlations, Classicism, the tradition, applied to *his* poetry? Surely you must have seen that he was one of the most subjective and daemonic poets who ever lived, the victim and helpless beneficiary of his own inexorable compulsions, obsessions? From a psychoanalytical point of view he was by far and away the most interesting poet of your century."

Yet Eliot still remained elusive and any putative connection between the poet's art and biography was off limits.

On her death in January 1947 Vivienne Haigh Eliot had bequeathed her papers, which included diaries, fictional sketches, poetry, correspondence and account books, to the Bodleian Library, Oxford, under the terms of her 1936 will. At first the Bodleian believed it held copyrights in the manuscripts,[7] and in the 1970s it was possible for Dr. Lyndall Gordon, who undertook valuable work on Vivienne's papers, to quote from them in her biography of T. S. Eliot, with the permission of Vivienne's brother, Maurice Haigh-Wood, to whom she was referred by the library. However, following the 1984 performance of Michael Hastings's play, *Tom and Viv,* and the subsequent film, the copyright in Vivienne's papers was claimed by Mrs. Valerie Eliot, widow and literary executor of T. S. Eliot. From that date the second wife was, in effect, able to silence the first. Legal opinion remains divided on the matter of ownership of the copyright.

When I began working on Vivienne's papers I was astonished to encounter an artistic, energetic, gifted woman, very different from the stereotype who lingered in literary history. I was touched by Vivienne's poignant love for Tom Eliot, her anguish when he left her, which leapt out from the pages of her diaries. In page after page of her notebooks lay irrefutable evidence of the close literary partnership she and Eliot shared, including drafts of her poems, prose sketches and short stories, which he published in the columns of *Criterion*. Although in the 1930s her voice became agitated and fearful, it seemed to me incredible that she should have been certified as insane.

Nor could I ignore the confession made by Vivienne's brother, Maurice, shortly before his death in 1980, to Michael Hastings:

> It was only when I saw Vivie in the asylum for the last time I realized I had done something very wrong . . . She was as sane as I was . . . What Tom and I did was wrong. And Mother. I did everything Tom told me to. Not ashamed to say so . . .

It was a statement which hinted at darker motives for Vivienne's committal, and suggested that it was she, no less than Tom, who was victim in the marriage.

The mystery intrigued me. But reading Vivienne's passionate diaries had stirred another emotion apart from curiosity or sympathy: anger. I became determined to discover the truth that lay behind her incarceration, to rescue her from ignominy and disgrace, and to restore her to her rightful place in the historical record. For the next five years I would be hostage to Vivienne and her story.

It immediately became apparent that substantial obstacles lay ahead. A number of people told me that the task would prove impossible. It was a David against Goliath battle which five biographers had allegedly already attempted without success. No co-operation would be forthcoming from T. S. Eliot's second wife, Mrs. Valerie Eliot, who was following the instructions given by her late husband in a letter to his previous literary executor, John Hayward: "Your job," wrote Eliot, "will be to suppress everything suppressible."[8] The pessimists seemed justified when my then agent declined to have anything to do with the project. But it was too late to give up.

Unearthing the sources for a life of Vivienne did indeed prove problematical. Material was buried in archives on both sides of the Atlantic, in university and private collections, but with the invaluable encouragement of librarians and literary executors, they yielded a far greater fund of new information than I had ever imagined. All the same, days sometimes passed as I waited to see letters of Vivienne's which seemed mysteriously to have vanished from the face of the earth. More than one assistant expressed surprise that a first Mrs. Eliot existed, assuming that it was to Valerie that Tom was married when he wrote *The Waste Land*. I realised that, unbelievable as it may seem, some readers might have understood the dedication "To My Wife" in *Ash Wednesday* (1930) to refer to the second Mrs. Eliot. In later editions of the poems the dedication to Vivienne was dropped, as Eliot eradicated his first wife from his history. It was time to redress the balance.

As I followed the twisted trail of Vivienne's life, I felt strangely close to both Eliots. But the longer I worked, the more sure I became that it was justified to view T. S. Eliot's poetry and drama, bedrock of the modernist canon, through the lens of his life with Vivienne; that the autobiographical and confessional element in Eliot's texts had been greatly underestimated, due at least in part to a paucity of information.

Vivienne Eliot was a major influence upon her husband. The Eliots' tragic and tempestuous marriage was both source and subject of his poetry and drama; together they shared one of the most neurotic partnerships ever recorded, the deepest and strongest of the "tentacular roots" of his work. Vivienne had a predisposition to instability but Eliot, also neurotic, brilliant, repressed, unable to accept himself, contributed to that instability by withholding love, and it was this unhappy combination of "Tom and Vivienne," this crucible of dysfunction which, rather than hindering the poet's creativity, provoked it. For Vivienne was Tom's Muse: she was "the true inspiration of Tom," said Virginia Woolf. Theresa Garrett Eliot, Tom's sister-in-law, wrote: "Vivienne ruined him as a man, but she made him as a poet." Without Vivienne, in all probability, Eliot would not have given the world *The Waste Land.*

The poet had thrown down the gauntlet to researchers when he admitted that *The Waste Land,* far from being an expression of horror at the fate of Western civilisation, "was only the relief of a personal and wholly insignificant grouse against life."[9] Was he challenging readers to search for a new, personal understanding of his poetry, I wondered. How much did he want me to know? He had left clues everywhere, in the early manuscripts in the Berg Collection, New York Public Library, in the vast Eliot collection at the Houghton Library, Harvard University, in the largely untouched Mary Hutchinson and Ottoline Morrell Papers at the Harry Ransom Center at the University of Texas at Austin, in the John Hayward Bequest at King's College, Cambridge, and, most revealingly, in the excised pages of the "lost" Notebook of his early poetry ("Inventions of the March Hare") preserved in the Ezra Pound Papers at the Beinecke Library, Yale.

It may seem that T. S. Eliot was determined to preserve his reputation at all costs. However, it is significant that he failed to destroy revealing evidence. Although he arranged for Emily Hale's letters to him to be burnt, he sold the early "Notebook," so indicative of his sexual orientation, to his agent, John Quinn. Perhaps Eliot was less concerned in 1922 about the verdict of history than he became in the homophobic 1950s. To eradicate all traces of his secret life was possibly too great a task. But as Joseph L. Sax writes in *Playing Darts with a Rembrandt* (1999): "The failure of the principal to destroy material during his or her lifetime at least suggests a willingness to abide posterity's judgement." The descendants of Oscar Wilde co-operated generously with biographers; the daughter of Charles Dickens allowed herself to be persuaded by George Bernard Shaw not to burn her mother Nelly's letters to the great author. They were acknowledging that time may change puritanical attitudes and justify a new openness about family secrets once thought shameful. But if an archive is destroyed by the caprice of heirs—as Stephen Joyce burnt his schizophrenic aunt Lucia's letters to her father, James Joyce—the chance is lost forever for the wider community to come to a new understanding of a great artist. In time, claims of public interest deserve to be set against the private claims of family.

If her husband's wishes were perhaps ambiguous, Vivienne's desire to have her story told is indisputable and provided my motivation:[10] "You who in later years *will read these very words of mine* will be able to trace a true history of this epoch, by my diaries and papers," she wrote on 1 August 1934. More than once Vivienne congratulated herself on having left her papers to the Bodleian, writing triumphantly to Lady Ottoline Morrell: "The truth will all come out, if not in *our* life—*then after it.*"[11] Certainly Vivienne never wavered in her determination to preserve those sources which would enable later readers to understand, in some degree, the causes of her deepening hysteria.

Vivienne longed for the sympathy which was denied her in her lifetime. Instead, silenced behind the bars of the asylum, she has waited over fifty years for her story to be told. Only part of her diaries were eventually delivered by Maurice to the Bodleian, where at first they mouldered in the basement; the rest had gone up in flames in a garage fire at the house of Mildred Haigh-Wood, widow of her nephew Raggie. Vivienne's Bodleian papers have been controlled by the Eliot estate since 1985; I record now my debt of gratitude to Faber & Faber, representing the Estate, for their generous permission to quote without restriction from the writings and papers of Vivienne Eliot, although I have been required to paraphrase all direct quotations from the writings of T. S. Eliot, except for passages considered fair dealing by Faber & Faber.

C.S.J.
July 2001

I

A Bohemian from Bury

Oxford was losing its young men. It was the winter of 1914, and the streets were unnaturally quiet, the quadrangles deserted by those undergraduates who had joined the British army. But the university was not entirely empty. A number of Americans had arrived to fill the gaps, to the extent that at Merton College the Junior Common Room proposed the motion, "that this society abhors the Americanisation of Oxford." The resolution failed by two votes, after a recently arrived graduate student in philosophy named Thomas Stearns Eliot pointed out to his fellows how much they owed to "Amurrican culcher . . . in the movies, in music, in the cocktail, and in the dance."[1]

As spring arrived, the presence of the Americans attracted eager young women, short of partners in the first year of the Great War. One such visitor to Oxford was Vivienne Haigh-Wood, a vivacious artist's daughter from Hampstead who, one sunny afternoon, hired a punt on the River Cherwell. She was a slight girl with huge grey eyes, a governess with pretensions to culture. As the boat glided under the willows, Vivienne bent over her phonograph and placed the needle upon the record. The sound of ragtime drifted over the water.

The familiar tune attracted the attention of Eliot, the tall, nervous young American from Merton who had also taken a punt on the river. It reminded him of home in St. Louis, Missouri, where as a child he used to listen to the music from the honky-tonks, and promised an antidote to the gloom of wartime Oxford where he had been "plugging away at Hüsserl" and finding it terribly hard.[2] To his old Harvard friend, Conrad Aiken, Eliot had written on New Year's Eve 1914, "I hate university towns and university people, who are the same everywhere, with pregnant wives, sprawling children, many books and hideous pictures on the walls . . . Oxford is very pretty, but I don't like to be dead."[3]

Now, catching sight of Vivienne, one of the "river girls," as the press of that time described such light-hearted young women, Tom Eliot saw a way out of his gloom.[4] For in the punt with her was another American he thought he recognised: Lucy Thayer, a cousin of Scofield Thayer, Tom's fellow alumnus from Milton Academy in Massachusetts, a young man who came from the same distinguished New England milieu as Eliot, and who was also studying at Oxford, at Magdalen College, conveniently close to Merton. And Scofield was about to give a luncheon party to which Eliot was invited. Watching Vivienne and Lucy, laughing in their white dresses, his spirits began to lift. It only needed a word in Scofield's ear . . .

This tale was related by Eliot's friend Sacheverell Sitwell, and may well be apocryphal, although Vivienne *was* introduced to Tom Eliot at a lunch party in Scofield's rooms at Magdalen.[5] And she *did* love the river. One of her only surviving sketches is of a punt moored under the willows. For Vivienne, it seems, one glance was enough. She fell in love. It was a violent love—fierce, uncompromising and loyal. "Father and Tom, Tom and father, those two of my heart," she whispered in 1934 as she walked by her father's grave.[6]

The attraction between Vivienne and Tom was instant—and mutual. She admired his accent, which she described in her diary as "the *real* middle westerner's deep and thrilling voice," although in fact Eliot had been at some pains to lose his childhood accent in favour of the clipped tones of Boston. To Vivienne, the handsome American symbolised the heroic spirit of the Wild West, "the call to the wild that is in men"; but she had mistaken her man. It was to be but one of several fundamental misunderstandings. Eliot, too, had misjudged Vivienne. Unschooled in the complexities of the English class system, however well schooled he was in philosophy, Eliot was as impressed by Vivienne's leisured and apparently wealthy background as he was by her lively personality: her father, Charles Haigh-Wood, a retired member of the Royal Academy, lived on his unearned income and was the possessor of several houses, in Hampstead, Buckinghamshire and Anglesey; his son Maurice, educated at public school, was at Sandhurst training to be an army officer. But Vivienne's roots were, in fact, very different from what Eliot imagined.

Born in Bury, amidst the factory chimneys of the booming Lancashire cotton town, Vivienne Haigh-Wood made an unexpected arrival into this world on 28 May 1888. Her parents, local-boy-made-good Charles Haigh-Wood and his wife, Rose Esther, had taken lodgings near the railway station at Knowsley Street, having travelled north from London to mount an exhibition of the artist's pictures at a gentleman's club in his home town.[7] It was a long journey for the pregnant Rose, and perhaps one which brought on the birth inconveniently early. Had time allowed, Rose might have preferred her confinement to take place in the comfortable villa owned by her in-laws, Charles and Mary Wood, in Walmersley Road, nearby. As it was, the small, dark-haired baby arrived to the sound of trains, loaded with bales of raw cotton for the mills, steaming into Bury from Liverpool.[8]

The artist was busy with his one-man show in Manchester Road, and not until 4 July did he find time to register the birth of his first child, "Vivienne Haigh in the sub-district of Bury South in the county of Lancaster." Charles gave his occupation as "Artist (Painter)." The entry suggests a certain desire on the part of Haigh-Wood, as the artist styled himself, to avoid any confusion with his artisan father, plain Charles Wood, a gilder and picture framer born in nearby Bolton. It also suggests Haigh-Wood's pride in his success, for by 1888 the boy from Bury had become a Royal Academician whose fame had spread far beyond the cotton town in which he grew up.

In later life, Vivienne was ashamed of her northern roots. Writing to her new brother-in-law, Henry Ware Eliot, in October 1916 as she sat on the train to Manchester on her way to stay with a childhood friend, she declared: "I know I shall hate it. I know my Father was (is) a Lancashire (and Yorkshire) man, and I was born in Lancs, altho' I only lived there three weeks! But we have a number of *old* friends who live in Lancashire and North Wales. They are the most dreadful people really—very *very* rich manufacturing people—so provincial . . ."[9] Yet Vivienne had spent many childhood holidays at the *"beautiful"* country houses of the Lancashire manufacturers she affected to despise, and her upbringing had greater significance for her than she acknowledged. Her childhood was split between north and south, as was Eliot's, and there is a genuine sense of "not belonging" in her confession to Henry that she is a different person from the girl who sat on the same train just two years ago, on her way to be brides-maid to her hostess: "I have got out of the way of these people now—(not that *I ever* was *in* the way—having lived in London and in such a different set all my life) but I was more used to them." Vivienne's upbringing left her self-conscious and snobbish, with an underlying sense of social inferiority when she mixed with "old money," such as that exemplified by Lady Ottoline Morrell, half-sister of the Duke of Portland. Yet Vivienne also in-herited northern grit and determination, of which she was to have need in the coming years, as she attempted to follow the path of Victorian upward mobility set by her grandfather Wood.

Vivienne's father, Charles, was born over the shop owned by his father in 22 Fleet Street, opposite the parish church in the centre of Bury. As a boy he heard the heavy tramp of the women's clogs on the cobbles below as they hurried to the mill. His father, also Charles, a master craftsman, had moved his workshop from Bolton to Bury, where business flourished as the looms whirred in the cotton factories and the mill owners embellished their homes with pictures framed by Wood.[10] A shrewd marriage consoli-dated Wood's position. His bride was Mary Haigh, an Anglo-Irish Protestant girl from Dublin with financial expectations, about seven years his junior,[11] who had sailed from Kingstown to Liverpool, sometime after the 1845 potato famine. It was a period of busy traffic between Liverpool, Holyhead and Dublin, where the British government maintained a mili-tary garrison; the Haighs were a family of means, and Mary Haigh's mar-riage may have seemed like a misalliance to her family. Nevertheless, by 1851, she and Charles Wood had set up home in the four rooms over the shop in Bury, where five children were born in quick succession. Young Charles arrived in 1856, three years after the birth of the couple's first child, Laura Amy. Another son followed, James, who died young, and two more daughters, Emily and Sarah. There was Kate, too, an Irish servant girl Mary had brought over from Kilkenny, and soon the cramped rooms over the shop were uncomfortably crowded.[12] But by the 1870s Charles Senior's business had prospered under the patronage of the mill owners, and he di-versified into picture-dealing; soon he was able to move into a substantial new house at 14 Albion Place, Walmersley Road.[13] He had laid the foun-dations for his rise from artisan to gentleman.

Young Charles Wood was not only as ambitious as his father, but precociously talented artistically. As a boy he was sent to nearby Bethel Sunday School in Henry Street, an independent Congregationalist chapel, and attended the local grammar school, but his sights were set on the world outside Bury. At some point in his upbringing he decided to combine his parents' surnames as Haigh Wood (later hyphenated), perhaps when his mother Mary inherited property in Kingstown (now Dun Laoghaire). The rents from the seven semi-detached houses made a difference to the family fortunes, and may have made it possible for Charles Wood to sign the 999-year lease on the house at 14 Albion Place for £780, a not inconsiderable sum in the late nineteenth century.[14] Wood sent his promising son to Manchester Art College, where he won several prizes. In 1873 Charles shook the dust of Bury from his feet, arriving in London at just seventeen to attend the Royal Academy School.

His rise in the art world was rapid. Charles later recalled how, when he was training at the Academy, he was noticed by the editor of the *Art Journal,* S. C. Hall, a "discriminating art critic," who praised his work; by the age of twenty-one he was exhibiting at the Academy and elected a member. Three years of travelling and studying the Renaissance masters in Italy followed, before he returned to settle in a little house at Taplow, on the upper reaches of the Thames. Nevertheless Haigh-Wood kept his links with the north. His ability to catch a likeness and his technical virtuosity brought him an increasing number of commissions from the local worthies of Bury and its neighbouring towns, Bolton and Rochdale, and he kept a studio at Castle Chambers in Market Street, Bury. His sister Sarah married into the Heap family, drapers in the same street as Charles Wood, and Mayor Heap was the subject of one of Charles's portraits in 1880. In 1899 he was still painting the aldermen and mayors of the neighbourhood, working on a portrait of Alderman Baron, who was about to be presented with the freedom of Rochdale. Three years earlier Charles had painted the portrait of Alderman Turner, Mayor of Rochdale.[15]

These portraits demonstrate Charles Haigh-Wood's ability to penetrate to the personality behind the mayoral robes, but he probably regarded them as bread-and-butter work. The pictures of which he was most proud were the drawing-room "conversation pieces" which made him a fashionable genre painter in the late nineteenth century—scenes of polite society in which gentlemen wooed elegant young ladies, and coy studies of children. His paintings carried titles like *Chatterboxes* and *The Old Love and the New*. So popular did this cloyingly sentimental style make him that all his pictures were sold before the doors of the Academy opened in 1899, two to the greeting-card manufacturers Raphael Tuck and Son for reproduction. Galleries from as far away as Australia were bidding for his pictures, the artist proudly recalled.

Despite his comfortable circumstances, Haigh-Wood complained to a reporter from the *Bury Times* in 1899 that although in France the government fostered art, "here in England the artist struggles on, sometimes receiving from purchasers the patronage necessary to keep him in comfort, but more often sighing for such assistance. An English artist, unless he is possessed of private means, can seldom afford to wait for the appreciation accorded to the highest form of art. He would be painting above the understanding of his public."[16]

These protests were hardly justified, for in fact Haigh-Wood had no need to live by his brush alone. On his father's death in 1881 the house in Albion Place passed to his mother, Mary, and on her death in 1890,[17] two years after Vivienne's birth, to his sister Sarah. But Charles, the only son, inherited the bulk of his mother's fortune. She left him her properties in Kingstown, then a fashionable watering place. Charles rented these properties out to the town corporation. "Dad collected and lived on the rent," remembered his son Maurice.[18] In addition, Haigh-Wood inherited Eglinton House, a substantial property in the same neighbourhood. He became, through this lucky legacy, not a struggling artist but an English Protestant landlord, living off the rents of his Irish tenants. As a fashionable painter with a private income, it was time to think about a change of lifestyle.

His first move was to leave Buckinghamshire for Hampstead, since "The Porch," his house at Taplow, though pretty, "did not in other respects answer my expectations."[19] Perhaps Rose, at home with the new baby, missed the proximity of her family. The couple moved to Hampstead in about 1891, taking a sixty-year lease on a house at 3 Compayne Gardens, the house which Vivienne was always to think of as home. Rose, *née* Robinson, had originally come from North London, and her sister Lillia Symes lived nearby, at Broadhurst Gardens. Soon the Haigh-Wood family settled into comfortable bourgeois life.

Charles no longer had the need to prostitute his art to the public.

Paintings such as *A Fisherman's Cottage, Runswick 1886*[20] show the social realism of which he was capable when he painted the Yorkshire fishing folk. This charming study of a young woman and her daughter, carrying apples down a path from their cottage, anticipates the Newlyn School. Yet Haigh-Wood never fulfilled his promise: he continued to churn out the mannered conversation pieces which reproduced so well as greeting cards, and when in 1910 his home town decided to honour him with a retrospective exhibition, it met with hostile reviews. The *Bury Times* said: "Mr. Haigh-Wood's art suffers much from the tyranny of fashion," while the *Manchester Guardian* was even more critical: " 'Is it Yea or Nay?' or 'Will He Come?' are the sort of questions the pictures ask; the trouble is that if the stories do not interest the spectator profoundly he is likely to find little else to satisfy him in the pictures."[21]

For Vivienne, however, her father remained a hero, the parent of whom she was so proud.[22] During her childhood his painting was at its most popular, reflecting the values of Victorian civilisation: she was born a year after Queen Victoria's Golden Jubilee when the imperialistic fervour which greeted General Gordon's death at Khartoum was still fresh in people's minds. Kaiser Wilhelm came to the throne a month after Vivienne's birth, and Arthur Conan Doyle had recently published his first Sherlock Holmes story. There were few doubts in British minds about the morality of empire, and such assumptions were reflected in Haigh-Wood's quintessentially Victorian style. When her father's reputation plummeted after the Tories fell from power and Liberal reforms began to chip away at the old capitalist class structure, it made no difference to Vivienne's cloistered world. Her father continued to paint in his studio at the top of the house, to make marmalade in the kitchen—cooking was one of his favourite ways of relaxing—and to conduct his peripatetic life between Hampstead, Bury and Buckinghamshire (where he had taken on another house to serve as a studio and picture store), and to spend summers with his family at Plas Llanfair, Llanfairpwll, a manor house on Anglesey. There was never enough money, yet in Hampstead Rose kept servants, ran an ordered household, took the children to the tennis club, and wintered abroad with Charles in the Alps and the south of France.

Vivienne was also her father's favourite model. One of his most dramatic portraits was of his daughter in a cape, exhibited at Bury Art Gallery in 1910[23] and at the Paris Salon. It was a painting he refused to sell. Rose also modelled for him, as did their son Maurice, who was seven years younger than Vivienne. She and Maurice are the subjects of a painting entitled *The Peace Offering,* or *I'll Be Sorry If You'll Be Sorry,*[24] painted in 1900 when Vivienne was twelve and her brother five. The room in which they stand, with its green patterned wallpaper and ornate fireplace, lined with blue and white Delft tiles, was probably the family drawing-room. The small boy, in frilled white shirt and breeches, holds out an apple to his elder sister, chubby and pretty in her smocked pink pinafore, with bows at the shoulders and long curling brown hair; the pair have clearly been squabbling, and a torn picture book lies open on the carpet. But the girl refuses the peace offering her brother shyly holds out to her.

This picture was originally entitled *Small Girl Sulking,* and is an early indication of the moods from which Vivienne suffered increasingly from the age of twelve. Identifying with her half-Irish father, she later described herself as "a tormented Celt" to Ezra Pound—but it was her other parent, Rose, who was called upon to provide the stable mothering Vivienne required as the father she adored was often absent. When Rose tried to deal with her high-spirited and sensitive daughter, mother and daughter often clashed.

In her early childhood Vivienne was infected in her left arm with tuberculosis osteomyelitis or tuberculosis of the bone, a common nineteenth-century disease. Treatment for TB of the bone was in its infancy in the 1890s, and there was little that the medical profession could do before the discovery of antibiotics. Patients were prescribed rest, fresh air and sunlight, and the infected parts were immobilised so that children whose spine and lower limbs were affected often spent years in plaster casts. Surgery was very limited, but Vivienne's parents insisted on the best for their daughter, calling in Sir Frederick Treves, Surgeon-Extraordinary to Queen Victoria, who became famous for treating the "Elephant Man." Although there is no record of his treatment of Vivienne, she may have been subjected to painful aspiration of any cold abscesses on her arm and possibly curetting of decayed bone. She later told Osbert Sitwell that she had had so many operations as a young girl that she had no memory of her life before the age of seven.[25]

Remarkably, Vivienne recovered from her illness well enough to excel physically in adolescence. It is possible that she made a spontaneous recovery; diagnosis was not always very precise. Her brother Maurice remembered that Vivienne was a good swimmer and reached a high standard at ballet. Brigit Patmore, a friend whom she met through Ezra Pound, wrote that "Vivienne had studied ballet technique—was expert at its many complications and yet it did not prevent her enjoyment of ballroom dancing."[26] Dance was always a powerful form of release for Vivienne. "Shut up, don't talk. Surely you know I can't dance and talk," she says in "The Night Club," one of her autobiographical short stories in which she calls herself "Sibylla."[27] Her admirer, probably one of the "pick-ups" whom she easily attracted, tells her that she dances better than anyone in the room. "You dance gloriously, you extraordinary little thing."

This portrait of a flapper, dancing deliriously to the new jazz tunes of the 1920s—and this story was written in 1924—encapsulates many elements of Vivienne's personality. The desire to shock, to be outrageous, the sharp wit combined with impatience with intellectual debate, the intense interest in clothes and making a dramatic appearance, were fundamental characteristics. Indeed, in Vivienne's story, "Sibylla" meets her brother "Horace," a barely disguised caricature of Maurice. "I like your surplice," he comments sarcastically, glancing down at her dress, which was presumably unwaisted. In fiction, as in life, Maurice was conventional like his mother, whose favourite he was, and frequently shocked by his impulsive, unpredictable sister.

On the surface Vivienne's adolescence seemed happy. The family often escaped London for Plas Llanfair, which Vivienne's father had taken on a ninety-year lease. The house was cold and hideous, thought Maurice, but for Vivienne, who liked nothing better than to walk the family dogs on a blustery day, the island of Anglesey was a haven from city life. The summer, she wrote, was the season for the country—the air, the wind tearing the hair and reddening the face as one tramped across the marshes. "Your scarf blows out like a flying jib behind you. Boots wet in the salt water puddles, one slips and slides across the rank grass—the seaweed slime. The sky is clear and scrubbed, reflected in blue pools." When a shower "stumps her," Vivienne shudders, eager to get home. But then the sun comes to laugh at her, warms her. "You smile and swing your stick, call the dog and push on towards the sea."[28] It may have been on Anglesey, or on holiday in Cornwall, that Vivienne first learnt to sail a boat and developed her love of the sea. And when the weather was so bad as to daunt even her, she put on plays for the family and entertained her bored brother.

Yet beneath the surface, Vivienne hid a shameful secret. For this energetic, sporty girl, the arrival of menstruation was truly a curse. She bled irregularly, probably as a result of a hormonal imbalance which today could be cured by the contraceptive pill. It is also possible that she might have had a polyp in her uterus, or cervicitis. Whatever the cause, the mood swings and abdominal pains and cramps which accompanied her all too frequent and unpredictable periods began to dominate her life.[29]

There was no treatment for the condition at this time. Vivienne became obsessional about washing her bedlinen herself, sometimes twice a day.[30] Nor could she turn to her father for help—women's problems were left to Rose and the doctors to deal with. Rose seemed to have little understanding of Vivienne's temperament, and wished only for her to conform to the mores of suburban Hampstead. She had no patience with Vivienne's rebellious urges to dance, to escape, to satisfy her frustrated creativity. In 1924 Vivienne wrote a sketch about her childhood in which she describes a family by the name of "Buckle": the Buckles were a local Hampstead family well-known to Vivienne, and in 1914 she became engaged to the son Charles. But her sketch, although possibly inspired by the Buckles, appears primarily to be a self-portrait as well as a vehicle for criticism of her mother. In the sketch she calls herself "Rosa," her mother's name. The family she describes hide their conflict behind laughter: "As a family the Buckles laughed too much. They were proud of their daughter. They thought themselves an exceptionally merry family . . . Unless they were laughing they were in the dumps . . ." The family were "all rather hysterical. Rosa was the only one with any character."

All Mrs. Buckle's children, declared Vivienne, suffered from having a mother with too strong a personality. "Her personality was so big that there was no room for any other personality at all in the crowded Kensington house." In the evenings she and "Rosa" sat together sewing, mending and darning for "the boys," making their own and other clothes. Mrs. Buckle liked her daughters to sing as they worked and she led the songs lustily: "She would be happy if her son brought home his friends, and there would be singing and playing the piano and laughter all evening." But if Maurice was allowed a certain freedom, Vivienne was not.

But even then [Mrs. Buckle] expected her daughters to go on with their sewing. She never liked it if one left the room. "Where are you off to?" she would say sharply. "Only to get a handkerchief, mother." "Then don't fiddle about up there, and don't leave the light on." The sisters would nudge each other, but they were too timid to disobey. None of them had ever been alone for a moment from their birth. They were anaemic and frequently painted. They were all pretty and healthy looking girls, and their brother was handsome.

It was an accurate self-description, and Vivienne knew also that she had a streak of wilfulness which "Mrs. Buckle" would be hard put to control. In "Rosa's" eyes, there is

A queer look, a fleeting expression of utter recklessness. It was a startling and disturbing look—unconscious and almost inhuman. It was not the recklessness of high courage and adventurousness but rather a wild expressive look of a secret urge towards self-destruction . . .[31]

In her struggle to control her determined and difficult daughter, Rose turned to the family doctor, Dr. Smith, who practised at Queen Anne Street, W1. Maurice subsequently recalled that Vivienne was about sixteen when her doctors began to prescribe drugs for her symptoms. Dr. Smith recommended bromide, the drug commonly used to treat hysterical or over-anxious patients. He probably diagnosed Vivienne as suffering from hysteria, a female malady in which the uterus was believed to work in opposition to the brain and cause irrational behaviour. It was a label often pinned upon young women who were unhappy and frustrated with their circumscribed lives in the late nineteenth and early twentieth centuries. Potassium bromide acts on the central nervous system. "By lowering the activity of both motor and sensory cells, the bromides are of great service . . . in the treatment of cerebral excitement," according to the British Pharmaceutical Codex of 1911. They "render the brain less sensitive to disturbing influences," reduce all reflexes and promote sleep. Bromide, often administered as a preparation dissolved in alcohol, was the drug of choice and habit for most general practitioners of the period, and was especially recommended for dysmenorrhoea, or irregular menstruation, as well as hysteria. And so the process of tranquillising Vivienne began. Her regular "doses," as she called them, were facilitated by Rose, who had an account as a private patient of Dr. Smith's at Allen and Hanbury, a pharmacy in the nearby Finchley Road. As well as bromide, the doctors prescribed Vivienne "Hoffman's Anodyne" and other powders. The anodyne was dissolved in spirit of ether, a powerful anaesthetic with a distinctive smell. Maurice believed Vivienne's medicines contained formaldehyde, and that she also took snuff. She was, he recalled, "stuffed with filthy drugs" by the time she reached adulthood.

As the medical bills for Vivienne's treatment mounted, so did Maurice's resentment of his sister. He became convinced that the heavy burden of her medical expenses on the family budget prevented him going to a first-rate public school. After Ovingdean Prep School, Maurice was accepted at Malvern College, which he complained was a "second-class school." It seems not to have occurred to Maurice, who spent thirteen years trying to find employment as a stockbroker after leaving the army, that he lacked the intellectual credentials for Winchester, or the social background for Eton. The difference in fees between one public school and another would not have been great, and it is more likely that this family with its roots in trade did not have the right connections for entry into the most privileged schools. But Maurice continued to bear a grudge against his sister, just as she continued to embarrass him, turning up at Malvern to take him out to tea, wearing a white shirt and tie above her long skirt—an outfit the seventeen-year-old boy considered unbecomingly masculine—and turning cartwheels on the headmaster's lawn.

A "double-binding" situation thus arose in which Rose and Maurice combined to designate Vivienne the "victim" in the family; she was the one they were permitted to harm, the scapegoat for Maurice's failings.[32] Vivienne's father Charles, her anchor, failed her; anxious for a quiet life, and dominated by Rose, he distanced himself from the situation both emotionally as well as physically, abandoning his vulnerable daughter to the mercy of his wife. For Vivienne, her family became the source of overwhelming stress, as her mother criticised her, controlled her, and bombarded her with conflicting commands. "Vivie," as Maurice called his sister, knew she resembled her bohemian father not her bourgeois mother, but her aspirations to become a dancer or an artist never translated themselves into a career. There seemed no alternative but to try to adjust herself to the standards of the mother she continually seemed to displease, but even at this she failed. Moreover, Rose told Vivienne, as she gave her her "doses," that she was sick. The label seemed to fit, and increasingly Vivie acted out this role by indulging in temperamental outbursts and crying fits.

Such symptoms are often protests against strict management, which may become pathological if they grow rigid, habitual and part of an illness pattern.[33] But Vivienne's "nerves," as she learnt to call them, by no means disabled her to this extent or became pathological. She was not only attractive but intelligent, describing herself later as "a *frightfully* mentally *over*developed child . . . and Oh what a child I was. Poor, wretched, *clever* child."[34] She longed to learn, although academies for young ladies offered "accomplishments"—piano, sketching and languages—rather than the classics or sciences which were only available to their brothers. At King Alfred School in Hampstead and later in Margate, where she boarded at Dulwich House School, Vivienne read Hardy and Swinburne and grew to love poetry; she also excelled at languages. Holidays in Paris and Switzerland with her parents gave her the opportunity to become a fluent French speaker and she regarded Paris as a second home. She wrote as quickly as she thought, and learnt to type to dictation. In London she regularly attended her beloved art school, and also sketched with her father at the seashore at Eastbourne, Hastings, and the Hampshire coast, as well as on Anglesey where Haigh-Wood obsessively painted cows. The few of Vivienne's watercolours which have survived are of boats and waterside scenes.

Brigit Patmore described Vivienne in 1914: "She was slim and rather small, but by no means insignificant. Light brown hair and shining grey eyes. The shape of her face was narrowed to a pointed oval chin and her mouth was good—it did not split up her face when she smiled, but was small and sweet enough to kiss. Added to this, she did not quiver, as so sensitive a person might, but shimmered with intelligence."[35] Such an attractive woman found many suitors among her brother Maurice's army officer friends, who were often her dancing partners. After Sandhurst Maurice had joined the Manchester Regiment; despite their differences, brother and sister both liked to dance, and Vivienne shone at the army balls. As she entered her twenties, marriage became her goal: it would give her status and identity and a way out of the family ghetto.

Once again the obstacle was her mother. Rose made up her mind that Vivienne was not fit to marry or have children, and stood in the way of her efforts to form a relationship which might lead to marriage. Rose believed that Vivienne suffered from "moral insanity," another diagnosis much in favour with doctors of the period, such as Sir George Henry Savage, who treated Virginia Woolf. Savage defined "moral insanity" as a condition in which "the moral nature or moral side of the character is affected greatly in excess of the intellectual side." Savage believed that a child might be born "prone to wickedness," and that "many so-called spoiled children are nothing more nor less than children who are morally of unsound mind . . . In many cases, doubtless, the parent who begets a nervous child is very likely to further spoil such a child by a bad or unsuitable education." It was a diagnosis which could be applied to Vivienne who, during long periods of illness, had been indulged. Such children, argued Savage, were "naturally unstable and unfitted to control their lower natures."[36]

"Moral insanity," a term more usually applied to women than men, was shorthand for a precocious sexual awareness leading to promiscuity.[37] There is little doubt that Rose feared her strong-willed daughter would lose her virginity and disgrace the family. In her diary Vivienne remembered her "young days, at Esher, when a whole gang of us . . . painted Esher red." The gang consisted of herself, Maurice, Lucy Thayer and "dozens of others."[38] Such wild partying aroused her mother's deepest apprehensions. Significantly the bromide prescribed for Vivienne was recommended to damp down sexual desire, and was labelled an anaphrodisiac by the Pharmaceutical Codex. In reality Vivienne may have had a predisposition to manic depressive illness, which would account for her uninhibited "manic" episodes which so alarmed Rose, alternating with periods when she preferred to withdraw from society. It was the secret fear of inherited insanity which lay behind Rose's determination that Vivienne should not marry. During her teenage years Vivienne was rebellious, but the question of marriage did not arise. In 1914, however, when she was twenty-five, she fell in love. It was time to challenge her mother.

2

The River Girl

Privileged, protected and popular, Vivien, as she now chose to call herself, lived the life of a social butterfly as the merry-go-round of balls and parties whirled ever faster in the shadow of war. Later she remembered how she

> started life as a beautiful Princess admired and worshipped by all men and living in a house of rosy glass through which one watched the envious world go by & how the glass house is broken and one wants to get back inside, safe & beautiful & secure.[1]

Vivien was "fresh, innocent, a chatterbox, pretty," said a friend of Stephen Spender's who used to dance with her at the Hammersmith Palais de Danse before the war. She was nicknamed "The River Girl," wrote Spender, by "Eliot's social friends (Lady Ottoline Morrell, St. John Hutchinson and his wife, Virginia and Leonard Woolf, the Sitwells, the Aldous Huxleys),"[2] although Eliot himself called Vivien and her friends "Char-flappers"; and, according to Osbert Sitwell, "River-Girl" was a term used by the contemporary press to describe "that kind of young person— the rather pretty young girl who could be seen, accompanied by an undergraduate, floating down the river in a punt on a summer afternoon."[3] It was a light, insouciant name, reflecting Vivien's supposed character, and suggesting the sparkle and mutability of water, that quality which led Brigit Patmore to describe her as "shimmering" with intelligence. But it is also derogatory, conjuring up the image of the only half-human naiad or water sprite who lives at the bottom of the river and lures men to fall in love with her. "There seems a trace of mockery in this name," said Spender, remarking damningly, "She had a history of illness and 'nerves.' "

But Vivien was neither as conventional nor as empty-headed as her nickname suggests. In the undated (early 1920s), prose sketch of George Bernard Shaw, in which she described feeling like a princess in the pre-war era, she also tells how she longs to hold Shaw's hand and "tell him all about the Firebird and cages . . ." The Firebird, flying free, symbol of escape from the confines of bourgeois life, inspired Vivien, and in 1914 it was escape from her golden cage on which she was determined. Under her fashionable flapper dresses beat a passionate heart, and inside her neatly bobbed head was a sharp brain eager to be of use. She had trained as a secretary and was proficient in shorthand and typing, and in the winter of 1914–15 she worked as a governess in a family in Cambridge as well as successfully tutoring backward children individually.

In early 1914 Vivien was twenty-five, and would be twenty-six in May. It was a critical age for any young woman, and matrimony was necessarily in the forefront of her mind. The alternative of spinsterhood was, in that period, too horrible to contemplate. The panic which such a prospect aroused in Vivien is shown in her portrait of the Buckle family in which she writes about herself and the young man with whom she fell in love in 1914, Charles Buckle. In her sketch, Vivien calls herself Rosa Buckle, is an indication that she liked to imagine herself as Charles's wife, even though her fictional little sisters tease her about her fiancé's lack of good looks: "Certainly Charles Spencer was neither fair nor tall nor handsome (but) Rosa was twenty-six and in 1886 that was very nearly an old maid."[4]

In January 1914, Vivien had bought herself a Boots' Lady's Diary and Notebook, and began recording the progress of her romance with "C.B.," as she usually referred to the young schoolmaster and occasional journalist. It seems that at first Charles and Rose Haigh-Wood had no objection to their daughter's suitor.[5] He came from a local family whom they knew, and seemed a suitable match.

Vivien's brief, excited entries for the month of February paint a picture of frequent, intense meetings with Charles Buckle. Proximity in North London made meeting easy, and the weeks flew by with almost daily outings together to tea-shops in Baker Street, dances at the Elysée dance hall, where she had a "perfect time," visits to Whiteleys, where

Vivien had her hair washed and waved, and lunches with her American friend Lucy Ely Thayer. At the Dutch Oven on 12 February Vivien and Lucy discussed the progress of the romance; afterwards Vivien rang up Buckle and was pleased to hear he had missed her and "hadn't liked it."[6]

Vivien and Lucy Thayer had met in Vevey in 1908 when the two families were holidaying in the Alps; the Haigh-Woods regularly visited Switzerland in the winter, perhaps on the recommendation of Vivien's doctors when she was recovering from TB of the bone. It was a time when Charles Haigh-Wood was forbidden by Rose to bring his paints, and the family could relax together in the mountains. Vivien was a bold and graceful skater; she and Lucy became firm friends, bound together by their love of sports and shared experience of "nerves."[7] Soon Lucy became a regular guest at Compayne Gardens, and her parents frequently took a house in London.

In the autumn of 1913 Lucy's cousin, Scofield Thayer, later to be editor of *The Dial,* also arrived in England, to study at Oxford. Scofield was the only child of Florence and Edward Thayer, and his father was the millionaire owner of several woollen mills in Worcester, Massachusetts. Thayer Senior had high expectations of his only son and intended that he should crown his successful academic career at Milton Academy and Harvard with an Oxford degree. Scofield, however, having no need to work for a living, had other ideas.

That Michaelmas term, Scofield took rooms in the cloisters at Magdalen, looking out on the lawn in the middle of the quad. Prince George of Teck had rooms nearby, and HRH the Prince of Wales on the opposite side. Thayer himself, wrote his friend Henry McBride, seemed "more than a gentleman, a prince."[8] He regarded himself as an aesthete, and at once joined the Nineties Club, a society dedicated to living by the principles of Oscar Wilde. "The society conceives of the world as having come again to the same condition as it found itself in the 1890s," said its manifesto. "Following the lead of the obscure young men who followed Oscar Wilde, they are busy marking time and making every effort to live only a sensuous life with no purpose in the future . . ." The "amusing" side of the club members was said to be their "odd costumes of long white cloaks, great rings on their fingers, rare flowers in their rooms etc."[9]

Scofield apparently began reading for a degree in English, before switching to philosophy in 1914, and registering for a BPhil, but there is no record of his ever taking a degree. Instead he began collecting pictures, laying the foundations for his great collection of modern art; shopping, visits to his tailor, and to his aunt Josephine, drew Scofield to London, where it was inevitable that he would one day meet Vivien.

Buckle, meanwhile, had been drawn into the friendship between Vivien and Lucy Thayer, taking both girls to the "kinema" on 18 February. On the 21st Vivien was invited to a dinner party Lucy's parents were giving in London. It was a high-point of the romance. Vivien wore her favourite yellow silk dress, which set off her shining brown hair; Buckle had sent her "dark flowers," and after the dinner party he took her dancing, before returning her to the Thayers, where she was staying the night. He did not leave till 2 a.m.; "Told me he loved me," wrote Vivien with satisfaction in her diary.

Vivien lay in late the next morning, and Lucy came to sit on the edge of her bed. No doubt they discussed C.B. and Vivien's hopes of a proposal. Vivien dressed and went out to lunch, followed by another intimate tea with her boyfriend, but hardly had love been declared than a quarrel followed in Holland Park. She gave him up. "Fearful nerves and depression," she confided miserably to her diary.[10] It is probable that she was suffering from pre-menstrual tension, for one of the stars which appear to mark the beginning of her period decorates the next day's entry.

Two days later the lovers made up. "Got engaged to C.B." wrote Vivien triumphantly, heavily underlining the entry in her diary for 26 February, the day of Buckle's proposal. In her excitement she fainted the next morning, but her recovery was swift; by that evening she was well enough to go dancing again with her new fiancé at the Savoy. The next day Buckle came to dine with the Haigh-Woods and asked Vivien's father for her hand in marriage. Vivien was apprehensive and nervous, fearful that Charles might not agree. But Haigh-Wood consented, offering to settle £500 on his only daughter, and to give her £50 outright. Overcome with joy, Vivien went to Silverman, her dressmaker, and ordered a new coat and skirt to celebrate her engagement.[11]

Her happiness was short-lived, however. Over tea on Sunday at Compayne Gardens, where Vivien and Buckle had an *"awfully* nice time," she persuaded him to tell his mother of their engagement that evening. Later he rang to say that Mama very much disapproved. Vivien was "very upset" and spent a sleepless night, and the next day, Monday, was "the most awful day." Rose Haigh-Wood decided to intervene. She summoned Charles Buckle and overrode her husband's decision, ordering the young man to break off the engagement. Vivien, she declared ominously, was unsuited for marriage and maternity. "Mother sent me away and talked to him and thoroughly upset him," recorded Vivien. "Mummy warned CB off," recalled Maurice,[12] relating how the engagement was broken off. According to Vivien's diary, Buckle stayed on and on and the row "got worse and worse." "When Rosa Buckle became engaged to Charles Spencer . . . Rosa was very angry and her cheeks were red," wrote Vivien in her fictionalised account of the event. "She tried to be dignified and scornful but her eyes filled with mortified tears . . . Mother herself felt a little blank on Rose's engagement . . . She still loved to see 'a fine tall handsome man,' if possible with brown eyes and a heavy moustache."[13] The ill-favoured Buckle was driven out, complaining that he felt ill as he left the house of arguments and tears. The family friction which had rumbled through Vivien's adolescence, as the Haigh-Woods found themselves divided, father and daughter ranged against mother and son, had culminated in the sabotaging of Vivien's hopes of independence by her mother.

Rose Haigh-Wood may have felt she had her daughter's interests at heart, but it is more likely that she was influenced by early twentieth-century hysteria over eugenics, and fears of the physical deterioration of the British race aroused by the fiasco of the Boer War. Fabians such as Sidney and Beatrice Webb and Bernard Shaw argued that "degeneracy" was inherited and the "feeble-minded" should be compulsorily sterilised. Doctors declared that "moral insanity" disqualified women from motherhood, and women who had illegitimate babies were confined to mental asylums as "morally insane"; the fear that Vivien might become pregnant was never far from her mother's mind. According to Maurice: "Mummy wasn't very clever," there was "something in her that made her fancify; Mummy got so worried she believed her own fears" of Vivien's "moral insanity," which she placed in a different category from "lunacy." His sister was never a "lunatic," emphasised Maurice.[14]

Another factor in the family opposition to the engagement, from Buckle's mother as well as from the Haigh-Woods, was the approach of war. Although there is no hint in Vivien's artless account of tea parties, balls, dinner parties, art and dance classes, of the escalating quarrel with Germany, the bubble was soon to burst. Charles Buckle had volunteered for the army and was waiting to hear if he had secured a commission. His thoughts were of politics, even of glory, as much as of marriage, and Rose's prohibition as well as his own mother's may have made him hesitate.

The morning after Rose's bombshell, Tuesday, 3 March, Buckle telephoned Vivien to say he was too ill to go in to school to teach. "It's *all wrong*," wrote Vivien miserably. Lucy had spent the night with her to comfort her and now Vivien went round to the Thayers' house for lunch, where she rang Buckle again, who would not come out to see her. "*Terrible*. Everything slipping away," wrote Vivien. As usual she cheered herself up by having a fitting for a new dress.[15]

Within a day the lovers were together again, although not harmoniously so. They met for tea and went to see *The Darling of the Gods*. The next night Vivien decided to escape her mother and went to stay with Lucy at 38 Inverness Terrace, Bayswater, a flat rented by the Thayers. Buckle took Vivien out for the evening, and there was a *"fearful* scene" in the bedroom. "I gave way altogether," recorded Vivien. "No good."[16] Did Buckle voice the fears put in his head by Mrs. Haigh-Wood? In any event, Vivien was too depressed to see "B" for several days. By Sunday, however, they were meeting again for tea at the Old Oak, and Buckle was in a "perfect mood." Vivien, in response, was "standoffish," which had the desired effect. The young schoolmaster asked her out to dinner, and she accepted. Over the meal at the Boulogne, he told her of his plans to give up his job and go to France. It was a *"perfect* evening," wrote Vivien happily. Everything seemed right again, and he was "splendid."[17]

Now their daily meetings restarted. Soon Buckle was again in a "vile mood." Mrs. Thayer came into the room in the middle of the argument, and was "very unpleasant. So was B!" Buckle went to meet his mother for dinner, and Vivien was trembling all evening. The next night she had to leave the cinema because of the "noises,"[18] an indication of the hypersensitivity to noise of which Vivien was to complain later to her friend Sydney Schiff. The couple returned to the Thayers' house at 10:45, and by the next day Vivien had decided the Thayers, who also disapproved of the engagement, were all "beastly" ("I hate it!"), and she would be thankful to leave, although that evening she went to the ballet with Lucy to see Nijinsky.[19]

Restless, volatile and upset over the deterioration of her relationship with Buckle, the next day Vivien decided on impulse to visit her friend Constance Darley at Bookham in Surrey. The Darleys were "perfectly sweet," and Vivien felt calmer in their company, sewing quietly all morning and motoring to Guildford in the afternoon. But she could not stay away from Charles Buckle. She decided to slip up to town the next day and sleep at Inverness Terrace: "A great risk—but still—."[20] After church the next day she took the train to Waterloo, and met her lover. As usual they dined in Soho and went to the cinema, returning to the Thayer residence at 11:30 p.m. where another "very great scene" took place in the bedroom. It is probable that by this time Vivien and "Charles" were having an illicit sexual affair, and Maurice later stated that "Vivie and Charles had a *real* affair";[21] if that were the case it would account for Mrs. Haigh-Wood's anxiety. Certainly Vivien's attachment to Charles Buckle was deep enough for her to risk disgrace, for as well as sneaking away from the Darleys, she seems to have met "B" at the home of his aunt, Lady Allen, who was away, as well as at the Thayers' residence, which she used with the increasing disapproval of Mrs. Thayer.

Early the next morning a guilty Vivien hurried back to Bookham, "glad to be back and to find that nothing had happened to discover me. I was so nervous."[22] That night she had a long talk with Mrs. Darley, who encouraged her to abandon the idea of marriage to Buckle. Vivien sent an express letter to Buckle, asking him to come and see her at home that evening; she was "dead tired," but knew "definitely what I wished to do. It is [for] the best."[23] Lady Allen was returning to her flat—"and of course that means the very end."[24] On 20 March, a cold snowy day, Vivien stayed indoors with a "fearful liver and very depressed." She had requested her father to write to Buckle, saying that "he prefers that all consideration of marriage shall for a time be set aside, and that we shall have no further opportunity of knowing each other better."[25]

Although Vivien had now broken off the engagement, she remained in love with Buckle. Gloomily she began to make herself a blue dress, but could not resist ringing Buckle to say she was "not very well." All the next morning she sewed and brooded about the affair, only emerging for a trip to Harrow with Lucy. That night she wrote Buckle a long letter.[26] On Tuesday he came in for tea, and her father joined them. The next day

Vivien could not resist ringing Charles up late that evening, who was *"very horrid."*[27] The young man must have been confused by Vivien's contradictory behaviour; for hardly had she rejected him than she was pestering him to meet her again. Her capricious behaviour continued; Vivien sent Buckle a wire demanding he come to tea again. He did so, and a "dreadful, awful time" ensued. She continued to nurse hopes of a reconciliation while Buckle went to the Boat Race, only to find them finally dashed when they met on Passion Sunday for tea at their favourite tea-shop, the Dutch Oven. "Really the *best, the very end,"* wrote Vivien in her diary. "Had a better talk, but it is all quite hopeless."[28]

After that meeting, there continued to be "no word or sign" from Buckle, and Vivien consoled herself with the return of her brother Maurice, now an officer cadet at Sandhurst. She took Maurice and her mother to watch her ballet class with her friend Iris. But on 2 April "bad neuralgia" did not prevent her from going dancing with Buckle, who had once again responded to her letters and telephone calls. It was, remembered Vivien, "an extraordinary evening," which renewed the affair. The couple came back through Holland Walk, the scene of a previous quarrel, "and here things happened." They kissed and petted; perhaps Buckle confessed his love again, but it was only, supposed Vivien cynically, because she was going away again to stay with the Darleys.[29]

"The happiest Easter Sunday I have had for years" followed, as Charles took Vivien for dinner in Soho, and after to the "kinema" and out to coffee. It was *"a perfect* evening" she wrote dreamily.[30] "Heavenly" days followed, as Charles continued to ring three times a day, to take Vivien to lunch, tea and the "kinema"; they visited St. Paul's, saw the play *The Melting Pot* ("rotten play but *lovely* evening"),[31] had innumerable cups of coffee in the Monaco, and while Charles was teaching, Vivien gardened or went to her dance class. Sometimes she lunched with him at Hammersmith, near his school, "hung about" while he taught, and met him at the end of school for tea at 4:30 p.m.[32] They had become inseparable.

This idyll was shattered when once again Vivien exploded on the day she began menstruating: "I made an awful row, and cried and screamed, and made myself ill." She lay down all afternoon and cried, but was well enough the next day to "bring Buckle round" over lunch, and to leave for

Surrey again where she spent the next five days on a walking holiday in the hills with Lucy. The two young women followed Vivien's favourite route from Chilworth to Shere, stopping for the night at the White Horse Inn, and tramping to Coldharbour, ten miles away, where they spent another night before walking back to Shere. Although "dreadfully tired" on Friday, Vivien sketched the stream and the church, before returning on Saturday to Hampstead.[33]

A day or two later, Buckle went down to Torquay with his aunt. It was in his absence that Vivien met Lucy's cousin, the princely Scofield Thayer, over tea on 30 April 1914. "Liked him very much," she recorded.[34] The next day, 1 May, Vivien and Lucy set off for a day in the Buckinghamshire countryside. Once again a ten-mile walk followed, and at Chalfont St. Giles, Vivien and her friend found "the most perfect cottage in the world," which, on impulse, they rented.

A week later, when the Haigh-Woods were out to dinner, Buckle came back to 3 Compayne Gardens at nine o'clock, and he and Vivien went into the tennis court for what seems to have been another romantic interlude. Vivien made no entries in her diary for the rest of May or June, but she was drawing closer to Buckle and his family. On 29 July she wore her new dress for the service of St. Paul's Apposition, and "sat with his people." Mrs. Buckle asked her to go back for dinner, and she ended up having "a *lovely* time" and liking his sister very much. Charles brought her home very late, and two days later took her dancing again at the Savoy with his sister.

On 3 August, the day before Britain declared war on Germany, Vivien made her first entry concerning the coming conflict: "Great suspense about the war." Charles came to tea, for the last time, although Vivien did not then know it. Her brother Maurice had arrived back from camp, "because of the war," but Vivien had to leave for a prearranged visit to Henley-on-Thames. She missed Buckle badly, and when on 6 August she received a letter from him, saying he had written to the War Office to offer himself as a "Galloper" or interpreter, she at once decided to come home, where she found "everything was wrong, as I expected."[35] For the next two days, Friday and Saturday, Vivien went to the town hall to do some work for Colonel Carpenter, perhaps typing or rolling bandages. On Monday she

quarrelled with Charles, probably over his decision to enlist. A brief interlude followed with Maurice at Esher, where she and her brother had "an
excellent time of tennis and golf—but for the trouble with CB,"[36] before returning to London to meet him at Victoria Station where they had an amicable tea. Vivien was by then resigned to his decision to serve in the army.

On 24 August, Charles rang to say he had been called to the War
Office, examined, and put on the shortlist. "He is certain to go in a few
days," wrote Vivien. "He is delighted."[37] The lovers spent the next two
days in each other's company, Charles accompanying Vivien to the town
hall to help with her war work. At lunchtime on Wednesday, 26 August,
Buckle's mother rang to say that the War Office had wired for him. "He
dashed out, had had no lunch, ate half a pork pie in an Express, and started
in a taxi." Charles would not let Vivien go all the way to the War Office
with him, and she was "fearfully upset and behaved stupidly." Her tears
had no effect. Caught up in the patriotic fervour of the time—the mood of
"dulce et decorum est pro patria mori"[38]—and the cheerful belief that the
adventure of war would be over before Christmas, Charles was "icy" in the
face of Vivien's pleas.

On 28 August she set out at quarter to nine to "see the last of CB."
Dolefully she watched him and his mother going into the War Office, and
then waited outside, joining Mrs. Buckle who was walking up and down.
An hour later Buckle came out, and said goodbye. He was "very cheerful,"
said Vivien. "I saw the last of him," she records proudly, for she went back
when his mother had gone and just caught a final glimpse of him jumping
into a taxi with another soldier. When they said goodbye, Buckle's words
were: "Goodbye child, for the present." "I hope it may be. But I am sure it
is for ever," wrote Vivien with a heavy heart.[39]

At this point, her diary entries ended. The fact that she kept an almost
daily record of her rollercoaster relationship with Charles Buckle is an indication of the importance of this love affair to her; after he left for France,
Vivien's mood must be gleaned from her letters to Scofield, to whom she
grew closer in Buckle's absence. A characteristic letter she scribbled at one
o'clock in the morning in February 1915 expresses the bubbling exuber-
ance, the teasing wit, the sharp mood changes which both bewildered and
fascinated the opposite sex. On 22 February, in a letter to Scofield only
dated "Sunday," she writes:

Dear Scofield

Is'nt [sic] it nice of me to write you this—out of a clear blue sky? Is'nt it *kind?* Please say—yes it is—Vivien. Tell me, did you think the half letter I gave you was beastly? Please say. I didn't mean it to be. Although this is Sunday, it is very early on Sunday, in fact, Scofield my child, it is 1 o'clock in the morning. I have just got back from the dance . . . and I am making a night of it as I usually do. If I don't go to bed at 10, I don't want to go to bed at all . . .

Vivien's late hours are, she remarks, a frequent and bitter cause of contention between Scofield's cousin Lucy and herself.

The dance was VERY nice, says Vivien in her letter. But, being a philosopher, she supposes he doesn't care very much. Vivien is obviously impressed that Scofield is a philosopher, although she doesn't even know the meaning of the word. "Do tell me what it is, will you?" she asks pertly. A friend of Scofield's called Parr has told Vivien that *everybody* has a philosophy, and it's no particular distinction. The subject both worried and intrigued her because Buckle, she says, had always told her that her problem was that she had no philosophy. He used to implore her with tears to try and get a little—"but where, and how do you get it?" Her own flippant creed, outlined to Scofield, is that whatever happens, you say to yourself— I don't care. I've got myself, what more do I want? Yet she feels this is not an attractive attitude. "Please tell, what's the truth of this philosophy business?"[40]

Vivien's naïve questions in this letter betray her lack of confidence about her education. She is curious, anxious to be better informed, and yet defensive in the face of the careless superiority of Harvard philosophy graduates who seem to have the key to the knowledge she covets. Even Buckle, who claimed to love her, criticised her for her thoughtless, irresponsible attitude to life before he left for the front, something she could not forget. She will write for support to Ellen Thayer (another cousin of Scofield's, who in March 1925 came to work on *The Dial* as Assistant Editor), says Vivien; Ellen thinks Vivien is *"very clever,"* she tells Scofield defiantly. "If you don't believe me, ask her."

Ellen Thayer had said, before their acquaintance, that she wished

Scofield and Vivien knew each other. However, after his last visit to town Vivien is inclined to doubt whether this is a point in her favour. Scofield was scolded for trying to "work her in" as well as a visit to his tailor and aunt, and still catch the 5:30 train back to Oxford. "You must remember I am English and not accustomed to being pushed about in a hurry," she informs him. Sitting at tea with a distraught American holding his watch in his hand and giving her so many minutes in which to eat her tea and so many in which to say what she has to say, unnerves her, and causes her to relapse into one of those "awful silences" which are the terror of her American acquaintances.

Yet despite her complaints about American habits, Vivien's closest friends after Buckle's departure were American: Lucy, Scofield, and his circle. "You do seem to have a lot of friends, which is one good point about you," she informs Scofield, only half-jokingly. She liked their self-assured manners and expensive clothes, remarking à propos of Scofield's friend Parr, whom she disliked because he was too "posy (and prosy)," that she did *hate* people who had no pose, though too much of it made them unreal and nauseating. Scofield responded to Vivien's flirtatious overtures, and by 3 March 1915 he was complimenting her on "the radiancy of her countenance," and comparing her flatteringly to the *Mona Lisa*.[41] "No, Scofield, you have never seen me 'divine' or 'exquisite' yet. But I hope you may some day," replied Vivien, who was in bed with "prosaic, recurring influenza" and not looking robust, merely "interesting . . . It is nice of you to compare me to the Mona Lisa. I wish she and I had anyhow one point in common, and that is that someone would cut me out of my frame too."[42]

Vivien's weakness for good dressing continued to make her susceptible to the charms of men in uniform. That spring (1915) she was badgering her brother to introduce her to an officer called Butler-Thuring: Maurice was going to "overcome his prejudice against opening his lips, and speak to Mr. B-T," she confided excitedly to Scofield. In March she was invited to dance at the Savoy with a Captain Holmes. But by this time Scofield had also introduced her to another friend from Milton Academy and Harvard days: Thomas Stearns Eliot, whose tall, dark good looks and languid poise were guaranteed to appeal to the eager, restless Vivien, disappointed in love and looking for a new boyfriend.

3

An Alien in America

Four months after Vivienne was born in humble circumstances in Bury, another baby was born to an older, wealthier mother in the booming city of St. Louis, Missouri, on the other side of the Atlantic. Thomas Stearns Eliot was the seventh child of his forty-five-year-old mother, Charlotte, who had assumed her child-bearing days were at an end. Nevertheless, a new son was welcome, for Charlotte's family was predominantly female: her daughters Ada, Margaret, Charlotte and Marian preceded Thomas, as well as her first son, Henry, eight years older than his little brother. "Lallie and little Thomas are well," read the telegram from the proud father, brick manufacturer Henry Ware Eliot Sr., to his brother, Pastor Thomas Lamb Eliot of Portland, Oregon, announcing the birth of the new baby on 26 September 1888. In a letter written the same day, Eliot *père* added: "Young Thomas Stearns (for his grandfather) came forth at 742 hrs am."[1] The birth must have seemed like a miracle to Charlotte Champe Eliot, a deeply religious woman who had lost another daughter, Theodora, in 1886, and Tom soon became her favourite.

At first the baby seemed healthy enough, but Charlotte's protective instincts were quickly aroused when it was found that he had a congenital double hernia, which she was afraid might rupture at any moment. As a result Tom had to wear a truss from boyhood. As late as 1905, when he was sixteen, she was writing to his prospective headmaster at Milton Academy, Massachusetts, a preparatory school for Harvard University: "Tom has never fully realised until now, when he is almost the only fellow debarred from football, his physical limitations. We hope in a few years he will be entirely normal . . ."[2] Her nervousness at allowing Tom independence was intensified by being an older parent, and he was rarely allowed out of the sight of the women who cared for him. Ada, the eldest sister, nineteen years older than he, became a second mother to the little boy who was so much younger than his brother and sisters that he had to play alone. Even when he was given sailing lessons at the family's summer house at East Gloucester, Massachusetts, mother came too.

Nevertheless Charlotte was not involved in the day-to-day upbringing of her children, preferring to immerse herself in social reform and campaigning for social justice for young offenders. "Well, she wasn't particularly interested in babies, that's the fact of it, and I don't think she petted her daughters at all," remembered Tom's cousin, Eleanor Hinkley. "But I think they were well taken care of—there was a nurse." Tom was a bright and bookish boy, who seemed not to resent his lack of playmates: "He could sit all day long in his little rocking chair, and he'd read anything; she never supervised his reading."[3]

Tom's nursemaid was an Irish Catholic girl, Annie Dunne, whom he accompanied to the Catholic Church on the corner of 2635 Locust Street where the family lived. Later Tom remembered Annie taking him behind a screen and talking about the existence of God. It was his first introduction to the comforting rituals and doctrines of Catholicism, and was to leave a lasting impression upon him, associated as the Holy Roman Church was with Annie, who was, in some senses, his "real" mother; Annie provided the warmth lacking from his preoccupied, rigidly Puritan mother and his deaf father, who found communication difficult and spent his leisure playing chess alone or drawing cats. Later Eliot recalled that both his parents, being so much older, were like "ancestors to him."[4] And so the Catholic Church became "Mother Church," while the cool creed of Unitarianism, to which his parents adhered, offered only a set of moral injunctions.

Unitarianism, exemplified in the life and example of Tom's paternal grandfather, the Rev. William Greenleaf Eliot, known as "the Saint of the West," dominated the Eliot household, and was responsible for the transplantation of this cultured New England family to a corner of the raw Midwest. William Greenleaf Eliot, a Unitarian minister who had left Harvard Divinity School in 1831 to found the Unitarian Church in St. Louis, had died in 1887—the year before Tom was born—but his presence was as vivid to the small boy as if he still lived. "I was brought up as a child to be very much aware of him," said Tom. "So much so, that as a child I thought of him as still the head of the family." The standard of conduct the children adhered to was that which their grandfather had set; and moral judgements, decisions between duty and self-indulgence, were taken "as if, like Moses, he had brought down the tables of the Law, any deviation from which would be sinful." Plain living was the order of the day: "I grew up," said Eliot, "in a family in which to buy candy for oneself was considered selfish indulgence."[5]

Henry Ware Eliot Sr. had not felt the call to follow his father into the church, complaining that "too much pudding choked the dog," and went into business instead, working his way up from clerk to become President of the Hydraulic-Press Brick Company. It was Charlotte whose personality responded to that of her father-in-law, and she began writing his biography. Her own Stearns ancestors had been preachers and theologians who lived by the "Good Book," and her mother, Charlotte Blood, was descended from General Thomas Blood.[6] On his father's side, young Thomas inherited the judgemental certainties of the Salem witch-finders. His ancestor, Andrew Eliot, had emigrated to New England in about 1668, and served on the same witch-trial as Nathaniel Hawthorne's great-grandfather; as Eliot later told Ezra Pound: "I just naturally smell out witches."[7]

His paternal grandfather's educational legacy also shaped Eliot's early life. Not only had William Greenleaf Eliot founded Washington University at St. Louis, but a preparatory school, Smith Academy, to which Tom was sent. And it was loyalty to Grandmother Eliot after her husband's death which kept the family in the "old Eliot place" on Locust Street, a substantial house around the corner from old Mrs. Eliot at 2660 Washington Avenue, as it gradually became a slum area from which other families of their social class fled to the west of the city. Henry Ware Eliot refused to sell up, and it was in the nearby commercial centre that Thomas first saw the name "Prufrock," over a furniture wholesalers;[8] but, as the neighbourhood went downhill, Tom's mother discouraged him from playing with local children. Instead, she talked to him "as I would with a man."[9]

A less introverted child might have made friends with the local boys, but Tom's own nature, and a mother who ensured that he was invariably dressed formally in a sailor suit, and was reprimanded for using the expression "OK," made him conscious of the gulf between himself and boys of a lower social standing, even at his private dancing school, "Mr. Mahler's Select Academy for the jeunesse dorée of St. Louis," as he later described it to his friend John Hayward: "How I dreaded those afternoons, and my shyness, and being chivvied about by my most loathed enemy, Atreus Hagadine von Schrader Jr." Nor did Tom much like the girls, "Effie Bagnall whose family were considered distinctly nouveaux riches," or the reigning beauty of the dancing school, Edwine Thornburgh herself, who subsequently became Lady Peek of Peek Frean & Co. Ltd. It was odd, re-marked Eliot, that Edwine's most assiduous admirer was Lewis Dozier Jr., "the small but pert and self-assured son of a biscuit manufacturer—I think his father made his fortune out of Uneeda Biscuit, which, as you must know, is a kind of cracker. Well, it seems Edwine got on by sticking to bis-cuits." Another youth Eliot disliked was Gerard Lambert, whose family made a fortune through the manufacture of Listerine; unlike Eliot, Lambert was good at mathematics and athletics.

Outside the dancing academy, Tom's childhood acquaintances at Smith Academy were, he later told John Hayward, more "mixed in origin than any of your playmates, I'm sure." There was Butch Wagner, Pat Sullivan, Snowball Wolfpert, Elephant-mouth Hellman, Gander Giesecke . . . "What has become of them?" But Tom congratulated himself that these early school days had not "corrupted my good manners," and once he arrived at Milton Academy, the society was "more select," being supposedly limited to scions of the best Unitarian families of Massachusetts, whose names, Dago Parker (who became Churchwarden of King's Chapel, Boston), Chicken Gilbert, and Doodle Page (son of an ambassador), he never forgot. Despite spending the first sixteen years of his life in St. Louis, Eliot became conscious at an early age that he sprang from that distinguished clan of Eliots who numbered themselves among the "best" Brahmin Boston families of New England.

In other ways, growing up in the American "South West, which was, in my own time, rapidly becoming the Middle West," as Eliot wrote in 1928, left its mark on him.[10] One of his strongest associations, he wrote, was that of the smell of grapes which greeted him on returning in the autumn to their house in St. Louis, after the summer at The Downs, the house his father had built at Eastern Point, Gloucester.[11] Another lasting memory was of the great Mississippi River in flood, a sight he was taken to by his nurse Annie as a treat. Like Krishna, the river was "a strong brown god"—both destroyer and preserver, thought Eliot, as he stared at the sullen, untamed Mississippi "with its cargo of dead Negroes, cows and chicken coops."[12] At night the sound of the St. Louis blues, carried on the warm night air through open windows, wove its way into his dreams. "Lincoln Snow, Negro Jazz Drummer" in *Sweeney Agonistes* comes from his childhood; there are curled snapshots of "Stephen" and other black servants, one of whom used to hold his foot in front of the fire until the small boy hopped up and down with alarm.

From his earliest years Eliot lived in an interior world. A friend of his brother Henry remembered Eliot "folded in a chair in the family library reading 'heavy stuff.'" He was a "tattle-tale, stingy (who wouldn't lend money); when a phone call came for Henry he would leave the receiver off the hook and go back to his reading without bothering to find Henry. But Henry, who was a regular guy ... was very fond and protective of his kid brother."[13] Tom's reading paid off and at Smith Academy he won the Latin prize in his last year. His mother was delighted to see him excel at school, as she herself had done, but it was not easy to escape her control or her anger, for Charlotte was a frustrated woman who had not been allowed to go on to university despite her intellectual gifts. "I should so have loved a college course," she confessed to her son, "but was obliged to teach before I was nineteen. I graduated with high rank, 'a young lady of unusual brilliancy as a scholar' my old yellow testimonial says, but when I was set to teaching young children ... I made a dead failure."[14]

Nor had marriage to Henry Ware Eliot brought Charlotte the intellectual companionship she craved. In his autobiography Eliot Sr. called himself a "Simpleton," and, handicapped by deafness as a result of scarlet fever, an affliction shared by his son Henry, he became a remote husband and father who left the upbringing of his youngest son to his wife.[15] Tom was forced to fill the emotional vacuum in the life of his mother, a woman whose personal characteristics were described as "sincere conscientiousness and great reserve."[16] The burden of Charlotte's thwarted aspirations lay heavily upon him, for although she taught unhappily at the Normal School in St. Louis, and sometimes substituted at the Mary Institute, a girls' school also founded by William Greenleaf Eliot, next door to the Eliot house, it was into religious poetry that she poured her heart.

But her verses, although employing many of the powerful themes of sacrifice and martyrdom which strongly influenced her son, met with little success. The journals to which she submitted her work invariably rejected them, and she was published only in religious journals of a Unitarian or religious complexion to whose editors her married name opened the door: *The Unitarian, The Christian Register, Our Best Words.*[17] Charlotte became increasingly embittered. She began to channel all her hopes and dreams through her talented son Thomas, writing: "I hope your literary work will receive early the recognition I strove for and failed." As her sense of failure grew, so did the fervour of her poetry in its exhortations to reject this sinful world and turn to God: "Loose the spirit from its mesh/From the poor vesture of the flesh," she commands the reader. Poem after poem hammered home the message of the saints, the examples of St. John the Baptist, St. Francis, or Savonarola, that it is better by far to endure the privations of the desert, or burn at the stake, than to enjoy secular pleasures.[18]

The prohibition upon pleasure was a lesson Eliot learnt young, and he said that it left him "permanently scarred."[19] Sex was equated with sin, his father in this instance joining with his mother to reinforce the lesson of the "nastiness" of sexual intercourse. Syphilis, said Tom's father, was God's punishment for sin, and he hoped that no cure would be found for it; otherwise he believed it might be necessary "to emasculate our children to keep them clean." Sex instruction for children meant "giving them a letter of introduction to the Devil."[20] Such opinions left a deep and lasting impression upon his son, who never forgot the lesson that the sexual act was unclean, often linking in his poetry "The coupling of man and woman/And that of beasts." Such couplings, wrote Eliot in "East Coker," come in the end to "dung and death."[21]

One childhood incident at the age of five or six affected him deeply. Tom was in the habit of playing in the schoolyard of the Mary Institute next door. There was a high brick wall which concealed the Eliots' back garden from the schoolyard. "There was a door in this wall and there was a key to this door," said Eliot sixty years later, recalling how the habits of voyeurism were learnt young. Over the wall he could hear the girls playing and laughing together; it was a forbidden world which the solitary boy longed to join, but from which he was shut out. Not until the girls had gone home did he dare unlock the door and enter the empty yard, some-times even exploring the deserted corridors of the school. A photograph shows young Tom in his sailor suit, standing alone in the schoolyard. One day, however, he miscalculated and unlocked the door too early. The girls saw him, but they did not invite him to join them; instead, they laughed mockingly and Tom "took flight at once."[22]

The theme of children's mocking laughter was to occur over and over again in Eliot's poetry: "The hidden laughter/Of children in the foliage," in "Burnt Norton" is but one example. The girls attracted Tom, but jeered at him, found him ridiculous and rejected him. It was a paradigm for many future encounters with women from which he was to flee. Another early memory of great significance for Eliot was his "first love affair at (as nearly as I can compute from confirmatory evidence) the age of five, with a young lady of three, at a seaside hotel. Her name was Dorothy; that is all I know . . ." Eliot "pined a bit" after he and Dorothy separated in the au-tumn.[23] That memory, he told John Hayward, was his preparation for reading the *Vita Nuova,* and it was one which led him to compare himself to Dante in his first sighting of Beatrice. In his essay on Dante, Eliot re-marked that: "The type of sexual experience which Dante describes as oc-curring to him at the age of nine years is by no means impossible or unique. My only doubt (in which I found myself confirmed by a distinguished psy-chologist) is whether it could have taken place so *late* in life as the age of nine years." The psychologist agreed with Eliot that it was more likely to have occurred at about five or six years of age. Emphasising that the *Vita Nuova* could only have been written based on a personal experience as, by inference, his own poetry also was, Eliot wrote, "I cannot find it incredible that what has happened to others should have happened to Dante with much greater intensity."[24]

"I was seven, she was littler," Eliot writes in French in the published version of "Dans le Restaurant," in which he describes an encounter with a small girl. "She got soaked, I picked primroses for her . . . I tickled her to make her laugh/I felt such power for a moment, such rapture."[25] An ear-lier English version which Eliot sent to Ezra Pound is more explicit than the sanitized French: "Down in a ditch under the willow tree,/There you go to get out of the rain/I tried in vain,/I mean I was interrupted/She was all wet with the deluge and her calico skirt/Stuck to her buttocks and belley [sic],/I put my hand up and giggled . . . That one can do at the age of eight,/I was younger." It was a "big poodle" which interrupted Eliot; the dog came "sniffing about" and scared him "pealess."²⁶ In the *dédoublement* of experience which Eliot learnt from the Symbolists, he is both protagonist and the observing waiter in this poem ("You crapulous vapulous relic . . . to have had an experience/So nearly parallel, with . . . /Go away,/I was about to say mine"). In this screen memory, rapture is mingled with frustration and rejection. Eliot remembered that he expressed his feeling of love for Dorothy by "bullying, teasing, and making her fetch and carry."²⁷ Underneath the surface of the "priggish little boy" Tom knew he had become, lay strong emotions.

Lyndall Gordon, Eliot's biographer, claims that he "accepted his mother's domination in good humour," but there is evidence that this was not so.²⁸ In "Animula" he is a perplexed and protesting child, who offends each day, and finds himself surrounded by fierce imperatives, the "may's and may not's" of control. The unhappy boy flees the mother he cannot appease: "The pain of living and the drug of dreams/Curl up the small soul in the window seat/Behind the *Encyclopaedia Britannica.*"²⁹ Resentful of a mother who lived only through her son, Eliot immortalised Charlotte as "Amy" in his most autobiographical play, *The Family Reunion.* Wishwood, the family house, is a "cold place," where nothing is allowed to change. "Were you ever happy here, as a child, at Wishwood?" Harry, Eliot's persona, is asked. "Not really," replies Harry, remembering that his unhappiness was viewed as naughtiness. His one memory of freedom is the hollow tree in the wilderness beside the river, and even this Charlotte/Amy destroys: "The wilderness was gone,/The tree had been felled." In its place a neat summer-house had been erected "to please the children."

The core revelation of the play is that Harry's father once wanted to kill his mother, the central character in *The Family Reunion.* Amy is seen as the root of Harry's neurosis. It is very possible that this was the interpretation Eliot later put on his own childhood, and that he believed that it was his dominating mother who crippled him in his later relationships with women.³⁰ Certainly Eliot's feeling for his mother was deeply ambivalent, love mixed with a fear which was replicated in the alarm, physical revulsion and violent misogyny which women were to engender in him.³¹ His brother Henry, by contrast, an unexceptional boy of quite different temperament and ability, shielded from Charlotte's possessiveness by sisters close in age, experienced no such difficulties.

Tom possibly exhibited some of the tendencies of obsessive-compulsive disorder from which, argued American writer Randall Jarrell, he suffered as a result of his upbringing, when he entered Harvard University from Milton Academy in 1906: fastidious cleanliness, secrecy, the desire for order, control and repetition as a defence against anxiety.[32] He was deeply inhibited and, on his own admission, extremely shy with girls.[33] His fellow student and friend at Harvard, Conrad Aiken, noticed him as "a singularly attractive, tall and rather dapper young man, with a somewhat Lamian smile."[34] Others called him a Buddha, for although his distant cousin Charles William Eliot was at that time President of Harvard, and he was a member of a distinguished New England family, Boston society presented an ordeal to a nervous Prufrock:

> In the room the women come and go
> Talking of Michelangelo.

Eliot's only thought was "Do I dare?" as he hesitated at the threshold. "Time to turn back and descend the stair."[35] Nevertheless, he dutifully joined university societies, took dancing, skating and boxing lessons, and worked on his accent.

As Eliot later explained to his confessor, the Rev. William Force Stead, "I was a nomad, even in America." His "real ancestral home" was Massachusetts, but his branch of the family had been settled in St. Louis for two generations, and although he was proud to be "a descendant of pioneers," the family jealously guarded its connections with New England.[36] The result was, "I was enough of a Southerner to be something of an alien in Massachusetts."[37] He was embarrassed by the divided existence he had led between Massachusetts and St. Louis, and one of his first tasks when he "came East" at seventeen to Milton Academy was to eradicate the southern drawl which he felt marred his speech, and to develop a "correct" accent acceptable to the young blades from the best Boston families with whom he was mixing. Nevertheless, he was conscious that on going to school in New England, "I lost my southern accent without ever acquiring the accent of the native Bostonians." Later he expressed to the poet Herbert Read his confused and bitter memory of how it felt to be "an American who wasn't an American, because he was born in the South and went to school in New England as a small boy with a nigger drawl, but who wasn't a southerner in the South because his people were northerners in a border state and looked down on all southerners and Virginians, and who so was never anything anywhere and who therefore felt himself to be more a Frenchman than an American and more an Englishman than a Frenchman and yet felt that the USA up to a hundred years ago was a family extension."[38]

Although there had been dislocation in Tom's youth, it did not trouble his brother and sisters to such an extent; the ready acceptance of his cousins, such as Eleanor Hinkley, with whom he played on the beach at East Gloucester during the family's three-month summer holidays, the sailing lessons arranged by his mother with an elderly mariner, the excursions in his brother's catboat *Elsa* in the waters off Cape Ann, should have smoothed the path to Harvard. Yet Eliot remained aloof and silent. In New England he missed the long, dark river, the ailanthus trees, and the flaming cardinal birds; in Missouri he missed the fir trees, the bay and goldenrod, the song sparrows, the red granite and blue sea of Massachusetts, comparing his own childhood, with a grandmother who shot her own wild turkeys for dinner, to that of a schoolfriend whose family had lived in the same house in the same New England seaport for two hundred and fifty years.

At Harvard Eliot chose to take courses considered conservative and relatively unpopular, Greek and Latin texts at first, inspired by his tutor, the fiery Irving Babbitt, whose defence of "Classicism" struck a chord with his student; he steeped himself in Dante, puzzling out *The Divine Comedy* with the help of a prose translation before he had any grasp of Italian. And then by chance he picked from the library shelves Arthur Symons's *The Symbolist Movement in Literature,* a book which introduced Eliot to the poetry of Jules Laforgue. Eliot felt an immediate sense of identification with the French poet, whose "bittersweet dandyism" spoke to him. Eliot was just twenty, and he said later that reading Laforgue "affected the course of my life." In the Symbolist poet he found not only an ironic, self-deprecating voice which reflected his inner feelings, but the use of idiomatic, everyday speech in poetry rather than the high rhetoric of the late

Romantics. Instantly Eliot abandoned the mannered, *fin-de-siècle* verses based on Tennyson and Swinburne which he had been publishing in the *Harvard Advocate,* and began to try something new.

Laforgue's most enduring image is that of Pierrot, the comic figure who hides his sadness behind a mask, and Eliot's first attempt at a pastiche of Laforgue, "Conversation Galante" (1909), was based on Laforgue's "Autres Complaintes de Lord Pierrot."[39] Masks offered Eliot the protection his sensitive spirit needed, and Pierrot promised the mask of the dandy by which the poet might distance himself from his fellow human beings. Laforgue had made a habit of dressing formally, in top hat, dark tie, English jacket, clerical overcoat, and carried his rolled umbrella over his arm. By January 1910 Eliot had completed his own transformation, expressed in his poem "Spleen," in which, "Life, a little bald and grey,/Languid, fastidious and bland,/Waits, hat and gloves in hand ... On the doorstep of the Absolute."[40] It had not been a difficult task, as Conrad Aiken recalled that from his first days at Harvard, Eliot carried himself "with enviable grace."

The Laforguean disguise fitted so well because Eliot did more than study the dead poet as a model: he felt an immediate sense of psychic recognition. In *The Egoist* he wrote later about "a feeling of profound kinship, or rather of peculiar personal intimacy, with another, probably dead author ... Like personal intimacies in life, it may and probably will pass, but it will be ineffaceable."[41] The young poet studied Symons for descriptions of Laforgue's personality as well as his dress. Laforgue practised, wrote Symons,

> An inflexible politeness towards man, woman and destiny. He composes love-poems hat in hand, and smiles with exasperating tolerance before all the transformations of the eternal feminine. He is very conscious of death, but his *blague* of death is, above all things, gentlemanly. He will not permit, at any moment, the luxury of dropping the mask: not at any moment.[42]

There were elements in Laforgue's life which caused Eliot to feel that the French poet's soul had passed into his own. Laforgue had died four days before his twenty-seventh birthday in 1887, the year Eliot was conceived.

This sense of synchronicity affected Eliot deeply; years later he would choose to be married for the second time in the same London church in which Laforgue had married.[43]

The balanced, chill, colloquial style of Laforgue with its "icy ecstasy" enabled Eliot to discard the pretentiousness of late Georgian poetry, and to reinvent himself. Laforgue led to Verlaine, whose translucency also attracted Eliot. Already well-read in Shakespeare, he discovered the late-sixteenth-century dramatists Marlowe, Kyd, Webster and Tourneur, writing: "The form in which I began to write, in 1908 or 1909, was directly drawn from the study of Laforgue together with the later Elizabethan drama; and I do not know anyone else who started from exactly that point." It was this cross-fertilisation of ideas from other languages and periods which was to revolutionise his poetry.

A second but equally significant effect of Eliot's sense that he was the reincarnated soul of Laforgue was to impel him to follow the course of the poet's life. Laforgue, born, like Eliot, outside France, in his case in Uruguay, had gone as a young man to Paris, and Eliot was determined to follow in his footsteps. The French capital was a mecca for artists and writers, and Eliot was attracted by the idea of "scraping along" there, and writing in French. His mother, however, was opposed to the idea: "I can not bear to think of your being alone in Paris, the very words give me a chill. English speaking countries seem so different from foreign. I do not admire the French nation, and have less confidence in individuals of that race than in English."[44]

This time, Tom was not prepared to accept his mother's decision without a fight. His rebellion had been germinating under the influence of Laforgue, and his scorn for Unitarianism found expression in a new poem, "Mr. Eliot's Sunday Morning Service," which satirised his uncle, Christopher Rhodes Eliot, a Unitarian minister, and his congregation filing into their pews like "religious caterpillars" along "the avenue of penitence," where "The young are red and pustular/Clutching piaculative pence."[45] Now the genteel aunts and cousins who had welcomed Tom into their houses at Cambridge were also made the subject of savage satire in "Cousin Nancy" and "Miss Helen Slingsby." Boston society was described as "a society quite uncivilised, but refined beyond the point of civilisation." Beneath his own refinement—for Eliot was always influenced by the standards of the society for which he professed disdain—lay barely contained hostility towards the hostesses who entertained him to tea.

In the *Harvard Advocate* Eliot spelt out these feelings in a series of poems between May 1907 and January 1909. Women humiliate, emasculate and disappoint men. "Circe's Palace" comes straight from Eliot's unconscious and is the product of the split vision which led him to see women as either saint or sinner, Madonna or whore.[46] Although such stereotypes are common in Western literature, Eliot's images have an intensity and violence which point to their childhood origins: although calm and compliant on the surface, beneath his painfully constructed "false self," he knew rage.[47] The dream sequence of "Circe's Palace," written when Eliot was twenty, represents in Freudian imagery his fears of women as he experienced them at Harvard: creatures who threatened him with impotence, engulfment and annihilation. Around Circe's fountain, which flows with "the voice of men in pain," are "flowers that no man knows." Their petals are "fanged and red/With hideous streak and stain." In the "forest" below, "along the garden stairs/The sluggish python lies."[48] The poem, writes critic George Whiteside, describes "a frightening hilltop fountain with a sinister garden around it, and a thick forest below—which in archetypal Freudian dream symbolism is obviously a mons veneris. Indeed one climbs to this mons on stairs 'along' which a phallic snake lies! The scene . . . clearly shows Eliot's fear of female sexuality."[49]

Eliot used myth to disguise fears he dared not face, but his flower metaphor works on different levels: "The flower's petals recall the women's lips, inviting but masking fangs . . . ; finally the petals suggest the lips of the vagina, whose stain reveals a revulsion not only from women, but from intercourse," writes American critic John T. Mayer. "We shall not come here again," is the poet's damning verdict.[50] In the next stanza the phallic python lies "sluggish"; the hidden message of the poem is that "sexual woman threatens man with a fundamental loss of maleness, of potency transformed and rendered impotent."[51] At first a panther, strong and "rising," man is transformed into a coiled and lazy python, and finally a showy and effeminate peacock, whose "eyes," an obsessional image for Eliot, appear here on the peacock's tails, watching the poet, as the little girls' eyes watched and judged him in the schoolyard. Eliot's grandfather had magnificent eyes that read one's innermost thoughts, according to his son. "One feels rebuked in his presence . . . How can one be familiar with the Day of Judgement? asked one of William Greenleaf Eliot's classmates."[52] Charlotte's eyes were equally penetrating.

Tom's urge to escape became all-consuming. Frustrated by the neat, white picket fences, the well-swept streets, the ordered rituals of Cambridge, with its tea parties and amateur dramatics, he persisted in his demands to go to Europe. Even sailing in the grey waters off Cape Ann only tempted him with the promise of freedom over the horizon. As his mother prevaricated, he collapsed with an undiagnosed illness. Charlotte hurried from St. Louis to nurse him, and finally gave in. Tom would have his way. Captain "Colombo," as Tom thought of himself in the ribald rhymes he was writing, might cross the Atlantic and begin his conquest of the Old World.[53]

Free at last from the shackles of family, Tom Eliot arrived in Paris in the autumn of 1910 to attend the Sorbonne, and found a room on the *rive gauche*. Settling into the pension at 9, rue de l'Université, his expectations were high; André Gide had founded the *Nouvelle Revue Française* only the year before, and as Eliot hurried out to buy the new review in its grey paper cover, he met Jacques Rivière, who was later to become its editor. He took lessons in French conversation from Rivière's brother-in-law, novelist Alain-Fournier, who introduced him to the works of Dostoevsky. He listened to the anti-democratic speeches of Charles Maurras, and met up occasionally for a *sirop de fraises* with Conrad Aiken, his old Harvard friend who was also in Paris. But none of these acquaintances, either old or new, wholly absorbed his thoughts.

Instead it was the vibrant life of the Parisian streets which cast its spell over him. Urban squalor was already familiar to Eliot, for his earliest memories were of the seedy poverty of St. Louis, and in New England he had penetrated beyond the privileged precincts of Harvard Yard to walk the slums of Roxbury in North Cambridge; two of his early poems had experimented with images of street pianos, dirty windows, broken glass, wailing children and tattered sparrows pecking in the gutter.[54] But now a new layer of experience was superimposed upon American decay: the squalor of Montparnasse, which became for Eliot a symbol of Paris.[55]

Ten years earlier, Charles-Louis Philippe's little-known novel *Bubu de Montparnasse*[56] had been published. The *quartier* had changed little in the intervening decade, nor had the trade for which it was infamous. *Bubu,* the story of a pimp and the prostitutes he controlled, opened Eliot's eyes to the life of the underworld. Repelled yet fascinated, he took to walking the streets at night, shadowing the women as they bargained with clients, darting into back alleyways when he was in danger of being seen. In his imagination he entered into the life of the young prostitute, the "pauvre petite putain," who flashed him a smile as she went about her work, and the business of the streets "où l'on vend son âme pendant que l'on vend sa chair."*[57]

In "Rhapsody on a Windy Night"[58] Eliot tells how every street light seems to beat like a drum in his head as he paces the streets: a fatalistic drum controlling him. Drums become a recurrent image in his poetry: elsewhere he writes of the "drums of life" which "were beating on their skulls/the floods of life . . . swaying in their brains."[59] The drumbeat of the streets impels him towards connection with people rather than the mandarin-like detachment he has so assiduously cultivated.[60] At half past one in the morning he imagines the street light is speaking to him: "Regard that woman/Who hesitates toward you in the light of the door/Which opens on her like a grin." For a moment he is tempted. But as he looks again he sees the corner of her dress is torn and stained, the corner of her eye is twisted like a crooked pin. Instead he passes on, past the scavenging cats, the nocturnal smells of chestnuts in the streets, and female smells in shuttered rooms. Sometimes he peers through lighted shutters at the people within, experiencing vicariously the warmth and companionship from which he is shut out. Finally, it is four in the morning, and he finds his front door, fumbles for the key, and mounts the stairs to his unmade bed and toothbrush hanging on the wall.

Eliot was lonely; it is the sense of his loneliness, as much as the scent of the working women, that rises from the pages of his poetry written in the first months in Paris. Uprooted from the familiar sights and sounds of New

*where one sells one's soul as one sells one's flesh.

England, the certainties of family and university life, the young American felt as much of a misfit, as much of an outcast, as he had done during his adolescence lived on the cusp of Missouri and Massachusetts. The intense sensitivity which caused him to feel deep embarrassment at an accent which seemed to fit him perfectly for nowhere—although to other relatives, speaking like a Bostonian in Missouri or a Midwesterner in Boston was simply an occasion for laughter—was intensified in Paris.[61] Added to it were the sexual urges which he found harder and harder to ignore.

The women of the streets seemed to promise an antidote to depression and loneliness. In "Prufrock's Pervigilium,"[62] an unpublished section cut from the "The Love Song of J. Alfred Prufrock," where "lonely men in shirtsleeves" smoke their pipes and lean out of windows, it is the women, spilling out of their corsets as they stand at the entrances to their flats, who symbolise a motherly rather than a seductive bosom, the female company to which Eliot had been so accustomed in childhood; the oil-cloth curls up the stairs and the gas-jet flickers, inviting him in. Did Eliot finally mount the stairs and take his chance with one of the prostitutes, or did he remain the irresolute voyeur as portrayed in "Prufrock"?

Perhaps the answer is to be found in the pages of the new notebook the young poet bought in 1909, a year before leaving for Paris. This notebook, with its stiff marbled brown cover, came from a bookstore in East Gloucester and cost only 25 cents, but it signalled a radical shift in Eliot's poetry. In a fine spidery hand, Eliot printed in black the title "Inventions of the March Hare."[63]

It was a title full of significance, for the "madness" of the March Hare in *Alice in Wonderland* expressed something of Eliot's feelings at the time, on his own admission. Images of *Alice* occur in his poetry, for example, the white rabbit hopping "around the corner,"[64] and the perennial tea parties. In *Alice,* it is the White Knight who claims, "It's my own invention," but Eliot's choice of title suggests that his inventions are peculiar to the March Hare, who in March is "raving mad." During the breeding season, hares are "unusually wild," says the *OED,* and the obvious sexual excitement of the twenty-two-year-old poet found expression in a series of obscene verses, relating the exploits of King Bolo and Colombo, a sea-captain in charge of a band of merry men, who has crossed the Atlantic to discover a new world as Eliot (and Christopher Columbus) did.[65]

Christopher Ricks, editor of *T. S. Eliot: Inventions of the March Hare—Poems 1909–1917,* suggests that Eliot may have been thinking of Rémy de Gourmont when he chose his title, with its implications of the madness of sexual desire. Of hares in heat, Rémy de Gourmont wrote: "Ce sont des animaux fort bien outillés pour l'amour, pénis très développé ... les mâles font de véritables voyages, courent des nuits entières, à la recherche des hases...."* [66] It was at about this time that Eliot composed "The Jolly Tinker," relating the adventures of the tinker who had "come across the sea/With his four and twenty inches hanging to his knee." In the second stanza the tinker is "in heat/With his eight and forty inches hanging to his feet." Finally, with "his whanger in his hand" the tinker walks through the hall. " 'By God,' said the Cook, 'He's a gone and fucked us all.' " [67]

In Eliot's verse, Colombo cries, on board ship: "I feel like frigging," before chasing the chaplain around the deck and "up among the rigging." Since the chaplain, "that good old man," had no one to protect him, Colombo grasped him "by the balls and buggered him up the rectum." In another unpublished "ithyphallique" verse Eliot sent to his confidant, Ezra Pound, Colombo comes aboard with a bunch of big bananas, takes the chaplain by the drawers and shoves "one up his anus." [68] Nor is King Bolo's big black queen safe from Colombo's attentions: when the queen calls Colombo a "dirty Spanish loafer," he terminates the affair "by fucking her on the sofa." Even animals are in danger from the captain; when the wind drops and there's no sailing to be done, the Captain suggests fucking a tortoise. "The beast was caught, the beast was fucked" and the merry men set up a cheer for their captain, "bold Colombo."

Phallic and scatological details sprinkle the verse. Feeling "rooty" after three weeks at sea, Colombo "took his cock in both his hands/And swore it was a beauty." Of Colombo's favourite, the cabin boy Orlando, or Orlandino, "whose language was obscene-o," we learn "his prick was 13 inches long/And wound around with marlin," while his role was of "backhouse darling." "Fry my balls!" exclaims Colombo, when he is feeling strong, ordering one of the crew to quickly go and fetch "my cabin boy Orlando." When full of rum, however, Colombo's role is a passive one:

---

*They are animals very well equipped for love, with a very large penis ... the males travel great distances, running all night in search of females.

after Sunday morning prayers, surrounded by the masturbating crew, he falls down in a stupor and turns "his asshole SSW."[69]

Eliot's poem "The Triumph of Bullshit," probably written in November 1910, gave rise to the earliest recorded instance of the word in the *OED*.[70] Written in pencil, like many of the verses on the eight or nine pages and half pages preserved from the Notebook, in the spiky hand Eliot developed during his year abroad which differed markedly from his earlier (and later) handwriting, it is an indication of the sudden release of feelings long repressed. Like his constipated hero (Colombo was constipated for forty days and forty nights at sea, praying to the Virgin for "a hundred shits a-piece from 100,000 assholes"),[71] the poet takes his revenge on the "ladies" who laugh at him, who consider his merits are "unmale . . . etiolated . . . crotchety, constipated, impotent galamatias," who find his attentions are ridiculous, his manner gauche, and that he is altogether as dull as an unbaked *brioche*. "For Christ's sake stick it up your ass," he commands.[72] At the queen's banquet Colombo "hoisted up his ass/And shat upon the table." The repetitive references to defecation reveal the fantasies of the anal character who, beneath the polished and exquisite exterior, longs to display the contents of the "shithouse" and to revenge himself upon the women who humiliate him, such as the "great big whore with bloodshot eyes" who "bitched him with a pisspot."[73] In his tinker rhyme, Eliot imagines the tinker's "john" mutilating the woman who falls in love with him and, in a reversal of the usual arrangement, offers half a dollar for sex: "he ripped up my belly from my cunt to my navel."[74]

Pound was full of enthusiasm for his friend's verses (he ticked the description of the crew—"the rest were jews and niggers") and responded in similar vein:

Sweet Christ in hell, spew out some Rabelais
To belch and fahrt and to define the day
In fitting manner and her monument
Heap up for her in fadeless excrement.[75]

The bawdy, lecherous sea-captain of these long-hidden verses of Eliot's presents a vivid contrast to the Prufrock who asks "Do I dare?" and "Do I dare/Disturb the universe?" (a question lifted directly from

Laforgue). This persona represents the dark, secret side of Eliot; he himself referred to the Jekyll and Hyde sides of his personality,[76] with the alter ego of "Captain Eliot" representing the secret life of Mr. Hyde, who dared to live differently from the repressed Dr. Jekyll, who was Eliot's public face. "Captain Eliot" was to be a persona to which Eliot clung tenaciously and acted out in fact as well as fantasy.[77]

Hugh Kenner has called Prufrock the "generic" Eliotic voice, the forerunner of Gerontion and the bisexual Tiresias in *The Waste Land*: the timid lover who hesitates and turns back, whose action dissipates in thought, when he comes face to face with a woman. Eliot began writing "The Love Song of J. Alfred Prufrock" in Paris in 1910, although it was finished in the summer of 1911 in Munich. An early draft of "Prufrock's Pervigilium" contained a passage, cut at the suggestion of Conrad Aiken, in which the protagonist visits a prostitute; Eliot's biographer Lyndall Gordon believes this to be only "the fantasy of a nervous Bostonian," arguing that it is unlikely that the deeply inhibited Eliot ever entered one of the whorehouses whose comings and goings he watched so closely. However, in one of the ribald Colombo verses he imagines himself going to the "whore-house ball" with a prostitute, "La Grosse Lulu." The text of the Pervigilium suggests that Eliot did enter one of the "evil houses leaning all together" but that the encounter was not a success. At dawn he feels a sense of nausea and fumbles to the window to experience the world and "to hear my Madness singing, sitting on the kerbstone." A blind, drunken old man sings below, and as he sings Prufrock's world began to fall apart. His only desire is to separate himself from the woman he has visited. His alienation from the female sex is expressed in the image of the crab, the nervous sea creature whose soft body is protected by its shell from attack as surely as Eliot's mask—the "envelope of frozen formality" noted by Virginia Woolf—protected him from the world of other people.

> I should have been a pair of ragged claws
> Scuttling across the floors of silent seas . . .

Eliot cannot even visualise himself as a whole crustacean; he is simply a pair of claws fleeing across the sea bed, isolated from marine life as surely as he is from human life.

Nor are the women who terrify the protagonist in the published verses of "Prufrock" only the brazenly sexual prostitutes of Montparnasse; the well-bred women of Boston society whose arms are "braceleted and white and bare," or decorously wrapped in shawls, also throw his "nerves in patterns on a screen," and cause him to turn back upon the stair. The contrast between the virile Colombo and the impotent Prufrock could not be greater.

In another poem, "Prelude in Roxbury," Eliot is again the observer who seems to be sitting in the bedroom of the "petite putain," watching her toss a blanket from the bed, fling out an arm, while in the dawn the light creeps through the shutters and the sparrows start to chirp. The girl sits up and takes the curl papers from her hair, clasps the yellow soles of her feet between the palms of her soiled hands. Most revealingly, it is her soul rather than her body which is the theme of the poem, which bears the epigraph "son âme de petite putain" from Philippe's *Bubu de Montparnasse*. For Eliot, her soul is constituted of "a thousand sordid images," and it seems likely that his relationship to the women of the street was as ambivalent as was the mother-dominated Baudelaire's, whose poetry also much influenced Eliot.

It was Baudelaire the Symbolist whose example suggested to Eliot that the world of prostitution was a fit subject for poetry. Later Eliot acknowledged that Baudelaire had taught him the poetical possibilities of the more sordid aspects of the modern metropolis, "the possibility of fusion between the sordidly realistic and the phantasmagoric." He said that Baudelaire's significance could be summed up for him in the lines:

Fourmillante Cité, cité pleine de rêves
Où le spectre en plein jour raccroche le passant . . .*[78]

If Baudelaire set a precedent for writing about the underworld, he also demonstrated to Eliot in his autobiographical *Fleurs du Mal* the predicament of the poet who is the prisoner of his doubleness, a *homo duplex,* to use Baudelaire's words: "always double," caught in the gap between "action and intention, dream and reality; one always harming the other, the

*Teeming city, city full of dreams,
  Where in broad daylight ghosts accost the passer-by . . .

one usurping the part of the other." As Baudelaire's biographer says, "the *Fleurs du Mal* is not merely the autobiography of a soul; it is the autobiography of the divided modern man, peering at his own reflection..."[79] Baudelaire dealt in polarities, in the oscillation between two simultaneous positions, one leaning towards God, the other towards Satan. In *Spleen et Idéal* the poet reaches towards God or the "Ideal" through art and through love, but is finally conquered by his own animal nature, falling back into *ennui* or *spleen*. This sense of paralysed inaction may have its roots in the love/hate relationship Baudelaire had with his mother. Although close to her after the death of his father when he was six, he bitterly resented her domination over him and expressed great hostility to women in his diaries; he compared the act of love to the "torture of a surgical operation" and although he had relationships with prostitutes they seem unlikely to have been consummated.[80]

Eliot, too, felt deeply equivocal towards women and was hampered by the same sense of guilt and revulsion from the female body as his mentor Baudelaire. Both men had mothers whom they considered as persecutory, and yet on whom they were dependent. For Eliot, the relationship with the mother is always the dominant one: "with a mother who becomes both the object of desire and the Divine Mother...the usual relationship with a woman is always the deeply wrong form of love and...the father-figures are disposed of..."[81] argues critic David Moody. Eliot escaped the "deeply wrong" heterosexual form of love through the creation of woman as an ideal-object, as in "La Figlia Che Piange," which describes an ethereal young woman.[82] And deeply embedded in his conscience also were the injunctions of parents and grandfather on the subject of sex. The equation between sex and sin is perhaps most clearly expressed in a poem of 1910, "The Little Passion: From 'An Agony in the Garret,'"[83] in which the poet imagines himself once again walking the streets on a stifling August night, following the lines of lights and knowing where they will lead: "To one inevitable cross/Whereon our souls are pinned and bleed."

So Eliot sat in the vacant square, watching other men come and go into the leering houses which "exude the odour of their turpitude." There was an obvious solution to his frustration: masturbation. In *Inventions of the March Hare,* Colombo's crew masturbate—on deck, and in their bunks. "Imaginations/Masturbations/The withered leaves/Of our imaginations," wrote Eliot in "First Debate Between Body and Soul," in which the conflict between the flesh and the spirit which had so preoccupied his mother is expressed. But such short-term satisfaction did not assuage his loneliness.

His overpowering need was to find connection with another human spirit who would provide the intimacy and emotional understanding he craved, without the female sexuality which repelled him. And then, most opportunely, his need was met by an encounter with a young medical student, born in Pau in the French Pyrenees in 1889. Jean Verdenal was also a resident at Mme. Casaubon's pension at 151 bis rue St. Jacques, a narrow street in the *quartier* of St. Germain des Prés on the Left Bank, where Eliot had moved. Tall, dark and cultured, Verdenal was exceptionally well read for a science student, and shared Eliot's interest in the philosopher Henri Bergson. The twenty-two-year-old poet and the twenty-one-year-old medical student struck up an instant friendship.

Meeting in the autumn of 1910, they shared a magical spring together in 1911, which Jean later recalled in the words of André Gide: "Ou d'aller encore une fois, O forêt pleine de mystère jusqu'à ce lieu que je connais où, dans une eau morte et brunie, trempent et s'amollissent encore les feuilles des ans passés, les feuilles des printemps adorables."*[84] Memories of their shared excursions were recalled by Jean in the spring of 1912, when he retraced their footsteps in the parks and woods they visited together. "Une vivace ardeur de soleil de printemps m'a poussé aujourd'hui à sortir dans les bois."† Full of nostalgia, he took the little boat to Saint-Cloud, drifting between the rows of translucent green shoots illuminated by the April light. In this fairy tale scene it was Tom's figure which appeared to him: "*Vous* me fûtes particulièrement évoqué par le contact de ce paysage senti ensemble,"‡ he wrote on 22 April.[85]

Jean expressed these memories in a series of letters written after Tom had left Paris for Munich and northern Italy in July 1911. There is no doubt that Tom replied to Jean's letters, for the medical student makes fre-

---

*"Or to go once more, O forest filled with mystery, to that place I know, where, in darkened, stagnant water, the leaves of former years are still steeping and softening—the leaves of adorable springtimes."
†"A bright blaze of spring sunshine impelled me to go out in the woods today."
‡*"You* were especially called to mind by this scenery we enjoyed together."

quent references to his friend's replies, which do not appear to have survived.[86] Immediately after Eliot's departure Jean wrote to him at the Pension Burger on Luisenstrasse, saying he is waiting impatiently for Tom to find some writing-paper in Bavaria "et d'en recevoir un échantillon couvert de votre *belle écriture* avant que la bière allemande n'ait engourdi votre esprit."*[87]

Later in July he writes again to say Tom's letter has arrived just as he is leaving Paris for the Pyrenees, and that he would be happy to see him in September.

It is possible that they met in Munich—where Jean urged Tom to hear some Wagner—he himself had just seen *Götterdämmerung*—or in Paris, before Eliot returned to America. Eliot's copy of a novel by Charles-Louis Philippe, *Mère et Enfant,* which Jean recommended to him, is marked "T. S. Eliot/Paris/September 1911."[88] It would have been their final meeting. "Ne croyez pas que je vous oublie" ("Don't think I'm forgetting you"), wrote Jean in October, explaining that he was cramming for his medical exams, studying twelve hours a day and had only time to write a quick letter; but he was pleased to receive Tom's, signing off: "Cordialement je vous envoie mille choses affectueuses." After Christmas Jean's mood seemed to change; exhausted by the drudgery of study—although he had passed his examination—he had returned to his family for a few weeks' holiday and was back in Paris in the New Year of 1912 before taking up a post as a surgical registrar. The shadow of war hung over the capital. Alain-Fournier wrote to Eliot that although four or five years ago he was an internationalist, now he would willingly march against the Germans, and he thought most French people felt the same way.[89]

In the pension at 151 bis rue St. Jacques, watching Mme. Casaubon mix the salad with her wrinkled hands for, he said, "the 2474th time," Jean was trying to pick up the threads of his life, not knowing to whom to attach himself, for his best friend was away ("mon meilleur ami est en voyage"). He missed Tom, and waves of nostalgia swept over him as he remembered the past. Apathetic and depressed, Jean decided to move into Eliot's old bedroom, although it was smaller than his own; he liked the

---

*"and to receive an example of it covered in your beautiful handwriting before German beer has dulled your wits."

way the bed was set into a small recess, he told his friend, "mais les dessins du papier (vous en souvient-il?) m'ont bien souvent exaspéré,"* an indication of shared times spent together in Tom's bedroom. "Zut," exclaims Jean, "je viens d'avoir l'idée de vous envoyer un tout petit bout de ce papier en question—au même instant je m'aperçois que l'idée n'est pas de moi et me vient d'une lettre de J. Laforgue, et je n'en ferai rien."†

Verdenal's deepest fear was that the bond between them was loosening: "Mon cher ami, nous ne sommes pas très loin, vous et moi, de la limite au delà de laquelle les êtres perdent, l'un l'autre, je ne sais quelle influence, quelle puissance d'émotion naissant à nouveau quand ils sont rapprochés."‡

Not only time but also space separated them. "Send me news of yourself," he begs, "avec détails suggestifs, comme vous savez; secouez votre gracieuse nonchalance et donnez-moi un peu de temps volé à vos études—si indigne j'en sois" ("with suggestive details, you know the sort of thing; shake off your elegant nonchalance and spare me a little time stolen from your studies—however unworthy of it I am"). Wistfully he wonders what kind of figure Tom cuts at home in America, where he had returned in the autumn of 1911, after a brief visit to England, to enter graduate school at Harvard; there must be a few Americans left in the States, jokes Jean, in spite of the number here in Paris.[90]

Jean Verdenal found consolation for his melancholy mood in music, particularly Wagner. In February 1912, he told Tom that he had been listening to *Tristan und Isolde* and was left "prostrate with ecstasy"; he hoped his friend would be able to hear a Wagner opera in America. It is likely to have been Jean Verdenal who put into Eliot's mind the quotations from *Tristan und Isolde* he later used in *The Waste Land:* in "The Burial of the Dead" the sailor ("Captain Eliot") longs for his loved one.[91]

As he lay on Eliot's bed, Jean brooded over the purpose of life. He had listened to Charles Maurras with Eliot in early 1911 and attended the

---

*"but the pattern of the wallpaper (do you remember it?) often gets on my nerves."
†"I just had the idea of sending you a little piece of this wallpaper—then I instantly realised that this wasn't my idea but came from a letter by J. Laforgue, so I won't do it."
‡"My dear friend, we are not very far, you and I, from the point beyond which people lose that indefinable influence and emotional power over each other, which is reborn when they come together again."

meetings of the Action Française; certainly, like Eliot, he was convinced that the latter half of the nineteenth century had seen a decline in materialism and a return to Catholic or evangelical Christianity. The criterion by which he judged a modern writer such as Verlaine or Huysmans was by how far he could influence the inner life towards the knowledge of the supreme good. Pious, sensitive and idealistic, Jean Verdenal may have been as important an influence on Eliot as his nursemaid Annie Dunne in leading him along the path which was to end ultimately in his conversion to the Anglo-Catholic Church.[92] Together Jean and Tom had queued for seats at the Collège de France, and listened to Bergson's message to cast aside intellectual analysis and to open oneself to the flow of immediate experience—to act rather than to observe.[93] Jean had responded to the call to action, berating himself for his lethargy: he was, he wrote, not made to be melancholy: "Je ne suis pas fait pour être mélancolique (et puis c'est trop romantique), je ne sais guère agir; et si j'agis (ô l'action, ô Bergson) je suis assez malin pour qu'un sincère regard vienne bientôt analyser la joie d'agir et la détruire."*[94] Caught up in the wave of patriotism which glorified the "joy of action" and cast aside doubt, Jean continued to philosophise along Bergsonian lines. In April 1912, eleven months before he renounced his deferment from military service and joined the 18th Infantry Regiment, he wrote to Eliot that he believed the "Ideal" to be an inner impulse, not an attraction from outside. So long as men live they will be inspired by the Ideal, since it is inherent in "l'élan de la vie" (the life force). This leads us to think of the finality of life and makes that end unknowable—"Et nous avançons, nous avançons toujours."[95] Carefully addressing the envelope to "Thomas Eliot Esq." (he had progressed from writing "Monsieur Thomas Eliot") at 16 Ash Street, Cambridge, Mass., Jean hoped that his friend was doing great things in America and "que germent des fleurs radieuses" ("that radiant blooms were germinating").

For Tom, too, Bergsonian exhortations to taste life to the full enabled him to cast off Bostonian inhibition and, free from the watchful eye of his mother and his classmates, to allow himself to create an emotional bond with Jean Verdenal. For a man who had no intimate friends previously, the

---

*"which is too romantic anyway, and I hardly know how to act; and if I do act I'm sharp enough to take a good look at action and destroy it by analysis."

relationship with Jean was a revelation. Full of conflict, ascetic, yet deeply sensual as his poetry reveals, Eliot discovered that his new-found intimacy with Verdenal crystallised the struggle between his instinctive sexual orientation, which seemed predominantly homosexual at that time, and the dictates of tradition and conscience, which demanded a conventional life. Although the relationship with Verdenal was unlikely to have been a physical one, given Eliot's inhibitions—notwithstanding the consistent homosexual theme of the Colombo verses—it was the knowledge that in this gay relationship alone he felt, for the first time, accepted and understood by another human being, which was to lead to a mental crisis after his return to America.[96]

That August, revising once more in Eliot's old room in Paris, Jean listened to the nearby bells chiming, just as he and Eliot used to listen together; first the distant bells, then the deeper note of one close by: "Do you remember it," he asks on 26 August 1912. Suddenly he thinks of Tom as ten o'clock strikes. "Et votre image est là devant moi"—"your image is before me."[97] Write to me when you can, he begs. As Christmas approaches, his defences fall away: on Boxing Day he expresses his innermost wishes for what might have been, and asks God's help in resisting them. Praising Tom's "delicate taste and clairvoyance" which will be put to good use in his study of philosophy, he wishes his friend for the new year "une ardeur souvent renouvelée—ardeur, flamme—mais c'est au coeur qu'en est la source et voici où nos voeux doivent être prudents. 'Amène sur moi les biens, ô Dieu, que je te les demande ou non, et écarte les maux quand même je te les demanderai.' "[*][98] It is possible that it was Jean who took the initiative in the relationship, who wished for "evil" and begged for divine help to resist his desires.

The emotional intensity of these long, sometimes seven-page letters, for whose style, crabbed handwriting and crossings-out Jean apologises, explaining that he was in the habit of coming down to Tom's old room in an old jacket, collarless and in slippers to write to his friend, indicate that Jean had given his heart to Eliot; it seems that Eliot felt the same way, for he continued to exchange letters during 1912 with Verdenal who was tak-

---

*"an oft-renewed ardour—ardour, flame—but its source is in the heart, and it is here that our wishes must be prudent. 'Bring good upon me, O Lord, whether I ask for it or not, and remove evil from me even though I ask for it.' "

ing his final medical exams before joining the French army on 18 March 1913. Their correspondence may have continued until Verdenal's death on 2 May 1915. One of Tom's most abiding memories was of Jean, with branches of lilac in his arms, bathed in the rays of the setting sun as he ran across the grass in the Luxembourg Gardens towards him; the gardens were near the pension in which the two young men stayed in Paris, as was the medical school Jean attended. Many years later Eliot recalled that day with deep emotion, and the friend who was "to be mixed with the mud of Gallipoli."[99] This undoubtedly was Jean Verdenal, *"mort aux Dardanelles,"* to whose memory Eliot dedicated *Prufrock and Other Observations* in 1917, later adding the epigraph culled from his pocket Dante which he had written out in the "March Hare" Notebook:

> . . . Tu se' ombra ed ombra vedi.
> . . . Puoi, la quantitate
> Comprender del amor ch'a te mi scalda,
> Quando dismento nostra vanitate
> Trattando l'ombre come cosa salda.*
>
> (*Purg., XXI*)[100]

As time passed, the memories of lost love became ever more vivid for Eliot, rather than fading. In 1925 he altered the epigraph slightly, and changed the dedication to "For Jean Verdenal, 1889–1915 Mort aux Dardanelles," rather than "To Jean Verdenal" as it stood in the 1917 *Prufrock and Other Observations.* Verdenal had feared that Eliot was forgetting him; in this epigraph the poet gave him his answer.

Back at Harvard in the autumn of 1911, Eliot decided to read for a doctorate in philosophy, studying Indic philosophy, Buddhism, and the philosophy of F. H. Bradley rather than literature as he had previously planned, a decision which his mother attributed to the influence of Bergson,[101] but which was undoubtedly connected with Eliot's sense of personal crisis. He appeared to Conrad Aiken to have gained a new veneer of European sophistication, hanging a print of Gauguin's *Crucifixion* in his

---

*. . . For thou art a shade and a shade thou seest . . . Canst thou comprehend the measure of the love which warms me toward thee, when I forget our nothingness, and treat shades as a solid thing.

room, adopting a malacca cane in imitation of Jules Laforgue, and snapping at Aiken with a waspishness that led him to nickname his friend "the
Tsetse."[102] Eliot also made a conscious effort to "discipline" himself to fit
into Harvard society, becoming an editor of the *Harvard Advocate,* joining
the Signet literary society, attending dances and taking boxing lessons with
a pugilist named Steve O'Donnell who may have been the prototype of
Sweeney.[103]

Yet underneath his apparent insouciance lay a soul in turmoil. Eliot
experienced a mysterious "personal upheaval" which, he later told Virginia
Woolf, turned him aside from his inclination to develop "in the manner of
Henry James" to devote himself instead to philosophy.[104] For almost two
years Eliot wrote no poetry except for "La Figlia che Piange" ("Young Girl
Weeping"), which may have been inspired by a young woman from the
same exclusive Boston society as himself, Emily Hale, whom he met at the
house of his cousin Eleanor Hinkley, probably in 1912. With Emily he participated in amateur dramatics, playing Mr. Woodhouse to Emily's Mrs.
Elton in a scene from Jane Austen's *Emma.* "Weave, weave the sunlight in
your hair," Eliot exhorts the young woman in his poem, but she remains
removed from him, "on the highest pavement of the stair," and already
wears an expression of "fugitive resentment." Eliot later came to believe
that at this point he fell in love with Emily, although "I cannot make that
assertion with any confidence," he wrote in the 1960s, unsure whether such
feeling was merely his reaction to later misery.[105] Certainly there is no hint
of fervour in his poem; instead, as if prophesying what was to follow, Eliot
imagines his protagonist "faithless," leaving "La Figlia" to stand and
grieve.

By contrast, in the poem "Do I know how I feel? Do I know what I
think?" Eliot expresses suicidal despair. In his desperation he asks the hall
porter to tell him what to think and feel. But he knows that to the porter
he is only the gentleman who lives on the second floor; and he dreads what
"a flash of madness" might reveal. Would the porter tell him how much
beauty is wasted in marriage? "If we are restless on winter nights, who can
blame us?" exclaims Eliot. Alone in his room he tries to masturbate, but
"something which should be firm . . . slips, just at my finger tips." He
imagines his own suicide, his brain "twisted in a tangled skein," he takes a
drug ("the sinking blackness of ether"), and finds release ("I do not know

what, after, and I do not care either"); finally the doctor with his black bag and a knife comes to investigate the cause of death.[106]

Eliot was struggling to repress sexual inclinations to which he could only give expression in his poetry. "The Descent from the Cross," in which the poet tells Conrad Aiken that he will go to the masquerade as St. John among the Rocks, dressed in his underwear,[107] reveals his innermost fantasies; while to outsiders he appeared the diligent doctoral student as he worked on his dissertation on "Knowledge and Experience in the Philosophy of F. H. Bradley." Lyndall Gordon asserts that at this point in his life Eliot was "circling . . . on the edge of conversion," citing the evidence of the "visionary poems" he was writing,[108] and asks why did he not make a "serious religious commitment in 1914?" Certainly Eliot was much preoccupied with mysticism and the lives of the saints—St. Theresa, Dame Julian of Norwich, St. Ignatius and St. John of the Cross—but Eastern texts interested him as much as Christian ones. He studied Sanskrit and Pali and read the *Bhagavad-Gita*. It is easy to argue with hindsight that the poet's psychological distress of the time,[109] the fears and night panics expressed in his poetry, were the product of a spiritual struggle, steps along the pathway of an aspirant saint to his God. But it is more likely this was a very different psychic crisis for Eliot, precipitated by the intimate relationship with Jean Verdenal, in which the poet was forced to confront his sexuality with all its implications for his future life.

The psychotic "Saint" poems Eliot wrote in 1914 must be seen within the context of the development of his intense anxiety, as he struggled with the knowledge of his aberrant sexuality (as he, his family and the society of which he was part would have perceived it) while turning a polished face to the world. Preoccupied with the journey towards self-understanding, immersed in both Western and Eastern asceticism, he at times apparently experienced his own hallucinations and visions and lived with "shadows for my company."[110] Far from being simple signposts along the path to sainthood, the "Saint" poems reveal Eliot journeying to the psychic edge as he experiments with heightened states of awareness.

Eliot was inspired to write "The Love Song of St. Sebastian" after seeing *"three* great *St. Sebastians"* as he travelled through Europe in the summer of 1914: Mantegna's in Venice, Antonello of Messina's at Bergamo, and Memling's in Brussels.[111] Eliot tells Aiken that he has studied St.

Sebastians, and asks why any artist should paint a beautiful youth and stick him full of pins (or arrows) unless he felt the same way as the hero of his verse—"only there's nothing homosexual about this." Since no one ever painted a female St. Sebastian, he had given the poem this title *faute de mieux.*[112]

It might seem that Eliot protested too much. St. Sebastian was already established as a gay icon in European art by the early twentieth century, and Eliot was unlikely to have been unaware of this, or to have missed seeing San Sodoma's famous *St. Sebastian* in the Uffizi in Florence. Following the example of Baudelaire, who developed the ability to observe himself objectively with the detachment of a scientist, and to heighten his own hypersensitivity through the technique of *dédoublement,* Eliot too developed "the sensual excitement of a voyeur." "I have cultivated my hysteria with delight and terror," wrote Baudelaire, insisting on "the supernatural sensual delight man can experience at the sight of his own blood."[113] Eliot's reading of Eastern texts opened his eyes to the development of trancelike mystical states, and at the same time the Decadent movement, which had grown out of the Symbolist movement, intrigued him with its interest in androgyny, perversion and pain. Like the aesthete Walter Pater he began to see ecstasy as a bridge between the physical and the spiritual,[114] and to aim for Eastern detachment through the surrender of self. In "The Love Song of St. Sebastian" the protagonist mortifies the flesh, coming in a hair shirt to flog himself until he bleeds. Hour on hour of "torture and delight" follow, until his blood "should ring the lamp/And glisten in the light." At first the poet is victim, dead between the breasts of a woman; then he murders her: "and you would love me because I should have strangled you . . . And I should love you the more because I had mangled you." Perhaps Eliot was influenced by Huysmans, who wrote of artist Gustave Moreau that he painted virgins who, under the pretence of prayer, appealed for "sacrilege, shameful orgies, torture and murder."[115] The theme of murder—an enduring one for Eliot—was already preoccupying him in 1914.

The mental crisis Eliot was experiencing, which he viewed as a conflict between body and soul, life and art,[116] expressed itself in "The Death of Saint Narcissus," a poem which Eliot cancelled just before it was to be published in *Poetry* in 1915, but later incorporated into *The Waste Land.*[117] The self-absorption of the poem reflects the poet's own narcissism. The same auto-eroticism surfaces: "With slippery white belly held tight in *his* own fingers/Writhing in his own clutch, his ancient beauty/Caught first in the pink tips of his new beauty."[118] The androgynous hero/heroine knows too that he has been a young girl, caught in the woods by a drunken old man—but he also knows that "his flesh is in love with the pentrant arrows," in a phrase which recalls the image of St. Sebastian. His punishment therefore is to be exiled to the desert, where he dances on the hot sand until the arrows come, and surrenders himself to them "until his white and redness" satisfy him.[119] Self-punishment has here become not only a habit, but a source of pleasure.

There is no doubt that this poem betrays the influence of Eliot's mother Charlotte, whose own poems related the ordeals of the desert fathers of the early Christian church. But a more significant reference may be to Dante. In Canto XV of the *Inferno,* it is the Sodomites, "the Violent against God," who are condemned to cross and recross the fiery sands beneath the rain of fire until they perish.[120] Eliot the puritan knew that if he followed the path of the Sodomites he would be condemned to the Inferno. In the poem, Narcissus, like the black moth in "The Burnt Dancer," is consumed by fire and becomes a "dancer to God." The image of the moth circling the flame, in the ecstasy which is a bridge to the spiritual life, is borrowed from the *Bhagavad-Gita;*[121] it represents Eliot's solution to the conflict between God and Satan, the Ideal and Spleen of Symbolist poetry. To take the path towards the phallic arrow was to risk divine retribution; to renounce it was an act of painful self-sacrifice. Such inner conflict was the root of neurosis and it was in this frame of mind that Eliot travelled towards England as the continent of Europe slipped into war.

4

A Clandestine Marriage

Tom Eliot cut an impressive figure when he arrived in England. To Vivien Haigh-Wood, meeting him for the first time in March 1915, he seemed an American "prince" in the same mould as Scofield, but his "deep and thrilling voice" with its slow drawl added a dash of glamour.[1] Vivien was a young woman who, as she wrote years later when attending historian Arthur Bryant's lectures on "The American Ideal" at London University, found "the shout of the baseball team . . . deep, stirring, madly exciting." She read Henry James, and her favourite entertainment, apart from dancing, was the "kinema" where Hollywood's silent stars aroused in her dreams of romance. In short, she was susceptible to all things American, and Eliot, unlike Charles Buckle, was "a fine tall handsome man" of the kind that "Rosa" preferred.

When she met him Eliot was twenty-six, as was Vivien. His appearance was strikingly feline: he had "peculiarly luminous, light yellow more than tawny, eyes: the eyes, they might have been, of one of the greater cats, but tiger, puma, leopard, lynx, rather than those of a lion, which for some reason, display usually a more domesticated and placid expression." His face, too, wrote Osbert Sitwell, "possessed the width of bony structure of a tigrine face, albeit the nose was prominent, similar, I used to think, to that of a figure on an Aztec carving or bas-relief." The impassivity of his face, the resemblance to a carved Aztec mask, was also noted by the artist Wyndham Lewis. This mask-like face enabled the poet to armour himself "behind the fine manners, and fastidiously courteous manner that are so particularly his own." In 1917, when Sitwell met him, "His air . . . was always lively, gay, even jaunty. His clothes too,—in London he usually wore check or 'sponge-bag' trousers, and a short black coat—were elegant, and he walked with a cheerful, easy movement." Speculating that a poet's technique was represented in his etheric body, Sitwell found that "Eliot's muscular conformation and his carriage and the way he moved seem to explain the giant muscular control of rhythm he has acquired." But although Eliot seemed patient and controlled, at his heart Sitwell detected "a tiger's fiery core of impatience."[2]

Astute, arrogant and determined, Eliot had made few moves that were not to his benefit following his arrival in England after an uncomfortable journey from Marburg in August 1914. It had "never entered his head" that England would declare war on Germany, and not until 2 August, two days before that declaration, did he take the decision to flee Marburg for London, piqued, as he told his mother, that the summer school for which he had gone to Germany *"expressly"* had been cancelled.[3] He was surprised to find the London in which he arrived "literally boiling with war," as his old Harvard friend, Conrad Aiken, who was also in the capital, described it. On 3 August Aiken was amazed to see the crowds coalescing like some animal force in desperate need of direction and unity, as they poured up the Mall to Buckingham Palace, where their prolonged cheers brought out the "little figures on the high stone balcony." Rumours of late wires and ultimatums flew around London. Sir Edward Grey, the Foreign Secretary, was speaking to the House, and "It looked like the real thing, yes, it looked like it." All day there was the tramp of feet towards the railway stations, the sound of bands playing (one of them playing a Harvard tune, thought Aiken) as men hurried to enlist.[4] The excitement made it impossible for Aiken to stay in his Bedford Place boarding house, where he was soon joined by Eliot, at number twenty-eight. But Eliot's reaction to British patriotism was rather different. He had found the evacuation from Germany "an intolerable bore," and felt the Germans were "perfectly justified" in violating Belgium. The war interested him little; it was of greater concern to discover whether, despite all the noise and rumour, he would be able to work. The commotion in Bloomsbury was like "hell turned upside down," as to the general hubbub of crying babies, pianos and street accordions was added the shouts of newspaper vendors proclaiming "GREAT GERMAN DISASTER" and an hour later selling the next extra, the list of English dead and wounded. However Eliot found the noise "depersonalised" and was able to detach himself from it.[5]

Nevertheless, as the days passed he became a little depressed. He continued to feel a barrier between himself and the English, and to be home-sick for Paris. He and Aiken had made a previous, brief visit to London from Paris in 1911, but Eliot considered that it was much easier to under-stand a Frenchman or an American than an Englishman; the English, he decided, lacked the intellectual honesty of the French. There was a "brick wall" through which he could not pass: something to do with convention-ality, he thought, not snobbishness, for "I am a thorough snob myself," he confessed to his cousin Eleanor Hinkley.[6] He was gloomily aware of "the damp souls of housemaids" brooding in the basements, of the brown fog tossing up twisted faces from the bottom of the street towards the window of his boarding house.[7]

Nor did things improve when he arrived in Oxford in October to take up his Sheldon Travelling Fellowship in philosophy at Merton College. The city was three parts deserted, as the majority of undergraduates had enlisted in the army; Eliot later recalled that, "I left with my only trophy a pewter mug obtained for stroking a college junior four at a time when all the real oarsmen were fighting for England and France." He was not able to meet the reclusive F. H. Bradley, a fellow of the college and the subject of his doctoral thesis, although he did like and respect his tutor Professor Harold Joachim, who taught him the importance of punctuation as Eliot worked on the text of Aristotle. "In criticising the papers I brought him, Joachim taught me what little I know of the art of writing English prose. It was a painful and humiliating experience," he recalled, declaring that no prose he had written justified the agony he had endured, although he did admit that practice in writing prose was necessary to those who wanted to write verse.[8] The food and climate were "execrable," he complained later to Aiken. "I suffer indigestion, constipation and colds constantly."[9] But when a telegram arrived from Harvard, notifying him that he had been nominated for his fellowship, it threw his mind into turmoil. Unsure whether he really wanted the academic career for which he was preparing himself, it became all the more important to find a toehold in English so-ciety and penetrate the closed world of Anglo-Saxon letters.

His first stroke of luck, or so it seemed, was to bump into Bertrand Russell in New Oxford Street. The philosopher recognised Eliot from an earlier encounter that spring at Harvard, where Russell had taught a post-graduate class of twelve, including the young poet, at that time president of the university philosophical club and an assistant in philosophy. Eliot, normally "extraordinarily silent," remarked when Russell praised the Greek philosopher Heraclitus, "Yes, he always reminds me of Villon." "I thought this remark so good that I always wished he would make another," said Russell,[10] impressed not only by the American's intelligence but by his appearance, which was "very well-dressed and polished with manners of the finest Etonian type,"[11] although Russell confided to his mistress Lady Ottoline Morrell that he feared that despite being "ultra-civilised" his pupil had "no vigour or life—or enthusiasm" and was unlikely to be very creative.

The English professor had made an impression on the young American too; Russell looked like the Mad Hatter from *Alice in Wonderland*, "his large head poised on a little neck with a high collar,"[12] but his clear mind and irrepressible laugh appealed at once to a young man who likened himself to the March Hare. In his poem "Mr. Apollinax," a satirical portrait of Russell, first published in 1916, the poet recalls that "When Mr. Apollinax visited the United States/His laughter tinkled among the teacups," on an afternoon visit to Harvard academic "Professor Channing-Cheetah" and his mother "Mrs. Phlaccus." Later Russell's laughter was to enrage Eliot, who compared it in his poem to that of an "irresponsible foetus," and hinted at the philosopher's satanical nature.[13] In October 1914, however, Eliot found "Bertie," as he was asked to call his new friend, very hospitable.[14] Russell was living near Eliot in Bloomsbury, and invited him back to his flat for tea. Eliot thought the flat was furnished in very good taste and its owner, although a pacifist, amusing as he compared the thoroughness of German war-making to their scholarship. Not for another year was Eliot to discover that Russell's friendship was a poisoned chalice.

A second contact of immense importance to Eliot was with another American expatriate, the poet Ezra Pound, to whom he was introduced by Conrad Aiken. Rabbi Ben Ezra, as Aiken mockingly called him in his autobiographical novel *Ushant,* was in some ways markedly similar to Eliot.[15] Pound, too, had felt an "alien" growing up in the suburb of Wyncote, near Philadelphia, dislocated from his roots in the pioneer town of Hailey, Idaho, where he was born on 30 October 1885;[16] he, too, seemed isolated and detached from his fellow students at the University of Pennsylvania.

Like Eliot he admired European literature, and in particular Dante, although Pound preferred the songs of the troubadors to French Symbolism as a source of inspiration. Like Eliot he left a woman behind in America who felt herself romantically attached to him: in Pound's case the daughter of the Professor of Astronomy at the University of Pennsylvania, Hilda Doolittle, who followed him to London, whereas Eliot's Emily Hale continued to languish in New England. Both men took enormous trouble with their appearance and although the images they so carefully crafted were very different, they served the same function: that of mask, behind which to hide from the human race to whom each found it hard to relate. As Pound expressed it in 1914: "I began this search for the real in a book called *Personae,* casting off, as it were, complete masks of the self in each poem. I continued in a long series of translations, which were but more elaborate masks."[17] The adopted persona was often a virile one but, despite finding comfort in the company of women, and flirting ostentatiously with a number of them, both Pound's and Eliot's sexuality was ambiguous, and both claimed to be virgins before marriage.[18]

Pound had arrived in London in 1908 with only £3 in his pocket. Unlike Eliot, he had left America under a cloud, having been dismissed from his university post at the Presbyterian College of Wabach, in Crawfordsville, Indiana, after a scandal in which he shared a meal with an actress in his rooms (although he slept elsewhere). "They say that I am bisexual and given to unnatural lusts," he confided to Hilda.[19] Never an academic star like Eliot, Ezra Pound struck people as being something of a charlatan, the small-town huckster brashly peddling his wares to a doubting crowd. He dressed to fit the popular idea of the bohemian poet, in a wide-collared shirt with loosely knotted tie, spats over his shoes, and a velvet coat, carefully combing his crinkled hay-coloured hair up from his forehead in a bird-like tuft. The buttons on his overcoat were replaced with new ones of lapis lazuli; he grew "a forked red beard" and a thin moustache, wore a pince-nez and carried a malacca cane. Egotistical, self-obsessed and impatient, he was known to eat tulips at a dinner party where he felt ignored, and to wear a single turquoise earring in one ear.

Pound's talent for self-publicity served him well in his pursuit of reputation.

'Tis the white stag, Fame, we're a-hunting,
Bid the world's hounds come to horn![20]

Although at first he was ignored, this "small but persistent volcano in the dim levels of London literary society," in Richard Aldington's words, began to be noticed.[21] Elkin Matthews, the literary publisher, stocked his first collection of poems, *A Lume Spento (With Tapers Quenched),* which Pound had self-published in Venice, and at Matthews's bookshop he met the charming novelist Olivia Shakespear, a solicitor's wife who had had a secret affair with W. B. Yeats in 1895. When Maud Gonne reappeared in Yeats's life, Olivia remained his friend and, as to meet "Bill Yeats" was one of Pound's chief reasons for coming to England, she introduced the twenty-three-year-old American to his hero. An instant rapport grew up between master and disciple; soon Pound had taken over Yeats's Monday evening salons at his house in Woburn Place, and during the winter of 1913 was employed as Yeats's "secretary" at Stone Cottage, Coleman's Hatch, his rural retreat in Sussex.

Another breakthrough for Pound was being published by Ford Madox Hueffer (who had changed his name during the war to Ford Madox Ford), influential editor of the *English Review.* Ford and his mistress Violet Hunt—often known as "Immodest Violet"—were the centre of a literary circle at South Lodge in Campden Hill, of which Pound soon made himself an indispensable part. Ford has described how Pound would walk up to South Lodge from his lodgings in Church Walk, Kensington: "He wore a purple hat, a green shirt, a black velvet jacket, vermilion socks, openwork brilliant tanned sandals, trousers of green billiard cloth, in addition to an immense flowing tie that had been hand-painted by a Japanese Futurist poet."[22] Despite Pound's bizarre appearance, Ford detected his talent and energy. His horror at Pound's "jejune and provincial" collection *Canzoni,* which left the editor rolling on the floor in protest at the archaic and over-blown language, stung Pound into new attempts at finding a modern poetic voice.

Establishment poetry was at that time represented by the Poets' Club, founded in 1908: "An arthritic milieu," said Pound, representing the "doughy mass of third-hand Keats" into which English poetry had degenerated, and against which T. E. Hulme and F. S. Flint were in revolt.[23] Hulme's group met in Soho on Thursday nights, and soon Pound was introduced to A. R. Orage, editor of the radical journal *The New Age,* who gave him a weekly column in which to express his evolving views about modern poetry. By the end of 1911, in a sequence of articles entitled "I Gather the Limbs of Osiris," Pound was working out his new principles: "As to twentieth-century poetry, and the poetry I expect to see written during the next decade or so, it will, I think, move against poppycock; it will be harder and saner . . . At least for myself, I want it so, direct, free from emotional slither."

An experiment became a movement with the unexpected arrival in England of Pound's former fiancée, Hilda Doolittle. Embarrassed by her presence, since he was by now involved with Olivia Shakespear's daughter Dorothy (whose devotion was more fervent than his own lukewarm courtship), Pound introduced Hilda to another young poet experimenting with *vers libre,* blond, nineteen-year-old Richard Aldington, the self-taught son of a Portsmouth solicitor with whom she duly fell in love.

Pound was as impressed by Aldington as Aldington was by Pound. The younger poet remembered that, "I showed him my *vers libre* poems over a beefsteak in Kensington and he said: 'Well, I don't think you need any help from me!' "[24] But Hilda—whom Pound had long ago nicknamed "the Dryad"—was more reticent. It was only over tea and buns in the British Museum tearoom that she shyly showed Pound a page of manuscript which seemed to meet his urgent need to find poetry for a new American journal. *Poetry* had been launched recently in Chicago by a middle-aged spinster named Harriet Monroe, who had accepted Pound's offer to become her overseas editor. "But Dryad . . . This is poetry." He slashed with a pencil. "Cut this out, shorten this line, 'Hermes of the Ways' is a good title. I'll send this to Harriet Monroe of *Poetry* . . ." Finally he scrawled "H. D. Imagiste" at the bottom of the page.[25] Not only had Pound launched a new movement, he had found a new *métier*—that of editor and impresario.

It was a role which Pound found much to his liking, and for which he had as great a talent as he did for creative verse. In *Des Imagistes,* the anthology of Imagist poems edited by Pound and published in 1914, "H. D." had seven poems. The edition sold out, even though neither the "Dryad"

nor Aldington (whom Pound nicknamed "the Faun") much liked the
label. "I didn't like his insistence that the poems should be signed: 'H. D.
Imagiste'" protested Aldington, "because it sounded a little ridiculous.
And I think (she) disliked it too. But . . . it was only through him that
we could get our poems into . . . *Poetry.*"[26] The *succès de scandale* of *Des
Imagistes* attracted another female American poet, Amy Lowell, the
wealthy and rotund lesbian author of a collection of poetry entitled *A
Dome of Many-Coloured Glass* (1912), whose energy rivalled Pound's.
Although Aldington condemned her book as "the fluid, fruity, facile stuff
we most wanted to avoid,"[27] Amy Lowell was not easily deterred; having
read about Imagism in *Poetry,* she crossed the Atlantic in July 1913 with an
introduction to Pound from Harriet Monroe and soon found herself accepted by the Imagist group. Although amazed by Pound's appearance
("never, since the days of Wilde, have such garments been seen in the
streets of London," she wrote to a friend) she allowed herself to be converted to free verse by the Imagist leader.[28] Returning in the following year
with her actress lover "Peter," Lowell challenged Pound's hegemony with
the publication of her own Imagist anthology, *Some Imagist Poets.*
Although another counterblast against the increasingly popular Georgian
poets, it led not only to a rift between her and Pound but between Pound,
"H. D." and Aldington, the junior two members of the triad resenting
Pound's "czarist" behaviour in trying to prevent them from contributing
to Amy's anthology.[29]

Pound was not overmuch concerned, for a new star had burst onto
London's artistic and literary scene: Percy Wyndham Lewis, son of an ab-
sentee American father and English mother, and friend of Augustus John,
with whom he had enjoyed the *vie de bohème* in Paris between 1905 and
1909. Lewis was an artist, writer and, in his own words, an "art politician,"
who had begun to be published by Ford Madox Ford in the *English
Review.* He had not much liked Pound when he first met him at South
Lodge, but he changed his mind when he encountered him at the Vienna
café in New Oxford Street. Pound, with his "fierce blue eyes and reddishly
hirsute jaw" was viewed by the other habitués of the café as a "bogus personage" and they were determined not to be taken in by this "tiresome and
flourishing, pretentious, foreign aspirant to poetic eminence," but Lewis
detected "a heart of gold" beneath Pound's eccentricity.[30] After being

shown Lewis's paintings, Pound christened his new friend "Vorticist." Lewis, who had quarrelled with the artist Roger Fry over an invitation to exhibit with the Omega Workshops, and regarded the Bloomsbury group with violent dislike as the province of perverse spinsters, was delighted with Pound's intervention. "We were a youth racket," remembered Lewis. "It was Ezra who in the first place organised us willy-nilly into that."[31] Lewis was at a point in his career when he was ready to launch a new movement. Like Fry, he considered himself in opposition to the Royal Academy, but the split with the older artist was the catalyst for Lewis to set up his own Rebel Art Centre in Great Ormond Street and to publish a sensational new review, *Blast.* This publication, which had bright puce pages, trumpeted the manifesto of the Great London Vortex, and was signed by Richard Aldington, Ezra Pound, Wyndham Lewis, and Pound's sculptor-protégé Henri Gaudier-Brzeska, among others. *Blast* made a splash when it was published in July 1914, and Pound's confidence grew in his ability to "puff" his friends.

Having cut his teeth on "H. D.," Aldington and Wyndham Lewis, not to mention his old friend from the University of Pennsylvania, William Carlos Williams, and another American poet, Robert Frost, whose work he sent to Harriet Monroe, Ezra Pound did not hesitate to "edit" Yeats's poetry, to the poet's initial fury, although even Yeats soon came to believe that Ezra had the magic touch. In 1913 Pound began to throw his formidable energies into promoting yet another new discovery, James Joyce, who regarded him as a "miracle worker" after Ezra accepted his poem "I Hear an Army" for *Des Imagistes* and followed it up with the decision to serialise *A Portrait of the Artist as a Young Man* in *The Egoist* (formerly *The New Freewoman*), a literary journal founded by two English feminists, Dora Marsden and Harriet Shaw Weaver. *The Egoist* served as a London platform for Pound—who became its literary editor in 1913—just as *Poetry* did in America.

No one, therefore, was in a better position to advance the career of Tom Eliot in 1914 than Ezra Pound, with his mission to modernise twentieth-century poetry and his sympathy for the "rebel." Pound had absolute confidence in his own literary judgement, dismissing those he considered unsuitable with the crushing remark: "Il n'est pas dong le mouvemong." But when Conrad Aiken showed Pound "The Love Song of J. Alfred Prufrock" his reaction was excited and determined. "I was jolly well right about Eliot," he wrote to Harriet Monroe in September 1914. "He has sent in the best poem I have yet had or seen from an American. PRAY GOD IT BE NOT A SINGLE AND UNIQUE SUCCESS."[32] What impressed Ezra most was that Eliot had "actually trained *and* modernised himself *on his own"*—something Pound was aware he had not been able to do himself. He brusquely overrode Miss Monroe's objections to the Laforgue-inspired poem which she was not sure she understood. "No, emphatically I will not ask Eliot to write down to any audience whatever . . . Neither will I send you Eliot's address in order that he may be insulted."[33] Harriet Monroe continued to protest at the ending: " 'Mr. Prufrock' does not 'go off' at the end" retorted Pound in January 1915. "I dislike the paragraph about Hamlet, but it is an early and cherished bit and T. S. E. won't give it up, and as it is the only portion of the poem that most readers will like at first reading, I don't see that it will do much harm."[34] His editor remained reluctant: *"Do* get on with that Eliot," wrote Pound in April.[35] Only in response to his threat to "quit the magazine" unless Monroe published Eliot did Prufrock finally appear in June 1915. And Pound was unrelenting; in August he sent Monroe "three jems of Eliot" for September, and this time Monroe acted quickly: three of Eliot's new poems appeared in the September issue of *Poetry,* "The Boston Evening Transcript," "Aunt Helen," and "Cousin Nancy."[36] Pound had launched his new protégé.

Eliot held less complimentary views about the merits of Pound's verse, which he confided to Aiken he found "well-meaning but touchingly incompetent,"[37] but he was grateful for his help, particularly as Harold Monro, owner of the Poetry Bookshop, which opened on 8 January 1913, and editor of *Poetry and Drama,* had previously been offered "Prufrock" and rejected it as "absolutely insane"—a decision neither Monro nor Eliot ever forgot.[38] Pound's support was deeply significant; his encouragement and example led Eliot to rethink his decision to continue with philosophy *faute de mieux.* Instead he began to contemplate an alternative course of action: to stay in England and make a reputation as a poet and editor, as Ezra had done.

Wyndham Lewis described his first meeting with Eliot in Pound's narrow triangular flat at 5 Holland Park Chambers, just up the road from

Church Walk. "A sleek, tall, attractive transatlantic apparition—with a sort of Gioconda smile" sat not two feet away from Lewis, and struck the artist as "Prufrock himself," only a Prufrock who had quite enough confidence to "dare" to eat a peach: "For this was a very attractive young Prufrock indeed, with an alert and dancing eye—*moqueur* to the marrow—bashfully ironic, blushfully *tacquineur.* But still a Prufrock!" At first Lewis eyed the stranger with contempt, for he was used to finding Pound's flat used as a *rendez-vous* for transatlantic birds of passage, and barely listened to "the prepossessing, ponderous, exactly-articulated, drawl [which] made a sleepy droning in my ear, as if some heavy hymenopter, emitting a honeyed buzz, had passed in at the Kensington window."[39] Pound showed him Eliot's poems in typescript, which Lewis barely glanced at; being one of Ezra's protégés himself, he had a healthy suspicion of rivals, and considered that his mentor "warmed, with alarming readiness, to almost anything that was immature, in the development and evolution of which he might masterfully intervene."

At the flat Eliot met Pound's new wife, Dorothy. Ezra had married Dorothy on 20 April 1914, and she was paying the rent of the new flat, which was in the same block as the Aldingtons', for Richard had married Hilda Doolittle the previous autumn, a match much encouraged by Pound.[40] Holland Park Chambers was therefore something of a nest of poets, although the Aldingtons soon fled from over-proximity to Pound. Both marriages united an Englishman or woman (Aldington, Dorothy) with an American. Dorothy, silent and submissive, must have appeared an excellent example of a wife to Eliot; not only did she design the covers for her husband's collections of poetry such as *Ripostes,* her private income also spared Pound the necessity of having to earn a living from his poetry.

Eliot's own thoughts now began to turn to women. Alone in Oxford on New Year's Eve 1914, he confessed to Conrad Aiken that he was experiencing "one of those nervous sexual attacks which I suffer from when alone in a city. This is the worst since Paris." He was, he explained, "very dependent upon women (I mean female society)" and felt the deprivation in Oxford. "One walks about the street with one's desires, and one's refinement rises up like a wall whenever opportunity approaches."[41] He felt the burden of his virginity, telling Conrad that he sometimes thought he would be better off if he had disposed of his virginity and shyness several years ago: "and indeed I still think sometimes that it would be well to do so before marriage."

Only the month before, Eliot had asked Conrad to order some red or pink roses for Emily Hale, who was appearing in a Cambridge Dramatic Play, probably at the house of Eleanor Hinkley at Berkeley Place, Cambridge, Massachusetts. Conrad was to send them to her for the Saturday night performance with a card he had enclosed.[42] But Emily was far away; it was time to meet some English girls. As ever, Eliot sought safety in numbers with women, in order to keep them at a distance. "I should find it very stimulating to have several women fall in love with me—several, because that makes the practical side less evident. And I would be very sorry for them too," he confessed to his friend, wondering what would happen if he gave a few lectures from the *Inventions of the March Hare* with wax candles. A new Colombo poem, transcribed to Conrad in the same letter—which had been turned down, so he said, by several publishers on the grounds that it paid too great a tribute to the charms of German youth—revealed desires closer to Eliot's heart. In this verse the captain is pacing the quarterdeck, parading in his corset, until the ship is sunk by a German warship; the cabin boy, saved alive, is "bugger'd in the sphincter."[43] Eliot also showed his Bolo and Colombo rhymes to Pound, who passed some on to Wyndham Lewis for inclusion in *Blast*. Lewis also refused them, writing to Pound: "Eliot has sent me Bullshit and the Ballad for Big Louise. They are excellent bits of scholarly ribaldry. I am trying to print them in *Blast;* but stick to my naif determination to have no 'words ending in -Uck, -Unt, and -Ugger.' "[44]

Despite Eliot's nervousness with the opposite sex and fear of the "practical side" of a relationship, there is plenty of evidence that women found the shy but handsome poet sexually attractive. Lewis's impression was of a Prufrock "to whom the mermaids would decidedly have sung, one would have said, at the tops of their voices—a Prufrock who had no need to 'wear the bottom of his trousers rolled' just yet."[45] In his Bloomsbury boarding house during the Christmas vacation Eliot was the object of attention from a "delightful" young woman from New Zealand, and attended "cubist teas" with Futurist novelists, Vorticist poets, and Cubist painters he had met through Pound. In Oxford and London his social life was expanding; by March 1915 he was planning to take a Miss Petersen punting in the summer, and telling his cousin Eleanor that he would like English girls better if they were not so completely managed by their mothers. Perhaps the ones he had been meeting were too young, he mused.[46]

A month later Eliot was putting on his dancing shoes and practising the ballroom dancing skills he had learnt at Harvard. He decided he much preferred metropolitan to provincial life ("the latter is so much like New England, and the former quite unique") now that he had met "several English girls" and been admitted to two dancing parties at the large hotels where one could dine and dance. These new lady friends were about his own age, and there were two especially who were very good dancers, although he found the English style of dancing very stiff and old-fashioned, confessing to Eleanor Hinkley on 24 April that he had terrified one poor Spanish girl by starting to dip in his one-step. "The two I mentioned are more adaptable and caught the American style very quickly." Fascinated by the difference between these "emancipated Londoners" and anything he had known at home or in England before, he speculated that his previous generalisations about English girls didn't apply to London girls over twenty-five. "They are charmingly sophisticated (even 'disillusioned') without being hardened; and I confess to taking great pleasure in seeing women smoke, even though for that matter I do not know any English girls who do not." The English girls had such amusing names, confided Tom to his cousin. One was named "Vivien."[47]

Vivien found her new dancing partner equally amusing. The first indication that she reciprocated Eliot's interest comes in a reproachful letter she wrote in March 1915 to Scofield Thayer, who had cancelled an invitation he and Eliot had extended to Vivien and Lucy (who were staying at Thyme Cottage, Upper Bourne End, Buckinghamshire), to visit them the following weekend at Oxford. Vivien had hinted on 22 February that she would like an introduction to Eliot—reported to be visiting Epsom races with another friend of Thayer's—as he sounded "a very nice person."[48] She wrote again on 3 March, but not until her third letter, which is only dated "Thursday," is it clear that Scofield had made the fateful introduction at a lunch party in his rooms at Magdalen.[49]

It is hard to know whether Vivien's irritation with Scofield, with whom she was involved in the kind of flirtatious relationship which both found amusing, was simply because he had stood her up, or because she was annoyed at missing the chance of getting to know his friend Tom better. Vivien writes haughtily that Lucy and she were given to understand by Eliot and Scofield, "severally and definitely," that they were expected to keep both Saturday and Sunday free, and if Saturday was wet they would come on Sunday. The young ladies had therefore refused an invitation to Cambridge for Sunday, and, even worse, said no to a particularly charming dance on Saturday. Vivien is at pains to emphasise her popularity to Scofield, and her irritation that he has cancelled as late as *Thursday,* accepting another invitation for himself on Sunday. Such casualness, she tells him, in the tones of Lady Bracknell, is "really not done." It is quite unforgivable to leave Vivien in the lurch for the whole weekend "to the horrors of unmitigated London."

Switching from petulance to threats, Vivien reminds Scofield of her specialist's words: "Do not be the instrument of pushing me more quickly than is necessary into an untimely melancholia, or else, as he also prophesied, an early grave." Then, with a swift change of mood, she begs "dear, kind hearted little Scofield," as the weather is obviously turning out cold, to come to her in London on Saturday instead of meeting in Oxford—"Please do." There is no better way to spend a wet Saturday, according to Vivien, than by coming to town and having a cheerful afternoon looking at pictures, watching an Irish theatre group, having tea at the Piccadilly Hotel, and going out to dinner with "little Vivien to jog along beside you and gaze lovingly upon you with her golden eyes. And you are *an awful* fool—my dear," she warns him, since in two weeks he is to return to America:

> When, like a rat, you desert a sinking ship—from that day I do *solemnly promise* you I will never have speech or correspondence with you, nor will I *ever* look upon your promising-much and fulfilling-little countenance. Never. I have made up my mind, really. And you will never meet another such as I—and one day, I assure you, you will grind your teeth at the raw, childish *folly* which prevented you distinguishing between a yellow diamond—a white flame—and an ordinary toy of coloured glass.

Why cast pearls before swine, demands Vivien: "Yellow diamonds and white flames before hide-bound, unawakened, limited savages?" You ought to snatch *every hour* in these last days, she exhorts her bemused suitor: *"Try,* try to burn just one of your fingers in the white flame—just for the experience, you know." Each hour is a pearl, each pearl a prayer, in Vivien's philosophy.

Mercurial, intense, albeit immature, Vivien was full of confidence in her powers of attraction: she was the "yellow diamond, the white flame," the pearl beyond price to which ordinary women could not be compared. Part coquette, part drama-queen, she alternates promises with threats. You *must* come to London, she commands him again. She will not forgive him if he does not. "I could have danced like a faun at the Savoy," she says in a reference to Nijinsky's performance in *L'Après-midi d'un Faune,* which she and Lucy had seen at the Palace theatre. "I have a new dress—and *what a dress!"* "You shall *not* spoil everything," she tells Scofield sulkily. Her final weapon is to cast the responsibility for her mental health upon her correspondent, complaining that she "Can't stand these things now, I can only keep going by the skin of my teeth—"

Despite this emotional blackmail, Vivien was far more in control than she suggests, and it must be emphasised that she believed herself in 1915 to be a far stronger and more stable personality than Lucy Thayer, who was also considered neurasthenic. "Nerves" were, it seems, a common bond between Vivien and Lucy, but in Vivien's opinion the two families took a very different attitude to their temperamental daughters. Lucy was not really weak, Vivien told Scofield in February, apologising if she had given the wrong impression about his cousin. "I never know myself how far nerves can be helped," she remarks thoughtfully. Although Vivie had been trained "to consider them a crime, to be concealed," Lucy had always been allowed to consider them "an interesting misfortune."[50] Enclosing a letter of Lucy's to help Scofield understand, Vivien gives him the benefit of her own experience:

> She will have to find out one day that no human being can ever really help another, & if you can't help yourself you are done for—won't she? But it's a nasty jar when you arrive at that conclusion! You will help me to drag her out and make her enjoy life a little when you are here—won't you?

This letter reveals Vivien's independence and determination not to allow a troubled adolescence to prevent her living the life she wants, as well as her protective attitude towards Lucy. There is no indication that at this point in her life she was dependent on drugs, although they had been prescribed in the past; certainly she was well enough to be working in January 1915 as a governess with a Cambridge family, with whom she lived at 26 Malcolm Street.[51] One beautiful Sunday afternoon in February Vivien was planting seeds at home in the Haigh-Woods' "half inch of garden": "Did ever you see such a day as this?" she asks.

But at the end of February, a bittersweet *rendez-vous* with Charles Buckle had left Vivien depressed, as she complained to Scofield on 3 March. Only ten minutes after Scofield had left her house the previous Thursday, while she was feeling ill with influenza, the telephone rang and it was *"Mr. Buckle!!!"*—home on four days' leave, who whisked Vivien away to the Savoy to dance. Despite her high temperature—"I guessed it would kill me"—she could not resist the invitation, although the next day she felt so ill that she could hardly stand. Vivien was disappointed that she was not able to see her former fiancé before he returned to the front on Sunday, or even wave him goodbye. For a short while Buckle's visit revived Vivien's old feelings for him; "Wasn't it queer," she asks Scofield, that Buckle rang just after she had been showing Scofield his photographs, and she confesses that "there is so much more to tell," which she will disclose when she sees him.[52]

But her hopes seem to have melted away again with Buckle's departing regiment, the Royal Garrison Artillery, in which he had been commissioned 2nd Lieutenant on 19 September 1914. As a "galloper" he would have ridden one of the horses pulling the 80-pound guns.[53] The rows of the past year which ended in their broken engagement probably convinced her that the relationship had no future. Despite the lengthening lists of soldiers killed in action, which might have alerted Vivien to the danger of marrying an officer—although it seems that Charles Buckle survived the Great War—she continued to divert herself with friends of Maurice's, particularly cavalrymen such as Butler-Thuring of the 5th Lancers, for whom she had a particular weakness, and Captain Holmes, who also took her dancing. But if Vivien seemed fickle, she was also determined; her thoughts were turning increasingly to the more exciting, and safer, option of an American. Disappointed that Scofield was about to return to America, she now had his friend Tom Eliot in view.

The development of Vivien's relationship with Eliot was stimulated by the long-standing rivalry between himself and Scofield. They had competed academically at both school and university in poetry and Latin, and Eliot had emerged triumphant, being chosen to declaim his "Ode to Fair Harvard" on Harvard Class Day at graduation in June 1910.[54] Now to academic competitiveness romantic rivalry was added. Vivien gave the impression of being Scofield's girlfriend in the months before she met Eliot, as her flirtatious letters demonstrate: Scofield is a "noble Roman" she tells him in February. "You had me in your . . . sight," she remarks teasingly in March 1915, and urges him to take "a batchelor's [sic] flat" at Queen Anne's Mansions: "You *must* go there, I want you to." Mischievously she attempted to arouse Scofield's jealousy, telling him that her brother Maurice had been beagling with Mr. Butler-Thuring, whom she would like *very* much.[55] At the Savoy again on 2 August, she is reminded of Scofield and "that very nice dinner which cost you such an *awful lot* that we had there."[56] Maurice remembered that "Scofield Thayer was going out with Vivie," and Ezra Pound also thought so.[57] The intimacy between Vivien and Scofield was evident to Eliot and spurred him to steal yet another prize from his friend. Vivien, of course, was never serious about Scofield, however much she valued him as a generous escort, friend and consolation for her hurt pride over the broken engagement.

Not only did Vivien's popularity in the set to which he himself now belonged increase her desirability for Eliot, she also appealed to his snobbishness. The dances at the Savoy, the dinners in Soho, seemed to promise a more upper-class lifestyle than the "Cubist teas" he attended with Pound or Wyndham Lewis. Vivien must have talked of her army officer brother, her father the Royal Academician, with a private income and several houses, who could be expected to settle a generous sum on his only daughter. On first acquaintance it seemed to Eliot that Vivien came from a social background equivalent to his own in New England, although to an English aristocrat such as Bertrand Russell, Vivien, only two generations away from her roots in trade, seemed "a little vulgar."[58] She made a similar impression on Aldous Huxley, who saw it as a point in her favour: "I rather like her; she is such a genuine person, vulgar, but with no attempt to conceal her vulgarity, with no snobbery of the kind that makes people say they like things such as Bach or Cézanne, when they don't." Another aristocrat, the generous-hearted Ottoline Morrell, could not help noticing in 1921 that Vivien was "really rather common."[59]

Vivien's eager response to Tom's poetry fostered their relationship. Her enthusiasm for her new suitor's poetic mission encouraged the astonishing but intoxicating thought that Tom might stay in England at the end of his year at Oxford instead of returning to a dull and predictable future in academic philosophy at Harvard. Together he and Vivien made secret plans. Perhaps Eliot detected in Vivien's bright, articulate manner a good, if untrained mind; certainly her secretarial skills would aid him in his career. Although no intellectual, in the months before their marriage Vivien was educating herself in the poetry of the Imagists. In February 1915 she visited the Poetry Bookshop, complaining to Scofield that bookseller Harold Monro was "rather haughty" about exchanging her book, demanding to "inspect it first"; Monro, a good judge of his customers, suspected that Vivien was trying to conceal the fact she had cut some of the pages. In March, Vivien confided to Scofield that she had read T. E. Hulme's poem "Conversion" while waiting in someone's drawing-room, which made her search for the book in which it was included, Pound's *Ripostes*. Her favourite poems were "Luies—Echoes II, and the *last* part of 'A Girl' *(I love that)*." Pound's poem "A Girl" is a verse of pagan sensuality, in which a girl is a spirit of the earth:

> Tree you are,
> Moss you are,
> You are violets with wind above them.
> A child—*so* high—you are,
> And all this is folly to the world.[60]

The appeal of the poem for Vivien reveals her innocence as well as her animism, the "child's eye" through which she viewed nature. She also liked Pound's "An Immorality," "A Virginal" and "Camaraderie" in *Personae*. The wistful sonnet "A Virginal" expresses the thoughts of a lover for the woman he has left behind, and reminded Vivien no doubt of Buckle, who had so lately left her to go to war. She hoped her soldier lover missed her as much as the narrator of Pound's poem:

> No, no! Go from me. I have left her lately.
> I will not spoil my sheathe with lesser brightness,
> For my surrounding air hath a new lightness;
> Slight are her arms, yet they have bound me straitly
> And left me cloaked with a gauze of aether;
> As with sweet leaves; as with subtle clearness.
> Oh, I have picked up magic in her nearness.

Another of Vivien's favourites, "An Immorality," from *Personae,* 1909, was also liked by Pound's mother, and was set to music by Aaron Copland:[61]

> Sing we for love and idleness
> Naught else is worth the having.
> Though I have been in many a land,
> There is naught else in living.
> And I would rather have my sweet,
> Though rose-leaves die of grieving,
> Than do high deeds in Hungary
> To pass all men's believing.

The troubadour's idealisation of love as the purpose of living, as interpreted by Pound, influenced Vivien and may have clouded her judgement of Eliot. He, finding Vivien as much an admirer of Hulme's "Conversion" as himself, and influenced by Bergsonian exhortations to cast oneself into the flow of immediate experience, began to feel "the magic of her nearness" in a way which gratified Vivien. But although Eliot was impressed by her interest in Imagist poetry, and saw it as an indication of shared interests, boarding-school education had left many gaps in Vivien's knowledge—"I have found out how to spell 'queu' [sic]. Isn't that it?" she writes hopefully to Scofield, explaining that she wasn't really referring to billiards and remaining just as confused between "cue" and "queue" as before.[62] This ignorance may have had its charm for Eliot. No doubt her naïve questions about philosophy fed his ego and gave him the confidence to overcome his usual Prufrockian paralysis in the presence of women. It must have seemed to Tom Eliot that Vivien, child-like, artistic and vulnerable, was the very opposite of his formidable, managing mother, and in this very weakness lay her attraction for him.

As he held Vivien's slim androgynous figure in his arms, an avenue of escape opened before him: escape from his mother's domination, provincial New England life and an academic career. With Vivien, emancipated yet seductive, he felt an unaccustomed sexual spark as they sparred in conversation, or quickstepped across the ballroom, a stylish couple who turned heads. Aldous Huxley believed there was a "sexual nexus" between them: "One sees it in the way he looks at her . . . she's an incarnate provocation."[63] Certainly Vivien, for her part, had fallen in love with the "thrilling" American from the Midwest. Tom seemed to have stepped straight out of the movies, putting in the shade the callow army officers who had formerly been her suitors. In her diary, she described Tom's clean-cut mouth, fine head and deep, hawklike eyes.[64]

Both Vivien and Tom carried an air of mystery; undeniably they mirrored each other, both *poseurs* who attached great importance to fashion and outward appearance. Each felt a Narcissus-like spark of recognition in the other's presence. Added to this subliminal attraction, which was the basis for physical desire, Vivien found in Tom Eliot someone who seemed to promise everything she had hoped for from Buckle and had lost: love, marriage and, most important, freedom from her mother. For Vivien, marriage was a revenge upon Rose Haigh-Wood as much as it was—for Tom—upon Charlotte Eliot.

Vivien's very vivacity seemed to breathe into him the life force her name promised: "adventurous, full of life," in Russell's words, she roused Eliot from the *aboulie* and nervous depression which had troubled him in the past, and offered an apparent solution to his sexual problems, an opportunity to normalise his life. She promised, too, an end to the loneliness he had experienced since coming to England, in a re-creation of the close family life he had known in St. Louis with his sisters. Perhaps most of all, his vision—and hers too—was of a literary and artistic partnership like the Pounds' and Aldingtons', at the heart of the vortex. The energy of this vortex, which Gaudier-Brzeska wrote from the trenches was "the vortex of will, of decision, that begins," caught Tom and Vivien in its tumbling centre and swept them towards action.[65] Rationality was lost as they spun in the whirlpool. Looking back, Eliot came to see Pound's role as fateful, both for his career and his marriage. Pound, he said, was the man who had "changed his life" by giving him the praise and encouragement he had long since ceased to hope for. "Pound urged me to stay ... and encouraged me to write verse again." Astute enough to realise that Eliot's future as a writer lay in England, Pound encouraged him to follow his example of settling in London and marrying an Englishwoman.[66]

It was an attack on two fronts, for in the same month, at Pound's insistence, "The Love Song of J. Alfred Prufrock" appeared in *Poetry*. Much later, Eliot came to believe that he had been in love with Emily Hale in 1915 and had only wanted a flirtation with Vivien: "I came to persuade myself that I was in love with her simply because I wanted to burn my boats and commit myself to staying in England. And she persuaded herself (also under the influence of Pound) that she would save the poet by keeping him in England."[67] Nevertheless, Pound the matchmaker cannot be blamed for the marriage: Eliot never loved Emily Hale enough to want to propose to her; when he had the opportunity later he failed to do so. It was Vivien's personality and position which seemed at that moment to meet his needs.

Vivien's restless energy may have been psychologically necessary to Eliot in May and June 1915, for he nursed a secret grief he could not share with her. His dear friend, the Frenchman Jean Verdenal, who had become a medical officer in November 1914, had been killed on 2 May in the Dardanelles. His service record contains a citation dated 30 April 1915: "Scarcely recovered from pleurisy, he did not hesitate to spend much of the night in the water up to his waist helping to evacuate the wounded by sea, thus giving a notable example of self-sacrifice." A later entry dated 23 June 1915 says: "Verdenal, assistant medical officer, performed his duties with courage and devotion. He was killed on 2 May 1915 while dressing a wounded man on the field of battle."[68] In his small library his brother Pierre later found volumes of Laforgue and Mallarmé.

Eliot never eradicated the memory of Jean, which became an obsession as time passed. In 1934, reminiscing in the editor's column of the *Criterion* about his year in Paris in 1910–11, he wrote: "I am willing to admit that my own retrospect is touched by a sentimental sunset, the memory of a friend coming across the Luxembourg Gardens in the late afternoon, waving a branch of lilac, a friend who was later (so far as I could find out) to be mixed with the mud of Gallipoli." Lilacs became Eliot's symbol of loss: "April is the cruellest month, breeding/Lilacs out of the dead land, mixing/Memory and desire." Eliot would have heard of Verdenal's death in May or June, and the shock and sorrow of this news may well have precipitated his proposal to Vivien. The poet's anguish was immense. It seems that Verdenal was later transfigured in his imagination into Phlebas, the drowned Phoenician in "Death by Water" in *The Waste Land.* "Gentile or Jew," he addresses his readers, "O you who turn the wheel and look to windward,/Consider Phlebas, who was once handsome and tall as you." It is a cry of grief which has given rise to the suggestion that *The Waste Land* is in essence an elegy for Jean. The medical officer, like Phlebas, was "a fortnight dead," when Eliot, on the rebound, proposed to the young Englishwoman he scarcely knew.

The war was also dividing Eliot from another close companion, a successor to Jean, at the end of the Oxford term. Just before his marriage Eliot was forced to part company with Karl Henry Culpin, an Anglo-German undergraduate, who was in his final year as an Exhibitioner at Merton College when Eliot met him; according to Eliot's confidant, New Zealand critic Robert Gordon George, who wrote as "Robert Sencourt," Eliot "shared one of the deepest friendships of his life"[69] with Culpin, who was nearly five years his junior. Karl Culpin had been educated at Doncaster Grammar School and was described by Eliot as "the most intelligent of the Englishmen at Merton"—he graduated with First Class Honours in Modern History in the summer of 1915; his warm appreciation of "Prufrock" made him an "ideal companion" for the poet, whom Culpin introduced to his sister, Mary. During the Christmas vacation Eliot and Karl and an American friend, Brand Blashford, had spent a fortnight's holiday together by the seaside at Swanage in Dorset. After graduation Karl entered the army and despite poor eyesight was commissioned as 2nd Lieutenant in the Gloucestershires.[70] Soon Eliot would lose this friend also.

Vivien seemed to promise life, whereas the love of men promised only death. Sencourt alludes to Vivien's "melancholy, disillusionment, fragility and sensitiveness": Eliot found her sensitive to his moods and his pain. It may have seemed to Eliot that the death of Verdenal represented punishment for a love that was sinful. Was he tormented by guilt, were his Unitarian grandfather's prohibitions ringing in his ears, when he took the fatal decision to propose to Vivien? Did she trap him into marriage? Sencourt suggests that Vivien seduced Eliot: "it is normal for a woman to enjoy her power to play upon the strings and nerves of manhood till they hasten the throbbing pulse with sensations of peculiar pleasure."[71] A myth was put about by Cyril Connolly that Vivien compromised Tom Eliot; that "the awful daring of a moment's surrender" took place in a punt, with Eliot playing "the young man carbuncular" and Vivien "the indifferent typist." Eliot then felt honour bound, as a New England gentleman, to propose: "In Richmond I raised my knees," run lines in *The Waste Land:* "Supine on the floor of the narrow canoe." Eliot's American biographer, T. S. Matthews, dismisses this theory, and the evidence suggests that Eliot was no victim.[72] He had told Aiken that he wanted to marry and lose his virginity; and in a letter to Scofield, congratulating him on his own marriage a year later, Eliot remembered how the two Americans took the initiative in "charming the eyes (and ears) of Char-flappers"; he recommends to Scofield the advice of Oscar Wilde that "only the soul can cure the senses, and only the senses can cure the soul."[73] If this is not sardonic—for Eliot was not to know that Scofield the aesthete's marriage to Elaine Eliot Orr was rapidly to collapse, although he might have guessed it—it suggests that in his girlfriend Vivien, Tom Eliot believed for a moment he had found a cure for his sickness of soul.

Eliot's willingness to marry without a formal engagement or introductions to either sets of parents was of vital importance, for Vivien knew she must keep her plans secret or else Rose Haigh-Wood would forbid marriage to Eliot just as she had forbidden marriage to Charles Buckle. And Vivien was resolved to be a bride; she was twenty-seven in May (although she gave her age as twenty-six on her marriage certificate), and did not want to spend the rest of her life as a spinster governess. Tom, too, knew his own mother would be opposed to marriage to an unknown English girl, but it was not only fear of his mother that drove him to hurry into this marriage. He could not afford to stop and think, for the only way to overcome the conflict between head and heart which up till now had left him paralysed and inhibited towards women, was to jump in with his eyes shut. Like Stephen Spender, who also married his first wife Inez on impulse, after knowing her for only a few weeks, Eliot felt that, despite the ambivalence in his attitudes towards men and women, he needed the "eternally feminine," the otherness of women which contrasted with the self-identification of male-male relationships. "I could not develop beyond a certain point unless I were able to enter a stream of nature through human contacts, that is to say, through experience of women," says Spender.[74] Like Spender, Eliot knew that if he did not act on impulse he could not act at all; and having reached a point in his life where work no longer filled the emptiness of living alone, where "friends had failed," marriage seemed the only solution.

On 26 June 1915, after knowing each other for three months, Vivien Haigh-Wood and Thomas Stearns Eliot were married at Hampstead Register Office, shortly after the end of the term at Oxford. Lucy Thayer was present, but the only member of either family to witness the marriage was Vivien's aunt, Lillia Symes. So ill-prepared were the couple for life together that neither had given the slightest thought to money or where they would live.

5

The Poet's Bride

B less war babies, Selfridges, The scaffolding around the Albert Memorial, All ABC Tea-Shops" and "BLESS the Poet's Bride (June 28th)"—the date was incorrect by two days—*Blast* exhorted its readers in July 1915. "BLAST Bevan, and his dry rot, and Birth Control . . ." An article by editor Wyndham Lewis congratulated his friend Eliot on his decision to marry: "There is nothing so impressive as the number Two," wrote Lewis. "For the Individual, the single subject, and the isolated, is, you will admit, an absurdity . . . Hurry up and get into this harmonious and sane duality. The thought of . . . Male and Female, Eternal Duet of Existence, can perhaps still be of help to you."[1] *Blast* published several of Eliot's poems in the July edition of the magazine: four "Preludes" and "Rhapsody on a Windy Night." But although recognition by an underground magazine might bring the white stag of fame a little closer, it did not pay the bills.

Eliot had taken lodgings at 35 Greek Street, Soho, for the week between the end of the Oxford term on 19 June and his wedding, but these were unsuitable for a new bride. The problem of where to live immediately presented itself. Vivien sent a telegram breaking the news of the marriage to her parents, Charles and Rose, who were staying in Lincolnshire, where Maurice's regiment was quartered. They returned directly and, to Vivien's immense relief, Rose's reaction to her daughter's shocking announcement—marriage without a previous engagement was scandalous behaviour for a girl of her social class—was more favourable than she expected. Instead of venting their anger on Vivien for presenting them with a *fait accompli,* Rose and Charles "very quickly recognized Tom's sincerity and high character and took him to their hearts as a son-in-law."[2] Vivien's new husband was, after all, no stranger to the Haigh-Woods, for he had been to stay at Compayne Gardens with Lucy Thayer, although he kept a poste restante address in London at which to receive his American post. Now Tom joined Vivien in the spare room at number 3, and Rose's warnings to Buckle that her daughter was not fit to marry or become a mother were quietly buried.

The truth was that Charles and Rose Haigh-Wood were relieved to have their problematical daughter taken off their hands in 1915, a year in which their financial situation was changing for the worse. With the onset of the First World War the "peripatetic ease" of their life, lived between London, Taplow, Anglesey, the Alps and the South of France, came to an end. According to Maurice, monies sent between Dublin and London were frozen and Charles and Rose Haigh-Wood "found themselves a little low on cash."[3] The careless extravagance of the *belle époque* was no longer possible, and Haigh-Wood began cutting the annuities he paid to a number of sisters and cousins. Apparently Aunt Lillia and cousin Cornelius refused to leave the outer hall of Compayne Gardens until they received the funds they believed were owed them. Although circumstances may not have been as straitened as Charles claimed (the manor house in Anglesey was retained and none of the Irish property was sold) he now made his "beloved" Rose "for whom I have thanked God every day during our married life" his priority.[4] After settling £1,000 on Vivien, which gave her an income of £50 a year, he made it clear to his son-in-law that henceforth his new wife was to be his own responsibility.

Maurice has said that his father "was not involved with Tom and Vivie: he only wanted what was best for her, and never enquired further. He never wanted to know much about her 'womanly problems.' "[5] Rose's attitude was equally detached, behind coaxing words, as a letter she wrote to Vivien from Plas Llanfair in Anglesey on her wedding anniversary shows:

[Friday, June 1916]

Dearest Little Vivie,

Of course I was delighted to have your nice little letter this morning . . . Now I want to hear you are *building* up. You know what I mean, dear. And you must do it with your own bricks and mortar. And your own trowel. Firmly lay your bricks with good strong cement. Each day adding one more. Till you build yourself a strong wall of defence. So I shall want your assurance that each day the brick has been truly laid.

Write me a *really* newsy letter. There's a dear little Vivie. So now darling with all my most loving wishes for many happy returns of the anniversary of your marriage and wishing you all good luck, your own loving mother, love to Lucy and Tom.[6]

It was a strange letter to write to a woman of twenty-eight, and gives an indication of why Vivien found independence so hard. But for both her children to be independent was Rose's desire. Maurice had been commissioned 2nd Lieutenant in the Manchester Regiment on 12 May 1915[7] and, aged only nineteen, left for France on the day Tom and Vivien were married. He and Tom formed a close friendship from the beginning, in which Maurice looked up to his older brother-in-law and accepted his judgement, even at the expense of his sister: "He is a very handsome boy, with a great deal of breeding," wrote Eliot to his mother. "Very aristocratic, and very simple too."[8] When Maurice returned from northern France on his first leave in November, Rose tried to give the early Christmas celebrations an American flavour: "There was cranberry sauce in my honour—they did not know that it ought to be served with the turkey! And had it as a dessert!" Eliot pretended this was right, as his mother-in-law had taken such pains with it, and the pudding came in "blazing properly," with an American flag on it. Rose did everything possible to show that she was fond of Tom, although he had expected to take a back seat when Maurice was at home, "but they all treated me with more cordiality than ever, and I felt very fond of them." Nevertheless, he began quite soon to realise that, for all their friendliness, the Haigh-Woods were self-preoccupied and would do little to help him. He was not told of his new wife's history of illness and dependence on doctors. "You must be kind to Vivie," was the coded message Maurice gave his brother-in-law.[9]

The only solution to Tom and Vivien's pressing financial crisis seemed to be to apply to Henry and Charlotte Eliot, who had supported their gifted son in the past through his years at Harvard, Paris and London, in the expectation that he would finally win a prestigious post at Harvard and bring academic glory to the family. More conventional than the Haigh-

Woods, the news of Tom's hurried marriage to an unknown English-woman hit them like a bombshell. Equally shocking was his proposal to abandon philosophy and stay in England to make his fortune as a poet. Such deviation from the path his parents had laid out for him demanded an explanation, and Tom knew that he must go to them in person if he was not to be cut off without a penny.

His first action was to turn to his old friend, Ezra Pound, who, only two days after the marriage, wrote to Henry Ware Eliot, defending Eliot's decision to devote himself to a literary life. He cited his own case as proof that it was possible to exist by letters: "I believe I am as well off as various of my friends who plugged away at law, medicine, and preaching. At any rate I have had an infinitely more interesting life." Unfortunately Pound's view of subsistence living was different from Tom and Vivien's: the $500 allowance for the first year "to begin on" and $250 for the second, for which Ezra pleaded, was far below the standard of living to which both the Eliots were accustomed.[10] Nor were the rest of Pound's arguments likely to carry much weight with the brick manufacturer to whom he was writing. Pound had paved the way for Eliot, he explained: "I have brought something new into English poetry; I have engineered a new school of verse now known in England, France and America," adding that he had cast his poetry in medieval Provence but Tom was doing the far more difficult job of setting his "personae" in modern life. "T.S.E. is . . . that rare thing among modern poets, a scholar," and thus a man with the mental stamina to finish "a distance race." Eliot needed to be in London, declared Pound with brutal honesty, because, "No one in London cares a hang what is written in America . . . London likes discovering her own gods."[11]

It was not a letter calculated to please a father who wanted his son to take a steady job, or a mother who wanted him to live out her own dreams of academic brilliance. Nor did Bertrand Russell's subsequent letter to Charlotte Champe Eliot, arguing that the "financial outlook"[12] for Eliot would be just as good in England as in America bring her round. Charlotte replied crisply that she did not see "any reason why if my son makes Philosophy his life work he should not write all the poetry he pleases, if not too much of the ephemeral *'vers libre.'* "[13] Charlotte was not impressed by Russell's praise of Vivien. "I have taken some pains to get to know [Tom's] wife, who seems to me thoroughly nice, really anxious for his welfare, and very desirous of not hampering his liberty or interfering with whatever he feels to be best," wrote Russell. "The chief sign of her influence that I have seen is that he is no longer attracted by the people who call themselves 'vorticists.' " The mention of the Vorticists was like a red rag to a bull to Charlotte. "As for the 'The *Blast,*' Mr. Eliot remarked when he saw a copy he did not know there were enough lunatics in the world to support such a magazine."

The announcement of the marriage in the *St. Louis Globe Democrat* of 16 July 1915 was heavy with disapproval. "Thomas Eliot of St. Louis Weds Abroad," proclaimed the headline: "Bride of Oxford Student was Miss Vivien Haigh-Wood, Daughter of Member of Royal Academy of Arts. The announcement of the marriage of Thomas Stearns Eliot, son of Mr. and Mrs. Henry Ware Eliot of 4446 Westminster Place, St. Louis, and Miss Vivien Haigh-Wood in London, England, on June 26, was made by the Eliots, who are at their summer house in Gloucester, Mass." Henry Ware Eliot Jr., notified by his mother, "said he knew little of Miss Haigh-Wood."[14] Between the lines of the local newspaper item we can read the horror of the Eliot parents that, as Henry's wife Theresa expressed it, "T.S.E. and Vivienne married in 1915 without prior announcement to their parents."[15]

A week after his marriage, Eliot sent a letter of explanation to his brother Henry. It reads as if he is still trying dazedly to convince himself that he has made the right decision. Henry knows what his younger brother has always wanted, writes Eliot, and so his sudden marriage will seem natural enough: "The only really surprising thing is that I should have had the force to attempt it, and when you know Vivien, I am sure you will not be surprised at that either." The responsibility of marriage, he declares, is just what he needs. "Now my only concern is how I can make her perfectly happy, and I think I can do that by being myself infinitely more fully than I ever have been. I am much less suppressed, and more confident, than I ever have been." After asking Henry to approach the editor of the *Atlantic Monthly* on his behalf if he happened to be in Boston, and telling him that "Portrait of a Lady" was coming out in a new publication called *Others* in New York, Tom repeats his conviction that he feels more alive than he ever has before.[16] Will Henry use his influence to persuade their mother and father to come over to see them, he begs. Vivien adds a postscript: "I am sure we can depend on you to help us. I read the letter you wrote to Tom and liked it so much, and I almost feel I know you. I should like it if you will write to me." She signs herself, "Vivien S. Eliot," proudly adopting Stearns as her middle name.

Eliot struck the same note of guarded enthusiasm in a letter sent in early July to Mrs. Jack Gardner, a Boston hostess and art patron whom he used to visit in 1912. He had not been secretive, or rash, he assured her, in marrying Vivien: "You said once that marriage is the greatest test in the world. I know now that you were right, but now I welcome the test instead of dreading it." Marriage, he had already discovered, is much more than a "test of sweetness and temper," as people think; rather it tests the whole character and affects every action. Simply saying this, rather than telling his correspondent about Vivien, or his happiness, will show her that he has done "the best thing."[17] Reading between the lines, Isabella Gardner might have detected signs that her correspondent was already finding the "test" of marriage a trying one.

On 9 July Tom invited Bertrand Russell to dinner to meet Vivien, and perhaps to ask the older man for advice as to how to solve some of the problems crowding in upon him. Russell instantly judged the marriage to be a failure. His interest was aroused by Eliot's pretty but discontented bride, however, and he encouraged Vivien to confide her secrets to him. "Friday evening I dined with my Harvard pupil, Eliot, and his bride. I expected her to be terrible, from his mysteriousness; but she was not so bad," he wrote to Ottoline Morrell. "She is light, . . . adventurous, full of life— an artist, I think he said, but I should have thought her an actress. He is exquisite and listless; she says she married him in order to stimulate him, but finds she can't do it. Obviously he married in order to be stimulated. I think she will soon be tired of him."[18] Eliot may have hoped marriage would restore the sense of Bergsonian *élan vital* which he had experienced in Paris in the company of Jean Verdenal, but for all his claims to Henry to be more "alive," he struck Russell as "listless." From her complaint that she was unable to "stimulate" Tom, Russell quickly scented that the couple's problems were sexual.

"He is ashamed of his wife," noted Russell, "and very grateful if one is kind to her." Within just two weeks of marriage, Vivien's mock-Cockney chatter and theatrical manner had begun to jar on her husband:

"Thanks very much for your cable—*and* for yr gratters and invitation," wrote Vivien to Scofield, who had telegraphed not only his congratulations but an invitation to stay with him at Edgartown, Massachusetts, if she came to America. "Charmed as I should be to avail myself of the latter, I fear it is impossible at present."[19] It was the kind of language which Eliot was to incorporate into *The Waste Land,* a task in which Vivien aided him, but although the rhythms of Cockney speech fascinated Eliot, his wife's affectations began to irritate him as his suspicion grew that nothing of substance lay beneath her lively chatter.

As Vivien poured out her feelings to Russell, who was sixteen years older than both the Eliots and presented himself as a father-figure and mentor, Eliot felt a surge of relief that someone seemed to understand his wife, and to sympathise with them both. Naïvely he believed Russell could solve the problem of what to do with Vivien while he was away, for he was due to sail for the U.S. on 24 July, for a six-week family reunion at the Eliot summer house at East Gloucester. Vivien refused to accompany him. "She refuses to go to see his people, for fear of submarines," wrote Russell to Ottoline.[20] Vivien expressed the same fear to Scofield, saying she was "much too frightened" of the voyage and the submarines, and did not want to go at all. Such fear was justified, for the *Lusitania* had been sunk in May 1915, only a month before the Eliots' marriage; it was an indication of Eliot's own sense of crisis that he braved the journey in obedience to his parents' summons. But Vivien's fear of submarines was not the only reason for her reluctance to accompany her husband. She wrote to Scofield on 2 August, the day that Eliot arrived in America, that "all the Eliots appear to have an overwhelming desire to see me, and have written me such charming letters of welcome into their select family, that I am sure I *shall* have to go over soon, probably in the spring."[21] It was an alarming prospect. Would they find her acceptable, she wondered apprehensively. "I hope you will repeat your invitation," she told Scofield, putting off the evil day, for her feelings about America were ambivalent. Although Vivien admired the novels of Henry James, likening herself to Daisy Miller,[22] the Rousseauesque "child of nature" in James's eponymous tale, and Eliot to Daisy's repressed suitor, Winterbourne, the United States seemed a "savage land" to her and she remained resolutely in London.[23]

The night before he sailed, Tom wrote a letter to his father, asking him to look after Vivien if anything happened to him on the voyage. Specifically he hoped Henry Ware Eliot would see she got the $5,000 insurance he had taken out for his son. Vivien would need it, he wrote. She would be in a most difficult position. Her own family were in straitened circumstances owing to the war, and he knew her pride would make her want to earn her own living. This would be very hard for her at first, with the weight of Tom's loss. He had taken on a great responsibility, he admitted, perhaps the first hint of Vivien's frail constitution, but he was also aware of all that he owed her:

> She has been ready to sacrifice everything for me . . . Now that we have been married a month, I am *convinced* that she has been the one person for me. She has everything to give that I want, and she gives it. I owe her everything.

Only too conscious that he was penniless, he burst out: "I have married her on nothing, and she knew it, and was willing, for my sake. She had nothing to gain by marrying me. I have imposed upon you very much, but upon her more . . . Your loving son, Tom." Vivien, he wrote, had not seen his letter.[24]

It was a generous letter, expressing Eliot's deep sense of obligation to Vivien for marrying him "on nothing," and for freely offering him her love and support at a critical time in his life. Had she not done so in June 1915, it is highly questionable whether Eliot would have stayed in London and made the career he did. Instead he would have obeyed his mother's summons to return to New England and philosophy. In 1915 his literary life hung in the balance, and Vivien tipped the scales. It was she who anchored him in England. Had Vivien sailed to America with Eliot, the increasing danger of submarines would have probably kept them both on the other side of the Atlantic for the duration of the war at least. Like Scofield, Eliot might never have returned to England. Vivien's refusal to accompany him to the family reunion in Gloucester gave Eliot both the courage and the excuse to do as he wished, to defy his parents and return to England and poetry.

Eliot's letter to his father to some extent contradicts Russell's damning and not wholly disinterested verdict on the marriage written in the same month. But although Eliot voiced his gratitude for Vivien's "sacrifice," he did not say he loved her. And it was certainly a very disgruntled bride he left behind. Vivien was annoyed that her new husband had left her to make the risky journey home, and did not understand the necessity for it. It seemed to her that no sooner had she captured a husband than he abandoned her. "Tom has gone to America without me," she complained to Scofield on 2 August. "Rather unwise to leave so attractive a wife alone to her own devices! However—I did not at all want to go," she wrote, explaining that as well as being afraid of the voyage, she "much preferred to play my own little games alone." It was an ominous portent for the events that unfolded during Tom's six-week absence.

Artlessly Vivien described her life since her marriage to Eliot to Scofield, painting an initial picture of charming bohemian poverty: "Do you remember my mentioning a studio flat which I rather hankered to take, while you were here? Well, Tom and I took it—furnished—& lived there for about 3 weeks before he went . . . It was a delightful place." Vivien kept the studio for another week after Tom's departure, and spent three days at home at Compayne Gardens before joining her friend Lucy at Thyme Cottage. Tom was supposed to be coming back on 1 September. "After we have had a second honeymoon!—we shall have to set up a house or a flat of our own—in London, of course. It is very nice being Mrs. Stearns-Eliot" (a name Vivien adopted in the first euphoria of marriage, later dropping the hyphen and the Stearns and reverting to her paternal grandmother's name, Haigh). She was seeing a good deal of the Pounds, of course, "and between ourselves, find them rather boring." However, they were very nice to her, and sought her out such a lot that she supposed she should feel honoured.

Teasingly Vivien tells Scofield something of the "little games" she is playing with the officers she knew before her marriage.

I was at the Savoy the other night with 2 male friends who are consoling the grass widow, so I thought of you Scofield . . . You really ought to be over here now, just think of the dinners in Soho we could do—and grass widows do seem, I find, to be so very *very* attractive, *much more* than spinsters! Now WHY is that? Butler-

Thuring is in the *5th Lancers!*—so is of course bucked to death.
But he has done well—It is a very crack regiment.[25]

There is no doubt that Vivien was extremely pleased to be married at last,
a change of status which encouraged her to play the coquette. "Have you
seen the new *Blast!*" she demands, gratified that she was featured in it as
"the Poet's Bride," although she found Lewis "an impossible man." Was
Scofield married yet, she inquires archly. If not, why not? "If you can manage to refrain from marriage (it is *so* catching I know!) do come over here
before long and let us resume our childish aquaintance [sic] and youthful
prattle." She wasn't really keen on meeting him in the United States, she
repeated. "London is far better—is it not?" Almost as an afterthought, she
remembered her husband, and asked Scofield to remember her kindly to
Tom if he should see him in Massachusetts.

There is an air of unreality about Vivien's "prattle," as she herself
called it. "What I want is MONEY! $! £! We are hard up!"[26] Tom was
writing to his old friend Conrad Aiken from The Downs, the large house
overlooking the sea which his father had built in 1896 at Eastern Point,
Gloucester; Vivien, meanwhile, was still dancing at the Savoy in the "snobbish, social sunset," in the words of Wyndham Lewis, of the pre-war
golden years.[27] Setting up a house in London, as she wished, would be impossible on a schoolmaster's salary, for by now Tom was planning to look
for a teaching job in a boys' school, a prospect which filled his mother with
horror: "It is like putting Pegasus in harness," she confided to Bertrand
Russell.[28]

Despite Vivien's bravado, she was lonely without Tom, and therefore
vulnerable. Her brother Maurice was away in France, and the officers she
saw briefly had to return to their regiments, but there was another man
who was interested, available, and as lonely as she was: Bertrand Russell.
He did not take long to strike. The first hint of Russell's pursuit of Vivien
comes in her boast to Scofield in her letter of 2 August that she is "very
popular with Tom's friends—and who do you think in *particular*? No less
a person than Bertrand Russell!! He is all over me, is Bertie, and I simply
love him. I am dining with him next week."

Flattered and excited by the philosopher's reputation and background, Vivien was easy prey for the fickle and predatory Russell, a man with a long history of broken relationships, who was as unwise a choice of guardian to a new bride as it was possible to make. It is difficult to believe that Eliot was unaware of Russell's reputation, through Pound and the Vorticists, when he left his lively wife in the mathematician's care: did *naïveté* have its secret intentions?

By 2 August, Russell's euphoric mood of early summer had evaporated. Born in 1872, Bertrand Russell was the second son of Viscount Amberley, heir to the Russell earldom, and grandson of Lord John Russell, twice Prime Minister and the architect of the Great Reform Bill of 1832. His childhood had been a tragic one, since he lost his mother, sister and father before the age of four. At the point in his life when he met Vivien, he was disillusioned with two important relationships in his life: his "blood-brotherhood" with D. H. Lawrence, with whom he had struck up an instant friendship when they first met in 1915; and his love affair with Lady Ottoline Morrell, wife of Philip Morrell, MP for Burnley.

Russell was an essentially solitary man, one of whose life tasks was to "escape from the inner life, which is too painful to be endured continuously." His first wife, Alys Pearsall Smith, from a distinguished Quaker family, never offered him the intimacy or sexual fulfilment he craved: "Alys, even when I was most in love with her, remained outside my inner life," he told Ottoline. "What I get from you is an intensification of it, with a transmutation of the pain into beauty and wonder."[29] From the moment Russell stayed at Ottoline and Philip Morrell's house at 44 Bedford Square in Bloomsbury on 19 March 1911, his marriage was dead; he and Ottoline resolved to become lovers, and his first hope was that she would leave her husband for him. Ottoline was not a classically beautiful woman but she had enormous appeal for Russell, as for many other men: "Ottoline was very tall," wrote Russell in his *Autobiography,* "with a long thin face something like a horse, and very beautiful hair of an unusual colour, more or less like that of marmalade, but rather darker . . . She had a very beautiful gentle, vibrant voice, indomitable courage, and a will of iron . . . We were both earnest and unconventional, both aristocratic by tradition, but deliberately not so in our present environment, both hating the cruelty, the caste insolence, and the narrow-mindedness of aristocrats, and yet both a little alien in the world in which we chose to live, which regarded us with suspicion and lack of understanding because we were alien."[30] Their shared background drew Ottoline and Russell together and ensured that even when they ceased to be lovers in 1916, they remained close friends. Both were sometimes regarded as figures of fun by those of a different social background, to whom both Ottoline and Russell displayed a curious blindness, never comprehending that a working-class protégé like Lawrence might feel patronised by the sudden interest of two aristocrats who took him up with great alacrity and then appeared to reject him.

Immediately after the *coup de foudre* from Ottoline, Russell told Alys their marriage was over. "She stormed for some hours," he reported matter-of-factly, but his wife's feelings aroused no pity in Russell, who had lost interest in her as long ago as 1902 when he had fallen in love with Evelyn Whitehead, the wife of the co-author of *Principia Mathematica*. Russell's remarks about his first wife demonstrate the coldness and detachment he displayed to most of his lovers, with the exception of Ottoline. His solipsism was all-encompassing. Relating how Alys used to come to him in her dressing-gown and beseech him to spend the night with her, Russell wrote that, "About twice a year I would attempt sex relations with her in the hope of alleviating her misery, but she no longer attracted me and the attempt was futile."[31] Unfortunately for Russell, Alys refused him a divorce and her brother Logan Pearsall Smith demanded conditions for not naming Ottoline, when Russell decided to end his nine years of "tense self-denial" with his wife: the most painful of these was that Russell and Ottoline were never to spend a night together.[32] After their first rapturous love-making at Studland Bay, Ottoline agreed to this embargo. Russell's pyorrhoea, about which Ottoline was too embarrassed to speak to him, may have had something to do with her decision. In a cruelly honest entry in her journal, Ottoline once wrote that she could hardly bear Russell's lack of physical attraction:

> Not that he was at all ugly—he is rather short and thin, rigid and ungraceful, and would be unremarkable in a crowd. Then the exceeding beauty of his head would arrest me, for it gave the impression of perfect modelling: the skull thin and delicate, and the shape, especially when looked at from behind, always gave me the thrill of a very beautiful object. His eyes are large, and hold a con-

centrated beauty of intelligence and passion, and at times great
tenderness. The chin is small and rather weak, and the upper lip
very long and straight.[33]

However, she induced Bertie to shave off his large moustache, which she
thought had the effect of changing his appearance from that of a
Cambridge don to a cross between an actor and Voltaire.

Hurt that Ottoline would not leave Philip, Russell had no compunction about having sexual relations with other women, although he never
wished these transgressions to endanger his relationship with Ottoline. In
March 1914 he travelled to America to lecture in logic at Harvard, and in
Chicago met Helen Dudley, the daughter of a distinguished gynaecologist.
"I spent two nights under her parents' roof, and the second I spent with
her,"[34] remarks Russell casually, justifying his decision as a form of philanthropy, for Miss Dudley was apparently "withering like a flower in
drought" for lack of love, and "the impulse that came over me was like the
impulse to rescue a drowning person, and I am *sure* I was right to follow
it,"[35] as he informed Ottoline. Russell invited Helen Dudley to come to
England as soon as possible, so that they could live together openly and
perhaps marry later if a divorce could be obtained from Alys.

Russell was hardly back in England before his ardour towards Helen
began to cool. Ottoline had written to him that henceforth she wanted
their relationship to be platonic, but on hearing the news both that he had
a new mistress and that his pyorrhoea had been cured in America, changed
her mind, exhibiting a new sexual passion which revived all Russell's love
for her. "My Heart, I cannot lose you . . ." he wrote to Ottoline. By the time
the unfortunate Helen Dudley and her father sailed for England on 3
August 1914, Russell had resolved to have nothing to do with her, making
the excuse of loneliness to Ottoline for his misdemeanour: "The actual bottom fact is that the lonely nights grow unendurable and that I haven't
enough self-discipline to overcome the desire to share the nights with a
woman . . ."[36] In his *Autobiography* Russell argued that it was "the shock of
war" that ended his love for Helen Dudley, but this was as much a lie as
his vows of love to Helen. When she came hammering on the door of his
flat he refused to let her in: "I shall break her heart," wrote Russell dispassionately.[37] Finally Helen returned unhappily to America.

A second abortive affair with his research assistant, Irene Cooper-Willis, to whom Russell was introduced by Ottoline through her friendship with the writer Vernon Lee, had an even more extreme effect on his old lover. Ottoline was witness to Russell's and Vernon Lee's struggle for ascendancy over Irene Cooper-Willis, who finally agreed in January 1915 to help Russell research his proposed book on British foreign policy from 1906. Every afternoon, after a day in the British Museum, Irene called in at Russell's flat nearby for tea and conversation. Ottoline, feeling guilty that she and Russell had only snatched afternoons together, encouraged Russell's growing intimacy with Irene, and he kept up the fiction that his assistant was susceptible to his advances, even when she made it clear that she had no interest in him. On 15 January Ottoline wrote to ask Russell to spend a night with her. Jealousy made her more passionate than usual. "Last night I could only go on my knees in deep awe and thankfulness that such wonders had been given to one," she wrote to Russell. "It was simply unearthly, wasn't it? Every moment of it up to the last . . . It is worth all the sufferings of hell to love like this."[38] Russell's response was even more ecstatic: "My Heart, my Life, how can I ever tell you the amazing unspeakable glory of you tonight? You were utterly, absolutely of the stars—& yet of the Eternal Earth too—so that you took me from the Earth & in a moment carried me to the highest heights." The next night he continued:

> I want the mountains & the storm & the danger, & the wild sudden beauty, & the free winds of heaven. I have all that with you . . . you have *all* that my soul craves—I can't tell you the depths & wildness & vastness of my love to you. We have had many many great & wonderful times, but yesterday was more than all of them—more full of flame & fire—with the wildness of our having meant to part—with all the pain of the war—with everything, everything, caught up & transfigured in a great world of love, love, love.[39]

Despite this outpouring of passion, by the late summer Russell felt that Ottoline was "completely indifferent" to him. The companionship for which he yearned was unavailable to him at Garsington Manor, even though Ottoline had prepared a flat at the Bailiff's House for him in which to write his lectures on Social Reconstruction. But his hostess was wholly absorbed in her new property. On her forty-second birthday and house-warming party on 16 June 1915, Bertie joined D. H. Lawrence, the painter Mark Gertler, and Gilbert Cannan, a friend of artist Henry Lamb, in painting the oak panelled drawing-rooms, one Venetian red and the other sea-green, but this camaraderie proved illusory. All summer Garsington thronged with guests, and Bertie suddenly jarred on Ottoline when compared with the Bloomsbury wit and gossip offered by Clive and Vanessa Bell, Duncan Grant, Lytton Strachey, and the Slade School artists Dora Carrington and Dorothy Brett, as well as Lawrence's friends John Middleton Murry and Katherine Mansfield. Those who had passed through Ottoline's green double doors to her Thursday evening parties at Bedford Square now followed her to Oxfordshire. They represented the world of art, beauty and feeling to which she felt she belonged, while Bertie was of that other culture—science. Bertie "gets dreadfully on my nerves," wrote Ottoline on 19 July. "He is so stiff, so self-absorbed, so harsh and unbending in mind or body, that I can hardly look at him, but have to control myself and look away. And of course he feels this, and it makes him harsher and more snappy and crushing to me. What can I do? . . . Bertie . . . would remake me . . . It is far better to be alone than to be false."[40]

But Ottoline was never alone. And Russell's depression deepened when he became the subject of an unexpected, "ferocious" attack by D. H. Lawrence, to whom he and Ottoline had become very close after they had both read Lawrence's *The Prussian Officer*. The triangular mutual admiration society which had developed between Russell, Ottoline and Lawrence had done much to heal the wounds suffered by Russell at the hands of Wittgenstein, whose criticism had dented his confidence in 1913. "Lawrence is wonderfully lovable," Russell wrote to Ottoline. "The mainspring of his life is love—the universal mystical love—which inspires even his most vehement and passionate hate."[41] Weekends at Garsington consolidated his admiration for Lawrence, and Lawrence's for Ottoline, whom he called his "high priestess," imagining she could form the nucleus of a "little colony" of people who would sail away from the world of war and establish their own Utopia called Rananim.[42] Lawrence's ideal was "*a religious belief which leads to action"* and for a time Russell too was caught up in Lawrence's energetic fantasies. In spite of difficulties created by Lawrence's wife, Frieda, who resented Ottoline's adulation of her "Lorenzo," Russell began to believe that in Lawrence he had found a man who could finally assuage his loneliness. And when Lawrence accepted Russell's invitation to Cambridge, where the miner's son railed against the homosexual culture of Maynard Keynes and Duncan Grant, comparing them to "black beetles . . . which are cased each in a hard little shell of his own," and telling his new friend, "You must leave these friends, these beetles,"[43] the philosopher was delighted. Lawrence "has the same feeling against sodomy as I have," he informed Ottoline: "You had nearly made me believe there is no great harm in it, but I have reverted; & all the examples I know inform me in thinking it sterilising." Lawrence encouraged Russell to dream of leaving Trinity College, Cambridge, and becoming an independent teacher like Abelard. Together they began to plan a course of lectures in London in the autumn of 1915—Lawrence discoursing on ethics and Russell on immortality.

Russell's biographer Ray Monk draws attention to the mood of euphoria in Russell's letters of the time. It was unlikely that the working man from Nottingham and the academic philosopher could collaborate, and when Russell finally apprehended Lawrence's philosophy he thought it "bosh." When Russell sent Lawrence the synopsis he had drawn up of their proposed joint lectures, his collaborator attacked him with brutal ferocity. Russell received the rejected synopsis from Lawrence on 8 July, the day before he met Vivien. His reaction was extreme. "I feel a worm, a useless creature," he told Ottoline.[44] On 10 July he met Lawrence in London and had a "horrid" day. "I got filled with despair, and just counting the moments till it was ended."[45] Bertie decided to go it alone with his lectures, and made alternative arrangements through C. K. Ogden, editor of *The Cambridge Magazine,* to hire a hall in London, while Lawrence too began to make his own plans to publish his views in a new journal called *Signature,* which he was starting with John Middleton Murry.

The final blow came on 14 September, when Lawrence responded with a vehement attack on an essay Russell sent to him, outlining the danger to civilisation of the war; the essay was a lie, countered Lawrence, and

Russell was a hypocrite posing as the "angel of peace," although Lawrence would prefer Tirpitz a thousand times in that role. "You are really the super war-spirit," wrote Lawrence. "You are simply *full* of repressed desires, which have become savage and anti-social. And they come out in this sheep's clothing of peace propaganda." Russell's face looked evil, said Lawrence, and he was "too full of devilish repression to be anything but lustful and cruel," a man inspired by "a perverted, mental blood-lust. Why don't you own it? Let us become strangers again. It is better."[46]

For twenty-four hours Bertie was stunned by this attack, and even contemplated suicide, although later he came to think that Lawrence was simply Frieda's mouthpiece. "He was like a mollusc whose shell is broken," wrote Lawrence in a 1920s story called "The Blind Man,"[47] which was a fictional account of their relationship. He had read Russell's weaknesses, the chief of which was his inability, in Lawrence's eyes, "ever to enter into close contact of any sort." Interestingly, Russell made a similar accusation about Lawrence's living in a "solitary world."[48] Part of Lawrence's bitterness came from the feeling that he had been the plaything of Russell and Ottoline, whom he now saw as "traitors" who used him for their own gratification as if he were a cake or a wine or a pudding. In the split which followed Russell broke with Lawrence and cooled temporarily towards Ottoline, who remained aloof at Garsington but continued to entertain Lawrence.

In this fraught emotional climate, Russell felt uncomfortable working at Garsington. An alternative occurred to him when he discovered that Vivien could type to dictation: he would return to his flat at 34 Russell Chambers, Bury Street, near the British Museum, and persuade Vivien to take up the role of research assistant recently vacated by Irene Cooper-Willis. She seemed to have everything that he needed and she was far prettier than Helen Dudley, who had struck Ottoline as "an odd creature of about twenty-seven, rather creeping and sinuous in her movements, with a large head, a fringe cut across her forehead, and thick lips . . . She did not at all belong to the self-assertive, strident type of American woman: on the contrary, she was languid and adhesive, sympathetic but insensitive and phlegmatic . . ."[49] Vivien was also twenty-seven, but small and slim, a better match for Bertie physically than Ottoline, who towered over her lover.

Vivien's youth was an added inducement to the forty-three-year-old Russell, whose overriding desire was to find a woman who would bear him a child. His marriage to Alys had been childless, and he felt an "intolerable ache" when he saw a child playing in the street. He had had hopes that Ottoline, who had a daughter, Julian, might be impregnated by him, but when he sent her to a gynaecologist for an examination on 12 February 1914 the report came back that "there was absolutely *no* possibility, or practically none" of Ottoline having a child. The fact that Vivien was just married was no more of a deterrent to Russell than it had been in the case of Ottoline; he saw the Eliots' difficulties as an opportunity to ingratiate himself with Vivien, suspecting that her "exquisite and listless" husband was unlikely to father a child by his wife.

On 12 August, only ten days after Eliot's departure, Russell wrote to tell Ottoline that he would not arrive at Garsington the following weekend until late on Sunday afternoon, as he was taking Vivien out to lunch. Although he gave the impression that this was the first time they had met alone, Vivien's letter to Scofield indicates that she and Bertie had already dined together the week before. In Eliot's absence their meetings grew more frequent as, despite his physical shortcomings, Bertie Russell had a charismatic personality which women found irresistible. As Vivien sat opposite him in Soho restaurants, the "intense, piercing, convincing quality" of his conversation had the same mesmeric effect on her as it had originally had on Ottoline. Bertie's technique was to concentrate the full force of his personality upon the woman he wanted: "He assumed at once that I was his possession, and started to investigate, to explore, to probe," until she felt she was in the hands of a "psychological surgeon investigating the tangle of thoughts, feelings and emotions which I had never yet allowed anyone to see," wrote Ottoline of an early meeting with Bertie. Now Vivien was the woman whose psyche was being probed, and she felt Russell's interest upon her like a searchlight illuminating her unhappiness. There could be no greater contrast to her silent, introverted husband. Like Ottoline, Vivien found herself carried into worlds of thought of which she had never dreamt, and was flattered that so remarkable a man should find her worth talking to. "Bertie had a wonderful clear mind," recalled Frances Partridge. "That was what fascinated me."[50] Vivien too was fascinated.

Soon she became a convert to his pacifist ideas; by 24 October Vivien was enthusiastically informing Scofield that she was going to bring "Bertie Russell's seditious writings" with her when she and Tom came to the United States in the spring, and try to place them in New York. "Will you help me, Scofield *deeear?*"[51]

The physical spark which was dying between Ottoline and Russell ignited rapidly between Vivien and her new admirer. Vivien's pride had been hurt by Charles Buckle's rejection of her, and the mortifying knowledge that she did not sexually arouse Tom. As Russell put it in a mollifying note to Ottoline, referring to Buckle and Eliot, "She has suffered humiliation in two successive love-affairs, & that has made her vanity morbid."[52] Russell, whom Irene Cooper-Willis named "Tom Wolfe" in a fictionalised account of her employer's pursuit of her, was known for the passion as well as the amorality with which he pursued women.[53] In 1916, in "Mr. Apollinax," Eliot likened Russell to a satyr in the shrubbery, or a centaur whose "dry passionate talk" devours the afternoon. The images of a lustful predator reflect the poet's reaction to Bertie's intimacy with his wife in the months following July 1915, as well as his memories of Russell at Harvard, for the poem was first published in *Poetry* in September 1916.[54]

Russell's pursuit of Vivien was tinged with a certain desperation after his rejection at the hands of both Ottoline and Lawrence. Fortunately for Russell, Vivien's excited response to his compliments rebuilt his shattered self-confidence and soothed his wounded pride, just as his interest in her restored Vivien's own self-esteem. Abandoning the lectures he was writing after completing only three of the series, Russell began spending the weekdays in London rather than Garsington. Within weeks of Eliot's departure, Vivien was helping Russell work on a reply to a pamphlet written by Gilbert Murray defending government foreign policy, "The Foreign Policy of Sir Edward Grey 1906–1915," which had been published that summer. Irene Cooper-Willis had already collected substantial material towards an analysis of British foreign policy for the book which Russell had been planning, and he now used this as a foundation. Vivien also began typing the collection of articles on the war Russell was writing, entitled *Justice in War Time.*

Despite Russell's attentions, Vivien was unhappy at Tom's absence and wanted him back. Although her letter of 2 August to Scofield bubbles with high spirits, her guilt, illness, or a determination to demonstrate her power over her husband against that of her mother-in-law ensured that by 16 August Eliot had received an urgent summons to return immediately to England. He wrote to his supervisor at Cambridge, Professor Woods, that he had just heard that his wife was "very ill in London," and he must sail at once for England.[55] After barely three weeks in America he left Massachusetts. Not until 1932 was he to return to the country of his birth.

The family reunion had been painful, and it left Tom with bitter memories. First, he had quarrelled with his old friend Scofield, who objected to Eliot's snatching Vivien from under his nose. Eliot wrote a smooth and insincere letter of apology, affecting to be surprised at how "nettled" Scofield was. "You had never given me the impression that your interest in the lady was exclusive—or indeed, in the slightest degree a pursuit: and as you did not give *her* this impression, I presume that I had wounded your vanity rather than thwarted your passion."[56] It was a shrewd thrust, but Vivien had probably been less than honest with Tom about how close she was to Scofield, whom she had begged not to return to the U.S. and its "savages of Wall Street calibre." She had castigated herself for wasting time on Scofield. "A fool there was, & *she* made her prayer—to a rag & a bone & a hank of hair . . . Oh God WHY?"[57] Eliot signed off, "Sincerely yours, Thomas Stearns Eliot," but on his return to England repented of his coolness and sent apologies for his "shabby letter."[58]

Secondly, arguments raged within his family. These were not so easily mended. The family reunion Eliot endured with his parents formed the basis of his later play of that name, a play to which in earlier drafts he gave alternative and revealing titles: *Follow the Furies,* or *Fear in the Way.*[59] The horror and fear the character Harry feels when he returns to Wishwood to confront his mother, Amy, mirrors the emotions experienced by Eliot when he returned to East Gloucester to confront Charlotte Eliot. All the buried resentment of the child who was denied his freedom spill out in this drama. It is "the stupidity of older people" which destroys happiness and brings "The sudden extinction of every alternative,/The unexpected crash of the iron cataract." "You do not know what hope is, until you have lost it," declares Eliot. "You only know what it is not to hope." Returning to the family home ("Wishwood") confirmed Eliot in his belief that to stay in America would mean the "crash of the iron cataract." Vivien represented a bridge to freedom, to enable him to roam in the wilderness of his imagination far away from his mother's "stupidity." Escape was the only possible choice he could make.

Charlotte also expressed her own expectations of her favourite son in her dramatic poem "Savonarola." In this drama the mother, Elena, Charlotte's autobiographical persona, is "of illustrious birth and a woman of great intelligence and force of character. Between her and the most famous of her sons there existed strong sympathy and affection." When Elena's son Savonarola leaves her, she asks in desolation:

> . . . Must we part
> And loneliness and longing in my heart
> Usurp love's deep content?

Savonarola answers that he must take the vow that separates him from his mother. The vow that Charlotte wished her son to take was to allow "the current of his being to be directed by the Lord."[60] In 1915 this was not the vow that Eliot made, although to do so became an increasingly insistent inner demand. His vow was to another mistress—Art—and for this his mother never forgave him.

Eliot left New England weighed down with sorrow and anger. Henry Ware Eliot had taken a hard line with his younger son, refusing to continue his allowance. Knowing that his father owned substantial property in St. Louis, as well as the single biggest block of shares in the Hydraulic Press-Brick Company (whose slogan was "Largest Manufacturers of Face Brick in the World"), Tom had not expected to be cut off. But his father had five other children to consider, and his brick firm had not paid a dividend since 1913, the year in which Henry Eliot Sr. had retired as President at the age of seventy. Eliot Sr.'s only concession was a grudging agreement to pay Tom's rent. In return his son was to finish his thesis on Bradley and present it to Harvard in May. They parted in bitterness, and Eliot never saw his father again. "Tom has always had every reasonable desire gratified, without any thought of ways and means, up to the present time,"[61] a resentful Charlotte complained to the duplicitous Russell. She was not to know that the decision she and Henry made was to have an altogether different result from that which they intended. It did not persuade their impecunious son to return to academic philosophy, as they wished, but instead increased his dependence on his benefactor, Russell.

6

Triple Ménage:
Bertie, Vivien and Tom

Bertrand Russell wrote Vivien out of his life in his *Autobiography*. Complaining of his fading intimacy with Ottoline in 1915, he confessed: "I sought about for some other woman to relieve my unhappiness, but without success until I met Colette [O'Niel],"[1] the aristocratic actress Lady Constance Malleson, with whom Russell fell in love in 1916. Economical with the *actualité,* Russell makes no mention here of his relationship with Vivien, the first "other woman" to console him for the fading of Ottoline's love, yet their intimacy lasted from 1915 until 1918, continuing after Russell began his affair with Colette, and was the product of an instant mutual attraction from which both found it hard to break free. Indeed, it left Vivien with lasting wounds.

Russell destroyed most of Vivien's letters to him,[2] although by nature he was an inveterate hoarder who preserved his correspondence with both Ottoline and Colette. What did he have to hide?[3] In Eliot's opinion, Russell undermined his wife's mental health: "He has done evil," he wrote to Ottoline. It became common literary gossip, as Evelyn Waugh recorded in his diary on 21 July 1955, "that Mrs. T. S. Eliot's insanity sprang from her seduction and desertion by Bertrand Russell."[4] For Eliot, to blame his former friend rather than himself for Vivien's psychological distress was a tempting salve to his conscience, but there is evidence that even Russell, for whom morality had little place in affairs of the heart, was left with deep feelings of guilt for his treatment of Vivien. Tampering with the truth in his *Autobiography* could not obliterate his memory of her. After Vivien's death in 1947 he fictionalised their relationship in an autobiographical short story, "Satan in the Suburbs," written in 1953 when he was eighty-one. His emotional account of the harm done to Mrs. Ellerker,[5] a woman married to a "pompous" and dull husband, Henry Ellerker, by his rival Mr. Quantox, who seduces her, indicates Russell's uncomfortable sense of responsibility for Vivien's ultimate fate, and links her story to his own fear of madness. His biographer Ray Monk associated this fear with Russell's recurring nightmare that he might suffer the same fate as his Uncle Willy who, as Russell discovered as a child, strangled a man in 1874 and spent the rest of his life in an asylum.[6]

In his *Autobiography,* Russell tellingly compares himself to Faust, betraying his awareness of his own sin, as well as of a sense of omnipotence: he often returned to the idea that there was something devilish within him (an accusation made by both D. H. Lawrence and Eliot). It has been assumed that it was Ottoline who awoke in the desiccated philosopher repressed desire, as Gretchen did in Faust, but in Ottoline's case her favours were rationed as she never found Russell physically attractive. It was in fact Vivien who not only aroused but responded to Russell's passion, and in return was betrayed.

In "Satan" Russell introduces a Mephistophelian figure, Dr. Mallako, who tempts the Faustian Mr. Quantox to talk Mrs. Ellerker into committing a murderous crime. When "Mrs. E." goes to the authorities to accuse Mr. Quantox, no one believes her for she is a "nobody"; but Mr. Quantox is "too valuable a public servant to be at the mercy of a hysterical woman, and Mrs. Ellerker, after being quickly certified, was removed to an asylum." The story can be read as Russell's confession as, like the "sneering ghost" Dr. Mallako, who will not leave Quantox alone until he succumbs to temptation, Vivien's ghost dwelt reproachfully in Russell's unconscious in his old age.

Russell draws a flattering self-portrait: Mr. Quantox is "sparkling and witty, a man of wide education and wide culture, a man who could amuse any company by observations which combined wit with penetrating analysis . . ." Perhaps this was Russell's answer to Eliot's unflattering description of his former tutor in "Mr. Apollinax," since he chose so similar a name. Confessing that "Mr. Quantox had a roving eye, and would have incurred moral reprobation but for the national value of his work . . . ," he describes Mrs. Ellerker (referred to as "Mrs. E." in Russell's letters to Ottoline), emphasising the sense of identification he felt with Vivien and the closeness which developed between them.

Mrs. Ellerker, in many of these respects, bore more resemblance to Mr. Quantox than to her husband ... Her neighbours in Mortlake were divided into those who enjoyed her sparkling talk, and those who feared that such lightness in word could not be wedded to perfect correctness in behaviour. The more earnest and elderly among her acquaintance darkly suspected her of moral lapses skilfully concealed, and were inclined to pity Mr. Ellerker for having such a flighty wife. The other faction pitied Mrs. Ellerker, as they imagined his comments on *The Times* leaders at breakfast.[7]

Once she has met Mr. Quantox, Mrs. E. "imagined what she would feel if Mr. Quantox's eyes looked at her with passion, if Mr. Quantox's arms were about her, if Mr. Quantox's lips were in contact with her own. Such thoughts made her tremble, but she could not banish them."[8] She dreams of Mr. Quantox: "How we should stimulate each other, how shine, how make the company marvel at our brilliance! And how he would love, with passion and fire, and yet with a kind of lightness, not with the heaviness of uncooked dough." Soon, "overcome by reckless desire," Mrs. Ellerker allows Mr. Quantox to kiss her in the library. She agrees to the crime he requires of her which results in loss of life and her husband's suicide; once it is committed, Mr. Quantox abandons her. He is rewarded in the Birthday Honours, "but to Mrs. Ellerker his door remained closed, and if they met in the train or in the street he gave her only a distant bow. She had served her purpose. Under the lash of his disdain, her passion died, and was succeeded by remorse, bitter, unavailing, and unendurable."[9]

In this story Russell spelt out his shame for having used Vivien; she too had "served her purpose" for him, restoring his confidence until he met someone he loved better—Colette—and finally someone who would give him the children he longed for—Dora Black, who became his second wife. In "Satan" Quantox allows Mrs. Ellerker to languish in the psychiatric hospital, even though he visits her and realises that she is perfectly normal and not suffering from "insane delusions." But Russell sets up his own imagined punishment: after murdering the evil Dr. Mallako, Mr. Quantox ends up in the asylum too; there he and Mrs. Ellerker dance together as they used to: "Once a year I shall meet my dear Mrs. Ellerker, whom I ought never to have tried to forget, and when we meet, we will wonder whether there will ever be in the world more than two sane people."

Vivien became Russell's guilty secret, just as his murderous Uncle William was his grandmother's, and the insistent image of himself as an insane murderer haunted his imagination. Rogojin, the murderer in Dostoevsky's *The Idiot,* was the character in fiction with which he felt most "intimate," Russell told Ottoline, as he brooded over the question of what constituted insanity. It is difficult to avoid the conclusion that Russell, who often felt suicidal, believed that he, like Vivien, sometimes teetered on a "knife edge" between reason and unreason, and was equally misunderstood by a society which judged them both unfairly. This was the bond that at times linked them together, and at times repelled Russell because of his fears for his own state of mind. For Vivien, the affair which developed became her guilty secret also, but she was left not only with the feelings of remorse with which Russell credited her, but also with profound regrets for lost love.

In September 1915, however, Russell appeared unselfishness itself as he wrote to Tom Eliot, who had returned from America on the 4th, and offered to share his Bury Street flat with the Eliots until Christmas. To Tom, beside himself with worry over his parents, his finances, his wife's poor health and his thesis, this plan, which Bertie and Vivien had hatched together while he was away, seemed manna from heaven. He had hurriedly accepted a teaching position at Wycombe Grammar School, which was still open at £140 a year with free dinners, to give lessons in French, mathematics, history, drawing and swimming, but until his salary was paid he and Vivien were hard up. "You will see that until January we shall be in urgent need of funds, and that we shall need some money very soon," he wrote in another begging letter to his father on 10 September, apologising for his "blunders" and explaining why he had decided to stick to his original plan of studying for his exams in England. "We have planned a very economical mode of life, and Vivien's resourcefulness and forethought are inexhaustible. We are not planning to make living easier: the question is how to live at all."[10]

Now Bertie's offer answered the question of "how to live," and obviated any need for thrift and "resourcefulness" from Vivien. The proposal had obvious advantages for Russell. He saw it as a way of continuing his delightful intimacy with Vivien at a time when he was bearing the full brunt of Lawrence's savage attack as a "super war-spirit," and feeling ever more divided from Ottoline, who was exhilarated by bringing in the harvest with the Garsington villagers (an occupation which bored Bertie immensely), and newly involved with her "adorable companion" Lytton Strachey, then writing *Eminent Victorians* in the bedroom set aside semi-permanently for him by his hostess. The luxury-loving Vivien also preferred to continue her agreeable arrangement with Bertie, rather than follow her husband to live in his rented lodgings in Conegra Road, High Wycombe, at the start of the autumn term. Nevertheless to leave Vivien in the flat made "nice and pretty" by Ottoline in the early days of her affair with Russell, rather than to set up home with his new wife, seems a strange choice for Eliot to make.

"Dear Mr. Russell," Eliot wrote from Eastbourne where he and Vivien had gone for a belated honeymoon in mid-September, although she was apparently still so "unwell" that he had sent for the doctor in order to put their minds at rest, "Your letter coming on top of all your other kindnesses, has quite overwhelmed me." Such generosity and encouragement, he wrote, meant a great deal to him, "above all coming from you." He was feeling quite exhausted each day at having to write so many letters to friends and family in America, but was "overpowered" by Russell's generous offer. Moving on to the practical details, he assured Russell that there would be no problem if their landlord wished to spend nights in London alone with Vivien: "As to your coming to stay the night at the flat when I am not there, it would never have occurred to me to accept it under any other conditions," he wrote. Such a concession to convention had never entered his head and seemed to him not only totally unnecessary, but also would have destroyed all the pleasure he and Vivien took in the "informality of the arrangement."[11] This letter demonstrates a curious blindness to the likely outcome of leaving Bertie alone with Vivien.

Why did Eliot acquiesce in the *ménage à trois* which ensued? It is probable that he grasped at the apparent solution to his difficulties without suspecting the older man's motives. At this stage Eliot knew little of Russell's private life. It is of course possible that the relationship which developed between Vivien and Bertie was as innocent as Eliot apparently assumed—or that Eliot was a cuckold. On the other hand, the triple *ménage* could in fact have been a far more complicated bargain, by which Eliot, for his own reasons, permitted Bertie to enjoy Vivien's sexual favours.

Russell himself later categorically denied to Eliot's friend Robert Gordon George ("Robert Sencourt") that he had slept with Vivien, writing: "I never had intimate sexual relations with Vivienne." Biographers have tended to believe him. Caroline Moorehead writes: "No one has ever been sure whether Russell, by this time something of a philanderer, actually slept with Vivienne."[12] "There can be no doubt . . . that he and Mrs. Eliot did not, in the expected progress of night following day, become lovers," states Ronald W. Clark, arguing that Russell told Ottoline, "to whom he never lied," "I never contemplated risking my reputation with her, & I never risked it so far as I can judge."[13] Peter Ackroyd describes Russell's relationship with Vivien as "intense but 'platonic.' "[14]

But Russell's letters to Colette and Ottoline are inconsistent, for he changed his story to suit his correspondent. On occasions he did lie to Ottoline, but there is little reason to doubt his confession to Colette in October 1916, a few months after meeting her, that he was already "intimate" with Vivien, a tell-tale word which for Russell implied full sexual relations.[15] He had already confessed to being "intimate" with Ottoline. Later, in October 1917, Russell gave Colette a blow-by-blow account of making love to Vivien, an account intended to bring his latest, but already wayward, mistress back to his side.[16] That particular night with Vivien had "a quality of loathsomeness about it which I can't describe," wrote Russell to Colette, but the "loathsomeness" should not be attributed to Vivien's menstruating, as Peter Ackroyd surmises, for Russell went on to say that the one and only thing that made the night loathsome was that it was not with Colette. He was in the habit of telling one of his girlfriends that she was better in bed than the other, remembered Dora Russell, his second wife.[17] Playing one off against the other usually resulted in a revival of passion from the mistress Russell felt was neglecting him, and presumably this was his intention in this letter to Colette, who described Russell as a "lover" of Vivien's in 1917. In 1972, Colette wrote to Kenneth Blackwell, Director of the Russell Archives, on the question of sexual relations between Vivien and Russell: "I always took it for granted that they had, & when I wrote so to BR, he never contradicted me."[18]

Another explanation for Eliot's enthusiastic acceptance of Russell's offer of accommodation may lie in the disastrous honeymoon he and Vivien spent at Eastbourne, a spot she probably chose for its happy memories of holidays there with her family and father, to whom she naturally compared her new husband. Vivien had looked forward to her "second honeymoon!" with Tom, as she told Scofield in an excited letter which suggests that her initial experience of marital relations in the three weeks she and Tom had spent together in the studio flat before he left for America were not an unmitigated failure. She hoped for a rapturous reunion with the bridegroom from whom she had parted so soon after their marriage, imagining that, having solved their money troubles and made his peace with his parents, he would turn to her with new ardour. She still had no idea of the value of money; still prattled of dances and balls; while Tom knew that his schoolmaster's salary of £140 a year could not possibly support the upper-middle-class lifestyle his new wife expected. Even £200 a year would not support such a lifestyle, although in socially divided England in 1910, 94 per cent of incomes were less than £160 a year. Nor did Eliot seem to observers to possess the energy and determination necessary to make a success of this new undertaking; in March 1914 Russell had judged him to be "very capable of an exquisiteness of appreciation, but lacking in the crude insistent passion that one must have in order to achieve anything."[19]

Bertrand Russell's report of the honeymoon suggests that it was not turning out as Vivien hoped. "I am worried about those Eliots," he wrote, with a hint of *schadenfreude,* to Ottoline, whom he had just left at Garsington:

> It seems their sort of pseudo-honeymoon at Eastbourne is being a ghastly failure. She is quite tired of him, & when I got here I found a desperate letter from her, in the lowest depths of despair & not far removed from suicide. I have written her various letters full of good advice, & she seems to have come to rely on me more or less. I have so much taken them both in hand that I dare not let them be. I think she will fall more or less in love with me, but that can't be helped. I am interested in the attempt to pull her straight. She is half-Irish, & wholly Irish in character—with a great deal of mental passion & *no* physical passion, and universal vanity, that

makes her desire every man's devotion, & a fastidiousness that
makes any expression of their devotion disgusting to her . . . She
has boundless ambition (far beyond her powers), but it is diffuse
and useless. What she needs is some kind of religion, or at least
some discipline, of which she seems never to have had any. At
present she is punishing my poor friend for having tricked her
imagination—like the heroine of the "Playboy."

Presenting Vivien as the disappointed heroine of J. M. Synge's *The Playboy
of the Western World* gave Russell the opportunity to make altruism his excuse:

I want to give her some other outlet than destroying him. I shan't
fall in love with her, nor give her any more show of affection than
seems necessary to rehabilitate her. But she really has *some* value
in herself, all twisted and battered by life, lack of discipline, lack
of purpose, & lack of religion.[20]

It was a letter which rang alarm bells with Ottoline, who was instantly
fearful that if Vivien and Russell had an affair it would create a scandal.
This might then reflect badly on the pacifist cause with which she and
Philip were increasingly involved as disaster unfolded at Gallipoli, where
her brothers Henry and Charles Bentinck were fighting. Russell's intention, as usual, was to provoke jealousy in Ottoline by hinting at Vivien's attachment to him, a technique which had worked well in the past.
Although Ottoline had been disengaging herself from Bertie as she compared him unfavourably to the "lovable" Lawrence, who continued his visits through the autumn of 1915, and to the stream of new friends such as
Aldous Huxley, Katherine Mansfield and John Middleton Murry, who
filled the manor house to overflowing, it was obvious to her from Bertie's
breathless and detailed analysis of Vivien's personality, that he, too, was becoming infatuated. His criticisms of Vivien, such as her lack of religion,
were calculated to appeal to Ottoline, who had a strong religious faith, but
his correspondent was not taken in. On 9 September 1915 she wrote an
anxious reply:

My darling,

I was awfully glad to hear from you this morning, but I am rather worried about the Eliots. I am so afraid of what might happen if she became in love with you, which is evidently quite likely . . . I feel you are running a very great risk and I beg and entreat you to be awfully careful—for if you want to do any lecturing or public work any scandal of this kind would entirely damage it and I don't suppose she is worth it.

Anyhow I don't think it would *help her* and help towards making the joint Eliot life happier to let her fall in love with you. I expect in a way it may have made her already more critical of Eliot. Don't think I want to interfere or stop you but I feel *very* strongly that in getting her confidence you are rather separating her from Eliot—and besides that running an awful risk to your reputation . . . Please don't think I am cross, for I am not one bit, only I know you are led on by yr. sympathy and by yr. longing to set people straight and the big things you *can* do are more important.

My Love darling.

Yr. O.

Ottoline's warning that to encourage Vivien to fall in love with Bertie would separate her from Eliot was altogether reasonable; and she may also have seen the ominous similarity between her lover's argument here and his excuse that sleeping with Helen Dudley was like saving a drowning woman. The pattern which Bertie's seductions followed was already apparent to Ottoline, who was unlikely to be convinced by his assurance that Vivien had "no physical passion." Ottoline had been deeply hurt to discover, when Helen Dudley showed her the love letters Russell had sent her, that he had used almost identical language to the young American as he had to her. She should, however, have guessed that the threat of scandal would do little to sway Russell; when in love, he was recklessness itself. His affair with Ottoline had already cost him his teaching post at Newnham College, Cambridge, where the college had decided to dispense with the services of an adulterer.

Russell hastened to reassure Ottoline. "There is no occasion for your fears," he wrote on 10 September. Eliot was not "that sort of man & I will be much more careful than you seem to expect. And I feel sure that I can make things come right. We can talk about it when I come. I would not for the world have any scandal, & as for the Eliots, it is the purest philanthropy—I am sorry you feel worried—there is *really* no need—I am fond of him, & really anxious to be of use to him. The trouble between them was already at its very worst before I came into the matter at all—it is already better, & when I saw him he was very full of gratitude. I must have given you quite a wrong impression when I wrote."[21] Nevertheless Ottoline remained unconvinced and declined to invite Vivien to Garsington. Russell meanwhile kept his two women separate and continued to lead a double life between Garsington and Bury Street.

Although Russell often dramatised the emotional situations in which he found himself, this time his description of Vivien's mood of suicidal despair seems to have been accurate. Maurice said later that the Eliots' honeymoon was "rotten," a euphemism for the sexual failure that had undoubtedly occurred. It cannot have been helped by Tom's emotional state on his return from what had been a painful confrontation with his parents; he was, said Maurice, "terrified" of his mother, this "tough old woman who wrote poetry." The fierce ticking-off he received for marrying Vivien may have made him reconsider the sudden decision he had made, and its economic consequences, as he brooded over his situation on the boat carrying him back to England. Certainly it was a shaken bridegroom who travelled down to Eastbourne with his sickly wife. In his absence Vivien had fallen under Russell's spell and must have looked with new, critical eyes at her nervous husband, embarrassed by his truss, who attempted to make love to her. "He was a virgin when he married," remembered Maurice (as Eliot himself confessed). "He had a hernia: this awful truss must have depressed him. Tom was convinced that his hernia was a form of tumor, cancer—and wouldn't let anyone look at it." In the hotel bedroom, Vivien, newly reunited with the husband she barely knew, was horrified by the arrival of her menstrual period, which embarrassed her as much as Tom. Maurice remembered that "both Tom and Vivie were so clean, both so worried about cleanliness." As he bluntly expressed it: "Viv's sanitary towels always put a man off."[22] It was not a stage set for passion.

In a confessional poem entitled "Ode on Independence Day, July 4 1918,"[23] published in *Ara Vos Prec* ("I pray you"), a collection of Eliot's poems published in February 1920, of which only two hundred and sixty-four copies were printed, and which he later suppressed, Tom recalled his honeymoon three years after the event and the long-deferred rite of passage he had endured at Vivien's hands. The title of the volume is taken from a speech from Canto XXVI of Dante's *Purgatorio* in which the poet meets the souls of the Sodomites and the souls of the Lustful, one of whom, Arnaut Daniel, a twelfth-century troubadour, speaks to Dante and Virgil in Provençal, regretting his sins. Eliot takes Arnaut Daniel's words, "Ara vos prec . . . ,"[24] asking his audience to be "mindful in your time of my pain," before diving back into the refining fire of purgatory; it was a canto to which he would frequently return. *Ara Vos Prec* also carried the Dante epigraph which Eliot later made an explicit dedication to Jean Verdenal in *Prufrock*: "Now you are able to comprehend the quantity of love that warms me towards you/When I forget our emptiness/Treating shades as if they were solid." The title of the poem, too, celebrating Independence Day, is surely ironic: in the trap of marriage the poet feels he has lost his freedom.

In "Ode" the poet mourns the "silence from the sacred wood," the source of his creativity, since he retired from "the profession of calamus." This is a reference to Walt Whitman's *Calamus* poems which celebrate the intimacy of man-to-man relationships. Whitman chose the Calamus, "a large and aromatic grass, or rush," for its value as a symbol of life associated with the phallus.[25] The friendship with Verdenal, transfigured in Eliot's memory, grew to have a significance greater than the reality of their association; the winter of their friendship, 1910–11, was a time of great creativity for Eliot, which he compared unfavourably to the negativity of life with Vivien.

The poet feels "tired," "misunderstood." The morning after his wedding night he is "Tortured/When the bridegroom smoothed his hair/There was blood upon the bed./Morning was already late." He feels revulsion at consummating the relationship with his bride, irritation at messing his hair and rising late because of her sexual demands. In his imagination the children sing a wedding chant: "(Io Hymen, Hymenaee)/Succuba eviscerate." Eliot may have had in mind the ironic reproach of Whitman's expression of sexual ecstasy in the *Children of Adam* poems which precede the *Calamus* poems. He may also have been thinking of Catullus's wedding chant, "Hymen to Hymenaee," in a poem in which the husband is reminded that he must give up his previous "Calamus-like" relationship with "a boyfriend favourite." The "succuba eviscerate" to whom the bridegroom refers is a female demon who has sexual intercourse with men in their sleep, disembowelling or castrating the bridegroom (who later becomes the sterile Fisher-King of *The Waste Land*).

Decoding this poem, with its vivid imagery of a castrating female, leads to the suggestion that Eliot was impotent, or partially impotent, with Vivien. Psychiatrist Dr. Harry Trosman has claimed that Eliot's deprived childhood left him "isolated and uncomfortable in his ill-fitting masculinity ... It is likely that ... unacceptable homosexual longings were activated. Such longings, to which he responded with panic, were transformed into aesthetic sublimations or dandyism."[26] Strongly fixated on his powerful mother, Eliot had followed the classic pattern of same-sex orientation in identifying with her in adolescence, and looking for love-objects in whom to rediscover himself.[27] His resulting profound fear of sexual relationships with women was not only expressed in early poems such as "Circe's Palace,"[28] but also in the *Prufrock* poems which he placed immediately after "Ode" in *Ara Vos Prec*.

The last stanza of "Ode" returns compulsively, through twisted paths, to the image of the dead Verdenal: "Tortuous/By arrangement with Perseus/The fooled resentment of the dragon," perhaps an allusion to the trickery by which Perseus slew the Gorgon, and Eliot's own resentment at being tricked into a marriage he regrets. "Sailing before the wind at dawn./Golden apocalypse. Indignant/At the cheap extinction of his taking-off./Now lies he there/Tip to tip washed beneath Charles' Wagon."[29]

Lyndall Gordon has interpreted these last lines as a reference to the bridegroom's disappointment as he, "sailing expectantly towards 'a golden apocalypse,' is frustrated by what appears to be a premature ejaculation. He is left a good way below the stars, 'Indignant/At the cheap extinction of his taking-off.'"[30] But the stanza must be read in conjunction with Eliot's sources: resonating with grief and anger, his lines also echo the lament for Duncan's death in *Macbeth* (Act 1, Scene 7) and Shakespeare's praise for his virtues which:[31]

Will plead like angels, trumpet-tongued against
The deep damnation of his taking-off . . .

Surely the "cheap extinction" is a reference to the needless loss of
Verdenal's life in the Dardanelles. Now his body lies beneath the waves, in
lines which serve as a prologue to *The Waste Land:* "Now he lies there/Tip
to tip washed beneath Charles' Wagon." Charles' Wagon is another name
for the constellation of Ursa Major, the Great Bear, visible over the
Dardanelles. "Washed" and purified by water, the body rests in its grave:
it is an image to which Eliot returned again and again in anguish, as he
turned away from the living body of his wife.

Eliot's response to the threat of Vivien's messy and demanding proximity was to escape, to withdraw into "icy urbanity." Maurice recalled that
Tom spent a night in a deckchair on the beach at Eastbourne, while a distraught Vivien locked herself in her bedroom and apparently damaged the
room. The couple returned early from Eastbourne, Vivien insisting on
bringing the soiled sheets home with her in a laundry basket to be washed
at home; the manageress of the hotel wrote to Charles Haigh-Wood to
complain that the sheets had been "stolen," but this was a habit Vivien had
developed while still at school at Margate, where she first acquired the
laundry basket. Since puberty she had become accustomed to taking the
basket with her wherever she stayed, filling it with the dirty laundry, and
having it sent home by rail. One of her maid's jobs was to collect the laundry basket from the station and have the contents washed. It was a habit
which irritated Eliot immensely, remembered Maurice: "Vivie stole sheets
from the hotels, had them washed and sent them back. Sometimes she
went along to the Post Office and posted the clean sheets back to the hotels. Tom went *mad.*"[32]

In the midst of this marital crisis, Tom turned in panic-stricken gratitude to Russell. The flat into which the newly married couple moved was
small, and the sleeping accommodation inconvenient; there was "just a *tiny*
cupboard room behind the kitchen, so small you couldn't swing a cat," remembered Maurice. "Tom slept in the hallway in a deckchair. Vivie used
a cot-bed she got from Compayne Gardens." The room in which Vivien
slept was in fact the former pantry. In such circumstances conjugal relations were well-nigh impossible, but this was no doubt a relief to Tom. The

rest of the flat was attractive, for Ottoline had spent three weeks in 1911 fitting it out for Bertie in the first flush of their relationship; she had bought a rug and filled the rooms with carnations and lilies of the valley, while Bertie moved in his grandfather's desk and a small table made from Domesday Book oak that had belonged to his mother and on which he had written most of *Principia Mathematica*. "It will be very nice—we shall have a great sense of liberty & I can have books there & means of making tea, & even some peppermints in some secret recess!" (Ottoline's favourite sweets were peppermints).[33]

Ottoline had found Bertie a demanding and dependent lover; he was so isolated from people in general that he once confessed he felt he had to speak to them in "baby talk" if they were to understand him. "How much emotion those little rooms in Bury Place held—intense and burning and very tragic!" she wrote. "Bertie demanded so much, and all I could give him was so inadequate to his desires. He would stand at his window look-ing for my coming, growing tenser and tenser, counting the minutes if I was late. As I hurried along the street I dreaded looking up, and seeing his face pressed against the panes looking for me. And then it was dreadful leaving him in those rooms, unsatisfied and tragically lonely. How could I satisfy him? The very intensity of his demands seemed to crush me." Sometimes when she was with him Ottoline had felt as if she were in prison, for his passion was so possessive and oppressive. On returning home she would "skip for joy, and often dance round my bedroom and fling out my arms and sing 'Free, free.' "[34]

Vivien, by contrast, had never been happier than she was with Bertie. And, instead of snatched hours in station waiting rooms, afternoons in Tottenham Court Road hotels at 2/6d a time, or brief trysts in Russell Buildings, which was all Ottoline would allow her lover, Russell had the relationship he had always wanted with a woman, in which domestic inti-macy and writing were shared in a companionable twosome. "Physical in-stinct, at least in me, is not satisfied by the physical act alone, but cries out for constant companionship, especially in the night,"[35] he had written to Ottoline during his affair with Helen Dudley, a bitter allusion to the prom-ise they had made to Logan Pearsall Smith never to spend a night together. Now he could climb into Vivien's little bed, or persuade her to move into his own much more comfortable bedroom, which Maurice remembered as well-furnished, while Tom was safely away in the country. He was no longer dependent on Ottoline for love; Vivien was dependent on him. She had moved into his home, and although he sometimes returned to Garsington, Bertie and Vivien lived contentedly in the flat while they worked. "The foreign policy of Sir Edward Grey 1906–1915" was published that summer[36] and *Justice in War Time,* the collection of his articles on the war, in November.

Tom left for High Wycombe almost immediately after his ill-fated Eastbourne honeymoon, taking lodgings during the week with a Mrs. Toone. Lack of money continued to worry him. On 27 September he wrote another anxious letter to his father, telling him that he was settling into school work and had two free afternoons a week in which to work for his degree, but his deposit was reduced to almost nothing and that was all he had to live on: "If no money comes from you at the end of the fortnight I shall be forced to cable, as I shall be reduced to the last pound by the time you get this. I hate to *cable* for money . . ."[37] He could be earning extra money by writing, he reminded Henry Ware Eliot Sr., if only his parents had not insisted that he finish his degree.

Eliot therefore eagerly accepted Russell's temporary gift of £3,000 of engineering debentures, used to fund the making of munitions; as a pacifist Russell felt he could not keep an unethical investment, but Eliot retained the debentures, which produced an annual income of £180 at 6 per cent, for nearly twelve years after the war.[38] Nor were these the only gifts the Eliots accepted, for Russell, increasingly attached to Vivien, kept her like a highly prized mistress. "I am getting very fond of Mrs. Eliot," he confessed to Ottoline on 13 October 1915. "Not in an 'improper' manner— she does not attract me much physically—but I find her a real friend, with a deeply humane feeling about the war, & no longer at all unkind to her husband. I feel her a permanent acquisition, not merely an object of kindness, as I thought at first."[39] As the months passed, he admitted "a very great affection" for Vivien. His feeling was, he told Ottoline, "utterly different from the feeling I have for you. What makes me care for her is that she affords me an opportunity for *giving* a kind of affection that hitherto I have only been able to give in a slight, fragmentary way to pupils—I don't mean that is the whole of it, but it is what is important." Vivien, needy, dependent, as lonely as he, was grateful for Russell's care, in contrast to the rich, socially successful hostess and politician's wife he had chosen before. He had loved Ottoline, but she never desired him as he desired her; now, with Vivien, he had found a woman to whom he could not only feel effortlessly superior but who also accepted the totality of his love without finding it oppressive. Insecure, and as alone as Vivien for all his intelligence, Bertie began to spend more and more time with her, returning to 34 Russell Chambers, Bury Street, after an abortive attempt to write his lectures on social reconstruction at Garsington, although to Ottoline he rationalised his feelings as paternal: "I shall be seeing a great deal of her—the affection I have for her is what one might have for a daughter, but it is very strong, & my judgement goes with it."[40] Since henceforth his relationships would invariably be with younger women, such professions of fatherly love on Bertie's side were never to be trusted.

Russell showered Vivien with presents, much to Ottoline's annoyance. By July 1916 she was writing in her journal: "I had a long talk with Bertie about Mrs. Eliot. I don't really understand her influence over him. It seems odd that such a frivolous, silly little woman should affect him so much, and she looks up to him as a rich god, for he lavishes presents on her of silk underclothes and all sorts of silly things and pays for her dancing lessons. It takes all his money . . ."[41] Vivien accepted his gifts without compunction. Like Tom, she had been used to a privileged lifestyle, and saw no reason to allow her standards to drop. A letter to Scofield Thayer in October shows an indulgent Russell funding her dream of becoming a professional ballet dancer like Karsavina in the Russian Ballet, or the English Jenny Pearl, despite his remarks to Ottoline that Vivien had "boundless ambition (far beyond her powers) but it is diffuse and useless." Vivien had a studio portrait photograph of herself taken, and sent a copy to Scofield:

> I must *insist* that if you do not like it you will return it. I will *not* allow my photograph to be retained out of politeness (Scofield was always so courteous!) . . . I am not at all sure that I like it myself—and now that I am the wife of a poet whose fame is rapidly increasing throughout the length and breadth of more than one land, *and* in order not to become merely "T.S. Eliot's wife"—am

embarking on the proffession [sic] of ballet dancing myself (shade of Jenny Pearl!)—I shall frequently present my features to the camera.

After telling Scofield that an anthology of poetry, including poems by Yeats, Pound, Eliot and others was coming out the following week— "Elkin Matthews, 3/6d!"—she confides to her old admirer that "We have been more or less of a triple menage. Bertie Russell has taken us to his bosom. I cheer him up, he says—and the flat rings with his raucous mirth. Bertie has rather an elementary sense of humour!" In the spring she and Tom are going to the U.S., she tells Scofield, where she will take Bertie's "seditious writings" and try to place them for him in New York. If they stay long she will want to take some ballet-dancing lessons there. "I am going in for it very seriously. Is there a school of ballet in New York," she asks. "I am a true JP [Jenny Pearl] now. Three times a week I descend into a subterranean hall in Carnaby Street, Soho, and there, in a little black skirt above my knees, and toe-blocked shoes, I leap & skip under the guidance of a massively-calved lady who calls me 'darling.' When Bertie and Tom come to watch me, as they often do, she calls them 'darling' too."[42]

High-spirited and happy in this strange, triangular relationship, Vivien contrasts the "slow, deep tones" of Tom, who remarks ponderously, "It *would* be nice to see Scofield again," with Bertie's reaction to Scofield's letter: "He enjoyed it, he laughed with joy . . ." What pleasure Scofield has given to more than one of them in this dark land, she tells him. "Send us another ray of light!" Bertie's neighing laugh was famous among Ottoline's cronies: D. H. Lawrence, caricaturing him as Sir Joshua Malleson in *Women in Love,* writes of "a learned dry Baronet of fifty who was always making witticisms and laughing at them heartily in a harsh horse-laugh."[43] Vivien, receptive and quick-witted, provoked such laughter; in return she received not only money but the concentrated force of Russell's charismatic and intense personality focused upon her. It is no wonder that Vivien did indeed fall in love with Bertie, whose high sex drive and determined charm was effortlessly to win him a succession of much younger wives, Dora, Patricia (Peter) and Edith, in the future. Vivien was attracted to highly intellectual men, and Russell and Eliot had much in common: both were brilliant, introverted and highly emotional. The difference lay in their attitude to women.

Vivien was not the first woman on whom Russell had secretly lavished presents, as a way of achieving intimacy, and perhaps also as a form of control. He had acted in a similar fashion with Evelyn Whitehead, wife of Alfred North Whitehead, paying her bills without her husband's knowledge.[44] But to Vivien he gave much more than silk stockings and dancing lessons: Maurice recorded that Russell gave his sister dresses and also "Russell family heirlooms." It was a mark of Russell's deep infatuation that he was prepared to give his mistress part of his inheritance. In the end, said Maurice, "Bertrand Russell got scared. His family asked Vivien for a ring back." Later, he reported, "Mummy made her give it back."[45]

Tom and Vivien continued to live in a state of dependency upon Bertrand Russell, and it is almost impossible to believe that Tom was unaware that Russell and Vivien were having a sexual relationship; he may have suppressed the knowledge, and no doubt it was never openly discussed, but from his unconscious came the poem which characterised Russell as a satyr, "Mr. Apollinax." Nevertheless, Eliot remained complaisant and grateful for several good reasons. First, although Russell could ill afford it, he was subsidising both Eliots because he had taken pity on his former pupil for being "desperately poor." "Eliot was not truly poor" writes Paul Delany, "but he certainly exuded an air of desperation,"[46] which caused Russell to write to Eliot's Harvard supervisor, J. H. Woods, that "It has driven me almost to despair to see his fine talents wasting."[47] It was to become a characteristic of the Eliots that they expected other people to subsidise their lifestyle.

Secondly, Eliot was relieved to turn over to Russell the conjugal duties he often found distasteful. "The difficult relationship with Vivienne served as a constant reminder of sexual failure," writes Dr. Harry Trosman. "Eliot's tolerance for and complicity in Vivienne's affair with Russell suggested an unresolved oedipal tie and a need to placate a sexually aggressive father surrogate."[48] While Russell took care of Vivien's demands for affection and sexual fulfilment, all three could be happy. A third reason was that Russell was an important literary contact for Eliot; he put his protégé in touch with the editor of the *International Journal of Ethics,* Sydney Waterlow, who commissioned two reviews from him in October, work which Eliot found more congenial as well as more lucrative than toiling over academic philosophy for his thesis. "The reviewing has cheered me up very much," he wrote gratefully to Russell from High Wycombe.[49] Russell was also attempting to mollify Charlotte Eliot, assuring her that the shortage of educated men who had now enlisted in the army would enable Tom to obtain "suitable work" once he had taken his Ph.D.[50]

However, it would be wrong to assume that Vivien and Eliot *never* had physical relations, as Ackroyd and Monk appear to do. Monk states that Eliot was "incapable of sexual relations with her," and this was the explanation for his acceptance of the triangular relationship.[51] Ackroyd also attributes this to the "physical failure" of the marriage. But Eliot's honeymoon nerves seem to have evaporated to some extent as the months passed, and it is perfectly possible that Vivien was intimate with both men in the autumn of 1915. By 8 May 1916 Vivien was writing a letter of congratulation to Scofield in which she implied limited love-making with her husband had taken place, although it appears she had to work hard to stimulate him. "How nice that you are going to be married!" she writes. "Nothing could be better! Try black silk sheets and pillow covers—they are extraordinarily effective—so long as you are willing to sacrifice *yourself.*"[52] Colette also remembered that Bertie "once appeared in my bedroom wearing black pajamas, saying that V.S.E. (Vivienne Stearns Eliot) likes them."[53] Black sheets and pajamas would not, of course, show blood stains, and were possibly Vivien's own solution to her problem.

As the term drew to a close, the *ménage à trois* began to unravel. Perhaps Vivien grew too demanding, and Russell's brother Frank began to protest at the disappearance of the family jewels. Perhaps Russell himself grew "scared," as Maurice believed. Eliot's conscience may at last have driven him to hunt for a flat for himself and his wife. What is not in doubt is the nervous collapse which the ending of this crucial love triangle precipitated in Vivien. "The situation is anxious and painful, although it is too interesting to be left alone, apart from kindness," wrote Russell to Ottoline on 10 November, apologising for being unable to come to Garsington. He had come to love Eliot "as if he were my son":

> He is becoming much more of a man. He has a profound & quite
> unselfish devotion to his wife, & she is really very fond of him, but

has impulses of cruelty to him from time to time. It is a Dostoevsky type of cruelty, not a straightforward every-day kind. I am every day getting things more right between them, but I can't let them alone at present, & of course I myself get very much interested. She is a person who lives on a knife edge, & will end as a criminal or a saint—I don't know which yet. She has a perfect capacity for both.[54]

This passage, in which Russell implies Vivien is mentally unstable, has been much quoted. It should be remembered that it was written to Ottoline, who was prejudiced against Vivien; it should also be compared to the letter Russell wrote on 3 December to Tom's mother, Charlotte Eliot, in which he praises Vivien's charm and ability:

I have continued to see a good deal of your son and his wife. It has been a great pleasure having them staying in my flat, and I am sorry to lose them . . . She has done a great deal of work for me, chiefly typing, and consequently I have come to know her well. I have a great respect and liking for her: she has a good mind, and is able to be a real help to a literary career, besides having a rare strength and charm of character.[55]

As the time of leaving approached, Vivien's illness necessitated her mother's presence to nurse her in 34 Russell Chambers, and Russell had to take refuge in the Waverly Hotel just around the corner. "I have been having a horrid higgedly-piggedly pillar-post kind of time," he complained to Ottoline on 8 December,[56] as he worried about completing the lectures on social reconstruction he was due to deliver in the new year. Finally he decamped to the house of his old friend Robert Trevelyan, at Holmbury St. Mary, near Dorking, and thence to his brother's in Sussex, where he found the necessary quiet in which to write. It was time for the Eliots to move on. By early December the Eliots had found a flat of their own in St. John's Wood, and by the 20th they had left. Such was Vivien's panic at the prospect of living alone with her husband that Russell was forced to promise to take her on holiday to the seaside after Christmas.

7

A Child in Pain

Early in the new year Bertie and Vivien travelled together to the Torbay Hotel, Torquay, where they stayed for five days, from 7 to 12 January 1916. It was a provocative move by Bertie, who had complained sulkily to Ottoline that he did not want to visit Garsington because it was full of "morbid corners," but instead mentioned in a letter of 3 December that he was planning to invite Vivien for a holiday before Christmas.[1] All he wanted, he told his old lover, was six months' sleep. The letter, meanwhile, had the desired effect, bringing fresh pleas from Ottoline to visit her.

"I *long* to be with you," replied Bertie, not altogether truthfully, on 1 January, "but I am afraid I can't . . . I made a beginning of an attempt to get out of it [the holiday with Vivien], but found I should hurt her feelings so I dropped it. Now she is well enough, and wants to go on Monday."[2] He assured Ottoline he was in no mood for a holiday and would have preferred to stay in London where the Military Service Bill, which introduced conscription for all single men aged between eighteen and forty-one, was making its stormy way through Parliament. As a leading activist in the No-Conscription Fellowship, and as an acquaintance of H. H. Asquith, the Prime Minister, an old admirer of Ottoline's whom he had met at Garsington on the occasion when he emerged naked from a pond to find Asquith on the bank ("the quality of dignity which should have characterised a meeting between the Prime Minister and a pacifist was somewhat lacking on this occasion," wrote Russell[3]), he might have been expected to stay in London to fight this extension of the powers of the state.[4] Yet Russell left the capital just as the bill was receiving its first reading on 6 January in the Commons, in order to take Vivien to the seaside.

Before his departure, Bertie teased Ottoline with excuses for his West

Country holiday. Vivien, he was sure, would "much prefer" to be with her husband, but Eliot needed to work on his thesis and was looking forward to the time alone: "She needs a change in order to get well, & Eliot has been so busy nursing her he wants solitude. So it seems inevitable." The conventions would be observed, Russell assured his former lover: "We shall be quite 'proper'—There is no tendency to develop beyond friendship, quite the opposite. I have really now done all I meant to do for them, they are perfectly happy in each other, & I shall begin to fade away out of their lives as soon as this week is over."

On 3 January Russell made another attempt to justify his holiday alone with Vivien, explaining that he had made "a valiant attempt" to get out of going away with "Mrs. E.," without success.

> The whole thing rather amused me, because it was so unlike the way things are conventionally supposed to happen. First I talked to him, & said I felt the responsibility of her health, & wished he were going as he knew better what to do. He was willing to take my place, but reluctant on account of his work . . . However, he would have gone; but when I said the same things to her, she wouldn't hear of it, again on account of his work. So I had to let the matter be . . .[5]

Clearly Vivien preferred to go on holiday with Russell rather than her husband, but as a sop to Ottoline, who was unhappy that she and Bertie had lost "the fine intense moments" of the past, and their affair was "fading out,"[6] Russell promised to make the break with the Eliots soon: "What I meant to do for these two is done, except to some slight extent as regards money (I must go on giving her my typing)," and assured her that the Eliot marriage was happier than it had been. But for all his promises, Vivien's vulnerability had touched Bertie's heart, for it stood in such contrast to the strong-willed Ottoline, whom he was determined to punish for rejecting his "oppressive" physical advances: "I don't quite know why, she appeals to me as a child in pain would," he wrote on 7 January 1916. "I hate to see her suffer. She has the one great thing, real love—She will endure anything rather than hurt people." Russell disliked Vivien's mother, Rose, who in his opinion was "odious, but Mrs. E. is always thinking how to keep her happy—For some reason she had no kindness to her husband at first, but now she is quite changed towards him."[7]

It is possible that for once Russell was telling the truth when he emphasised the innocence of his relations with Vivien at Torquay to Ottoline, and that Vivien had taught him why women found him oppressive. "I have been quite fantastically unselfish towards her, & have never dreamt of making any kind of demands." Russell claimed to have discovered that a "clash" existed between artistic people, those like Ottoline and Vivien who took pleasure in "things of sight," and the inartistic, like himself, those who lived *"exclusively* in thoughts & purposes." It was hardly a profound insight, but Russell attributed the lifting of his mood to this lesson learnt from Vivien's conversation and company. Now he understood this, wrote an exuberant Russell, and realised that such personality clashes could not be cured, he was no longer in a state of depression at all, but was simply trying to see things clearly. "I simply *must* understand, & avoid getting into such a state again."[8]

Whether Ottoline believed him is unlikely; certainly she had heard from Aldous Huxley that Vivien was a flirtatious and seductive woman, and she had no reason to trust Bertie's fidelity in affairs of the heart; past experience had taught her that he could lie when he felt it necessary. She responded, however, with dignity:

> I feel you think I am hurt that you are with Mrs. Elliot [sic]. You must not *please* think so, for I am not a bit. I am only sorry that it is such a mere health sojourn & that it is very little rest or relaxation for you, but I hope in spite of everything that it may rest you . . .

But despite her brave protests, Ottoline *was* hurt. She knew that Russell, who lived "entirely mentally," was critical of her longing to live what she described as "the simple instinctive life" at Garsington, although few of her guests would have recognised in those terms the lifestyle she had created at the Oxfordshire manor house. Ottoline could not help confessing to her "darling Bertie" her disappointment that she had failed "so lamentably lately to make you *at all happy* & that you dread to come here—to a place I Love. Please dont think I am *hurt*—about it—only it *is* a disappointment

& I feel—really—discouraged—about the future." In future, said Ottoline, they could only meet in London.[9]

Ottoline knew that Russell had been in a state of nervous tension before leaving for Torquay. The decision he made in 1915 to devote himself to anti-war propaganda had made him an increasingly hated figure in the country. Under suspicion by the government, he was about to give the first of his lectures on social reconstruction on 18 January, the preparation of which, he complained to Ottoline, "nearly drove me into insanity." In fact Russell had felt so distressed before leaving London that he had discussed with Ottoline the possibility of consulting her "nerve doctor," the Swiss psychiatrist Dr. Vittoz, asking if he could cure "despair." Vivien's health was allegedly equally precarious: "Coming here is merely a question of health—Mrs. E. fancied it would do her good," wrote Russell. "She is too ill for any thought of real enjoyment in the place." On the day they arrived, 7 January 1916, he told Ottoline, "I detest it but she seems to like it. However, she is not any better so far."

Alone in each other's company, in a climate so warm that they could sit out without a coat, "warmer than Rome" in fact, Bertie and Vivien found "very lovely places" near the coast to explore. Soon Bertie was feeling quite fit, "and Mrs. E. is better, I no longer feel anxious and weighed down with responsibility." What exactly was wrong with Vivien? Ottoline had enquired; Russell had told her in December when Vivien was laid up in his flat that "Mrs. Eliot's illness is not serious in itself, but she has been threatened since childhood with tuberculosis in the bones, and it means everything has to be treated very carefully. All through her childhood she has been kept alive by Sir F. Treves, gratis, because the case interested him. I had always thought he was a brute, but her experience of him is quite the opposite . . ."[10] As Russell's correspondence makes clear, Vivien was "delicate," an easy prey to influenza and chest infections, but her ill-health was largely "nervous," as was his.

Ottoline urged Russell to see Dr. Vittoz at the Villa Cimerise in Lausanne, explaining that he need only be away just over a fortnight, and the doctor was not very expensive. But by 12 January Russell, like Vivien, was feeling so much better that he saw no need to visit Dr. Vittoz—not that the Foreign Office would have allowed him to leave the country. Ottoline was magnanimous: "I am *so* glad Mrs. E. is better," she replied the next day. "It is really a great comfort to feel you have been such a help to them, & it was well worthwhile."[11]

The same afternoon, 12 January, Eliot arrived at Torquay, "as happy as a boy escaped from school," said Russell, who paid both the Eliots' expenses. Russell's revealing phrase, "Eliot replaced me,"[12] suggests that he had, in some sense, fulfilled the role of husband until Tom, who had journeyed down through Somerset, passing East Coker, from where his ancestor Andrew Eliot had emigrated to Salem, was reunited with his much recovered wife. Russell reluctantly returned to London, still struggling to analyse the mystery of Vivien's attraction for him: "I can't quite make out why I like her, & feel you wouldn't, & I couldn't defend her," he told Ottoline. "I believe I like her really because I can be useful to her, so I get over the sense of being a failure & making people unhappy when I want to make them happy." It was, he wrote, a sort of comfort to him to think that the Eliots were happier than they would have been if he had not known them.[13] "Mrs. E does for me what the Germans did last Xmas," implying that Vivien roused him from torpor and depression to a sense of purposeful activity.

In Vivien and Russell's absence Eliot had been staying alone at 34 Russell Chambers, looked after by Russell's charwoman, Mrs. Saich. As ever, he had no qualms about accepting Russell's offer of free accommodation at Torquay, and the alacrity with which he agreed to take his benefactor's place suggests that Eliot's need to work on his thesis, most of which had been completed at Oxford before he sent it to his supervisor Professor James H. Woods at Harvard in February, was not as pressing as Ottoline had been given to understand. "This is wonderfully kind of you—really the last straw (so to speak) of generosity," wrote Eliot. He was very sorry Russell had to return to London—"and Vivien says you have been an angel to her"—but of course he jumped at the opportunity of a holiday. "I am sure you have done *everything* possible and handled her in the very best way—better than I. I often wonder how things would have turned out but for you—I believe we shall owe her life to you, even."[14]

It was a letter of heartfelt gratitude, but one which carries an air of desperation. Eliot may have believed that once again Russell had saved Vivien from suicidal despair,[15] but the miracle Russell had worked required no great skill: essentially it was to make Vivien, a feminine and dependent woman, feel loved and desired. Eliot's true agony sprang from the knowledge that when his wife was with Bertie her health improved, and when she was alone with him it deteriorated.

Eliot hinted at his marital disharmony in a letter to his old college contemporary Conrad Aiken, with whom he often employed a vivid homosexual imagery he did not share with his new English acquaintances. On 10 January, while Vivien was away, Eliot listed his tribulations, cursing the Boston publishers who had refused to publish his poems "on account of his being an Englishman: If you are in with them you might tell them to butter their asses and bugger themselves . . . ," complaining that the *Catholic Anthology,* the collection of modern poetry edited by Ezra Pound, which included some new poems of Eliot's, "Miss Helen Slingsby" and "Hysteria" as well as "Prufrock" and "Portrait of a Lady," was not selling well (it was condemned by critic Arthur Waugh in the *Quarterly Review* as "the unmetrical incoherent banalities of these literary 'Cubists' "),[16] and that his only paying publications were *Poetry* and the *International Journal of Ethics.* But it was not only uncooperative publishers and unkind critics who frustrated Eliot. "I have *lived* through material for a score of long poems, in the last six months," he exploded to Aiken.[17] It was a prophetic remark if, as early as 1916, Eliot was aware that his calamitous marriage could be the raw material for a masterpiece. Certainly the comparison between himself and Russell the womaniser was a cruel one. Now Bertie had gone and Tom and Vivien were left alone in the quiet desperation of an unhappy marriage.

Eliot struggled to put the best face possible on their holiday: "Vivien is massaging my head, so my writing will be rather scrawly," he wrote to his father two days after his arrival in Torquay.[18] The West Country was lovely, rich and green, with bright red soil, and had one of the "loveliest bits of shore" he had ever seen. "I was in raptures over it," he wrote to Russell. "It is wonderful to have come out of town and been bathed in this purity." In front of the hotel was a little harbour. Reminded of his sailing days with Henry in the *Elsa,* off the coast near East Gloucester, Tom was tempted to seize a boat and put to sea—"except that Vivien couldn't come with me."[19] The little boats symbolised the freedom he had so impetuously sacrificed, as the poet stared out to sea and dreamed of escape.

Alone with Tom, Vivien's maladies multiplied. Although when

Russell left she was about to start typing a manuscript he had left her, within two days of his departure she was having bad nights, bad stomachs, headaches, and feeling tired and faint. Even so Torquay was idyllic. "You could not have chosen a better place for Vivien: it's a sign how badly she needed it, when even under the absolutely *perfect* conditions you have provided for her, she is still so weak and fatigued," reasoned Tom, unwilling to admit that Vivien's collapse was due to her change of companion rather than any disease. "I am convinced that no one could have been so wise and understanding with her as you. She was very happy." The past tense is significant.

The Eliots had intended to return in time for Russell's first lecture at Caxton Hall, but Vivien was, according to Tom, too "tired and low" to travel. They stayed an extra night, at Tom's expense *("Of course . . . I insist on that")*, although Vivien was anxious to attend her admirer's debut. Tom had begun to take control of the situation, laying down for his wife "a very strict regimen, with very clear limits of exertion [which] will be imperative for the rest of the winter."[20]

Conscription was the issue of the moment when Tom and Vivien finally returned to London, and Russell was fast becoming the man of the moment, as his revulsion at the slaughter of young men at the Battles of the Marne, Ypres and Gallipoli in 1915 inspired his lectures with new passion: "When the War came I felt as if I heard the voice of God . . . As a lover of civilisation, the return to barbarism appalled me. As a man of thwarted parental feeling, the massacre of the young wrung my heart." Appalled at the apparent eagerness with which parents such as the Whiteheads offered their sons to be sacrificed, Russell took to watching the troop trains steam out of Waterloo and began to experience strange visions of London. In his imagination he saw the bridges collapse and sink, and the city vanish like a morning mist. Its inhabitants began to seem like hallucinations to him, a product of his nightmares. These illusions he described to Eliot, who later used them in *The Waste Land,* or so Russell believed.[21] The need to stiffen pacifist resistance roused Russell to action, as it did most of Bloomsbury. The Derby Scheme, whereby unmarried men of military age "attested" their willingness to serve, had failed in the autumn of 1915 as the roll call of the dead lengthened and the enthusiasm of young men to enlist palled. Men who did not wear the prescribed armband were open to the gift of the white feather, but still the war machine remained short of numbers. Public feeling grew against men of military age who were still in "civvies," and in November 1915 Duncan Grant was arrested at Folkestone for not being in uniform.[22]

When the First Military Service Bill became law in March 1916 the government joined battle with the pacifists. Lytton and James Strachey, Duncan Grant, Vanessa Bell, her brother Adrian Stephen, David "Bunny" Garnett and Bob Trevelyan all volunteered for work at the Fleet Street headquarters of the National Council for Civil Liberties, and many joined the NCF, the other centre of opposition to compulsory military service. Old friends were divided by the war; Lytton sent his former lover, Maynard Keynes—a fellow member of the Apostles, the élite Cambridge *conversazione* society—the "conscientious objector's equivalent of a white feather," when he posted to him a newspaper cutting of a militaristic speech by Edwin Montagu, Foreign Secretary to the Treasury, with a note saying: "Dear Maynard, Why are you still at the Treasury? Yours, Lytton."[23]

To Russell fell the task of defining the arguments against militarism in his lectures, which proved a huge popular draw.[24] Lytton, also a member of the NCF, attended every lecture, finding that, as he wrote on 16 February 1916:

> Bertie's lectures help one. They are a wonderful solace and refreshment. One hangs upon his words, and looks forward to them from week to week, and I can't bear the idea of missing one—I dragged myself to that ghastly Caxton Hall yesterday, though I was rather nearer the grave than usual, and it was well worth it . . . He . . . plants it down solid and shining before one's mind. I don't believe there's anyone quite so formidable to be found just now upon this earth.[25]

Lytton Strachey needed the support of Bertie's philosophy as well as the presence of his friends for his tribunal hearing which took place in March. With Philip Morrell in attendance as chief character witness, carrying the air cushion upon which Lytton sat, for his piles, Lytton gave his celebrated answer to the tribunal's question: "What would you do if you saw a

German soldier attempting to rape your sister?" "I should try and come between them." Rejected as medically unfit, Lytton retired to Garsington to recover.

In the weeks after her return to London Vivien remained on intimate terms with Bertie, despite the "strict regimen" prescribed by her husband, and Bertie continued to bait Ottoline with news of his encounters with Vivien; on 30 January he informed her that Mrs. Eliot had dined with him, "which I enjoyed. She is living a more or less invalid life, going out very little, & going to bed at ten—but she is getting much less ill, especially nervously. Her husband is out all day at his school, & works all evening, so her existence is very dull, but I am sure it is good for her."[26] As Russell continued to lunch and dine with Vivien twice a week, his relationship with her became an increasing bone of contention with Ottoline, who complained in February that Bertie now only wrote her "very meager letters . . . I suppose you are tired and busy."[27] Moreover she firmly declined to meet her rival, writing at the beginning of the year: "I had felt it rather better not to meet her as it might complicate matters, especially if I didn't like her much—but—if it was any use or help to her of course I should be delighted to ask them both here, a little later on, when the spring comes— just Now I am feeling tired and want to be quiet."[28] Instead she suggested that Bertie should introduce Dorothy Brett to the Eliots, or Carrington or Gilbert Cannan—"I'm sure he would be delighted to know Mrs. Elliot [sic]."

But Russell continued to put pressure on Ottoline to receive his new mistress at Garsington until she finally capitulated: "My darling, I am delighted to have Mrs. E. here. I wrote to her yesterday. I hope she will come for I should like *very* much to know her." Would Bertie come for the weekend, she asked, suggesting Maynard and Lytton as fellow guests.[29] However, a reply from Vivien, which has not survived but which Ottoline found over-emotional, prompted the chatelaine of Garsington to withdraw her invitation. Bertie accused her of being unkind to his "child in pain." "My darling, I am very sorry you thought me unkind. I *really* didn't mean to be—nor did I realise that I had been," replied Ottoline on 3 March. "I *really* don't mind yr. friendship with The Eliots, quite the contrary, for I am sure it is an *enormous* help to them both & incidently [sic] to you too. I hope you don't think me unkind about *her*. The effect of her rather exaggerated letter made me draw in . . ."[30]

Ironically, Vivien's epistolary style could resemble Ottoline's with its dashes, capitals, underlinings and misspellings sprinkled haphazardly through the text. Under particular stress, her letters become confused and incoherent, yet in conversation Vivien did not suffer from the inarticulacy for which Ottoline was often mocked by the literati she patronised. Lawrence, for example, satirises Ottoline as Hermione Roddice in *Women in Love* whose tendency to "rumble" and inability to complete a sentence is a source of amusement to her guests. It is possible that Ottoline recognised a certain similarity in style, indicative of a shared emotionality and nervous temperament, between herself and Vivien, which at first influenced her against receiving her rival at Garsington. Under Bertie's relentless pressure, however, Ottoline finally agreed to meet Vivien on neutral ground, in London. Bertie owed her a favour in return, implied Ottoline, asking him to keep Wednesday afternoon free for her alone. In exchange she would ask a few people in on Thursday evening: "You could ask the Eliots to come too—and they could meet a few others Thurs."

Three days later Ottoline and Philip came up to London for Russell's final lecture. Ottoline was delighted to be back at her "dear old house" in Bedford Square, the top floors of which were let out during the war, although she and Philip retained the drawing-room and dining-room floors for themselves. Many of Bertie's old friends came to the lecture, including Desmond MacCarthy, Clive Bell and his mistress Mary Hutchinson, wife of barrister St. John Hutchinson, and artist Merk Gertler. The next evening the long-awaited meeting took place: Ottoline and Philip dined with Bertie, Tom and Vivien at a restaurant in Soho. Ottoline had already read some of Tom's poems in "a little American magazine" *(Poetry),* and they had struck her as "very remarkable," but she remained reluctant to condone Bertie's meddling in the Eliots' marriage. He "was convinced that the Eliots were not really happy together, but by a little manipulation on his part everything would come right between them," she wrote in her journal. "By what he had told me I was not convinced of this and felt doubtful as to whether he would not make things much worse."[31]

The dinner was not a success. "T. S. Eliot was very formal and polite, and his wife seemed to me of the 'spoilt-kitten' type, very second-rate and ultra-feminine, playful and naïve, anxious to show she 'possessed' Bertie, when we walked away from the restaurant she headed him off and kept him to herself, walking with him arm-in-arm," wrote a resentful Ottoline. "I felt rather *froissée* at her bad manners." Nevertheless, the next day she gave a tea-party at Bedford Square, to which she invited the Eliots and Russell. Ottoline had turned one of the drawing-rooms into her bedroom, in which stood a large four-poster bed, hung with cardinal-coloured silk curtains trimmed with silver. It was, she remembered, very lovely looking into that room from the great drawing-room. Molly MacCarthy, wife of journalist Desmond MacCarthy, and Dora Sanger, wife of Thoby Stephen's old friend Charles Sanger, and artists Dorothy Brett, Carrington and Mark Gertler came too, and the afternoon was a happier gathering than the evening before. To Tom Eliot, anxious to meet people of influence in English society, it must have seemed like entering Circe's cave. At last he had the introduction to Bloomsbury's powerful high priestess,[32] who could open the door to acceptance by the most exclusive and influential literary clique in England.

The next prize to be won was a visit to Garsington, for if Bedford Square remained magnificent despite being half-shut down in wartime, it could not match the Tudor manor house about whose exotic house parties Eliot had heard so much from Russell. Vivien, however, was too agitated by late March to care whether or not she received an invitation. A new crisis had arisen. Despite the German wartime blockade of allied Atlantic shipping, Tom was due to sail for America on 1 April to present his "decidedly anti-Russellian" thesis at Harvard, and take the oral exam for his doctorate. Vivien was afraid he would be putting his life at risk.

Throughout March Vivien's panic increased. Despite having told Scofield that she was planning to visit America that spring, when the moment came her fear of submarines led her to change her mind. Once again she refused to accompany Tom. Her apprehension was not without foundation, for on 24 March 1916 the cross-Channel steamer *Sussex* was torpedoed off Dieppe with the loss of fifty lives, including those of three Americans. "Mr. Eliot did not believe it possible that even the Germans (a synonym for all that is most frightful) would attack an American liner," wrote Charlotte Eliot in indignation: "I am glad all our ancestors are

English with a French ancestry far back on one line . . ."[33] On 23 March, the day before the *Sussex* was sunk, Russell received a worried postcard from Eliot; once more he stepped into the breach, cabling to Tom's father: "STRONGLY ADVISE CABLING TOM AGAINST SAILING UNDER PRESENT PECULIARLY DANGEROUS CONDITIONS UNLESS IMMEDIATE DEGREE IS WORTH RISKING LIFE."[34] "He will probably not go to America—she is probably not really ill—she wasn't before—but her nerves are all to pieces," Russell explained to Ottoline. "It is the way of his going that upset her. She is afraid he would be sunk by a submarine."[35] Henry Ware Eliot Sr. was "not greatly pleased" with the language of Russell's cable, but he was helpless in the face of circumstances when Tom's boat was cancelled. A relieved Eliot posted his thesis,[36] which was received as the "work of an expert," and promised to come *"at the first opportunity"* when the war was over. "Naturally I do not like to leave my wife here, or venture the waves myself, while it is still on," he told Professor Woods. Having failed to present himself for the viva voce, Eliot never did receive his doctorate.[37]

The prospect that she would be left alone to manage their forthcoming move from their old flat at 3 Culworth House, Henry Street, St. John's Wood, to a new one in Marylebone, added to Vivien's worries. She poured out her troubles in excited letters to Ottoline, who took fright at Vivien's near-hysteria. "I hope Mrs. Eliot will be able to array her affairs—Does she often write like that—I couldn't make out how substantial it was or if it was exaggerated—I felt it was so . . ." wrote Ottoline to Bertie on 28 March. Her natural sympathy for a fellow sufferer, and the shared experience of having been Bertie's lover, which was to form the basis of the future bond between Ottoline and Vivien, was tempered by the lack of understanding of a wealthy aristocrat for the difficulties of an impoverished young couple:

> I don't know what to say about Mrs. E. She is evidently overwrought by the pain—& rather hysterical. Isn't her letter rather exaggerated? Perhaps she will feel better in a day or two. Has she got another flat that she can send her furniture into? If she has, I should advise her just to Tilt into the new place & Lock the door & either go home to her people to rest for a week—or if she would

like to come down here I should be delighted to have her Next
week—on Monday, for a bit.

Ottoline's letter suggests that Vivien's doctor was prescribing medication
for the pain from which she was suffering, probably bromide to calm her
and counteract her migraines and abdominal discomfort. Ottoline understood the side effects of the tranquillisers of that time, and was sympathetic
to Vivien's case: "The *Numbness* comes frm thgs she has taken fr the Pain,
I expect—I always feel that—Perhaps a rest in this warm house would do
her good. Couldn't her mother help her to arrange for her furniture to be
moved?"[38]

By the next morning, however, Ottoline had thought better of her rash
invitation:

It is snowing *& so so cold here*—that I feel rather nervous of asking Mrs. E to come here until the weather is better—I think she
would hate it—& be miserable so perhaps better *not* suggest her
coming just yet—she was coming on Thursday—Of course tho if
it is any good I would have her just to rest—Do you think she
would like to go to a Nursing Home for a *rest*—I know of quite
a nice one—but after she would hate it. Are her own people horrid?[39]

On 7 April Ottoline wrote to enquire of Bertie whether Vivien was better,
but the highly coloured letters she had received from Vivien had confirmed Ottoline in her decision to entertain Tom only. Four days later she
wrote that she would be pleased to have Mr. Eliot, who she thought would
get on with Lytton, but she had cancelled Vivien, who was to have come
the following week. "I suppose it would rest him more to come alone."[40]
And although she remarked to Bertie on 19 May that she had had a "nice
letter from Mrs. Eliot," she remained determined after her initial poor impression in London not to receive her at Garsington in the coming months,
despite Bertie's pleas: "Yes, I am *sure* Mrs. Eliot is nice," she responded
tartly. "I hope she will come some day & that I shall know her a little—I
rather wish I hadn't seen that letter—It was so like my sisters-in-laws' letters . . . I am sure you can help her. Please don't think I grudge that at all."[41]

The day of Eliot's spring visit to Garsington arrived finally in April. To her journal Ottoline confided her excitement that Russell was bringing Eliot, but, unlike his hosts the Morrells, Russell, and the majority of the guests, Eliot was not in sympathy with the pacifist movement. When asked by Russell in October 1914 what he thought of the war, he had replied: "I don't know. I only know that I am not a pacifist." "That is to say, he considered any excuse good enough for homicide," commented Russell.[42] Their lack of agreement did not, however, divide them as it did Lytton and Maynard Keynes.[43] As an American there was as yet no question of Eliot confronting his conscience, although the question of whether the U.S. would be drawn into the war, and whether or not he should volunteer at some time in the future was beginning to weigh on his mind, stimulated by the conversation at Garsington, which had become a rallying point for "conchies," whose work as farm labourers exempted them from military service.

This time the meeting between Tom and Ottoline was less successful than in London. Russell was irritating Ottoline more than usual, despite their common opposition to conscription and the fact that her husband, Philip "Pipsey" Morrell, was risking his seat at Burnley by speaking against the war in Parliament. "I never feel my best with Bertie. I cannot tell why. He always quenches my lightheartedness and gaiety and puts a blight on me," wrote Ottoline. As for his new friend Eliot, she found the poet "dull, dull, dull":

> He never moves his lips but speaks in an even and monotonous voice, and I felt him monotonous without and within. Where does his queer neurasthenic poetry come from, I wonder. From his New England, Puritan inheritance and upbringing? I think he has lost all spontaneity and can only break through his conventionality by stimulants or violent emotions.[44]

Anxious to impress his aristocratic hostess, Eliot was at pains to suppress any traces of his hybrid American accent, but, despite his erudition, his carefully enunciated English sounded false to Ottoline. "Eliot spoke English very beautifully and deliberately," recalled Helen Gardner, but he "lost his American accent without ever developing English speed and

English slurring or English speech rhythms."[45] Struck by the poet's formality and ignorance of England, Ottoline tried talking French to Eliot in the hope of breaking down the barriers between them. He seemed to imagine that it was essential to be polite and decorous, and she hoped that he might feel freer in another language. Again she failed, although he was "better" in French than English. "He speaks French very perfectly, slowly and correctly . . . It shows how very foreign Eliot seemed to me then; but I generally found that Americans are as foreign to us as Germans are."[46] Ottoline found no reason to change the nickname she had given Eliot: "The Undertaker."

While Russell's affairs galloped towards a crisis with the circulation of his "seditious" leaflet protesting against the sufferings of Ernest Everett, a conscientious objector condemned to two years' hard labour, and his provocative letter to *The Times* in May 1916, inviting prosecution, Vivien was feeling calmer now that the move had taken place on 12 March into the new flat at 18 Crawford Mansions, Crawford Street, Marylebone. Her pride in their first real home together was immense, as she experimented with interior decoration: "It is the tiniest place imaginable," she wrote to Tom's brother Henry Ware Eliot Jr. in June. They had just a dining-room, a drawing-room, a large bedroom, a kitchen and a nice bathroom. "We have constant hot water, which is a *luxury* in England." The building was quite new with "every modern convenience," and Vivien chose all the wallpapers herself. Among the "rather original effects" was an *"orange paper"* in the dining-room ("which is also Tom's dressing room and study!") and black and white stripes in the hall.[47] The orange paper, Vivien's pride and joy, featured in another letter to Scofield Thayer, in which she sent "congratulations of the most fervent" on the occasion of his marriage to Elaine Eliot Orr in New York. "I was never more delighted than when I heard you have an orange wallpaper," she wrote, telling Scofield that they had one in the dining-room. He was to come and see them when he brought his bride to see Europe. "You can do us and the Tower of London on the same day."[48]

The news that his old friend was also marrying aroused surprise and nostalgia in Tom, who could scarcely believe that it was only a year since he and Scofield were charming the eyes and ears of "Char-flappers" from their virginal punt at Oxford. Had Scofield, the Magdalen aesthete, "the connoisseur of puberty and lilies . . . about to wed the Madonna of the mantelpiece," discovered the Fountain of Eternal Youth not in Florida, but in Troy (New York), he asked ironically. Quoting Oscar Wilde to his old friend, Eliot prayed that domestic felicity might not "extinguish the amateur" in Scofield, nor the possession of beauty quench the passionate detachment which his friends admired and admirers envied. He hoped that "within an interior of dim light drifting through heavy curtains, by a Buhl table holding a Greek figurine, and a volume of Faust bound in green and powdered with gold, with a bust of Dante, and perhaps a screen by Korin, a drawing by Watteau—a room heavy with the scent of lilies," Scofield would enshrine such a treasure as that with which he rightly credited Eliot—"a wife who is not wifely."[49] It was perhaps as hard for Eliot to imagine Scofield, described as "strikingly pale, with coal-black hair, black eyes veiled and flashing, and lips that curved like Lord Byron [who] seemed to many the embodiment of the aesthete with overrefined tastes and sensibilities,"[50] settling down to marriage, as it had been for Scofield to imagine Eliot as a bridegroom, and it was therefore with a degree of fellow feeling that Eliot enquired into Scofield's domestic arrangements. Although Eliot declared that when Mr. and Mrs. Scofield Thayer came to visit London, "Mr. and Mrs. Stearns Eliot will be outraged if they are not the first to entertain them," his doubts proved well founded: Scofield returned to his bachelor flat in Washington Square within months of his marriage, and his wife had a baby daughter, Nancy, by the poet e. e. cummings, whom she later married.[51]

Vivien, lover of "pose" and fashion, shared Scofield and Tom's aesthetic values and aspired to create a similar beauty in her flat. The following year she describes herself to Scofield in her drawing-room: upon an inlaid Renaissance chest two mysterious faces confront her, two inscrutable smiles. One is that of a Burmese buddha, curiously carved in green jade, the other that of a young man still in his prime, whose eyelids are heavy with the languor of those upon whom the gods have lavished knowledge too early. He is "one of those mad amateurs of beauty," a strange figure of the late Empire who in the midst of corruption preserves a childlike grace. "Quis desidirio aut pudor aut modus/Tam cari capitis?" ("Unshamed, unchecked, for one so dear/We sorrow") murmurs Vivien, between "half-open lips," misquoting Horace's "Ode to Vergil on the Death of

Quintilius,"[52] as she lies on her divan, burning incense of cloudy Gold Flake.[53] The head of the youth standing on her cabinet reminds her of Scofield: "Behold thou are overfair, thou are overwise," she quotes, recalling "vanished days and evenings to one who is grateful for these memories." It was a letter designed to impress Scofield, who had always made Vivien feel horribly uneducated, but it also conjured up a heartfelt nostalgia for pre-war gaiety.

Despite their aspirations to luxury, both Tom and Vivien were obliged to face the painful business of trying to balance income and expenditure during the course of 1916. Henry Ware Eliot had agreed to pay the rent of their flat, but told Tom that he should "get some work to support his wife."[54] After only one term in Buckinghamshire Tom had found a new post in London at Highgate Junior School, teaching the boys French, Latin, mathematics, drawing and baseball, at a slightly increased salary of £160 a year; he also earned a little money from literary journalism, but *The Monist* and the *International Journal of Ethics* paid poorly for book-reviewing. Tom was once again grateful to Russell for an introduction to Philip Jourdain, editor of both periodicals, who commissioned two articles on Leibnitz.

Vivien believed fervently in her husband's poetic genius, and thought him *"too* good and *not* fitted" for school teaching: "Tom is *wonderful"* she enthused to Henry in June. Never had she met a man who impressed people so much with the feeling that he was *worth* helping. But if Tom went on teaching he would throw away innumerable chances and openings for writing, and would only be able to do "the little scraps" that he had time and energy for after school. "And school tires him very much—and chances don't come twice." The question was, did they dare gamble on giving it up? "He would win in time, but in the first year or two—how should we live?"[55] Henry responded to this begging letter as Vivien hoped, by sending money, one of the "constant five poundses" that he sent during the year. By October, Vivien confessed to Henry, they had only twenty-two pounds in the bank, and Tom wouldn't get any more till Christmas, so they were in a "fairly tight place." This, unfortunately, meant "writing to your father for help again."[56] Eliot Senior responded with cheques, despite the fact that he was "very despondent" about the brick business which he feared would go downhill if Woodrow Wilson lost the coming presidential election. Tom was duly grateful, remarking to his brother that he certainly had every reason to be proud of his family: the way they had accepted the responsibility for helping him—"without a single murmur"—was wonderful.

Vivien's letters to her mother-in-law paint a picture of a self-sacrificing, frugal and devoted housewife: "Darning alone takes me hours a week." Tom needed a new suit, "and I think *must* have one. His pyjamas are all very old and need constant mending." Tailoring her prose to Mrs. Eliot's own puritan standards, Vivien assured her that she was a careful manager, often sending the receipts for the clothes she had bought for Tom: "I *would* get Tom some new vests myself but I really *do* think the old ones are quite good for the rest of this winter." He was wearing his flannel shirts all the time, she promised Charlotte, albeit "under protest!"[57] Vivien of course omitted to mention that she and Tom had been subsidised by Russell while staying in his flat, and were still receiving help, as he admitted to Ottoline on 26 January 1916. Russell was thankful that his successful lectures had made him "rich," having earned £65 from his writing in the last few weeks: "I needed it, as I spent a lot on the Eliots. I don't need to spend much more, as they are now safely established."[58]

Both Tom and Vivien's letters to the Eliot family are notable for what they leave out rather than what they put in and, taken alone, provide a distorted version of their early married life. There is only thrift, never overspending, although we have Maurice's evidence that Vivien was still extravagant; she "lived" in the shops in the Finchley Road, where her mother had several accounts. In October 1916 Vivien returned to Lancashire for a week to ten days to stay with a girlfriend to whom she had once been bridesmaid; it was a trip which entailed "getting more clothes than I should have needed otherwise."[59]

Nor do these letters give an accurate picture of the Eliots' health problems. The emphasis was always on Vivien's illnesses, which appear mysterious. In 1970, Theresa, Henry Eliot's widow, recalled: "Henry, my husband, sent money to Tom for some years, but Tom never said anything to his family about Vivienne's ill-health and the doctor's bills."[60] But, although Vivien had been prescribed tranquillisers such as bromide from adolescence, her letters show that she could be happy and high-spirited with Russell; nor does the evidence of her 1914 and 1919 diaries and the letters of her early marriage suggest that her use of drugs was continuous. It is more probable that under the stress of living with Eliot, depressed by their sexual problems and incompatible temperaments, Vivien developed a range of psychosomatic symptoms for which her doctors on occasions prescribed drugs. She was far from being always incapacitated, as her lively letters to Scofield show.

Nevertheless, the angle presented by Tom, from his earliest letters home after his marriage, is that Vivien is invariably the "invalid" ("my invalid dependent wife") and he the devoted caregiver. This was the version of events Eliot was to promulgate until it became widely accepted as the truth. He plays down Vivien's own important role in nursing him through his own frequent bouts of influenza, bronchitis and episodes of paralysing depression, which culminated in his nervous breakdown in November 1921. Apologising to Conrad Aiken in August 1916 for not having written for so long, Eliot writes: "My wife has been very ill all the winter . . . This was not a case of maternity in any degree. Most people imagine so unless I explain. It has been nerves, complicated by physical ailments, and induced largely by the most acute neuralgia."[61] In reality, however, Vivien was sometimes the stronger of the two in this co-dependent relationship in which she also nursed Tom, as she did in early 1917 when he was ill for weeks with influenza, and in 1921.

In many of his letters home Eliot exaggerates Vivien's condition. With Russell he was more honest. In March 1916 Tom sent Russell a long and agitated account of Vivien's visit to the dentist which is notable for what it reveals about Eliot's state of mind rather than Vivien's teeth. According to Tom, Vivien was upset by this visit and as a result was in great pain, "both neuralgia and stomach." The dentist himself made light of Vivien's toothache, saying the problem "meant no great pain or risk"; significantly, he thought Tom was the person to be calmed down, and that he had communicated his own fears to Vivien. Sensing Tom's terror, for Eliot suffered as much as Vivien with his teeth until he had them all removed in later life, the dentist decided not to alarm him by mentioning that Vivien might develop an abscess (although he trusted Vivien with the truth). When Tom discovered this, he panicked: Vivien, who had been typing up some work for Russell all afternoon, was allegedly "very ill tonight, and I am very, very sorry that she went through this. It has been too great a strain upon

her will . . . The mistake was in letting her go at all—the effort and the anticipation during the last weeks . . . have taken every ounce of strength out
of her. Don't expect her to lunch to-morrow. I am sure it will be some days
before she can go out to lunch or dinner."[62] Did Eliot exaggerate Vivien's
symptoms in order to prevent her seeing Russell? It would appear that he
was taking back control of the situation now that he and Vivien were in
their own flat and it could be that his wife's "invalidism" suited Tom, for
it was the best possible excuse to keep her at home.

A typical letter of October 1916 from Vivien to Henry, in whom she
frequently confided, listed her symptoms: migraines, neuralgia and sinus
problems, but there is no clue as to *why* she is suffering so acutely. Vivien
explains she is trying not to spend too much money on doctors: "I shan't
have my sinus trouble touched until I simply have to." Three weeks before
"they" had sent her to the doctor for her headaches, which were quite separate from her sinus pain and "much *more* horrible." The doctor concluded that in the first place, she was undernourished—one of the first
mentions of the anorexia nervosa from which Vivien probably suffered.
"The headaches are called hemicranial migraine, and they are really 'nerve
storms' affecting one whole side of me—they make me sick and feverish
and they always last fifteen to twenty-four hours." When they pass, she
rises up "weak and white" as if she has been through some long and dreadful illness. Her headaches are "rather rare . . . *no drug touches them*"—fifteen to twenty grains of phenacetin bring not the slightest relief, she tells
Henry.[63]

In Tom and Vivien's misleading letters to his family from 1915,
Bertrand Russell is to be the missing link. Henry and Charlotte Eliot were
not to guess that Vivien was deeply in love with the man who featured only
in their letters as a respected friend, rather than as Vivien's lover, benefactor and counsellor to the couple ("You are a great psychologist," wrote
Eliot in 1925). Russell continued to be a key figure in the Eliots' lives, existing with them in a state of intimate interdependence throughout 1916.
In May, for example, Russell was writing to Ottoline from Leith Hill in
Surrey: "I have unexpectedly come down here for Sunday with Mrs. Eliot
(she is in the hotel and I am in the cottage) . . . I am enjoying this little
plunge in the country."[64] The triangle, wrote Robert Sencourt, "was to alter
drastically both Vivien's hopes for the future with Tom, and her already

fragile grasp on sanity [and was] the background of everything that Eliot wrote in verse or prose from 1915 onwards."[65] The pattern of Vivien's illnesses in 1915–18 is explicable within the context of her relationship with Russell: when he withdrew, she sickened; when he returned, she revived.

Russell himself was in collusion with Tom in writing himself out of the Eliots' personal history, and creating the myth of Tom, the capable caregiver of a sick wife, although he was aware of the fragility of Eliot's own conflicted personality. Russell writes to J. H. Woods that Eliot "has spent his spare hours in looking after his wife, with the most amazing devotion and unselfishness . . . Except in the one matter of health, his marriage is a very happy one and altogether desirable."[66] This was far from true, but both Eliot and Russell—although a personal and intellectual rift widened between them in later life—remained united in the belief that concealment was necessary in their private lives, although they approached this objective in different ways: Russell laid a false trail in his autobiography while Eliot, like his creation Eeldrop, sought to protect himself by an embargo on biography. "Such is precisely the case," returned Eeldrop (to Appleplex, the Russell persona), "but I had not thought it necessary to mention this biographical detail."[67]

During the spring of 1916 Russell's provocative anti-war propaganda continued to bait the government. Eventually it had no option but to bring him to trial on 5 June over his No-Conscription Fellowship leaflet attacking the sentence handed out to conscientious objector Ernest Everett. The trial took place at the Mansion House, attracting widespread publicity. Russell was fined £100 by the Lord Mayor, but pleaded that he could not pay; Ottoline began raising a fund to meet the fine: "His goods and furniture at Cambridge are to be sold to pay for it, but his friends have offered to buy them and restore them to him: I am busy collecting money for this purpose," she wrote, irritated that this job should fall upon her because Bertie had spent all his money on Mrs. Eliot.[68] At the subsequent auction of his belongings Philip and Ottoline bought most of his possessions, thus saving him from going to prison. Even in the midst of this crisis, on 6 June, Russell was writing tactlessly to Ottoline that "Mrs. Eliot makes it much easier for me not to mind not seeing more of you . . . I am really very devoted to her."[69]

Worse was to follow. On 11 July 1916, Russell was removed from his lectureship at Trinity College, Cambridge. His notoriety was such that the Foreign Office denied him a passport, thus making it impossible for him to recoup his financial position by teaching at Harvard, where he had been invited to return. Financially Russell's fortunes took a sharp downturn, although he professed to feel exhilarated at the prospect of devoting himself entirely to the peace movement. He was forced to let his London flat and move into his brother's flat at 57 Gordon Square, before setting off on a lecture tour of South Wales for the NCF.

In these difficult economic circumstances, Bertie could no longer afford to help Vivien financially. It was a mark of his deep infatuation with her that he nevertheless continued to pay for her dancing lessons and provide the other frivolous gifts jealously chronicled by Ottoline in July. In the face of Ottoline's remonstrances that he was ruining himself, he took Vivien out to dinner again "& discussed money."

> The passion of her life is dancing & ever since I have known her I have paid for her dancing lessons whenever she has been well enough. I don't suppose she will ever be any good, because of her health, but it is such a passion that I can't bear to baulk it if I can possibly help it . . . Of course, it would save my pocket if her husband got better-paid work . . .

Praising Eliot's reviewing ("it has quality & distinction, although it is done in the evenings after a full day's work at school"), Russell asked Ottoline if she would persuade Desmond MacCarthy to get his protégé published in the *New Statesman* or the *Guardian*. Making the extraordinary confession that he had not only paid for dancing lessons and other luxuries but was subsidising the Eliots' ordinary living expenses, Russell wrote, "So if you can see any way of helping me it will relieve me of a great anxiety."[70]

Dancing continued to be the great joy of Vivien's life, not only ballet but ballroom, an interest she shared with Tom. In November 1915 Eliot had excused himself from a meeting with Wyndham Lewis as "we have got to go and dance on Saturday."[71] Brigit Patmore, a member of the South Lodge Circle and later the lover of Richard Aldington, remembered frequent outings to a dance hall at Vivien's suggestion, soon after the Eliots had moved into their own flat. "You see, I'm very anxious to get Tom to take some exercise and there's a hall in Queensway where a small band plays on Sunday afternoons for people to dance to; very respectable, all that it should be. If you'd come and perhaps a few other friends sometimes— the quieter we begin the better, I believe Tom might come and not be bored." They danced with "unostentatious pleasure" on those Sunday afternoons. "Tom was an adequate performer, held one lightly and gracefully," Brigit recalled. "There was no agitated under-the-breath counting of *one*-two-three, *one*-two-three, but it might not have been a long time back and perhaps kept him silent . . ." She found Tom charming but unnerving. "His slow way of speaking in a slightly booming monotone, without emphasis, was quite beguiling." Yet she also sensed he was "pleased with nobody" and was always judging people.

> His mouth had turned-up corners, not with merriment, but with some kind of restriction—perhaps the bit between his teeth—for he was careful never to say anything indiscreet. Yet how winning and cordial he could be when the wide mouth smiled and the lines from both sides of the strong, well-shaped nose looked humorous and really genial. But the eyes, not yet inquisitorial as they became later, but cold dark grey, wide open and suiting finely the forehead so wide and high, but not too high . . . He was distinguished in appearance, perhaps handsome, but one longed for a grace, a carelessness which would have let him approach beauty.[72]

Those afternoons at the dance hall brought out the best in Tom and Vivien. One day, remembers Brigit, they went into a chemist's shop after the dancing. "Vivienne was talking about a ballet and said, 'I think I can do what Karsavina does at that moment.' And she held on to the counter with one hand, rose on her toes and held out the other hand which Tom took in his right hand, watching Vivienne's feet with ardent interest whilst he supported her with real tenderness. From him it was unexpected. Most husbands would have said, 'Not here, for Heaven's sake!' But he looked as if he did indeed want to help Vivienne in her chosen work."[73]

Another pleasure Tom and Vivien allowed themselves, despite their straitened finances, were seaside holidays, which they had both enjoyed as children. In August 1916 they left London for Bosham, in Chichester Harbor, taking a cottage in an area already favoured by Bloomsbury: Mary and St. John Hutchinson rented a farmhouse named Eleanor House at West Wittering, and invited Clive and Vanessa Bell and Duncan Grant. The indispensable Russell had already supplied Eliot with an introduction to Clive Bell in June, through whom it was inevitable he would meet Mary Hutchinson, as well as Roger Fry and Goldsworthy Lowes Dickinson, a Cambridge don. "Bloomsbury on sea" provided Tom and Vivien with rare hours of happiness. "We are vegetating and gaining health against the coming term on a backwater near Portsmouth harbour, where the tide is either very much in or very much out; the place alternates between mud and water, and is very charming," wrote Eliot to Conrad Aiken,[74] describing a routine of mornings spent working, afternoons bathing, boating and bicycling, with occasional trips up to the British Museum to prepare the lectures he was to give at Southall in the autumn term. As so often, Russell came too, preferring to spend time at Bosham with Vivien and Tom than at Garsington, where he would have to face the exhortations of Ottoline to give up Mrs. E. In the weeks after returning from his lecture tour in Wales he holidayed with the Eliots, apart from two or three days a week in London or staying with his brother at his country house near Chichester. "Mrs. E's brother is here—invalided home," he wrote to Ottoline on 20 August. "I like him—he is very like her in temperament, but a gentleman" (the implication was that Vivien was not a lady). Making the first of many promises on the subject of Vivien's allowance, he said: "I told her a definite date (not far off) after which I can't undertake to find any more money, explained how hard up I am, which I had not done before. She accepted it without demur."[75]

Vivien was more tenacious than Bertie would admit. Throughout August Ottoline increased her pressure on Bertie to end his affair with this "frivolous, silly little woman," but he refused to do so. Two years later Ottoline may have been thinking of Vivien when she mourned the decline of love in her life: "Isn't it sad that no one *really* falls in love nowadays?" she said to Virginia Woolf. "Its the rarest, rarest thing . . . Bertie does of course—but then his choice is so often unfortunate."[76] For there is no doubt that in 1916 Vivien's star was in the ascendant, as Ottoline's was waning, and it was to Vivien's pleas that Russell listened. He protested to

Ottoline that he had promised "Mrs. E." he would meet her that week, and he was afraid of a "violent quarrel" if he acted on Ottoline's suggestions, although he assured her they had influenced him. "But it is difficult to act on them without cruelty. The only part in the matter that I feel on my own account to be wrong is the spending of money. Quite at first, that was justifiable, but it has ceased to be. At the same time, having created the expectation, I can hardly stop suddenly . . . You were *quite right* to speak," he told Ottoline. "I am *sure* it will work out as you think right but I ought not to do anything violent or sudden."[77]

It was Russell's payment of the Eliots' everyday bills, as well as the "extras" they both considered essential, which subsidised a lifestyle well beyond their means and enabled them to mix with the Bloomsbury group, many of whose members practised a similar "open marriage" to that of Tom and Vivien. There was Philip Morrell turning a blind eye to Ottoline's lovers, although she was ignorant of his; Vanessa Bell living with the homosexual Duncan Grant while Clive was the lover of Mary Hutchinson; and the Strachey-Carrington-Partridge triangle, all of which made the Eliots' arrangement seem perfectly natural. It was a bohemian ethos in which the Eliots felt comfortable, one in which bourgeois conventions had long ago been abandoned; honesty in personal relations, based upon the ideas of G. E. Moore, was the ideal; and homosexuality or bisexuality was as acceptable as it had been to the Apostles at Cambridge under the leadership of Lytton Strachey and Maynard Keynes. The Eliots, therefore, could not give up Russell's allowance without a fight—too much depended on it. Given Russell's poverty, his generosity seems inexplicable but, cast adrift from his academic milieu and his old friends, uncomfortable with new suburban allies like Clifford Allen, chairman of the No-Conscription Fellowship, he needed Vivien, and was therefore unable to refuse her demands.

In his letters to Ottoline, he agonised over the strange hold Vivien had over him, and he over her. "She is trustful & thinks of me as wise & good—at least as regards her—& as regards her I have been," he wrote on 20 August 1916. "Partly this satisfies my love of despotism, partly it makes me feel not such a wretch as I have always felt for a long time in relation to you." That Vivien might be flattering her older lover, and even manipulating him, Russell seems not to have realised. All Vivien's faults were "gradually improving," he wrote, congratulating himself on his successful therapy, and the fact that

> I have made her . . . look up to me & care for me to a considerable extent. In spite of her faults I have an affection for her, because I feel they spring from a root of despair & that she might become different. And apart from affection, I have incurred responsibility.

Pleading with Ottoline that he could not abrogate this responsibility, he continued to play for time: "I don't want to quarrel—I think with time I can avoid giving her the feeling that I have played her false, without getting into a permanent entanglement. But it will want time."[78]

Russell's promises that he would see Vivien just once more, and then the long-awaited "readjustment" would come when he would finally break with her, must have brought a weary smile to Ottoline's lips, as she read page after page of excuses from her former lover. "I am going . . . to Bosham for a few days," he wrote on 22 August. "After that I don't expect to see Mrs. E. again at any rate till the spring; but I can't be sure. There has been no quarrel of any sort . . ." The next day he was still "unhappy" about dashing Mrs. E's hopes.

> One thing that attracted me to her was that it seemed clear one could make her happy by the very simple method of spending a certain amount of money. If I had succeeded I should have got rid of a morbid oppression. As it is, it has come back. It would have been worth a good deal of money to get rid of it . . . I can afford the money, but it seemed clear that it was wrong to spend so much on a matter of no real importance, & also that I ought not to have to think too much about making money. I said all this to her. She took it very well, but on my side it makes trouble—the pleasure I had was in giving things.
>
> (undated, ?23 August)

By 26 August a quarrel had taken place. Vivien was upset that Bertie was stopping her money and pleaded with him to reconsider. "Mrs. E. and I are drifting apart," wrote Russell. "We have practically agreed not to meet during the winter. My feelings on the matter are very complex."[79] Two days later his financial situation had improved, as Helen Dudley and her sister agreed to rent his flat in Bury Street at £3 a week, and Russell began to relent. It is remarkable, however, that Russell was prepared to sacrifice having a home of his own and to make himself dependent on the generosity of his brother Frank, in order to subsidise his mistress.

Nevertheless it was the price Russell had to pay if he wanted Vivien, as Tom now made clear to him. There had been a hint of blackmail in Tom's earlier demand that Bertie "fix" some lecturing work for him. In June Russell had rushed to Ottoline a letter from Eliot "à propos of University Extension lecturing which he wants to get." Did *she* know anyone with influence, as he did not. "He wants everything done before Saturday. If you *do* know anyone & can write, I should be *infinitely* grateful."[80] Eliot's lecturing posts were arranged for him, but it was not enough; Vivien's "allowance" must continue if Bertie wished to enjoy her favours, and he was forced to concede:

> Yesterday I came up by way of Chichester, & had a talk with Eliot there (I didn't see Mrs. E. who was ill). It was rather gloomy, but I got quite clear as to what must be done . . . It is fixed that I go to Bosham Monday to Friday; . . . I shall go on doing what I have done in the way of money during the winter, but beyond that I have said I can't foresee what will be possible.

Promising to come to Garsington after his week with the Eliots, Russell told Ottoline: "Matters with Mrs. E will be decided then. I never contemplated risking my reputation with her, & I never risked it as far as I can judge."[81]

For the moment Vivien had won the battle. Astonishingly Russell had agreed to continue to pay up. Such a change of heart must have aroused suspicion in Ottoline's mind as to the nature of his relationship with Vivien. Vivien's collapse with "neuralgia" had been the weapon she used in the battle over money, one which led Bertie to change his mind after a discussion with Tom, who probably accused him of ruining Vivien's health.

The decks cleared, Bertie was intending to make a final visit to

Bosham the following Monday, he told Ottoline on 28 August.[82] Tom had apparently returned to London, so he and Vivien would be alone together, just as they had been in Torquay in January. Perhaps both hoped for an amorous reconciliation after the dispute which had soured the relationship. But at this point the government intervened. According to a second letter Russell wrote to Ottoline on 1 September, headed "Gordon Square," two men in plain clothes appeared on behalf of the War Office at twelve o'clock and served a notice on him, ordering him not to go into any prohibited areas, which in effect meant the sea coast, from where it was suspected Russell could signal to submarines. He told Ottoline that he had to give up going to Sussex on Monday ("It makes my blood boil") but in his *Autobiography* he gives a contradictory account: "At the moment when the order was issued I had gone up to London for the day from Bosham in Sussex, where I was staying with the Eliots. I had to get them to bring up my brush and comb and tooth-brush, because the Government objected to my fetching them myself." As so often, Russell was lying to Ottoline in order to play down the relationship with Vivien.

Nevertheless, the ban ended his chances of any more holidays with "Mrs. E." Forced to stay in London, Russell threw himself once more into NCF work. Within three weeks an event occurred which was ultimately to spell the end to all Vivien's hopes. In August, at Lavender Hill police station, Battersea, when Clifford Allen was arrested, Russell had seen a striking young woman. She, too, had noticed him: "A small man, with a fine brow, aristocratic features, silver-grey hair, and a passionate expression." He was conventionally dressed, "but all the furies of hell raged in his eyes."[83] She was Lady Constance Malleson, an actress generally known by her stage name, Colette O'Niel, and married to the actor Miles Malleson. Both the Mallesons supported the NCF, where Colette was working in the office. She caught Russell's eye for the second time at Gustave's restaurant in Soho, at one of the Wednesday night meetings of Left-wingers, which included Philip Snowden, Ramsay MacDonald, George Lansbury and Gilbert Cannan. Perhaps not wholly by accident, Colette found herself placed next to Russell at dinner; afterwards he escorted her through the quiet Bloomsbury squares to her attic flat in Bernard Street, saying good-night on the doorstep and walking off, a "curiously lonely figure," in the direction of Gordon Square.[84] Intrigued, she came ten days later to hear

Russell speak at the NCF Convention in the Portman Rooms, Baker Street, on 23 September. Afterwards he took her out to supper in the restaurant opposite and she invited him up to her flat. They talked half the night. "In the middle of talk [we] became lovers," wrote Russell, in words almost identical to those relating how he fell in love with Ottoline. "I clung to Colette. In a world of hate, she preserved love."[85] Within the next few months Russell was to have eyes only for Colette.

8

Wartime Waifs

Vivien returned from Bosham to war-ravaged London on 18 September 1916, and lunched with Russell that day. On his return from Bosham Russell had gone to stay at the Eliots' flat, as his own was still let to the Dudley sisters, and Gordon Square was occupied by his brother Frank and his wife, Elizabeth, Countess of Arnim (author of *Elizabeth and Her German Garden).*[1] "It is all right *really* about the Eliots," Russell reassured Ottoline, who remained concerned about the state of his finances as well as his relationships, perhaps not realising that Bertie enjoyed being a cuckoo in other people's nests. "I shan't get more involved—there is no expectation of my going on indefinitely. After this winter it will be all right—you were *quite* right to speak." He and Vivien were simply "very good friends." As if to underline this statement, five days later he consummated his love for Colette. Vivien was, it seemed, to be pushed into the margins of his life.

In Crawford Mansions the Eliots' memories of Bosham faded to "a beautiful dream."[2] The air raids over London intensified, and the night sky was red with the flames of burning Zeppelins. Vivien felt that Tom's family in America did not understand the ordeal they were enduring. Public feeling was running high against America for remaining out of the war. "It is horrid, I hate it," wrote Vivien to Henry, enclosing one of her brother Maurice's letters to help her brother-in-law appreciate that "England is *all* army now"; Maurice was not one of Kitchener's Army, who were put in khaki directly they joined, she explained, but a member of the regular army ("Of course there is some feeling of class distinction").[3] Only twenty, Maurice was commissioned as a 2nd Lieutenant in the Manchester Regiment on 12 May 1915,[4] had already served in France and, said Eliot, was used to the sight of corpses and sitting up at nights shooting rats with a revolver.

All the "Bloomsberries" who could manage it deserted the capital in favour of the country: Ottoline dug in at Garsington, while that other unconventional *ménage à trois* of Vanessa Bell, Duncan Grant and Bunny Garnett, were moving from Wissett Lodge to Charleston Farmhouse, near Firle in Sussex, close to Virginia and Leonard Woolf at Asheham.[5] But the Eliots were trapped in London. In their cramped, noisy flat near Paddington Station, with slums and "low streets and poor shops" close by—although within a stone's throw of great squares and big houses—Vivien felt as if she were in a wilderness. To her mother-in-law she complained: "We are just two waifs who live perched up in our little flat—no-one around us knows us, or sees us, or bothers to care how we live or what we do, or whether we live or not."[6] She missed the green Hampstead suburb in which she had been brought up, where there were familiar faces, even a need to keep up appearances, and began to feel miserably isolated. Incarcerated with her husband, bereft of Russell's presence to defuse the tension, Vivien was forced to face the inescapable fact that her marriage to Tom was deeply troubled.

"Hysteria," the prose poem Eliot wrote in the summer of 1915, reveals that despite his earnest desire to make a success of the marriage, he could not suppress his negative emotions towards Vivien.[7] The poem may be interpreted autobiographically in the light of Eliot's remark to Henry in January 1916 that he had *"lived* through material for a score of poems in the last six months." Eliot's statement that there should be a separation in the artist between "the man who suffers and the mind which creates"[8] formed the cornerstone of his impersonal theory of poetry: the poet, he wrote, surrenders himself in the act of creation: "The progress of the artist is a continual self-sacrifice, a continual extinction of personality." He emphasised this "process of depersonalization" by which "art may be said to approach the condition of science,"[9] and warned off critics who were tempted to make connections between art and life. For at least a generation, readers obeyed his stern injunction to concern themselves with the poetry not the poet.

Yet Eliot's critical writing expresses a contradiction, for he also believed that "what every poet starts from is his own emotions,"[10] and for him the struggle, one which he believed he shared with his idols Dante and Shakespeare, was "to transmute his personal and private agonies into something rich and strange, something universal and impersonal." His poetry begins, like Yeats, "In the foul rag-and-bone shop of the human heart," writes A. David Moody. "His method is to observe himself and the whole world of his experience with passionate detachment and to fashion out of his observations 'an individual and *new* organisation.' "[11] In *The Sacred Wood* Eliot quotes Rémy de Gourmont's view that the artist "se transvasait goutte à goutte" ("decanted himself drop by drop"). Even in his favourite analogy of the chemistry experiment, in "Tradition and the Individual Talent," in which Eliot describes himself as scientist *qua* artist, it is the poet's feelings which form the basis of a new compound.[12] It was a largely unconscious, subterranean and unpredictable process, which Eliot compared to the gradual accumulation of a tantalus jar.[13] The incubation period could not be hurried, but the poetry ultimately created, issued from "the deeper, unnamed feelings which form the substratum of our being, to which we rarely penetrate."[14]

In the poem "Hysteria," as so often with Eliot, it was an encounter with a woman which spurred him to transmute life into art.[15] This word-painting of a nervous young couple seated tête-à-tête at a rusty green table, the elderly waiter with trembling hands serving them tea in the hotel garden, provides several clues as to why Eliot perceived Vivien as a threat. She is laughing. He is silent, his silence "an in-gathering against that threat." He watches her open mouth, her "shaking . . . breasts," and imagines himself being "drawn in by short gasps, inhaled at each momentary recovery, lost finally in the dark caverns of her throat . . ."[16] Such a fear of being swallowed up has been described in *The Divided Self* by R. D. Laing as the schizoid fear of engulfment, or loss of autonomy. For someone as ontologically insecure as Eliot, who daily wrestled with the task of preserving his sense of identity and selfhood, Vivien's nervousness and the sense that the afternoon was splintering into "fragments" would have created immense anxiety. But Eliot's fear was not only the dread of intimacy which such a person is liable to feel in almost any relationship, however "harmless,"[17] but a sexual one also: "One cannot avoid the conclusion that he is frightened of her sexuality," writes critic George Whiteside, who argues that the mouth, with its "squad drill" of teeth, implies an overwhelming sexual as well as a schizoid threat: "There may be a terror, hardly recognized by him, of an imagined *vagina dentata,* into which one's penis can be 'drawn . . . lost finally . . . bruised by the ripple of unseen muscles.' "[18] The "hysteria" of the poem's title is primarily the poet's, as he strives to "collect" the afternoon in the face of the woman's nervous laughter; but it is also hers, as her laughter becomes hysterical in the face of his icy silence. The latent hostility expressed in the final lines of the poem becomes a threat, as the poet concludes that the only solution open to him is to silence the woman: "I decided that if the shaking of her breasts could be stopped, some fragments of the afternoon might be collected, and I concentrated my attention with careful subtlety to this end." It was an ominous omen for the future.

If Vivien had tried to "stimulate" Tom physically with her seductive sexuality, and to coax or even goad him into opening up emotionally, the experiment had failed: his defence was to close up even more tightly, like the crustaceous Prufrock. A symptom of Eliot's acute distress was that he stopped writing poetry. This creative paralysis worried Vivien intensely; one of her prime reasons for marrying Tom had been her belief in his genius and, if Russell is to be believed, from the unspoken recognition of their unhappiness had come a new resolution on her part to stop "punishing" Tom verbally. United in their belief in Tom's destiny as a poet, both Vivien and Tom suffered when he felt that his creative spring dried up, as it did at least three times in his life. These were periods when he became convinced that he would never again be able to write anything worth reading. Consumed by self-doubt, he attempted unsuccessfully to keep his fears secret from Vivien: "I often feel that 'J.A.P.' is a swan-song, but I never mention the fact because Vivien is so exceedingly anxious that I shall equal it, and would be bitterly disappointed if I did not," he confided to Henry in September 1916. "The present year has been the most awful nightmare of anxiety that the mind of man could conceive, but at least it is not dull and has its compensations."[19]

Meanwhile, Vivien opened Henry's reply while Tom was out ("We always do this with *family* letters") and read the postscript which was intended to be private; it did not matter that she had seen it, she said, for Tom knew perfectly well that she shared his feelings over his poetry:

I look upon Tom's poetry as real genius—I *do* think he is meant to be a great writer—a poet. His prose is very good—but I think it will never be *so* good as his poetry. Anyhow, it is a *constant* canker with me that it is at a standstill—and every time the thought is in Tom's mind I see it. I know how he feels—he has told me more than once—he feels *dried up*.[20]

What Vivien did not realise was that in one hidden corner of Tom's mind he blamed her for his barrenness; in "Ode" he had linked his being "now retired" from the "Profession of the calamus," to the loss of the male comradeship which he associated with poetic inspiration. But Vivien's identification with Tom's despair led her to push him into any action she felt would cause the spring to flow again. With considerable foresight, Vivien diagnosed that journalism was bad for Tom. Although he loved it, she wrote to Henry, "I am sure and certain that it will be the *ruin* of his poetry—if it goes on. For him—he ought never *to have to write.*" One of her more impractical ideas was that Henry, who also nursed literary ambitions, should come and live in London and take over Tom's journalistic work, while Tom concentrated on lecturing. Tom had taken on a much larger risk a year ago, she told Henry, for he had her to keep as well— "And I can swear he has never regretted it." It was a defiant remark and, one suspects, one she did not wholly believe; what is more pertinent is Vivien's proud boast, "Of course, he has had *me* to shove him—I supply the motive power, and I *do* shove." As she later told Jack Hutchinson: "As to Tom's *mind,* I am his mind."

Vivien's "shove" may have encouraged Tom's apparently rash decision to give up his teaching post at Highgate Junior School. There, despite the attentions of a young pupil named John Betjeman, who presented "the tall, quiet usher" called "the American Master" with a manuscript entitled "The Best Poems of Betjeman," he found the work intolerably draining. His mother Charlotte, who had taught unsuccessfully in a girls' school, felt only contempt for Eliot's teaching post, believing that "the male teachers in secondary schools are as a rule inferior to the women teachers, and they have little social position or distinction." She wrote to Russell: "I hope Tom will not undertake this work another year."[21] But it was not only to appease the two women in his life that Tom gave up teaching: he found the effort to control the boys "altogether too exhausting."[22] As he later told his Harvard classmates, "I stayed at that for four terms, then chucked it because I did not like teaching."[23]

Eliot's prospects were now uncertain. Optimistically he believed that he could make a living through journalism and lecturing. Before abandoning the task of teaching small boys, he had, with Ottoline's help, applied to the Oxford University Extension Delegacy, and to the University of London Joint Committee for the Promotion of the Higher Education of Working People, for a post in adult education. The rewards were meagre; he was paid only £60 a year with £3 expenses for his Monday night lectures on modern English literature to working people at Southall, a course which was to last for three years, and see a £10 rise to a salary of £70. He also found employment in Ilkley, Yorkshire, as an Extension Lecturer on modern French literature from 3 October to 12 December 1916; it was his first introduction to the north of England, and to Yorkshire's manufacturing class, whom Vivien despised. Its members were, she told Henry as she travelled north for the first time in two years in October 1916, "So *provincial* that my American friends tell me that they are very much like Americans!! Tom has met just a few at Ilkley (in Yorkshire) when he went for his first lecture—and *he* says the same—he was struck with how much more like Americans they are than the South of England people."[24]

Lecturing may have released Eliot from the classroom, but it brought him little more free time. His syllabuses reveal the extent of the reading required to prepare for his lectures; although his Yorkshire lectures—on Romanticism and the reaction against it, sketching the life of Rousseau, the rise of Charles Maurras and royalism and the return of French intellectuals to the Catholic Church—covered ground already familiar to him, his Southall classes, which Vivien attended, required a plunge into less familiar Victorian literature.[25] But whatever lecturing lacked in remuneration, it made up for in interest, and he became a keen advocate of the working classes for their enthusiastic response to his "personal magnetism," as he described the experience to his cousin Eleanor: "My greatest pleasure is my workingmen's class in English literature on Monday evenings. I have steered them through Browning . . . Carlyle, Meredith and Arnold, and am now conducting them through Ruskin."[26] The class was in fact largely composed of women, elementary school teachers bent on self-improvement, but their "unabated eagerness to get culture in the evening" built up Eliot's confidence after his failure as a school teacher, as well as setting him on a path of self-education which stimulated him to write poetry again, albeit at first in French. His poem "Mélange Adultère de Tout" reflects his pleasure in these different roles: "En Amérique, professeur;/En Angleterre, journaliste" and "En Yorkshire, conférencier."[27]

Literary journalism paid equally poorly. The *Westminster Gazette* gave him no more than half a crown per review, but, he told Charlotte Eliot, the editor had said she could read and review six novels in an evening and he could do the same ("and Vivien can do some of them for me"). In addition he could sell the novels (published at six shillings) for two shillings each. "At that rate one would take in one pound and seven shillings for an evening's work!" He was learning, said Tom to his mother, the "ins and outs of journalism," proudly enclosing a complimentary review in the *Nation* of his poems in the *Catholic Anthology,* although he suspected it was a word in the ear of the editor Henry Massingham from his friend Ottoline which had made the difference. "This is Fleet Street!"[28]

Despite his creative crisis, Eliot knew he had to take a gamble. "I think everybody gets the kind of life he wants, and that if he doesn't know, or doesn't want strongly enough, he will never get anything satisfactorily," he had written to Henry on 5 November 1916, at the end of his last term at Highgate. Teaching, as well as being uncongenial, had prevented him pursuing his literary connections, and was "telling on the quality of my production," so it had to be abandoned: "The only recklessness, I think, consists in taking a risk when your will is not strong enough in that direction to carry you through." The financial risk was, however, rather less than Tom explained to his family, since he had succeeded in persuading Russell to continue supporting them, although he forbore to mention this fact.

Eliot's originality and relentless ambition had already brought remarkable results for an American who had arrived unknown in England in 1914. Nineteen fifteen had been "the year of his flowering," as Cyril Connolly[29] described it in 1963, when "The Love Song of J. Alfred Prufrock" had finally appeared in *Poetry* in June, to be followed by the two "Preludes" and "Rhapsody on a Windy Night" in the second or war number of *Blast* in July, and "Portrait of a Lady" in *Others* in September. Three

more short poems appeared in *Poetry* in October, and Pound's determination "to get Eliot between hard covers" had borne fruit in the *Catholic
Anthology* in November. Nevertheless Eliot was still comparatively unknown, as a letter from Ottoline demonstrates: "Huxley said there was
some *very* good poetry by Elliot [sic] in an American Chicago paper called
Poetry," she wrote in surprise to Russell in February 1916. "It is your
Elliot."[30]

As the citizen of a neutral country, Eliot was able to benefit from the
war. He was adept at networking: Pound attributed Tom's ability to befriend those who would enhance his own status and position to his aptitude for "playing possum." By showing as few signs of life as possible he
did not alarm people, and therefore could get away with revolution. Eliot
adopted this stance intentionally, staking out his strategy in "Prufrock":
"No! I am not Prince Hamlet, nor was meant to be;/Am an attendant
lord . . ." His behaviour was "deferential, glad to be of use,/Politic, cautious, and meticulous."[31]

Certainly there was little danger of Eliot alienating people with rash
outbursts of temper like Ezra Pound.[32] Instead, Eliot's watchful charm and
sharp insight into the location of the citadels of power enabled him to
profit from the increasing shortage of journalists, many of whom were
now in the forces. Unemotionally Eliot listed the Vorticists leaving to fight:
Wyndham Lewis, Wadsworth, Ford Madox Hueffer, T. E. Hulme,
Aldington, for there were no conscientious objectors among that group.
Already Hulme and Gaudier-Brzeska had been killed. The Imagist and
Vorticist movements, which had been gathering momentum in 1914, spent
its energies on the battlefields of France, or was scattered abroad; James
Joyce remained in Trieste and Zurich, although *A Portrait of the Artist as a
Young Man* continued to be serialized by *The Egoist.* This left the papers
"rather hard up for reviewers," Eliot explained with satisfaction to his
mother, and as a result he was also hired by the *New Statesman,* whose literary editor was J. C. Squire.[33]

In this critical period Tom still depended on Pound's support, even
though he was skilfully laying the foundations for a Jamesian "conquest of
London" and had already outstripped the reputation of Pound who, ignored by the reviewers and "killed by silence,"[34] continued to work inde-
fatigably and unselfishly to "puff" his protégé, Eliot. In January 1917

Pound wrote to Margaret Anderson, editor and founder of the Chicago-based periodical *The Little Review:* "I want an 'official organ' (vile phrase). I mean I want a place where I and T. S. Eliot can appear once a month (or once an 'issue') and where Joyce can appear when he likes, and where Wyndham Lewis can appear if he comes back from the war . . ."[35] By May Pound had become foreign editor for Anderson, and was placing the remaining modernist poets, "H. D.," Amy Lowell, even Yeats, as well as Aldington, Lewis and Ford Madox Ford, whose poetry appeared in its columns with Eliot's. Margaret Anderson was braver than Harriet Monroe—editor of another Chicago-based journal, *Poetry*—who had "loathed and detested Eliot" when first she read "Prufrock," as Pound reminded her in April. She had published James Joyce's *Ulysses* in March 1918, an action in keeping with her masthead slogan: "A Magazine of the Arts Making No Compromise with the Public Taste." Boldly she declared that "the ultimate reason for life is Art. I don't know what they mean when they talk about art for life's sake. You don't make art so you may live; you do just the reverse of that. . . . Art uses up all the life it can get—and remains forever."[36]

It was a philosophy with which Tom and Vivien agreed in principle, but living for art became increasingly hard to practise by January 1917. Tom's income was substantially reduced. The Yorkshire lectures had ended, and he had not yet begun another course on Victorian literature he was to give on Friday evenings at the County Secondary School, Sydenham, from 28 September. Even then, the fee was a mere one pound a lecture, with no travelling expenses.[37]

Not only did the Eliots keep a servant, Rose, but food prices were rising week by week; every day "the strain and difficulty is a *little* increased, and the screw turned a little tighter," said Vivien. She adopted her own *"rigid,* locking-up-everything principles," as she explained to her mother-in-law:

> In the flat, if we have a woman, I lock up every mortal thing, and not a grain of rice or a crust of bread is eaten without my knowledge. Naturally one does not enjoy practising such parsimonious ways, but when it is a choice between that and practically starvating [sic] as it has been with us—there is of course no question.[38]

Tom hastened to assure his mother that he did not think anyone could manage more economically than Vivien did, and that she had Rose "very well in hand." Vivien was a good cook, he told Charlotte, and wanted to give up her charwoman and do the housework herself: "Of course when I think of all the clothes she needs—she has not had any for a long time, and I have my new suit [which his mother had paid for] I see advantages in giving up the woman, but I do not like it."[39]

Behind the harmonious façade they presented to Tom's family, in reality the Eliots were facing a personal and financial crisis in early 1917. Tom found the life of a freelance journalist more taxing than he had imagined. Enforced domesticity brought on black moods ("It is terrible to be alone with another person"). So inhibited that he would never dream of shaving in front of his wife, as he later confessed to Leonard Woolf, Tom found Vivien's very femininity abhorrent. Her physical presence, her smell, her clothes, her bodily functions, all repelled him, as a savage line in "Lune de Miel" (July 1917) reveals. Speaking of a young couple on honeymoon, as he and Vivien had been eighteen months ago, he comments on "une forte odeur de chienne" ("the strong stink of bitch") rising from the open thighs of the woman lying on her back.[40] It was an expression of a primitive instinctual revulsion. Filling the empty hours became a torment. "But what is there for you and me/For me and you/What is there for us to do?" he asks, "Where the leaves meet in leafy Marylebone?"[41] (from "Death of the Duchess").

Tom missed his mother Charlotte, the ageing matriarch on whose love and guidance he depended: "I long to see you, every day," he wrote in June 1917. Separated by the war, now entering its third year, Charlotte had begun to fear she would never see her favorite son again. "Don't talk about not seeing me again; it is too painful, and besides you *shall* see me again," he reassured her, nostalgically recalling his childhood when she used to sing him nursery rhymes like the "little Tailor."[42] "He was most gloomy and depressed and very irritable and I know he felt that life was simply not worth going on with," wrote Vivien to Charlotte on 8 March 1917. Eliot's depression at this point was such that he even lost confidence in his ability to write philosophy, feeling that an article he sent on 13 March to Russell to criticise was "too scattered and incoherent" and he had better keep it in his drawer for a year or two.[43] When Russell replied reassuringly, Eliot repeated that "what I have said is too negative and perhaps looks obscurantist." He wanted to discuss authority or reverence, "But this is a task which needs impulse and hope, and without more peace of mind and contentedness, better nerves and more conviction in regard to my future, I do not feel capable of satisfying myself."[44]

Following the bouts of influenza through which Tom and Vivien had nursed each other that winter (1916–17), Vivien was left anxious and insomniac: "I worry a great deal, and my brain is restless and active," she confessed to Charlotte. "Often when I lie down to sleep I feel that a wheel is going round in my head, and although my body is dead tired my brain gets more and more excited . . . my migraines are coming back and I don't feel nearly so well."[45] Tom wrote to his father: "When she worries she bleeds internally, in a metaphorical sense, as well as other internal pains, like migraine and stomach trouble, in a literal sense."[46]

Vivien's own mother, Rose, seems to have done little to help her distressed daughter and son-in-law, a neglect which perhaps bears out Russell's comment that Rose was "odious." "Couldn't her mother help her?" Ottoline had enquired of Bertie in March the previous year when the Eliots were struggling to move flats.[47] "Are her own people horrid?" In fact Rose Haigh-Wood often invited Vivien and Tom to Sunday lunch and tea, but otherwise left her daughter and son-in-law to their own devices, perhaps feeling that, at nearly thirty, they should be able to manage on their own. In this terrifying vacuum Tom began to feel he was staring failure in the face. If the "silence from the sacred wood" of which he wrote in "Ode," and which he associated with his marriage, and Russell's intrusion in it, continued for many more months, the gigantic gamble he had taken to abandon family and country for an English wife and the hope of fame would be in vain. He began to think of himself as another Coriolanus, an identification which found expression in 1921 in *The Waste Land* as "a broken Coriolanus." In Shakespeare's *Coriolanus* the mother "breaks the hero's iron spirit," and in Eliot's "Coriolan" poem, written after his mother's death in 1929, the same utter dependence upon her is voiced: "What shall I cry?/Mother mother . . ." The poet, "I a tired head among these heads," utters his lamentation: "Mother/May we not be some time, almost now, together" repeating: "O mother/What shall I cry?"[48]

The Eliots' mutual misery, in which neurosis fed off sexual incompatibility, can in part be attributed to the withdrawal from their lives of Bertrand Russell in September 1916. Both Tom and Vivien experienced this trauma in their different ways. Eliot had lost his mentor, but for Vivien the agony of Bertie's abandonment was magnified by the knowledge that he was rhapsodizing over his new love affair with Colette, a woman who had many advantages over Vivien. First she came from a similarly aristocratic background to Russell's as the younger daughter of the fifth Earl of Annesley by his second marriage to Priscilla Cecilia Moore. Born in 1895, Constance had been brought up at Castlewellan, a grey granite castle looking out over the mountains of Morne in Northern Ireland, and despatched to boarding school at Downe House in Kent, which she nicknamed "Damned Hell." After her father's death she begged her mother to allow her to join her sister at school in Dresden and, at only fourteen, she began training for the theatre in Germany and later Paris; only reluctantly did she return for the London season, striking a bargain with her mother that she would become a débutante on condition she was allowed to train at the Royal Academy of Dramatic Arts. Constance had beginner's luck, and soon after taking the stage name Colette O'Niel found herself understudying Yvonne Arnaud for £2 a week.[49] She had a firm idea of her vocation and a professional training in contrast to Vivien's ever-changing aspirations to paint, dance or act. Again in comparison to the sickly Vivien, Colette enjoyed vigorous good health as well as unbounded confidence, which led her to being described as "imperious" as well as striking. Like Russell's other lovers, Ottoline and Vivien, Colette was married, having eloped in her teens with the dramatist and actor Miles Malleson, to whom she was married in 1915. Both had joined the Independent Labor Party and the No-Conscription Fellowship after Malleson was invalided out of the army, and Colette was working in the NCF office on the index of conscientious objectors by day and acting at the Haymarket by night when she met the "brilliantly witty" Bertie.

Russell could scarcely believe that the twenty-year-old Colette returned his love, but his fiery eloquence had made an indelible impression on the young actress. After he walked away from her attic flat at 43 Bernard Street (only round the corner from Frank Russell's at 57 Gordon Square, so the lovers never needed to use the post) she dissolved into tears:

"I was crying. The moon shone down through my window. I cried and cried, but I knew I had found myself."[50] The next day Russell wrote her the first of many passionate and lyrical love letters, in language similar to that he had used in the early days of his affair with Ottoline: "Colette, my soul & my life. I love you every day with a deeper love. I feel you the embodied hope of the world—the youth & life with new promise, like the first flowers of spring . . ." He had grown weary in the struggle, he said, but with her he felt full of vigour and strength. Colette replied that she felt unworthy of Russell, of whose reputation she was in awe: "Strength you seem to have and courage. Then I can only add joy. But perhaps, from all the inward striving, something will grow. I stand with empty hands. Colette."[51] Touched by this answer, Russell ran out into the street early the next morning and bought red roses from a man who used to "haunt" the Bloomsbury streets calling out, "Sweet roses, sweet lovely roses," and had them delivered to her door.

Only by degrees did Russell reveal to Colette the web of relationships in which he was caught. By 2 October Colette was thanking Russell "very specially" for telling her about his relations with Ottoline, whom Colette had met once at Garsington, remembering her "splendid bearing and real kindness." Of Vivien Russell at first said nothing, for she belonged in a very different compartment of his life.[52] Comradely fervour and pacifist convictions united Russell and Colette, something with which Vivien, who identified with her young brother in the army, had no sympathy. Sending her new lover a Hoppé photograph portrait of herself, Colette asked for one of him when his "heathery head hasn't been all shorn off by the damn'd barber—I'd like it looking robustious [sic] and revolutionary."[53] As the NCF split into two factions, the Absolutists or extremists, which included Clifford Allen, Russell, the Mallesons and the NCF founder Fenner Brockway, and the Alternatives or moderate wing, Colette turned to Russell to save the situation. He wrote an article in the NCF magazine which she found "marvellously good": "I want your humanity, your radiant tenderness, your golden wisdom, the lightening [sic] flash of your mind," she told him, humbled to be the object of love of the NCF's most famous activist. But she was conscious of their age difference: "I'm just twenty. You beloved, are . . . forty-five? To me it seems that your life must have been a wonderful tapestry, rich in experience, a glorious feast of adventurous thought; and now I come along like a sip of wretched after-dinner coffee."[54]

There was more in the tapestry of Russell's life than Colette suspected and, after they had spent her birthday on 24 October together in Richmond Park, where they were caught in a storm and forced to shelter under a giant oak, he decided to tell her something of Vivien. His opportunity came on the long train journey to Manchester, where he was due to speak for the NCF. Painfully he struggled with the words, writing page after page as the train puffed northwards: he had meant to tell her many things about his life, and every time the moment had conquered him. He was old and she was young, and

> because with me passion can seldom break through to freedom, out of the net of circumstances in which I am enmeshed; because my nature is hopelessly complicated, a mass of contradictory impulses; & out of this, to my intense sorrow, pain to you must grow.

It was an honest attempt at self-analysis, as he tried to explain the "terrible pain" at the centre of his being as he searched for "something transfigured and infinite, the beatific vision—God," which he was unable to find. "It is like the passionate love for a ghost."

At last he comes to the point of the letter: his relationship with Vivien, of whom Russell sounds as ashamed as Eliot seemed to be when first he introduced his wife to his former tutor:

> I began telling you about my friends the Eliots. I have a very great affection for them both—my relation with her especially is very intimate. If you met her you would be utterly unable to understand what I see in her. You would think her a common little thing, quite insignificant. But when I first knew her, which was 14 months ago, after her marriage, I found her so bruised and hurt by various people that I couldn't bear it, & I felt only a great deal of affection would cure her—The result is responsibility. I thought lately that I had come to an end, as there had been a long

disagreement. But I find her mood quite changed, and all that I had tried to do for her has at last succeeded . . .

The root of Vivien's troubles, wrote Russell, was that she had become filled with fear through having been hurt, and out of defiance had become harsh to everyone, including her husband, "Who is my friend, whom I love, & who is dependent on her for his happiness. If I fail her, she will punish him, & be morally ruined." Russell thought this had happened during their last disagreement, and although it had turned out otherwise, he still felt he was essential to the Eliots' happiness. "I am really vitally needed there, & one can't ignore that . . ."[55]

Colette responded generously to this confession, even though Bertie was saying that he was now reconciled with Vivien and would continue to see her, for reasons which he asked Colette to believe were therapeutic. "I cannot give you a *simple* happiness," he wrote. "I can give you moments of heaven with long intervals of pain between—if you think them worthwhile." It was a prophetic remark which was as true of Russell's relationship with Vivien as of that with Colette. But, in the first flush of love, Colette had no inkling of the complicated nature of her new lover's relationships with women: "Of course, Beloved, you mustn't neglect other people, neither women nor old friends, on account of our two selves. It would be entirely against my creed and against your own . . . Freedom must be the basis of everything. And that *is* so. For my part I'd rather cut off my right hand than not live by my creed."[56]

A few days later Colette told her husband Miles about Russell. Miles took the news that his young wife was passionately in love with another man well enough for, like Colette and Russell, he believed in an open marriage, the "new morality," which was intended, as Russell's daughter Kate later wrote, "to be joyful and positive, but no less demanding than the old . . . They believed it would be easy to live without jealousy, but it turned out the new morality was no easier and no more natural than the ideal of rigorous life-long monogamy it was intended to replace."[57]

For the moment the creed of free love seemed an intoxicating one which would allow Colette a tolerant husband and a devoted lover, and Bertie the thrill of a new mistress while retaining the old, as well as continuing his long-standing relationship with Ottoline. Vivien's despair in

October 1916, when she suffered from "nerve-storms" and acute migraine, is easily understood in the context of Russell's withdrawal from her as his passion for Colette reached a new pitch of intensity: "We seem to enter some world beyond passion—more passionate than any passion," he wrote at midnight on 29 October. "My Beloved I feel we are one eternally—I want to travel with you through all the lands of the spirit—heights & depths & wildernesses—to pierce with you to the mystic heart of the world—I long to be with you in wild & lonely places—to gather up in one eternal moment all the ages of man & all the abysses of space."[58]

In the face of Vivien's desolation, Russell could not avoid meeting her. "I am dining with Mrs. Eliot to-night," he told Colette on 2 November 1916. "I rather dread it. I don't *wish* to take less interest in the Eliots than I have done, but unavoidably it works out so. You fill my heart & mind so full that it is very difficult to find room for anything else." No doubt there was a tearful scene, and Vivien protested that Bertie was deserting her, for he wrote guiltily to Colette: "I had a painful time with Mrs. Eliot & am very worried. I *can't* make myself feel the Eliots' affairs at all vividly any more—it seems so cruel."[59] By now Colette's sympathy for Russell began to run thin:

> Beloved I'm terribly sorry that your evening with Mrs. Eliot turned out painful. What can I say? You write that you're very worried. But you've known her for more than a year, and I've never met her; and I've never really been in the sort of situation in which you find yourself; and I don't suppose there's anything useful I can say.

Stung by Russell's accusation that she did not understand complex situations, she added: "I also suspect you'd find any remedies of mine far too simple . . . When you first wrote me about her, you said I'd see nothing in her and would think her an ordinary little thing. You may be right, but I mostly *like* people . . ."[60]

Vivien's misery would have deepened had she known that Russell and Colette were about to leave for a three-day "honeymoon" in mid-November 1916, at the Cat and Fiddle, a rough stone pub in the Derbyshire Peak district. "The 'Cat and Fiddle' sounds *too* delicious. I want to be the dish,"[61] was Russell's response to Colette's suggestion. It was a bit like *Wuthering Heights,* said Colette, imagining herself and Bertie as Cathy and Heathcliff. The bleak moors suited their mood, remembered Bertie, even though it was bitterly cold and the water in his jug was frozen in the morning. "We spent our days in long walks and our nights in an emotion that held all the pain of the world in solution, but distilled from it an ecstasy that seemed almost more than human."[62]

For Colette, too, the days with Bertie had been wonderful "beyond mortal words . . . the evenings sitting by the fire, the wonder and joy of the nights, the untellable joy of sleeping in your arms." He was her "dear dear Love, heart's comrade as never before," she wrote from Manchester. The brief interlude on the moors was to remain the high point of their relationship, which soon began to run into difficulties. One reason was yet another new female interest in Russell's life that autumn (1916): Katherine Mansfield, a cousin of his sister-in-law Elisabeth. He had met the young and gifted writer from New Zealand at Garsington, and she had asked him for a reference for a flat, having been refused by St. John Hutchinson on the grounds that she was living in sin with John Middleton Murry, whom she was to marry on 3 May 1918. Happy to oblige, Russell was soon entertaining Katherine to dinner; by October Katherine was living with Murry, Dora Carrington and Dorothy Brett in a house they nicknamed "The Ark" in Gower Street, just round the corner from Russell at Gordon Square, and her influence over him began to grow.

Colette was very hurt when Russell announced that his work and other engagements would prevent him from seeing her for "some very considerable time." Although she did not yet know it, this was a phrase he used when considering breaking off relations with a woman. "I shan't lose foothold in the storm," she wrote bravely.[63] For Russell, Katherine's allure lay primarily in her mind: "Her talk was marvellous, much better than her writing," he recalled in his *Autobiography.*[64] "I want to get to know (her) really well," he wrote to Ottoline. "She interests me mentally very much indeed—I think she has a very good mind, & I like her boundless curiosity."[65] "My head aches with a kind of sweet excitement," responded Katherine to one of Russell's letters in December 1916,[66] suggesting the interest was mutual.

At Garsington, where they met at Christmas 1916, Russell listened to

Katherine's envious, dark, penetrating talk about her hostess, Ottoline, whom Katherine detested because she believed, without foundation, that Ottoline had made overtures to her lover, Middleton Murry. Although Russell professed to believe very little of what Katherine said, her malicious conversation encouraged him in the disengagement from Ottoline which he believed was necessary to his happiness, since she no longer returned his feelings. In his *Autobiography* Russell writes that after Christmas he saw no more of Katherine, but was able to allow his feelings for Colette full scope. In fact he continued to meet Katherine throughout 1917, just as he continued to dine with Vivien. Colette disliked Katherine intensely, and was shocked by her disloyalty towards Ottoline, who had entertained her generously. "Beloved, if you feel you want to see a good deal of her, of course you must do so; but I wouldn't be honest if I didn't say that, if anybody spoke of you in the way she speaks of Ottoline to you, I'd think they'd gone clean off their head—or, the quicker they got out of my Attic the better," wrote Colette in September 1917. "But as *I* don't have to know K.M., my feeling is beside the point."[67]

Katherine Mansfield's "dark hatreds" bore fruit: Russell ceased to think of Ottoline as a lover, but only as a friend—and even his friendship wavered over the months. He had finally confessed to her, in the same sentence in which he admitted that he liked Katherine, that "In a gay boyish mood I got intimate with Constance Malleson, but she doesn't suit serious moods."[68] In June 1917 he blamed Ottoline for the fact that he and Colette nearly broke up in the winter of 1916–17: it was Ottoline's criticism which influenced him too much, whether of people or his work:

> I wanted to tell you more about Constance Malleson—I began to know her well in the autumn, & meant to tell you, but your attack both made me afraid of you & set me to thinking I wanted to break with her. I set to work to withdraw, & almost completed the process. It was at that time that I hated everybody—& I found it set me against you too. At last I came to the conclusion that I didn't really want to withdraw . . .

Russell's need to find an outlet for his libido and Ottoline's failure to return his passion was a recurring theme with him, highlighted by her recent infatuation with a young army officer and poet, Siegfried Sassoon: "Nearly a year & a half ago now I realised once for all that I *must* detach my *instinct* from you, because otherwise life was too painful to be borne. That left me with a feeling of grudge, unless I could let my instinct go to someone else."[69] Both Vivien and Colette were outlets for Russell's frustrated "instinct," implied in his admissions of "intimacy," as he turned against Ottoline, complaining that she had found fault with him for becoming absorbed in writing, and as a result his "impulse" to write his lectures on Social Reconstruction had "stopped dead . . . It was only after I got interested in the Eliots, & by means of that interest, that I was able to get back to the lectures. I do not think you know at all how vehemently you find fault, or how it kills one's impulse when you do it . . ." It is a letter which reveals Russell's egotistical attitude to the women in his life: Vivien, like Ottoline, was there to serve *his* needs, to overcome *his* sense of failure: "Mrs. E. happened to turn up . . . and I used her for my purpose," he confessed with no hint of shame.[70] Later, Colette was to write in her novel *The Coming Back* a thinly disguised account of her relationship with Russell, whom she describes as

> a man exhausting other men by his intellect; exhausting women by his intensity; wearing out his friends, sucking them dry, passing from person to person, never giving any real happiness—or finding any.[71]

Ottoline, already reeling from the blow of finding herself cruelly satirised by D. H. Lawrence in *Women in Love,* needed Bertie's understanding rather than his criticism. "Lawrence has sent me his *awful* book," she complained on 2 January 1917. "It is so loathsome that one cannot get clean after it—& a most insulting Chapter with *minute* photographs of Garsington & a horrible disgusting portrait of me making me out as if filled with cruel develish [sic] *Lust* . . . It is of course Frieda's revenge."[72] She was quick to forgive Bertie: "Perhaps after all Lawrence's view of me in his book is partly True," she wondered sadly.[73] But as her depression deepened ("All Life came shattering down about me—and all that I had been trying to build up—came grinning in mockery at me—")[74] she began to withdraw from Bertie and his volley of grievances, and warn him that her patience had limits: "You have battered me hard—for many months indeed years now—and even the poor rag doll will turn someday."[75]

Insensitive to the needs of individuals, Russell remained deeply touched by the plight of millions.[76] His role in the NCF was becoming ever more vital as the original leaders of the movement disappeared behind prison bars, including Fenner Brockway, the original founder of the Fellowship in 1914, and he began to withdraw from both Colette, whom he now only saw once a week, and Vivien. "The ghosts from the Somme & the Dardanelles & the blood-drenched plains of Poland come & call me not to forget them," he told Colette. "I think of Allen and Fenner & all the rest of them—& I feel ashamed."[77] On 3 January 1917 Russell dined with Vivien, afterwards assuring Colette that he had told Vivien he wouldn't see her again "for an indefinite time."[78]

He did not keep his promise. Although in January 1917 Russell became acting chairman of the NCF, and was actively involved in furthering the cause of peace by lobbying President Woodrow Wilson of the United States,[79] who had been elected as the "peace candidate" in November, he continued to meet Vivien frequently. In March he told Colette:

> Practically the only people I see nowadays except on business are the Eliots—She is rather dependent on me in a variety of ways—I took on the responsibility of her when she was in a bad way, and the responsibility remains. I have an affection for her, but almost entirely because of her dependence. My affection for both of them grows less as time goes on.[80]

Colette's acceptance that Vivien was a fixture in Russell's life is clear in a letter in which she asks him to accompany her and Miles to the great celebration to mark the Russian Tsar's abdication and the Kerensky Revolution in March 1917. "On Saturday there's the Albert Hall, 7 oc. Aren't you coming? I know you were by way of dining with Mrs. Eliot, but if Sunday happened to suit her just as well, you could come?"

"I find I must dine with Mrs. Eliot on the Saturday or the Sunday, to make up for last Saturday," replied Russell, after the "electric" meeting at the Albert Hall on 31 March, at which his euphoria rose to such dizzy heights that he longed to call on the audience to follow him and pull down

Wormwood Scrubs. "If I made it Saturday, I could (if you are free) go away Sunday morning & stay away the night. If you are free Sunday evening, I will see Mrs. E. later, and keep Saturday dinner for you as planned."[81]

This careful dovetailing of Vivien and Colette in Russell's diary demonstrates the falseness of the impression he gives in his *Autobiography* that his love affairs were sequential. Vivien was the ever-present backdrop to his affair with Colette, remaining in the shadows only because so little of her correspondence with Russell appears to have been preserved. In her letters Colette makes many references to her lover's "complicated tangles."[82] Years later, writing of Vivien's importance in Russell's life, Colette commented, "I was . . . very surprised when, in his autobiography, he made it appear that none of his women overlapped with each other; which, so far as I knew, they all did."[83] Nor do the facts bear out Russell's dismissive comment that he merely used Vivien for the "purpose" of freeing himself from Ottoline, for he continued to see her long after he had broken with Ottoline as a lover; once released from the influence of her hostile judgment on Vivien and Colette, Russell followed his own inclinations.

In March 1917 the Eliots' fortunes at last took a turn for the better. Charles Haigh-Wood took pity on his daughter and son-in-law and introduced Tom to L. E. Thomas, chief general manager of the National Provincial Bank. He in turn put Tom in touch with the Colonial and Foreign Department of Lloyds Bank at 20 King William Street, in the heart of the City; Eliot was taken on as a bank clerk at a starting salary of £2.10s. a week, on the false assumption that he was a linguist, his task being to tabulate the balance sheets of foreign banks and make digests of the foreign language press. Soon he was using his French and self-taught Italian, and picking up Spanish and Danish in his lunch hour. To Vivien's surprise, her husband's depression at once began to lift: "His health is *much* improved," she wrote to her mother-in-law on Easter Sunday. "There is a marked change in him. Everyone notices it. His nerves are so much better—he does not have those black silent moods, and the irritability. Those months when he was entirely at home were very very trying . . ."[84]

The assurance of a regular salary ("However *little*"), and the prospect of a pension which would provide for Vivien in the event of his death, removed a burden from Tom's shoulders. Like his father, who had started life as an agricultural clerk, he enjoyed the routine of work and the department in which he was "petted" by the female staff, as well as finding the "science of money" to be extraordinarily interesting.[85] Vivien could hardly contain her delight that Tom had taken so extraordinarily to the City: "He is considering, to my *great* astonishment, taking up Banking as his *money-making* career!" she confided to Charlotte. "We are all very much surprised at this development, but not one of his friends has failed to see, and to remark upon, the great change in Tom's health, appearance, spirits, and literary productiveness since he went in for Banking." Amazed that Tom was so interested in finance and found it a congenial career, which left his mind fresh enough to write, she was relieved that he would no longer have to depend on journalism for a livelihood.

> This is what he has *always* been hoping for—he has never al-
> tered . . . So far the Bank *seems* to be the thing. No one could be
> more surprised than I am. I shed *tears* over the thought of Tom
> going into a Bank! I thought it the most horrible catastrophe.
> Most of Tom's friends agreed with me. We all wrung our hands
> and lamented . . . Only when he began to be more bright and
> happy and boyish than I've known him to be for nearly two years,
> did *I* feel convinced.[86]

Not only did life as a bank clerk free Eliot from the stress of freelancing, it relieved him of the daily company of his wife; soon his writer's block had vanished and he had written five "excellent poems," finding that writing in French helped his "spring" to run again. He was now "A Londres, un peu banquier," as he described his new situation with relief in "Mélange Adultère de Tout."[87] And in June Ezra Pound was able to do Tom another favour which turned his financial fortunes around, as well as giving him an important leg-up on the literary ladder. Richard Aldington, assistant editor of the fortnightly *Egoist,* joined the army and Pound persuaded the editor, Harriet Shaw Weaver, who had founded the review in 1913, to take on Eliot in Aldington's place. The salary was £36 a year, of which Pound secretly contributed half. It was Harriet Shaw Weaver's readiness to publish *Prufrock and Other Observations* under the banner of the Egoist Press in June 1917, when no other publisher was forthcoming, for which Eliot was always to remain grateful, which made possible his initial breakthrough in poetry.

Provided Russell's help continued, and the cheques for the rent and extras such as clothes (a black quilted satin chest protector for Tom to wear when he went out in evening dress) continued to arrive regularly from the Eliot family, Tom and Vivien were now much better off than previously. However, in May a financial tug-of-war took place between Vivien and Colette. Brought up to a life of privilege, Colette was extravagant by nature and, despite having an unearned income of £500 a year, £100 more than was now available to Russell, she was always short of money. "We lived mostly on tuppenny fish cakes from a shop up the back street, and scrambled eggs concocted by me out of a horrid looking orange powder called somebody's 'best dried eggs,' " wrote Colette of early 1917.[88] It was hardly true. In reality the aristocratic actress was more likely to abandon her gas ring in the attic for Gustave's or Canuto's restaurants where she and Bertie and the NCF activists liked to plot and dine. Miles did not earn more than £1 a week acting, and so both of them were dependent on Colette's unearned income. As a result Colette poured out her financial troubles to Russell, who in April offered to sell his debentures (already passed to the Eliots) to help her. "Now listen, Beloved," replied Colette on 2 May. "You are on no account to sell your debentures for me. It was an adorable thought, for which I love you, but I would *hate* you to do it."[89]

On 1 April, shortly after Eliot had joined Lloyds Bank, Bertie had entertained Vivien to dinner. She was unable to hide her affection for him, and her consequent unhappiness. "Mrs. Eliot yesterday assured me that she is perfectly happy, & finds her life quite satisfactory," he told Colette. "She lied quite bravely and convincingly." Russell was touched by Vivien's plight and, if he had been planning to remove the debentures which had been put into Tom Eliot's name and realise the capital in favour of Colette, he changed his mind, perhaps at Colette's insistence, perhaps because Vivien pleaded with him that she still needed the money. "The matter of the debentures is fixed in my will and cannot be altered," was Russell's excuse to Colette on 4 May. He continued to help both Vivien and Colette, to whom he often advanced small sums which she repaid punctiliously.

Russell's relationship with Ottoline had deteriorated further since a comment he had made on leaving Garsington after one of his visits: "What a pity your hair is going grey." "My rapier is out," recorded his hostess. In July he would write her a letter which marked the end of their affair: "It is true that I am not in love with you now." His roller-coaster relationship with Colette did not seem to promise lasting happiness, as he begged her to leave the stage to join him in political work, and she refused. After a holiday together near Ludlow, Shropshire, he had hoped she would leave Miles for him, but instead Colette hesitated. Frustrated, and growing bored with revolutionary politics, Russell's thoughts were turning inwards once again to philosophy. On Good Friday, 6 April, the United States declared war on Germany, and the possibility that Eliot would enlist drew nearer. Meanwhile, as other doors closed to him, Bertie began to feel it was time to woo Vivien again.

9

Priapus in the Shrubbery

The prospect that Tom might have to fight filled Vivien with dread. On the "eventful day," 4 April 1917 (in fact 6 April)[1] which she believed to be that of the United States' declaration of war, Vivien wrote to her sister-in-law, Charlotte Eliot Smith, the third of Tom's sisters: "Today's news is very exciting—rather unpleasant—but exciting to one personally."[2] Vivien was sure that Charlotte, like herself, would hate the thought of her husband going to fight. She hoped and prayed that the married men would not be conscripted for a long time, and that the war would be over before their turn came. Returning to her recurrent theme, that many Americans simply "don't know what war means—I mean what *this* war means. I dont suppose you ever will, as we have known it," she apologised for her depressing letter. "I have got a bad sore throat, & it does not help towards looking on the bright side of things—if there is such a side!"[3]

By 1917 the euphoria of the early days of the war had evaporated. Vivien had seen too many cases of the "bad and dreadful" effect of the war on young men to have any illusions left: "If they are nervous and highly-strung (as Tom is, and also my brother) they become quite changed. A sort of desperation, and demoralisation of their minds, brains, and character. I have seen it so, so often."[4] Tom shared her scepticism. He was distressed to learn in May that his closest friend from Merton, Karl Culpin, was critically wounded and not expected to live.[5] It was one more blow, coming after the death of Jean Verdenal, which made him see the war as simply "sordid," even if the cause were righteous. As well as Culpin, who died a few days later, the fiancé of one of Vivien's friends had just been killed. "You cannot realise what it is to live in the midst of alarms of war!" Tom told his mother, confessing that he didn't envy his Harvard contemporaries who were patrolling the seas, and hoped that he would not be called up for a couple of years and by then the war would be over. "I certainly do not feel in a position to go until 'called out,' though Vivien has been rather troubled. I should go then, but not till then."[6] Tom wondered hopefully whether his hernia might affect his medical.

Ezra Pound, meanwhile, sent his name to the American Embassy in May, only to be cautioned by John Quinn, the wealthy American lawyer and patron of the arts, against foolhardy patriotism: "I would let it go at that, let it be pigeon-holed . . . Don't be in a hurry about getting to France. This is not lack of patriotism, it is just horse sense."[7] Safe in his subterranean cubby-hole beneath the London pavements, sitting at his mahogany desk surrounded by tall filing cabinets, in the office he shared, with another clerk, Mr. McKnight, who lived in a suburb and cultivated his kitchen garden, Tom expressed his reluctance to exchange his balance sheets for the trenches to his cousin Eleanor. "I have been living in one of Dostoevsky's novels, you see, not in one of Jane Austen's," he wrote. "If I have not seen the battle field, I have seen other strange things, and I have signed a cheque for two hundred thousand pounds while bombs have dropped around me."[8]

Now that Tom was settled at Lloyds Bank, Vivien also tried to look for work. "She is possessed with the idea that she ought to earn money, and if she had average health and could find congenial work, I should not object," Tom told his mother.[9] He was against the plan, feeling that it would be impossible for Vivien to work in a noisy office after the sleepless nights and headaches from which she suffered. But in the autumn of 1917 Vivien did apply for a position in a government office where she could use her secretarial skills, and was called for an interview in November, only to be rejected outright as the wife of an American. To be refused on the grounds of her "nationality" was a great disappointment to her. Vivien longed to exchange the isolation of her flat for a busy office, and to feel she was participating in the war effort. It would have given her life some purpose and probably improved her health, as it had done for Tom. Her failure to find war work was a key factor in the increasing separation of her life from Tom's.

Thrown back on her own resources, Vivien took pride in homemaking at Crawford Mansions: "I should like you to see our flat," she wrote to Charlotte Eliot Smith. "It is the one thing I do really take a pride in—I mean seem to have succeeded in. It means an extraordinary lot to me—I am a person who simply does not exist without a home, & am always fussy with it." Nevertheless, life in wartime London was hard, not only for Vivien: "Hell is let loose on earth this Christmas—all around me the devil-world is whirling, swaying, reeling. Somewhere, through the madness, you are . . ."[10] Colette had written to Bertie at the turn of 1916 and, as Russell's despair deepened at the failure of revolutionary politics to bring about peace, he spoke of looking "only into horror and black darkness and the red pit of hell."[11] Even in the quiet of the Oxfordshire countryside, Ottoline too, sheltering the "nervy" Sassoon at Garsington, felt the horrors of war had worn away all feeling. "Ones nerves are rampant and one is all raw," she comforted Bertie, feeling that "*extreme* nerve fatigue" was affecting them all.[12]

Temporary respite of a sort came when Vivien's parents offered Tom and herself the use of their house in Compayne Gardens for a fortnight in June. They were able to exchange their "scrambling, overworked, hand-to-mouth sort of existence" for the large, airy rooms and quiet greenness of the Hampstead square, where Rose Haigh-Wood's two servants kept everything running smoothly, and Vivien was able to sink back into the easy comfort of her life before marriage. It seemed very strange to her to return to her childhood home with Tom, after two years of noisy struggle in a working-class area of central London. "I had almost forgotten that life could be so pleasant, so smooth," she wrote wistfully to her mother-in-law. "It is the old tale, I suppose, of no-one's ever appreciating anything till they have lost it."[13] Tom, Vivien's brother Maurice (who was at Chelsea Barracks), Ezra Pound and a civil servant friend named Arthur Dakyns played tennis together, and soon both Tom and Vivien were "doing better" than in their flat, Tom told his mother. But despite the fact that the Haigh-Woods paid £1 a week for their servants' food while the Eliots were staying at their house, Vivien found it cost considerably more to live in Hampstead than in Marylebone. It was becoming more and more difficult and harrassing to procure proper nourishment on Tom's salary of £2.10s. a week, which Vivien thought an absurdly low salary for the work he was doing, she confided to her mother-in-law: "I dont know what will happen if he does not get a rise soon."

Vivien worried as much about Tom's health as he did about hers. "It seems he has not average strength," she wrote, "and added to that he lives as no average man does. The incessant, never ending grind, day and evening—and always *too* much to do, so that he is always behind hand, never up to date—therefore always tormented—and if *forced* to rest or stop a minute it only torments him the more to feel that inexorable pile of work piling up against him."[14] Vivien continued to type Tom's articles on her Corona typewriter, often to dictation which saved time when he had many reviews to do; she bought his clothes with the money his mother sent—two pairs of pyjamas, one shirt, and six pairs of socks in June, all "absolute necessities"; she ran the household as economically as possible, for example, bringing back quantities of blackberries from Bosham to make into "delicious" jam, and faithfully attended Tom's Friday night lectures on Victorian literature. But as his reputation grew, so did the demand for his services as a journalist and literary critic.

In June 1917, *Prufrock and Other Observations* was published, subsidised by the kindly Pound, which was unknown to Eliot.[15] Tom himself felt it was only a *réchauffée,* and that his friends were growing tired of waiting for something better from him,[16] but *Prufrock* sold well and brought his name before a wider public. "I have read Eliot's little book of poems with immense enjoyment," wrote publisher Alfred A. Knopf to John Quinn. "I do not know whether it is great poetry or not. I do know that it is great fun and I like it."[17] It was a typical reaction. Quinn, who had already offered to repay Pound the cost of the *Egoist's* printing bill for *Prufrock* ("No-one would know about it, neither Eliot nor anyone") became an important patron of Tom's work, which he "boomed" at every opportunity.[18] Meanwhile Clive Bell recalled—probably incorrectly—that he had that Easter taken a dozen copies of *Prufrock* to Garsington which he distributed "hot from the press" like so many Good Friday buns to the assembled guests of Lady Ottoline Morrell, who included Mrs. St. John Hutchinson, Katherine Mansfield, Aldous Huxley, John Middleton Murry, Lytton Strachey and Mark Gertler. Katherine read aloud "The Love Song of J. Alfred Prufrock" from the badly printed book, bound in its "trashy yellow jacket": it caused a stir, remembered Clive.[19] There was much discussion and some perplexity; but the Bloomsbury audience knew instinctively that the verse they were hearing was as revolutionary as the music of Stravinsky or the paintings of Picasso.

Vivien's stay at Hampstead was followed by another summer holiday at Bosham, where she and Tom sailed together every day despite having a rainy week. Returning with reluctance from Sussex, she succumbed to influenza; ill and feverish, Vivien was forced to stumble downstairs from their top-floor flat to take shelter in the cellar for two nights running because of the air raids—even though the doctor had forbidden her to get out of bed. It was the last straw. She resolved to find a country cottage to live in for the remainder of the war, where the laryngitis, catarrh, neuralgia and migraines which made her life miserable in London might improve. In October 1917 Vivien told Charlotte Eliot that she had spent nearly eight weeks in the country during the summer, and "I'm so *much* better for it. I have not felt so well since we were married."[20] Tom, too, longed for the peace of nights undisturbed by air raids. "We are going to try and find rooms outside of London, not too far for me to come up every day," he wrote. "It is absolutely imperative; we cannot stand the strain of moonlight nights in London."[21]

Vivien struggled to justify the expense of renting a "cheap" cottage to Charlotte, while at the same time keeping on the flat at Crawford Mansions, despite the fact that she and Tom were, almost by the same post, asking for money from his parents for the rent and clothes. A cottage was essential, and would become more so, she said, wishing she could describe conditions at home without fear of the censor: "I am sure if you were here you would urge us to find something in the country." As to the flat, they were bound to keep it on to store Tom's books—"to say nothing of papers—typewriters, and all the other business!" He needed somewhere to stay for two nights a week after his lectures, from which he did not return till eleven at night. In any event, argued Vivien, the flat was unlettable, being on the top floor.[22] Tom added his voice to hers: "She is ever so much healthier in the country, and I should be delighted if we could find a small cottage, such as she and Miss Thayer had before quite near town at 8/- a week. And of course she is very nervous in town," he told his father.[23]

The truth was somewhat more complicated. Vivien's conviction that her health was better out of London was undoubtedly sincere, but what she left unsaid to her mother-in-law was, once again, the significant part played by Bertrand Russell in the Eliots' lives. For Vivien's desire to escape London coincided with a crisis in the relationship between Russell and Colette, which led Russell to feel the time had come to breathe new fire into the embers of his affair with Vivien. His sudden desire to resurrect the old arrangement of a "triple ménage" with Vivien and Tom came at a particularly vulnerable time for the Eliots, when they were making an attempt to work out their own *modus vivendi*. Their mutual concern and loyalty is evident in their letters, but it was to be freshly destabilised by Russell's selfish attempt to assuage his misery over Colette in the arms of Vivien.

Russell's desire for a child had also grown stronger with the passing of time. After an ecstatic interlude with Colette in August 1917 at the Feathers Inn, Ludlow, when they made up their quarrel over her refusal to give up her stage career, his love for her seemed to reach new heights. Colette was equally fervent: her love, she said, was, "minted like a gold coin which may become rubbed, worn thin, deformed with incrustations, but will last till the end of our lives. Let tempests rage, let cities crumble, my small gold coin will outlast them all."[24] But the demands of her increasingly unhappy husband Miles, who also wanted to have a child with her, cast a shadow over their relationship, just as Philip's terms to Ottoline had put constraints on *her* affair with Bertie. Russell must have wondered whether Colette, like Ottoline, would ultimately choose the status quo rather than passion out of wedlock when she wrote: "The long and short of it is that [Miles] is now *minding* that he is no longer the *central* person in my life." As to children, in response to the urging by both the men in her life to be allowed to impregnate her, Colette wrote crisply: "Well—I've sometimes thought that my parents had no business to have children. And if that should be so, it's a thing I wouldn't want to repeat in my own life."[25]

Bertie found it hard to reconcile his emotions with his belief, reiterated to Colette in August, that "one must follow love freely wherever it leads one,"[26] when she accepted an offer to star in a film called *Hindle Wakes,* based on a Lancashire play about a mill girl who is seduced by her employer's son. When Colette left for Blackpool and began filming in the cotton mills with director Maurice Elvey, Russell's jealousy was inflamed.

"B.R. thought acting was a worthless sort of occupation," remembered Colette. "He thought it brought out the worst in one's character: personal ambition, love of admiration."[27] Vituperative letters followed Colette: "The whole region of my mind where you lived, seems burnt out," wrote Bertie on 23 September. "There is nothing for us both but to try and forget each other. Goodbye."[28] On 25 September he sent her a letter containing a harsh character analysis, accusing her of being a personality whose happiness depended on "an unusual amount of sexual adventure . . . for the satisfaction of sexual vanity." Colette's energy, he said, made her enjoy an element of roughness and fierceness in love and her vanity led her to seek notoriety and luxury, and the path of commercialism, "With all its attendant evils of competition, envy, shoddy work, and possibly prostitution . . . She is almost entirely destitute of self-control . . ."[29]

Insecure in his relationship with Colette also because of the age difference, Russell was convinced that she was about to have an affair with Elvey; and Colette's husband Miles Malleson, who was looking after the philosopher in London, believed he was on the verge of a nervous breakdown. "I don't need to tell you that Maurice is not my lover in the sense that you are the lover of Ottoline and Mrs. Eliot," retorted Colette on 28 September 1917, another indication that Russell's tie with Vivien was a sexual one.[30] Colette was irate at Russell's double standards, since on 21 August and 6 September he had dined with Katherine Mansfield, unwisely confessing to Colette on the latter date, in words almost identical to those he had used to Ottoline previously: "She doesn't want a love-affair . . . I don't *at all,* but her mind is very interesting & I should like to see a fair amount of her, so long as there is not too close an intimacy . . ."[31] As well as suspecting Bertie of sleeping with Katherine, Colette was annoyed that he had spent time with Vivien in the country during the summer—Vivien had stayed at the White Horse in Shere, near Guildford, for part of the time.[32] Russell was feeling "completely set up," he had told Colette, after two days' walking with Vivien, and lunch with Bob Trevelyan in late June. It is very probable that Russell helped Vivien in her search for a cottage in the vicinity. On 3 September he told Colette that he was planning to find a country cottage in the spring, not too far from London, as he was thinking of returning to philosophy after finishing *Mysticism and Logic.*

Colette was therefore not in the mood to abstain from a "minor adventure" of the sort designed to arouse wild jealousy in her lover, and by 11 October 1917 was on the verge of breaking with Bertie. "I'm sorry I've understood so little," she wrote. "First, that you care nothing for me; second, that you don't believe in my love; third, that you hate my work. I've not known these things before. I know them very well now . . . I hope to God that we shall never meet again. I shall of course break with Maurice . . ."[33] Bertie rushed over to see her that night in her new attic in Mecklenburgh Square, where she and Miles had moved that summer, and attempted to make up. Five days later he analysed the problem of his jealousy: "Possessiveness in sex-relations is clearly an evil; it makes them something of a prison," he wrote to Colette on 16 October. "I must get rid of *all* possessiveness to you." Because jealousy robbed him of any sense of rest or peace, he could not be with her constantly—"only as much as will not leave me tired out."

Now that Russell felt "cold" towards Colette, he found his own solution to his need for peace: to be with Vivien, who did not exhaust him like Colette. Although he made his work needs his excuse, Russell was using Vivien to punish Colette for her intimacy with Elvey.

> I found accidentally that the Eliots don't want to go on being always together, & that she was looking out for a place where she could live alone in the country & he would come for week-ends. So I suggested that, as I too wanted to live in the country, we might be less dreary if we lived in the same house.
>
> She was pleased with the idea, & no doubt it will happen. I want, for every day, reliable companionship without any deep stirring of emotion; if I don't get it, I shan't do any more good work. I feel this plan may hurt you, & if it does I am sorry; but if I let myself grow dependent on you, we shall have all the recent trouble over again next time, & I can't face that, & I don't suppose you can. So I must have a life which is not fundamentally shaken by your moods . . .[34]

Although Russell presented his plan to set up house with Vivien as a new idea to Colette, it had probably been germinating in his mind as long as it had been in Vivien's. In July he had been shaken by the experience of mob violence in London, when "drunken viragos" with boards full of rusty nails attacked him in the Brotherhood Church, Southgate Road, Islington, at a meeting of sympathisers with the Kerensky Revolution. Shocked and frightened, he resigned from the NCF in the autumn, and began cutting his ties with pacifist politics. This left the question of where to live, and with whom, as Russell had to have the companionship of a woman in order to keep his demons at bay, and he never lived alone by choice. Garsington was no longer congenial; his sister-in-law Elizabeth had returned to Gordon Square from America, and this did not provide the quiet refuge he required for a return to his work on logic. Once more Russell started gravitating towards Vivien and Tom.

October found Vivien settled in the Surrey hills, in a farm four miles from the village of Abinger Common. Tanhurst Farm was in a little hollow in the hills, surrounded by a ring of pine woods, and broken only by a narrow winding road wandering down into the valley. It was "completely in a forest," wrote Tom, but after walking two miles you emerged suddenly on the top of Leith Hill, with a view over the Surrey and Sussex downs.[35] The owners, a farmer and his wife, did not normally take lodgers, but they had been gardeners to Lord Russell and the Trevelyans; Bob Trevelyan lived only a few hundred yards down Tanhurst Lane, at Shiffolds, and a word from him or Russell persuaded the farmer to take in the Eliots as lodgers. Tom and Vivien spent the weekend of 20 October together there: "It is the sort of country where old farmers touch their hats and call you 'gentry,' " noticed Eliot approvingly, as he prepared his lecture on William Morris.

On 22 October Vivien wrote to her mother-in-law, Charlotte, from Tanhurst Farm, explaining that she and Tom had decided to search ("probably in vain") for a "tiny cottage" within easy reach of town:

> The only way to do that was to take some neighbourhood as a centre and to stay there for a time, hunting all around. I spent much time and money in correspondence, trying to get rooms near enough for Tom to go up and down each day while I hunted but of sixteen addresses I had not one could take us, except this one—which we discovered, *when* we arrived, to be six miles from

the nearest station!!! It was a great disappointment, for of course
it means that Tom can only be here at weekends.

It was a disingenuous letter, for Vivien knew the Surrey countryside well
from her childhood, including the triangle between Coldharbour, Abinger
Common and Holmbury St. Mary. Both she and Bertie were aware how
far Tanhurst Lane was from Gomshall and Dorking stations, and that
commuting would be impossible for Tom. Vivien may have longed to introduce Tom to the area in which she had walked and sketched before her
marriage, one which was, "In my opinion, and in Tom's too, now—the
most beautiful country in England. It is all hills and miles and miles of pine
forests—with stretches of heath—heather and bracken and bushes—in
between. It is very wild although so near to London, and very *very*
healthy,"[36] but she had other motives for finding a sequestered spot in
Surrey.

Vivien stayed on at the farm, ostensibly to house-hunt while Tom was
in London. She had engaged a new servant to look after him during the
week, a hard-working woman and an excellent cook ("a most finished servant altogether"), and professed to feel perfectly confident that Tom was as
well looked after and fed as if she had been at home. The farm was like the
setting for a fairy tale, with its pine trees surrounding the large old house
which could only be reached by a cart track. Pigs rooted among the trees,
and the farmer's wife fed Vivien on fresh milk and homemade butter.
Vivien waited there, like Rapunzel in the tower, until Bertie, who was feeling deeply misanthropic and claimed he longed to mix with "very simple
country folk who live with the seasons," came to visit her on the Tuesday
or Wednesday after Tom's departure.

Bertie's arrival filled Vivien with joy, and her calmness seemed to
soothe him. Colette was still touring in the north and had written to him
that she wished them still to be together, *"but not as lovers."* Convinced his
relationship with Colette was over, Russell made overtures to Vivien, who
was, he claimed, very "happy" at the resumption of relations. Nevertheless
the unexpected result for Bertie was a sudden shame at the revenge he had
wrought on Colette, with whom he was still in love. "I intended to be (except perhaps on very rare occasions) on merely friendly terms with Mrs.
Eliot," wrote Bertie in an emotional confession to Colette on 25 October:

But she was very glad that I had come back, & very kind, & wanting much more than friendship. I thought I could manage it—I led her to expect more if we got a cottage—at last I spent a night with her. *It was utter hell.* There was a quality of loathsomeness about it which I can't describe. I concealed from her all I was feeling—had a very happy letter from her afterwards. I tried to conceal it from myself—but it has come out since in horrible nightmares which wake me up in the middle of the night & leave me stripped bare of self-deception. So far I have said not a word to her—when I do, she will be very unhappy. I should like the cottage if we were merely friends, but not on any closer footing—indeed I cannot bring myself now to face anything closer.

It was not the experience of love-making with Vivien in itself which filled Russell with self-loathing, only his betrayal of Colette: "I want you to understand that the one & only thing that made the night loathsome was that it was not with you. There was absolutely nothing else to make me hate it."[37] For once Russell's guilt seemed genuine: "I wish there were monasteries for atheists," he wrote.[38] "Such people as I am ought not to be left to live. I have spread pain everywhere—because of a devouring hunger which is ruthless and insatiable."

But if, as he said, Russell felt guilty over his unfaithfulness towards Colette, he displayed remarkably little guilt at leading Vivien on and using her as the tool for his revenge on the actress. Instead, he speculated on the impact his decision to abandon "Mrs. E." for the second time will have on her:

> The plan of the cottage with the Eliots was an attempt to make myself a life more or less independent of you, but it has failed. If the plan goes through, I shall be more dependent upon you than ever. Apart from you, life has no colour & no joy. A sort of odour of corruption pervades everything, till I am maddened by nausea. I have to break Mrs. Eliot's heart & I don't know how to face it. It mustn't be done all of a sudden.[39]

His letter crossed with one of Colette's written on the train heading south from Manchester: "To-morrow I will be in your arms. Our big moon will look down through the window, and I think he will be glad to see me in your arms—I love you, love you, love you."[40] The intensity of Bertie and Colette's relationship, with its peaks of passion and troughs of misery, explains Russell's reference to "an odour of corruption" pervading everything, a euphemism for his revulsion at his own moral degradation: he had played one woman off against the other. Moreover, his letters had intended to deceive: "Pride has led me a strange dance since you went to Blackpool," he confessed, "but what I am writing now is the real truth," an avowal which Colette may have found hard to believe.

Vivien stayed three weeks at Tanhurst Farm, and Bertie may well have spent more time with her than the single night to which he confessed to Colette; certainly he had promised Vivien more: "I led her to expect more if we got the cottage," implies that Vivien was anticipating a full-scale resumption of the affair. But now that Bertie had decided it was Colette's love he wanted after all, despite her "insolent triumph" at capturing Elvey, he barely gave a thought to the necessary consequence: breaking Vivien's heart.

In the rapturous reunion which followed, Vivien was forgotten. She was still in the country ("so I shan't have to see her to-night") and Russell could meet Colette instead: "I am coming back to you to-night with all my heart and with all my soul," he wrote. "I want your hand in my hair—my arms about you—the love in your eyes . . . I have been numb & now I am not. O Love, my love, my love—B."[41] Since his flat was unavailable, still being let to Helen Dudley, and there was no privacy at his brother Frank's, the lovers decided to find a place of their own. "To-morrow morning at eleven sharp I'll be waiting on the doorstep for you," wrote Colette, "and we'll walk out together to find a home."[42] They took a studio in Fitzroy Street which she began to redecorate and furnish for herself and her lover.

Meanwhile Russell had an appointment with Vivien. His task was to shatter her delight in their revived romance. It was not an encounter to which he looked forward, but Vivien behaved with a dignity and understanding for which he was grateful: "I had a *very* satisfactory time with Mrs. Eliot last night—got out of the troublesome part of the entanglement by her initiative," he told Colette on 7 November, apparently thankful to be released from any sexual obligation to Vivien. "She behaved very generously—it is a great relief."[43] Colette may have wondered, like Ottoline in the past, why so many meetings with Vivien were necessary to release Bertie of his "entanglement," but then he had told her that breaking Vivien's heart could only be done slowly. On the 13th he was writing that he dreaded seeing Vivien that evening: "Nevertheless, the relief of having done something irrevocable persists, though I feel this is shameful."[44] Yet again Vivien acted with a generosity and diplomacy which kept Bertie within her orbit: "Mrs. E behaved like a saint from heaven," he wrote on 14 November after his second tête-à-tête. "She put away her own pain & set to work to make me less unhappy—she succeeded."[45] There were no recriminations; Vivien kept Bertie on a long leash while she continued to hunt for a permanent place in the country. Although she seemed content to leave her lover to Colette, her rival may have wondered whether, for all his protestations of love, Bertie was not still keeping his options open.[46]

Yet again Colette began to withdraw from Bertie. Puzzled by her sudden and mysterious coldness, he confessed that he was now dreading spending a night with her (rather than Vivien). He suspected her of still being attracted to Elvey: "I keep wondering—I imagine Maurice cares less for you than you for him?"[47] Russell's suspicions were well founded. In November Colette discovered she was pregnant. The father was Maurice Elvey, who had shared a house with her, his leading lady, in Blackpool. Colette was resolved to have an abortion but there remained the difficult task of telling Bertie.

On 29 November Bertie and Colette spent their first night together in the studio in Fitzroy Street. Colette had bought a new bedspread and "the very softest Johnny pillow for your heathery head. Everything is longing for you to see it. And so is your Colette."[48] But the evening proved a fiasco: the lovers quarreled violently over Maurice, and no doubt over Colette's condition. Distraught, Russell asked her to meet him there four days later, on 4 December: "I may be all raw nerves . . . I desperately want just *time* with you. I would rather you did not try to talk about Maurice . . ."[49] Deeply hurt by Colette, Bertie turned again to Vivien. Once again he put the suggestion to her: could she find a cottage for the three of them to share?

In the tug-of-war for Russell's heart, Vivien knew that Colette's pregnancy by Elvey had given her the advantage. For a moment caution made her hesitate, but Russell's attraction for her was too strong. In an excited letter to her new friend, Mary Hutchinson, she wrote:

> Bertie says he wants to go shares in a country cottage. That will probably mean being out of the frying pan but *in* the fire! However, as I have NO money, and insufficient energy, the plan has its merits. We are going forth to hunt in a few days.

Vivien could not disguise her triumph at her victory over Colette, quoting to Mary a comment by Mark Gertler which Aldous Huxley had just repeated to her: "viz, that the Mallesons might be said to keep 'open bed.' It's true, from all I hear!"[50]

In the first week in December Vivien was able to give Russell the good news: she had at last found a pretty terraced Victorian house to rent in Marlow, not far from the river.[51] Russell was delighted; he planned to live harmoniously with Vivien during the week in Buckinghamshire, a county which she knew well, enjoying rural peace while he worked on his new book, *Roads to Freedom*.[52] The couple planned to leave Eliot alone to occupy Crawford Mansions from Monday to Friday. Eliot, hard-pressed by his assistant editorship of *The Egoist*, twice weekly lecturing, nightly book reviews, on top of daily labour at the bank, was relieved to fall in with a plan which in effect restored the *ménage à trois* they had enjoyed in Russell Buildings. Vivien and Bertie wasted no time in taking out a joint five-year lease on the Marlow house.

In a letter of 22 November 1917 Vivien had told her mother-in-law of Russell's offer to share a country cottage, "as he needs some quiet place of refuge himself." They did not intend it *instead* of living in town, she wrote cautiously: Tom found it essential to have his headquarters in London, but they all three longed for a bolthole, "somewhere we *could* go to at any time when things are bad in town. For weekends too."

Having decided to move in with the Eliots, Russell faced several tricky obstacles. First there was the task of moving his furniture out of the studio to Marlow, without letting Vivien know that he had ever shared a love-nest with Colette. Secondly there was the problem of stripping the studio of the furniture he had bought for Colette without causing a scene.

"Nothing but financial necessity would have made me suggest moving the studio furniture to Marlow—I don't want to tell Mrs. E of the Studio if I can help it—still less to take her there—but the saving of money is important—," a heartless Bertie wrote to Colette on 13 December. "I think perhaps I can manage it without telling her."[53] "Beloved, you must do just whatever you think best about the Studio furniture and Mrs. Eliot," replied a weary Colette. She had troubles of her own. The termination of her pregnancy had just taken place and had been "very painful"; Bertie came to visit her in the nursing home. "I remember being surprised that he didn't seem upset by my . . . abortion," recalled Colette. According to Russell's biographer Ray Monk, the philosopher paid for the operation, but Colette denied this, writing in 1975: "I had a number of abortions in my youth; but I'm almost certain that B.R. did *not* pay for any of them."[54] In keeping with her code of freedom, she believed that abortions were a woman's choice, and "need not be secret"; she chose never to have children and continued to make her career her priority.

"I got out of telling Mrs. E more than that there was furniture available," wrote a jubilant Russell, congratulating himself on having covered his tracks. "I found I would have died sooner than take her to the Studio. I can't think how I fancied I could do such a thing. I promised to see to getting it sent."[55] By 1 January 1918 he had moved to Marlow with Tom and Vivien, but was reluctant to "drift apart" from Colette, who "froze up" over dinner when he let slip that he was spending New Year's Eve with the Eliots at Marlow. "You had given *all* your *real* free time to Maurice (Sundays), & had only allowed me to see you at times when you were too tired for it to count . . . I can't bear the suspicion that when you are with me you are wishing you were with him . . ." Bertie reproached her, justifying his cohabitation with Vivien on the grounds that Colette was too "upsetting" for a long-term relationship.

> I come now to another matter: Mrs. Eliot. I am not in love with her, & I do not care whether I have a physical relation with her or not. But I am happy in talking with her & going about with her. She has a very unselfish affection for me, & but for her I don't know how I should have lived through the unhappiness of these last few months. I am intensely grateful to her, & I expect

that she will be an essential part of my life for some time to come . . .[56]

Colette replied with a spirited defence of her own actions, coupled with an attack upon Vivien—and indirectly upon Bertie:

> You say she (Vivien) has a very unselfish affection for you. I'm quite prepared to take your word for it. I don't know her and I can't therefore judge in any way. But what I do know is that you've been, times without number, involved in the most complicated tangles with her (dreading meeting her and so on), which would seem, perhaps, quite as upsetting to your work as the things you hold against me. I also know that you quite frequently find your relations with her oppressive . . .

Colette argued that personal rage of the sort Russell was feeling could not be squared with her creed of freedom for others. *"Freedom for oneself only is no creed* . . . I don't feel personal rage against Ottoline or Mrs. Eliot." Mrs. Eliot might be an essential part of Russell's life for some time to come, but Colette had no such expectations of Maurice.[57]

But Bertie's sense of humiliation that Colette had become pregnant by Maurice in preference to himself runs through his letters. On Sunday, 6 January, he set out his vision of the future: "My work-a-day life will be at Marlow, with Mrs. E. I shall come up to London one or two nights a week, according to how busy I am. If you are prepared to give me those nights & a day, we shall keep in touch . . ."[58] There was a gulf between himself and Colette which Russell found impossible to bridge, and he clung to Vivien as a haven in the storm. "When I took up with the Marlow plan, one of my chief reasons was so as to make myself an existence in which I should not demand of you more than you could give," he wrote. "We shall be much happier with each other if I want rather *less* of your time than you could give me if I am always wanting more."[59]

Bertie's resentment towards Colette, and his continued co-existence with Vivien, only broken by visits to Garsington, where he had been working on his lectures on logical atomism, led Colette to bid him another bitter farewell. Predictably her letter provoked an emotional declaration of love, written in the large scrawling hand which Bertie used when exceptionally distraught: "Colette, we *must must* not break with each other," he pleaded. "I must *must* have you or life is hell."[60] She relented, and they continued to meet on Sundays for walks in the country, of which her favourite was that between Dorking and Merrow Down. But his "work-a-day" life continued to be with Vivien at Marlow, where a comfortable routine had evolved. Russell had finished his book, and Eliot, too, was working well in the peaceful atmosphere; he wrote a perceptive review of Russell's *Mysticism and Logic,* which was published in January 1918. Russell was anticipating a productive summer working on philosophy in the company of his prize pupil when a new bombshell fell. Ironically, at the point when he was severing all connection with the NCF, and had decided to abandon political propaganda, he wrote a final editorial, "The German Peace Offer," in *The Tribunal,* in which he remarked that the American army might shoot down strikers in Britain; on 17 January this article landed on the desk of the Home Secretary.[61]

This final, foolish—as Russell admitted to Ottoline—act of defiance would abruptly curtail Russell's Marlow idyll with the Eliots; but the damaging impact on the Eliots' marriage of his affair with Vivien was not so easily overcome.[62] From Tom's point of view, she had cuckolded Tom with "Mr. Apollinax," as Eliot named Russell after his visit to the United States, a man old enough to be her father: "I thought of Fragilion, that shy figure among the birch-trees," wrote the poet. "And of Priapus in the shrubbery/Gaping at the lady in the swing." Russell as Priapus among the Surrey birch-trees, or in the shrubbery, gaping at Vivien, mocked Eliot with his rude heterosexuality, his virility as insistent a reproach to the limp poet as his neighing laugh. Outraged, Eliot visualised Russell dead and dismembered, "the head of Mr. Apollinax rolling under a chair . . ."[63] There is, the poet implies, something mad about "Mr. Apollinax," who, like the devil, has "pointed ears . . . he must be unbalanced," and does evil, a charge whose accuracy Bertie himself sometimes acknowledged in those rare moments of insight when he believed that, like Satan, he should not be allowed to live because he too "spread pain everywhere."[64]

But Eliot's reaction was a complex one. Although his Puritan code led him to condemn the very behaviour in which he had colluded, and to feel disgust at Vivien's adultery, he had cooperated for the second time in a convenient *ménage à trois* which continued to bring him not only financial benefit, including the debentures which he was to retain in his name for many more years, but also introductions to key figures in Bloomsbury such as Ottoline and Clive Bell, as well as to editors and journalists essential for his conquest of literary London. Opportunistically, while he needed Russell's support, Tom had offered Vivien as bait. Eliot, as much as Russell, had used Vivien for his own ends. Now both men would together grow tired of Vivien, as together they had once wanted her. For Vivien it was to be a painful and double rejection.

There is a sense too, in which the most significant relationship in this bizarre triangle was not between Russell and Vivien, or between Vivien and Tom, but between Tom and Bertie. Sometimes it operated as a substitute father/son relationship, on another level there was an element of homosexuality by proxy in the way in which Eliot offered Vivien to Russell.[65] It is possible that Eliot made no objection to Russell's physical relationship with Vivien for fear of abandonment by Russell. Certainly Eliot's passivity in the face of Russell's sexual aggression is remarkable.[66]

That Eliot and Russell discussed Vivien in a derogatory fashion is evident in a rare prose sketch Eliot wrote for the *Little Review,* "Eeldrop and Appleplex" (September 1917). It is an autobiographical piece: Eliot refers to himself as "Eeldrop" in a letter to Ezra Pound dated 23 September 1917,[67] in which he said he had "Appleplex on the brain."[68] "I am, I confess to you in private, a bank clerk," says Eeldrop to his friend Appleplex, another version of "Apollinax," or Russell. The two men are close friends and live together, although their philosophical positions are dissimilar: Eeldrop is "a sceptic with a taste for mysticism," an accurate representation of Eliot's religious attitude in 1917; Appleplex, by contrast, is "a materialist with a leaning toward scepticism." "Eeldrop was learned in theology, and . . . Appleplex studied the physical and biological sciences," writes Eliot.

Eeldrop and Appleplex discuss marriage together, and Eeldrop the clerk relates the story of his friend, Bistwick, who has married a housemaid, "and now is aware of the fact"; his relatives are moved by "their collective feeling of family disgrace . . . Bistwick is classified among the unhappily married." But what does Bistwick feel when he wakes up in the morning? He feels "the ruin of a life." At this point in his sketch Eliot juxtaposes a newspaper report of a man who has murdered his mistress. It is another early indication of an interest in the theme of murder, particularly of women and wives, which was to dominate much of his future drama. The murderer, remarks Eliot, has crossed a frontier: "The act is eternal, and that for the brief space he has to live he is already dead." He acknowledges the truth of the medieval belief that punishment lasts for eternity— but he understands the murderer's motives.

In Part II of "Eeldrop and Appleplex" the two men are again in their South London suburb, discussing a woman called Edith, alias Scheherazade. For both Tom and Vivien the name "Scheherazade" would have conjured up images of Nijinsky dancing the Golden Slave in the Ballets Russes production of Rimsky-Korsakov's ballet in London in 1912.[69] *Scheherazade* was inspired by the sexuality and exoticism of *fin de siècle* decadence, and by assigning the name "Scheherazade" as well as "Edith" to a character which had elements of Vivien, Eliot was telling his readers that his wife was sexuality incarnate, a woman whose powers of seduction as well as her wit enabled her to escape death at the sultan's hands.

"Edith," murmured Eeldrop, . . . "I wonder what became of her. 'Not pleasure, but fullness of life . . . to burn ever with a hard gemlike flame,' those were her words. What curiosity and passion for experience! Perhaps that flame has burnt itself out by now." His words bear a striking resemblance to those of Vivien to Scofield, whom she had taunted for leaving her, the "yellow diamond" who burns with a "white flame." Eeldrop speaks of "Edith" with withering scorn: "the passion for experience" is "a creed only of the histrionic." Appleplex defends her, saying he finds she has "a quantity of shrewd observation," and an "excellent fund of criticism," although he cannot connect them to any peculiar vision. "Her sarcasm at the expense of her friends is delightful, but I doubt whether it is more than an attempt to mould herself from outside, by the impact of hostilities, to emphasise her isolation." Eeldrop replies that he tests people by the way in which he imagines them waking up in the morning; he imagines "Edith" waking "to a room strewn with clothes, papers, cosmetics, letters and a few books, the smell of Violettes de Parme and stale tobacco. The sunlight beating in through broken blinds, and broken blinds keeping out the sun until Edith can compel herself to attend to another day."

It is a contemptuous portrait which anticipates that of Fresca in the original unedited version of *The Waste Land,* and may have been partly based on Katherine Mansfield,[70] whose short story "Prelude" (1916) was the second publication of the Woolfs' Hogarth Press, and of whose sudden success Eliot was jealous.[71] Scornfully Eeldrop remarks that he thinks of "Edith" as an artist without the slightest artistic power, and when Appleplex protests, Eeldrop interrupts him to declare that there is no such thing as artistic temperament. What holds the artist together is the work which he does; by this criterion Edith fails to be an artist.

Eliot's misogyny, which found expression in his struggle while editing the *Egoist* to "keep the writing as much as possible in Male hands, as I distrust the Feminine in literature,"[72] would have fuelled his criticism of "Edith," but the virulence of this portrait suggests that his emotions were engaged. Vivien's pretensions to be an artist—a dancer, artist, or actress, in all of which spheres she had talent—had impressed Tom when he first met her, but after two years of marriage he considered her to be the possessor of nothing more than a histrionic temperament. Certainly, Vivien's ambitions were always more grandiose than her achievement, and by 1917 her adultery with Russell was the subject of gossip in literary London, and probably at Garsington too. For so private a man as Eliot this was deeply painful; he must have suspected that people were laughing at him. In addition, Vivien's erratic moods and non-specific, but expensive, ailments, took their emotional and financial toll. How often Eliot must have wished his conscience would allow him to leave the wife for whom he had lost respect. As Eliot witnessed the unprincipled behaviour of Russell, he must have envied the older man's insouciance, while condemning his amorality. For every day the knowledge must have tormented Eliot, like Eeldrop, that he had made a marriage of which his family was ashamed; every day he must have berated himself for his impetuous and unwise choice. If only he had chosen a different path, to be able to say when he married, like another character in the sketch: "Now I am consummating the union of two of the best families in Philadelphia." Perhaps Eliot's thoughts turned nostalgically to Emily Hale, the well-connected, well-behaved young woman who had participated in amateur dramatics at Harvard with him. Instead he was locked into marriage with an Englishwoman whom most observers considered vulgar. Was Eliot's fate, too, to be "the ruin of a life"?

10

Bloomsbury Beginnings

For many months in 1918, and indeed for the rest of their marriage, Vivien and Tom harvested the bitter fruits of Vivien's affair with Russell and Tom's complicity in it. For his part, Russell was
forced to withdraw from the Marlow triple ménage so harmoniously re-
constituted with the Eliots, when on 1 February the police demanded to
know if he was the author of the offending article in *The Tribunal* which
suggested that an occupying "American garrison" might intimidate British
strikers. Forced to acknowledge that he was, Russell found himself summoned to appear in court, charged with making statements prejudicial to
His Majesty's relations with the United States of America; on 9 February
he was found guilty under the Defence of the Realm Act and sentenced to
six months' imprisonment in Brixton Prison.[1] Russell at once appealed; urgent negotiations began for his sentence to be commuted from the second
to the first division. He was obliged to spend less time at Marlow and,
while waiting for his appeal to be heard on 12 April, again became reconciled with Colette, spending a nostalgic week with her at the Cat and
Fiddle in the Peak District, before entering prison the following month.

It was a double blow to Vivien. Not only was it blindingly clear that
she would always be second string to Colette, but Bertie's imprisonment
ended Vivien's dream of riverside domesticity with him in the terraced
house with the pretty black-and-white canopy over the step, at 31 West
Street (the same Marlow street in which Shelley had lived), only ten minutes' walk from the banks of the Thames and Marlow Lock. There would
be no summer days spent gardening—a favourite hobby—while Bertie
wrote. Instead she was left alone with a resentful husband who expressed
his stark feelings of disgust for his wife's body in the repressive "Ode,"
written in May 1918, the month in which Bertie entered Brixton. The

poem's title, "Ode on Independence Day, July 4th 1918," was a sarcastic allusion to his bondage to Vivien, while the accompanying epigraph from Shakespeare's Coriolanus:

> To you particularly and to all the Volscians
> Great hurt and mischief

has been rightly described as a curse as much as an avowal of guilt.[2]

In the spring of 1918, however, Vivien proved more resilient than might have been expected in the face of Bertie's disappearance from her life—a disappearance which allowed a new chapter in her life to begin. Vivien had recently acquired a new and stimulating friend who was already replacing Lucy Thayer in her affections: Mary Hutchinson. Mary was the stylish, self-assured, unconventional but well-connected wife of Jack (St. John) Hutchinson, a wealthy and eminent liberal barrister. "She was," remembered Frances Partridge, "clever and plain. She always managed to say, 'I'm a jolie laide.' It was all too true—apart from the jolie part. She was very neatly dressed—great care was taken. She was sharp and witty, but not creative."[3]

The Hutchinsons lived on the banks of the Thames at River House, Upper Mall, Hammersmith; there Mary gave parties which were the talk of London society. She was linked to, although at first only tolerated on the margins of, the Bloomsbury Group, by virtue of her liaison with art critic Clive Bell, who had attended Trinity College, Cambridge, with Thoby Stephen—brother of Vanessa and Virginia Stephen—Lytton Strachey and Leonard Woolf, in 1899. Clive, with his pink complexion and sporting friends, was never elected a member of the Apostles, who formed the nucleus of the group of friends known as "Bloomsbury." "They didn't care about what people thought," remembered Frances Partridge. "They only thought about each other. They were not deliberately shocking." Frances compared Bloomsbury to a "fringed jellyfish," the fringes representing those who belonged to "outer Bloomsbury." "Old" Bloomsbury was an élitist group; in 1921 Frances was struck by the Strachey accent, a particular, languid, overemphasised way of speaking peculiar to Lytton Strachey's family, which was adopted by other members of the group. The members could be intimidating; Frances recalled as a young woman receiving an envelope covered with "beautiful handwriting," and realising that it was a letter from Virginia Woolf: "I was terrified."[4] Bloomsbury could sting those who came too close; it could even kill.

Clive's apparent lack of a first-class intellect disbarred him from the Apostles, but he was a founder of the Midnight Society, a reading group so called because its members met on Saturday nights at twelve o'clock. His acceptance by the small membership which included Lytton Strachey, Leonard Woolf, and Saxon Sydney-Turner is perhaps evident in an anecdote concerning one evening meeting, at which, after whisky and beefsteak pie, Lytton recorded of Bell: "He was *divine*—in a soft shirt, & hair and complexion that lifted me and my penis to the heights of heaven. Oh! Oh! Oh!"[5] But, according to Frances Partridge, many members of Bloomsbury found Bell and Mary, nicknamed the "parakeets" by Virginia, an irritating couple: "We'd arrive at the Ivy, where we often lunched," recalled Frances, "and I'd say, 'Oh bother! There they are again.' "

Mary Strachey Barnes was born in India on 28 March 1889, daughter of Sir Hugh Barnes and Winifred, daughter of Sir John Strachey, and was thus a half-cousin of Lytton Strachey; she was largely brought up in Florence by her maternal grandparents. By 1908 she had settled in London with her brother James, and had developed an appetite for culture and ideas and joined the Fabian Society. In 1910 she helped St. John Hutchinson fight the General Election as the candidate for Rye, Sussex. On the eve of the poll he proposed, and although the electors of Rye rejected him, Mary did not.[6] Her brother Jim thought they made a strange pair: "The one, smallish, palish, Parisian, pliable like a reed that never breaks, possessed of a roguish and naif humour . . . he, immense and Pasha-like . . . at once both judge and advocate, all rolled into one, sarcastic, mordant, witty . . ."[7]

The Hutchinsons moved in artistic circles. Henry Tonks showed a pastel of Mary in a red jacket at the 1913 summer exhibition of the New English Art Club and, after Tonks rented a farmhouse named Eleanor House that year at West Wittering on Chichester harbour, Mary and Jack took it the next spring. Clive Bell's affair with Mary began in 1914, following his prolonged flirtation with Virginia Stephen and an affair with Molly MacCarthy. Bell had married Virginia's sister Vanessa in 1906, but by 1911 Vanessa had begun an affair with Roger Fry in Turkey after he nursed her through a serious miscarriage. Two years later Vanessa fell deeply in love with homosexual artist Duncan Grant, a love which was to be lifelong, although she had to share her lover with David "Bunny" Garnett. It was in 1914 also that Clive made his reputation with the publication of *Art,* his first book, and he and Mary soon became inseparable. In July 1918 Clive took his lover to Richmond to meet Virginia, who spoke "perfect literary sentences." It was strangely like being in a novel, thought Mary, unaware that before many years had passed Virginia would have used her as the basis for the character of the socialite, Jinny, in *The Waves.*[8] Vanessa meanwhile took her revenge on her errant husband by painting an unflattering portrait of his new mistress, in which Mary's full mouth is exaggerated into a sulky pout.[9] Nevertheless, by May 1915 Vanessa was lodging in a cottage near Eleanor House with Duncan and his boyfriend Bunny, while Clive squeezed into a caravan in the garden in order to be near Mary. Bohemian tolerance had won the day. When Jack and Mary moved into River House in 1916, it was Vanessa and Duncan whom Mary commissioned to decorate it. Their work was featured in *Vogue,* for which Mary wrote on fashion and interior design under the byline "Polly Flinders."

Bloomsbury's disdain for middle-class morality had its antecedents in the Apostles society. By 1904 homosexuality was in fashion among the Apostles, personified by Lytton Strachey and Maynard Keynes, who had superseded G. E. Moore as leaders of the society. Of this change in ethos former member Bertrand Russell wrote:

> The tone of the generation some ten years younger than mine was set mainly by Lytton Strachey and Keynes . . . We were still Victorian, they were Edwardian . . . There was a long-drawn out battle between George Trevelyan and Lytton Strachey in which Lytton Strachey was on the whole victorious. Since his time, homosexual relations among the members were for a time common, but in my day they were unknown.[10]

Maynard Keynes was elected an Apostle in February 1903, and became Lytton's able lieutenant. The frankness of their correspondence, with its "frequent references to buggery and rape, its oscillation between higher and lower sodomy, was part of the new Apostolic code," wrote Strachey's biographer Michael Holroyd.[11] This frankness was carried into the Stephen sisters' drawing-room at 46 Gordon Square, Bloomsbury, where they moved after the death of their father, Sir Leslie, and where they began the Thursday evening *soirées* at which they entertained their brother Thoby's former Cambridge friends, including Strachey and Woolf. "Isn't that semen on your dress?" enquired Lytton of Vanessa, and with that infamous remark another barrier fell. "One can talk of fucking and Sodomy and sucking and bushes and all without turning a hair," remarked Vanessa to Maynard.[12]

Mary's "role in Bloomsbury has dwindled to little more than a walk-on part as 'Clive Bell's mistress' " writes David Bradshaw, editor of Bell's letters to Mary.[13] Richard Shone simply describes her as "a cousin of Duncan Grant . . . the lover of Clive Bell for many years . . . and a valuable patron of the Omega Workshops,"[14] but Mary's significance was greater than this. She was a key figure in the lives of Tom and Vivien Eliot over a period from 1916 to, in Vivien's case, 1936[15]—the trusted confidante to whom both wrote hundreds of spontaneous and amusing letters.

Although never a creative artist to bear comparison with the "great figures" of Bloomsbury—Roger Fry, Virginia Woolf, Vanessa Bell, Lytton Strachey and Duncan Grant (followed by a "sub-rout of high-mathematicians and low psychologists, a tangle of lesser painters and writers")[16]—Mary, as a successful hostess, straddled the worlds of Georgian society and Bloomsbury, and few in either world refused her invitations. Her guests marvelled at her dress sense and her parties. Mary in turn expected much of them:[17] "No-one should go to a party as he is every day," she wrote in *Vogue*. "He must be changed—touched by a little frenzy. Remembering that night permits of extravagance and excess . . . the witty must be wittier, the gentle more insinuating, the fat much fatter, the pale paler, a flirt more flirtatious . . . Like tropical plants all should extravagantly flower."[18] Katherine Mansfield was no more impressed than she had been with Ottoline at Garsington: "Oh God! Those parties. They are all very well in retrospect but while they are going on they are too infernally boring."[19]

It was not an opinion shared by the Eliots. For Vivien, Mary was an enviable woman of fashion, socialite and cultural touchstone. She cultivated Mary's friendship eagerly, and Mary in turn saw that Vivien could be useful to her. She showed her new friend Mrs. Eliot a short story she had written, inspired by the war. "Dear Mrs. Hutchinson," Vivien wrote in September 1917, "I am not sending back your story to-day, because I want to show it to my husband." The story ["War"] was "so vivid and amusing . . . You *must* let me show it to him."[20] A day or two later, Vivien returned Mary's story, telling her that her husband was "ever so pleased with it. He is going to write and tell you so. I admire you very much."[21] Shortly afterwards Eliot agreed to publish "War" in the *Egoist*. A shared interest in literature drew the two women together, and Vivien's own wit and vivacity appealed to Mary, who wasted no time in adding the Eliots to her guest list. At River House, Vivien's world began to open up in a fairytale fashion, as she and Tom mixed with the *beau monde*. Vivien felt like Cinderella, as she was transported from her tiny flat near Paddington Station to the glamour and glitter of Mary's drawing-room. The evening, she wrote, was "unreal, dreamlike," although at the same time Vivien was forced to apologise for "one of my indiscretions," towards Lytton Strachey. Vivien had probably repeated gossip concerning Lytton, to his annoyance, but it was only the first of many such indiscretions which were to create difficulties for Vivien with the Bloomsbury group. To become the object of Lytton's scorn was a foolish move, as Ottoline had discovered. "I feel it's my fault," Vivien wrote apologetically to Mary, "But I knew Tom rather wants him. He's lonely. How could he be otherwise? And Lytton is such a dear, *surely* they could be friends?"[22]

Vivien shared Mary's enthusiasm for parties because of her love of dance. In the physicality of dance she forgot the "troubles" which dogged her days and, although Tom could be leaden-footed, she knew that together they looked superb. The autumn of 1917, when the Eliots' fortunes took a turn for the better as Tom thrived unexpectedly at the bank, found Vivien often encouraging her friends to give dances. Their friend Arthur Dakyns was dragging his heels over arranging a dance, so, she urged Mary, "If he won't, I wish you would have one! I can imagine it being a wonderful occasion—You *must* like dancing." She and Tom were going to a dance that night in a studio in Kensington, wrote Vivien, and to another dance on Wednesday night.[23]

Mary's *soirées* also provided a valuable *entrée* to the world of wealthy literati. There Vivien met the Sitwell trio, Osbert, Edith and Sacheverell, to whom Eliot was first introduced in the autumn of 1917, when he was invited to read his new poems for charity at the house of another fashionable hostess, Sybil Colefax. "Osbert and Edith Shitwell [sic] will be there," he told Pound, wondering if he might not shock the bigwigs with "our old friend COLOMBO? Or Bolo, since famous."[24] It was just as well that Eliot did not recite his ribald rhymes about Colombo who couldn't "stop a-pissin" in front of the distinguished audience, including chairman Sir Edmund Gosse who publicly rebuked Eliot for arriving a few minutes late after a day's work at the bank. But Eliot showed no sign of annoyance at this reproof. His good manners impressed Osbert, and his reading of his satirical poem "Hippopotamus" delighted Arnold Bennett.[25] Vivien, meanwhile, was making friends with Edith. "I liked Miss Sitwell much better yesterday," she wrote to Mary, taking back her earlier poor opinion of Edith: "We both positively loved your party. I have seldom seen Tom so stimulated by anything as he was last night."[26] Soon she was inviting Mary and Edith to tea at 18 Crawford Mansions to meet the Pounds.

The gaiety which at first made Vivien a popular new arrival in Bohemia is evident in an undated letter to Mary which bubbles with high spirits as Vivien anticipates the summer in the Marlow house in 1918. She compares the "remote tower" of their Crawford Street flat, "secret and shut off" from the street noises which surround it ("You know I have *loved* this flat") to the house they have taken in Marlow, which she will like so much more if Mary will come to visit her and Tom. "You must come alone sometimes, when it is very *hot,* and we can be just three by ourselves," pleads Vivien. She is planning

> a very ripping weekend party, if only people don't mind the scarcity of furniture *and* the food. We could go on the river in punts in the day, and perhaps we should dance in the evening . . . One day you must try Tom's negro rag-time. I know you'd love it.

The Sitwells are coming today, writes an excited Vivien. *"He* says you are to give a dance!"

Tom Eliot had met Mary Hutchinson as early as 1916, the result of

Russell's initial introduction to Clive Bell that summer.[27] Mary was instantly impressed by the handsome and erudite American poet. If Clive was sometimes dismissed as third-rate, too "wordy and gossipy" in Ottoline's words,[28] to be taken seriously, no one could make the same criticism of the silent, brooding Eliot. Clive, whose thinning ginger hair and pot belly reminded Ottoline of a balloon rather than Prince Charming, had first been spotted by Lytton Strachey walking through the Great Court at Trinity, Cambridge, in full hunting-rig, including a hunting horn and the whip carried by a whipper-in.[29] He could not compare in elegance with the dandyish Eliot, whose letters to his mother reveal his preoccupation with fashion. Dutifully Eliot acknowledged the hand-knitted sweater and woollen muffler Charlotte sent as presents, but he preferred his own recent, well-cut purchases: a light overcoat, bought "at Vivien's earnest solicitation . . . as an investment," a new pair of shoes ("fearfully expensive"), and a new suit—"very nice, very dark gray, almost black . . ."[30] Like Vivien, Eliot was prepared to spend extravagantly in the pursuit of fashion, justifying his new clothes by the argument that the price of wool was going up due to the war. It was another example of Tom and Vivien's shared tastes, as each dressed to impress their new Bloomsbury friends.

But it was not only Eliot's immaculate *extérieur pimpant,* as Aldington described it, which so powerfully attracted Mary, but his personality. The luminous light yellow eyes were as mesmeric as those of his grandfather or his formidable mother; the beautiful but impenetrable features and the controlled, muscular body suggested a powerful will hidden beneath fastidious courtesy. Eliot was, wrote Sitwell, "a most striking being." Instantly captivated, Mary had invited him to Eleanor House in September 1916, an invitation he smoothly declined, yielding precedence to Roger Fry's boating party.[31]

On 16 January 1917, when Mary was in London rehearsing in one of the private, often transvestite plays which Lytton wrote for performance by members of the Bloomsbury group, and Clive was at Garsington, he wrote:

> I daresay you will be gay at your rehearsal, but I shall take care
> not to think about that . . . To-night when I return from my party
> I can either read Thucydides by candlelight like a Renaissance

grammarian or write to you like a Petrarchian lover: but you will be flirting with Eliot! . . . I'll write a better letter to-morrow night if I'm not feeling too jealous.[32]

Mary, meanwhile, was joking to Lytton about writing and relationships, and how the latter got in the way of the former. During the rehearsals of the play, in which both Eliot and Lytton's brother James had parts, she claimed to have lost hope of writing an "immortal work." How could she invent a character with her head so full of "charming and subtle flirtations," of the sort which she had practised with an elderly gentleman in the shape of Lytton? Shouldn't she always be wondering whether she was ready to give Mr. Eliot "a prolonged kiss," or whether James would expect her for certain to embrace him in return? "No! No!" cried Mary. Such rehearsals were far too distracting.[33]

The following year found her demanding a new play from Lytton, one with a part for her husband Jack. This play was not to be one of Lytton's usual transvestite farces like *The Unfortunate Lovers or Truth Will Out,* which dramatized Bloomsbury's liaisons of the moment and had been performed at a private party in 1914 at which Duncan Grant came dressed as a pregnant whore and Majorie Strachey wore nothing but a miniature of the Prince Regent round her neck.[34] It was to be for public performance, said Mary, and must be "fairly convenable—*no mixing of skirts and trousers.*"[35]

Clive Bell's insecurity grew as the months passed. "Darling, how delicious it will be—like a summer's day—when one has almost forgotten what summer is—to see you again, and catch hold of you and kiss you and walk along with you, chattering and commenting, and kiss you again," he wrote from Garsington on Easter Day 1917. "But I had forgotten, you have probably been kissing Elliot [sic], or at least squeezing his hand, and my ecstasies are a little mistimed." Frustrated at his confinement as a "conchie" in the Oxfordshire countryside, which kept him apart from Mary, Clive was, he confessed, only in a moderate humour.

What about you? O Mr. Elliot is come to call after his dinner party, and you are getting on very well talking about his verses. Pray make him tell you exactly what it means, word for word, as

they used to construe Greek in the Lower School; and a little later
get him to show you how the footman sat on the dining-room
table with the second housemaid on his knees . . .[36]

Clive seethed with jealousy as he pictured Mary on Eliot's knee. Why did
Mary send her story to "Mrs. E," he demanded from Garsington on 20
September 1917. "Doesn't mean I hope that you're not going to send it to
Virginia . . . I wonder, what this great secret attraction in Mr. T.S.E., beyond his beaux yeux and his plus beaux vers may be, and in Mrs. Eliot too,
beyond her confidences: the plot thickens."[37] Three days later he was asserting his prior claim to his "dearest Polly," his nickname for Mary, for the
weekend: "I shall fix nothing with Vanessa till I know . . . I am very much
in the mood for a romance in spite of all your wicked sidelong glances at
Mr. T.S.E. and his obliging criticism; but if you can't choose but go to River
House I will acquiesce with the best grace possible."[38] Magnanimously he
conceded that Mary would do better to publish in the *Egoist* through Tom
than in the Hogarth Press, which was taken up with Virginia's novel
(Night and Day). Others, however, beside Clive had noticed Mary flirting
with Eliot. Katherine Mansfield recorded that Mary, at one of her parties
in June 1917, had "an *eye* on Greaves [Robert Graves] and an *eyebrow* on
Eliot."[39]

Eliot, too, found in Mary a cultured and sympathetic personality,
a woman with a gift for friendship, well-bred, well-read and robustly
healthy, whose capable and resilient character presented a refreshing contrast to Vivien. She was already the mother of two children, Barbara and
Jeremy, but remained *soignée* as well as sexually adventurous. Maurice
Haigh-Wood believed that Mary, like other women in Eliot's life, took the
initiative in her flirtatious relationship with the poet: "Tom was always in
demand," he said. "Mary and Nancy [Cunard] both made a pass at him."[40]
Behind flirtation, however, lay more serious business, on both sides. Mary,
for her part, was in earnest about her writing despite the "correspondence,
door-bells, telephone, sentimental journeys, and other extravagances"
which came between her and the immortal work she dreamed of composing. It was she who had first approached Eliot in 1917 to congratulate him
on *Prufrock* after Clive brought copies to Garsington, and in September
when Eliot read "War," he was genuinely impressed by her ability to get

inside the feelings of her characters, even if she had not quite got *out* again. "I like to feel that a writer is perfectly cool and detached, regarding other people's feelings or his own, like a God who has got beyond them," he told her, promising to publish her story in his journal.[41] The intellectual bond which developed between them was a genuine one.

But the maternal role Mary filled for both Vivien and Tom was paramount. Mary, like Ottoline, helped at first to launch the Eliots in society, manage their lives and straighten out their "muddles." It also amused her to be the confidante of both Eliots in their quarrels as each turned to her for sympathy. "Tom is impossible at present—very American and obstinate!" Vivien confided to Mary in March 1918.[42] In the beginning Mary was kind to Vivien. She genuinely liked her, writing to Lytton that she had gone out sailing with "my friend Mrs. Eliot."[43] To be "kind"—in other words tolerant—of Vivien's moods and muddles, was essential to the friendship. Vivien was afraid of those who were not "kind" to her, and it was a major cause of her later withdrawal from society. Accepting an invitation of Mary's to a party much later, in 1921, she invited Mary to lunch: "Do Mary, there's a child," she wrote. "Be kind to me as ever: Very much love—V."[44] And, years later in 1929, as the Eliot marriage disintegrated, Vivien wrote that she rather dreaded Barbara, Mary's daughter, coming to visit with her mother: "You must tell her not to be unkind to me, and that you and I must go on being friends."[45] In the event, Barbara turned out to be "charming."[46]

Meanwhile, Mary's encouragement, and the competence of Vivien's new servant, Ellen Kelland, prevailed on Vivien to invite the Hutchinsons to a lunch party in the flat in March 1918. It was the most ambitious attempt she and Tom had ever made, and the small dining-library was packed. "But it went off very well," Eliot told his mother proudly. "We are excellent hosts, I think, and our servant did admirably." It was easier to have people to lunch rather than dinner, he explained, because of the wartime restrictions on meat, but at lunch fish and spaghetti sufficed.[47]

There was another reason for Vivien's new confidence that spring. Her long-standing ambition to act or dance at last bore fruit. Vivien was given a part in a play in Hampstead, and was able to tell Mary that she had been quite busy and happy recently with her "suburban performances."[48] Soon she was so occupied with acting that she was forced to decline one of

Mary's invitations. On 31 March 1918 Vivien wrote that she had never disliked having to refuse an invitation so much as she did that one: "It was so tempting to me. Dances are so few, and as you know, they mean a lot to me," but she was still trying to earn an honest penny acting and had achieved some unexpected success. She explained that she had had to refuse the Sitwells the night before for the same reason. (Osbert was at this time living in Swan Walk, Chelsea, and entertaining frequently.) "I do not like it," wrote Vivien. "But we must do something, and I have been spending recklessly lately." She apologised for being "a wretched crock" who could only do one thing at a time.[49] However, it was unlikely that Vivien could earn enough by acting to pay for her impulsive purchases in the north London shops; certainly Colette never made a living from the stage. But Vivien's intentions were laudable, if unrealistic.

Vivien's admiration for Mary grew as their intimacy deepened: "I love you more than ever," she wrote. "I turn to you with thoughts of joy and relief . . . I am very fond of you and I think you are wonderful. And *wonderful* you are." It was a similar emotional attachment to that which Vivien had had with Lucy Thayer, who remained in America during the war, nursing her sick mother. Vivien was to give the name "Félise" or "Felice," probably inspired by Swinburne's eponymous poem, to the character of a close friend and companion in many of her fictional sketches; it is a name which bears witness to the importance of such relationships to her, although later Vivien would be horrified by Lucy's apparently lesbian advances to her. In Swinburne's Félise, a lover laments a lost "lifelong" love:

> Kiss me once hard as though a flame
>   Lay on my lips and made them fire;
> The same lips now, and not the same;
>   What breath shall fill and re-inspire
> A dead desire?[50]

But Vivien's affection for Mary was also founded on trust. Her references to Mary's visits to Marlow so that the three of them might be alone together demonstrate the happy intimacy which at first existed between Vivien, Tom and Mary, before jealousy came between them.

When Russell's prison sentence at Brixton began in May 1918, Mary's support was vital to Vivien. Although T. S. Eliot's name was upon the list of visitors whom Russell might see in prison, Vivien's was missing. Bertie's brother, Frank, Earl Russell, who had already served a sentence for bigamy in Brixton, persuaded the authorities to allow three visitors a week, who were to arrive together. Russell drew up the list of "compatible" visitors, such as Elizabeth Russell and Clifford Allen, ensuring that the visits of Colette and Ottoline were on alternating weeks. Apart from T. S. Eliot, other old friends on the visiting list included Gilbert Murray, Charles Sanger and Desmond MacCarthy,[51] but it was for Colette's visits that Russell longed most eagerly. Although forbidden to write to him, she sent him messages through the agony column of *The Times,* and soon Russell perfected a method of smuggling love letters out to her written in French, which the warders assumed to be part of his research. "Dans l'amour, la terreur cesse parce que la solitude n'existe plus. Il est difficile de trouver un amour réciproque si intime qu'il fasse cesser la solitude, mais il est possible. Tu l'as fait pour moi. Je ne sais pas si je l'ai fait pour toi . . ." ("In love, terror ceases because loneliness no longer exists. It is difficult to find a mutual love so intimate that it can banish solitude, but it is possible. You have done it for me. I don't know if I have done it for you.")[52]

Busily he began to straighten out his tortuous property arrangements, which reflected the emotional "tangles" in which he had found himself, and plan for his release in September. "I will not go to T.H. (Telegraph House) when I come out," he wrote. "I want to be with you. I cannot wait. I will make it all right with my brother. Here is everything cut & dried:

> You take my flat Sp 1, & let the Attic.
> My nominal residence is still Gordon Sq.
> ?We go 1st for 1 week to Ashford if they can have us & you have
>   no work?
> LET US NOW TREAT PLANS AS SETTLED.

His sister-in-law, Elizabeth, in flight, as so often, from her disastrous marriage to Frank Russell, decided to rent Colette's attic, and Colette prepared to move into Bury Street to make it ready for Russell. He had given notice to his tenant and former mistress Helen Dudley, to whom he allowed a solo prison visit to bid him goodbye. She sailed for the United

States on 15 August, leaving Russell temporarily remorseful over his treatment of her.[53] "I was upset about Helen Dudley," he told Colette. "I have broken her life and I suffer when I think of it."[54] Helen's subsequent mental deterioration and breakdown present interesting parallels to that of Vivien.[55]

There remained a final adjustment for Russell to make. So confident of his love for Colette and hers for him as to write that he could "live through fifty Maurices now,"[56] Russell decided to eradicate Vivien from his life, finally and irrevocably. In July Tom sent a message to Russell that he was having difficulty finding someone with whom to share the cost of the Marlow house. Russell responded by asking his brother to tell Tom that he would probably have to give up his share in it. It was a coded farewell.

Russell's sudden withdrawal increased the financial burden on the Eliots, and necessitated their letting their London flat. Instead of staying in Crawford Mansions during the week, Eliot was forced to commute over the summer of 1918. At first he did not mind. The relief of being out of London and getting away from it all at the end of the day was very great, and he found the train journey restful too. During May and June he wrote several poems, sitting in the back garden among the roses.[57] One was "Ode," in which he alludes, in one version of the poem, to the "sullen succuba suspired," suggesting Vivien sighing gloomily after the departed Russell.[58] The use of the word "succuba"—in the final version "succuba eviscerate"—alludes to the witch-craze which lasted for three centuries in Europe; sexual assaults by succubi and demons, who associated with the devil at nocturnal witches' sabbaths, is a constant theme of the 1486 *Malleus Maleficarum* or *Hammer of the Witches,* the handbook of persecution. In this period women were generally seen as more sexually voracious than men: "Of women's unnatural, insatiable lust," wrote an Englishman, Robert Burton, in 1621, "what country, what village doth not complain?"[59] In seventeenth-century England the word "succuba" also meant "strumpet" or "whore," a fact which would have been known to Eliot, whose knowledge of Jacobean drama was extensive. If Vivien existed in a hidden corner of Tom's imagination as a succuba, a female witch who threatened his potency, might he not also have believed that her diabolical compact was with Russell, who described himself as Satan in his own short story?

But any such feelings Eliot may have had towards his wife remained hidden to visitors. When in May Aldous Huxley paid a call on the Eliots, he found the poet "in excellent form, and his wife too."[60] However, as the summer progressed Tom discovered that the cost of the season ticket to Marlow was an added burden on his expenses, and he began to resent the hours spent in slow suburban trains.

During a summer heatwave, Vivien invited Brigit Patmore to stay.

The cab drew up beside an old-fashioned house—one of half a dozen or so with front doors opening straight onto the pavement, so no matter how quiet life in this little town was, you were right in the midst of it.

"Did you mind the journey?" asked Vivienne. "Such a funny little end-of-the-rail station! . . . Come upstairs. You're at the back. I do hope you don't mind. I'll be downstairs."[61]

After unpacking, Brigit went downstairs, carrying notepaper and envelopes. "Vivienne was in the sitting room which had a window opening onto the street. She looked well and young and said at once, 'I'm so glad you're here. Let's have tea at once. Don't you hate keeping to formal mealtimes?' "

Fortunately neither Brigit nor Vivien wanted to walk a great deal, punt on the river, or bother with people. "We lived seemingly by exchanging quiet moods, a little dreamily, a little melancholy. My writing case was old and ragged and apparently got on Vivienne's nerves, for she constantly referred to it as 'that horrible old thing,' 'your disgusting writing—flummery.' I said I liked old things and took it up to my room." It was an example of the obsessional tidiness and cleanliness which Maurice considered characterised both the Eliots.

"There sometimes seemed to be nothing that she and Tom did not take with terrible seriousness," recalled Brigit, who found it slightly exhausting. "It explained why Vivienne said, with a sigh, 'The frightful time I have with Tom.' " Yet, Brigit observed, Vivienne "could make him gay at times—even with a schoolboy sense of humour." Tom confessed to Brigit that one of their amusements on summer evenings in their flat in London had been to watch the two prostitutes in a flat across the road get dressed to go out or come in to undress.[62] Such voyeurism may have inspired one of the quatrain poems Eliot wrote that summer at Marlow, "Whispers of Immortality," although Ezra Pound took the credit for introducing Tom to the uncorseted woman of easy virtue whom he claimed was the model for the cat-like Grishkin, whose "friendly bust" promises "pneumatic bliss" in the poem, but whose female body odour also offends the poet. Even the "sleek Brazilian jaguar" says Eliot, does not "distil so rank a feline smell/As Grishkin in a drawing-room."[63]

In his garden Eliot brooded on death, and read Webster, the Jacobean playwright whose *Duchess of Malfi* was to be a potent source of inspiration for *The Waste Land.* "Webster was much possessed by death/And saw the skull beneath the skin," noted Eliot: "Daffodils bulbs instead of balls/Stared from the sockets of the eyes!" Identifying with John Donne, who knew that "No contact possible to flesh" allays the "ague of the skeleton" or "fever of the bone," and dehumanising the beings about whom he writes, Eliot's sexual imagery encompasses skull, eye socket, bust, part-objects of whose Freudian significance he was aware, having praised in a book review the Freudians' study of "the influence of the sexual instinct."[64] In the final verse Eliot makes his own confession: "instead of circumambulating 'her charm' like a tom-cat before it mates, 'our lot' (i.e. 'our kind' of men) do not circumambulate such women; instead we 'crawl between dry ribs' (. . . read books)," argues George Whiteside. "One cannot, I believe, escape the implications of the circumambulation image and the 'But our lot' phrase immediately consequent. They inescapably imply that Eliot is saying: our kind of men stay away from desire-filled women."[65] In his twenties, it seemed, Eliot struggled with contradictory urges, to confess and yet to repress his homosexual feelings: it was a kind of torture, but one which explains to some extent the obscurity of poetry in which so many secrets demanded concealment.

Among those secrets was his grief for Jean Verdenal, to which he had referred earlier in "Portrait of a Lady" (1915). In that poem it is once again April, the month Tom associated with his friend's death. Watching the "Lady" of the poem twisting a lilac stalk from the bowl of lilacs before her, Tom remembers Jean, and addresses a silent remark to the woman before him: "Ah, my friend, you do not know, you do not know/What Life is, you who hold it in your hands." He smiles and sips his tea: "Yet with these April sunsets, that somehow recall/My buried life, and Paris in the

Spring . . ."[66] He tells himself that now he is at peace; but, three years later in 1918, in the Marlow garden, Eliot returned to the theme of Jean's death, writing "Dans le Restaurant," which, like "Whispers of Immortality," was published in the *Little Review* that September.[67] Eliot's water poetry is some of his most beautiful verse; in his treatment of death by water he returns repeatedly to images of drowned men, sea voyages and shipwreck, the source of which lay partly in his childhood sailing experiences, but which also held for him the deepest personal meaning. Distancing himself from his emotions by writing in French, he transposes the image of Jean— "Phlébas, le Phénicien . . . quinze jours noyé?" (fifteen days drowned)— from the Dardanelles to an English sea: "oubliant les cris des mouettes et l'écume de Cornouaille"* where Jean will be carried far away by the current. The poet's own cry is one of pain: "Cependant, ce fut jadis un bel homme, de haute taille."†

As the weeks passed and Russell's release from Brixton approached, he demanded that Vivien and Tom return his belongings from Marlow: "Has Eliot brought the things I sent for?" he asked Colette in July. "If not, please make Miss Rider (of the NCF) write to him & remind him. I shall give you the Persian bowl, if it survives unbroken . . ."[68] Having settled, as he thought, the problem of his discarded mistress, he was content to dream in his prison cell of the work he would do under the inspiration of Colette's love:

> I want to stand with you at the rim of the world, and peer into the darkness beyond, and see a little more than others have seen of the strange shapes of mystery that inhabit that unknown night— terrible shapes, which the touch of your hand makes bearable. I want to bring into the world of men some little bit of new wisdom. There is little wisdom in the world . . . I want to add to it, even if only ever so little.[69]

*forgetting the cries of the seagulls and the sea-foam of Cornwall
†However, he was once a handsome man, and tall.

He would kiss her lips until their souls touched, he told her, as he waited impatiently for his sentence to end.

But for Colette the temptations of London nightlife had proved irresistible since she had left the NCF. "Dashing around between the Carlton, the Berkeley and Ciro's was a sort of reaction from the very rarified, elevated atmosphere of the N.C.F.," she wrote. "I was always a person given to bouts—of one sort or another."[70] As Russell's initial mood of euphoria switched sharply to a depression which led him to threaten a hunger strike in July, Colette sought for light-hearted diversion from her lover's profoundly gloomy letters. Not only did she see Maurice Elvey again, but she began to dine with an American colonel by the name of Mitchell, whose appearance intrigued her, his "sad, honest brown eyes" reminding her of a St. Bernard mastiff. It was a sympathetic portrait calculated to arouse the usual suspicions in Russell's mind.

In July 1918, meanwhile, an event occurred which was to affect Vivien and Tom profoundly: the call-up of all Americans in Britain was announced. Vivien's reaction was one of panic and she wrote at once to Mary, begging for help. Within eight weeks all Americans must either have gone to America to enlist, or be enlisted in England, "presumably as privates," she wrote inaccurately on 30 August. Tom was "rushing about the embassy."

> You know we have *no* influence here, American or highish political. Do you think yr husband could give him any useful introduction, or any help? *Or can you?* I mean to get him into a job *here*—propaganda or something.

Vivien's fear of losing Tom communicates itself in her rising hysteria:

> If he goes to America he will not be able to come back while the war lasts. That means years. If he stays here he will be killed, or as good as. If we don't save him, he'll never write again. You know how bitter he is *now*.

Desperately Vivien asked Mary to "be a friend" and communicate at once with anyone who could help. "Get Tom at the *Bank*—it's quicker (17

Cornhill—Avenue 6430)." Finally she passed on Tom's plea not to let word of their difficulties be passed on to Ottoline—"This is important. Will explain later. Do do *something,* please. Yrs, V.E."[71]

"Saving Tom" in August 1918 became the first of several such projects undertaken by the Eliots' friends over the next few years. Vivien and Tom were both alarmed at the prospect of his being passed fit for active service, and Vivien pressed her husband to find a commission rather than enter the forces as a private. To his correspondents, Eliot stressed his need for a rank high enough to support him and Vivien financially. "With an invalid dependent wife it is obvious that I should suffer very badly on a private's pay," he complained to his brother.[72] To John Quinn, too, he explained that "my wife (who is an invalid) is entirely dependent upon me, which I believe makes a difference . . ."[73] At thirty Tom was of draft age, and as the date of his medical examination approached his apprehension increased. Vivien related the outcome to Mary:

> I am too restless and unhappy to write much. It was a shock to both of us that Tom was graded so high in the medical exam. I did not realize until then how much I had *counted* on his being passed quite *UNFIT.* I can't understand it. He took a very strong certificate from our doctor, and he had been *fearfully* ill over the weekend so that he was *obviously* in a wretched state . . .

Vivien was also ill, she told Mary. She had been to a specialist just before the call-up, as she was getting "iller and iller all this summer. He gave me a lot of fearful directions . . ."[74]

Vivien had done everything possible to prepare her nervous husband for the medical examination on 12 August, coaching him carefully for the ordeal ahead: "I write out what he is to say under every conceivable situation, but it always happens that some unexpected twist occurs which throws him off his balance in the entire interview," she lamented to Mary. "Tom is *fearfully* vague, one can never trust him to be worldly wise and to say the inspired thing or to suppress the unfortunate truth, you see."[75]

But Vivien's coaching was not completely wasted. Fortunately, as the Eliots perceived it, Tom was eventually graded unfit for active service on account of his hernia, which his mother had explained to him was congenital (he had thought it was due to an accident), and tachycardia. His call-up was deferred, affording him the time to go about procuring a non-combatant commission through his connections. Eliot set to work soliciting testimonials to send in to the Quartermasters' Corps or Interpreters' Corps; he had by now learnt enough Spanish to read a newspaper, had been having lessons in Danish for his bank work, and was already fluent in French and German, and had some Italian. An even more attractive prospect was a commission in the U.S. Navy Office in London, perhaps in the Intelligence Department. Eliot turned to his old friends Wyndham Lewis, and Osbert Sitwell, at that time an officer in the Grenadier Guards, to intervene on his behalf. Osbert spoke to Lady Cunard and introduced Eliot to Arnold Bennett via the journalist Robert Ross. But in the third week in August a cable arrived from Washington forbidding any more naval commissions for Americans in England. Disappointed, Eliot renewed his efforts to become a non-combatant army officer.

Friends and strangers alike rallied round in his support. Quinn informed Major Turner of the U.S. Information Department that Eliot was "a man of ability, a good patriotic loyal American, a man of keen intelligence and of the right age . . . a desirable acquisition for the information department."[76] The artist Edmund Dulac, who had corrected Eliot's French poems, vouched for the poet's knowledge of French, as did Arnold Bennett. Hugh Walpole, Ezra Pound, St. John Hutchinson, Osbert Sitwell, Sir Alfred Zimmern, Graham Wallas, the Fabian leader, and Harold Joachim, Eliot's tutor at Merton, were among those who wrote between 22 and 27 August recommending him for non-combatant military service, while from America his relative Charles William Eliot, President of Harvard, chimed in with one of the three American testimonials Eliot also needed.

The more he thought about it, the more attractive the prospect of such a commission began to seem to Eliot. There were many points in its favour. Not only would such a role demonstrate to his family and Harvard contemporaries that he was finally prepared to serve his country, but it occurred to him that it might be a more restful form of occupation than the continual grind of bank work, editing and reviewing. As an officer, he could find more time for poetry than as a bank clerk. Despite the warm summer, and a garden bright with foxgloves, lupins and larkspur, his and

Vivien's mutual ill-health had persisted at Marlow. The dissatisfaction with each other's company which inevitably led both Tom and Vivien to dislike their residence of the moment, however apparently suitable it was for their needs, stirred Tom to hint to his mother on 7 July that "we long for Bosham and the sea." Three weeks later, on 28 July, he stressed Vivien's toothache, and begged for funds to allow them to go to the seaside, where Mary and Jack were holidaying at Eleanor House: "I think a week at Bosham would do her much good, and if father sends the money I think we can do it."⁷⁷ It would put Vivien in shape for the winter, he pleaded, but advised his mother to write to him at the bank as he did not know how much longer they would be able to stay at Marlow. Economical with the truth, as usual, Eliot did not admit the fact that Vivien had signed a five-year lease on the Marlow house, lest his mother think a seaside holiday as well as a riverside one an extravagance in a country at war.

The army also seemed to promise an enticing avenue of escape from Vivien. Tom wrote to "Dear Mary" on 25 August (the first occasion he used her Christian name), saying that although he hated a situation which made him force his personal affairs upon his friends to the exclusion of everything else, and he felt quite as she did "about khaki; at the same time I think that this is the moment for getting into it to the best advantage . . ."⁷⁸ Mary helped him with the "strings" he had out, and as the flattering testimonials continued to arrive, joining up became an increasingly agreeable prospect. Patriotism did not motivate him, for his disillusionment with the war was total, but, so long as there was no need for heroics in the trenches, the vision of "more leisure for serious work and (more) freedom from anxiety in the Army than out of it" opened up a new prospect of freedom. Soon Vivien was agreeing that "nearly *anything settled* would be less unpleasant than the present incessant strain."⁷⁹

In August Eliot also had a meeting with Russell in which he told him that he refused to be a conscientious objector, and asked Russell to add his name to those working on his behalf. "At present what I want are names which would carry instant conviction to *anybody*—celebrities, and people with official or social titles," he told Mary.⁸⁰ Russell passed on the request to Colette: "Tell me, did you accomplish anything for Eliot?" he asked three days later. "Don't bother yourself about it too much. I expect he will manage all right. She [Vivien] always gets in a fuss."⁸¹ Colette offered to ask her new American admirer, Colonel Mitchell, who was General Biddle's Chief of Staff, to pull strings: "Abt. Eliot. I daresay it might be quite easy for Col. M. to help him with a job more suitable to the special Eliot talents."[82]

On 11 September Colette invited Eliot, whom she had never met, to tea. He arrived at Russell's Bury Street flat, into which Colette had moved. "I gave him tea on yr. kitchen table," reported Colette. "He sat with his back to the bathrm, looking as if just put through a mangle & come out all smooth . . ."[83] She noticed the same feline quality as Osbert Sitwell had, finding the poet

> reserved and rather shut up in himself—remote. Extraordinarily erudite, of course. His eyes were most remarkable. One felt they might spring out on one at any moment—like a cat. His manner was detached and there was a certain frigidity about him. But underneath that frigidity, one felt there lurked a curiously deep despair.[84]

By September Eliot had eighteen letters of recommendation. He was waiting for a post in Army Intelligence when the U.S. Navy Intelligence suddenly offered to make him a Chief Yeoman with the promise of a commission in a few months. At once Eliot left the bank and waited for two weeks without pay, only to find that "Everything turned to red tape in my hands," as he complained to John Quinn.[85] The promised post never materialised. At last Eliot was ignominiously forced to ask the bank to take him back again. It was an anti-climax which he found exceptionally irritating. The number of detailed letters he wrote explaining that it was not *his* fault that he was not able to make himself useful to his country indicate his sensitivity on the point: "Possibly in the course of time the army will discover that they need me to peel potatoes," he wrote sarcastically to an American friend.[86] The armistice of 11 November ended Eliot's abortive attempts to join the forces and left him feeling decidedly anti-American. Having seen more of his countrymen in the last three months than he had done for four years, he wrote disgruntledly that he got on much better with the English. "Americans now impress me, almost invariably, as very immature."[87]

In Trafalgar Square the crowds danced under the lights, turned on for the first time in four years. On the evening of 4 August 1914 the crowd had "cheered for its own death," remembered Osbert Sitwell. By 1918 most of the men who had made up that crowd were dead. Now "their heirs were dancing because life had been given back to them."[88] Ironically, Eliot's call-up papers from St. Louis, requesting him to report for immediate military service, were issued on 25 November 1918, fourteen days after the armistice, but by then he had already returned to his office beneath the London pavements. Unlike Osbert Sitwell, who felt the "startling joy" of peace, with its promise of deliverance from the mud, poison-gas and sodden trenches of France, Eliot's chief emotion was one of gratitude to the bank, who had signed his appeal for exemption and raised his salary to £360 a year. But it was hard to let go of a lingering sense of bitterness that the avenue of escape from office drudgery—and from Vivien—had been suddenly blocked.

Vivien felt equally numb. "I really have not been able to rejoice much over Peace!" she wrote to Henry Eliot on 21 November. "In the abstract I do, and I try to make myself *realise* it." She was afraid that conditions would be harder than ever for a long time. "Poor Tom's disaster over his Navy job very nearly did for both of us. It was indeed the last straw."[89] By December Tom was in a state of collapse after his "exhausting year" of alarms, illness, moving house, and military difficulties.[90] His doctor advised him to rest. Pound, newly alarmed, wrote that Eliot's health was "in a very shaky state. Doctor orders him not to write any prose for six months." Eliot temporarily gave up writing for the *Egoist,* and found a colleague to undertake his reviewing for several months.

At this point Vivien took control of the situation. Of the two of them, she was sure she was the stronger. "Tom takes cold *very* much more easily easily than I do," she explained to Henry. "Most of *my* colds are caught from him." Troubled by "splitting headaches" and feeling "very very weak" so that he had to postpone his lecture, Tom continued to worry about his mind not working properly, and to feel that his writing was deteriorating. Vivien was convinced that he needed "a complete *mental* rest." After a good deal of argument, she persuaded Tom to sign a contract with her, saying he would do no writing of any kind, except what was necessary for the one lecture a week he had to give, and no reading, except poetry and novels for three months from December. She also made him promise her he would take a walk every day. "I am sure you will be glad to hear this," she wrote in a firm letter to her mother-in-law on 15 December. "When one's brain is very fatigued, the only thing to do, I think, is to *give up* the attempt to use it."[91] Vivien was certain that if Tom continued to tax his brain and felt it did not respond, he would collapse in despair. Her priority was to avert a breakdown. Three days before Christmas Tom had a sharp attack of sciatica, and Vivien administered cod liver oil.

Her firmness had the desired effect. By Christmas Day Tom was feeling better. He put up a small Christmas tree, and he and Vivien gave each other stockings full of nuts, oranges and candies. He gave her a coal-scuttle for the drawing-room, and she gave him some books. Aunt Lillia presented Vivien with a turkey, which she cooked for Charles and Rose Haigh-Wood, and although the little party missed Maurice, who had returned from leave to Italy, where he was directing railway operations, Vivien organised a cheerful Christmas dinner in the "dining-library" at Crawford Mansions. Tom had responded well to Vivien's care, and on Boxing Day he was well enough to rise early with her to watch American President Woodrow Wilson drive through the streets of London to Buckingham Palace. It was fine and sunny, "Wilson weather," said Vivien, and she and Tom stood for over two hours waiting for the president to pass. Vivien was too small to see over people's heads, as the spectators were thirty rows deep, but, as the carriage came in sight, Tom lifted his wife up high. "It was a most moving and wonderful sight to see him sitting next to the King," wrote Vivien to Charlotte Eliot.[92]

Tom had attributed his acute anxiety at the time of the armistice to the strain of military uncertainty, but this was not the only reason for his nervous terror. Vivien admitted: "As soon as I can, I *really must,* I *ought to,* go to America. I say I, but I mean we." Overnight the armistice had removed their most powerful excuse for not visiting Tom's family, and now nothing stood in the way of the long-overdue introduction of Vivien to her in-laws. Despite Tom and Vivien's constant protestations to the contrary, there was nothing they feared more than a family reunion. "You are certainly the most wonderful woman of seventy-four I have ever heard of," Tom had written to his mother in November 1917; but fear was mingled with the admiration he felt for the formidable Charlotte, now President of the St.

Louis branch of the Colonial Dames of America, who never failed to reprimand her son if he failed to write his weekly letter.

Vivien was equally apprehensive. She could not fail to realise that her mother-in-law regarded her as a rival, if not an enemy, for having married Tom in 1915. She guessed that Charlotte held her responsible for her son's failure to return to America and philosophy. She confessed her part in this to Richard Aldington in 1922: "Once I fought like mad to keep Tom here and stopped his going back to America. I thought I could not marry him unless I was able to keep him here, in England."[93] In addition there were particular reasons for Vivien's nervousness over meeting Charlotte. First she was afraid of Tom's parents discovering her "invalidism," although she felt close enough to Henry to be painfully honest: "I am always now in such wretched health, and I am simply ashamed of it," she wrote in October 1918. *"I don't want them to know* . . . I wish something would bring you over here. I do wish it."[94]

There was another reason for Vivien's terror at the prospect of visiting America: she was afraid that Tom's family would consider her socially inferior. From 1936 Vivien signed her letters "Daisy Miller," taking the name of Henry James's heroine; she could not have failed to have read James's novella by 1917, when Eliot was working on the *Egoist*'s Henry James issue which came out in January 1918 and was written almost exclusively by Eliot himself. "Read *The Europeans* and *The Americans*, . . . and *Daisy Miller*," Tom told his cousin, explaining that he had a great admiration for James.[95] When Vivien read James's tale of a fresh, innocent "child of nature," who attracts a stiff young New Englander called Winterbourne, she immediately identified with the character. "I'm a fearful, frightful flirt," says Daisy. "Did you hear of a nice girl that was not? But I suppose you will tell me that I am not a nice girl." Winterbourne, whom Daisy notices is as stiff as an umbrella when she first meets him, is too well-connected to contemplate marrying someone who is not a "nice girl"—and his suspicions of Daisy are confirmed when Mrs. Costello, who comes from a distinguished New York family, declares of Daisy and her mother: "They are very common . . . They are the sort of Americans one does one's duty by not—not accepting."[96] This helps Winterbourne make up his mind about Daisy: "Evidently she was rather wild . . ." and, as Daisy compromises her reputation by going out unchaperoned with young men of dubious reputation, he concludes that she is not someone he wishes to know. James articulated Vivien's own deepest fear: that she was too "common" to be acceptable to Tom's family. "Daisy" is the name of a common flower; the surname "Miller" betrays roots in trade like those of Vivien's picture-framing grandfather. And Daisy's impropriety was another characteristic with which Vivien identified, and for which her husband condemned her. Although amusing in other members of the Bloomsbury group, immorality in his own wife had shocked Tom; after the end of her affair with Russell he no longer trusted Vivien although he remained protective of her, weighed down by a growing sense of responsibility for her ill-health, and the conviction, as he confessed to Russell, that living with him damaged her.

The events which followed Russell's release from prison compounded Vivien's unhappiness. His rapturous reunion with Colette, his "lamp in this dark world," had failed to take place as anticipated. Although the actress had written on 7 September 1918 that she longed for the moment when Bertie would stand at the door of his flat: "I'll put my arms round your dear straight shoulders & stroke yr heathery hair, & kiss you like a starving man & love every bit of you,"[97] in the event she was caught unawares by his early release. Russell left Brixton three weeks earlier than expected, on 14 September, due to remission for good behaviour. That evening found Colette dining with her new boyfriend, Colonel Mitchell, at Bury Street. Bertie was mortified. A jealous scene took place, the holiday at Ashford was cancelled, and he flounced out of his flat to sleep at his brother Frank's.

Disappointments crowded in on Russell thick and fast. He was no longer welcome at Frank's as a permanent house guest. Ottoline declined to come on holiday with him to Lulworth. Plaintively Bertie asked if he could stay at Garsington for four days a week. He even regretted leaving his wife Alys in 1911, who had been a faithful companion, complaining that, "Of course what I *really* want is a wife . . . I need looking after . . . Since I quarrelled with Alys I have never found anyone who would or could take me away on holidays."[98]

As other doors closed to him, Russell, at Colette's instigation, turned to the "suburban" Clifford Allen, who was struck by his guest's self-centredness: "He is very child-like in his engrossment with his own emotions, virtues, vices, and the effect he has upon other people," he noted in his diary. "The oddest mixture of candour and mystery, cruelty and affection . . ."[99]

It was inevitable that as soon as Russell had quarrelled with Colette, he would turn again to the Eliots. Colette was annoyed: "Eliot's prospects are clearly of far greater importance to B than the damage done between us,"[100] she wrote to her mother, Lady Annesley. But although Tom was prepared to accept Russell's help in September, when military service still seemed a likely prospect, Vivien was no longer inclined to co-operate. Bertie had hurt her deeply by the cavalier and insensitive fashion in which he had pulled out of the Marlow house, leaving Tom to find a tenant at short notice. She felt Russell had ignored her at a time when she and Tom were caught up in the "storm" of problems over his call-up. And now, having decided to share a flat with Clifford Allen at 70 Overstrand Mansions, Prince of Wales Road, Battersea, he was making peremptory demands for his furniture to be returned from Marlow.

Ten days after disturbing Colette's dinner with Mitchell, Bertie repented: "My dearest, I cannot clip your wings and put you in a cage. Go back to Mitchell if that is what you feel right."[101] Colette, on the other hand, seemed willing to give up her American colonel. The usual reconciliation took place at Lulworth, and during a holiday at Abinger with Allen, Bertie took Colette walking in the same Surrey hills in which he had taken Vivien, retracing the steps they had taken together over Leith Hill. "Gomshall is the station," wrote Russell. "I would meet you there, and would lunch with C.A. . . . You can do your walking here, where it is beautiful."[102] He bought Colette a stout pair of leather boots for £3 in preparation for his Christmas holiday with her and Allen at Lynton, North Devon, and sent her 10s. "allowance" as well.[103]

On 26 November Bertie took Vivien out to dinner. Writing from the studio, he related confidently to Colette: "My dinner with Mrs. Eliot passed off without disaster—she has been going through a rest-cure—I told her I should probably not be able to see her again for a considerable time."[104] It was his usual brush-off until such time as he needed Vivien's company again, but it met with a different rejoinder than he had anticipated. This time Vivien was no longer prepared to be kept dangling at

Russell's pleasure. Disillusioned by past disappointments, she took the initiative at last. In January 1919 she wrote to Russell saying that she disliked fading intimacies, and must therefore break off all friendship with him.[105]

"I do hope you aren't very distressed about Mrs. Eliot," wrote Colette. "I really don't know what to say about her letter—except that I'm distressed if *you* are."[106] It was not perhaps a wholly sincere remark. Colette must have been relieved to have, as she thought, at last disposed of her rival. On 22 January Bertie replied that he was not in the least distressed at the break with Mrs. Eliot. He too was being evasive. In February Colette was horrified to discover the extent of her lover's domestic and financial involvement with the Eliots, as Bertie was forced to tell her the truth about Marlow. "Mrs. Eliot's country house . . . had been let at a reduced rate to tenants who maintained that it was only half furnished," recorded Colette.[107] The tenants were moving out, and therefore Eliot wrote that he wished to see Russell, as the house would be left on his hands. Russell then suggested to Colette that he might take over the house himself.

It was not a proposition which pleased Colette. It was difficult to give an opinion about Mrs. Eliot's house, she wrote sarcastically,

> mainly because I know so little about it. I quite see all the points you make, but I also see things against them. As her house is in a town, it wouldn't be a decent substitute for real country holidays; and I think your summer would be more fruitful for work if you were in peaceful country or in a farm by the sea. I'm not much in favour of business and property involvements; and I think you've enough of them already.

Russell was, as Colette emphasised, already over-extended. He was "not *completely* free of the Studio" (which was let to author Frank Swinnerton from 2 December 1918). "Were I run over tomorrow, you'd have this flat (Bury Street) on your hands; half of Allen's flat is still on your hands. I grant you that Battersea was my idea; but I didn't know then that you were still involved with Mrs. Eliot's house . . . I think you are really trying for two birds with one stone."[108]

Colette's judgement was more accurate than she realised, for Russell had continued to write to Vivien despite having assured Colette he was no longer seeing Mrs. E. Colette wrote loyally to Russell that "I think Eliot has no right to worry you. He's known, ever since Brixton in July, that he'd have the house on his hands. And if, as you say, houses are hard to get, then they're not hard to get rid of."[109] Eliot was furious that Russell had refused to abide by Vivien's decision that there should be an end to the relationship. He had begun to blame his wife's ill-health on Bertie: "It is not the case that Vivien 'won't reply'—I have taken the whole business of Marlow into my hands, as she cannot have anything to do with this or with anything else that would interfere with the success of her doctor's treatment," he wrote sharply. He had heard from the tenants who had at first offered to keep on the house at a lower rent because of the lack of furniture, but had decided on Saturday to leave on 29 March—"So after that date I shall be able to get at your things."[110]

"Sorry about Marlow but it can't be helped," wrote Russell airily on 27 February, explaining that he could not meet Eliot as requested because Allen had influenza and so he had been "forced back" to Garsington while he recovered. With breathtaking insensitivity, Russell continued to harass Eliot for his possessions, requesting that he return his copy of Synge to Gordon Square. "It is a book I value, & I had often wondered what became of it."[111] Colette, meanwhile, had organised the moving of Russell's other books, and his favourite "green Brixton vase" from Bury Street to Battersea in December.[112]

In February the meeting between Eliot and Russell finally took place, but not until the Eliots' servant Ellen, who was ill with pneumonia, had gone to hospital, did Tom have an opportunity to discuss with Vivien the future of the Marlow house. She was distraught at the prospect of losing it: "Dear Bertie," wrote Tom on 14 February 1919, "I am afraid that night I was only thinking of my own point of view towards Marlow. The idea of parting with the house altogether had not before occurred to me; with so many worries on my mind I lost sight of how attached Vivien is to the house and garden . . . I found she was extraordinarily upset at the thought of parting with it. She worked very hard at it during the spring and summer and put so much thought and so many hopes into it. The garden in particular is such a great joy and source of activity to her that now there are so few things she may do, as you know, I am sure it would be a mistake to deprive her of this interest."

Vivien was always thinking about the garden, said Tom, and even while the tenants had been in residence she had visited several times to look after it.[113]

Russell brushed aside Tom's concerns for Vivien and her garden. His mind remained focused on his own needs. On 19 March he sent Tom a list of his possessions he wished returned at once, asking him on no account to send anything to Gordon Square. Tom was to inform him when he was sending the things, and how, as "I don't want to have to go to Marlow myself if necessary . . . I should like the tea-table & coffee-grinder as soon as possible. Love to Vivien. How are your troubles?"[114]

The Eliots' "troubles" had taken a new turn on 7 January 1919 with the sudden death of Tom's father, aged seventy-six. "A fearful day and evening," wrote Vivien in her diary. She wisely withheld the cable until Tom returned from the bank. His first thoughts were of his mother, and he wrote at once to tell her how much he loved her. The death of Henry Ware Eliot Sr. heightened Tom's desperate need to prove himself to his family. Only the day before the news of the death of his father had reached him, Tom had written to John Quinn asking him to chase up the manuscript of prose and poetry he had sent to Knopf two months earlier. "You see I settled over here in the face of strong family opposition, on the claim that I found the environment more favourable to the production of literature," he wrote. "The book is all I have to show for my claim." It would, he argued, go some way towards satisfying his parents that he had not made a mess of his life.[115] His father's death made his task more urgent, as he explained a few days later—"This does not weaken the need for a book at all—it really reinforces it—my mother is still alive."[116]

Tom's sense that his father had died disappointed in his son weighed heavily upon him. In February he again had "a sort of collapse," nursed once more by Vivien as Ellen was still recovering from pneumonia. Eliot's doctor ordered him to spend a week in bed, where he slept almost continuously. "I am so tired now that it has ceased to be becoming," Vivien told Mary, explaining that she had not been able to get outside the door to telephone as she was nursing Tom continuously. "You see Tom depends on me for every meal, and I am cooking, cleaning and nursing all day long."[117] As he slowly recovered, Tom agonised over the failure of his relationship with his parents, two lonely people who had little connection with each other.

Fretting also over his inability to publish more poetry ("I have written so little, I have so little time to write"), he confessed to his brother Henry, "I feel very played out."[118]

The bickering over the furniture continued, and the Eliots' dilatoriness—as Russell perceived it—in this respect became the rock on which their mutual friendship finally foundered. Tom decided to keep on the Marlow house, in view of Vivien's dismay at the prospect of its loss, and told Russell he hoped that there would be fewer misfortunes in the future. He promised that, if the weather was moderate, Vivien would go down next week to fetch Russell's furniture,[119] but when she made the journey in April Vivien could find no one to help her carry the tea-table to the station. She wrote to him apologetically that she was going again the next day— "unless my cold turns to influenza"—to try to bring up the table and whatever else she could carry. Then there was the problem of getting "this first collection" conveyed to Bertie's address in Battersea. "I am sorry it has been so long, & I am afraid it will take a good many journeys before you have everything. So please have patience!"[120]

"I will call for the small tea-table at Crawford Mansions on Monday afternoon with a taxi—it can be taken loose," replied Russell in a frigid note to Tom, for he no longer communicated with Vivien. "Please mention that I shall be coming for it between 3 & 4." The triple *ménage,* which had once been so close, had finally unravelled. Once Tom would have turned to Russell, his surrogate father, on the death of his own father, but it was a role that Russell was no longer prepared to fill. Instead of benefactor he had become importunate and impecunious, an ageing Romeo whose prolonged and painful affair with Vivien had done irreparable harm to the Eliot marriage, and whom Tom wished only to forget. And, since Bertie had already served his purpose in Eliot's ascent of the literary ladder, his former student had few regrets over the withering of the friendship. Moreover, John Middleton Murry, the new editor of the *Athenaeum,* had just made Tom "the very flattering offer" of the assistant editorship of the literary weekly at £500 a year. It offered him social prestige, more leisure and more money.[121]

Vivien, on the other hand, was left with a lacerating sense of failure. "Like the sunshine," wrote Russell's daughter Kate of her father, "he could be loved while his warmth was upon you, but he could not be grasped to hold. Those who tried found themselves with a shadow upon their hands; the sunshine had escaped and was shining on someone else."[122] Like Colette and Helen Dudley, Vivien found it hard to dwell in the light without him. To be loved by Bertie was an intense experience none of these women found it possible to replicate and, despite his solipsism, they often remained devoted. Although Russell cannot be blamed for Vivien's subsequent mental deterioration, his acrimonious desertion of her destabilised her and contributed to her later depression and neurotic fear of abandonment. Had he remained her friend, as he did with Ottoline, she would have been better placed to overcome the trials ahead.

Now, though, a new triangle was forming. On 4 March 1919 Tom wrote to Mary, who he had heard was lunching with Vivien the next Thursday. Would she come on later and dance with him at a place near Baker Street, he asked. They could learn the new steps together, and dine afterwards. "I think it would be rather fun ... Do come."[123] In this new threesome Vivien was to be the dupe.

II

Possum's Revenge

In the immediate post-war years Vivien entered a new phase of gratifying social success. Those qualities which had attracted the attention of two of the most brilliant men in England,[1] her husband and Bertrand Russell, contributed to her popularity and Tom's. The Eliots' penetration of Bloomsbury as well as the acquisition of new friends such as the Sitwells and Sydney and Violet Schiff, is reflected in Vivien's "busy" 1919 diary: teas with Ottoline, outings to the Russian ballet with Sachie Sitwell for the first night of *The Three-Cornered Hat,* a literary party at Edith's, dinner parties for Aldous Huxley and picnics in Itchenor woods with Mary and Jack Hutchinson filled her often "perfect" days.[2] It seemed that Vivien had found the acceptance she had sought and, in her affectionate friendship with Mary, consolation for her break with Russell.

The three Sitwells, Osbert, Edith and Sacheverell, began to meet the Eliots regularly in the afternoons in "dank London tea-shops, seemingly papered or panelled in their own damp tea-leaves" near Marble Arch or Oxford Street. Vivien would be the first to arrive, and then Tom would come from his bank by Underground, and join them in consuming hot tea and muffins. "Tea-drinking is not a habit of Americans," remarked Osbert, who concluded that for Tom it possessed an exotic charm that it lacked for the English. But it was very noticeable how, though obviously very tired, Tom at once made an effort to stimulate the party. Osbert was struck by the contrast between his diction, the slow, careful, attractive voice, "which always held in it, far down and subjugated, an American lilt and an American sound of r's," the sharp observation evident in everything he said, and his old-fashioned courtesy.

In the early days of Osbert's friendship with the Eliots Vivien was kind and attentive to him. "I could not but like her," he recalled later. "She was slightly built, and had brown hair, and eyes which ranged from blue to green and were her chief attraction, being very expressive of her moods . . . Certainly her gaiety made her good company."[3] It was a description similar to that given by Richard Aldington in *Stepping Heavenward,* a satirical short story in which Vivien is lightly disguised as "Adèle Paleologue," a governess, and Eliot as Jeremy Cibber, a young American from Colonsville (St. Louis) in the Midwest who has come to Europe. It is Adèle's "deep grey eyes [which] were so effective under her neat black hair"; the "emotional spotlights" of her large eyes arouse Cibber's sympathy although the match is an unhappy one.

Aldington, who became bitterly jealous of Eliot's fame in the late 1920s, defends Adèle who he considers has, like the wives of many great men, been severely blamed.

> Enthusiastic admirers . . . forget that in these days the hero's inevitable valet is nearly always his wife. And they forget that Adèle was one of the earliest to proclaim Cibber's genius and to push him on in the world. Is she really to be blamed because she, an ordinary woman, could not dwell happily on the austere mountain heights of spiritual elevation? Could she help it if his presence— owing to the will of God, no doubt—drove her into neurasthenia? After all, it must be rather a shock to think you are marrying a nice young American and then to discover that you have bedded with an angel unawares.[4]

Aldington implies that Eliot was impotent, and the pair "though wedded in the sight of God and man, grew more hysterical daily simply through having to inhabit the same tank-like flat."

The Sitwell trio also often lunched with the Eliots in the "tank-like flat" in Crawford Mansions. Osbert experienced the same sense of confinement as Aldington in the grey distempered drawing-room, sparsely furnished and cramped. On the walls there hung a cluster of small outline drawings of elephants, executed in green ink, drawn by Eliot's grandmother. Osbert was struck by the "shrine" to Tom's family which grew in size over the years: old photographs, silhouettes and miniatures of the Eliot and Stearns families hung over the chimneypiece, until it seemed that something begun in mockery had established a genuine hold on Tom. "Vivienne's taste was not shown in the decoration of the flat," observed Sitwell: her early efforts to impress her personality on the flat gradually became subsumed under his, and it was Eliot's character which pervaded his surroundings.[5]

Noise they still found difficult to tolerate, although the flat was on the top floor, since both suffered from insomnia. There were the nightly shouts of "Hurry up please, it's time," from the pub opposite, lines which found their way into *The Waste Land,* and in the flat below the Eliots lived two sisters, "actresses," who occasionally appeared in suburban pantomime but spent most of their time playing the piano, singing, or playing loud records on the gramophone. About midnight the women would throw open their windows and call down to their "gentlemen friends" standing on the pavement several storeys below. This disturbance often continued into the small hours, interrupting Eliot's efforts to write or sleep, until at last, after several bouts of illness, he wrote to the landlord to complain. This gentleman came to see him in person, and reproved the poet: "Well, you see, Sir, it's the Artistic Temperament: We ordinary folk must learn to make allowances for artists. They're not the same as us!" Although the sisters prevented Eliot working, Osbert conjectured that they supplied much of the material for *Sweeney Agonistes.* Similarly, in this dark, cramped flat Osbert listened to two voices, one "querulous and insistent," the other, he considered, "patient and wise," which he later recognised in *The Waste Land.*[6]

In 1918 Osbert Sitwell had become an editor of the quarterly *Art and Letters,* which was financed by Sydney Schiff, his Holy Ghost, as he dubbed the wealthy patron of the arts who wrote novels under the pseudonym Stephen Hudson, and to whom he had introduced Tom and Vivien. Osbert invited Eliot to contribute to the new periodical, a compliment which Eliot returned by publishing the Sitwells in *Egoist.* The second number of *Art and Letters* in spring 1919 carried prose by Eliot and Wyndham Lewis, as well as poetry by Siegfried Sassoon, Herbert Read and Osbert; and in the summer "Burbank with a Baedeker: Bleistein with a Cigar," and "Sweeney Erect" were published. Neither Schiff himself, Osbert, nor the other editors, Frank Rutter and Herbert Read, troubled to censor Eliot's contemptuous anti-Semitism, expressed in lines such as: "The rats are underneath the piles./The Jew is underneath the lot./Money in furs."[7]

Anthony Julius, a lawyer and critic, has written that "Burbank resonates with anti-Semitic scorn."[8] Bleistein walks "with the palms turned out./Chicago Semite Viennese." He is, suggests Eliot, as parasitic and diseased as a rat:

A lustreless protrusive eye
Stares from the protozoic slime

These verses were written during the period 1917–22, in which the bulk of Eliot's anti-Semitic poetry was composed, years in which his long-established misogyny also took on a new virulence. Misogyny and anti-Semitism were historical partners in nineteenth-century Europe, expressed in the Symbolist and Decadent movements; and this historical linkage formed part of the context for Eliot's writing. However, Julius argues that Eliot had another purpose in combining the Jewish and the female, as he did in a string of names which resonate with disgust: Rachel née Rabinovitch, Lady Kleinwurm, and Lady Katzegg, "whose names are ugly and betray their owners." Unlike the women in *Prufrock*, however, "these Jews do not intimidate. By making women Jewish, Eliot overcame them; by subordinating them to Jews, he diminished them."[9]

Vivien seems to have shared Eliot's prejudices, which were deeply ingrained in British society at the time: Virginia Stephen was conscious of her own anti-Semitism when she married Leonard Woolf. Vivien later reviewed in the *Criterion* a book by G. B. Stern, *The Tents of Israel,* under one of her many pen-names, Irene Fassett, and stated that "no Jew can ever be a great artist:" the best a Jew can do by dint of cleverness and hard work is "a marvellous imitation of art."[10] She would have read "Burbank," for Tom respected her literary judgement but in any case, as a future member of the British League of Fascists, Vivien was unlikely to have made any objection.[11] Neither she nor Tom saw any contradiction in accepting the hospitality of Jews such as Schiff, who with his invalid wife Violet became close friends of the Eliots, or Leonard Woolf in 1919, and writing (in "Gerontion"):

... the jew squats on the window-sill, the owner,
Spawned in some estaminet of Antwerp,
Blistered in Brussels ...[12]

As Eliot's fame spread, even more illustrious literary allies than the Sitwells decided they wished to know the poet. Virginia and Leonard Woolf had made their first approach in the autumn of 1918 after reading *Prufrock and Other Observations:* they invited Eliot to Hogarth House, Richmond, and offered to publish his new poetry under the imprint of their fledgling Hogarth Press. It was to be a prestige project for the Woolfs, who considered it their best work yet, owing to the quality of the ink as well as of the poetry.[13] When Eliot visited the Woolfs on 15 November, he impressed Virginia as

a polished, cultivated, elaborate young American, talking so slow, that each word seems to have special finish allotted it. But beneath the surface, it is fairly evident that he is very intellectual, intolerant, with strong views of his own, & a poetic creed.

Virginia disagreed with Eliot's view that Ezra Pound and Wyndham Lewis[14] were "very interesting" writers, and was horrified that he admired James Joyce, whose novel *Ulysses* she considered "filth" and had already refused to publish.[15] But these differences did not prevent the Woolfs' printing nearly 250 copies of Eliot's poems on 12 May 1919 at 2/6d each.[16]

The publication of *Poems* was an important landmark in Eliot's ascent of the literary foothills, although he was still far from being the social lion that Lytton Strachey had become with the publication of *Eminent Victorians* in 1919. Such recognition perhaps gave Eliot the confidence to turn down Middleton Murry's offer of the assistant editorship of the *Athenaeum* at £500 per annum, but it was far from being the only reason for his decision. Eliot's inherent caution led him to distrust the prospects of a new literary weekly, for the paper had lost its character as a monthly under the old ownership and there was no guarantee, even with Murry at the helm, that it would succeed. In that case he calculated that he would be left in difficulties after his two-year contract expired. But Eliot's chief reason for turning down the offer, despite the higher salary, was the "drudgery" of journalism. "The constant turning out of 'copy' for a weekly paper would exhaust me for genuine creative work," he wrote to his mother on 29 March 1919.[17] Finance he could attend to "mechanically" but review-writing he could not, and so he chose to remain in the bank, where a new department was being opened which offered him the chance of more interesting economic work connected with the German war debt, and where he was certain of regular increases in salary. He was earning £360 a year, and was now, he told his mother, almost self-supporting.

Eliot's rejection of Murry's offer appeared a strange decision to the couple's friends, and it is one for which Vivien has been blamed. One of the charges laid against Vivien was that she pressed Tom to stay at Lloyds with its promise of a pension and medical benefits.[18] In fact, if Vivien had had her way Eliot would have left the bank in 1919. Nevertheless, Osbert Sitwell represented the commonly held point of view when he wrote:

> Never was there such a waste of a poet's days. In order to find money for the household, he was obliged to follow the, to him, exhausting and uncongenial profession of a clerk in Lloyd's Bank in the City.

Aldington was scornful rather than sympathetic. "With superb energy, Cibber made a decision—and what a mad world it was!—accepted work as the guiding spirit of a haberdashery department, where his courteous manners and distinguished appearance found full scope."[19] Yet in 1919 Vivien was in favour of Tom accepting the post Murry had offered him on the *Athenaeum,* as Eliot confirmed to Aldington in 1922.[20] It was Tom's choice to stay at Lloyds.

During 1919 Vivien's health was generally good. She was fit and extrovert enough to socialise four nights a week; in one week in November she had the Pounds to dinner on Monday, Ottoline on Tuesday, dined at Pagani's and went to a concert given by the Syncopated Orchestra on Wednesday, had tea-parties on Thursday and Friday, entertained the Pounds to dinner again on Friday, and had Schiff in for coffee afterwards, attended her dress-making class and went for the weekend to the musician Arnold Dolmetsch and his family at Haslemere.[21] Within the household

Fleet Street, the birthplace of Charles Haigh-Wood in Bury, Lancashire.
Vivienne was born in nearby Knowsley Street.

Rose Esther Haigh-Wood with Vivienne in
1898. Maurice, age three, stands behind.

Family group: Charles Haigh-Wood
with Rose, Vivie and Maurice.

(*right*) *The Peace Offering*, 1900:
a portrait of Vivienne and Maurice by
their father, Charles Haigh-Wood, at
their house in Hampstead. Maurice has
torn up Vivie's reading book and offers
her an apple as a peace offering. Vivie
often modelled for her father, whose
paintings were reproduced as greeting
cards.

(*below*) Vivienne in 1900. As a child she
was ill with TB of the bone.

(*below right*) Vivie visiting Maurice, age
seventeen, at Malvern College.

Henry Ware Eliot Sr.,
brick manufacturer.
He was profoundly deaf.

Charlotte Champe Eliot;
Thomas Stearns was her
seventh child.

Tom Eliot at four years old.

Tom Eliot with his mother, his sister Margaret and cousin Henrietta
outside 2635 Locust Street, St. Louis, 1896.

(*left*) T. S. Eliot as a young man.

(*below left*) Jean Verdenal, Eliot's close companion in Paris.

(*below right*) The announcement of the marriage of Thomas Eliot and Vivien Haigh-Wood in the *St. Louis Globe Democrat*, 16 July 1915.

THOMAS ELIOT OF ST. LOUIS WEDS ABROAD

Bride of Oxford Student Was Miss Vivien Haigh-Wood, Daughter of a Member of Royal Academy of Arts.

Announcement of the marriage of Thomas Stearns Eliot, son of Mr. and Mrs. Henry W. Eliot of 4446 Westminster place, to Miss Vivien Haigh-Wood in London, England, June 26, was made yesterday by the Eliots, who are at their summer home in Gloucester, Mass.

Henry W. Eliot, Jr., said last night that he had been notified of his brother's marriage, through his mother. He said that Thomas Eliot had been in London taking a year's course in philosophy at the Oxford University. He said he knew little of Miss Haigh-Wood, but understood that she was a daughter of a member of the Royal Academy of Arts.

Eliot, who is 26 years old, was graduated from Smith Academy in 1905 and Harvard in 1910. He went to London more than a year ago and entered Oxford. Eliot's father is chairman of the Board of Directors of the Hydraulic Press Brick Company.

A stylish couple. Tom and Vivien in the early years of their marriage, *c.* 1920.

Tom has gone to America
without me, & arrived
yesterday. Rather
unwise perhaps to leave
so attractive a wife
alone & other new
devices !. However —
I did not at all want
to go - I am much too
frightened of the voyage
& the submarines — &
preferred to remain & play
my own little games
alone.

Tom is supposed to be coming
back by September 1st, & after we
have had a second honeymoon! we
shall have taken up a house or a flat
of our own - in London of course. It is
very nice being Mrs Stearns-Eliot (notice
the hyphen) — I am very popular with
Tom's friends - & who do you think
in particular? No less a person
than Bertrand Russell !! He is
all over me, is Bertie, & I simply
love him. I am dining with him
next week. I see a good deal
of the Pounds, of course, & between
ourselves, find them rather boring.

Two extracts from a letter from Vivien to Scofield Thayer, 2 August 1915,
announcing Bertrand Russell's interest in her.

"Mr. Apollinax": Bertrand Russell, Lytton Strachey and Lady Ottoline Morrell, at the time of Russell's affair with Vivien, 1916.

Bertrand Russell in 1916. Vivien worked as his secretary during his campaign against conscription in the First World War.

Lady Constance Malleson, the actress "Colette O'Niel," who was Russell's mistress.

Maurice Haigh-Wood, age twenty-four.

American poet and critic Ezra Pound sitting on his bed in his Paris studio.

Mark Gertler (*behind*), Philip Morrell, Lady Ottoline and Vivien at Garsington, August 1921.

Vivien, in dance costume, playing croquet.

Ottoline and T. S. Eliot at Garsington.

her role was often that of caregiver rather than patient. For several weeks in February and March Vivien had nursed Ellen, her servant, through the first stages of pneumonia ("very fatiguing and unpleasant" in Tom's eyes) as well as caring for Tom himself, who had collapsed at the news of his father's death. She also nursed her mother, who had no servants and was ill in bed. In addition, she was responsible for all the housework and laundry. "Vivien is very tired and looks very ill," Tom told Henry on 27 February:[22] "I have been and am still very afraid of Vivien's breaking down," he confessed in a letter to his mother on the same day—as so often, projecting his own fears of nervous collapse onto Vivien.[23]

Vivien nevertheless found both time and energy for pleasure. It was the birth of the jazz age and, only a few days after Tom's letters to his family, on 2 March, her diary records an outing to the Elysée Galleries to dance with a friend named Hawkinson and "the boy," with whom she had "a splendid time."[24] The next day she was very tired, but still went over to Compayne Gardens to lunch with her parents and help them, before hurrying back to "get T's meal" and doing housework all evening. At the beginning of November she was nursing their friend and neighbour, Arthur Dakyns, at Marlow with Tom, returning to London when her aunt Emily, Charles Haigh-Wood's sister, fell seriously ill, taking her mother to Victoria Station, travelling to Eastbourne for Emily's funeral, and still finding time for another outing to the dance halls the next day. "Went to dance at Caxton Hall with Freddy," recorded Vivien. "Much against the grain, but enjoyed it."[25]

Vivien's courage and physical stamina in a crisis is underlined by an admiring letter of Tom's which relates the events surrounding a sailing expedition which took place in Chichester harbour in June 1919. Eliot and Dakyns had driven down for the weekend in Dakyns' motor car to Bosham, where Vivien was spending the summer. On the Sunday the party hired a boat and sailed with Sacheverell Sitwell and Mary Hutchinson down Chichester harbour to Wittering, where the Hutchinsons lived. There they had a picnic lunch, and Vivien took some photographs. The sailing, confessed Tom, was "rather disastrous." There was no proper place to land and the crew was forced to put the boat up on a beach. Tom was at the helm and, attempting to sail into the wind, got stuck on a sandbank on a falling tide. Soon they were left "high, but not very dry." "Captain" Eliot broke the boat hook trying to push off, eventually throwing out an anchor and wading ashore with his crew on planks because of the soft sinking mud. "Vivien is splendid in a boat, she took off her stockings and jumped off and tried to push," Tom told his mother.[26] It seems he played the incident down, for Sacheverell later often related the tale of how he and Eliot nearly drowned in Chichester harbour.

On occasions Vivien ventured alone in a sailing dinghy to visit Mary at Eleanor, with apparently more attention to the tide and fewer accidents than her husband. On one "wonderful day" in July she started in the boat early, rowed from Bosham all the way to Eleanor to pick up Mary, and sailed to Hayling Island, where they bathed and picnicked together and, as they lay on the sand, Mary told Vivien the story of her life; afterwards Vivien landed Mary back at Itchenor before sailing the boat back to Bosham at 6 p.m. Although she was exhausted by the outing, Mary had been "delightful."[27] The normality, even heartiness revealed in Vivien's diary, in which she records swimming even when it is very cold, sailing and walking, getting "soaked" in damp woods, but having successful picnics[28] contradicts the myth of her constant illness.

Anne Olivier Bell, editor of Virginia Woolf's diaries, comments with reference to a remark of Virginia's that Vivien looked "washed-out" in April: "She suffered increasingly from psychotic illness and this began to show in her appearance."[29] Judging retrospectively, many commentators forgot that Vivien did enjoy periods of good health during the earlier years of her marriage. Nor should the evidence of a novelist such as Woolf, who had her own reasons for distancing herself from Vivien, be accepted at face value. In 1919 Vivien speaks for herself. It is the only year of her marriage for which her diary survives, and it serves as a warning against accepting the judgement of biased observers.

Meanwhile Tom, free of the daily intrigues and demands of journalism, was able to write what he wanted. "There is a small and select public which regards me as the best living critic, as well as the best living poet in England," he proudly informed his mother. As contributor to the *Athenaeum,* where Murry, the editor-in-chief, was one of his most cordial admirers, as assistant editor of the *Egoist*[30] and with the new outlet of *Art and Letters,* which was glad to take anything he gave it, Eliot's position was a privileged one. He had more than enough prestige to satisfy him, he told Charlotte: "I really think that I have far more *influence* on English letters than any other American has ever had, unless it be Henry James. I know a great many people, but there are many more who would like to know me, and I can remain isolated and detached. All this sounds very conceited but it is true . . ."[31]

To his brother Henry, Eliot repeated Vivien's argument that he must conserve his creative energy for his own writing: "My reputation is built on writing very little, but very good." He calculated that he probably had more influence, power and distinction "*outside* the journalistic struggle" than within it.[32] To J. H. Woods he made the point that a poet's best work, the only work that counts in the end, is written for oneself. If one had to earn a living, therefore, the safest occupation was that most remote from the arts. Eliot's carefully thought-out strategy, designed to keep up his reputation as the "best living" critic and poet, was to keep his public hungry: his plan was to release only two or three new poems a year. The only thing that mattered was that these should be perfect in their kind, so that each should be an event.[33]

Money was also a factor in Eliot's decision. He was "deeply affected," believed Stephen Spender, "by the fact that his father left his family money in trust so that if he, Tom Eliot, died, it could not be inherited by his wife."[34] Henry Ware Eliot Sr. did not leave Tom a direct legacy, but this did not mean his son derived no benefit from the will. Eliot's habit of financial dependency on others continued after 1918, just as it had when, writes Paul Delany, he "came close to being paid for being a complaisant husband" by Russell. Delany estimates that Eliot and Vivien received about £100 a year from Charlotte and Henry from 1916 to 1919; in this period they "received twice the amount of Tom's earnings as gifts from his parents, Vivien's parents, and Russell." On Henry Ware Eliot's death on 7 January 1919, he left his silver cane to Tom, and about $3,000 worth of shares in the Hydraulic Press-Brick Company to each of three daughters and the residue to his widow to provide for his two sons. Delany writes that the probate value of the estate was $258,159 net, divided between $117,807 in shares (mostly in Hydraulic Press-Brick preferred) and

$128,000 in real estate. "As befitted a brick-maker, Henry Ware Eliot had been an inveterate buyer of building-lots in St. Louis,"[35] which featured in his son's early poems.

Soon after Henry Ware Eliot's death, his elder son, Henry Ware Eliot Jr., began selling off the family shares in the Hydraulic Press-Brick Company and moving into a portfolio of stocks and tax-exempt bonds in order to provide income for his mother and his siblings. Charlotte Eliot gave each of her six children 225 preferred shares of Hydraulic Press-Brick early in 1920, when they had already risen from the $30 probate valuation to $55 because of the postwar housing boom. Tom sold his shares in November at that price, and turned over $12,000 to Henry to invest for him. Henry invested the money at seven per cent. Charlotte gave Tom another 120 shares in the summer of 1923, which he sold at $64. "He now had an inherited capital of about $19,000, on which he earned $1400 a year." When his mother died Tom had expectations of receiving about another $35,000.

Charlotte's disapproval of Vivien was thus "the only blemish on Tom's rosy prospects." After the estate was settled Charlotte decided to give Tom further shares in trust rather than outright, against her son Henry's urging. In October 1920 Tom wrote a strong letter to his mother, telling her that if he died he wanted Vivien to receive his inheritance, but Charlotte pursed her lips and reserved judgment; she would wait until she met her English daughter-in-law. Meanwhile, Tom's sense of injustice grew: out of the other siblings only his sister Margaret, who was mentally handicapped, was to have her shares in trust; Henry and his other sisters were given their shares without restriction. This discrimination rankled with Tom, who deeply resented being treated in the same way as Margaret, on account of his marriage to Vivien.[36] Not until his mother had visited England would he know whether he could persuade her to change her mind.

Nevertheless, Eliot's sister-in-law, Theresa (wife of Henry Eliot), confirmed in 1970 that Tom had received a private income from the family trust. She did not know exactly what Tom's was, "but Marian (Tom's sister) yielded Eighteen hundred a year, and the estate was about 350,000 my husband told me. So Tom had additional financial help in 1919."[37] The pity that Tom's friends felt for his apparent financial plight was ill-founded. Pound, who later crusaded to raise funds in order that Tom might leave the bank, "did not know that Eliot was already endowed with a private income larger than his own," writes Delany.[38] Poverty and the "burden" of Vivien were, therefore, never the deciding factors in Eliot's decision to stay in Lloyds.

It was not long after meeting Leonard and Virginia Woolf that Tom and Vivien became drawn into the quarrels and intrigues of the Bloomsbury group. Vivien, emotional and sharp-tongued, was ill-fitted for the jealous squabbles of a self-regarding clique who thrived on gossip and mystery. Tom's cat-like stealth, his aptitude for "playin' possum," for smiling as he stalked his prey, was more suited to these ephemeral but fierce battles of will.

The honeymoon period between the Woolfs and the Eliots lasted into the spring of 1919, as Virginia and Leonard laboured to print and cover Eliot's *Poems* and Virginia's *Kew Gardens* on the hand-press at Paradise Road, Richmond. Both were to be published on the same day, 12 May.[39] On 6 April 1919 Tom and Vivien dined with the Woolfs and chose the cover for *Poems*. Subsequently, on 12 April, Eliot sent Virginia a list of people to whom he wanted a circular advertising the book to be sent prior to publication. But no circulars arrived. Vivien and Tom grew agitated. From 39 Inverness Terrace, W2, where she was lodging while their flat was being redecorated, Vivien wrote to Mary, asking what they should do:

> Tom has for a long time been very much worried, puzzled, and *annoyed* at the Woolfs' behaviour about his poems which they were, as you know, printing ... *No one* has received a circular about the book. This is very awkward ... He gave them several poems to print which are *not* published elsewhere, and has been counting on this book of the Woolfs' for showing them. *I mean* certain people are *asking* to see these poems in order to publish them, and Tom has been waiting and waiting for this Woolf book, to show them.

Vivien suspected the worst: "Now Mary, do you think that out of revenge, the W's are actually going to shelve the whole of those books of Tom's which they have printed? If they do, what a humiliation for Tom!" She was angry and unhappy on Tom's behalf: "If a man is sensitive and an artist, he can't stand these people."

If Leonard and Virginia were going to throw up the book, threatened Vivien, she would go round and have it out with them.

> Yet, *if* I *did,* I believe that Tom would never speak to me again. He would *hate* me. He hates and loathes all sordid quarrelling and gossiping and intrigue and jealousy *so much,* that I have seen him go white and *be ill* at any manifestation of it.

Ezra Pound had been ruined by literary feuds and see what he has become, said Vivien—a laughingstock. Only "a person of coarse fibre," like Wyndham Lewis, could stick it and remain undamaged. As for Mary, who had gossiped indiscreetly to Clive Bell over Tom's problems with the Woolfs, she must say nothing more to her lover, declared Vivien. "If you do the whole matter will end in complete estrangement between us. *I know it.* Leave Clive *out of it* . . . If you do not do what I say *about this*—I will never be a friend of yours again. I will not . . . Goodbye dear Mary I am not angry with *you,* but I am very much worried."[40]

Tom appears to have been speaking equally wildly against the Woolfs to Mary, and she had repeated his remarks to Clive who, jealous of Tom, had not hesitated to pass them on. Soon Tom's criticisms of the Woolfs reached Virginia's ears: "By the way, Mary rang me up yesterday in great agitation about Eliot, imploring me to say nothing, denying the whole story, and insisting that he only abused Bloomsbury in general, and not me, and that Clive had completely misunderstood!" Virginia told Vanessa.[41] The situation was complicated by the fact that, as Eliot explained to his cousin, Eleanor Hinkley, "A" (Mary) hated "B" (Virginia), of whom she was jealous; "A" therefore repeated Tom's remarks to "D" (Clive), who disliked him because "A" (Mary) liked him. "The sequel is that 'G' (Ottoline) is jealous of 'A.'[42] She hears that I spent a weekend at 'A's house. She promptly invites me for a weekend . . ." In associating themselves so closely with Mary Hutchinson the Eliots ran the risk of incurring the same hostility she encountered from other members of Bloomsbury, who were irritated by Clive's constant praise of his mistress. In October 1918, it had been reported, Mary had been "conveyed about London in a fainting condition in taxicabs,"[43] and Duncan Grant explained why in a letter to Lytton Strachey:

> That idiot Virginia went and told Gertler that we all despised and disliked Mary and only put up with her as a concubine of Clive's, which is perfectly untrue but which of course Gertler immediately tells Mary and she of course bursts into tears in the Cafe Royal and had to be taken home in a cab and you are thought to be the only person to cheer her up. Really Virginia and Ottoline are almost as bad as one another.[44]

That crisis blew over. By February 1919, Clive, Mary and Virginia were all three "chattering like a perch of parrakeets," although Virginia took a malicious delight in April in telling Duncan how Vanessa snubbed Mary at a party given by Roger: Vanessa approached the sofa where Mary was sitting, "decked like a butterfly in May—and said 'Its time you got off that sofa, Mary.'" This snub became part of the Bloomsbury repertory: "Katherine (Mansfield) acted it too yesterday," wrote a gleeful Virginia: "Its time you got off the sofa, Mary."[45]

Eliot enjoyed these spats, which he found an intellectual challenge, despite Vivien's claim that he hated gossip and intrigue. It was, he said, the sort of thing that was going on continually in a society where everyone was very sensitive, very perceptive, and very quick, and a dinner party demanded more skill and exercised one's psychological gifts more than the best fencing match or duel. "It does use one's brains!"[46] Vivien, as a very new acquaintance of Bloomsbury's founders, but one who wore her heart on her sleeve, was rash to criticise the Woolfs so openly. In May Vivien told Mary that Leonard had written very curtly to Tom to say he had lost the list. "I saw the letter, It could not have been curter . . . I really always rather hate a man who takes up his wife's feuds, don't you?"[47] Virginia, needless to say, could take offence as quickly as Vivien. After entertaining the Eliots in early April, she wrote: "I amused myself by seeing how sharp, narrow, & much of a stick Eliot has come to be since he took to disliking me." She laughed at Vivien's snobbery, judging her guest to be a "worn looking little woman, who was relieved to find Walter Lamb with his stories about the King provided for her."[48] This Bloomsbury imbroglio took an unexpected twist on 17 April when Virginia told Duncan that "the mystery of Eliot was further thickened by hearing how he'd praised me to the skies" to the Murrys. Now she had a letter from Eliot asking her and Leonard to dinner, and was determined "to draw the rat from his hole."[49]

Vivien could never outsmart Virginia, but her blood was up. She accepted an invitation from Ottoline to Garsington, intending to gather ammunition against her new enemy. On 10 May, on the train to Oxford, she scribbled a note to Mary: "Everyone seems to be hanging on my experiences at G! . . . I am going to throw out a few feelers at G. [and] try to trap O. into saying something to V's disadvantage. I like to go about collecting evidence, which I may not use for years perhaps never."[50] Vivien had an appointment with her then ally, Edith Sitwell, at four o'clock on Monday to give her her report. Although at this time Vivien felt herself to be a match for Bloomsbury, she failed to recognise the fundamental fact that it was Tom whose genius it recognised, and with whom its loyalties would ultimately lie. Bloomsbury, said Vivien's brother Maurice, destroyed her. Yet in 1919 it seemed to offer Vivien the hand of friendship, and so she felt herself to be among friends. Hot-headed and unfounded accusations were not the best way of keeping them.

Vivien's meddling extended to the romantic arena also. Mary's liaison with Clive left St. John Hutchinson out in the cold, so Vivien decided to pair him up with Brigit Patmore. On her way to Garsington that May Vivien planned a dinner party the following Tuesday to bring Jack and Brigit together. "Last time it did not come off," she told Mary, but she had not given up hope of a diversionary affair which would help her new friend. Perhaps Vivien was unaware that Tom was himself writing to Brigit, arranging discreet dinners with her while Vivien was at Marlow.

In May, Brigit accompanied Tom and the Hutchinsons to watch Diaghilev's Ballets Russes perform *Carnaval, The Firebird,* and *The Good-Humoured Ladies,* and he pressed her to dine again before she went to stay with Vivien. In the early summer of 1919 London was in a fever of excitement as it greeted the arrival of "Diaghileff's troupe" for the first time since the war. Diaghilev had brought two new dancers who rapidly created a sensation—Léonide Massine and Lydia Lopokova—who danced the new repertoire which included *La Boutique Fantasque,* which Vivien much preferred to *Le Tricorne (The Three-Cornered Hat)*. "Suddenly the arts became the preoccupation of Society . . . French became the language of the Savoy where Diaghileff, Massine, Stravinsky, Picasso, and Picasso's very beautiful and aristocratic wife were staying for the season," remembered Clive Bell. Picasso "dwelt" in the Savoy. "Madame Picasso had no notion of joining in the rough and tumble of upper Bohemia," and would only allow her husband to attend fashionable parties, dressed "en smoking." It was to Clive, then living at 46 Gordon Square with Maynard Keynes, that Picasso turned when he needed fitting out in white tie and tails; Clive was happy to oblige the painter.[51]

While it amused Tom to flirt with Brigit, Mary was the bigger prize. His invitation to Mary in March that year to dance at a club near Baker Street where they could learn the new steps together and dine afterwards was not an isolated occurrence. In part it was revenge on Vivien for her liaison with Russell. Tom and Vivien now danced less together than in the early days of the marriage when Aldous Huxley described Tom rolling up the carpet in the flat, and seriously fox-trotting with his wife to the strains of the gramophone.[52] Tom no longer met Vivien's demanding standards. In "Thé Dansant," one of Vivien's sketches published in the *Criterion* in 1924, she describes a wife trying to energise her husband on the dance floor: "Now *dance* for a change," she commands. "You never do dance, you know, you simply march about. *You've got no energy.*"[53] Vivien did not hesitate to find herself more skilful partners than her husband, who still needed to count under his breath as he danced. On 2 March, the same month in which Eliot was meeting Mary to learn the new steps, Vivien, in no need of such lessons, recorded that she went to the Elysée Galleries to dance with two of her usual companions and was "Picked up by three Canadian flying-men, all exquisite dancers—Danced as I never have since before the war."[54] Maurice considered that Vivien was a more gifted dancer than his wife, Ahmé Hoagland, who danced professionally in cabaret. It is then hardly surprising that rather than face Vivien's scorn, Tom preferred to dance with Mary and Brigit; but part of the excitement of these illicit encounters lay also in deceiving his wife.

Mary was a willing partner in the game of love. Soon she began inviting Eliot to parties alone. "Vivien would have made the party brighter/It's a Pity you didn't invite her," responded Tom, remarking that Vivien wouldn't have come anyway. He added a rhyming envelope, inviting the postman to "take your little skiff/And ply upstream to HAMMERSNIFF, there to rest an oar ('nay but you shall') at River House, Upper Mall."[55]

Vivien had no suspicions at first. She was unaware of the number of secret meetings which took place between her husband and Mary. Often Mary wrote directly to Tom, enclosing a letter for Vivien; sometimes he, knowing the extent of Vivien's dependence upon her, reproached his correspondent for not writing often enough to Vivien. His deception was made easier by the fact that in June Lloyds Bank sent him into the provinces on a business tour which lasted several weeks, and Vivien had little idea of his whereabouts.

On 16 May 1919 Tom had accepted an invitation from Mary to come alone to Wittering for Whitsun, assuring her that Vivien had made alternative arrangements.[56] "Please dont have anyone else—flattery quite apart!" he wrote to Mary. "I should like best to be the only guest . . . So you see I can be seduced. I am looking forward to it very keenly."[57] "So Tom is coming to you at Whitsun!" Vivien remarked with surprise, as she remained in Crawford Mansions, signing herself "Your devoted friend, Vivien."[58] Mary awaited her guest with anticipation. She had decided to ask Roger Fry for Sunday, but would give Tom an afternoon and evening alone with her first. Anxious as ever to be correctly dressed, Eliot decided to bring his flannels, as well as an account of the "provincial amours," which he provocatively claimed he had enjoyed while travelling for Lloyds, for his hostess.

The spell Eliot cast over women is apparent in Mary's memoir of her first meeting with the poet:

> The first time I saw my friend T. S. Eliot he was sitting alone on a sea-wall in the estuary of Chichester Harbour. It was in August 1916 . . . Eliot was dressed in white flannels and was looking out to sea. He says that I had in my hand an unusual flower picked in the woods through which my husband and I had been walking . . .

In his pockets Eliot carried a "very small Virgil and a very small Dante and read them by the water's edge." He told Mary that "Baudelaire and Dante are the two poets of whom I cannot have enough copies about." "Soon after our first meeting Eliot took a house near the Estuary, from different sides of which we could see white sails and sometimes a red one, 'sea-ward flying.' The oak woods which line the shores—as George Moore described them—became the meeting-place for picnics, and the ferry boat at Itchenor a bridge between his side of the water and ours."[59]

Mary's favourite poems became those in which Eliot captured "water in poetry." "The river sweats/Oil and tar" lines from *The Waste Land,* which describe barges drifting with the turning tide on the Thames, suggested to her Chichester Harbour, and the "Red sails/Wide/To leeward" reminded her of the dinghies she and the poet watched together from the windows of Eleanor.[60]

Strangely there is no mention in Mary's memoir of Vivien, her "devoted friend." It is Eliot only who lives on "his side of the water," Eliot to whom she sends tamarisk and sea lavender to be woven into laurels and roses of Pireira "with which his head will be crowned." Certainly Vivien was not much in either Mary's or Tom's mind when he arrived at Eleanor at Whitsun 1919. Mary, later immortalised as Erato, the Muse of Erotic Poetry, in Boris von Anrep's mosaic floor at the entrance to the National Gallery, was skilled in the arts of love, but it is significant that it is she, not Eliot, who he assumes will take the initiative in any love-making which may ensue. Whether the anticipated seduction took place is not known, but if so, Eliot's heart was not stirred. The world-weariness of the poem he was composing at the time, "Gerontion," dubbed the "new Byronism" by Middleton Murry in his review, speaks of Eliot's very different mood that summer. The poet is "an old man in a dry month,/Being read to by a boy, waiting for rain." Military and amatory progress are compared in the poem, argues Eliot's biographer Tony Sharpe;[61] it is replete with sexual innuendo: "I was neither at the hot gates/Nor fought in the warm rain." The last lines of "Gerontion" enact a sexual crescendo and diminuendo, but its protagonists end as fractured atoms whirling in a dissolving cosmos. The poet returns to the thoughts of "a dry brain in a dry season."[62] There may have been, from Eliot's point of view, a cold coupling at Eleanor, but the aridity of his mood at the time, which found expression in "Gerontion," revised in France that August, suggests anti-climax and disillusion rather than rapture by the water.

Nor is Tom's bread-and-butter letter to Mary after their Whitsun rendez-vous the message of a lover. Eliot speaks instead of being at cross-purposes, and hints at a disagreement. It is Mary's independence and self-sufficiency, and the mysteriousness which made her appear "incomprehensible and unaccountable," which he stresses. His inquiry: "Do you insist on being a very superior woman?" reflects distance rather than intimacy; his stay had not ignited the fires of passion, but instead served to highlight the gulf which existed between the lifestyle of the wealthy lawyer and his confident wife, and the Eliots' own misery.[63]

Nevertheless, rumours about Tom and Mary were now flying around Bloomsbury. On 19 May, a week after the Hogarth Press had published Eliot's *Poems,* Virginia and Ottoline met to "talk personalities," and discuss "the case of Mary Hutch and Eliot."[64] There was more trouble, too, with Virginia, who had heard the latest gossip that Tom thought her new novel, *Night and Day,* was "rubbish." Ottoline was in her turn jealous of Tom's new-found intimacy with Mary, and Clive was more green-eyed than ever when he heard that Tom had spent the weekend with his girlfriend Mary, and Roger Fry. Ottoline at this point invited Tom and Virginia for the weekend at Garsington, without Mary or Vivien. "Tom is going to Garsington; think of Virginia, Tom and Ottoline!" wrote Vivien to Mary. "O think of it."[65] But Vivien's efforts to trap Ottoline into speaking ill of Virginia had backfired and, although she had written "most sensibly and friendly with all due regard to her hothouse feelings," Ottoline was furious with her. "I am cast into outer darkness, so I can join you there," joked Vivien to Mary.[66] Tom, meanwhile, basked in being the centre of attention; "So I must go smiling on Saturday" to Garsington, he wrote to his cousin Eleanor Hinkley, who must have found Bloomsbury feuds as childish as they were confusing.

Unfortunately at this juncture Harold Peters, an old sailing friend of Eliot's, arrived from America, and the poet was forced to give up his weekend at Garsington in order to entertain him. On Saturday, 14 June, Tom brought Vivien to Bosham to spend the weekend at South View, the cottage they had rented for the summer. "Beautiful day," recorded Vivien in her diary. "It is almost too much for one." But by Sunday, despite the hot weather which allowed them to lie out in the grass near Itchenor ferry, her terse entry read: "Didn't get on."[67] Tom returned to London to continue his tour of the provinces and Vivien remained alone in Bosham. Although at this point Vivien still trusted Mary, she was becoming increasingly anxious as she lost track of her husband's whereabouts. The London flat was shut up, Ellen having gone to Margate for her own holiday. Vivien wrote several wistful and placatory letters to Ottoline. "I am awfully happy here, and never want to go back. It is so nice to have Mary so near too. We have glorious picnics together," she wrote, begging Ottoline, however, not to invite Tom to stay again too soon. "*Please,* my dear, don't ask him until *after* the weekend July 5th–7th, as a favour to me, because I do want him to come down here and stay with me. I never see him now."[68]

That June Vivien suffered another disappointment. Russell had arrived early one morning at the flat in Crawford Mansions to collect another instalment of his possessions which she had brought up from Marlow. Vivien had not been dressed when Bertie arrived, and had been forced to shout to him from the bathroom, as cheerfully as she could. She had met with a brusque response, and was left full of regrets, having hoped that she and Bertie might have talked over tea and come to an amicable truce. "But it is no good. I will make no more attempts at all. But it is strange how one does miss him! Isn't it hard to put him *quite* out of one's mind?"[69] Perhaps Ottoline, who had just had Bertie for the weekend at Garsington, was mollified by Vivien's evident unhappiness that Russell was no longer part of her life, as he was part of Ottoline's, and began to repent of her anger.

As the days passed Vivien waited anxiously for her elusive husband to return to her at Bosham. He was due to arrive on 28 June. "Tom is coming here and WE MUST HAVE A GOOD TIME," wrote Vivien to Mary. "It will be the only weekend he'll come, I think."[70] Vivien hunted unsuccessfully in Chichester for partridges and grouse, not realising that they were out of season. She settled for crabs, 6/6d for two, and lobsters, 4/9d for two, to bring to Mary. "If the crabs are *doubtful,* the *middle* parts might be taken out of the shell and kept on a plate. Then they will keep. I hope Jack will not be cross . . ." Envying Mary her children, whom she met on her visits to Eleanor, Vivien wrote a letter apologising for not saying goodbye to Jeremy and Barbara, and sending them some chocolate.

Vivien professed to be delighted with the "glorious" sailing expedition which ensued, after Tom's arrival, with Mary and Sachie Sitwell, although as this was the occasion when Tom ran the boat aground, she was unsure whether anyone else felt the same way: "It's possible that some people thought the boat adventure was boring & silly, I suppose! To me it was pure joy. Tom too, liked it." But her exasperation was growing with Tom, whom she blamed for the growing frostiness with the Woolfs, Clive Bell, and others. He had only asked Mary to arrange the outing as a mark of comradeship, Vivien said: "He thinks it is friendly to ask people to clear up his muddles for him."[71]

Alone again at Bosham, Vivien continued to ask Mary to join her for picnics in the woods, or, if wet, at the inn at Itchenor. However Mary, as hostess to Roger Fry and other guests, was not always available. "I love to get you *away* from everything," wrote Vivien. "I will be on this side of the ferry, waving, at 12.30." By this time Vivien seems to have heard the rumours linking Mary and Tom, signing one letter, "Your loving Vivien, The Woman's Friend, Damn you."[72] But she felt no real cause for concern, believing that Tom was unlikely to relish a physical union with Mary.

By mid-July Tom and Vivien were quarrelling vociferously. Vivien had come up to town to see de Falla's *The Three-Cornered Hat,* but Tom refused to take her to the ballet a second time as she wished: "Tom is *Im*possible—full of nerves . . . very morbid and grumpy. I wish you had him!" Vivien complained to Mary. Money troubles kept cropping up, and Tom reproached Vivien for spending too much, while his own "muddles" over conflicting invitations continued. "He gets angry and stubborn," Vivien confided to Mary. In contrast to her husband, Mary seemed perfect to Vivien after another wonderful day out together. "You are all that I admire," wrote Vivien on 19 July; "you are such a *'civilised'* rebel."[73]

That month an unexpected event occurred which was to change Vivien's view of events. Sydney and Violet Schiff invited the Eliots to spend a weekend at Eastbourne, and, although Vivien recorded in her diary that she found the Schiffs "fatiguing and irritating," she told a different story to Mary, and one with a purpose. As for Tom, she wrote, a lot seemed to happen in the time between her leaving Bosham and his going to France, where he was about to take a walking holiday with Ezra Pound in the Dordogne.

I had rather an affair with him for one thing. It began when we were staying with the Schiffs for the Peace Weekend. Don't you yourself find that staying in people's houses together is very conducive to reviving passions?

The novelty of sexual relations with her husband surprised Vivien. Was Tom's "affair" with her stimulated, perhaps, by his rumoured affair with Mary? Or did Tom find Vivien's own intimacy with Mary an aphrodisiac? The spark of passion, so briefly inflamed, was extinguished, however, when the Eliots left Eastbourne. Vivien remained frustrated by the quarrels she considered to be Tom's fault, telling Mary, "In future I am going to simply wash my hands of Tom, and refuse politely to explain him or influence or direct him. Tom must manage his own muddles." Mischievously Mary enquired whether Tom had many "enemies." "Has Tom enemies? You ask me, but I think you know better than I," replied Vivien. "Anyhow, it doesn't matter now, for I think enemies stimulate him. The important point is—friends . . . You do stand alone . . . Goodbye, darling Mary."[74]

In this Bloomsbury triangle, Mary may have wanted Tom, but he never felt as at ease with her as his polished exterior suggested. To his brother Henry, Eliot complained that summer of still feeling a foreigner among the English. "Don't think that I find it easy to live over here," he wrote. "It is damned hard work to live with a foreign nation and cope with them." He confessed that the English had a knack for making him feel humiliated and lonely, always on "dress parade," and unable to relax. People sought you out because they wanted something from you, and if they didn't get it, they dropped you and quickly became enemies. "London is something one has to fight very hard in, in order to survive."[75] His preservation would be due to luck, said Tom—"or Vivien's assistance, in large part." Even to Mary, Eliot made the same point: that he was a "métic" or foreigner.

Although it might appear that Mary and Vivien were in jealous competition for Eliot, in fact it was Mary whose attention both Tom and Vivien individually craved. Unhappy together, both wanted to be alone with Mary and experience what Vivien described as the "exciting joy" of her conversation, as well as her sympathy in the Bloomsbury squabbles which each tended to blame on the other. As Eliot put it to Mary, "We are both grateful to anyone who is intelligent enough to take us as individuals."[76] This Mary well understood.

The intense friendship which developed between Vivien and Mary in the summer of 1919 presaged that which developed in the 1920s between Maria Huxley and Mary. Indeed, Mary subsequently had relationships with both Aldous Huxley and his wife Maria, as well as with Vita Sackville-West.[77] As early as 1918 Clive was writing to his bisexual lover: "I often envy you your catholicity,"[78] and in 1922 he referred to an affair Mary might be having with a woman.[79] But it would be a mistake to assume that Vivien stepped into a lesbian nest when she spent the night with Mary, as she did on 18 September 1919, and possibly on other occasions. In her diary Vivien recorded that she and Mary stayed up till one o'clock talking, and she was afterwards "frightfully tired." It was probably on 9 July, when Mary had told Vivien the story of her life as the two women lay together in the sunshine on the beach at Hayling Island, that the relationship moved into a different phase. It was very bold of her to ask Mary to invite her to stay when she was alone, wrote Vivien on 1 September, "But you must not let me get too excited! Do you know I always get too excited when I see you & am very ill afterwards. This is true. That heavenly picnic we had nearly killed me."[80] Mary, sensual and self-indulgent, was tolerant of Vivien's quirkiness and mood swings. She wrote in 1927 to Lytton Strachey that she found exhilarating satisfaction in personal relationships, especially in those which one might describe as

> truthful, unbinding, courageous—"a l'état pur" of impurity . . . I think it is fatal to wish for any particular state or particular development—when one is provoked, one should adjust oneself very ingeniously—(the more complicated the character probably the more exciting) and develop by peculiar jumps![81]

During another later summer at Wittering, on 1 August 1925, Mary wrote to Maria Huxley of her memories of her lying in her "chaste, narrow bed" at Eleanor; she recalled the "gay and intense days and exquisite nights" she spent with Maria,[82] whose sweetly scented, oiled body Mary loved more than that of Aldous.[83] Bloomsbury's encouragement of bisexuality was fast breaking down old taboos against such relationships. In the 1920s lesbianism was the new chic, and the dual-sexed figure of the androgyne a central figure of revolt against bourgeois morality.[84] But there is no evidence that Vivien was lesbian, and her documented affairs were only with men, although she may have been tempted to experiment.

At one point during the summer of 1919 it is clear that Mary was setting up a meeting between Vivien and her brother Jim, whom she hoped might console Vivien for Tom's neglect and Russell's disappearance. Vivien was apparently not averse to the scheme. "Don't tell Jack about Jim, it wouldn't do, I assure you," she implored Mary. She was planning to buy a new wardrobe for the coming season, but didn't know what would please Jim most. "Do begin laying foundation stones for me with Jim," she begged.[85]

In August Tom left for his French holiday with Pound. This came as a welcome relief to Vivien and, combined with Mary's friendship, resulted in a dramatic improvement in her health. The migraines which often prostrated her, as on 1 January, when she had lain in bed all day without moving, with "very bad head pains," and was disturbed by Pound visiting after dinner ("their voices drove me mad as I lay in the dark"), vanished. There was no longer the strain of managing Tom's health and his moods, so carefully charted in her diary: for Saturday 21 June, "T. looking very ill"; Saturday 5 July, "Tom had a cold and was cross"; Monday 21 July, "T. went to Dr." Her own maladies seemed to disappear during these separate holidays. Having seen Tom off at Waterloo in "boiling and roasting heat," Vivien dined with her friend Freddie at Lyons Corner House, before leaving the next day for Eastbourne to spend a fortnight with another old friend, May Pacy. She was pleased to have the same bedroom as the year before at the Lansdowne Hotel, and to find a Colonel and Mrs. Ashe they had met last summer were again at the next table. The next day her brother Maurice arrived and they all went dancing and had "a roaring time." But as the time of Tom's return drew near Vivien again collapsed with premenstrual tension; she was in bed on the day he arrived home from France with several days' growth of beard. It was a starred day in her diary: "Tom came home . . . Very nice at first. Depressed in evening,"[86] she recorded.

Briefly the Eliots drew closer over the illness of their beloved Yorkshire terrier, Dinah, one of many they were to keep during their marriage. Tom had queued for many hours earlier that year to buy a muzzle for Dinah when there was a rabies scare. For three days at the beginning of September they nursed the dog, until on the Friday Vivien and Tom together took Dinah to the vet in a taxi. Nothing could be done and she was put to sleep at once. "Frightful day of misery," recorded a heartbroken Vivien.

Another picnic at Itchenor with Jack and Mary raised their spirits a little, and Vivien and Tom dined together that night at the Anchor at Chichester, before Tom took the train back to London. The following week Vivien's father Charles came to stay with Vivien in Bosham. Father and daughter sketched together and Vivien swam daily, as well as spending many hours blackberrying. It was an idyllic time. But Vivien's conscience pricked her when Tom's birthday arrived on 26 September and found her still in Bosham; once again her period arrived accompanied by a migraine, and a railway strike frustrated her efforts to return to London. When finally she managed to find a seat in a motor car for 30/– to take her as far as Putney Bridge, a typical Eliot muddle occurred: she had wired for Tom to meet her at Putney, but he went instead to London Bridge. She had to wait two hours, and finally abandoned her hamper of blackberries. "We both wept," she recorded.[87]

After Tom's return from France relations between Vivien and Mary were at first peaceful. "Although I've been trying hard to quarrel with everyone else, succeeding too, I *never* want to quarrel with you . . . Yr. devoted V," Vivien had assured Mary in May, but she found it hard to restrain her pen: "I will write a letter from Eastbourne, if I CAN write the sort of letter one woman likes to get from another."[88] Mary remained tactful, assuring Vivien of the "amiability of her savagery."[89] But, as the weeks passed, heightened emotions threatened to burst out into open warfare. On 26 September Vivien exploded with anger after missing Mary in Chichester. Annoyed at waiting three hours in vain, she wrote an "unfortunate" letter to Mary telling her she had "a good store" of things ready to be said to her, and accusing Mary of selfishness.

> About giving oneself up to people. I had never seen before we
> spoke how much I have done that with Tom. And how little *you*

were prepared to do it with anyone. Also how much one gains by doing it, how much one loses; and how much one *loses by not ever doing it.*[90]

Mary sent a cool reply, and on 29 October Vivien, who had returned to London, thanked her sarcastically for her "nasty letter," calling her "little cat." But it was Vivien who had her claws out, for Tom as much as for Mary. Hoping to see Mary at the lecture on "Modern Tendencies in Poetry," which Tom had given on 28 October as part of his Monday evening classes on Elizabethan literature in Southall,[91] Vivien had been disappointed when she failed to turn up; she had hoped to sit by Mary and poke her in the ribs. Instead, Vivien was left playing the Dormouse to "Pasha Schiff's Mad Hatter in the front row"; however, she wrote crossly, "As Tom is not a French artist, or a Flirt, or Amusing or even Rather Fun, your absence from his lecture was no surprise to him." Her barbed remark revealed the extent of the Eliots' disharmony, and it was in search of diversion that Vivien accepted another invitation from Mary to a party at River House, reminding her that she would see her at Edith Sitwell's party, and this time there would be no excuse to miss her: "You will know me by my paisley shawl." When might she stay the night with Mary, begged Vivien. "I embrace you."[92]

But Mary's own marriage was under stress. In late 1919 she temporarily left her husband Jack, who had become growingly resentful of his wife's affair with Clive Bell. Mary found refuge with Roger Fry at Durbins, his new house near Guildford. For once Clive was not his usual gossipy self, writing to Vanessa:

> You will see that if they are ever to live together again it is really important that you should be absolutely secret. Above all, I beg you, if anything does come out to make it quite clear that it didn't come from me. Knowing what Jack's feelings in the matter are, I do think it would have been disgraceful in me to have talked. I don't know what will happen, but I think it likely that there will be a partial separation, and that in a short time Mary will ostensibly go back to their house.[93]

So indeed it proved, and later in life Jack would jokingly refer to Mary's lovers.[94] In the interim, however, Mary turned her attentions to another admirer, Tommy Earp, before travelling to Paris in pursuit of Clive. Vivien was grimly amused to hear that her friend had a plot to reawaken Clive's affections. "I also have a gunpowder plot in preparation, but mine is not timed to go off until the New Year," she threatened Mary. "So perhaps it will be a case of he who laughs last laughs loudest."[95]

12

Breakdown

From the time of Henry Ware Eliot Senior's death, Vivien and Tom's lives were dominated by Tom's overriding desire to see his mother. He and Vivien fretted over plans: should Tom go to America for a short visit, which would use up all his leave from the bank, or could he persuade his mother, Marian and Henry to come for two or three months to England? "I want to see you *soon*," he begged his "dearest Mother," in February 1920. "Unless I can see you *once* again . . . I shall *never* be really happy unto the end of my life. Is anything so important as that? Does anything else really matter?"[1] Tom's longing for his mother became the perpetual theme of his letters home, intensifying as Charlotte Eliot appeared impervious to his pleas, protesting that she must first settle her business affairs, sell up in St. Louis and find a new house in Cambridge, Massachusetts.[2] Vivien began to feel she took second place to her mother-in-law during these long months of waiting for the American relatives to arrive. And although Eliot remained "devotedly your son, Tom," finding consolation in the pyjamas Charlotte sewed him for Christmas, the clothes, books, silver cane, his father's chessmen and even the mounted Eliot arms she sent were no substitute for her physical presence: her touch, the sound of her voice, her approbation. His wish that he and Charlotte might "live together a little bit" in England began to take on a neurotic and obsessional quality.

Nevertheless there were fears inherent in the prospective visit. Eliot worried whether his family would detect the falsehoods upon which his marriage was based, the contradictions which lay behind the "envelope of frozen formality" which seemed to Virginia Woolf to encase Eliot's personality, and the wildly glittering eyes she also noticed in 1920.[3] Tom thought of cutting out the page with "Ode" on it in *Ara Vos Prec* ("Now I

Pray You")—which was published in February by the Ovid Press at 15s. a copy—and sending the book thus mutilated to his mother, rather than allow her to see a poem so revealing of his and Vivien's disastrous honeymoon. "The 'Ode' is *not* in the edition that Knopf is publishing," he explained to Henry on 15 February, relieved that his family in America would not see the revealing poem. But although he had suppressed "Ode," he still worried about the other poems in his new collection: "I suppose she will have to see that book. Do you think that 'Sweeney Erect' will shock her?"[4] Tom asked, imagining his mother's reaction to a profoundly misogynistic poem in which a naked, broadbottomed and erect Sweeney shaves while on the bed a prostitute has an epileptic fit. Contemptuously Sweeney ignores her "Gesture of orang-outang" as she flails the steaming sheets, her shrieking mouth (an "oval O cropped out with teeth"), her jackknifing hips (a parody of intercourse) as she claws at the pillow slip, while he tests the razor on his leg. Hysteria might easily be misunderstood, observes Eliot: "It does the house no sort of good."[5] It was an observation which could as easily be taken as an allusion to Vivien as to the inmates of a brothel.

Eliot had made a proud, if premature, boast to his mother that he was England's greatest living poet and critic. Now, with her impending arrival, he had to prove it, and during 1920 he plunged into a frenzy of activity designed to ensure he had enough published work to impress her. Vivien helped with the typing, as Eliot struggled to finish *The Sacred Wood,* his collection of *Egoist* critical essays first suggested by Harriet Shaw Weaver; he hoped to have it ready in April for Methuen but it took until August to complete. Meanwhile he continued writing articles feverishly. He had fallen out with Middleton Murry at the *Athenaeum,* but Richard Aldington came to his aid. Aldington enabled Tom to step onto "the top rung of literary journalism" through his introduction in 1919 to Bruce Richmond, the powerful editor of the *Times Literary Supplement,* at that time the Delphic shrine of literary criticism.[6] Although, relates Aldington (who was the paper's French literature correspondent), Eliot nearly sabotaged his opportunity by arriving fresh from his holiday "wearing, if you please, a derby hat and an Uncle Sam beard he had cultivated in Switzerland," his erudite conversation saved the situation and on 13 November 1919 his first leading article on Ben Jonson appeared.[7] He was also contributing to

Harold Monro's *Chapbook*. Yet Eliot's sense of victimisation remained great. "Getting recognised in English letters is like breaking open a safe— for an American, and . . . only about three have ever done it," he confessed in a sudden burst of honesty to his mother,[8] admitting the magnitude of the task he had set himself as leader of the Modernist revolution.

Eliot found the success of lesser poets exasperating, especially his American contemporaries. Conrad Aiken was in London, "stupider than I remember him; in fact, stupid," he brusquely told Ezra Pound, although he lunched with Aiken two or three times a week in the City. Aiken had won a reputation as a poet in America, but he, Osbert and Sacheverell Sitwell, Aldous Huxley and Herbert Read all seemed children to the hard-pressed bank clerk, who suspected both Aiken[9] and Osbert Sitwell of copying his style and even the content of his poetry.[10] Eliot was angry that Sitwell seemed to be attempting "clever imitations" of his own poems, and was horrified at the prospect that Knopf might publish him and Sitwell simultaneously. *"Would I think of contributing to Wheels?"*—a poetry anthology edited and published by Edith Sitwell and Nancy Cunard between 1916 and 1922—"And so give the S(itwells) a lift and the right to sneer at me?" he demanded scornfully of Wyndham Lewis,[11] urging the painter to keep away from these second-rate, "Chelsea people." Eliot despised the wealthy Sitwells as amateurs, "weekend poets" who did not work for their living; Aldous Huxley also sneered at the family he called "Shufflebottom, one sister and two brothers . . . each of them larger and whiter than the other,"[12] who considered themselves revolutionaries but whose verse differed little from the neo-Georgians against whom they affected to rebel. Although Eliot did not object to accepting the Sitwells' hospitality, he felt embattled, envious of the wealth and leisure of literary dilettantes, bitter at the traditionalists who stood in his way.

In December 1920 a new blow came for both the Eliots when Ezra Pound finally abandoned London for Paris, "killed," in Eliot's view, by the British literary establishment. Pound had been a good friend to Vivien, but it was Eliot who most missed his compatriot and mentor, who now believed Paris to be the "centre of the world" and found in Dadaism a substitute for Vorticism.[13] Although only three years older than Tom, "Ez" had behaved like a father-figure or elder brother to his inhibited protégé, whom he cossetted and protected; when Tom visited him in France Pound fussed over his health, took him for long walks, and "put him through a course of sun and sulphur baths."[14] Pound's absence highlighted the loneliness of Eliot's struggle, and the triumphs of those whom he felt were inferior to himself and Ezra. The financial precariousness of the literary and artistic journals which sprang up and as quickly died, such as *Art and Letters* and Wyndham Lewis's ill-fated *Tyro*, confirmed the wisdom of Eliot's decision to turn down the *Athenaeum* job, as Vivien now acknowledged; nevertheless his work at the bank had become far more onerous since being put in charge of the settlement of pre-war debts between the Germans and Lloyds, despite a new salary increase to £500. When the Cambridge don I. A. Richards met Eliot at the bank he described him as

> a figure stooping, very like a dark bird in a feeder, over a big table covered with all sorts and sizes of foreign correspondence. The big table almost entirely filled a little room under the street. Within a foot of our heads when we stood were the thick, green glass squares of the pavement on which hammered all but incessantly the heels of the passers-by. There was just room for two perches beside the table.[15]

Lloyds, however, were pleased with Eliot's efforts: "If you see our young friend, you might tell him that we think he's doing quite well at the Bank," a senior official told Richards. "In fact, if he goes on as he has been doing, I don't see why—in time, of course, in time—he mightn't even become a Branch Manager." Horrified, like so many other of Eliot's friends and disciples, Richards tried to persuade the poet to find some alternative occupation—this time to accept an academic post at Cambridge—but, "like a wary animal sniffing a trap," he declined.[16]

Although a perverse caution kept Eliot at Lloyds, the price he paid was high. Proud of his new appointment, for he now had several assistants, he nevertheless felt chained to a treadmill with only the distant promise of retirement; Vivien, who had pleaded with him to leave in 1919, worried constantly about his health. Observer of Tom's bitterness and resentment, her own anger grew at the mother-in-law she blamed for their poverty and her husband's unhappiness. She was convinced that with one stroke of her pen Charlotte could change their lives, if she would only give them enough of the shares Tom felt were his by right, and which would release him from the bank. Vivien knew that Tom hungered for editorship of his own journal, envying the ease with which their rich friend Scofield Thayer was able to buy *The Dial,* which Eliot condemned as merely a "very dull" imitation of the *Atlantic Monthly,* although Thayer's generous rates forced him to agree to contribute a "London Letter" to his old Harvard rival's periodical.[17] Pound was even ruder about Scofield's new venture, finding it no better than the *London Mercury* "or one of those other mortuaries for the entombment of dead fecal mentality."[18] As the months passed, Eliot's paranoia increased alongside his unwavering determination to win the battle for literary supremacy in London.

Eliot felt the battle he was fighting was for high standards in the midst of the contemporary "putrescence" of English literature and journalism; he wanted to wipe the smile of imbecility from the face of London. Was he not a Puritan soldier fighting post-war degeneracy, of which modern journalism was simply one symptom, just as his Blood ancestors had struck down deluded witches? His sense of persecution, however denied, was intensified by his continuing sense of alienation: "I have got used to being a foreigner everywhere," he told Maxwell Bodenheim, an American poet then in London, in similar words to those he had used to Mary, "and it would fatigue me to be expected to be anything else."[19] The effort of disguise, of fitting himself to a post-war culture so different from the familiar certainties of Unitarianism, was commented on by Henry Eliot to their mother: "The strain of going out among people who after all are foreigners to him, and, I believe, always must be to an American—even Henry James never became a complete Englishman—has, I think, been pretty heavy." Tom had confessed, his brother said, to "always having to be alert to appearances, always wearing a mask among people. To me he seemed like a man playing a part."[20]

Acting the part of an Englishman might have been less of a burden, had not Eliot carried the heavier weight of feeling misunderstood by his family in America. In July 1919 a distant relative, Charles William Eliot, President of Harvard 1869–1909, wrote a severely critical letter to Tom, who had earlier solicited his help when attempting to enter the American armed forces in 1918. It was unintelligible to him how any young American scholar could forego the privilege of living in the genuine

American atmosphere, wrote the President sternly. Tom's duty was to be of use primarily to Americans of the present and future generations, as Emerson had been. The poet would find, like Henry James, that English residence contributed "neither to the happy development of his art nor to his personal happiness." If he wished to speak through his work to people of the "finest New England spirit," declared this elder of the Eliot clan, he had better not live much longer in England. "The New England spirit has been nurtured in the American atmosphere."[21]

Such reproaches weighed heavily on Eliot. His inherited sense of duty, the family "Fear and Conscience," which he believed was still keeping his mother in America since she refused to travel until her late husband's estate had been settled, conflicted with his burning desire for literary success, the quickest route towards which—he was certain—lay in London, in his eyes the literary capital of the world, even if Ezra had awarded that crown to Paris. There was no alternative. Eliot would play his part and bide his time. Ezra had failed and was out of the race, but Tom would pick up the baton his intemperate friend had dropped in anger, and do what no other American had done—impose "his personality, taste and even many of his opinions on literary England." His weapons were, as Aldington noted, "merit, tact, prudence and pertinacity."[22]

The "character armour" Eliot wore did not go unnoticed. Aldous Huxley observed to Ottoline that Eliot had created a character for himself, a wooden armour inside which he hid.[23] Virginia Woolf found him "sinister, insidious, eel-like, also monolithic, masked, intensely reserved."[24] Ottoline herself often found it impossible to penetrate the smooth, impervious surface of Eliot's personality. Vivien's emotions, by contrast, were transparently open, and this was the secret of her initial popularity, although she could not help responding to the hypocrisy and inauthenticity of her life with Tom, on both a social and sexual level, by sometimes losing control. The infiltration of Bloomsbury, so necessary for the fulfilment of Tom's ambition, the cultivation of men she knew he despised, the pretence of marriage, became impossible for her to sustain because of the falsity of her position.

Eliot's mind was like a Chinese puzzle, as Ottoline noted. He revelled in Machiavellian diplomacy and manipulation, and lived by the family motto, *"Tacuit et fecit"* ("Be silent and act"). Vivien, despite good intentions, could not keep a secret, and was too impulsive to play the games at which Mary excelled (to Tom's admiration). Mary was "as mute as a trout" when prudence demanded, a woman who "though silent . . . has the swift composure of a fish," the observant Virginia Woolf recorded;[25] Mary successfully handled the triangular relationships at which Vivien had failed, winning her errant lover Clive back from a new affair in 1920–21 with a Spanish beauty, Juana de Guandarillas.[26]

Nevertheless, there is no doubt that in 1920 Vivien was still a considerable asset to Tom in his pursuit of power and position. Despite, or perhaps because of her *naïveté,* she sparkled at literary gatherings, her spontaneity a refreshing contrast to the thrusts and parries of most of the guests. Herbert Read, then a civil servant, remembered Eliot bringing "his pretty . . . wife" to the Saturday afternoon tea parties given by Edith Sitwell and her companion Helen Rootham in their Bayswater flat. "Posterity will probably judge Vivienne harshly," he wrote, "but I remember her in moments when she was sweet and vivacious."[27]

Vivien's path through the salons of London was smoothed by the warm friendship she now shared with Ottoline Morrell, with whom she had become reconciled after their quarrel the previous year. Dependent, as always, on other people to make her marriage to Tom bearable, Vivien had written in December 1919 that she wished *ever so much* that she could see Ottoline at Garsington for the Christmas festivities: "Xmas is awful, *awful."* She was longing for Ottoline to come to London. "I keep saying to Tom, 'when Ottoline is here we will do so and so . . .' You do not know how I admire you, my dearest Ottoline. I hope we shall always be friends." Innocently Vivien urged Ottoline to become closer friends with Mary, whom she believed Ottoline would like very much if she liked Vivien. Although Ottoline would not think it, wrote Vivien, she and Mary were very much alike—"Leaving out the sex business which of course makes a vast difference"[28]—an allusion to Mary's promiscuity. Vivien was probably unaware that Ottoline and Virginia had been gossiping over Mary's relationship with Tom[29] and that Virginia had taken perverse pleasure in seeing the "poor parakeet fallen off her perch, or left to preen & prink in solitude," when Clive strayed in the direction of the beautiful Spaniard.[30]

Ottoline responded to Vivien's pleas by taking Ethel Sands's house at 15 Vale Avenue in Chelsea for six weeks from the end of January 1920, and was touched to find that Vivien was the first person to welcome her back to London. Vivien's obvious affection appealed to a woman who felt neglected by her unfaithful husband Philip, now father of two illegitimate sons, and who shared a bond with Vivien as a former lover of Bertrand Russell. A common love of the ballet also drew Ottoline and Vivien together, for Vivien was as impressed with the Russian stars as the rest of High Bohemia, noting in her diary in July 1919: "Massine really wonderful."[31] In addition, shared maladies, migraine, insomnia, gastric attacks and "nerves" led to mutual understanding of the difficulties of being "delicate"; with Vivien too, whose education had been as sporadic as her own, Ottoline felt none of the intellectual inferiority induced by the acid tongue of Katherine Mansfield or Virginia. Ottoline was still the target of criticism by ungrateful Garsington guests such as Clive Bell, who was liable to lose his temper with his hostess on account of "her confounded stupidity," writing, "I wouldn't mind her utter inability to see the point when it becomes the least bit difficult—Philip is almost as bad—but she's so damned pleased with herself and feels so noble and idealistic when she reaches the heights of imbecility—that it is hard not to let her see the least little bit what one thinks."[32] With relief Ottoline turned to the unpretentious Vivien, who seemed to have more sensibility than brains, a fact Ottoline put down to her being partly Irish, like herself.[33] The impression Vivien gave was also noted by Ottoline's daughter Julian, who described her as "coy, actressy, flirtatious, amusing."[34]

Vivien and Ottoline soon became inseparable. On Wednesday, 18 February 1920 the Eliots dined together with Ottoline. Tom then left Vivien to spend the night with their hostess; the next day Vivien gave a dinner party for Osbert and Sacheverell Sitwell and Aldous Huxley, and afterwards the party went on to Ottoline's Thursday night reception, where a Japanese performer did a hara-kiri dance, pretending to disembowel himself with a fan, and uttering horrid cries until the duchess who had brought him calmed him down with a cup of tea.[35]

Relations between the Eliots and the Woolfs had also improved: Eliot's *Poems* had met with poor reviews, a particularly severe one entitled "Not Here O Apollo" appearing in the *Times Literary Supplement* in June 1919.[36] Critics and readers alike agreed with Aldington, who had written crushingly to the poet that July, "I dislike your poetry very much; it is over intellectual and afraid of those essential emotions which make poetry."[37] Leonard attempted to rescue the situation by writing a favourable review which was published in Murry's *Athenaeum* (although it was awkward for Leonard to review their own publication, confessed Virginia), and Tom was grateful for his words of praise. Clive Bell also gave Tom and Virginia a "puff" in *The New Republic* (New York) in the same month in an article condemning English critics for ignoring the young Bloomsbury writers, Tom, Virginia and Murry.[38] United in their loathing of the middle-class literary establishment, which was headed by J. C. Squire, editor of the newly founded *London Mercury,* and which seemed blind to the merits of the modernists, Bloomsbury began to close ranks. Virginia confessed to her diary that she was a snob: "The middle classes are cut so thick, & ring so coarse, when they laugh or express themselves. The lower classes don't do this at all," she wrote at the end of January 1920,[39] sentiments with which Tom and Vivien entirely agreed. Tom's idealistic view of the English working class, which he considered less "aggressive and insolent" than the same class in America, had grown since he lectured to working people in Ilkley and Southall: "This class of person," he had written to his cousin, "is really the most attractive in England . . . it is not so petrified in snobbism and prejudice as the middle classes."[40] The "hopelessly stupid" middle class, whose family life was, said Tom, "hideous" and whose only motive in sending their sons to public school he believed to be snobbism, attracted nothing from him but contempt.[41] Ignored by readers, under attack by the "squirearchy," it was with new-found relief that Tom, and Vivien too, dined with the Woolfs on 20 February 1920, in the company of Sydney Waterlow, Lord Robert Cecil's right-hand man at the Foreign Office, to whom Tom had escaped for Boxing Day after the "awful" Christmas Day alone with his wife.

A few months later Vivien, repenting of her former feud, invited Leonard and Virginia, who was working on *Jacob's Room* (1922), to dinner. They declined, but Virginia sent a kindly note to Vivien, saying she hoped Tom's new book *(The Sacred Wood)* would have poems in it. "I have been wanting to say how much I enjoy his poems—but I never know whether it is better to say so or not."[42] In July Virginia issued a tentative invitation to both Eliots to stay for the weekend at Monk's House, Rodmell, the cramped, damp house beside the water meadows of the Ouse which the

Woolfs had bought in 1919, partly because it was near enough for Virginia to stride over the Downs to her sister at Charleston. "We would like to ask you and Mrs. Eliot here for the weekend," Virginia wrote to Tom. "The only thing is that the discomfort is so great and arrangements so primitive that I dont think she would find it possible."[43] Tom assured Virginia that Vivien would find conditions perfectly comfortable, and despite Virginia's sense of inadequacy over her "tiny" house compared to Charleston,[44] an invitation for September was despatched. "Please bring no clothes," commanded Virginia, alarmed that Eliot might appear in a "four-piece suit." "We live in a state of the greatest simplicity."[45]

In September 1920 Eliot came alone to stay with the Woolfs. When the three of them were walking across the fields, Woolf fell behind to relieve himself. On catching up with Tom and Virginia, he noticed that the poet seemed uncomfortable and even shocked. A frank conversation about conventions and formality followed, in which Eliot admitted that not only would he not have urinated himself in similar circumstances, but that he would never dream of shaving in the presence of anyone else, even his wife.[46] The anecdote illustrated the extent of Eliot's inhibitions and the difficulties faced by Vivien, frozen out when she attempted to overcome them. Eliot was defensive about criticisms of his coldness: "The critics say I am learned and cold," he told Woolf; "the truth is I am neither," but although Virginia felt sympathy for the poet, she still found him as chill as marble.[47]

Social success only made the contrast between the privileged lifestyle of so many of their friends and the sordid flat the Eliots inhabited more insupportable. They decided they could no longer tolerate living in a neighborhood full of prostitutes, which they "loathed." Tom began flat-hunting, encouraged by the prospect of dividends from the first tranche of 225 Hydraulic Press-Brick Company shares which his mother gave him in early 1920. But a bigger flat meant sacrificing the house in Marlow, much against Vivien's will. She had refused to let it to a prospective tenant the previous year: "I will not let them have it," she confided to Ottoline. "I should be *wretched* without it,"[48] but in 1920 the Eliots surrendered the lease. Rents outside Paddington were much higher than they had expected, and by May 1920 Vivien and Tom were both in a state of prostration. A brief visit to Paris for Easter, a treat promised to Vivien who had not left

England for six years, proved a disappointment as Tom collapsed again with flu: "It was very worrying and exhausting to Vivien having me on her hands in Paris, and having to fetch a doctor, get medicines etc., and the journey back was trying for her," Eliot explained later to Ottoline.[49] Even as close a friend as Herbert Read could not but admit that Eliot "had a streak of hypochondria and was addicted to pills and potions."[50] That summer Vivien worried about Tom's health, as he continued tired and low-spirited.

Working against the clock to finish *The Sacred Wood,* Tom began to make excuses to see less of Mary, who attempted to provoke him with an account of her stay with Lytton. "Glad . . . to hear Lytton's life is so perfect," responded Eliot. They dined out together and Eliot wrote that although he was ashamed of the quality of the meal, he was very happy to see her and hoped it would happen again.[51] But his heart was not in the relationship. He began to backpedal, encouraging Mary, who continued to press invitations upon him, to see Vivien as well as himself. "Can you come to lunch with Vivien on *Saturday,"* he asked. "I will hope to see you afterwards when I get in?"[52] Mary, who was still having difficulties with Clive, seems to have suspected Eliot of having a new lover, and he accused her of having "a very suspicious nature."[53] When Mary asked him to dinner, he replied that they would *both* enjoy seeing her again: "Vivien is not here just now, and she will grumble if I go without her . . . so will you please not be nasty and invite us for next week," he begged.[54] He was relieved when she agreed to postpone dinner. Would she wear her cotton earrings, he asked, and look nice and be nice and they would talk a great deal.[55]

Vivien had communicated her growing fears for Eliot's health to Ezra Pound while they were in Paris. As a result, in June, Pound wrote to John Quinn in New York, who had begun to act as Eliot's agent, to propose the scheme which became known as "Bel Esprit," by which subscribers would contribute to a fund to allow Eliot to give up the bank. It was "a crime against literature," declared Pound, for Eliot to stay at Lloyds.[56] But his friend's terms were steeper than Pound anticipated: Eliot wanted £800 a year, a flat in London and six months abroad, and was not prepared to go back to lecturing which he found "much *more* fatiguing" than banking.[57] Meanwhile, unknown to Pound, Eliot received the first dividend cheque for $225 from the $900 promised by his mother from the Hydraulic Press-

Brick Company, and decided to take a walking holiday in France to restore his health after the "depressing adventure" which Paris had turned out to be.[58]

Before leaving he and Vivien spent the weekend of 6 August 1920 at Eastbourne with the Schiffs ("very nice Jews"); the weather was beautiful and the party, which included Wyndham Lewis, went motoring along the cliffs, and in the evening performed amateur dramatics in which both Vivien and Tom excelled. Momentarily they drew closer. Vivien's vivacious performance as an actress was remarked on by Sydney Schiff, who paid her gratifying attention. A few days later Tom sent his mother some photographs of Vivien taken by Ottoline at Garsington, telling her Vivien looked "very attractive."[59] It was not a comment calculated to please Charlotte, however hard Tom tried to bring his mother round to the idea of accepting her daughter-in-law.

On the 15 August Eliot and Wyndham Lewis—who had decided at the last minute to accompany the poet—arrived in Paris, leaving Vivien in the care of Violet and Sydney Schiff. The two men visited James Joyce in Paris, Eliot carrying a heavy parcel which he had been entrusted by Pound to hand to Joyce, who on first acquaintance struck Lewis as an oddity in patent-leather shoes, large powerful spectacles and a small ginger beard. Joyce accepted Eliot's invitation to meet at their small hotel on the Left Bank of the Seine. The parcel was placed in the middle of a large Second Empire marble table, standing upon gilt eagles' claws in the centre of the apartment. Joyce cut the string with Eliot's nail scissors and unrolled the damp brown paper. "Thereupon a fairly presentable pair of *old brown shoes* stood revealed." "Oh!" exclaimed James Joyce faintly. " 'Oh!' I echoed and laughed, and Joyce left the shoes where they were . . . ," wrote Lewis. Eliot, in his "still-trailing Bostonian voice . . . asked our visitor if he would have dinner with us."[60]

After this interlude, Eliot and Lewis continued on to the Loire and Brittany together. Lewis noted with surprise that his companion entered most scrupulously in a small notebook the day's expenses. "This he would do in the evening at a café table when we had our night-cap. There was not much more he could spend before he got into bed."[61] Eliot, however, found Lewis an intellectually stimulating companion, enjoying their stay in Saumur, where the artist sketched the old houses and they both drank copiously, until Lewis fell off his bicycle on the road to Chinon and bruised his hand so he could no longer hold a pencil; Eliot then left him in Dieppe to return to Vivien.

Eliot's holiday resolved him to try again for a new flat: Henry had sent £90 which encouraged his brother to look for something more expensive, and by September he thought he had found a property but, as he lamented to Henry, John Quinn and his mother, what he really longed for was a period of tranquillity to "do a poem that I have in mind."[62] Negotiating with the vendor, an "insane she-hyena," left him feeling maddened. Like every house-move the Eliots made, it was a fraught business, made worse by Eliot's impracticality and indecision, the *aboulie* or paralysis of will of which he complained throughout his life. As in the previous crisis over his son-in-law's unemployment, it was Charles Haigh-Wood who saved the situation. Haigh-Wood stepped in and took charge of the negotiations, which Eliot thankfully placed in his hands while he hurried to correct the proofs of his book.

It was not an opportune moment for Mary Hutchinson to renew her reproaches to Tom for ignoring her, and he responded touchily when she enquired in September whether he had forgotten her. No doubt Tom had heard the gossip about Clive's affair with Juana, although, according to Vanessa Bell, it was "on its last legs and . . . Mary will probably triumph after all,"[63] and about Mary's own latest love affair with Thomas Earp, the *Daily Telegraph* art critic. Oddly, in view of his own behaviour, Clive could not get over Mary's affair, writing sarcastically to enquire whether "to round the matter off," Mary was going to bed with Mrs. Earp as well.[64] "It is the only thing that really prevents Clive from returning to her," reported Vanessa.[65] But Tom was too preoccupied to be any sort of substitute for Clive. It would be more reasonable to ask if Mary had forgotten him, he retorted huffily. What had suddenly recalled him to her memory? As to her questions, he was not well and was about to have an operation; he had been engaged in activity towards a new flat, varied by agreeable weekend visits; his "pamphlet" *(The Sacred Wood)* would "emerge into obscurity in October *höffentlich*." As for writing, said the frustrated poet, I am only signing my name to leases.[66]

Eliot's irritation mounted at Mary's complaint that he and Vivien had not visited West Wittering that summer. Vivien had suggested September, said Tom, and neither of them had heard anything from her. Mary was still able to live her life on pre-war terms, and did not understand the difficult choices he and Vivien had to make between town and country, because he could not afford both. Mary, with her fine houses in London and Wittering, was insulated against the "horrible waste of time, energy, life, of the struggle with post-war machinery of life."[67] Mary's uncomprehending letters brought Tom face to face with the contrast between their lifestyles, hers that of a leisured wife, his that of hard-pressed City office worker.

Mary subsequently changed her line of attack, inviting Vivien to bring Tom to Wittering to convalesce from the operation on his nose, which was to be cauterised. In a dignified letter, Vivien declined the invitation, explaining that she could not possibly come with Tom to Eleanor, which she now believed had been the scene of Mary's seduction of Tom the previous summer, as well as of her own quarrel with Mary in autumn 1919. "It is a pity, but there are some things I can't do, and that is one of them." Magnanimously Vivien agreed that it might do Tom good to stay at Eleanor, if someone in the village could come in and cook his meals, but she herself could not be Mary's guest. "I do not bear you a grudge," wrote Vivien, but she had not forgotten her threat that he who laughs last laughs loudest. Like Eliot she would bide her time, and work on her "gunpowder plot," although not until 1925 was she to explode her "bomb" and betray her true feelings towards Mary, the wealthy and duplicitous hostess she believed had betrayed her friendship, in a malicious portrait intended to make Mary the same object of ridicule as she had made of Vivien as a deceived wife.[68] Sometimes Tom felt equally hostile towards Mary, writing to "Dearest Mary" as "Mrs. H (tho' rich)/A dreary kind of bitch."[69] What an extremely fine actor Tom is, noted Ottoline astutely, for he hates Mary and yet he is attentive to her.[70]

At the end of September 1920 Vivien asked Mary to meet her in London. "It would have been nice if you had come to Eastbourne to find me," she reproached her. "I wish you had."[71] Not for the first time, Vivien felt Mary neglected her when Tom was away. That summer Abigail Adams Eliot, Tom's first cousin, who was spending a year in Oxford, had asked Vivien to travel to Holland with her, but Vivien was obliged to stay at home; she had to prepare for the move into the new flat, and save money while Tom was abroad with Wyndham Lewis. Abigail was disappointed. In 1965 she wrote

> I have thought many times about Vivienne. You know I knew her quite well in the 1920s and I saw her once even after Tom had separated himself from her . . . I knew her as a charming, sensitive, affectionate person. I never doubted Tom's love for her and hers for him. I have been distressed by statements about . . . Vivienne as a person which have appeared in the press.[72]

In mid-October the long-awaited move took place to 9 Clarence Gate Gardens, a more spacious London flat, and the Eliots finally gave up Marlow. They were "moving in 2 peices" [sic] explained Vivien to Mary on 25 October. "Moving, especially double moving, is a great event,"[73] which was to take several weeks, as they lingered on in Crawford Mansions awaiting the arrival of Wyndham Lewis, who was taking it over. Vivien lost Mary's letter inviting them to dinner, because the confusion was immense in both flats; there was no place to be civilised in, she complained. "And Lewis sits here, in the wreckage. With a black patch on his eye."[74]

Just as the Eliots were completing the move, a new crisis occurred: Vivien's father Charles fell dangerously ill with what appeared at first to be food poisoning from some tinned sardines. An emergency operation was performed in the house in Compayne Gardens. Vivien was told by the surgeon that her adored father would have died within ten minutes, as there was an abscess in his abdomen which was on the point of breaking. Haigh-Wood was not expected to survive the night. Vivien, Tom and Rose sat up with him till daybreak, and for many days afterwards shared his care with two hired nurses. Although the abscess had been removed, the surgeons said they would have to operate again as soon as Charles was stronger. Vivien lent her mother her servant Ellen, as Rose's servant was ill, and then collapsed with a migraine. Forced to return to the new flat in the evenings, because there was no room for her to sleep at her parents' house, she remained anxious because she and Tom had no telephone. "Vivien is particularly fond of her father," explained Tom to his mother on 31 October, describing Charles Haigh-Wood as a "sweet, simple man" who was perfectly happy in the country, drawing and painting. "She takes more after him and his side of the family, and understands him better than the others do."[75]

Somehow Haigh-Wood survived a second operation, even though the surgeon was apparently so horrified by what he found that at first he simply wanted to sew the patient up and let him die. Weeks of worry followed for Vivien, as her father slowly convalesced. She wrote:

> We have been fighting every minute a long losing battle against *horrible* illnesses, unimaginable pain, doctors' mistakes—obstinacy—stupidity—delays—family's blindness. The only thing on my side has been my father's courage and determination. But I am afraid we're going to lose after all, & after so much fighting it will be very hard to bear.

Anxious to stay in touch, Vivien had a telephone installed. On Boxing Day Haigh-Wood's life was again despaired of. Vivien told Mary:

> I can't make an engagement more than an hour ahead. There are changes every few hours, and every single complication and misadventure happens. I never go to bed without fear, & to ring up first thing every morning takes all one's courage . . .

Vivien asked Mary to ring her at two o'clock, and if she felt "secure enough to leave Father," she would come over. She had been out of the "great world" for so long, she wrote, that before long she would fade away altogether.[76]

By February 1921 Haigh-Wood was convalescing in Tunbridge Wells. Vivien was deeply grateful to Tom for his support in this crisis, telling Mary that her husband had been simply wonderful, doing everything and making everyone adore him. "We should never have come through without him," she wrote. Her father was still alive, but in great danger and great pain. "I am so fond of him," she told Mary; it was the utmost torture to see people one loved in pain, or to think of doing without them.[77] Eventually Haigh-Wood made a miraculous recovery.

As Vivien continued to nurse her father, Tom felt his own brain had become numb. The upset of the move to Clarence Gate Gardens and the strain of his father-in-law's illness had prevented him from writing for two months, despite trying to seal himself hermetically against the "domestic weepies." Now, the move completed, Eliot decided to take his remaining holiday from the bank in Paris. It was a nostalgic trip. He returned alone to the Pension Casaubon in rue St. Jacques, where he had stayed with Jean Verdenal in 1910–11. The old proprietors were dead, but their grandson had kept on the pension. Perhaps Eliot stayed in his old bedroom, which had been taken over by Jean when he left, and wandered again in the nearby Luxembourg Gardens where Jean had picked lilac. Certainly his thoughts were of the medical student as he at last set to work on the "long poem," provisionally entitled "He Do the Police in Different Voices," a quotation from Charles Dickens's *Our Mutual Friend* which expresses Eliot's intention to weave together a pattern of voices both personal and impersonal.[78] This poem, which would become *The Waste Land,* had been in his mind since November 1919,[79] when he had been attending séances conducted by a mystic, P. D. Ouspensky, in London, in a possible attempt to communicate with his lost friend.[80] The city "would be desolate for me with pre-war memories of Jean Verdenal," Eliot confessed to his mother, but for the company of Vivien's brother Maurice, who joined him in Paris, and the new acquaintances he made—writers and painters who had heard of him even if they did not read English. For Vivien, left at home, he bought "very cheap" a drawing by Raoul Dufy.[81]

Many months of caring for her father without respite took its toll on Vivien, and when he was finally out of danger in February, she collapsed with influenza. Tom professed to feel sorry for her, but he remained detached. "Do come on Monday if you don't mind Vivien's being shut in her room," he wrote to Mary.[82] Vivien developed neuritis, in her arms, legs, feet and back. "Have you ever been in such incessant and extreme pain that you felt your sanity going, and that you no longer knew reality from delusion? That's the way she is," Tom informed Brigit Patmore on 17 March 1921. "She is in screaming agony."[83] The doctors were unable to help Vivien's pain, which may have been in part a psychosomatic expression of her longing for some sympathy from Tom. Instead he sent Vivien to a nursing home for several weeks until the mounting expense made it necessary to bring her home again. A specialist treated her for nervous exhaustion, and her "stomach trouble" had become so alarming, despite massage, that she was allowed to see no one but Tom. As soon as she was up, he resolved to send her to the country for a month, gloomily confiding to Sydney Schiff, whose wife Violet had just had an operation, that he did not expect his wife to be really well for another year or two.

Banishing Vivien to the country, whether to an institution or a cottage, was Tom's frequent response to her illnesses, and one liable to increase her sense of rejection and abandonment. Aldington speculated in his novella that Eliot's attempts to free himself temporarily of Vivien came about at the suggestion of Ezra Pound, who had watched his protégé's dissension with his wife with growing dismay:

> "You can't go on like this. You're driving each other crazy."
>
> "Ye-es," said Cibber.
>
> "Well, can't you do *something*?"
>
> "What is there to be said, what is there to be done?" Cibber retorted languidly . . .
>
> "Look here, what I mean is, why don't you send her to the country for a month?"
>
> "What! In cold weather like this?"
>
> "Why not?"
>
> "She wouldn't like it."
>
> "Well, she'll have to lump it."
>
> "But she wouldn't go."
>
> "Damn it!" exclaimed the irascible Cholmp, "make her go."
>
> "But I don't know where to send her."
>
> "Hell! You've got the whole miserable little island!"
>
> "Ye-es, ye-es."
>
> ". . . Try Cheltenham."
>
> "Yes," Cibber agreed, "one might do worse than Cheltenham."[84]

By 1921 the cracks in the Eliot marriage were becoming chasms. Eliot began to think of himself and Vivien as Paolo and Francesca, Dante's doomed lovers, buffeted for eternity by the "warring winds" of hell as punishment for their carnal sins.[85] In Tom's eyes, he and Vivien seemed to be suffering a similar fate: to inhabit their own hell, to wage their own war of words. In their unhappiness both Eliots had looked outside the marriage for comfort, each becoming acutely dependent on an aged parent for the love and affection missing in their own relationship; it was the frailty of Vivien's father, and the prospect of his loss, which had triggered her breakdown, for only her father offered her the love and devotion her husband denied her. Tom's own despair was expressed in his choice of pseudonym, "Gus Krutsch," under which he contributed a poem, "Song to the Opherian," published in Wyndham Lewis's *Tyro* in May 1920. It is an ugly name, not only suggesting deformity,[86] but, in its resemblance to "crotch," also an apt one for the protagonist of a sexual story. "Krutsch" also resembles Conrad's "Mr. Kurtz" in *Heart of Darkness,* a novel which influenced Eliot so profoundly that he chose a quotation from it as the original epigraph for *The Waste Land* until dissuaded by Pound. For Kurtz, "nerves went wrong"; he is possessed by the "powers of darkness." Among the "subtle horrors" of the jungle, he discovers he is "hollow at the core." Did Eliot, like Kurtz, feel "I am lying here in the dark waiting for death?"[87]

Certainly the effort of creativity implied self-sacrifice: "It is a sacrifice of the man to the work, it is a kind of death," Eliot wrote in a letter to the *Athenaeum* published on 25 June 1920, in which he voiced the same conviction expressed in his most famous essay in *The Sacred Wood,* "Tradition and the Individual Talent," that what the poet experiences "is the continual surrender of himself as he is at the moment to something more valuable. The progress of an artist is a continual extinction of personality."[88] Each poem was a little death, the depersonalized mind of the artist operating as the catalyst through which emotions were transmuted into new combinations; sometimes Eliot felt himself to be like a scientist with his test-tube, creating new acid from old gases. But as he gestated his greatest poem, he was preoccupied not only with transforming his own creative death into life, but with the theme of the death of a woman: Eliot had recently seen Webster's *The Duchess of Malfi* at the Lyric, in which the lustful duchess is strangled by her brother's agents as punishment for her immoral marriage.[89] For the Duchess, like Francesca, death was, it seemed, the karma she deserved.

By midsummer 1921 all Tom's hopes were centred on the arrival of his mother, Charlotte, who he believed would magically heal his unhappiness. His spirits rose as the date of her arrival drew close, while Vivien's sank at the prospect of finally coming face to face with her rival. Charlotte, who had now moved to 27 Concord Avenue, Cambridge, sailed with her un-married daughter Marian Cushing Eliot, and Henry, on the *S.S. Adriatic* at the beginning of June; Tom had insisted that Charlotte should not book rooms in an hotel or take lodgings, but accept his offer of their own com-fortable flat and servant during their stay. Vivien and Tom in turn would move in with Lucy Thayer, Vivien's American friend, who had returned to England after the death of her mother, and was renting a much smaller flat at 12 Wigmore Street. Vivien had no desire to leave her new home in Clarence Gate Gardens so soon after moving in, but the arrangement met Tom's own need to re-create his childhood proximity to his mother: "I should keep my books here and should often work here in the evenings, and I should be dropping in of course all the time . . ." he wrote happily.[90] Conscious of his mother's age, he implored her not to start the holiday fa-tigued. Ellen, their servant, would bring her breakfast in bed every morn-ing, and she was to rest in the afternoon.

Vivien was determined to be on her best behaviour for her mother-in-law, despite her ambivalent feelings towards the woman she felt was de-priving Tom of his rightful inheritance. She returned from the sanatorium full of good intentions. Much depended on the visit, for if Charlotte could be persuaded to like her English daughter-in-law, she might agree to hand over to Tom outright, as she had to Henry, the rest of the Hydraulic Press-Brick Company shares, which were holding up well despite the industrial depression. Henry had been trying to convince their mother to take this step, but she refused to make a decision until she had met Vivien. Tom, who was conscious that Vivien had made a financial sacrifice in marrying him, was also anxious to know whether Charlotte would agree to his ear-lier strongly worded request for his wife to receive his inheritance on his death. Eliot had also asked Charlotte to keep up his life insurance, arguing that Vivien would only receive £60 a year from Lloyds in the event of his death.

Vivien's inheritance from her father would not support her, argued Tom, because of heavy death duties and the division of the estate between her and Maurice, who was unemployed after his discharge from the army. In any case, Vivien and Maurice would receive nothing until both parents were dead. Vivien could not support herself, Tom explained, because her eyes were so weak that her oculist only permitted her to do close work for two hours a day—not a convincing excuse in view of the secretarial work she was accustomed to doing.[91] Peter Ackroyd has speculated that Eliot's preoccupation with the possibility of his own death, despite having no serious disease, indicates his suicidal feelings at this time. But it is more likely that Eliot's depression sprang from his fierce sense of injustice at being treated the same way as his mentally handicapped sister, Margaret, was—her shares were also put in trust—as well as his frustration at the lack of time to work on the important poem which it had been his New Year's resolution as long ago as 31 December 1919 to complete.

When she finally disembarked at Southampton on 10 June 1921, the seventy-seven-year-old Charlotte proved not to be the frail old lady her son anticipated, but a "terrifyingly energetic" personage who demanded every moment of Tom's time; of whom, in fact, Tom was "terrified," said Maurice, when he saw his brother-in-law with this "tough old woman who wrote poetry."[92] Coming face to face after six years with this formidable matriarch, the model for Amy in *The Family Reunion,* was a considerable shock to Tom, banishing the false and sentimental memories of childhood recalled from the safety of England, and reviving the fear and sulky obedience of the years in St. Louis. He had to take "Mother dearest" sightseeing, to Stratford and Kenilworth; he was forced to devote weekends to introducing his family to Ottoline at Garsington in August, instead of going to the seaside at Bosham. Despite the poet's handsome presence, which caused Ottoline to remark admiringly to Vivien, "Isn't Tom beautiful, Vivienne, such a *fine mind,* such a grand impression. Such a good walk,"[93] as he escorted Charlotte through the Italian garden created by Ottoline, Virginia sensed the suppressed rage which lay behind Tom's "grim marble face: a mouth twisted & shut; not a single line free & easy; all caught, pressed, inhibited; but great driving power somewhere."[94] To Tom, his mother, sister and brother appeared not as the intimate family members he had anticipated, but as strangers who interrupted the creative solitude for which he longed.

On 7 August, Vivien, Tom and Charlotte Eliot were entertained by Ottoline, and six days later, on the 13th, Vivien and Henry Ware Eliot Jr. visited Ottoline again at Garsington. Tom was present the day after, on the 14th.[95] It was on one such evening, when Tom was talking to Siegfried Sassoon, that Vivien began gossiping to the artist Mark Gertler, whose patron Ottoline had become since meeting him in 1914. Gertler, a frequent Garsington guest, was known for his malicious tongue and self-interest; he and Vivien dashed off arm in arm into the garden and Ottoline suspected that they were laughing about herself and Philip. It was a subject on which she was particularly sensitive after D. H. Lawrence's cruel portrait of her as Hermione Roddice, and Ottoline began to sense that Vivien could be indiscreet. Their friendship, which had been so close, was no longer unsullied.[96]

Nor was there a happy resolution to the financial problem. During July, Vivien and Tom sweltered in the tiny flat in Wigmore Street, "an attic with a glass roof." Vivien asked Charlotte to tea and, anxious to make a good impression, invited the Sitwell brothers to help her manage her guests. "Mrs. Eliot senior, and her daughter were polite, formal, even stiff, black-clothed New Englanders by style and antecedents," remembered Osbert. Vivien had given Osbert the impression that she "bitterly resented" her mother-in-law, explaining that since the death of his father, Tom's mother was well enough off to help her son, and could "spare him the necessity of being a bank-clerk," but that she would not come to his aid owing to her scruples of conscience, "knowing that, because Tom was a poet and not a business man (though he had been forced to become one), his father would have strongly disapproved of any effort that she might make to ease the burden." Osbert was impressed that Vivien seemed "immensely, genuinely, and without selfishness, to resent this treatment of her husband." But he remarked that "when you met old Mrs. Eliot it was difficult to think any ill of her. She appeared to be a strait-laced, straightforward, conventional, but kindly lady."[97]

Mrs. Eliot Senior was not as kindly as Osbert supposed. She blamed and disliked Vivien as much as Vivien blamed and disliked her. She was not convinced that Vivien was really ill. "I am afraid [Tom] finds it impossible to do creative work (other than critical) at home," commented Henry. "Vivien demands a good deal of attention, and I imagine is easily offended if she does not get it well buttered with graciousness and sympathy."[98] In addition she was deeply suspicious of Vivien's brother Maurice, now a louche "young man about town," who would soon leave for Kenya's Happy Valley to make his fortune.[99] The following year, on 8 April 1922 Mrs. Eliot wrote to Henry that she feared that Maurice "would sponge off his sister and brother-in-law."[100] She made up her mind not to transfer the shares, writing her decision into her will in 1923. Charlotte's malevolent jealousy of Vivien can be understood in the words of condemnation Amy, mistress of Wishwood in *The Family Reunion,* delivers on the dead wife of her son Harry: "She never would have been one of the family,/She never wished to be one of the family,/She only wanted to keep him to herself/To satisfy her vanity." Vivien never accepted, says Amy/Charlotte "Harry's relations or Harry's old friends;/She never wanted to fit herself to Harry,/But only to bring Harry down to her own level."[101] The character Mary, for whom Eliot's Cambridge friend Emily Hale was probably the inspiration, talks revealingly of the effect Amy's hatred has on Harry's wife: "And even when *she* died: I believed that Cousin Amy—/I almost believed it—had killed her by willing." Mary asks, "Doesn't that sound awful?" but the strength of Mrs. Eliot's disapproval of Vivien was such that Tom felt able to imagine such a result.[102]

Charlotte Eliot defended her decision not to transfer the Hydraulic Press-Brick Company shares to her second son in a Memorandum summarising Tom's life, which she wrote in 1921 on her return from the fateful visit to England. Her disappointment is evident that her son "unfortunately" postponed his examination at Harvard for his doctorate in philosophy, not literature as he originally planned, until after his return from Göttingen and Oxford; that the war then intervened, and that in the summer of 1914 "he met and married an English lady." Vivien is not even named in this account of Tom's life. Were she able to afford it, wrote Charlotte, she would settle on Tom enough to enable him to devote his entire time to literature, but "this is impossible."[103]

At this juncture, in July 1921, Vivien retreated again to the country, ostensibly for the sake of her health, but Tom urgently summoned her back to help him. It seemed that at last his luck had changed: an opportunity had arisen to crack the safe of English letters. The proposal, brokered by Scofield Thayer and Sydney Schiff, was to establish a new literary quarterly to take the place of the now defunct *Art and Letters;* Eliot was to edit it, and Lady Rothermere,[104] wife of Harold Sydney Harmsworth, first Viscount Rothermere, the owner of the *Daily Mirror,* was to finance it. It was the chance for which he had been waiting, but the negotiations required "exceptional tact," Eliot told Ottoline, and Vivien was *"invalu-*

able."[105] However, as Lady Rothermere continued to stall, Vivien became pessimistic, writing to Scofield Thayer on 20 July that Lady Rothermere "does *not* wish . . . to spill her cash for the cause of Literature . . . I am sorry and Tom is sorry." They were in the midst of a heatwave in London, and Tom had had his family on his hands since early June. Tom was so "tired and hot" that she was taking over his business correspondence, despite joking to her old admirer that her mind had left her and she was gradually becoming insane:

> So you see other people have troubles as well as yourself, and I believe you invited me to come and drown myself with you, once. I am ready at any moment. T. says delighted to review Joyce . . . Well, go and frizzle—we shall be in Paris in *October,* many D's V.[106]

Just before the Eliot party left, Vivien's control snapped. Intuitive enough to sense Charlotte Eliot's implacable hostility towards her, and irritated by her mother-in-law's puritanical manner and financial control over their lives, Vivien at last gave way to her emotions. To Henry, whom she regarded as a friend, although she was disappointed not to see more of him during his visit (perhaps he chose to avoid her), she wrote on 23 August 1921:

> Dear Henry.
> Now I want you to tell me something truly. You are not to lie. Did your mother and sister show, think say or intimate that I behaved like "no lady," and just like a wild animal when [we] saw you off? I was perfectly stunned on that occasion. I had no idea what I was doing. I have been more or less stunned for many months now and when I come to, I suppose it seems dreadful, to an American. I have worried all the time since. Tom said it was perfectly allright etc. but I am sure he has lived here so long he hardly realises how *very* much less English people mind showing their emotions than Americans—or perhaps he does realise it so perfectly. But I was extremely anxious to show no emotion before your family at any time, and then I ended in a fit!

I found the emotionless condition a great strain, all the time. I used to think I should burst out and scream and dance. That's why I used to think you were so terribly failing me. But I won't talk about that now, except to ask you if ever two people made *such* a fearful mess of their obvious possibilities ... Goodbye Henry. And *be personal,* you must be personal, or else it is no good.

Nothing's any good.

Vivien.[107]

Although Henry's loyalties lay with his family, he was discerning enough to detect some of the psychological motivation behind Vivien's "invalidism." "I have a feeling that subconsciously (or unconsciously) she likes the role of invalid, and that, liking it as she does to be petted, 'made a fuss over,' condoled and consoled, she ... encourages her breakdowns, instead of throwing them off by a sort of nervous resistance," he wrote to Charlotte on 30 October after his return to Chicago. Henry thought that it was hard to tell how much of Vivien's illness was physical and how much mental and controllable by will power, but if she had more of "the Will to Be Well" she would have less suffering. She needed something to take her mind off herself, something to absorb her entire attention.[108] Henry thought he had discovered the key to Vivien's breakdown after her father's near-fatal illness: that it was the only way she knew of penetrating her husband's remoteness and formality, of reaching a man who otherwise ignored her. He did not see that Eliot, in starving Vivien of affection, was unwittingly contributing to her hysteria.

After Charlotte, Henry and Marian left, Tom and Vivien both became deeply depressed. They lingered on in Wigmore Street, lacking the energy to move back to Clarence Gate Gardens, their only consolation Henry's typewriter, which he had left for his brother to use. "You are ... an angel. A bloody angel ..." wrote Vivien in thanks. Henry's roses were dying miserably in their vase, as she confessed, "We miss you dreadfully." She and Tom did not even have the spirit to buy wine, yet when the evening came they cursed and abused each other for not having gone out to get it.

Quarrels and migraines punctuated their lives. "I feel you are right about Tom. He must somehow be *tamed*," Vivien wrote to Mary

Hutchinson, warning her not to say anything to Jack. "You don't know it, but he is often very unkind to me in a way, and often makes me wretched."[109] Tom's expectations of his family's visit had been unrealistic; when they left he blamed Vivien for the fact that nothing had changed. They were still trapped in this misery. Overpowered by a sense of anti-climax, he complained to his friends that he was exhausted, "paralysed" by his reaction to his family's departure, although by the end of August he had signed a contract with Lady Rothermere and was plunged into business calculations. Surprisingly, in view of her lack of experience, he turned to Mary Hutchinson for advice, asking whether she thought a new literary periodical the size of *Art and Letters* was possible or worthwhile. Were there enough good contributors, or enough possible subscribers, and what would it all cost? The biggest question of all was, "Whether I am competent and have time enough . . . *Please keep it to yourself till I let you know it may be revealed* . . . Write and comfort me," he begged.[110] Mary offered to meet him—they had not met since April—and they made an assignation at the Piccadilly Hotel for 5:15 p.m. "I will look out for you inside the Regent Street entrance," wrote Tom.[111]

But neither old friends nor society could mend his "emotional de-rangement." On the verge of collapse, Eliot turned to Richard Aldington, whose own experience of war-shattered nerves and marital problems in-clined him to sympathy. Aldington was at the time consoling the Imagist poet and translator Frank Stuart Flint, who was depressed, Harold Monro, who had problems with alcohol, and Frederic Manning (a con-tributor to Monro's *Chapbook*), complaining to Amy Lowell that his own work was delayed "because of having to rush off from time to time to save people from nervous breakdowns,"[112] but he invited Eliot to Malthouse Cottage, near Reading, where he was living. Even a weekend in September at Aldington's "cottage for neurasthenics"[113] did nothing to re-store Tom's spirits, although his friend had written a generous review of *The Sacred Wood,*[114] perhaps in an effort to cheer Tom, who was depressed by the book's generally disappointing reception since its publication in November 1920.

Eliot continued to go downhill rapidly: "I have been feeling very ner-vous and shaky lately, and have very little self-control . . . Your not being here but in Chicago seems as unreal as death . . ."[115] he told Henry. Vivien was seriously worried, writing to Mary: "Tom is ill. He is overworked and tired of living . . . I wish he could break his leg, it is the only way out of this that I can think of."[116] Fearful that her husband was indeed suicidal after his separation from his family, Vivien decided to take matters into her own hands. At the beginning of October she made an appointment for him to see a celebrated nerve specialist, who, shocked at his patient's mental state, immediately prescribed three months' complete change and rest. The bank agreed to give Tom three months' leave. By now Eliot was barely able to function, sleeping all day and struggling to write the few essential letters before his departure. Asking St. John Hutchinson to write his "London Letter" for *The Dial,* he left on 14 October for Margate with Vivien. "I am supposed to be alone, but I could [not] bear the idea of starting this treatment quite alone in a strange place, and I have asked my wife to come with me and stay with me as long as she is willing,"[117] he explained to Richard Aldington, asking him to house their small cat (a good mouser) while they were in Margate.

The day before Vivien had written to explain the situation to Scofield Thayer:

> Tom has had a rather serious breakdown, and has had to stop all work and go away for three months. He has to follow a strict regimen, and may only read (for pleasure, not profit) two hours a day.

Could Scofield wait for Tom's review of Marianne Moore's poems until February, she asked. She had written to Seldes, Thayer's partner, to tell him that Tom had "fortunately" secured St. John to do the "London Letter." Would Scofield (who was in Vienna) write to Seldes for her about the review, she pleaded. "You have nothing to do, I presume, and look at *my* position. I have not nearly finished my own nervous breakdown yet."[118] It was an ironic letter which demonstrates that Vivien managed to retain a sense of humour in the midst of her trials. She was suffering "hateful stupid temperatures" for no real reason at all, as she confided to Violet Schiff, who had the same troublesome symptom, and had so many business letters to write for Tom.[119]

At Margate, on the Kent coast, Vivien and Tom stayed at the

Albemarle Hotel, Cliftonville, "a nice, comfortable and *inexpensive* little hotel," and Vivien bought her agitated husband a mandolin. Sitting in the shelter on the promenade, he began to pick out the notes. The days passed in walking by the sea and enjoying the air. "You will be pleased to hear that Tom is getting on *amazingly,"* wrote Vivien to Violet. "It is not quite a fortnight yet, but he looks already younger and fatter and nicer. He is quite good, and not unhappy, keeping regular hours and being out in this wonderful air nearly all day."[120]

Nevertheless Tom's psychological distress was extreme, and required more than physical exercise and a healthy diet. He and Vivien discussed the idea of consulting Dr. Roger Vittoz, the Swiss psychiatrist who was a favourite of Ottoline Morrell's, whom she had recommended for Bertrand Russell and was now strongly advising Tom to visit. "I want a specialist in psychological troubles," Eliot wrote to Julian Huxley, whom Ottoline had also sent as a patient to Vittoz in 1918, after Huxley had collapsed with a nervous breakdown following his honeymoon.[121] Meanwhile Vivien reported to Mary: "I have started Tom well and he shows great improvement already." After two weeks she returned to London.

Tom continued to sit in the shelter on the promenade, to sketch the passers-by and practise scales on his mandolin. At last there was time to turn again to the manuscript of *The Waste Land* on which he had been working sporadically between crises for the last two years. He told Schiff on 4 November that he had done "a rough draft of part of Part III," calling it "The Fire Sermon." "I do not know whether it will do & must wait for Vivien's opinion."[122]

While Tom remained in Margate, Vivien wrote to Russell to congratulate him on the arrival of his first son, John Conrad, following his marriage to Dora Black. "As you know, Tom is having a bad nervous—or so called—breakdown . . . He is at present at Margate, of all cheerful spots! But he seems to like it," she wrote. In an allusion to Tom's poem "Mr. Apollinax," in which Russell's satanic aspect is stressed, she wrote: "Tom says he is quite sure the baby *will* have pointed ears, so you need not be anxious. Even if not pointed at birth, they will sharpen in time."[123] It was a painful letter for Vivien to write. Bravely she hid her true feelings, for she often missed Bertie's companionship in the days of misery since the end of their affair. In a revealing undated letter to Ottoline she had written:

About Bertie, you know he was *extraordinarily generous* to me. I mean in *giving* things. So much so that it will always make me feel mean for talking against him. I know you understand perfectly. But I think he was more generous to me than he has ever been to anyone. He really made a sacrifice. I shall never forget that, and it makes a lot of difference to *everything*. I have really suffered awfully in the complete collapse of our relationship, for I *was* fond of Bertie (I think I still am). But it is of course hopeless. I shall never try to see him again.[124]

On 18 November 1921 Vivien escorted her husband across the Channel to Paris, where she and Tom stayed with Ezra and Dorothy Pound at 70 bis rue Notre Dame des Champs. A few days later Tom travelled on alone to Lausanne to meet the psychiatrist Roger Vittoz.

13

The Waste Land

Vivien found it difficult at first to get "a clutch on Paris." After being immured in England for seven years, it was painful to be torn up by the roots, and "thrown, hurled, alone & stunned, into such a strange way of living." The first few days alone with Tom were perfect, she told Mary, but then the moment came when she was forced to take her husband to the station and watch him climb onto the "dreadful Swiss train." Vivien was left alone on the platform at 9:20 in the evening, feeling as if someone had taken a broomstick to her and knocked her on the head.

The empty weeks stretched ahead. She had no idea when Tom would return to Paris. "I was so *absolutely* alone," she wrote to Mary on 16 November 1921: "All the French I knew deserted me." But gradually, like someone slowly coming back to life after a long hibernation, Vivien forgot London and became absorbed in Parisian life. It was a relief to leave behind the Bloomsbury backbiting and literary feuds which she had come to detest, to forget the " 'intellectual' party" given by Lady Rothermere ("What a woman"), and the last evening at the Huxleys which epitomised everything she disliked about "the whole stupid round": the monotony, the *"drivel,"*[1] which had given her "an awful down on London." Mary would disagree with her, acknowledged Vivien, but she was glad to turn her back on it all. Yet even from the safe distance of the Hotel du Pas-de-Calais, 59 rue des Saints-Pères, a narrow turning off the Boulevard Saint-Germain, she could not help worrying if the Eliots' "enemies" were talking behind their backs. "Stick up for me if you hear nasty things (they will be lies) and also for Tom," she begged her friend.[2]

Although Vivien professed to miss Mary, the Pounds' kindness compensated for her absence. Ezra and Dorothy had made their home on the Left Bank, renting an "exquisite" studio, with two rooms on rue Notre

Dame des Champs, the street where Whistler had lived as a young man. The studio was not far from Vivien's hotel and the fashionable bohemian bar Les Deux Magots, and only cost £75 a year. Vivien herself was marooned in a "high up little room" and having meals *en pension,* which she loathed. She envied the Pounds their snug nest, for she had already decided that she would prefer to live in Paris rather than London. "For Tom, I am *convinced,* Paris!" Although the city was incredibly dear—"it costs *fortunes,*" she complained, it had a vibrant artistic life, to which Vivien had the entrée through Pound, who performed the same role of impresario to impoverished and undiscovered artists and writers in Paris as he had done in London, bringing James and Nora Joyce to a supper party where the Irishman met Sylvia Beach, publisher and owner of the famous bookshop Shakespeare and Company. Pound, as flamboyant as ever in his velvet jacket and "open road shirt," his jutting red beard reminding one writer of a fox's muzzle, had persuaded Ernest Hemingway, W. B. Yeats, and André Gide to subscribe to Beach's costs in publishing *Ulysses.*[3] In between writing his Cantos and encouraging the sculptor Constantin Brancusi, Pound made his own furniture and cooked over an oil lamp, producing, declared Wyndham Lewis, better suppers than in London.

Pound took Vivien three times to meet the thirty-eight-year-old Joyce, but although she admired him as a writer, she did not find the "cantankerous Irishman," in his long overcoat and tennis shoes, an agreeable acquaintance. The attraction of Paris for her lay not in the presence of Hemingway, Ford Madox Ford, Lewis, Aldington, or even Gertrude Stein, but in the prospect of a *rendez-vous* somewhere on the continent with her close friend and former suitor, Scofield Thayer, who had arrived in Paris in July 1921 with e.e. cummings. While Pound had stayed at the cheap hotel on the rue des Saints-Pères that he recommended to Vivien, Thayer had been able to afford the luxurious Hotel Continental on the rue Castiglione. But by the time of the Eliots' arrival in November the bird had flown. Scofield had left for Cologne, having told Vivien on 27 July that he preferred the "coolth" of Germany. His plan was to move on to Vienna sometime in October: "If en route to Paris you should get the wrong train and get out at Vienna, be sure to look me up,"[4] he wrote.

Scofield's sympathy meant a great deal to Vivien; there was no one else apart from Ezra Pound whose friendship predated her marriage, and who she felt understood her troubles. "Yes, drowning just now should certainly be the thing," he had responded ironically to her last letter offering to drown herself with him. Scofield was sorry that Vivien and Tom were so troubled, remarking that to have one's family on one's hands in midsummer struck him as no less appropriate than to wear mittens. "Goethe once observed, speaking of his love affairs, that it was pleasant to see the moon rise before the sun set," he wrote on 20 October in another attempt to comfort Vivien. "But such is not I presume the case with nervous breakdowns, especially when they are both in the same family."[5] Vivien applied for a German visa, as Thayer was still in Cologne, but then as the value of the Deutschmark fell, she decided to wait for Scofield's return. Meanwhile she exhibited few signs of mental strain: to the concert pianist Olga Rudge, Vivien, to whom she was introduced by her friend Pound, seemed "very charming, perfectly normal."[6]

While she waited at the Hotel du Pas-de-Calais for the return of "the man from Cologne," as she discreetly described him to Mary, anxious no doubt that Clive's wagging tongue would not broadcast tales of her meeting with Thayer to Bloomsbury ears, Vivien began to record her impressions of Paris in a notebook. It was not the first time she had considered writing creatively, for she was a "reckless" letter-writer already, as Virginia and Brigit Patmore both noticed, as well as a diarist, but while she still hoped to dance or act professionally it did not occur to her to think of writing for publication. Nor were the war years in London conducive to writing: in 1918 Vivien had written that "life is so feverish and yet so dreary at the same time, and one is always waiting, waiting for something. Generally waiting for some particular strain to be over. One thinks, when this is over I will write. And then there is something else. For *months* now I have waited for T. to be settled [over joining the army]. I am also waiting to be well."[7] Later, Virginia Woolf was to claim that she was the person who had first suggested to Vivien that she might write, but it is possible that Vivien had begun recording her thoughts in her writing book in adolescence, during the long days of being confined to bed for treatment of TB of the bone. She has been "writing for a long time," Tom admitted to Ottoline, who challenged him over Vivien's authorship of a poem in the *Criterion* in May 1925, "and I have always suspected that you knew it!"[8]

Ottoline herself was an example to Vivien. Ottoline confided to

Dorothy Brett as early as 1916 that she was writing her memoirs, and showed her extracts from her journal;[9] Vivien may also have seen Ottoline's work in about 1919 when they became intimate, and felt encouraged that her friend, despite being "very diffident" at any thought of competing with her celebrated guests, nevertheless dared to record her own opinions of the authors who rarely hesitated to caricature her. But it was Mary Hutchinson, a published writer, who was Vivien's prime inspiration; fashionable, flirty Mary, rather than the cool Virginia or "acid" Katherine Mansfield, served as her role model. However, there is also little doubt that in 1921 Vivien, just as much as Tom, felt a compelling need to express her despair with her tormented marriage. To do so was a form of therapy. In addition, both the Eliots were suddenly free from the domestic responsibility for which they were singularly ill-fitted, and had the time and solitude necessary for creativity.

The prospect of the launch of Lady Rothermere's new review may have been an added inducement to Vivien. The *Criterion,* a name which Vivien suggested,[10] inspired by a hotel at which she and Charles Buckle used to dine, could provide her with an outlet for the prose sketches with which she was experimenting. Her husband, as editor, might be persuaded to give her the same chance as he had given Mary at the *Egoist.*

Whatever her reasons, Vivien's prose sketches were autobiographical, a fact which was to be her undoing. In "A Diary of the Rive Gauche," she writes in the first person, painting a vivid picture of herself, aimlessly walking the streets of the Latin Quarter. For three days it had been raining, "the cold hard venomous rain of Paris. Very different from the soft enveloping moisture of London where often one can hardly tell if it is raining or not. Wet English weather, and a wet wind, say I. Steam heating and harsh winds soon take the bloom off poor thin-skinned English faces." At last the rain stopped, to be replaced by a fierce, drying wind which cut through the narrow streets and blew full blast over the bridges. Vivien took refuge in the pension's salon, bringing her writing materials downstairs because the chambermaid Victorine and her husband were cleaning her room. The salon was so small that only four people could sit in it, and anyone could read what Vivien was writing unless she hedged the paper with her left arm like an awkward schoolgirl over a letter. No light penetrated into the room except that from the open door into the hall, and the radiator heated it to suffocation; but she found the warmth comforting and began to write. The theme she took was one much on her mind: the relationship between an American man and an Englishwoman.

> There is a strange man in the salon, who is obviously waiting for someone. He holds his hat in his hand. He is American, I think. He looks at me from time to time and I feel sure that he contemplates asking me a question. But why me? Although of course the others are obviously French: the pale, austere old lady, and the uncomfortable-looking middle-aged woman who glares at me so indignantly. So many people look at one indignantly here. One gets used to it. Hardened.[11]

Vivien sympathises with the other guests' disapproval. She is, after all, in loose shabby clothes with no hat and slippers on her feet, daring to sprawl at the writing-table and write on and on without stopping or looking up or making any of the impatient clicks or ejaculations that they do. The middle-aged woman is wearing "black bombazine or some such harsh material, made very tight and fitting to her figure—a *real* figure, not a few bones with rags hung on, like mine. No wonder she is indignant." At this point the stranger addresses Vivien:

> "Pardon me!—but do you happen to be acquainted with Miss Newton who is staying in this hotel?"
> "No," I say flatly.
> "You will excuse me addressing you, I hope; but I took you for English—" he looks at me hard.
> "Yes—?"
> "I'm an American," he tells me, most unnecessarily; "and I made the acquaintance of Miss Newton at the Soirée last Friday at the Consulate. I asked her if she would like to go to one of these Latin Quarter balls."

His next question provokes Vivien's irritation: might he take Miss Newton to the ball without a chaperone?

Now is this fair? First of all, I have seen his "American girl"—an arch miss of about forty, fresh from Main Street, and I am only—well, never mind, but that's that. Why should *I* know? Why ask *me*? *I* am indignant now. There are three indignant people in this salon now . . .

At this point the middle-aged person in black begins to tremble with disapproval. The old lady comes out of her swoon, and with one look of horror swoons again. Vivien gathers up her writing materials. "I am sorry," she says, "but I have never been to a ball in Paris." The American actually dares to appear incredulous. "I know nothing whatever about balls in Paris," she continues coldly, leaving the salon with all the dignity she can muster.

On the way up the five flights of stairs Vivien reminds herself that she has always found Americans to be a mystery:

I simply do not understand Americans. When I see an American coming I ought to say immediately, "Please do not speak to me, because if you do I shall not understand you. I shall never understand you, so will you please pass on." For instance, why do Americans insist that all European women are *au courant* with every form of vice (to them all pleasure and amusement really means vice, so far as I can see) whereas they insinuate that the female of their own species is supremely innocent and unsullied. They actually appear to be trying to protect their own women from *us!* Why? Because they cannot cope with European women. Ha! They can't cope with us!

The note of personal resentment in this description in "Diary of the Rive Gauche" of the American male suggests Vivien was brooding over Tom and the nostalgic feelings she believed he still harboured towards Emily Hale, the refined New England drama teacher he knew at Cambridge; Emily was a woman of whom Vivien would have heard much from her indiscreet friend Lucy Thayer, although Tom's sister Marian may have proved more reticent when she came to stay. But Vivien was already sensitive to any hint that she did not measure up to the standards of purity and education of a young woman such as Emily, who remained on the other side of the Atlantic, unmarried, forlorn, waiting. Vivien's barbed remark that to an American all pleasure means vice, was no doubt aimed at Tom, who she felt had misled her. When they met had he not delighted in dancing, smoking, talking with her? And yet by 1921 he condemned such pleasures as "vice," although he was prepared to practise them with alternative companions. Vivien may have felt that it was her affair with Russell—although he did not object to it at the time—which had altered her husband's perception of her morals and had a disastrous effect on their relationship.[12]

While Vivien remained in Paris, struggling to exist on £5 a week, for she was paying her living expenses out of her own small income from her father, Tom had put himself into the hands of Dr. Vittoz at his sanatorium in Lausanne. In Margate Tom had reassured himself that he was not psychotic, telling Richard Aldington that his "nerves" were "a very mild affair, due not to overwork but to an *aboulie* and emotional derangement which has been a lifelong affliction. Nothing wrong with my mind."[13] Certainly Eliot's hesitancy and slowness, which he described as *aboulie* or want of will, was noticeable to observers who invariably commented on it. Russell, for example, wrote to Ottoline that Eliot's "slowness is a sort of nervous affliction due to lack of vitality. It *is* annoying—it used to drive his wife almost to physical violence—but one gets used to it."[14] It was this paralysing indecisiveness which led Vivien to write to Jack Hutchinson: "As to Tom's *mind, I am* his mind,"[15] and to claim that she gave him the "shove" responsible for his success.

Yet had Eliot's psychiatric illness been as mild as he implied to Aldington, he would have accepted Lady Rothermere's offer of the free use of her villa above Monte Carlo, as he first intended, rather than travelling to the sanatorium which he knew to be expensive.[16] It was his knowledge that he was in urgent need of help which drove him to seek Vittoz, a "specialist in psychological troubles." The insistent "voices," both male and female, which Eliot heard talking to him when he tried to sleep, and which concerned him enough to complain of them much later on, in the 1950s, to Mary Trevelyan, a close friend at the time, may have troubled him earlier in life, and triggered fears for his own sanity.[17]

The therapy offered by the Swiss psychiatrist was simple, and in all probability his apparent success in Eliot's case was due to the transference which occurred between therapist and patient. The poet's symptoms and their causes were manifold, suggests the psychiatrist Dr. Harry Trosman:

> Depression with exhaustion, indecisiveness, hypochondriasis, and fear of psychosis. His personality had been aloof and distant and he guarded himself against the intrusions of others with icy urbanity. Compulsive defences enabled him to isolate his emotions. Sexuality was a potent danger not only because of intense conflict but because instinctual forces threatened him with loss of ego control and dominance.[18]

Trosman argues that Eliot's equilibrium was easily vulnerable to injury as a result of his deprived childhood, in which he felt "isolated and uncomfortable in his ill-fitting masculinity . . . His illness can be characterised as a transitory narcissistic regression with partial fragmentation and loss of ego dominance." This diagnosis accords with Eliot's own sense of a disintegrating self, and Trosman's theory that *The Waste Land* served as a form of "self-analytic work" is supported by Eliot's own confession, when he writes towards the end of the poem: "These fragments I have shored against my ruins." He was, according to Trosman, describing "a process of partial integration."

Eliot acknowledged the creative and therapeutic aspect of his psychological illness, writing that some form of ill-health, such as debility or anaemia, might produce "an efflux of poetry." What one wrote in this way gave the impression of having undergone a long incubation—"though we do not know until the shell breaks what kind of egg we have been sitting on." Such moments "are characterised by the sudden lifting of the burden of anxiety and fear which presses upon our daily life so steadily," and the accompanying feeling was one of "a sudden relief from an intolerable burden."[19]

The programme of "cerebral re-education" to which Eliot now submitted himself was a treatment plan devised by the Swiss psychiatrist, who laid his hands upon the patient's forehead in order to feel the disordered vibrations of the "cerebral hemispheres" before setting simple mental exercises intended to relax him. Vittoz would ask Eliot to look at a rose in a vase or a hat on a rack, and to concentrate on the sensations aroused; with eyes shut the patient would retain the image, and then eliminate it. "Be like a photographic plate," commanded Vittoz. "Eliminate thought." One also had to practise eliminating letters from words, or one number from a set of numbers, recalled Ottoline. "Julian would laugh at me when, perhaps in the train, she would see me gazing into space—'There is Mummy eliminating.' "[20] The emphasis was on calmness and rest, as the patient gradually learnt to exercise and master the will. Vittoz compared his treatment to the tuning of a piano, bringing harmony and control to an over-anxious mind and, as Eliot settled into Ottoline's old room at the Hotel Ste. Luce, and enjoyed the "excellent" food, he was reassured by the psychiatrist's diagnosis, writing to Ottoline: "I never did believe in 'nerves,' at least for myself!"[21]

Vittoz's success owed more to his personality than to any magical ability to detect brain vibrations. "I like him very much personally," wrote Eliot, "and he inspires me with confidence."[22] The psychiatrist urged his patients to follow the model of Christ, to take the path of sainthood and self-control, moral exhortations which to Eliot's ears echoed those of his grandfather, William Greenleaf Eliot, and his mother, and would also have appealed to Ottoline, who was deeply religious. "I am trying to learn how to use all my energy without waste, to be *calm* when there is nothing to be gained by worry, and to concentrate without effort," Eliot wrote to his brother on 13 December. "I hope I shall place less strain on Vivien, who has had to do so much *thinking* for me."[23]

It is likely that Vittoz functioned as a paternal figure whom Eliot felt able to idealise and obey, for he told Ottoline that although he could not tell *much* about the method yet, he felt much calmer than he had for many years since childhood. "That may be illusory—we shall see." Certainly the sanatorium provided the ambience, free of the multiple pressures of banking, literary journalism, Bloomsbury parties and domestic demands, in which Eliot was able to complete *The Waste Land*. "This is Tom's autobiography," exclaimed Mary Hutchinson, when she first read *The Waste Land*.

The poem's intense emotion, so tightly controlled, its springs disguised by a trail of footnotes which lead away from the source, led the critic Edmund Wilson to hail Eliot's greatness despite the poem's obscurity. "The acuteness of his suffering gives poignancy to his art," he wrote in *The Dial*.[24] "These drops, though they may be wrung from flint, are nonetheless authentic crystals. They are broken and sometimes infinitely tiny, but they are worth more than all the rhinestones on the market." Wilson's thesis in "Philoctetes: The Wound and the Bow" (1929) that it is the suffering of the artist which inspires creativity, was true of Eliot, who, like Sophocles' Philoctetes, had a wound which would not heal; like Philoctetes the wounded archer of Wilson's essay, Eliot's genius became "purer and deeper in ratio to his isolation and outlawry."[25] The poet's anguish was as complex as the man: its roots lay in his grief for Jean Verdenal and a love cut short by death, the cruel comparison to an unloved wife who reproached him with sexual failure, and his disillusion with the post-war world.

From Joyce, Eliot borrowed the idea of myth as the starting point for his work. Just as Joyce had based *Ulysses* upon the *Odyssey,* so Eliot took the Arthurian legend of the Holy Grail and the impotent Fisher King who rules a waste land, a desolate and sterile country in which not only have the crops ceased to grow, the animals to reproduce, but even human beings no longer bear children. The wound of the Fisher King can only be healed by the success of the Knight who has come to find the Holy Grail, which will allow the land to be renewed.[26] For Wilson, like other contemporary readers of Eliot's poem, the meaning behind the myth was not altogether clear. Virginia Woolf spoke for many when she commented after a visit from Tom during which he read his new poem aloud to her: "I have only the sound of it in my ears, when he read it aloud; and have not yet tackled the sense. But I liked the sound."[27] But Wilson, in his review in *The Dial,* was the first to interpret the poem as social criticism. He saw the waste land as a concrete image of spiritual drought, the action of the poem taking place half in the real world of London, half in the wilderness of medieval legend: "The Waste Land is only the hero's arid soul and the intolerable world around him, our post-War world of shattered institutions, strained nerves and bankrupt ideals." The poet's sense of futility is expressed in the words of the Cumaean Sibyl, who was condemned to live for as long as the number of grains of sand in her hand; when asked by little boys what she wanted, she replied only, "I want to die."[28] It was one of the layered meanings behind the declaration, "I will show you fear in a handful of dust."

The obscurity of the poem, whose four hundred lines contained quotations from, allusions to, and parodies of a daunting list of earlier writers from Buddha to Wagner, led critics away from any attempt to relate the poem to the facts of Eliot's life.[29] It continued to be viewed as the expression of the disillusionment of a generation; Hugh Kenner, for example, wrote that Eliot went to Margate "preoccupied with the ruin of post-war Europe."[30] But the footnotes were a carefully laid wild-goose chase, the scholarship much more than the "peevish assumption of superiority" of a "timid and prosaic" poet noted by Wilson.[31] Together they functioned as a smokescreen behind which Eliot hid his need to confess, while over future decades his impersonal theory of poetry put an embargo on decoding a poet's work as a personal statement. Yet Eliot tapped into the mood of despair and disillusion of 1921 precisely because he was writing about his own inner despair and disillusion. He used the material of his own life and made it universal, as has been recognised by some later critics, transmuting his "personal and private agonies into something rich and strange."[32] "It is an anguished personal revelation and an austere cultural monument," argues John T. Mayer.[33]

Later, Eliot repented of having sent his readers in the wrong direction, and wished to correct the poem's reputation, writing: "Various critics have considered it, indeed, as an important bit of social criticism. To me it was only the relief of a personal and wholly insignificant grouse against life; it is just a piece of rhythmical grumbling."[34] This disclaimer was almost as far from the truth as some early critics' comments. Valerie Eliot's publication of the original drafts, showing the radical revision made by Ezra Pound, which removed much of the personal element from her husband's writing and made it more opaque, gives a tantalising glimpse of what he longed to reveal.

In Lausanne, "this decayed hole among the mountains," Eliot ruminated over his past life, "in every detail of desire, temptation and surrender during that supreme moment of complete knowledge," as he put it in the words of Conrad he originally chose as an epigraph. In a flash of insight he saw "The horror! The horror!"—and felt a sense of identification with the dying Kurtz.[35] It was an extreme state of mind, one he would later describe as the poet "haunted by a demon, a demon against which he feels powerless, because in its first manifestation it has no face, no name, nothing; and the words, the poem he makes, are a kind of form of exorcism of this demon."[36]

Conversation with the other patients, the "people of many nationalities, which I always like," penetrated his gloom, and perhaps stimulated him to write—just as writing in French had done previously—and a *mélange* of foreign phrases found its way into his poem.[37] Memories of his visits to Germany flooded back to him, of the Hofgarten in Marburg, of the Starnbergersee near Munich and of a Lithuanian girl he had met there, originally from Russia, who claimed, to Eliot's amused surprise, that she was a "real German"—"Bin gar keine Russin, stamm' aus Litauen, echt deutsch."[38] A remembered conversation with Countess Marie Larisch, niece of the Austrian Empress Elizabeth, whom Eliot apparently met in 1911, also worked its way into the poem; as a child she had stayed with her cousin, the archduke: "he took me out on a sled,/And I was frightened. He said, Marie,/Marie, hold on tight."[39]

But most of all Eliot's thoughts returned to his last summer trip to Munich, on which Verdenal may have accompanied him, and to that Paris winter of 1910–11 ("Winter kept us warm") in the pension with Jean. Trosman speculates that during periods of "regressive isolation," such as in the confinement of the clinic, Eliot was flooded with "unacceptable homosexual longings . . . To such longings Eliot responded with panic." In 1952 a Canadian critic, John Peter, suggested in *Essays in Criticism* that *The Waste Land* was indeed written as an elegy for Jean Verdenal. Peter's reading of the poem was breathtakingly simple:

> At some previous time the speaker has fallen completely—perhaps the right word is "irretrievably" in love. The object of this love was a young man who soon afterwards met his death, it would seem by drowning. Enough time has elapsed now since his death for the speaker to have realised that the focus for affection that he once provided is irreplaceable. The monologue which, in effect, the poem presents is a meditation upon this deprivation, upon the speaker's stunned and horrified reaction to it, and on the

picture which, as seen through its all but insupportable blackness, the world presents.[40]

A later critic, James E. Miller, has compared *The Waste Land* to Tennyson's mourning for the dead Arthur Hallam in *In Memoriam;* in a revealing comment, Eliot praised Tennyson's poem as "a long poem, made by putting together lyrics, which have only the unity and continuity of a diary, the concentrated diary of a man confessing himself."[41]

John Peter's homosexual interpretation of the poem brought an angry response from Eliot, who threatened to sue the editor of the journal; as a result the remaining copies of the offending issue were pulped. Not until after Eliot's death in 1965 was the critic able to restate his case. In 1969 his article was republished with an interesting "Postscript" in which he identified Phlebas the Phoenician as Jean Verdenal, and described how he was obliged to tender an apology to Eliot through his solicitors. The poet accepted his apology, indicating that "he considered it neither necessary nor desirable for a public retraction to appear" but that he would take "the very gravest view of any further dissemination of this article or the views expressed in it." Eliot's solicitors informed Peter that their client had read his essay and found it "absurd" and "completely erroneous."[42]

Nevertheless Peter's case is a convincing one. The recurrent image in *The Waste Land,* to which Eliot returns obsessively, is of Verdenal walking towards him in the Luxembourg Gardens, his arms full of lilacs. Eliot's memory forces him to a bitter contradiction of Chaucer, who had welcomed April with its "shoures sweete":

> April is the cruellest month, breeding
> Lilacs out of the dead land, mixing
> Memory and desire, stirring
> Dull roots with spring rain.

Eliot never knew exactly how Verdenal died on 2 May 1915, remaining uncertain whether he was "mixed with the mud of Gallipoli."[43] Was Jean drowned ("those are pearls that were his eyes") or did he die on land? Influenced by the army citation dated 30 April 1915, which describes the young medical officer up to his waist in water, helping to evacuate the wounded by sea, Tom came to believe that the sea had claimed Jean, even if the officer's bones were left in the mud of Gallipoli. In the poem there are images of death on land: "White bodies naked on the low damp ground . . . Rattled by the rat's foot only, year to year." None, however, are so powerful as the lines in "Death by Water" commemorating "Phlebas the Phoenician, a fortnight dead . . . /A current under sea/Picked his bones in whispers." The repetition of earlier lines from "Dans le Restaurant," which mourned "Phlebas" in almost identical phrases in French—the heartfelt plea to the reader to remember Phlebas, "once handsome and tall as you"—supports the contention that Verdenal is central to *The Waste Land*.[44]

The "dull roots" stirred by the spring rain suggest a reawakening of Eliot's repressed sexuality, the mixing of memory and desire as he relives the sweet spring shared with Jean. Since April, in its cruelty, has deprived him of his companion, he is cast out in the stony desert ("Come in under the shadow of this red rock") in a fragment of verse taken from his own earlier poem, "Saint Narcissus," in which the saint is transformed from a beautiful youth, entranced with his own physicality, into a young girl who is raped in the woods. In that poem, because "he could not live men's ways," the poet-protagonist becomes "a dancer before God," dancing on the hot sand, in a poem which anticipates both the homoerotic imagery of *The Waste Land* and the androgyny of Tiresias.[45]

The anguish of the poet's situation in the shadow of the rock melts into fresh memories of the past, evoked by a verse from Wagner's *Tristan und Isolde: "Frisch weht der Wind/Der Heimat zu./Mein irisch Kind,/Wo weilest du?"* (The wind blows fresh homeward, my Irish child, where do you tarry?). The sailor is singing with an ardour once shared by the speaker.[46] The poet then returns to the ecstatic moment, ". . . when we came back, late, from the hyacinth garden,/Your arms full, and your hair wet, I could not/Speak, and my eyes failed, . . . and I knew nothing,/Looking into the heart of light, the silence."

These lines evoked a mood of bliss and transcendence, shattered by the second fragment of the opera, which Jean and Tom saw together in Paris; its message is brutal: *"Oed' und leer das Meer."* The sea is empty and desolate, the sailor drowned, a message reinforced by the fortune-teller Madame Sosostris, who deals the tarot cards (a practice to which Eliot had been introduced in Primrose Hill in north London). Here, she says, is your card, the drowned Phoenician Sailor. The accompanying quotation from *The Tempest,* "Those are pearls that were his eyes," is repeated, the reprise in Eliot's tale of lamentation. But the next card dealt by Madame Sosostris (another incarnation for the satanic Russell, derived from Aldous Huxley's *Chrome Yellow*)[47] is Belladonna, the amorous "lady of situations."[48] She is juxtaposed, in the original draft, with the Fisher King, symbol of impotence and sterility, and only in the cut version is the less revealing card, the "man with three staves," substituted. "Fear death by water," is the fortune-teller's prophecy to the protagonist, underlining the bereavement to come.[49]

Was "the moment's surrender," to which Eliot refers with such emotion in a later passage, to the "seductive" Vivien—as Sencourt argues—or to Jean Verdenal? Or was it indeed to the Virgin, in spiritual surrender, as Helen Gardner believed?[50] Eliot wrote in his original version of this irrevocable moment of fulfillment: "We brother, what have we given?/My friend, my friend, beating in my heart,/The awful daring of a moment's surrender/Which an age of prudence can never retract—"[51] Clearly his partner here is masculine. The facsimile edition of the poem, which includes the cuts made by Ezra Pound, confirms the homosexual theme eliminated from the 1922 version.[52] This is underlined by Eliot's final benediction: "Those are pearls that were his eyes. See/Still and quiet brother are you still and quiet."[53]

The image of eyes associated with a lover lost to the "kingdom of the dead" is one to which Eliot returns in three poems he entitled "Doris's Dream Songs," which were published by Harold Monro in his *Chapbook* in 1924 and later incorporated into "The Hollow Men." He speaks of "Eyes that last I saw in tears/Through division." In his "dream kingdom/The golden vision reappears."[54] The eyes are "eyes of decision," perhaps after Verdenal decided to enlist. The poet mourns the fact that they are "Eyes that I shall not see unless/At the door of death's other kingdom." As in *The Waste Land,* the protagonist now exists in "the dead land . . . the cactus land" (perhaps derived from memories of the desiccated landscape of Arizona or Texas), his mind circling around the "golden vision" of Verdenal, lit up by the "sentimental sunset" of their tryst in the

Luxembourg Gardens. "This is my affliction," confesses the poet, a reminder that inversion, although acceptable to Bloomsbury, was considered by society at large to be a deviant sexuality, and in his own mind perhaps remained so. He asks poignantly whether it is like this in death's other kingdom, walking alone "At the hour when we are/Trembling with tenderness/Lips that would kiss/Form prayers to broken stone."[55] The same lyrical and sensual mood celebrating an "angelic" lover is expressed in Eliot's earlier "dream poem," "Song to the Opherian,"[56] in which the "golden foot" he may not kiss or clutch glows in the shadow of the bed "Waiting that touch—that breath."[57]

The memory of Verdenal may have been transfigured in Eliot's imagination into something of far greater significance than the bare facts of the relationship warrant. The dedication of his first volume of poems to his friend in 1917, rather than to his parents, to Vivien, or indeed to Pound; the repetition of that dedication in *Ara Vos Prec* in 1920, linked to the passionate Dante epigraph ("Now you are able to comprehend the quantity of love that warms me toward you . . .")[58] was not only an affirmation of love, but a tribute to the powerful spell the dead can cast over those who survive.[59] W. H. Auden speculated that even as late as 1942, Eliot was thinking of Verdenal when he wrote the Dante section of "Little Gidding": "Of course Dante was meant, but he probably had something more personal in mind."[60]

It is difficult to imagine a more powerful contrast to the tremulous tenderness of love directed towards a "brother" than the deep hostility of the verses whose subject is a woman. Eliot's fantasy of wife murder is expressed in "The Death of a Duchess," a section of the original *Waste Land* text, which he modelled on John Webster's *The Duchess of Malfi,* precisely because both the "breathless tension" and the plot of the Jacobean dramatist mirrored Vivien's and his own situation. Just as Webster's Duchess has married her steward, Antonio, a misalliance which leads to her misery and death, so this modern Duchess and her husband are "bound forever on the wheel" in Hampstead, where even the aspidistra grieves at the entrapment of marriage. "It is terrible to be alone with another person."[61] This flat statement of despair resonates with the "cold fury" of "André," the scowling husband in one of Vivien's most powerful short stories.[62] The poet's feelings are angry, confused and primitive: they have tails and hang like monkeys from the chandelier. The woman brushes her hair in fierce strokes so that under the brush her hair is spread out in "little fiery points of will" and glows into words almost identical to those of Webster, who wrote originally:

> You have cause to love me, I entered you in my heart
> Before you would vouchsafe to call for the keys.[63]

It is a reproach which underlines Eliot's indebtedness to Vivien who gave him her love when he was penniless and unknown: "She has everything to give that I want and she gives it. I owe her everything," he had written to his father in 1915.[64]

As in Webster's original scene, the woman in "Death of a Duchess" turns her back, giving her husband the opportunity to leave. "Time to regain the door," writes Eliot, echoing Antonio's desertion of his wife. Should he feign love, he wonders, say "I love you." What would be the point? "If it is terrible alone, it is sordid with one more." Whether he pretends love or not, the meaningless routine of their lives will continue, the daily drives, the games of chess which fill up the hours. It was Vivien who asked Eliot to delete the line "The ivory men make company between us" (from "A Game of Chess"), so revealing their incompatibility, although her first instinct had been to scribble an enthusiastic "Yes" against the chess verses. Eliot did as she asked in the first printed version, but in 1960 restored the line from memory.[65]

In "Death of a Duchess," an importunate, vulnerable woman meets a similar fate to Webster's Duchess, who is stabbed by her brother Ferdinand. Eliot's Duchess pleads despairingly with her husband: "But I know you love me, it must be that you love me." Grimly the poet disposes of his victim: "Then I suppose they found her/As she turned/To interrogate the silence behind her." The cancelled lines which follow—"I am steward of her revenue/But I know, and I know she knew..."[66]—imply the wife may guess the fate she is about to meet, and emphasise the connection between the monologue and its original source in Webster's drama. Eliot's continual rehearsal of a wife's desertion and death prepared his mind for the desertion of Vivien, which he was probably already considering; his belief that he would in some way cause her death may also be foreshadowed in *The Waste Land.*

"Death of the Duchess" was in the end sacrificed by Pound, with only a few lines being incorporated into Part II of *The Waste Land,* originally entitled "In the Cage" (perhaps inspired by the Henry James novella "In the Cage") and later changed to the less revealing "A Game of Chess."[67] Vivien also used the metaphor of a cage to describe the entrapment of marriage. "Now one begins to beat against the bars of the cage. One's soul stirs stiffly out of the dead endurance of the winter—but toward what spring?" she would write in "Letters of the Moment—1," in the *Criterion.*[68] The image of the captured bird, trying to fly, was one with which she identified in Stravinsky's *Firebird:* "It tries to fly, over and over again, wings beating."[69] The sibyl of Eliot's epigraph, from the *Satyricon* of Petronius, is also in a cage, waiting to die, and it can be no coincidence that Vivien chose the name "Sibylla" for the unhappy wife in several of her short stories, for there were occasions during her own marriage when she felt suicidal.[70]

Eliot's lines in "A Game of Chess" describe a woman imprisoned, and the cage metaphor is appropriate to the animalistic passions of the scenes which follow, in which woman is no longer Madonna or muse, but *femme fatale,* enslaving men through her seductive arts in whatever class of society she finds herself. The opulent description of Belladonna—a beautiful but poisonous woman—sitting on her throne is sardonic in its intention; marble, gold, glitter, and overpowering perfume surround her, tempting and even inviting the rape which is the fate of Philomel, at the hands of her brother-in-law Tereus. Mutilated, her tongue ripped out, Philomel is transformed into a nightingale whose cry, "Jug Jug," is as ugly as the tales of lust from the "bloody ends of time."[71]

In *The Waste Land* facsimile edition, Belladonna is powerful, phallic, castrating, her hair as fiery and venomous as Medusa's snakes. The atmosphere is oppressively sexual: the woman's desire is clear as she demands of the protagonist "the bestial act rudely forced on him by his marriage, and his unwillingness or inability to comply turns their relationship into a parody of marriage." The language hints at his impotence or "withered stumps" in the face of what all "the world pursues/Jug Jug"—a sex act which repels him. The gorgon's scornful gaze "deadens him for he has lost his bones, his erections."[72] The connection between the panic aroused by his wife's sexual demands, and the "accents of neurasthenia" which follow, are no coincidence. Freud claimed that frustrated sexuality bred anxiety neurosis, like wine turned to vinegar:

My nerves are bad tonight. Yes, bad. Stay with me.
Speak to me. Why do you never speak? Speak.

"What are you thinking of?" demands the wife. "What thinking? What?" "I think we met first in rats' alley," replies the poet, "Where the dead men lost their bones." "What is that noise?" Her voice is querulous. "The wind under the door." "What is that noise now? What is the wind doing?" His unspoken reply is: "Carrying/Away the little light dead people," a reference once more to Paolo and Francesca, Dante's doomed lovers.[73]

"WONDERFUL" wrote Vivien, who was closely involved in the editing of *The Waste Land,* and suggested three lines of her own. In front of her was a virtual transcript of her own nervous assaults upon her husband, echoing one particular letter to Mary Hutchinson in 1928: "Of course, he is *so* reserved and peculiar, that he never says anything and one cannot get him to speak. That makes one much more lonely."[74] The insistent questions of the wife in the poem, "What shall I do now? What shall I do?" and the answer, "I shall rush out now as I am, and walk the street," mirrors an invariable response of Vivien to the stress of her marriage. Her own frustration and rage led her once to throw her nightdress out of the window onto the pavement below. In 1942 Eliot pointed out to Mary Trevelyan the building near Trafalgar Square in which this happened.[75] Pound, too, recognised the verses' origins, commenting: "PHOTOGRAPHY."

Belladonna steps down from her throne. "Do you know nothing? Do you see nothing? Do you remember nothing?" she demands. The poet blots out his wife's voice, remembering only the moment of rapture in the "hyacinth garden." In the first section of *The Waste Land,* "The Burial of the Dead," Eliot again makes it clear that his remembrance is not of a "hyacinth girl" with whom he is in love, but of a male partner, who may indeed be symbolised by the god Hyacinth, killed by Apollo when the two are playing at discus. The allusion is to ecstatic male love which ends in tragedy.[76] The girl in the garden may be the poet himself, in another sex-

ual transfiguration, as in "Saint Narcissus" when he changes sex; Eliot's remark that Tiresias, in whom the two sexes meet,[77] is the "most important
personage in the poem, uniting all the rest," stresses the androgynous impulse which is central to the poem. The image of transfiguration is one
Vivien herself used in 1936, writing *"Tiresias"* above her announcement
that she had "become" Daisy Miller.

Androgyny continued to be fashionable in Bloomsbury in the 1920s,
part of the revolt against middle-class morality by the self-consciously
decadent; Viola Tree sneered at George Moore, so old-fashioned that at a
Phoenix Society performance he was surprised that "the Silent Woman
was a boy; his conception of woman is so womanish, and of man so mas-
terful, no wonder he fails to believe that there could in this strange age be
any mistake!" In their boyish flapper dresses, in which barely a hint of
breast or hip dared break the line, and in make-up which could be "dead
white or putty colour," with touches of orange or mauve, women, in their
common desire to defy English dowdiness, could easily be mistaken for
men.[78] Aldous Huxley wrote poetry celebrating the role of the androgyne.
"One arrow and two pierced hearts," was the emblem of his 1927
Valentine tribute to his two Marias, his wife and Mary Hutchinson: "Soft
androgyne on androgyne/Using hermaphrodite arts."[79] Virginia Woolf
also acknowledged the creativity of the androgyne, writing: "It is fatal for
anyone who writes to think of their sex. It is fatal to be a woman pure and
simple; one must be woman-manly or man-womanly," perhaps proving
her own point when she found *Orlando* to be a book she was able to write
at great speed. And there is evidence that Eliot enjoyed challenging accepted gender roles too, performing in Lytton Strachey's transvestite
plays.[80] Not only Vivien (in "Fête Galante"), but several of his contemporaries bore witness to his use of cosmetics in the 1920s.[81]

The poet's disgust for heterosexual love is expressed in a different milieu, that of the working-class, in lines in *The Waste Land* describing the
marriage of a Cockney couple, Lil and Albert. The dialogue was based on
many conversations with Ellen Kelland, the Eliots' maid for many years,
to whom Vivien was devoted. The grim future Vivien predicted for Ellen,
who was later to marry one of her "followers," is captured in lines given to
"Lil" and her friend, and edited by Vivien, whose ear for dialogue was
acute: "Now Albert's coming back, make yourself a bit smart," says the

speaker. Albert's out of the army and wants a good time; Lil has spent the money he gave her for a new set of teeth, and is looking "so antique." If she doesn't please him, there's plenty of others who will. "Hurry up please, it's time," the landlord's cry from the pub opposite the Eliots' first flat in Crawford Street, is followed by a Cockney line of Vivien's own invention: "If you don't like it you can get on with it." Lil looks old, despite being only thirty-one, because she has had five children and an abortion: "It's that medicine I took, to bring it off." Thoughtfully Vivien changed "medicine" to "pills," and the final line reads: "It's them pills I took, to bring it off, she said." "You *are* a proper fool," replies the speaker. "Well, if Albert won't leave you alone, there it is." Again Vivien added to Eliot's typescript her own revealing line which he retained: "What you get married for if you don't want to have children?" Lil's tale of mechanistic copulation and squalid abortion ends with the landlord's "Good night, ladies," a phrase which echoes Ophelia's unhinged "good night, sweet ladies, good night, good night" in *Hamlet*. "Splendid last lines," wrote an impressed Vivien.[82] But Eliot's cry to his wife, like that of Hamlet to Ophelia, was one presaging flight: "Go to, I'll no more on't; it hath made me mad."

Vivien's own longing for a baby may have contributed to the Eliots' marital problems; Maurice remembered that his mother had said that Vivien had been pregnant at one time and had had an abortion, but he did not believe the story. There is no way of confirming whether or not Vivien had an abortion (took pills), and if so whether Eliot was the father. The line which asks, why marry if you don't want to have children, suggests a reproach to a husband who cannot satisfy his wife: the Fisher King of Jessie Weston's myth. And in an undated letter to Mary, Vivien makes the suggestion, tragic in its impracticality, that the enemies of the Left and Right in literary London should unite and live in a utopian community in which she might have an adopted child.[83] For Vivien, as for Virginia Woolf, motherhood denied may have had a more harmful effect upon her mental state than a pregnancy which Virginia's, and possibly Vivien's, doctors, advised against.

In his original manuscript, the poet-protagonist began Part III of *The Waste Land*, "The Fire Sermon," with his starkest statement so far of revulsion against women's physicality. James E. Miller writes that "there is passion throughout 'The Fire Sermon' but it is the passion of a misogynist, burning with a hatred that seems almost inexplicable, except in the context we have already encountered, the protagonist held in the grip of a paralysing memory of a dead and deeply beloved friend."[84] Interestingly, however, the couplets describing a privileged woman, Fresca, being brought tea or hot chocolate in bed by her maid may have originated in a poem reclaimed by Vivien as her own and published under the initials "F.M." (one of her pseudonyms) in "Letters of the Moment—II" in the *Criterion* in April, 1924.

> When sniffing Chloe, with the toast and tea
> Drags back the curtain to disclose the day,
> The amorous Fresca stretches, yawns and gapes,
> Aroused from dreams of love in curious shapes.
> The quill lies ready at her finger tips;
> She drinks, and pens a letter while she sips;
> "I'm very well, my dear, and how are you?
> I have another book by Girandoux.
> My dear, I missed you last night at the Play:
> Were you there? Or did you slip away? . . ."
> Her hands caress the egg's well-rounded dome;
> As her mind labours till the phrases come.[85]

These lines were possibly written by Vivien originally, and edited by Tom in Lausanne, only to be cut by Pound; neither of the Eliots liked to waste material, which may account for the publication of Vivien's "few poor verses" in 1924. However, the transformation of the "Fresca" verses in Tom's hands gave them a misogynistic twist. Now she awakes, dreaming of "pleasant rapes." "Leaving the bubbling beverage to cool,/Fresca slips softly to the needful stool." His contempt for woman is, once again, all the greater when she is Jewish: Fresca writes her letter, as in Vivien's verse, but relates how "out of dull despair" she went to "Lady Kleinwurm's party." "Who was there?/Oh, Lady Kleinwurm's monde—no one that mattered—/Somebody sang, and Lady Kleinwurm chattered."[86]

Eliot was possibly satirising Violet Schiff, a musician who studied singing under Tosti, and gave many parties at her house in Cambridge Square, even on occasion including Rose and Maurice Haigh-Wood.

"Fresca," also in Eliot's version reading a book by Girandoux, asks her correspondent to tell her all about herself, Paris, and her new lovers. Nancy Cunard or Mary Hutchinson may also have been Eliot's sources, but the contemptuous lines which follow were based on his revulsion at enforced cohabitation with Vivien. "Odours disguised by the cunning French/ Disguise the hearty female stench."

The diatribe which follows encompasses all women: Fresca, says the poet, in another time or place, had been a "weeping Magdalene" or prostitute: "The same eternal and consuming itch/Can make a martyr, or plain simple bitch;/Or prudent sly domestic puss puss cat./Or strolling slattern in a tawdry gown." One definition fits all women, he declares: "Unreal emotions and real appetite./For women grown intellectual grow dull,/And loose the mother wit of natural trull."[87] Women, believes the poet, have a "consuming itch," the insatiable appetite for sex which revolts him. And should they attempt to educate themselves, reading, like "Fresca," the Scandinavians who "bemused her wits," or the Russian novelists who "thrilled her to hysteric fits," they lose the "mother wit of natural trull"— the quick repartee of the barmaid or prostitute. Vivien might have recognised this savage portrait of herself, for she too read Dostoevsky and, like "Fresca," scribbled verse.

The Fresca couplets express, in an extreme form, Eliot's belief that "the love of man and woman (or for that matter of man and man) is only explained and made reasonable by the higher love, or else it is simply the coupling of animals."[88] The revelation he had experienced in the Hyacinth Garden had sanctified a relationship which, without such "higher love," was otherwise bestial. Nevertheless, the homosexual encounter between the poet-protagonist and the unshaven "Smyrna merchant," which follows, is treated with amused tolerance rather than the scorn reserved for male/female relationships. In the "Unreal City" of London, where people are "bound upon the wheel" and "phantasmal gnomes" burrow in brick and stone and steel, the speaker is approached by a Mr. Eugenides, who asks him "in abominable French/To luncheon at the Cannon Street hotel/And perhaps a week at the Metropole."[89] According to an informant of Edmund Wilson's, John Peale Bishop, this brief encounter under the "brown fog" of a winter afternoon, was based on real life. "Mr. Eugenides actually turned up at Lloyd's with his pocket full of currants and asked

Eliot to spend a weekend with him for no nice reasons," writes Bishop. "His place in the poem is I believe as a projection of Eliot however . . . the one-eyed merchant is homosexual. Thomas's sexual troubles are undoubtedly extreme." This supposition is chiefly of interest as an example of the gossip which was circulating about "Tears Eliot" (as a Parisian wit christened him) by November, 1922.[90]

At this point the poet adopts a new and prophetic voice: that of Tiresias, the mythical blind figure who can see, who has exchanged "eyesight for insight." Tiresias, the androgyne, "Old man with wrinkled female breasts, can see" the truth. Eliot emphasises the centrality of Tiresias. "What Tiresias *sees,* in fact, is the substance of the poem." Tiresias's insights relate to sex, which in Ovid's *Metamorphoses* he experiences first as a man, and for the next seven years as a woman, before changing sex once more. "Wise Tiresias' knows what love is like, from either point of view, declares Ovid, and the seer repeats the message that human sex is no better than that of coupling snakes: mechanistic, casual, unfulfilling, as Eliot's parade of typists, clerks, and young men carbuncular illustrates. Even the ironic pageant of historical romance which follows, Elizabeth and Leicester in their "gilded shell" on the Thames, underlines the sterility of heterosexual relationships. The question Jove asked Tiresias to settle was whether females gained more pleasure from loving than males do; Tiresias, having tasted the pleasures of both sexes, agreed with the male god against his wife Juno, that women had the better side of the bargain, an opinion shared by the poet.

Eliot can no longer maintain the pose of detachment. In a new metamorphosis as St. Augustine, he is "burning" with pain and passion: "To Carthage then I came/Burning burning burning burning/O Lord Thou pluckest me out."[91] Eliot explains, in a note which he attaches to this quotation from St. Augustine's *Confessions,* that the saint came to Carthage where "a cauldron of unholy loves" sang in his ears. But, argues John Peter, Eliot's note does not make clear that St. Augustine travelled twice to Carthage, the second time to escape from the misery into which he had been plunged at the death of a friend, one with whom he had enjoyed a friendship he described as "delightful to me above all the delights of this my life." It is in this context that the visit to Carthage can be understood as a prayer for release from attachment and the agony of human love. "Like

Augustine at this stage of his life the speaker is not yet able to accept Christianity, despite the craving for consolation and forgiveness that he endures," writes Peter. "At least his repetition of the word 'burning' seems to imply that he is still caught in the trammels of the senses." Eliot seeks for release from suffering through the Fire Sermon of Buddha, who taught his disciples to divest themselves of passion in order to become free.[92]

Like Baudelaire, Eliot struggled to escape from *ennui* and anguish towards a spiritual life. In 1930 he wrote of Baudelaire: "He could not escape suffering and could not transcend it, so he *attracted* (it) to himself. But what he could do, with that immense passive strength . . . was to study his suffering" (Eliot's italics).[93] In *The Waste Land* Eliot, too, studied his suffering and made art of it; but the struggle he chronicled by speaking in different voices, which enabled him to express and observe his own pain as his own analyst, was by no means over. He remained "bleeding between two lives," in the words of "Song for the Opherian," still casting backwards looks towards Hades like Orpheus in search of his Eurydice. "Who is the third who walks always beside you? . . . I do not know whether a man or a woman/—But who is that on the other side of you?" is the insistent question of "What the Thunder Said," the final section of *The Waste Land*.[94] Whether it was the shrouded shade of Verdenal, the hooded figure of Christ on the road to Emmaus, or simply an illusion, its ghostly presence in the marriage ensured Eliot's rejection of his wife; for Vivien, there was always a third person in her marriage.

Eliot longed for "Shantih," the peace of Eastern ascetism, but he burnt still with longing for his sailor "brother": "The sea was calm, your heart would have responded/Gaily, when invited, beating obedient/To controlling hands." Datta, Dayadhvam, Damyata: Give, sympathise, control, is the prayer he takes from the Thunder fable of the *Upanishads* and adapts to his own personal drama. "DATTA my brother, what have we given?/My friend, my friend, beating in my heart,/The awful daring of a moment's surrender." The memory of exaltation is ineradicable. "DA/Dayadhavam, friend, my friend I have heard the key/Turn in the door, once and once only."[95] But the finality of death is the lesson given in the Chapel Perilous, one which the poet must learn to accept if he is to exorcise his demon and find release and renewal, both physical and spiritual.[96]

Death into faith is a step he is not yet ready to take. His prayer collapses in a kaleidoscope of quotations. "London Bridge is falling down falling down falling down./*Poi s'ascose nel foco che gli affina*." He speaks with the voice of Arnaut Daniel, the Provençal poet, who is weighed down with guilt, a guilt explained by the provenance of the quotation from Canto XXVI, "The Reign of Lust" of Dante's *Purgatorio,* which relates the sins of a band of sodomites. *"Nostro peccato fu ermafrodito"* (Our sin was hermaphrodite), cries Daniel, as he plunges into the purifying fire.[97] It was the critic I. A. Richards who observed that this canto of the lustful sodomites illuminated Eliot's "persistent concern with sex, the problem of our generation, as religion was the problem of the last." Eliot observed that it was "very shrewd" of Richards to notice this, but that "in his contrast of sex and religion he makes a distinction which is too subtle for me to grasp."[98] It was a disingenuous rejoinder, but Richards's barb had indeed been a shrewd one. Sex lies at the heart of much of Eliot's poetry, becoming his personal synonym for sin. Sex attracts and repels, its urgency creating in the poet the same engulfing horror that he feels he, like Kurtz, deserves for breaking moral rules. For sinning brings in its wake a Calvinistic fear of punishment. "Elegy," part of *The Waste Land* original 1,000-line typescript cut by Pound, which closely resembles Charlotte Eliot's religious poetry, portrays a judgemental God who "in a rolling ball of fire" pursues the poet's errant feet in "flames of anger."[99] However, the conflict between sex and spirituality, body and spirit, was by no means over. Eliot could only cry in agony: "Hieronymo's mad againe."[100]

14

A Wild Heart in a Cage

"Complimenti, you bitch," wrote Ezra Pound after reading Tom's typescript. "I am wracked by the seven jealousies." Recognising that the sprawling, chaotic poem was enough "to make the rest of us shut up shop," Pound set to work with his blue pencil to cut the poem by nearly half, while Tom waited with Vivien in Paris for a fortnight. "The thing now runs from April . . . to 'shantih' without a break," Ezra wrote on 24 December, 1921. "That is 19 pages, and let us say the longest poem in the English langwidge. Don't try to bust all records by prolonging it three pages further."[1] Feebly Eliot protested at some of Ezra's cuts. Could he not work "sweats with tears etc" into the nerves monologue, the only place where it could go?[2] Pound was firm: "I dare say sweats with tears will wait." Discouraged, Eliot wondered if he should leave out Phlebas altogether. No, replied Pound, Phlebas was an integral part of the poem. "The card pack introduces him, the drowned phoen sailor. And he is needed ABSOlootly where he is. Must stay in."[3] In essence, Eliot abandoned the poem to Pound, whose aim was to make it the justification for the Modernist movement.[4] Addressing his compatriot as "Cher Maître," Tom allowed the personal element in the poem to be sacrificed, while Pound for his part claimed that "on each Occasion/Ezra performed the Caesarian Operation" which allowed the poem to be born.[5] Gratefully Eliot wrote: "Complimenti appreciated, as have been excessively depressed."

On 12 January 1922, the day on which Tom returned to England, Vivien wrote to Mary that she thought he was much better, although "you must judge for yourself."[6] Unwilling to return to London after two months in France, she lingered a few days in Lyons. Perhaps Vivien still hoped to meet Scofield, who continued to edit *The Dial* from Vienna, but he was busy establishing the *Dial* Award, as well as collecting pictures and entering analysis with Freud, and seems to have eluded Vivien. Finally, reluctantly, she crossed the Channel to join Tom. The weather was vile and he had collapsed with influenza. Both Eliots subsequently became severely depressed. They felt persecuted by their enemies as they struggled to launch the *Criterion* from their flat, find a publisher for *The Waste Land,* decide whether Tom should leave the bank, and rent a country cottage. "If Vivien had realised how bloody England is she would not have returned," wrote Tom to Ezra.[7] None of these problems would have been insuperable, had it not been for Eliot's acute sexual conflict which by 1922 urgently demanded resolution. In the anonymity of Paris he had socialised with artists and intellectuals: "May your erection never grow less," wrote Pound. "I had intended to speak to you seriously on the subject, but you seemed so mountany gay while here in the midst of Paris that the matter slipped my foreskin." Eliot was tempted to send his bawdy Bolo verses to James Joyce, but Pound cautioned him against doing so: "You can forward the Bolo to Joyce if you think it wont unhinge his somewhat sabbatarian mind. On the hole he might be saved the shock, shaved the sock."[8]

The 1920s were tempting yet dangerous times for homosexuals and members of the *avant garde.* "Kicking the corpse of Oscar," as Robbie Ross, Wilde's friend, described the homophobia of the time, reached fever pitch with the belief that the Germans held a "Black Book" listing the names of the "First 47,000" homosexuals in British society. Homosexuals were viewed as potential traitors, because they were open to blackmail in a Britain which outlawed the "invert," the "urning" or third sex, as sexologist Richard von Krafft-Ebing described gay men in his *Psychopathia Sexualis* (1886). Such "experts" viewed same-sex desires as an aberration from the procreative norm required by society. One such was Christopher Millard, Wilde's biographer and Ross's secretary, who in 1918 was prosecuted for a second time for indecent assault.[9] The need for discretion had never been greater, yet eighteen years after his death the cult of Oscar Wilde refused to go away.

The First World War had been a powerful catalyst in creating a homosexual sub-culture in Europe's cities, particularly Berlin and London, as recruitment into the armed forces had for the first time mixed together large numbers of men from different social classes in a heady cocktail of danger and proximity. Fears of German decadence infecting British soldiers led to calls for punitive measures against homosexuals, and Lord Alfred Douglas, Wilde's former lover and now a married man, exhorted the nation to unite against "The foe without, the foe within," declaring in verse:

> Two filthy fogs blot out the light:
> The German and the sodomite.

Within the armed forces a conviction for sodomy was punished by a minimum sentence of ten years, and a maximum of life. Nevertheless, this was no deterrent to the élite Guards regiments within which the attraction and availability of other ranks—"a bit of scarlet"—for officers and other members of the upper classes was well known. Mary Hutchinson, confidante of many homosexuals, related with glee to Lytton Strachey a visit from civil servant Monty Shearman, who told her that since time immemorial there had been a connection between the Foreign Office and the Horse Guards: "He described the tradition—when you have noticed your Horse Guard you walk past him and drop half a crown into his boot with a note fixing a *rendez-vous*—you then hope he will turn up—but imagine the state of the boots of a very handsome guard . . . When and how does he drill? . . . Imagine his state of mind—does he look to see who has made the chink or does he stare straight ahead of him?"[10]

A new sense of identity was also germinating among homosexuals. Michel Foucault argues that the category of homosexual has been culturally constructed. In the Renaissance sodomy had been condemned by the Church and prohibited by law as a shameful sexual practice which its practitioners were urged to confess to their priest, but not until the late nineteenth century did homosexuality finally metamorphose from the practice of sodomy into something new: "a kind of interior androgyny, a hermaphrodism of the soul. The sodomite had been a temporary aberration; the homosexual was now a species."[11] As the negative aspects of homosexuality were emphasised, the "invert" was increasingly seen as a suitable case for treatment, one who should undergo the "talking cure" of psychoanalysis and confess his aberrant sexuality to the new authority figure—doctor rather than priest. Thus Ottoline Morrell was instrumental in taking some of the young homosexuals who gathered at Garsington to see her favourite physician, the German Dr. Marten, to be cured of their "disease" at his clinic in Freiburg. Lytton was sceptical about these expeditions, especially after meeting Marten at Garsington in 1923: "Psychoanalysis is a ludicrous fraud," he told Dora Carrington, "the Sackville-West youth was there [at Freiburg] to be cured of homosexuality. After 4 months and an expenditure of £200, he found he could just bear the thought of going to bed with a woman."[12]

By the 1920s the homosexual was increasingly subject to social control. Tabloid newspapers had informed a fascinated public of accusations made during the notorious 1918 Pemberton Billing trial that dancer Maud Allen, who lost her libel action against Billing for describing her performance of Wilde's *Salome* as lesbian, was also enjoying a lesbian relationship with Margot Asquith, wife of the former Prime Minister, H. H. Asquith.[13] In 1885 the law against buggery had been strengthened by Henry Labouchère's amendment to the Criminal Law Amendment Bill, which criminalised all sexual acts between men including fellatio and mutual masturbation, and led to Wilde's conviction.[14] In 1921 the government attempted to extend the law to include lesbianism. The Lords threw out the Bill, protesting that it would bring such an offence to the notice of women who had never heard of it.[15] Indeed, Lord Albemarle was alleged to have walked into the Turf Club and asked who was "this Greek chap clitoris" everyone was talking about.[16]

Foucault argues that power produces but cannot contain resistance. Increasingly defined and categorised as perverse, homosexuals began to fight back:

> The appearance in nineteenth century psychiatry, jurisprudence and literature of a whole series of discourses on the species and subspecies of homosexuality, inversion, pederasty, and "psychic hermaphrodism" made possible a strong advance of social controls into this area of "perversity"; but it also made possible the formation of a "reverse" discourse: homosexuality began to speak on its own behalf, to demand that its legitimacy or "naturality" be acknowledged . . .[17]

Many homosexuals went abroad to indulge their tastes: Montague Shearman boasted to Mary Hutchinson that on the ship to Naples in 1927 he had a boy in every port, and the swimming instructor at Toulon, as well as "complicated affairs" in hotels. In England, W. H. Auden recalled, the 1920s were a period of decadence when he first became aware of the "undercurrents of homosexuality" at Christ Church, Oxford.[18] Nor were the universities the only area of escape from heterosexuality; in London, where society and Bohemia made common cause in the pursuit of pleasure, the worlds of the arts and theatre offered the "invert" an acceptance missing in mainstream culture. Nevertheless, homosexuals still walked in fear: of the hundreds of prosecutions each year for "unnatural offences" between gay men, nearly half resulted in custodial sentences.

Back at home, and still buried in the bowels of Lloyds Bank, in 1922 Tom Eliot's mood was bitter. He was aware that he had written his masterpiece: "A long poem of about 450 words [lines] which, with the notes that I am adding, will make a book of 30 or 40 pages. I think it is the best I have ever done, and Pound thinks so too," he confided to John Quinn on 15 June, explaining that Pound had introduced him to the publisher Liveright in Paris, who offered him a 15 per cent royalty and $150 in advance. Eliot had given first refusal on the poem to Knopf, who had published the American edition of his *Poems,* but Knopf told him his offer came too late for inclusion in the autumn list. Liveright then agreed to take the poem for his own autumn list, but the "extremely vague" contract he sent displeased Eliot, and he asked Quinn to renegotiate it. On 19 July Eliot sent Quinn a typescript of *The Waste Land* to hand on to Liveright, apologising that he was too busy to "type it out fair . . . I shall rush forward the notes to go at the end. I only hope the printers are not allowed to bitch the punctuation and the spacing, as that is very important for the sense."[19] In the same letter Eliot offered to present Quinn with the original MSS of *The Waste Land:* "When I say MSS, I mean that it is partly MSS, and partly typescript, with Ezra's and my alterations scrawled all over it." Whilst waiting for this famous gift, Quinn sat up on the night of 27 July reading the typescript. "*Waste Land* is one of the best things you have done," he reassured the anxious poet, "though I imagine Liveright may be a little disappointed at it, but I think he will go through with it . . ." Quinn thought the text was too short to make a book, and too difficult. It was a poem for "superior guys" only, he wrote, anticipating a "small number of readers."[20]

Eliot encountered the same muted enthusiasm for his masterpiece from Scofield Thayer, to whom he had written on 20 January 1922 asking whether *The Dial* wished to print his new poem ("*not* to appear in any periodical on this side"), and what he might pay. He offered to postpone all arrangements for publication until he heard from Scofield, and explained that as *The Waste Land* was in four parts, it could easily divide to go into four issues. The poem "will have been three times through the sieve by Pound as well as myself so should be in final form."[21]

Scofield's response to this generous offer was grudging. His own mental state was precarious: "As I am half dead already I beseech you not to counsel my coming to London" he had gasped to Tom the previous July, despite his anxiety to discover what plans his old rival was making to start a periodical with Lady Rothermere.[22] By December a row had blown up over the "horrid and vulgar and tedious and totally impossible London Letter" which Thayer's business manager Gilbert Seldes claimed to have received from St. John Hutchinson, who had written Eliot's Letter for him during his breakdown. Seldes and Watson sent Hutchinson $25, two thirds of the amount due, as the article was unusable. "Prevent the man from sending any more," wrote Scofield sharply from Vienna, informing Eliot that he had hired Raymond Mortimer instead until Tom could send a new Letter. "At least it will indicate that you are again well."[23] It was an embarrassing situation for Eliot and he stiffly informed Scofield in January that he wished Seldes to deduct $25 from his own next payment, to be given to Hutchinson—unless Thayer preferred to keep on Mortimer in his stead.

Scofield replied with heavy sarcasm on 22 January: "It is good to know that you have again taken up the old-fashioned custom of answering letters. I hope I shall not have to await another case of influenza before receiving another letter . . . You seem to take ill my frankness in re the lad Hutchinson." He offered Eliot an extra $25 for the next London Letter: "Then you and Mr. Hutchinson and *The Dial* and Mr. Seldes and the mad hatter will no doubt be tutti contenti . . ." Seemingly unaware of the herculean task which *The Waste Land* represented for the poet, he wrote coolly: "I thought you were aware that we pay fixed rates always and that therefore it is not for us to bargain. . . . We pay for verse that has been unpublished elsewhere 10 dollars the page which is something more than double our rates for prose. 450 lines will take something more than 11 pages. *The Dial* when dealing with famous writers may offer round sums rather than split figures. Can we have the poem? *The Dial* would pay $150." Pound's "sieving" would, he suggested, have eliminated any impropriety which might have got by Eliot's own censor.[24]

It was an offer which Eliot found insulting and when, a few days later, he heard "on good authority" that the editor of *The Dial* had paid £100 to George Moore for a short story, he exploded with rage. "Cannot accept under 856 pounds," he wired Thayer. "I presume there is some error upon the part of the telegraph service," replied his urbane correspondent, pleading that he and Watson ran *The Dial* on a very large annual deficit and had to make personal sacrifices to keep it going.[25] Knowing that Thayer was a millionaire, Tom refused to be mollified, and on 16 March repeated that he must decline "$150 for a poem which has taken me a year to write and which is my biggest work . . . Certainly if I am to be offered only 30 to 35 pounds for such a publication it is out of the question."[26] A stalemate resulted which would last for months.

Tom's fury and bitterness spilled over into the London Letter he sent to *The Dial* that spring, in which he described the "particular torpor or deadness which strikes a denizen of London on his return" after three months' absence. Tom, and Vivien too, knew he had broken the mould of twentieth-century poetry with *The Waste Land,* yet his work seemed to meet only with obtuse incomprehension. His sense of being misunderstood and unappreciated was never greater. "I am about ready to chuck up literature altogether and retire," he burst out to Sydney Schiff. "I don't see why I should go on forever fighting a rearguard action against time, fatigue and illness, and complete lack of recognition of these facts."[27] Jealously he hit out in his "London Letter" in the May issue of *The Dial* at the "moral cowardice" of English poets, with their instinct for safety, who were indistinguishable, in his view, from "the decent middle-class mob." Even the war poems did not represent a revolt, he wrote, but paid tribute to "all the nicest feelings of the upper middle-class British public schoolboy."[28]

Tom was living on the edge, and Vivien became fearful once more for her husband's mental health. She explained to Mary, whom she met at the Gimpel Galleries followed by a two-and-a-half-hour chat in a tea-room, that he was too sensitive: "Tom is *all* Achilles heel. That is the point, the trouble, the complex, the unhappiness." Other people had at least one *"hard spot"*—indeed, most of them were all "hard spot," but Tom had not one.[29] Tom, however, continued to believe that it was Vivien who was thin-skinned and needed protecting. "*Please* don't mention it to Vivien," he wrote to Ottoline in October 1923, the following year, in the middle of another Bloomsbury tiff over an article by Clive Bell which Eliot found "vulgar and tasteless," and which left him feeling as if he were covered with lice. He would not show Vivien the article, because "I don't feel these things but she does."[30] They were united in dislike of the London literary mafia, of whom Eliot wrote to Richard Aldington: "You know that I have no persecution mania, but . . . I am quite aware how obnoxious I am to perhaps the larger part of the literary world of London, and that there will be a great many jackals swarming about waiting for my bones."[31] Tom and Vivien longed to get away and have solitude and peace: "People won't let us alone and won't understand and take offence," Tom complained to Ottoline in the summer of 1922. He and Vivien felt "exposed . . . If only we could go abroad for a long time and hide and forget everything."[32]

Fortunately Eliot was not without friends who believed in his genius, although some of them blamed Vivien for being a burden on her delicate husband. "Eliot ought to be private secretary to some rich imbecile," Pound had written to Quinn in February 1922. "Failing that you might send someone over to elope, kidnap, or otherwise eliminate Mrs. E." Like Eliot himself, Pound partly blamed Eliot's American nationality for the fact that he was trapped in the bank: "Eliot has beautiful manners, wd. adorn any yacht club, etc . . . If he wuz English he wd. be stuck into some govt. sinecure . . ."[33] Learning that Eliot was in a bad way mentally from Richard Aldington, and perhaps also from Gilbert Seldes, to whom Eliot confessed that his mind was "in a very deteriorated state, due to illness and worry,"[34] Pound decided to relaunch his Bel Esprit scheme from Paris. His generosity was remarkable, for he himself was so hard-up that he had had to accept a loan of $250 from Quinn that October.

The aim of Ezra's scheme was "the release of captives," beginning with Eliot: "Only thing we can give the artist is leisure to work in. Only way we can get work from him is to assure him of this leisure . . ." "Eliot is at his last gasp," he wrote to William Carlos Williams on 18 March 1922. "Has had one breakdown. We have got to do something at once."[35] The circular Pound sent secretly to his and Eliot's friends stated the case even more baldly: "Eliot in bank, makes £500. Too tired to write, broke down . . . Returned to bank, and is again gone to pieces physically." Pound hoped to find thirty guarantors who would pledge £10 a year, as he and Aldington had already done: "NOT charity, NOT 'pity the poor artist.' Eliot wd. rather work in bank than do poor work. Has tried to live by pen and can't. (Poor health, invalid wife.)"[36] Quinn at once offered to take six or seven shares, and to find other American donors. On 30 March Pound went public with the scheme, to Eliot's acute embarrassment, appealing openly for funds for the poet in the *New Age.* The public appeal "took my breath away," wrote Quinn, more sensitive than Ezra to Eliot's feelings that he was being shown up as a charity case, and fearing that the bank might come to hear that the young man marked down as a future manager was in reality yearning for his freedom.

The mystery of Vivien's poor health had for a long time puzzled Pound, who had suspected she was suffering from syphilis. He continued to discuss the problem with Quinn by letter: "Eliot has always been very reserved about his domestic situation, so much so that I thought Mrs. E. had syph; and marveled that they didn't get a dose of 606" [an arsenical compound].[37] In the end Ezra got down to "brass tacks" with Tom, who told him that "the girl really has a long complication of things, tuberculosis in infancy *supposed* to have been cured. Symptoms, so far as I now see, point to pituitary trouble . . ." Rather than blaming Vivien, Pound now grew more understanding, as Eliot told him that she had "all along behaved very finely," even offering to live separately.

so that she shouldn't get on T's nerves, *and* prevent his working, is ready to live by herself if it will help T. to write etc. And in general ready to do anything she can to help his work, he can't simply chuck her in the Thames, even if he were so disposed, which he aint.

Pound, aware of how reliant he was on his own wife, Dorothy, whom he had married thinking she had £50 a year, but who in fact received an allowance of more than £150 from her family (bringing his total income up to barely £300 a year), sympathised with Vivien's own lack of support from her family. "Eliot's wife quite honestly expected to get something when she married, but they didn't get it fixed up, went off and married in haste, and then her old Member of the Brit. Academy father pled poverty, and hard times due to war. Has never done a damn thing so far as I know."[38]

By April 1922 Tom was going rapidly downhill, to Vivien's growing alarm. Vivien and he had suffered incessant illness since a week before Easter, Tom told Ottoline, who asked them to Garsington. Could Ottoline recommend a hotel in Brighton, so that they might get "braced up"?[39] A week or two later found them sheltering at the Castle Hotel in Tunbridge Wells, having given up the idea of Brighton because it was too far for Tom to commute from. Vivien was "very seedy" with an attack of neuralgia, having cut short a trip to Paris because of a temperature, and returned to England. Tom, Aldington told Amy Lowell on 5 May, "is very ill, will die if he doesn't get proper & complete rest . . ."[40]

That spring Vivien wrote Aldington—who was to become assistant editor of the *Criterion*—an agitated letter which suggested that Tom was on the verge of collapse. Vivien had read a letter from Aldington to Tom, criticising an article of his in *The Dial*.[41] Tom was, she said, "so *ill*" that it was she who had had to write the article: "He *asked me what he should say* and I told him what to say, and he just wrote it down, *anything,* not caring, for he felt too ill and in despair. So the article is more mine than his. I wd. be glad if everyone knew that." Tom always left his letters behind for her to read, said Vivien, which precipitated her protest:

> It is not easy for me to write to you in this way but I feel for once I must come out of my obscurity and say something. I think your letter is unkind . . . It is exactly the letter to upset Tom, and to harden his pride, and to help precipitate the disasters we all foresee and which you cheerfully say he is asking for. At this moment I know he *cannot stand* a letter like this from anyone he actually *did* look upon as his friend . . . Quarrel with me if you like, and

send me any kind of letter, or no letter at all—show your scorn for my interference.

Aldington had criticised the Eliots' choice of name for the quarterly review, which he thought pretentious, and Vivien robustly defended their decision:

> And as for the title—the *Criterion,* I am responsible for that too. It would be nice if you had offered some good suggestions for the title yourself in time. Perhaps you did not know how many were tried and discarded, and how much worry and bother even the stupid naming of the Review caused us. Anyhow, I thought of the *Criterion* out of my own head . . . and Tom, too tired—*too tired* to bother very greatly once an apparently harmless title had been found, which pleased Lady Rothermere, agreed, and was glad to get the matter settled.

The emotional tone of this letter reveals the paranoid state of mind of both the Eliots at the time, as well as the extent of Vivien's involvement in the creation of the *Criterion.* She fretted that now the title must be changed once more, even though the notices were being printed, and the headed writing paper. "I don't see what to do—Tom won't care, he will say let the wolves get him. You little understand his state of mind," she wrote despairingly.

> I am English, and once I liked England—once I fought like mad to keep Tom here and stopped his going back to America. I thought I could not marry him unless I was able to keep him here, in England. Now I hate it. I hate the word. I hate the people whom you explain so well and so truly. I think Ezra is lucky and wise to have got out. And it is an everlasting stain on the English that he did get out. I hope Tom will soon get out.[42]

Reminding Aldington that she was ill and an "endless drag" on Tom, Vivien begged him to remain the real friend he had always been. Tom would stand or fall by the new review. Could he not understand that?

"Each person who gives him a push now gives him a push out of England. And that will be damned England's loss." Defiantly she signed herself: Vivien Eliot.

Vivien could fight like a vixen on her husband's behalf, and her fierce, almost maternal devotion explains in part the strange and powerful bonds which tied her and Tom to each other. They existed in a state of co-dependence in which psychological need and distress played a large part in illnesses which often had no organic basis. Many letters bear witness to the dance of disease the Eliots shared, taking it in turns to be ill, as one led and the other followed in a flight into hysterical illness which served a particular purpose for each partner in the marriage. For Tom, illness was an escape from the demands of marriage, for his breakdowns in 1921 and 1922 were not simply due to the pressures of work. Vivien's own illnesses were in part an unconscious attempt to hold on to the husband she idolised, even if she could not live with him in harmony, in the face of her escalating fear that he would abandon her.

Some psychiatrists today argue that so-called "mental illness," and in particular hysteria, is a form of language ("protolanguage," which is more primitive than speech) by which the sufferer attempts to communicate with the caregiver or love-object through iconic body signs. "In general, whenever people are unable to prevail by ordinary speech over the significant person in their environment, they are likely to shift their pleas to the idiom of protolanguage," for example, weeping, tantrums or seizures, writes the psychiatrist Thomas S. Szasz. A hysterical symptom, such as a seizure, paralysis or pain, has meaning and transmits a message. The hysteric's goal is to arouse emotion in the listener and induce action. The message is, "You should be ashamed of yourself for making me suffer so," or "Take care of me!"[43] By communicating through such "symptoms" as migraine or backache a woman who is dissatisfied with her life may be able to make her husband more attentive towards her, or, if not her husband, her doctor. Thus Szasz points out that we find "human beings in complicated patterns of paired activities characterised by the helplessness of one member and the helpfulness of another." His game-playing model of human behaviour provides useful insights into the kind of situation which Eliot and Vivien created. One of Bertrand Russell's most perspicacious remarks was that after endeavouring to help the Eliots in their troubles, he found that "their troubles were what they enjoyed."[44] Tom and Vivien perfected the "routines of torment" which bound them together and in which there may have been more collusion than is immediately apparent.[45] It is significant that after leaving Vivien, Eliot moved in with another invalid, John Hayward, and his leaving Hayward was marked by as much stealth and emotional difficulty as was his abandonment of Vivien. It is probable that Eliot chose Hayward, as he did Vivien, because he detected a frailty, both physical and psychological, which met his own need for control, as well as a readiness to give total devotion to the service of genius.

Vivien's love, so freely given when Tom was most in need of it, laid a crushing burden upon him which he grew increasingly to resent during the 1920s. Since she had no sexual hold over him, so was unable to withhold sexual favours as a weapon in their marriage, she had to use hysteria to gain his attention. She probably did not do this consciously—though Szasz argues that lying can be part of the hysteric's armoury—but through "conversion hysteria," as Freud dubbed it, somatising her own pain.

Breuer and Freud, in their *Studies on Hysteria,* cite the case of a woman who, after a quarrel with her husband which felt like a "slap on the face," developed facial neuralgia, demonstrating how through symbolisation an insult can be converted into a symptom.[46] It is a case which bears a resemblance to that of Vivien, who often developed neuralgia, one may surmise, after angry exchanges with Eliot, and earlier with her mother.

But Eliot could play the hysteric too when circumstances demanded, and in this case his illness had the desired effect. Far from never doing "a damn thing," as Pound believed, Eliot's father-in-law, Charles Haigh-Wood, probably at Vivien's instigation, invited him to take a fortnight's holiday at his expense in Lugano, Italy. "I think this visit to Italy will just save me from another breakdown," wrote the relieved poet to Ottoline. Vivien could not decide whether to cross the Channel again and wait in Paris for her husband while he holidayed from 20 May to 4 June, or go "miserably to the seaside" in search of better health.[47] In the event she stayed behind, struggling alone to move their belongings back to 9 Clarence Gate Gardens from the flat at 10 Wigmore Street where she and Tom had been living temporarily. There was the usual Eliot confusion and muddle: they had quarrelled with the landlord at Wigmore Street and were trying to extract damages from the tenant in their own flat. Tom, meanwhile, recuperated in the heat and sunshine of Italy, confessing to Ottoline that he had *never* felt *quite* so lazy and languid as in his lakeside hotel "smothered in roses," and wished he could stay in Italy for six months.[48]

On Tom's return, Vivien's health became much worse, "accelerated in its decline," noted her detached husband, by the horrors of moving and the fatigue and strain of interviewing two Harley Street specialists. At this point Ezra Pound, following a heart-to-heart with Tom in Verona, decided to add a new role to his repertoire: that of medical expert. He would now take Vivien in hand. The work of Dr. Louis Berman, a New York endocrinologist, who claimed that most illnesses could be attributed to malfunctioning glands, had attracted his attention. In March 1922 he wrote about Berman's book in *New Age*, and when he met Berman in Paris, consulted him about Vivien's case. "I am sending him to Eliot, and hope he will get best gland specialists onto the job," he told Quinn on 5 July. "Of course if the poor woman has a cramped cella turcica [the bone over the pituitary gland], the job is nearly hopeless. Only one wd. at least KNOW what one was fighting."[49]

Grateful for Pound's interest, Vivien wrote to him on 27 June 1922 listing her symptoms: colitis, raised temperature ("I very often have a temperature of 99.4 for two or three days at a time for no obvious reason"), insomnia, which had lasted eight years, migraines, physical exhaustion, and increasing mental incapacity ("I have a horror of using my mind and spend most of my time trying to avoid contact with people or anything that will force me to use my mind.")[50] The "hateful, stupid temperatures" of which Vivien had complained in 1921 to Violet Schiff, who was similarly afflicted, refused to go away.[51] They may not, however, have always had a physical cause: sometimes Vivien's emotional storms could lead to a raised temperature. She used to become so upset that after two hours her raised temperature would necessitate calling in her doctor, she later recalled in her diary. Tom added a postscript to Vivien's letter: "Vivien has shown me this letter and I think it is *quite inadequate* as a description of her case, but she is *very* ill and exhausted, and I do not think she can do any better now." Pound had surmised that Vivien might have syphilis, because the symptoms of the secondary stage include malaise, headaches, sore throat and low irregular fever, as well as a rash, but if he was as indiscreet about his suspicions of the cause of her illness as he was about his fund-raising activities on the Eliots' behalf, it is no wonder Vivien felt like hiding away.

In fact the skin rashes which were also troubling Vivien had already sent her to a new specialist, at the urging of Ottoline. Thanking her, Eliot gloomily confided that this specialist, a biologist named Lancelot Hogben, had immediately diagnosed Vivien's "whole trouble as *glands. Most of her glands are not working at all.*" In addition Vivien's system was poisoned by colitis and, according to the specialist, these two problems accounted for all her problems. She was to start a new and violent cure at once.[52] Vivien did not think the treatment would be any use, although she agreed to try it; she was to take "some glands called ... Ovarian Opocaps" in sachets for a month. The doctor told Vivien that his treatment was a shot in the dark. "I think that English doctors are more fond of 'shots in the dark' than any treatment based on scientific knowledge," wrote Vivien to Ezra. "It appeals to the 'sporting' side of the English character."[53]

After a fortnight she noticed no improvement. Taking the glands of animals was of course purely experimental, explained Eliot to Ottoline, who was also putting herself in the hands of a new specialist: "It may take a long time before they find the right glands." In addition, Hogben prescribed "a very strong internal disinfection" for Vivien, who was to go without food completely for two days a week. Vivien hoped that this cure would prove scientific enough, wrote Eliot, seemingly unaware of his wife's scepticism as she obediently began fasting.[54]

In the summer of 1922 the Eliots again returned to Bosham. The peace of mind for which they yearned was symbolised for them by the idea of a country cottage by the sea, the possession of which became the focus of a vain but obsessive two-year quest assisted by Mary Hutchinson, as well as by Virginia Woolf and Richard Aldington. "Although we cannot in the least afford it, we are frightfully keen to get a tiny country cottage," Eliot had written to Aldington the previous April. "It would be very good for both of us ... a country cottage might just be the saving of my wife's health."[55] Southview, the cottage the Eliots had formerly rented, was no longer available, so instead, in July 1922, they took a two-month let on 2 Creed Cottages, on the outskirts of the village. The 300-year-old labourer's cottage, with its low ceiling, beams, inglenook and bread oven, was full of charm, but it had an outside privy and was not ideal for a "scientific" cure. Bravely Vivien followed her doctor's orders. She had benefited in some ways, wrote Tom doubtfully to Ottoline, but at the same time the cure was so drastic that it made her feel extremely ill and indeed caused her a great deal of pain.[56] In two or three weeks they hoped to know definitely how sound the treatment was.

Vivien put a brave face on conditions at 2 Creed Cottages to Mary Hutchinson: the first weekend was "ghastly" without any servants, but soon she had engaged two, one for the mornings and one for the evenings. Vivien took pride in her treatment of servants: although she did not like to pay a woman more than £1 a week, she gave them plenty to eat and sent their print dresses and aprons to the laundry,[57] and in her close relationship with faithful retainers such as Ellen, who became devoted to her mistress, she found a substitute of sorts for the affection missing in her life. But the furnished cottage was "inconceivably tiny," she complained to Mary, although the south-facing upstairs bedrooms looked out towards the sea, and offered a peaceful spot in which to rest and write. Vivien longed to find somewhere where she could put her own furniture and make a real home; then "how happy I should be!" Bosham seemed so lovely, she told Mary, and even if Tom did leave the bank at Christmas, as seemed likely, and they went to live in Paris, there was no countryside she liked better than English countryside—although she would cheerfully exchange London for Paris.[58]

As time passed—with Tom remaining in London during the week allegedly "head over heels in work"—Vivien's weakness increased under Hogben's fasting regime. She was at a very low point where "all weak spots break out—neuralgia, neuritis, eye trouble, etc," Eliot told Pound on 19 July, and had now started on a new diet for colitis which involved great care in the preparation of food: all meat had to be minced three times, only the "best sealed medical milk" allowed, together with "vitamins and proteids [sic] daily." He did not want Vivien to break the diet, which seemed to be "the best so far and really doing her good," although he agreed to see Berman if he came to London. "I should like to put her in your hands," Tom assured Pound, but for the time being she was not well enough to bring to Paris. In a postscript, Tom added the most significant diagnosis yet made by Hogben: that Vivien's colitis was not a disease but a symptom of a more deep-seated malady. The sharp-eyed doctor had observed the tensions between the couple, the source of which he could only guess at, and was aware of the link between anxiety or depression and disorders of the digestive system such as colitis or irritable bowel syndrome.[59] There seems little doubt that Vivien was depressed: in a letter to Ottoline written in pencil because of the pain of neuritis in her right arm, she complained of "extreme dejection . . . I long to see you. Yet I often get into a condition of such apathy that I can scarcely lift my head. I get long periods of this inertia and I simply dread it."[60] Tom, however, clung to the idea that Vivien's colitis was a symptom of "glandular trouble" and she continued to take Hogben's animal gland capsules thrice daily.[61]

Vivien's condition was far more severe than her husband admitted. The starving regime had been disastrous, inevitably increasing the effect of any drugs she was taking for insomnia and the pain of neuralgia in her right arm. The poor skin of which she complained to the Harley Street specialists was very probably a symptom of bromism caused by overdosing on the bromide and chloral sleeping draughts which she had been taking for many years. Taken in excess they caused crimson blotches on the face and hands, as Evelyn Waugh noticed to his horror when he began mixing his undiluted sleeping draught with crème de menthe and taking it in larger and larger quantities as an antidote to insomnia and depression. His face, like Vivien's, developed a "congested, mottled hue," and he began hearing voices. Paranoia was another side effect vividly described by Waugh in his novel, based on his experiences, *The Ordeal of Gilbert Penfold;* he began to feel he was being spied on. "The doctor has you under observation," whispered the voices. "He'll keep you in a home because you're mad, Gilbert." Not until his doctor informed him that his was a "simple case of poisoning" did Waugh/Penfold find relief from the fear that he was going insane.[62]

But drugs could be "comforters" to someone as unhappy as Vivien, as Muriel Spark related in her first novel, *The Comforters,* which in 1957 took a similar theme to that of Waugh's, in this case revealing how dexedrine caused her to have hallucinations.

Vivien's own "Nightmare figure" visited her at night with "strange looks and horrid glares," she confessed in 1924 to Sydney Schiff, who suffered a similar affliction.

I am no more responsible for him than you are, I take it, for your particular Nightmare. I mean your pet bogey, your tame Superman. But if we are to accept them, and you say in your letter we must, we shall I suppose have to accept all their accoutrements—their moods and fancies, their flights, their disguises, their *armaments,* their chains and padlocks & their groans, shrieks and imprecations. And why not?[63]

Vivien's vivid imagination may have been the source of these nightmare figures, but it is more likely that drugs caused her to hallucinate. In a painting by Henry Fuseli, *The Nightmare,* demons and goblins appear to a young woman who seems drugged. The culprit in Vivien's case was probably chloral, a commonplace drug of the time: Virginia Woolf found "Prince Chloral" a seductive comforter in her battle for sanity, claiming in her essay "On Being Ill" that we need a new "hierarchy of the passions":

> Love must be deposed in favour of a temperature of 104; jealousy give place to the pangs of sciatica; sleeplessness play the part of villain, and the hero become a white liquid with a sweet taste— that mighty Prince with the moth's eyes and the feathered feet, one of whose names is Chloral.[64]

Illness, such a constant presence in Vivien's life, inspired some of her most vivid and forceful writing. In a striking, semi-autobiographical sketch, "The Paralysed Woman," written in 1922, she describes "Sibylla," an unhappy wife living at the seaside, awaiting the return of her husband, André. In the house opposite is a paralysed woman. Sibylla observes her closely. The paralysed woman dines with an attentive man in grey. Sibylla feels she is more disabled, more unfortunate than the woman in the bath chair.

> On Saturday came André, wearing a bowler hat, with an anxious expression, and carrying as usual two large suitcases—one filled with books and periodicals and the other with medicine bottles . . . Felice, the help, is wearing her overall; she puts a kettle on the gas fire with a fat, helpless hand, spilling a little water as she

does. Her short-sighted eyes hold the expression of a worried monkey . . .[65] André scowled at her: "Are you quite certain that the milk is 'certified' "? he asked with cold fury, removing the cardboard disk from a milk bottle and peering down at the contents . . . André slept till three: he rose liverish and bad-tempered and ate a combined meal of stale lunch and early tea . . . He poked about the medicine chest, collected empty bottles, made copious notes, and packed and unpacked suitcases.[66]

André/Tom brings supplies of drugs for his wife from the London specialist, and the tranquillising compounds Sibylla swallows must have seemed a necessity, for her behavior is irrational and bizarre. Half-jokingly she threatens "Mike," another resident who claims to feel a Proustian indifference for life; carelessly picking up a knife, she asks if he cares whether he is dead or alive.

She stood the knife upright on its handle, and tapped it on the table. She glanced at the knife, and then again at Mike, who did not answer . . .

"Answer me," said Sibylla in a loud and martial tone. Mike hung his head.

"No," he said.

"Ah," said Sibylla, "so you are not indifferent to everything." She played with the knife. "You would not be indifferent for instance, if I were just to wipe this knife round your throat."

Vivien presents "Mike" as an obtuse character forever being set "traps" by Sibylla, Felice and André. Mike tries to laugh: "You know you look so awfully fierce, dear, sitting there." Sibylla ignores him; and only a few pages later she explodes with rage when André, Mike and Felice bring her the laundry to sort as she lies in bed; Felice has been using Sibylla's Sunlight soap without permission. Sibylla screams at Felice. She asks everyone to leave her room. With bowed heads they creep out. Left alone, Sibylla falls back exhausted on her bed, surrounded and covered with piles of linen, half-open parcels and paper and string.

"I can't bear it. I can't go on." She relaxed her body and appeared dead: but her mind went on as fast as ever.

Covering her face with her hands, she repeats to herself like a lesson—"I must be independent. I must. Somehow I must be independent."

Framed in the window opposite she sees the paralysed woman, wearing white, taking tea with the man in grey and a little boy. She has a son; she is surrounded by love. Sibylla locks her suitcase and lies flat on the bed. Her aching back eases a little as she puts her legs up over the end of the bed . . . "She'll probably get better anyhow," thinks Sibylla impatiently. She lies inert, waiting for André to come with the car and take her away.[67]

It would be possible to interpret this sketch as an indication of Vivien's inherent instability, manifesting itself in psychotic behavior, but there is no need for such a reductive reading of the piece. Vivien, like Tom, was neurotic but not psychotic. There are many references in Vivien's diaries to her feelings of depression, insomnia and lethargy, as well as to her hyperactivity or mania, when she could not stop writing, shopping or socialising, and experienced feelings of omnipotence. But in different marital circumstances her highly strung temperament might have found the calm and stability she required.

The hysteria from which Vivien suffered was the most common form of neurosis exhibited by women at that time. Hysteria, like "witchcraft," is a pejorative term, taking its name from *hystera*, the Greek word for uterus; its wide variety of symptoms was blamed by classical healers on the supposed ability of the uterus to travel through the body. Viewed throughout history as a women's disease, subject to punitive treatments, it can also be read as the "body language of powerlessness," the only outlet for frustrated libido and talent in a prefeminist era. Vivien, trapped in her marital cage, is like Hedda Gabler, of whom Ibsen wrote: "It is Hedda's repression, her hysteria that motivates everything she does."[68] Vivien is as much a paradigm of hysteria as Hedda when she writes to Mary from her cottage: "I felt like a wild heart in a cage."[69]

Hysteria as a response to the immobilising and silencing of women is a thesis which illuminates Vivien's case. Like Freud's patient, "Anna O," she cannot communicate with a man she perceives as hostile; yet "Sibylla" writes feverishly. Although unable to walk in "The Paralysed Woman," her typewriter sits in her bedroom. She plucks the last page of her story from it. "It was finished. She was sorry in a way." There is nothing more she can do to it, and it must stand or fall on its own. "Her back ached now, and suddenly she was aware of that, and of her fixed tense face and of the old dull pain." Writing is her rebellion as she fumbles to find a voice which will not only express her pain and anger but transcend it, for in her imagination she is not a sick woman but an exhibition dancer who is dancing in her yellow knitted dress to the applause of the audience. "It's the only thing to be," she cries to André.

> Don't you see? You simply dance and then you are finished. You
> don't have to think. You don't have to act. All you have to do is
> dance . . . and everybody claps.[70]

Significantly, both in folklore and in medicine, dance was seen as an imitation or representation of female hysteria, occupying the shadowy place between theatrical and histrionic frenzy.[71]

In reality, in August 1922, when she was writing "The Paralysed Woman," Vivien was struggling to regain enough strength to visit her friend Mary, who was recovering from a mild case of mumps. If she could walk as far as Eleanor, wrote Vivien, she would come and speak to Mary through the door, or climb up to the window. "I should love to do that. But I cannot walk so far, walk such a long way. It is so long now since I walked at all." She passed the time rereading Mary's letters, which she had meant to destroy, because she had "a mania for destruction." But they were so nice, so charming, that she kept them, so that they might go into "someone's biography." It is significant that as early as 1922 Vivien was concerned with preserving evidence for the future; as the years passed she took increasing care in dating her letters, although the recipients often failed to take equal care in preserving them. "I am not liking it here *very* much," she confessed sadly to Mary. "I try to like it. But something is wrong. I cant *relax*. What is it?"[72]

Bloomsbury, meanwhile, was taking Eliot to its very heart. At Hogarth House Virginia Woolf set up the type for *The Waste Land* with her own hands, as she had done with his *Poems*.[73] She now felt that the poet amused her more than old friends such as Clive Bell: earlier that year, in March, Virginia found Tom had grown "supple as an eel," positively familiar and jocular. She enjoyed the clash of steel with him as they crossed swords over *Ulysses,* a work about which they still held very different views.[74] And when, in July 1922, Virginia discovered the talk at Garsington was of the subscription Ottoline was getting up "to give Tom £300, & so free him from journalism," she decided to help rally supporters for The Eliot Fellowship Fund, as the English arm of Bel Esprit was known. Richard Aldington, with whom the scheme had originated in England, was a mere "greasy-eyed" tradesman, in Virginia's eyes. It was she and Ottoline, both of whom felt increasing sympathy for "great Tom," as Virginia dubbed him, who hastened to rescue their protége.[75]

Nevertheless Bel Esprit was beginning to look an increasingly precarious and undignified scheme: Eliot snapped at Pound that he strongly objected to any mention of Lloyds Bank in the circular: "*Please see my position—I cannot* jeopardise my position at the Bank before I know what is best."[76] His mood with Aldington was irascible, as he laid his plans for the *Criterion;* secrecy was imperative. His editorship was to be hidden from readers: "I shall initial my editorial," he informed Aldington, promising to arrange the division of labour between the two of them in "an orderly way."[77] The first issue was to kick off with some contemporary criticism from Aldington, and the first two sections of *The Waste Land;* he did not intend to launch the review with an attack on his enemy, Middleton Murry, he explained: "I wish to be very careful at first not to appear to use the paper as a weapon."[78] But behind the "softly, softly" approach, Eliot was in deadly earnest. The jackals were snapping at his heels, and he knew that his reputation would stand or fall by the success or failure of the new periodical which he intended to rival or surpass Scofield's *Dial.* Angry words were exchanged when Aldington's article did not come up to scratch, and when Herbert Read seemed to have let the cat out of the bag about his editorship, Eliot's fury was so great that he threatened legal action against his old friend: "I don't want *anyone* to write of me as the editor, and I am very angry that he [Read] has done so," he spluttered to Aldington. "I am seeing my solicitor . . ."[79]

Eliot's quarrels with Vivien and his short temper with male colleagues betrayed the stress of maintaining a mask which had never fitted and had now become an intolerable burden. Although to friends he appeared preoccupied with the *Criterion* launch and Vivien, the astute Virginia noticed that all was not as it seemed. When Tom visited her at Gordon Square in early August she no longer found him approachable but rather "sardonic, guarded, precise, & slightly malevolent . . ."[80] Clive Bell had confirmed her suspicions in March 1922 that Tom was wearing face-powder, explaining, via Mary, that Tom "uses violet powder to make him look cadaverous."[81] "I am not sure that he does not paint his lips," she recorded in September.[82] A few months later she noted with growing disillusion: "He dreads life as a cat dreads water. But if I hint so much he is all claws"; Tom was "broken down," unable to speak for tears when he telephoned her, distraught, peevish, egotistical.[83]

The pull of that other twilight world had become too great to be resisted. The conflict which brought Eliot for a second time to the verge of breakdown, before he fled to Lugano, had found its own resolution with the discreet help of Mary, always sympathetic to the needs of her friends. That year the Russian ballet had returned to the Coliseum for another triumphant season, its stars Lydia Lopokova and Léonide Massine delighting Ottoline Morrell, the Sitwell brothers, Roger Fry, Duncan Grant and other members of Bloomsbury, who were devoted adherents of the Ballets Russes. Ottoline entertained Diaghilev and Massine to tea at Garland's Hotel in Suffolk Street, where the dancers could be found after the first house eating strawberry or raspberry jam in silver spoons, dipped in black tea; she entertained them at Garsington too, impressing the snobbish Diaghilev, threatened with boredom among the shaggy writers in the garden, by announcing of Dorothy Brett: "That woman is sister to a Queen." "It is true that the Queen in question was Queen of Sarawak, but the words nevertheless produced a tonic effect," recalled Osbert Sitwell.[84]

Massine and Ottoline exchanged photos, and he signed himself "votre très dévoué Léonide."[85] Although London was at the feet of the "fluttering, pink-petticoated, mischievous Lopokova, and her . . . sinister-looking partner," as Massine described himself and Lydia, they looked for social life to Bloomsbury, and Lydia eventually married Maynard Keynes.[86] Massine, maître de ballet and principal choreographer of the Russian Ballet, had made his début in *La Légende de Joseph* in 1914, returning after the war in the role of Amoun in *Cléopatre,* in which he was naked except for a loincloth. His dancing had "a dark, grotesque quality," to which his partner Lydia, "fair, with the plump greenish pallor of arctic flowers," was the perfect foil.[87] Eliot had watched many performances of the Russian Ballet, both in Paris and London, but it was not until April 1922 that he asked Mary to find out whether Massine, who was starring in *La Boutique Fantastique, Le Tricorne (The Three-Cornered Hat)* and *Parade,* would be prepared to meet him. Her reply was encouraging, and he responded with excitement. "I hope your news of Massine at the Coliseum is true, as I have been to see him and thought him more brilliant and beautiful than ever— if what you said was sincere it is I consider a great compliment as I (never having been so close before) quite fell in love with him," he wrote to Mary on 28 April 1922. "I want to meet him more than ever—& he is a genius." Thanking her for one of their "Piccadilly teas," he repeated that he hoped to see Massine with her.[88]

Three weeks after returning from his Italian holiday, Eliot's wish was granted. He met the dancer—who at that time was still married to Vera Savina (formerly Clark—it was the custom of the Russian Ballet to give English dancers Russian names)—at a restaurant. "I liked Massine very much indeed—with no disappointment—and hope that I shall see him again," he wrote to Mary, thanking her for being "very sweet" in arranging a perfect evening. He was feeling rather tired, explained Eliot, for while Vivien starved, he had been out to a dinner and dance the night before, "and enjoyed myself and got off with the Aga Khan, and finished the evening at Wigmore Street where I ended the vermouth and packed my clothes, rather fun . . ."[89] Tom had made a decision: he would not yet abandon Vivien, but the time had come to lay the foundations for his secret life.

15

"Fanny Marlow"

By September the roses were fading around the door of the Bosham cottage. After a farewell picnic with Mary, Vivien reluctantly left the windswept shores of Chichester Harbour for London. But her heart remained in Sussex: she pined for her seaside cottage, whose lease was up, she told Ottoline, and wished she could make her home in the country. "London is so horrible . . . I certainly do wish that there was not so much hatred, and when one gets right away from everybody one cannot see what it is all about." Nevertheless, Vivien's mood was collected, her letter neatly typed and accurately spelt. Determined to act unselfishly towards Tom, she told Ottoline on 15 September 1922, in what may be a coded message of understanding, that she longed for him "to have a freer life and a less ugly one."[1]

From Clarence Gate Gardens Vivien continued her restless search for a replacement cottage. "Please please find me a cottage, house, bungalow, anything, *unfurnished*," she begged Mary on 23 September.[2] Messages flew to Mary at both Eleanor and River House on French postcards Vivien had bought in Paris in January. Still "starving and helpless,"[3] Vivien was frustrated by the difficulties of house-hunting from a distance. It was "terrible" when one could not *go and look*. Did Mary think a cottage on the main road to Selsey would be any good? Or a bungalow at Clymping, near Littlehampton—or even a fine Georgian residence in Chichester itself? There seemed to be so many properties, but they were *never* quite right. In response Mary showered Vivien with flowers—pink carnations for her bedroom and chrysanthemums for Tom's study—but kept her distance. Vivien remained the supplicant, asking herself to tea, complaining that they were "indeed behindhand" in seeing each other: "I want to see you, if you want to see me," she told Mary, enquiring whether next Saturday afternoon would be any good, for Vivien never went out in the evening.[4]

No such difficulties presented themselves to Mary when it came to meeting Tom. While Vivien remained in bed with a "strained heart," under doctor's orders, trying to reduce her blood pressure after a bout of bronchitis which had nearly turned to pneumonia, Tom asked Mary and Jack to dinner at the Café Royal as his guests. "I want very much indeed to see you, both—don't disappoint me," he wrote to Mary on 7 October.[5] His busy social life, which had crossed the increasingly blurred line between Bloomsbury and the drawing-rooms of high society, left little time for rest. Tom apologised to Mary for not being "at home" when she had called early one evening: he was in a very deep sleep, he explained, snatching a few hours before his new secretary, a young woman named Irene Pearl Fassett, came to the flat at eight. As his nights were seldom more than five hours, he usually took a nap before dinner.[6] Sometimes Mary complained that she could not reach him on the telephone: "O la, my dear Mary, and so I am not the only person who cannot be got on the telephone." He had tried her twice that evening and got "no reply." Well, he was glad she also understood that one *need not* respond to the busy bell. He hoped she was not also in bed with an aching head and back and an exasperated liver, after a night on the town, and that the next time he rang she would be "sweetly present."[7]

There is no doubt that Mary remained more than a little in love with Tom, as were Edith Sitwell and Nancy Cunard. Nancy never forgot the evening she met Tom in 1922 at a ball at her mother's house: he in a dinner jacket, she in a panniered Poiret dress, "gold with cascading white tulle on the hips." Although she had danced that night with the Prince of Wales, Nancy was bored until the moment when she met Eliot; they had had supper alone together, she recalled, and talked about poetry. She had suggested a *rendez-vous* the following evening. The poet agreed. They met, drank together and talked into the night. Nancy remembered that they were both engaged to dine at the Hutchinsons', but "I begged you not to get us there, and in the end I won."[8]

Eliot enjoyed flirting with amusing and decorative married women (Nancy was at this time married to Sydney Fairbairn). It is possible that he may have fallen prey to the seductive and promiscuous Nancy, who prided herself on demonstrating the pleasures of heterosexual relationships to otherwise confirmed homosexuals.[9] Certainly Maurice Haigh-Wood remembered that Nancy, like Mary, "made a pass" at Tom. But it is more likely that Tom continued to meet Nancy at Lady Cunard's box at the ballet because of his intense interest in the Ballets Russes, and in particular in his new friend, Léonide Massine, whom he had reviewed with unusual effusiveness in *The Dial* in August 1921. Eliot greeted the second, post-war "golden age" of the Ballets Russes, a period in which Massine's ascendancy was complete, with acclaim. In his view it surpassed the pre-war era of Nijinsky and Pavlova, both in simplicity and in sophistication.[10] In April 1923 Eliot would go on to claim that Massine was "The greatest actor . . . in London . . . the most completely unhuman, impersonal, abstract," observing in the dancer the same "mask-like beauty" he had noticed in another actor, Ion Swinley, of the Phoenix Society company, whose productions Tom, Vivien, and other members of Bloomsbury attended. Massine's training in movement and gesture, declared Tom in "Dramatis Personae" in the *Criterion,* allowed the Russian to transmute personality into art as only the greatest artist could do: "The difference between the conventional gesture of the ordinary stage, which is supposed to *express* emotion, and the abstract gesture of Massine, which *symbolises* emotion, is enormous." For the poet it was the ritualistic quality of Massine's performance which moved him: "For the stage . . . always . . . is a ritual, and the failure of the contemporary stage to satisfy the craving for ritual is one of the reasons why it is not a living art."[11]

Eliot was influenced by Clive Bell in his praise of the modernist "impersonality" of Massine's performing style, which echoed the qualities he and other "Bloomsberries" valued in poetry and literature. Yet, as Lynn Garafola, historian of the Russian ballet, points out, Eliot's enthusiasm for Massine's performance was "most astounding," when one considers the production in which he was dancing. This was George Robey's *You'd Be Surprised,* a "tinned" New York revue, as Eliot himself described it, which led Massine to cross the line dividing ballet and variety, and work with Noël Coward and C. B. Cochran.[12] Nevertheless, after sitting through an hour of this "cold-stored humour," Eliot discovered "life" as well as machinery: "We move toward satisfaction in the direction which moves Leonid [sic] Massine."[13]

The Russian ballet had become a cult with High Bohemia. Edward J. Dent, music critic of the *Athenaeum,* had written in June 1920 that the Diaghilev audience was dominated by the "intellectual-smart":

> musicians who know all about painting, painters who know all about music, poets who like to be men about town, men about town who like to be poets . . . M. Diaghilev understands them as if he were himself the *maestro* whose immortal hand had framed their sawdust and tinsel anatomies.[14]

If, as is likely, Eliot and Osbert Sitwell recognised themselves in this hostile portrait of "poets who like to be men about town, men about town who like to be poets," neither was unduly concerned. Both were committed to living beyond their means in the pursuit of pleasure. Hedonism and aestheticism were their natural values and, under the guise of robust heterosexuality, married women their confidantes. The difference between them lay not only in talent but in fortune; in his pursuit of a single social life apart from Vivien, Tom was forced to amuse himself largely at other people's expense, in contrast to Osbert, who could borrow on the security of Reninshaw, his future inheritance. But Tom, the handsome poet-about-town, was a welcome guest in many salons, and in the Rothermeres he had the good fortune to find a couple whose patronage linked the worlds of literature and dance: the press baron Rothermere was as devoted to dancers (Alice Nikitina, a Ballets Russes dancer, was his mistress) as his wife was initially to her lion cub Tom at the *Criterion,* and in the late 1920s would become financial backer of Diaghilev's company.[15]

In the final run-up to the *Criterion* launch on 15 October 1922, however, pleasure had to take second place to the pains of editorship. Fortunately Tom's problems over the publication of *The Waste Land* had melted away. The diplomatic John Quinn had resolved Tom's quarrel with Scofield over payment by hosting a lunch for Gilbert Seldes and Liveright at which a face-saving formula was found: Eliot was to be awarded the *Dial* prize of $2,000 for services to letters in America. This allowed *The Waste Land* to appear, without Notes, in *The Dial* in November 1922, a month after its first publication in the inaugural issue of the *Criterion*. The Boni & Liveright edition, with the "solemn mockery" (in T. S. Matthews' words)[16] of the added Notes suggested by Roger Fry, was published in mid-December, to be followed by the Hogarth Press edition in September 1923. When Quinn received the bundle of manuscripts from Eliot (which included the "unpublishable" 1909 notebook of Bolo poems) on about 15 January 1923, he commented that he himself would not have agreed to the cuts to *The Waste Land* made by Ezra Pound.[17] Nevertheless Eliot inscribed the copy of the Boni & Liveright edition he sent to Ezra in Paris with a graceful dedication: "for E.P./*miglior fabbro*/from T.S.E./Jan. 1923." The quotation was again from Canto xxvi of the *Purgatorio* in which Dante says of Arnaut Daniel: *"Fu miglior fabbro del parlar materno"* (he was the better craftsman in his mother-tongue). Eliot repeated the compliment to Pound when *The Waste Land* was reprinted in his *Poems 1909–25* with the dedication: "For Ezra Pound/*il miglior fabbro.*"[18] Eliot's gratitude for his friend's critical ability was genuine, but the dedication perhaps assuaged his guilt at receiving the *Dial* prize, which he felt should have gone to Pound, languishing in obscurity in Paris.

It is worth considering why Eliot took the decision at this point in his life to commit to Quinn's safe-keeping the notebook containing his early poems, and in particular the revealing Bolo and Colombo verses with their homosexual and scatological themes. By contrast it seems that Eliot arranged for Emily Hale's letters to him to be burnt by Peter du Sautoy, a director of Faber & Faber and one of his executors, as in March 1963 he gave du Sautoy a tin-box containing papers which he had, he said, "for a long time been meaning to destroy." Du Sautoy duly burned the papers in the coal-burning furnace in the block of flats where he was living.[19] The question remains, why Eliot did not also consign his "Bolo" notebook to the flames, since its repetitive tales of Captain Colombo, "the great big bitch," reveal inclinations which he had kept secret during his lifetime.[20] Surely the answer has to be that Eliot, like other great artists, intended such "sensitive" material to be read after his death. Arguably he wanted future generations to know the private man who sheltered behind the grave public persona, and we can only be grateful for his foresight in appreciating that a later generation might be less judgemental than his own.

Nervously Vivien awaited the publication of the first part of *The Waste Land* in their new quarterly. To Sydney Schiff, who expressed his appreciation of the poem in an "unexpectedly moving" letter, she wrote on 16 October, the day after the publication of the *Criterion* No. 1:

> Perhaps not even you can imagine with what emotions I saw *The Waste Land* go out into the world. It means to me a great deal of what you have exactly described, and it has become a part of me (or I of it) this last year. It was a terrible thing, somehow, when the time came at last for it to be published. I have been distracted these last 2 days . . .[21]

She need not have worried. The poem was an immediate financial and critical success, even if her prosaic brother-in-law Henry found that it seemed to be written in a "cipher" he could not understand. "Probably no poem of comparable length was ever more promptly, more variously, or more copiously rewarded," writes Professor Reid.[22] The evidence of genius needed to attract subscribers to Bel Esprit was there for all to see, argued Pound, who was now comparing Eliot to Keats, Shelley or Browning.[23] As Cyril Connolly realised, Eliot and Joyce had broken with nineteenth-century Romantic models and surpassed them in originality: 1922 was "the *annus mirabilis* of the modern movement, with *Ulysses* and *The Waste Land* just around the corner, and the piping days of Huxley . . . and the Sitwells, of the Diaghilev ballet . . ."[24] And Eliot, with the birth of his new quarterly, had taken yet another step up the pyramid of fame.

But barely was the *Criterion* born, than it seemed in danger of choking. Lady Rothermere complained that she was displeased with the first number, writing Tom three "offensive letters" from La Prieuré, a former Carmelite monastery at Fontainebleau which had become the Institute for the Harmonious Development of Man. Run by a Russian mystic, the

Institute was, wrote Vivien to Ezra Pound, an "asylum for the insane," where Lady Rothermere was doing "religious dances naked with Katherine Mansfield," who was also an inmate. Vivien worried that Mansfield was influencing their patron against Tom: " 'K.M.,' " Lady R. was writing in every letter—"is *the most intelligent* woman I have ever met," she told Pound. " 'K.M.' is pouring poison in her ear (of course) for 'K.M.' hates T. more than anyone."[25] Tom and Vivien began to panic that "Lady R." would "shipwreck" the quarterly, despite its instant "SUC-CESS," as Tom explained to Ezra in a letter written a day after Vivien's on 3 November. He had had nothing but good notices, and nearly all the six hundred copies printed were sold, but now he was afraid he would be forced to abandon the paper.[26] What were they to do?

Vivien's plan was a bold one: she proposed somehow to raise the money to buy out Lady Rothermere, whom she believed would take £500 for the journal now, although she would not sell it later if it began to pay. "Do you think this is a *possible* idea? If so, how shall we do it—and *can you get that money?*" she demanded of Ezra. Her belief in Tom was absolute. "I know he could make the *Criterion* a success," she wrote, offering herself to provide £500. It would halve her income from the capital her father had given her, but she would do it "gladly."[27]

Tom agreed with Vivien's idea. It would be "the thing of our lives," Tom told Ezra, if he and Ezra could get the *Criterion* into their own hands and run it for a couple of years. Come over to London for a weekend and see me, he pleaded. Ezra's reaction was unenthusiastic: "I think both you and V. are in delirium," he wrote, "thinking of paying £500 for the privilege of having worked six months. Bring out another number . . . Dear ole SON. You jess set and hev a quiet draw at youh cawn-kob." The *Criterion's* only asset was Tom himself, he told the anxious poet. "If you quit, *it* quits." And why would one story from Katherine M. really "queer the review? . . . I dare say K.M. IS the most intelligent female she [Lady R.] has ever met."[28]

This defence of Katherine Mansfield aroused a furious reaction from Tom two days later. K.M. was not by any means the most intelligent woman Lady Rothermere had ever met: "She is simply one of the most persistent and thickskinned toadies and one of the vulgarest women Lady R. has ever met and is also a sentimental crank."[29] (It was an opinion at odds with his expression in April 1923 of the *Criterion's* "profound regret"

at Katherine Mansfield's death, and the subsequent "loss to English letters.")[30] Vivien's own hostility towards Katherine may have had its roots in
her resentment of Katherine's brief liaison with Russell, as well as in
Vivien's protective feelings towards Tom. Yet at the same time Vivien's
own work showed signs of Katherine's influence: Vivien's story "Mrs.
Pilkington," which she wrote for the *Criterion* in October 1924 under the
pen name Felix Morrison, as well as her "Diaries of the Rive Gauche," resemble in both style and content Mansfield's "Je Ne Parle Pas Français."[31]

Pound's advice to Eliot regarding Lady Rothermere's vociferous complaints that the paper was "Dull" and looked like a corpse, was astute.
"She's right, mon POSSUM," he wrote in a letter which reached the Eliots
on 5 November 1922, the anniversary of Guy Fawkes's Gunpowder Plot.
How could Lady R. be expected to see what was scarce discernible to the
naked eye, that "the Crit . . . is *supposed* to be PLAYIN' POSSUM."[32]
Pound had detected Tom and Vivien's intention: to blow up the literary establishment and make of Tom a new, puritan leader in the mould of Oliver
Cromwell. It was a "plot" of long standing, first mentioned by Vivien to
Mary as long ago as November 1919, after Mary had asked, in apparent innocence, whether Tom had many literary "enemies." "You ask me, but I
think you know better than I," Vivien had retorted, worried that the
Woolfs were being influenced against Tom.[33] "I also have a gunpowder
plot in preparation," she had written to Mary, who was busy with her own
scheming, "but mine is timed to go off in the New Year."[34]

Tom also confided the Eliot "Gunpowder Plot" to his friend, the poet
Herbert Read, a contributor to the *Criterion*.[35] They would aim for a
"softly, softly" approach, as he explained to Ezra in July 1922, at first keeping the "jailbirds" behind the scenes, and only cautiously allowing Pound
and Wyndham Lewis into print.[36] Tom would, as Pound put it, play
Possum. And indeed the 1920s were the period in which Eliot amused
himself in the Possum role, signing his letters to Pound with his own logo:
a cross whose four corners were inscribed "POS SUM HIS MARK." The
Latin meaning of "possum"—"I can, I am able"—indicated perhaps that
Eliot knew that he had within his grasp the power he had always craved.[37]
Nearer a cat than a possum, as Osbert Sitwell had instantly discerned, Eliot
stalked his prey with stealth and patience, beginning with Middleton
Murry, his chief rival and intellectual antagonist in a war of words waged

on the battlefield of the *Criterion*. But such was Eliot's cunning in disguising the *Criterion,* so that it looked "so heavily camouflaged as Westminster Abbey,"[38] that few realised that they were living through a revolution.

If Eliot was the general, Vivien was his aide-de-camp in this struggle for ascendancy. She hatched a scheme, in collusion with Tom, whereby she could earn extra money to supplement his salary from Lloyds. She would write for the paper under a variety of pseudonyms, the most popular of which was "Fanny Marlow," sometimes reduced to the initials, "F.M." Vivien also gave herself two male pen names, Felix Morrison and Feiron Morris, as well as writing under the name of her close friend, Irene Fassett, who was Eliot's secretary. "Fanny Marlow" has interesting psychological associations, for it was during her stay at Marlow that Vivien's "fanny" was the object of Bertrand Russell's attentions. "I *MUST* explain that I have been riting (writing!) for a long time under various names and nomenclatures," she confided to Ezra in 1924.

> Have written a lot of stories . . . I wrote nearly the whole of the last "Criterion"—except anything that was good in it, if there was such—under different names, all beginning with F.M. I thought out this scheme of getting money out of the Criterion a year ago. Because was always annoyed by spouse getting no salary. So thought what a good idea will receive money for contributions. Have received money. No one knows.[39]

Vivien knew her education at private ladies' academies had left her lacking in the skills of her university-educated male colleagues on the *Criterion*. Watercolour sketching, sewing and dancing were not the best preparation for journalism, but she was encouraged by Tom's vigorous support. "My wife . . . [has] been working very hard for some months, doing a lot of the Criterion work and also writing," he wrote to Richard Aldington in April 1924. "She is very diffident and is very aware that her mind is quite untrained, and therefore writes only under assumed names, but she has an original mind, and I consider not at all a feminine one; and in my opinion a great deal of what she writes is quite good enough for the Criterion." Tom intended to see that Vivien got "training and systematic education," because there were so few women who did have what he considered to be an "un-feminine mind" that he thought they ought to be made the most of. Richard was the only person, confessed Tom, apart from two of Vivien's friends, who knew of her writing.[40]

One good reason for Vivien's money-making plan was the shortcomings of the Bel Esprit scheme: first, the five-year time-limit put on the scheme, after which Eliot "OUGHT to be self-supporting . . . BUT in all probability he *won't* be," as Pound was forced to admit to Quinn, recalling that Yeats at the age of forty-seven had been forced to draw out his last £5 from the bank;[41] secondly, the size of the proposed income: £300 might be acceptable to Ezra, but for Eliot, a tolerable life demanded £600 a year at least, preferably £800, a comfortable flat in London, and six months abroad. Too reticent to speak plainly, he allowed confusion to grow among his English supporters.

In September 1922 Ottoline had written to Vivien to ask her to suggest more subscribers to the Eliot Fellowship Fund; Vivien replied enigmatically that she had a lot to say on that subject, more than she could write in a letter. "As for giving you a list of names of people who would be interested, I do not know of one person outside of those who have already been approached . . . who would be likely to take the slightest interest in the subject."[42] Vivien had her reasons for this brush-off, for she knew better than Ottoline her husband's true financial position, although Ottoline was soon to be privy to secrets of Tom's which he did not choose to share with his wife.

Richard Aldington had seen the rapids ahead in the summer of 1922, when Amy Lowell refused to contribute to Bel Esprit. Pound's article in the *New Age,* publicising the scheme, had proved disastrous. "The publicity he has created (revolting to the last degree) makes [it] impossible," Aldington explained to Amy on 7 July. American supporters began writing in, demanding that Pound contact the press with photographs of Eliot. Horrified, Aldington proposed to withdraw from fund-raising, although he had already gathered promises of £100 a year for his own "private scheme" with Ottoline and Virginia. He made a statement in the *Literary Review,* attempting to correct Ezra's mis-statements, and to clear Eliot and himself from "the inevitable ridicule and odium. I don't mind very much myself," he confided to Amy, "but I do mind for Eliot's sake."[43]

The damage, however, had been done. Whispers were growing about the poet: it was said that his family were wealthy, that he earned £600 a year at Lloyds—and was not prepared to give up his job. There were jibes that he was a hypocrite, a miser even. It was probably known—for Pound was notoriously indiscreet—that Eliot had agreed to accept £20 from his impoverished compatriot; Eliot was to solemnly receipt the gift in clerkly hand: "Received from Bel Esprit per Ezra Pound Esq £20 (twenty pounds)," signing himself "T. S. Eliot" across two one-penny stamps.[44] People marvelled that Aldington, scraping a living doing translations at Malthouse Cottage, near Reading, was collecting for the author of *The Waste Land,* who had just won the *Dial* prize of $2,000. Tom's anguish grew, as the gossip spread.

On 16 November 1922 the story broke. The *Liverpool Post* printed a garbled but damaging piece about the collections being made for him:

> As the amusing tale went at the time the sum of £800 was col-
> lected and presented to Mr. Eliot there and then. The joke was
> that he accepted the gift calmly, and replied: "Thank you very
> much; I shall make good use of the money, but I like the bank."
> That was two years ago, and he held out until last spring, when
> he suffered a severe nervous breakdown which necessitated three
> months leave of absence. Thereupon the society of "Bel Esprit"
> was hatched in secret and carried through, the poet's own wishes
> not being consulted.

The long poem by Eliot in the first number of the *Criterion* was, said the newspaper, the "initial result" of "a considerate and generous scheme with excellent possibilities."[45]

Tom's fury at these "calamitous falsehoods," as he described them to Richard Aldington, knew no bounds. Certainly the paper's claim that Eliot had received £800 was erroneous, but his anger was due chiefly to the knowledge that the *Post* had made him a laughingstock. Tom was tempted to blame Aldington for leaking the story—although there is no reason to suppose the latter was to blame—and wrote to him on 18 November, de-termined to discover the source which had made possible the appearance of "such a libel . . . As I want to *track it down* and not merely secure an apology from the L. Post, please DO NOT MENTION THIS TO A *SIN-*

GLE PERSON until I have seen my solicitor. I pledge you to secrecy." But no sooner had Eliot called in a King's Counsel to help draft a letter to the *Liverpool Post,* than he received an anonymous letter from "Your Wellwisher," stating that the writer had heard that a collection was being taken for the poet and that although the writer's means were small no claim on his charity was ever in vain and he therefore enclosed four postage stamps in the hope that this would help to strengthen Tom's poetry until he became Poet Laureate. It was the last straw. Tom felt "utter exhaustion," as he complained to Aldington.[46]

Such mockery of their protégé evoked sympathy from both Ottoline and Virginia Woolf, who remained committed to the Eliot Fund. Virginia, in particular, was determined to come to Tom's rescue. Although their relationship was a complex and ambivalent one, and at times she did not wholly trust Tom, she nevertheless had felt peculiarly close to the poet ever since their encounter in a taxi in March 1921 on the way to the Lyric, Hammersmith, to see Congreve's *Love for Love;* there, in the dark interior of the cab, they had confessed to their mutual "vices" and acknowledged that they were both trying to write something harder than the classics, something "streaked with badness." "But I plunge more than he does," decided Virginia. "Perhaps I could learn him [sic] to be a frog."[47] Convinced now that if he would only allow her to organise affairs, she might instead make a prince of him, Virginia laboured assiduously to raise money. Her novel *Jacob's Room* was going into a second edition, and her reputation was well established. People did not like to refuse her, but nevertheless it was an uphill struggle. By December 1922 she, Leonard, Ottoline, Aldington and the Cambridge mathematician Harry Norton, who together formed the committee, had, despite paper promises, raised only £77. Of this they gave Eliot £50. Was he to receive an annual sum in future, enquired Tom delicately, or was the committee to continue just giving him "presents"?[48]

A month later Virginia was still waiting for Tom to leave the bank. He had told her "in confidence" of his decision to do so in December. Still he hesitated, "full of scruples." "He is about ready to leap," Ezra had written optimistically in July 1922. Instead Eliot did just as the *Liverpool Post* predicted, and in January 1923 put the £50 into the bank "to invest it," together with the *Dial* prize of £400 ($2,000). Harry Norton, irritated by the poet's procrastination, urged Virginia and Ottoline to get Ezra Pound to take over the fund.[49] Tom could not be blamed for his caution, for the Eliot Fund had given him no guarantees of an income which would match the bank's. A few days later Virginia attempted to clarify the situation with Richard Aldington. Would Mr. Eliot object to her mentioning the possibility that he might leave the bank, she enquired. "I find that when I ask people to subscribe, many of them object that he is staying in the Bank and drawing what many of them consider a good income."[50] She drew Mary Hutchinson into the scheme, too, asking her to persuade Sydney Schiff, who had already subscribed, to circulate the appeal. Mary in turn tried to persuade Vivien of the merits of the fund, but she remained reluctant; *if* the fund offered Tom a guaranteed sum, and *if* the *Criterion* succeeded, Vivien agreed Tom would automatically leave the bank, but in the meanwhile she was sure that any "forcing or pressure to *make* him leave the Bank at *this* point would be very tactless, and bad policy. *So much depends on the* Criterion."[51]

Vivien knew her husband better than Virginia, but she did not interfere. In early February 1923 Tom again visited Virginia at Hogarth House, Richmond; she was ill with a cold which was "a match for any in Bloomsbury." "We had a sitting: costive, agonised . . ." she told Clive Bell.[52] She and Leonard were too ill to penetrate Tom's sphinx-like reticence, but by 12 February Virginia had had an inspiration: since it was obviously impossible to collect enough money to provide Tom and Vivien with a sufficient income, she would pull strings to find him a more congenial job than the bank. She wrote to Maynard Keynes, who had taken over the *Nation* from its former editor, H. W. Massingham, asking whether he would employ Tom as literary editor:

> He would prefer not to teach, but would do secretarial or librarian's work. He is clearly getting into a bad state of health, and the efforts of the Eliot Fund are so slow that it is useless to wait . . . If he could rely on a small certain income from regular work he would risk giving up the Bank. If it were not for his wife's constant illness he would have left the Bank before now.[53]

Keynes's fellow directors were disinclined to give the post to Eliot, since "none of them ever heard of him," and Virginia was forced to plead with Lytton Strachey to promise to write for the *Nation* if Tom were appointed literary editor. "The poor man is becoming (in his highly American way, which is tedious and longwinded to a degree) desperate," she explained.[54] To her diary she confessed to growing boredom with Tom's troubles: "I could wish that poor dear Tom had more spunk in him, less need to let drop by drop of his agonised perplexities fall ever so finely through pure cambric. One waits, one sympathises, but it is dreary work . . ."[55]

By 17 March 1923 Tom could not speak for tears, as he agonised over whether to accept Keynes's offer to become literary editor. "He is broken down, & yet must buckle to & decide: shall he take the Nation?" wrote a weary Virginia in her diary,[56] meanwhile ordering "cheap" paper from which to make covers to bind *The Waste Land,* and arranging the marbling with Vanessa.[57] She consulted Bruce Richmond, editor of the *Times Literary Supplement,* who said emphatically, "He's not the man for the job." Virginia could not help agreeing, as Tom prevaricated over the question of guarantees (the *Nation* could not guarantee more than six months' employment). He was on the verge of collapse, she told Maynard, begging him for at least a two-year contract for Tom;[58] Maynard rang back to say that Tom seemed "distraught." "Whether distraught people can edit the Nation lit. sup. I doubt," mused Virginia.[59]

On 23 March Tom finally turned down the *Nation* job, which Maynard then unexpectedly offered to Leonard Woolf. "Here have I been toiling these 3 weeks to make Eliot take it; finally he shied; & this is the result," exclaimed Virginia, happy that her husband, who had formerly been a contributor to the *Nation* under Massingham, would be earning a regular salary. To the Woolfs it meant "safety . . . indeed luxury."[60] The Eliot Fund was subsequently wound up, as Tom decided he could not accept any more money while he remained at the bank. There was now, as Virginia told Ottoline, no prospect of his being able to leave it.

It is all too easy to follow in the footsteps of Tom's friends and blame Vivien for Tom's decision not to accept Maynard Keynes's offer, and for his consequent unhappiness. The problem was, according to Lyndall Gordon, "Eliot's obligation to secure the future for a wife who would never manage to shift for herself, or endure any privation . . . a vengeful muse who dragged him down to her dark seabed."[61] Tom himself complained to Ezra

Pound that, at the age of thirty-four, the prospect of staying in the bank was "abominable" to him, miserably comparing his own situation with Vivien to that of Ezra with Dorothy: "Dorothy has comparatively good health, a family who can help her, and prospects of enough money to live on afterwards," he had written on 15 November 1922. "Vivien has none of these things. Her father's property . . . is all tied up in Irish real estate, which he has been trying to sell all his life, has never paid much, now pays less . . ." It was, argued Tom, nothing but an encumbrance on Vivien and Maurice, although in the end Vivien's inheritance would prove sufficient to pay the fees of her mental asylum. Vivien was, in fact, as Henry Eliot realised, not penniless "as we once supposed."[62]

Vivien "will *never* be strong enough to earn her own living," insisted Tom, ignoring the fact that he, as editor of the *Criterion,* was about to start paying his wife for her journalism. The only reason he had asked for guarantees, he claimed to Ezra, was because of Vivien, for whom he felt a particular responsibility: "I have made a great many mistakes, which are largely the cause of her present catastrophic state of health, and also it must be remembered that she kept me from returning to America where I should have become a professor and probably never written another line of poetry, so in that respect she should be endowed." At the bank he was assured of a widow's pension for Vivien; outside it there was no security.[63]

It was a touching letter which nevertheless omitted several important facts. First, there was the question of Eliot's portfolio; only a few weeks earlier he had thanked his brother Henry for the "exceedingly welcome dividend," and instructed him to hold on to the Hydraulic stock while the market rose, looking for an opportunity to sell when sterling was low.[64] Eliot's interest in the stock market was a growing one: he was later in discussions with a very successful bond broker in New York, writing to Aldington in April 1924 that he could put him in touch with "a good broker" if he wished, although Tom himself had an aversion to "foreign securities."[65] Vivien's autobiographical sketch "On the Eve," which appeared in the *Criterion* under T. S. Eliot's name in January 1925, but bears all the marks of his wife's writing and his editing, indicates her knowledge that Eliot, by the mid-1920s, was not as poor as he claimed. The sketch pokes fun at a group of wealthy friends concerned about the possibility of being "completely and utterly ruined" if an extreme socialist government comes to power. "My few bits of stuff which pay me about twopence a year are all *absolutely* unsaleable," complains Agatha (perhaps based on Mary Hutchinson, whose husband "Alexander" resembles Jack). If only they could *sell* their horrible stocks and get the *cash* to invest in America: "We shall be destitute," she complains. Vivien's brother Maurice makes an appearance as "Horace," exclaiming that there are a few "stoutish fellows" left to save England, before departing for his club after a spirited rendition of:

> It's the sime the whole world over—
>   It's the pore that gets the blime,
> It's the rich that gets the pleashur:
>   Isn't it a ber-loody shime![66]

"Ow-ee, it's ni-eece to be rich, isn't it," remarks Lizzie the lift-girl to Rose, Agatha and Alexander's maid.

Eliot was more honest to Ezra than he ever was to Virginia about his real reasons for choosing to stay at the bank: "I don't want to write, no sensible man does who wants to write verse . . . It is preferable to run a review and be paid for letting other people write than to write oneself."[67] The editorship of the *Criterion* was demanding enough without the added burden of being literary editor at the *Nation;* he preferred the mechanical routine of Lloyds.

There was another factor in the equation which Eliot took care to keep hidden from Ezra. Only Ottoline was at first privy to this latest secret expense, which made it even more difficult to leave the bank. In January 1923 Vivien, whose vision had been so badly affected by the "starving" regimen that she could barely read, was sent "into exile" at Eastbourne, where her doctor had found her a flat without telling her the address.[68] Vivien had been sleeping worse than Tom had ever known her to do, he confided gloomily to Ottoline.[69] The intense strain of the "two very nasty personal affairs"—the insulting anonymous letter enclosing 6d in stamps, and the attack by the *Liverpool Post*—which she was to keep "absolutely to yourself" had worn them both out: no damages he might get could possibly compensate him for the strain and worry of bringing the case, he complained. He had retreated for a fortnight in November to Worthing himself, prostrated and unable even to write a letter.[70] As to Vivien, Tom expressed to his brother Henry on 31 December his anger at the damage done by her four months of dogged efforts in following the most severe and Spartan regime that he had ever known, one far more difficult than any cure in a nursing home or sanatorium: "Living in the midst of ordinary life imposes much more responsibility on her and requires infinite tenacity of purpose," he wrote. Vivien had not been able to deviate in the slightest from the most limited diet, she had followed special exercises prescribed for her and she had hardly seen anybody. "I have never known anybody stick to a thing with such persistence and courage, often with relapses which made her feel that the whole thing was useless."[71] On Christmas Day 1922 Vivien sat up to dinner for the first time for many months; by the first week in January 1923 she was in Eastbourne, beginning yet another "experiment."

Tom, meanwhile, took tea with Ottoline. A plan had been forming in his head which was facilitated by Vivien's absence. On 5 January he wrote Ottoline a confidential letter: by "an extraordinary stroke of good luck" he had come across a "tiny suite" of two rooms, amazingly cheap, which he intended to take. The idea, he said, was to use them as an office for the *Criterion* work, and when the lease of 9 Clarence Gate Gardens was up, to give that flat up. He and Vivien wanted to decrease their living expenses and settle themselves in a way that would be "adaptable to any kind of life," a hint that he and Vivien may have already discussed living separately. Tom had taken the liberty of giving Ottoline's name as a reference, knowing he could depend upon her not to mention this to *anyone at all*—and there were few of his friends of whom he could be sure in that way. The arrangement he was entering into was "so personal" that he did not want anyone to know of it. He asked Ottoline to reply at once to his agent, and be *very* quick about it.[72]

The flat Tom rented in early 1923 was to be the hub of his secret life, a place where he could throw off conventionality. Burleigh Mansions, a block of portered flats on Charing Cross Road, looked out on St. Martin's Lane, and was favoured by actors. Ellen Terry and Donald Wolfit both at times lived there. Eliot rented number 38, thus securing for himself a *pied à terre* in the heart of theatreland. At Burleigh Mansions he underwent a metamorphosis: here he was no longer "Mr. Eliot," banker and dutiful husband, but "Captain Eliot," hero of the Colombo verses, captain of his crew. Among that crew was in all probability Léonide Massine, who danced the French sailor in *Les Matelots,* a "light-hearted romp" which he choreographed for Diaghilev after divorcing his wife Vera in 1924 and returning to the bosom of the Ballets Russes and a bed-sitting room in Bloomsbury.

Osbert Sitwell noticed, when he visited Eliot in the "bizarre" atmosphere of the Charing Cross Road flat, that "Visitors on arrival had to enquire at the porter's lodge for 'The Captain,' which somehow invested the whole establishment with a nautical—for I cannot say why, I took the title to be naval rather than military—a gay, a gallant feeling." The room in which Osbert and Sacheverell dined was high up at the back of the block, looking down on the revolving glass-ball lantern of the Coliseum music hall, where the Russian ballet performed. Osbert sat next to Tom on one side, Sachie on the other:

> Noticing how tired my host looked, I regarded him more closely, and was amazed to notice on his cheeks a dusting of green powder—pale but distinctly green, the colour of a forced lily-of-the-valley. I was all the more amazed at this discovery, because any deliberate dramatisation of his appearance was so plainly out of keeping with his character, and with his desire never to call attention to himself, that I was hardly willing, any more than if I had seen a ghost, to credit the evidence of my senses.

Osbert was almost ready to disbelieve what he had seen, but he went to tea with Virginia Woolf a few days later. "She asked me, rather pointedly, if I had seen Tom lately, and when I said 'Yes' asked me—because she too was anxious for someone to confirm or rebut what she thought she had seen—whether I had observed the green powder on his face—so there was corroboration!" Osbert and Virginia were apparently equally astounded, and although they discussed Tom's use of cosmetics at considerable length, could find no way of explaining his "extraordinary and fantastical pretence," except on the basis that the great poet was expressing a craving for sympathy in his unhappiness.[73]

It was a cold summer evening, but the light lingered. After dinner

Osbert and Sachie sat in low armchairs; conversation did not flow. After a long silence Sachie remarked, as the golden globe of the Coliseum shone its beam on them, "What is so nice for you here, Tom, is that you're right in the centre of everything." Tom agreed, "in a tone of enthusiasm which lacked his usual wariness": "Yes. Near all the theatre." This amused Osbert, who did not find it easy to imagine Eliot hurrying out to see any of the popular successes of the moment, one of Noël Coward's plays or a current musical comedy, the electric signs for which could be distinguished if they walked to the window.[74] He remained mystified: "Osbert never did discover why T. S. Eliot called himself 'The Captain' and wore make-up," writes John Pearson, biographer of the Sitwells. Osbert, who himself found happiness in his relationship with David Horner after Sacheverell's marriage in 1925, seems to have had no inkling of Eliot's own inclinations, for the poet never took the Sitwells into his confidence as he did Ezra Pound. Osbert was only aware that there was some mystery about the Eliots, around whom there was "an ambience permeated with tragedy, tinged with comedy, and exhaling at times an air of mystification."[75]

Few people knew of Tom's new hidey-hole, certainly not those like Aldington and Norton who had so generously collected for him. Mary Hutchinson was, however, a guest, receiving in 1923 a postcard printed "from T. S. Eliot, 9 Clarence Gate Gardens, London NW1," with the handwritten message that the poet expected her at nine o'clock, Monday, at 38 Burleigh Mansions, almost over the publisher Chatto & Windus. She was to ask the concierge to take her to "Captain Eliot's" as the rooms were difficult to find. "Knock at the door three times." The card was unsigned.[76]

Barely had Eliot taken on the rooms in Burleigh Mansions than another financial burden fell upon him: in March 1923 Vivien discovered a tiny but south-facing labourer's cottage at 2 Milestone Cottages, Old Fishbourne, a mile or two from Bosham. She was eager to rent it, and Tom agreed, despite the cost. Vivien probably learnt in early 1923 that her husband had taken the flat on the fringes of Soho; later she visited it occasionally and wrote there but, despite its ostensible purpose as an office, the rental of the rooms in Burleigh Mansions marked a critical point in the Eliots' relationship—forcing Vivien to face the fact that Tom was creating an alternative life in which she had no place. Her response was panic, as her fear of abandonment mounted, a panic which is profoundly implicated in her acute illnesses of 1923. And, although renting both the extra flat and the country cottage created a practical *modus vivendi* which preserved the outward appearance of the Eliots' marriage, it was not a cheap arrangement. Vivien had acted generously in her tolerance of Tom's separate life, and yet she remained the object of his resentment and frustration at the "burden" she represented. The gay Captain longed to be rid of his sick, unhappy wife, and the situation was complicated by the fact that no one but Tom, and possibly Vivien, knew the truth about their financial affairs. It partly explains a confused "letter of denunciation" Vivien wrote to Osbert Sitwell and, so he claimed, similar letters she wrote to Ottoline and Virginia regarding their efforts to help Tom. Vivien also had her own resentments: she felt unfairly blamed for costing Tom the few shillings rent (Aldington was paying 3/6d a week for a similar cottage)[77] on a two-up two-down semi-detached cottage with an outside privy, which was less than the rent of a flat in central London, and for incurring doctors' fees to treat illnesses certainly exacerbated by her marital misery. She was caught in a web of Tom's weaving for, knowing that her husband was both richer and more extravagant than he admitted, she was forced to keep his secrets, live with his rejection, and accept that it was he, not she, who was generally the object of pity.

To Virginia Woolf Tom posed as a dutiful husband, expressing his regret at not being able to visit the Woolfs at Rodmell because he could not leave Vivien to "stick it out" in the country at the weekends.[78] To Mary he expressed a different mood: it was sweet of her to ask them to the Boat Race the next day, he wrote grumpily on 23 March, but they would be busy moving into their "tiny" country cottage. He was spending all his time packing furniture, and the next day he and Vivien were going down early before the van and furniture arrived. "It will be such a day's work."[79] Vivien was still very weak, exhausted by the fashionable but "most disagreeable" "Plombières treatment" (possibly enemas for constipation) which she had begun in early March in order to be ready to go to the country. It was, Tom feared, "too desperate a treatment for her," and he never knew, as he told Ottoline, whether the benefits of this sort of thing compensated for the strain, especially as Vivien was being given "electric treatment" in addition.[80]

On 5 March Vivien had written sadly to Mary that she was too ill to see her, but if anyone asked what was the matter with her, Mary was to reply that Vivien had—"in crude words—'catarrh of the intestines, with occasional enteritis'; that is, if your delicacy will allow you to frame such an intolerable statement of fact." If Mary could not bring herself to utter such indelicate phrases, she was to refer enquiries to Vivien, to whose cynical and unromantic mind such a statement of fact presented no difficulties.[81] Still, as the days passed amidst the horrors of "Plombières," and Vivien grew weaker, she began to feel anxious at the thought of being deprived of the care of her London doctors:

> It is my opinion that Tom is right in refraining at this point from taking steps which would make our common dwelling place a 4 roomed country cottage or an attic in London, and which would deprive me of medical assistance . . . Indeed, if he did take such steps I should bear him a considerable grudge. I know, too well, that in your eyes the poet's wife dying in a humble cot would be a pretty sight—almost a nosegay. Alas! That you should never have to experience such a pathetical [sic] situation . . .[82]

Vivien's terror mounted as Tom pressed her to leave London for the new cottage. Finally it precipitated "a terrible crisis": Tom had engaged a car to take Vivien down to Chichester on Tuesday, but postponed it to Thursday because she was too ill. As he explained to Ottoline:

> On Wednesday she had the worst crisis, after tea, that I have *ever* seen, the worst she has ever had. *I am sure she was on the point of death.* She went completely numb, terrible palpitations, and gasping for every breath.

Tom telephoned four doctors, who were all out. Finally one came. "But before he came she suddenly had a terrific colitis explosion—poison that must have been accumulating for two or three weeks, owing to the terrible strain of the *Nation*." According to the locum doctor, and also the Eliots' own doctor, Dr. Higgins, who came later, "*This saved her life.* Otherwise she would have died of acute toxaemia, or of the strain on the heart from the effort to resist it."

Both doctors advised Eliot that the danger was over for the moment, and Vivien had better get away at once. He therefore took her down to Milestone Cottages on the Thursday as arranged, but instead of the crisis being over, "Vivien had two more, all Friday night and on Saturday." Tom at once sent for Rose Haigh-Wood. That night, exhausted by the sequence of crises which meant, as he told Ottoline, that he had had hardly a moment to *read* a letter, much less write one, he was at last able to give her the latest news of Vivien in a long, undated letter written from the cottage: "Tonight for the first time she begins to show a little sign of being alive. She has not had any meal at all since last Thursday and for the last three days has been fed on little drops of milk and teaspoons of brandy to keep her alive. I *think* we are through now, but she has wasted in this week to an absolute skeleton so it will take weeks to build her up."[83]

There is little doubt that Vivien's "crises" were severe panic attacks and that her "colitis" or irritable bowel syndrome was also triggered by the acute fear that Tom was on the point of leaving her. Vivien's unconscious attempt to keep her husband with her was successful in the short term. Thanking Ottoline for sending him some of her favourite "hectine," a new "remedy" which she had recommended should be taken by injection as a cure for nervous trouble, he set off to Chichester to buy a syringe, promising Ottoline a cheque soon. He had not dared, he explained, to "try Vivien with any new thing during this crisis," but she would begin taking it directly she was able.[84]

Vivien was never well enough to try Ottoline's home cure. In the "humble cot" in Fishbourne she caught "malignant influenza" which turned to a "devastating" pneumonia. She hovered between life and death, once more "a wild heart in a cage," the trapped bird in whose body life only flickered faintly. Outside, the wind cut like a knife across the muddy fields. Tom's irritation grew. "We [heavily crossed out] *I* have only pitched the furniture into the cottage so must start without V.," he complained to Mary, absconding after Easter to holiday alone with the Schiffs at Hindhead.[85] By 26 April 1923 it was still "extraordinarily uncomfortable and inconvenient for a case of serious illness" in the cottage, and they had not even been able to arrange the furniture. Vivien was being kept going on "serum and Bulgarian bacillus"; the doctor from London had stayed for two weekends and was still visiting twice weekly, with the local man coming in daily and possibly a nurse in attendance too. His "successful holiday," wrote Tom sarcastically, would soon be at an end.[86] Barely had he returned to London than he too fell ill, taking another fortnight's leave "by the kindness of the bank."[87]

As her physical and mental state deteriorated, so Vivien's dependence grew upon the doctors who, whatever their faults, at least offered her attention and a measure of comfort. Her neediness made her vulnerable to exploitation. Such exploitation was difficult for Eliot to resist, as his own personality, combined with 1920s medical ignorance, predisposed him, even more than Vivien, to assign magical powers to the medical profession.[88] As Vivien spent more time alone with her caregivers in the isolated cottage, in conditions in which her liberty was almost as limited as if she had been in a sanatorium, she began to form a new dependent relationship to rival that which she had with Tom: she and her physician became a "doctor-patient couple," as Foucault terms it in *Madness and Civilization:* "In the patient's eyes . . . the authority [the doctor] has borrowed from order, morality and the family, now seems to derive from himself; it is because he is a doctor that he is believed to possess these powers . . ." According to this theory, the physician seems to possess an almost demonic knowledge. "Increasingly the patient will accept this self-surrender to a doctor both divine and satanic; beyond human measure in any case . . . submitting from the very first to a will he experienced as magic."[89]

The doctor in Vivien's case—as her Harley Street doctors in London no longer visited—was "a *very good* Scotch doctor in Chichester." Recovering from the pneumonia Vivien was left with a "depression of mind"[90] so severe that she was threatening suicide, as Eliot confided to Pound: she was too weak even to sit up. To her dearest Ottoline, Vivien confessed on 28 May that she still felt so ill,

> so intolerably unsteady, weak, dizzy, *reeling,* that life is a fearful burden. I hardly know where I am, now. After so great a shock— so many shocks—it is coming back from death and I am still

gasping for breath—just *hanging on.* It is not life, I don't know what it is. Time passes, it seems the summer is going—and I cant grasp it . . . I don't feel I could ever pick up the old life again. I feel so many hundred miles now from everyone and everything. You understand this, don't you?

Vivien reminisced that one of the very few *"really happy, stable* memories" she had to hang on to was Garsington. "You and Garsington, there is something definite there. *You* have *made* something real, comforting . . . Excuse incoherence."[91]

In mid-April Vivien received a charming letter from Virginia, who sensed something of Vivien's ordeal.[92] On 18 May, after entertaining Eliot to dinner, Virginia wrote: "I feel that he has taken the veil, or whatever monks do. Mrs. Eliot has almost died at times in the last month. Tom, though infinitely considerate, is also perfectly detached. His cell is, I'm sure, a very lofty one, but a little chilly."[93] But if Tom felt cool towards Virginia, as his obituary of her later demonstrated he did, and he practised a chilly detachment from Vivien, he retained warmer feelings for Mary Hutchinson, who continued to send Vivien presents—perhaps as a salve to her conscience. Touched by gifts of a lilac sun-bonnet and several copies of the *Nation,* Vivien roused herself to pencil a note to her "darling friend" Mary. "One feels & is—so unkempt, untended, ugly and in despair that one needs the stimulus of pretty things to remind one that life is not so barren," she wrote. "As Virginia so cleverly says—there is some romance in being very ill, but getting well is sordid misery. *It is.*"[94] Vivien's depression was possibly not unconnected with the uncomfortable knowledge that Tom preferred Mary's company to her own. While putting Mary off on 9 August with the news that Vivien was too "dizzy and weak" for a visit from her friend,[95] Tom did not hesitate to send his confidante an urgent telegram from London the following day, inviting her "if alone" to meet him on Sunday at three-thirty at the Black Boy pub, Fishbourne, for a picnic.[96]

A week or two earlier, however, Vivien *had* felt well enough to make her first drive into the country. She and Tom took tea with the Woolfs at Rodmell on 17 July. Virginia, who noticed Vivien was "very nervous, very spotty, much powdered ... overdressed, perhaps," watched with interest as Tom pressed alcohol on his reluctant wife, and recorded the conversation in her diary:

> Tom: Put brandy in your tea, Vivien.
> No, no, Tom.
> Yes, you must. Put a teaspoonful of brandy in your tea.
> Vivien: Oh all right—I don't want it.
> Virginia: One doesn't like taking medicine before one's friends ... (pause) I've been setting up your poem. It's a good poem.
> Vivien: A damned good poem, did you say?
> Virginia: Well, you've improved what I said. But it is a d—d good poem.

Virginia's impression was that the Eliots were nervous, but compared themselves with herself and Leonard, and liked them and their surroundings. "And on the drive home, I daresay Vivien said 'Why can't we get on as the Woolves do?' I think they meant us to feel them in sympathy together. Certainly they were lighter, more affectionate."[97] As she slowly convalesced, Vivien, despite her poor eyesight, began trying to learn Italian, in order to converse with the "foreign young gentleman" whom, she told Mary, was staying at the cottage with them.[98]

Eliot himself had felt exhilarated earlier in the summer to be invited by Ottoline to lecture to a group of Oxford undergraduates. "One has hopes of undergraduates," he wrote, "almost the only kind of audience that is interesting to talk to." He spent the night at Balliol, before coming on to Ottoline's, where he sang comic songs on the lawn with six of the students; the freshness of youth, noted his hostess, was like wine to him. Afterwards Tom hastened to tell her how "very keenly I enjoyed meeting the young men—all of them—I enjoyed every minute. I wish I might see them all again!" Finding "fresh and untried minds and unspoiled lives" appealed to him so much that he longed to give a whole course of lectures at Oxford.[99] Among the young, often homosexual, men Ottoline gathered about her at Garsington, such as "pretty" Lord David Gascoyne-Cecil, Puffin Asquith and Eddy Sackville-West, heir to Knole, Eliot often found a receptive audience, as Virginia confided to the poet on 2 June: "I sat next to a young Lord (Sackville-West) at Oxford, who said Mr. Eliot was his favourite poet, and the favourite of all his friends."[100] So effeminate was that "tiny lap dog called Sackville-West" that when he came to visit Virginia, her cook asked: "Who was the lady in the drawing-room?" "He has a voice like a girls, and a face like a persian cats, all white and serious with large violet eyes and fluffy cheeks," reported Virginia to the French painter Jacques Raverat, wondering whether her correspondent had any views on "loving ones own sex. All the young men are so inclined, and I cant help finding it mildly foolish . . . For one thing, all the young men tend to the pretty and ladylike, for some reason, at the moment. They paint and powder, which wasn't the style in our day . . ."[101] On this occasion Virginia had travelled to Garsington with Lytton Strachey, but was dismayed to find Ottoline had invited a "bunch of young men no bigger than asparagus," and that she had to walk around the vegetable garden with Lord David while Lytton flirted with another undergraduate, James Byam Shaw, on a green seat in a corner.[102]

It was on this particular visit to Garsington on 17 June 1923 that a fateful conversation took place between Eliot and Ottoline. The high priestess of Bloomsbury had herself come close to breakdown after her husband Philip's "brat" by her parlourmaid had been born.[103] Tom had been all sympathy: "It's like a horrible treadmill, isn't it?" he wrote. "Going on struggling and fighting for health only to be knocked over and to begin at the beginning. And how few people understand what delicate people have to put up with, & how much courage and *character* they have to exercise at every minute."[104] Expressing her own sympathy for the Eliots' predicament, Ottoline suggested her pet doctor, the German Dr. Marten, as the ideal specialist for Vivien. Tom was reluctant, for Vivien's colitis had almost gone under the care of the "Scotch doctor." Weakly Vivien protested that she knew she just needed a quiet, sensible life, and no "*mental* conflicts or worry," but Ottoline continued to urge her that it was "a chance not to be missed."[105] Finally Tom took Vivien to London: it was to be the beginning of yet more "magical" pseudo-science.

By mid-July the Eliots had had two long interviews and "three analyses" with Dr. Marten, who was, reported Tom, very much interested in

Vivien and talked to her for a long time. "He has discovered, by having bacteriological analyses made, an extraordinary excess of streptococcus fecalis, and other mischievous cocci. He has promised to send over cultures from Germany. But he says that it cannot be *properly* done in this country . . ." The only hope of a cure was for Vivien, despite the "ruinous expense," to go to Freiburg in the autumn.[106]

16

Deceits and Desires

Dr. Marten wasted no time in taking control of Vivien's case. Discerning in his new patient and her husband a gullible couple whose marital situation and neuroses predisposed them, as did Ottoline's, to offer themselves as his willing victims, he imposed a bizarre experimental regime upon Vivien. "My new cure," she informed Mary, in a faint pencilled note, "is to spend half my life upside down. *Do* come to tea, if you don't mind my having tea standing on my head."[1] The forced jollity was short-lived. Soon Vivien was again so weak that she could only "totter" through the days.[2]

In spite of Vivien's relapse, Tom's enthusiasm for Dr. Marten grew apace. When in October 1923 Dorothy Pound asked him for the name of Vivien's gland specialist, Dr. Hogben, Eliot joked that he wouldn't give it unless Dorothy wanted to do somebody in. *That* specialist had nearly put Vivien in her grave, and she had only just escaped at the moment of expiring—hence their year of disasters. But now she had an *excellent* man in Marten, whom he would recommend to anyone who was willing to go to Freiburg, and was, very slowly, fighting her way up.[3]

Before long Eliot was recommending the German doctor to his Bloomsbury friends as keenly as Ottoline. The following year he pressed Virginia Woolf to consult the "very remarkable Dr. Martin [sic]" who was staying in London in Eaton Square, and whom Eliot considered a "first rate physician." He also had the additional merit of being very accommodating about his fees. Tom liked him more than any physician he had ever had dealings with, he confided to Virginia, and claimed the doctor had brought about a turning point in Vivien's illness.[4] As a result, Tom was now consulting Dr. Marten himself. Ominously, the German was in reality not a medical specialist but simply "a Doctor of . . . wide special knowledge." Soon Virginia, in her turn, was urging Roger Fry to consult the fashionable Dr. Marten.

Fortunately for her health, perhaps, Vivien never reached Freiburg. During the summer of 1923 Ottoline made energetic but ultimately futile attempts to find Tom a lecturing post at Oxford University as an alternative to Lloyds. If Ottoline could fix it for the winter term, Eliot told his patron, he would take Vivien to the German clinic in September, "If she would go with me. But I feel so little hope of eligibility that I do not think of it." Plaintively he explained to Ottoline that the expenses of Vivien's illness were already so high that he saw little hope of affording the trip.[5]

Illness was not, however, the only cause of Eliot's spiralling costs during that summer. He had begun a relationship with a young man which was also to prove expensive, both to his purse and his temper. In May 1923 he invited the "foreign young gentleman," to whom Vivien referred in an undated letter to Mary, to stay at 2 Milestone Cottages, Old Fishbourne ("During May/J. came to stay.")[6] Ostensibly the young man had come to lend a hand during Vivien's illness, but there is little doubt that he was, in fact, romantically and sexually involved with Tom. The youth's name was Jack and he was German, recalled Vivien, who recorded the eventful summer in the "stunning sort of instant doggerel" with which, remembered Maurice, she had been accustomed to amuse her family at Anglesey.[7] At first the handsome young German, whom Eliot may have met at Garsington, made an excellent impression, as Vivien recalled in rhyming couplets written in pencil because she was too weak to hold a pen:

> His manners were good
> He *never* was rude
> His *expression* was sweet
> His ways were quite neat . . .

"That boy has a beeootiful nature," remarked Vivien's mother Rose, who was also a guest at the cottage. "He looked very *young*/And his praises were sung" enthused Vivien; she and Jack read Shakespeare aloud together, and practised Italian, and Vivien at first found the pliable young man an agreeable companion.

In July, though, the mood in the cottage turned ugly. A quite different Jack returned for a second stay. This time he looked "old, ugly and *bad*" in Vivien's eyes. There was "Not a trace of the lad/Who had helped us in May." Jack had "nothing to say/He was glum, never gay." The party in the cottage had also changed. In place of Rose Haigh-Wood was Eliot's new secretary, Irene Pearl Fassett, a fiery woman who idolised her employer, and who had joined the Eliots to help with the *Criterion* workload the previous year when Vivien was ill. Pearl Fassett had quickly become an intimate friend of Vivien's, and the two women soon began to collaborate on those reviews published under the name "Irene Fassett" in the "Books of the Quarter" in the *Criterion*. Pearl and Vivien, equally protective of Eliot, watched in horror as the friendship between Tom and Jack deteriorated. Jack's

> . . . incessant insistence
> Upon *passive resistance*
> Made an unhappy house
> With nothing but rows.

As the weeks passed, the young German grew "more *secretive* and bitter and rude/More lazy and obstinate, *ugly* and crude." His insulting manner towards Eliot infuriated Pearl, and filled Vivien with fear as tension mounted in the cramped two-bedroom cottage, in which the sleeping arrangements allowed for little privacy. (Eliot never shared Vivien's bedroom during their marriage, choosing to sleep in a deckchair in the hallway in Russell's flat rather than with his wife, and having a separate room in their subsequent flats and houses, as photographs taken by Eliot's niece, Theodora Eliot Smith, demonstrate.) It is probable that at number 2, Milestone Cottages, Vivien shared a room with Pearl, and Tom with Jack. Vivien could not have failed to be aware of the erotic nature of Jack's attraction for Tom, but she turned a blind eye to this unwelcome fact. She had no alternative but to remain a tolerant, if increasingly nervous, observer of the fury smouldering dangerously between the two men.

Finally, as autumn turned to winter, Jack's sneers and tantrums escalated to a pitch which the two women found unbearable. Vivien and Pearl watched in horror as Tom, a man of nearly thirty-five, silently put up with Jack's open rudeness. "[Jack] behaved in a way that Pearl *never* expected," wrote Vivien.

> To see Tom endure it detracts from the awe,
> Indeed, veneration, she gave him before . . .
> And worse & worse this matter grows
> Tom makes no move
> Pearl's fury glows
> While V. quite ill becomes like ice . . .
> Oh what a hell it all is *now*
> Xmas comes near, and then the row.
> Tom blacks Jack's eyes
> But does no good—

Tom's outburst of violence ended his countryside idyll with Jack. "In sullen mood," Tom threw Jack out of the house. In this breakdown of what was clearly an intense emotional relationship between the two men, Tom, believed Vivien, was incited to extreme behaviour by Pearl ("Who is, at least, a 'vengeance girl' "). The next day Jack returned, bruised and angry at the physical abuse he had suffered. He was determined to justify his behaviour towards Tom, and Vivien listened as the youth poured out his story: Jack declaimed his "views and griefs and aims," explaining that he had been happy enough in May to come to the Eliots' aid, but by July had grown tired of being at Tom's beck and call; he felt "a fool," as "Eliot's tool," a sexually ambiguous remark by Vivien which hints at reasons for Jack's indignation other than a reluctance to help around the house: it seems that Jack had grown to resent the older man's attentions.

Vivien, nevertheless, loyally judged that it was Jack who had abused his position. Convinced that Jack himself was too weak and unformed a character to have resented his situation, she was sure that his mother, who ruled "this stupid, stubborn, *witless mule,*" had told him to make a stand. Vivien—"Our wily Vivien," as she described herself—infuriated by Jack's growing meanness during his visit of many months, then decided to search his room. Rifling through the possessions the young man had left behind when he was abruptly turned out, she discovered letters which proved that he had been sending money home to his German aunts and friends.[8] Jack, it seemed, had been helping himself to the housekeeping money, feeling perhaps that he was owed payment for services rendered.

"We are now out of love with young people," confided Vivien to Virginia, in a masterly understatement. Young people with literary aspirations were especially out of favour, she said. Such guests used to go about harmlessly with a box of watercolours and a sketching block: now they immersed themselves in ink and shouted their ideas at meal times, giving their wan hosts no chance to digest their food.[9] Tom had hurriedly and thankfully returned to London; Vivien could not wait to follow him.

This emotional and pecuniary disaster with Jack affected Eliot deeply and he began to drink heavily. Virginia was surprised to see "poor Tom" getting drunk at Burleigh Mansions when "the Captain" invited her to a small Christmas party, probably the same occasion attended by Lytton Strachey on 17 December 1923.[10] The party had taken weeks of preparation, with all the food set out on little tables, Leonard Woolf remembered later; the Hutchinsons and Roger Fry were also invited.[11] Two days later Virginia recorded:

> We went to a flat in an arcade, & asked for Captain Eliot. I noticed that his eyes were blurred. He cut the cake meticulously. He helped us to coffee—or was it tea? Then to liqueurs ... There was a long pale squint-eyed Oxford youth on the floor. We discussed the personal element in literature. Tom then quietly left the room. L. heard sounds of sickness. After a long time, he came back, sank into the corner, & I saw him, ghastly pale, with his eyes shut, apparently in a stupor. When we left he was only just able to stand on his legs.

The next day Virginia spent ten minutes on the telephone receiving Eliot's apologies—"How distressing, what could we all think? Could we forgive him—the first time—would we ever come again? No dinner, no lunch—then sudden collapse—how dreadful—what a miserable end to the evening—apologise please to Leonard, to your sister ..." It was, thought Virginia, one of those comedies which life sometimes does to perfection.[12]

It would appear that Jack had successors. The Hon. Philip Ritchie, eldest son of Lord Ritchie of Dundee, a beautiful and gay young man to whom Lytton Strachey was attracted, stayed on occasions at Burleigh Mansions with Eliot, so Frank Morley, a Faber director, admitted to playwright Michael Hastings;[13] in 1923 Ritchie was an Oxford undergraduate, but he was not the "squint-eyed Oxford youth" noticed by Virginia on 17 December, for Ritchie was a friend of the Woolfs and Roger Fry and would have been recognised. The homosexual novelist C. H. B. Kitchin was also reputed to be a guest of "Captain Eliot's," as was Roger Senhouse, the art critic.[14]

Eliot's physical abuse of Jack may have been an isolated incident, but it explains Vivien's later fears, which she expressed to Ottoline, that she too would be battered by her husband, although there is no record of such marital violence taking place. There are, however, many references to Eliot's rages by those who knew him well. Throughout his adult life Eliot found it difficult to control his explosive temper. Vivien's personal account book for 1930 records "A FRESH START" on 24 October, and on Monday, 23 February 1931, a "Prize to Tom for keeping his temper."[15] In January 1935, recalling visits with Tom to the Haigh-Wood family solicitors, James and James, Vivien related that Tom was "livid with savage fury" on many occasions, particularly when the issue under discussion was the "mistake they [Tom, Maurice and the solicitors] all made" in keeping her in ignorance of the size of her private income. James, apparently arguing Vivien's case, was "very insulting" to Tom. Eliot responded with "a very real grudge and hatred" towards the solicitor.[16]

There are similar incidences in Mary Trevelyan's revealing memoir of her twenty-year friendship with T. S. Eliot, "The Pope of Russell Square 1938–1958," in which she documents the numerous occasions when she experienced Tom's "FURY," and had to plead with him not to upset her and John Hayward, whom he often snapped at in public.[17] On 16 August 1954, for example, the poet was in "one of his most towering rages, white with anger, and practically non-speaking," banging the door of Mary's car shut and creating "a high state of tension" for his sister Marian and niece Theodora, whom Mary was driving to the Prospect of Whitby. The ostensible reason for this angry outburst was that Eliot blamed Mary for arranging the party on a Monday, without consulting him, although the outing had in fact been Theodora's idea.[18] Many times Mary was left wondering, "Why the rocket?" only to learn that she had once again transgressed the obsessional "Rules" to which Eliot insisted she conform.[19] Mary, the inspiration for "Julia" in *The Cocktail Party,* was left with a lasting impression of a man who sometimes acted in a way which was "cruel and incompatible with his professed 'way of life.'" She concluded that Tom was quite blind to people—"perhaps because he doesn't love them."[20] Her accusation echoes that made by Lavinia, the wife in *The Cocktail Party,* against her husband: "You *are* cold-hearted, Edward." To the psychiatrist, Harcourt-Reilly, Lavinia confides, "My husband has never been in love with anybody."[21]

As the months passed it became clear that, despite Eliot's faith in him, Dr. Marten's spurious science was not, after all, improving Vivien's health. In May 1923, when Jack had been staying with the Eliots at Fishbourne, Tom complained to Ezra Pound that he was having "a hell of a time" with Vivien; she was contemplating suicide and "was going to leave you a letter."[22] Ottoline herself noted in her journal in June 1923 her opinion that Eliot was afraid Vivien would commit suicide, and this was why he was protective of her.[23] Did Vivien threaten suicide to keep Eliot at her side, as she competed against the lure of the beautiful young men to whom Ottoline introduced him at Garsington? Much later Eliot shared his memories of Vivien with Mary Trevelyan: "The dreadful nights when she would say 'I ought never to have married you' or, 'I am useless and better dead'—and then my disclaimers and her floods of tears—but the next morning that would be quite forgotten."[24] The horror of those nights of reproach and torment worked their way into Eliot's drama in 1923, as he began writing *Sweeney Agonistes;* his night sweats and nightmares resembled Sweeney's:

> You've had the cream of a nightmare dream and you've got the
> hoo-ha's coming to you.

During those stormy nights when a weeping Vivien played on his conscience, Tom in turn blamed himself for his wife's misery and psychological distress. "I thought it was my fault for a period," he told Mary in 1950. "I got away by going to America and not coming back."

In Eliot's imagination Vivien had become strongly identified with "wrong'd Aspatia," the heroine of Beaumont and Fletcher's play *The Maid's Tragedy,* a play Eliot knew well, having set it for his night class of Extension students in 1918. In the drama, Aspatia, deserted by her lover, engineers her death at his hands; there is one scene which particularly struck Eliot, in which the betrayed Aspatia hysterically laments her abandonment by her lover and compares herself to Ariadne, similarly abandoned by Theseus on the "cavernous waste shore" of Naxos. Eliot had already borrowed lines from this scene as the epigraph for "Sweeney Erect" (1919).[25] Aspatia commands her needlewomen to rework their tapestry of Theseus and Ariadne, in order to make it truly reflect Ariadne's sorrow.[26] "Make all a desolation," Aspatia commands. "Paint me the bold anfractuous rocks/Faced by the snarled and yelping seas," are the words Eliot himself gives Aspatia in "Sweeney Erect."[27] Eliot knew that he, like Theseus, had been false to the woman who loved him.

By 1921 Eliot's perception of Vivien had undergone a second metamorphosis: in the original manuscript of *The Waste Land* he portrayed her as a reproachful gorgon, whose hysterical complaints follow him night and day. She shadows his dreams, the "injur'd bride," issuing from sepulchral gates as in a tale by Edgar Allan Poe, as Eliot wrote in "Elegy," lines cut by the cautious Pound. In Eliot's nightmare Vivien is no longer muse but Medusa: "Around that head the scorpions hissed!/Remorse unbounded, grief intense/Had striven to expatiate the fault—" He implores the vision to keep its distance: "Poison not my nightly bliss," he begs, "Keep within thy charnel vault."[28]

Eliot's conscience tormented him. He could not repress the knowledge that he had rejected Vivien within weeks of his marriage to her, and that Vivien's affair with Russell, rather than being, in Ronald Schuchard's words, a vicious sexual betrayal of Eliot,[29] had in fact been one in which he had knowingly colluded in order to further his career, relieve himself of conjugal responsibilities, and to gain financial advantage. Nor could Eliot deny the strength of his own homosexual desires, which were leading him into a web of deceit. Those desires are powerfully documented not only in the Colombo verses torn from "The Inventions of the March Hare" notebook which Eliot sent to John Quinn, but in later pornographic verses Eliot attached to a letter he sent to Ezra Pound on 3 January 1934—verses which leave no doubts as to "Captain Eliot's" sexual orientation. Writing in the first person, Eliot boldly exhorts his reader to buggery, "again and again and again." Proclaim to the morning, he cries, that "a r s e spells arse."[30]

Eliot's obscene verse testifies to the violence of his feelings, and it is hard to believe that they were never acted upon. But, even if the strength of the poet's will, inhibition, or fear of exposure ensured that his desires remained in the realm of sexual fantasy, they affected both his and Vivien's lives powerfully. Eliot's secrets shaped his biography and his poetry. And the balance of probability seems to lie with the argument that Eliot, like Lytton Strachey and other members of the Bloomsbury Group, had a physical relationship with the young men like Jack or Ritchie with whom he consorted. Why should he have felt such a degree of shame and self-loathing had he not sinned—in his own eyes at least? Eliot's grinding sense of his own sexual sinfulness overwhelmed him, a legacy of his puritanical upbringing and the prejudices of the period in which he lived. It was Vivien's misfortune that not only did her very femininity repel him, simply looking at her reminded Eliot of the Russell affair, and of her immorality which he later roundly condemned. In his eyes Vivien was the harlot who bewitches, emblematic of Eliot's own immorality and sexual betrayal. Vivien now represented for her husband his shadow side, the dark anima behind Eliot's urbane exterior of which he speaks in "The Hollow Men" (1925): "Between the desire/And the spasm . . . Between the essence/And the descent /Falls the Shadow."[31]

For the hollow men, their heads stuffed with straw, the satisfaction of desire is annihilated by the falling Shadow. The epigraph Eliot chose for "The Hollow Men," taken from Conrad—this time he would not allow Pound to change his first choice—was "Mistah Kurtz—he dead." It speaks of Kurtz's end, in the heart of darkness, all civilised values abandoned. Kurtz is dead to God, and in the early 1920s Eliot began to feel he was too, as he abandoned his lawful wife to live an alternative life in Burleigh Mansions whenever the opportunity presented itself. At times the pricking of his conscience urged him to connect with the spiritual and let "the darkness come upon you/Which shall be the darkness of God."[32] Other voices spoke louder, as Vivien struggled with all the weapons at her disposal in the tug-of-war for her husband's love. Hysteria and illness were in the forefront of her armoury, and Eliot could not gainsay his Ariadne. He was unable to refuse Vivien her doctors, whatever they cost, and guilt and a desire to pass on responsibility to the "experts" drove him to acquiesce in whatever cure they suggested.

In 1924, Eliot decided to call in yet another fashionable London physician, Dr. James Cyriax. Cyriax was an orthopaedic surgeon who had trained at Cambridge and practised spinal manipulation; he was on the staff of St. Thomas's Hospital and had a reputation for being able to treat seemingly intractable back pain. He began to work on Vivien's "permanent spinal injury," as she later described it; but he was not, perhaps, as accommodating about his fees as Marten had been.

By 27 August 1924 Tom was bitterly bemoaning his financial position to Mary Hutchinson, whom he and Vivien had asked to help find them a house in London. Their latest whim was to exchange their flat in Clarence Gate Gardens for a house with a garden. Eliot explained that a garage selling "B. P. Motor Spirit" at all hours had opened beside their cottage at Old Fishbourne, and there was a lemonade stall opposite, so he and Vivien had decided that it was uninhabitable, and given up the lease.[33] In June they considered moving close to the Woolfs, and Tom enlisted Virginia's help to find a cottage on the Downs. As usual, plans failed to materialise. Tom fell ill again, and he and Vivien moved to Eastbourne, which became their base during another six-week visit from Tom's mother. "I have been boiled in a hellbroth," Tom complained to Virginia on his return from putting Charlotte on the transatlantic steamer on 27 August. He then bolted back to Burleigh Mansions, claiming his tax return was overdue, leaving Vivien alone in Eastbourne.[34]

On the same day that Eliot thankfully bade goodbye to his mother, he asked Mary to view a house on Chiswick Mall for himself and Vivien, assuring his correspondent that when they found a property they would depend upon her to get them into it: "You are an angel and give me confidence that we *shall* get a house." However, Eliot was in an agitated mood. He could not possibly afford a house unless he could sell the lease on their flat, he told Mary, and he lacked the time to attend to the business of buying and selling: "You see, Mary, I *must* settle down and write a *lot* of articles at once, because I *must* find the money, and I cant do anything else . . . I have been living beyond my income for 5 months, and eating up my savings. Vivien's illness and the cost of running *two establishments at once,* doctors, food, medicines, constant railway fares etc. have run me into colossal expense." He had to try to make £50 a month by writing, said Tom, something which it had been impossible to do for the last few months—"and I must do it *now.*"

Vivien, meanwhile, was working her way through a reading list which, in the interests of self-education, she had asked Mary to compile for her. "Don't feed her too fast," instructed Tom, saying that Vivien's vitality was so low that she could only read a very little at a time, as reading was too tiring and exciting. He preferred her to do manual work, when she could not be out of doors: she had been painting furniture very beautifully and this, while physically tiring, was mentally restful. Her mind was still "utterly worn out and *ruined"* by his indecision over the *Nation* job, he confided to Mary. "No-one will know what she went through."[35]

Eliot's anxiety as usual attracted sympathy from his correspondent, but the picture he painted was, as so often, not wholly truthful. "Tom is a 'great runner-away,' " wrote Mary Trevelyan in 1958 in a perceptive analysis of Eliot's character. "He is extremely deceitful when it suits him and he would willingly sacrifice anybody and anything to get himself out of something which he doesn't want to face up to."[36] Although in August 1924 Eliot wrote as if he were financially *in extremis* to Mary Hutchinson—who probably believed him—a far simpler solution to his over-expenditure presented itself than she realised. In the spring of that year Eliot had wired to his brother Henry to send him $2,000 as he was desperately short of money. This Henry did, as he informed Charlotte Eliot in a letter dated 15 March 1925.[37] The sum sent enabled Eliot to settle his doctors' bills and pay the rent on not two but three dwellings: Clarence Gate Gardens, Milestone Cottages, and Burleigh Mansions. As Henry later related, when he arrived in England in 1926 he found that the Eliots had committed themselves to several different leases, and it was his task to negotiate with landlords and extricate his brother from his legal tangles.

The real reason for Eliot's irritation over money in the spring and summer of 1924 was the mistake he (and his mother) felt Henry had made in deciding to sell 120 of Eliot's Hydraulic shares too early—at $63 in 1923—although by January 1924 they had soared to $80,[38] reaching $94 in February 1925. "Do not worry about Tom's stock. It is all right," Henry wrote defensively to Charlotte Eliot, saying that he had reinvested the proceeds in "good bonds." Although "stocks are irritating things," he wrote, Tom was still getting dividends from his investments. This was small consolation to Henry's younger brother, left out in the cold as he watched the rest of his family make money at the rate of $3,000 to $4,000 a month, just by holding their rocketing shares, as Henry was forced to admit on 17 February 1925.[39] Tom's jealousy over the disparity between his own and his brother's situation would have intensified had he learnt that Henry was also earning $8,000 a year as a partner in the advertising agency David C. Thomas of Chicago,[40] even though at this period the U.S. dollar was standing at about $4.90 to the pound so that a dollar was worth only one-third as much in sterling as it is now. Henry, then a bachelor, was able to save most of his salary; Tom was unable to live within his. By 16 March 1924 Henry was confessing to Charlotte that he regretted selling Tom's stock so soon, assuring her that there was however "no breach" between himself and Tom,[41] who was getting a return of 7.37 per cent on his capital of $19,000, giving him an income of about $1,400. Tom's total income, Henry estimated, was about $5,000 (£1,000) a year, made up of the $1,400 on his capital, $3,000 (£600) from the bank, and $600 in literary earnings. £1,000 a year was a comfortable income: a maid in London in 1925 might be paid £35 a year, and the Eliots had two maids.[42] But to normal upper-middle-class expenses Eliot had to add Vivien's medical bills and the costs of his other, secret life.

To add insult to injury, Henry continued to push Tom towards agreeing to the trust which Charlotte had set up in his name, and from which Tom would derive income only from a mixed portfolio of shares and bonds; not only was she refusing to hand his shares over to him directly, she was also cutting him off from the potential capital gains to be made on the substantial real estate she owned in St. Louis and Kansas City.[43] Undoubtedly Tom felt aggrieved; Henry and his sisters had the best side of the bargain. In addition, Henry continued to press his younger brother to make a will, arranging to have the proceeds of the trust distributed to "our family" in the event of Tom's and Vivien's deaths.[44] Tom, scratching a living editing an experimental quarterly in the spare time he could snatch from the bank, felt jealous of his shrewd brother, who in his turn envied his handsome and increasingly famous sibling. It was this sibling rivalry which lay behind Eliot's outburst to Mary as much as any costs of Vivien's.

Nor did Eliot give Mary a wholly accurate picture of Vivien's health as, far from her mind being so "ruined" that she could only paint furniture, his wife was quietly laying the foundations of a new career as a writer. As Tom had let slip in another letter on 2 January 1924, she was making "an exhaustive study of Clive's work, in her thorough way";[45] Vivien added that she was also reading law books, which she found more interesting than novels, apart from her beloved Hardy. And there were moments when Vivien and Tom were both fit enough to pursue their favorite hobby of viewing houses, which provided an escape from London, although they continued to expect Mary to do the real work of finding a suitable property. In a cheerful letter to Sydney Schiff on Boxing Day 1923, Vivien had said that she and Tom had spent "a queer sort of Christmas" wandering around the country in a borrowed car, in search of a more convenient country cottage.[46] Their quest took them to Surrey. From Dorking Vivien sent Mary a postcard of an open tourer in the front of the White Horse, inscribed "En auto—Vivien!"[47] Although she told Virginia that she and Tom had given up their dream of a Citroën car now that they were convinced that they must have a house in London with a garden[48]—a decision which did not stop the unending search for the mythical, ideal country cottage— her improved health is confirmed by Eliot's remark to Schiff that Vivien had stood the winter in London better than the year before, and had "kept up remarkably well," enabling her to go out and see her friends.[49]

As Vivien, encouraged by Tom, made tentative attempts to begin writing, she turned to her closest friend, Mary, as her model for a writer's life. Vivien had always occupied a position of deference towards Mary, but although she hoped to garner a few tips, she was anxious not to give away her own aspirations. On 29 December 1923 Vivien had written a disingenuous letter to Mary, enquiring what sort of life she was intending to lead until, say, April (1924): "What routine—what foundations—what reading—and what (of course) pleasures? And may I add, altogether towards

what end?" inscribing herself "Your curious friend, Vivien."[50] Fear of failure and of ridicule led Vivien to disguise her identity behind pseudonyms
when first she began to be published in the columns of the *Criterion.* She
was concerned that Mary should not discover her secret, for not only was
Mary likely to gossip to the indiscreet Clive, and expose Vivien to the scorn
of Bloomsbury, but Mary had already preceded Vivien along the path of
women's journalism, being published by the *Nation* and *Athenaeum* in July
1923. What could be more embarrassing for Vivien than to be found to be
challenging her accomplished, well-connected *confidante,* and to provoke
her mockery—or even her jealousy?

But Vivien was in need of advice in her new endeavour. Tom was the
first to encourage her, as she had encouraged him. Tom's belief in Vivien's
creative ability was the significant factor in developing her gift, and she
knew she could trust him to keep her secret, as she kept his. There was also
one other person she could trust: Sydney Schiff, whose novels Vivien
admired profoundly. Schiff, too, took Vivien seriously from the first.
Together they discussed style and the creation of character in the novel. He
advised her on no account to reveal her authorship. On 31 March 1924
Vivien replied that she was sure he would not give her away: "You do not
need to persuade me that anonymity is vital; the more so as I have a very
strong feeling that this is a sort of flash in the pan—that it won't go on—
that, in fact, it is being done *faute de mieux."* What is *mieux,* she asks. "Why,
Life of course, dear Sydney. No-one will persuade me that writing is a substitute for living," and yet, she confided, her "temporary aberration" was
making her very happy.[51]

Vivien was aware that what she and Mary were attempting was a
daunting enterprise: to write for publication in a male-dominated literary
world, to sup with giants at whose feet even the confident Mary trembled.
Self-consciousness and a despair of ever being able to express herself inhibited Mary in April 1924 from sending, even to Lytton, her cousin and
close friend, a report she had written of Virginia Woolf's speech to the undergraduates at Cambridge.[52] Mary believed that her inhibition was largely
due to Proust, "who," she wrote, "after so much pleasure, nevertheless
leaves one a nervous wreck—with this lack of simplicity—this sense of
being a hundred eyes instead of two." It was "this modern wretchedness of
feeling one is a slightly transparent ghost" which made Mary tear her re-

port up.[53] Vivien's own rebellion was to remain private. She would tear up her own first drafts in secret.

Virginia Woolf was not so easily deceived however. She was in close touch with Tom, who was continually badgering her for a contribution to the *Criterion,* and he at the time was grateful to the Woolfs for publishing *Homage to John Dryden: Three Essays on Poetry in the Seventeenth Century* in November. In 1924 Virginia was still Tom's "admiring and attached old friend, Virginia W"[54] and, although Tom joked that Virginia could only stand nineteen and a half hours with "the Prince of Bores" when he visited Rodmell, he valued her "timeless and generous friendship and understanding" as well as respecting her genius.[55] It was not, however, a genius he found easy to penetrate. *Jacob's Room* required "superhuman cleverness" on his part to review for *La Nouvelle Revue Française,* he wrote on 1 May 1924.[56] Neither Virginia nor Tom wholly understood what the other was seeking to achieve. Virginia confessed to the poet that she could not summon enough faith in her own judgement to criticise his poems to him: "Such radiance rises from the words that I can't get near them." Critics would call it enchantment, incantation, but she could only testify that she was held off understanding by magic.[57] But if neither comprehended the other's creativity, they each feared the other's judgment. Tom found Virginia's contempt an uncomfortable experience, he confessed to Ottoline.[58] Running the gauntlet of Virginia's biting wit was not a risk Vivien was prepared to take, even though it was the novelist who first recommended that Vivien should take up writing, probably as a form of therapy. When Virginia suspected her of contributing to the *Criterion* in June 1924, Vivien's reply was oblique: "Writing—!? Editing, perhaps."[59]

Disease and disharmony made demanding friends of the Eliots, as Tom spent his evenings struggling to bring out the new periodical on the dining-room table at Clarence Gate Gardens, on top of a full day's work at the bank, and Vivien typed to his dictation and suggested pieces of her own to fill gaps in the paper. Apart from a weekend in Paris in November 1924, there was no escape from the grindstone. Early in the new year of 1925 Tom again fell ill with influenza. That January he felt like a shell with no machinery in it; Vivien, as usual, nursed him through the "anxiety and strain" of the first ten days of his illness before collapsing herself with flu. Eliot was forced to take a month off work, and their mutual desperation was expressed once more in their longing for a country cottage, one near the Woolfs, whom the Eliots were still pestering as often as they did Mary "Hutch" to find them a place in the country. A cottage, a barn, a stable, a shed, even a bit of land on which to put up a bungalow, no matter so long as it was in the *country* and *cheap,* begged Tom. Ever since leaving Fishbourne they had pined more and more for the country, and if only Lady Rothermere would pay "a possible salary" they would move out at once. Of his unearned income Tom, of course, made no mention to Virginia: it was no good offering to lend Rodmell, he warned her. "We want a *hovel* of *our own,* not the house of friends."[60] Vivien chimed in with identical demands to Virginia to find them a cottage near the Downs— "and quickly."[61]

By February 1925 Vivien was again critically ill, laid up with "violent neuralgia and neuritis," Tom told Virginia. "Only her brain was alive."[62] At this moment of crisis Eliot finally exploded. Angry that his wife was once again stricken with a "near-fatal" illness, despite the haemorrhaging of his income into the pockets of fashionable doctors—the very predicament portrayed by Vivien in her satirical sketch "Médecine à la Mode"— he turned on the practitioners he felt had duped him, and on Ottoline. His fury precipitated a rift with the chatelaine of Garsington. Vivien's illness was Ottoline's fault, insinuated Eliot, since she had recommended Marten, whose bogus doctoring was responsible for Vivien being brought to the brink of death. Tom's rage also encompassed Dr. Cyriax, who had been no more successful than Marten in restoring Vivien to health. In an accusatory letter written in April 1925, in which Tom said Vivien was still paying for the effects of the Cyriax osteopathic treatment, he made his own diagnosis of Vivien's condition: "These people have done her damage that will take a *very long* time to repair, irritating and weakening the stomach, overstimulating & exhausting the nerves. Her stomach is now *persistently* relaxed and *out of place,* pressing on the heart and the nerves, and I think thereby causing the neuritis." Furthermore, Vivien was, he related, "in *agony* with neuralgia of the sinus and antrim," which was making her "almost *blind.*"[63]

On 1 May Tom complained again to Ottoline that Vivien was in continuous torture with a peculiar neuralgia which came from the base of the neck and affected all one side of her face, and had not left her for three weeks. It was impossible for her to stir out of bed. The simple truth was that "the Cyriax treatment" had exhausted every nerve in her body to breaking point, and had she gone on much longer she would have never recovered. "What doctors *can* do, in the way of criminal maltreatment is incredible—and one can never prove it in a court of law!" Ominously he wrote that he would explain more fully about both the Cyriax treatment and Dr. Marten when they met.[64]

What ill luck Tom and Vivien seemed to have with doctors, remarked Henry Eliot with a degree of *schadenfreude* to his mother in May 1925:

> They thought this Dr. Cyriax was such a wonder at the time. Tom has indeed a dreadful time. I suppose it is cruel and unsympathetic to think of Tom's troubles more than Vivien's, but it is of course natural.[65]

But Eliot refused to confide in his brother or mother, to Henry's annoyance. Instead he increasingly turned to Leonard Woolf for advice, rather than the disgraced Ottoline, or his family. There were obvious parallels in Tom and Vivien's situation and that of Leonard and Virginia. Eliot began lunching regularly with Leonard, and in April 1925 wrote to ask him for advice on how to deal with Vivien. Should she be allowed to write, did Leonard think? Leonard replied tactfully that it depended on the actual cause of the nervous disturbance, but if it was nervous exhaustion, then "anything which excites or tires the brain is bad and that therefore writing is bad." Tom was to begin with food and rest alone which would produce stability: "When the stability begins, then a little work like writing is good, but at first only in minute quantities." When Virginia was recovering from acute nerve exhaustion, wrote Leonard, she began by limiting her writing strictly to half an hour a day and only increased it months later when she was sure she could stand the strain. If, on the other hand, the cause of Vivien's nervous trouble was not exhaustion but something entirely different, wrote Leonard, he imagined that writing might "do good."[66] Woolf recommended that Eliot consult Sir Henry Head, a strange choice considering that Virginia was Head's patient when she attempted suicide in 1913, and one that Eliot rejected; Woolf agreed that Head was "too brusk in manner."[67]

Ottoline was deeply hurt by Eliot's accusations. Her journal demonstrates how her sympathies shifted over the years between Tom and Vivien, to both of whom she at times exhibited generous friendship, before withdrawing in exasperation from their unceasing and often unrealistic demands. Eliot hurried to placate his old friend, explaining in a quickly pencilled note that he assigned the blame for Vivien's illness equally between "Dr. Marten, the Cyriax, and myself" and *by no means* threw the whole blame on Dr. Marten: "He was a factor in a terrible nexus of misfortune," he wrote, "which has dogged Vivien for years. I blame him as much for urging her to go on with the Cyriax treatment, when she was already showing its ill-effects and on the verge of a nervous breakdown, as I do for anything else, because I think this shows *really bad doctoring.*" Tom only went to Leonard Woolf for advice, he protested, because he was "a very nice and clever man."[68]

It is doubtful whether Woolf's advice would, in any event, have been helpful to Vivien's condition. Vivien's predisposition to mental illness, complicated by her dependence on prescription drugs—a dependence which increased in the 1920s—the bizarre experimental treatments imposed upon her, and a toxic marriage which in itself produced neurotic symptoms, proved a deadly combination. And Eliot, like Woolf, had no option but to put himself and Vivien in the hands of doctors, who were themselves handicapped by the limits of medical knowledge of the time. It is probable that the tranquillising drugs prescribed for Vivien were similar to those prescribed for Virginia Woolf. For women who suffered mood-swings typical of manic-depression, chloral hydrate was a "chemical restraint" given to the neurotic patient which, wrote Sir George Savage, Physician Superintendent at Bethlem Royal Hospital, and physician to Virginia Woolf, could itself "produce physical ill-health, hypochondriasis, and insanity." Another, even more dangerous drug was hyoscyamine, which, as the drug trials which Savage carried out on patients at Bethlem in 1879 demonstrated, had serious side effects. Even a tiny dose could induce collapse. Serious loss of appetite followed, together with an inability to read, loss of power in the limbs, great mental depression, "dread" of death, confusion, hallucinations of sight and touch, and "a dry, unpleasant feeling in the throat which drinking did not relieve."[69] Patients detested being given hyoscyamine, and one accused Savage of being a poisoner. Yet

Stephen Trombley suggests, in his study of Virginia Woolf's doctors, that hyoscyamine was prescribed for the novelist, who complained of a bitter taste in the mouth during a fainting fit in 1930.[70] Given the widespread influence of Savage, an "expert" on psychoneurosis and author of a standard textbook on the subject, it is possible that hyoscyamine was also a drug of choice for Vivien, and was implicated in her loss of appetite and subsequent emaciation, weakness, weak eyes and difficulty with reading, and episodes of depression in the 1920s. For Vivien, Virginia and Ottoline, the "cure" was often more disastrous than the illness.

During the 1920s, Henry Eliot came to believe that both Tom and Vivien were hypocrites as well as hypochondriacs, who exaggerated both their illnesses and their poverty. "Vivien always recites some account of her migraines and malaises in her letters," he had remarked to his mother in 1921. "But I suppose it is natural; it is a relief to talk about one's pains." Henry considered that Vivien encouraged her breakdowns, which he thought were both mental and physical in character, and which she could control if only she had the motivation to do so: "I think some strong impulse from outside, some change in her circumstances, might call forth the necessary power to be well. She needs something to take her mind off herself; something to absorb her entire attention."[71]

His diagnosis was more accurate than that of many of the expensive professionals the Eliots consulted. When Vivien began to write and be published, she did at last find something which absorbed her entire attention and, as Henry predicted, her health improved. Yet writing and illness were parallel dramas, inextricably linked, and the attempt to make sense of her own situation gave Vivien one of her most recurrent themes, just as it became an excuse to avoid the people and parties she disliked. Illness therefore served as a spur rather than a restraint upon her creativity in the early 1920s. Her awareness of her own situation, and ability to find comedy in the midst of tragedy, is remarkable. Vivien's sketch "Médecine à la Mode" is full of insights as, with wry humour, she depicts both her dependence upon fashionable doctors—for example, the black-eyed Dr. Papadopoulos, vast and loose-jointed, who smiles kindly at Vivien when they meet in the corridor (a portrait perhaps based upon Dr. Cyriax)—and her bitter experience of financial exploitation at their hands.

In this unsparing portrait of herself, written in pencil in 1923–24 in the second of the exercise books with stiff black covers which Vivien bequeathed to the Bodleian Library at Oxford, "Sibylla," Vivien's autobiographical protagonist, has just come from the treatment room at the clinic after a sadistic session at the hands of the lady doctor with cold blue eyes. Sibylla stands outside the open door:

> Her short dark hair untidily disposed on her head . . . & her thin hands clasping and rubbing her emaciated body in the places where the treatment had been most severe. She looked a strange little bony object in her shrunken grey flannel dressing gown with all her life in her small, keen face, & her startled grey eyes.

Emerging into the corridor, "big Dr. Papadopoulos" regards Sibylla with a slight smile under his untidy mustache; his large comfortable body is reassuring, he jokes with the patients and makes them laugh: "I may be a good doctor—yes, but I am absolutely hopeless, my dear lady. Mad, that's what I am. Mad as a hatter . . ." he seems to be saying. He and Sibylla have a special understanding. "His black gypsy eyes" take in Sibylla, who receives their "full message." He makes a semi-humorous bow to her, remarking that they always seem to meet in the corridor. Sibylla, who is being addressed by the lady doctor, cannot escape. In some "deep down and suppressed agony" she allows the large untidy figure to pass behind her and on down the corridor without another sign. But the suppressed urge becomes too strong. Casting prudence to the wind, she turns her head and deliberately looks after the doctor:

> She met his eyes as he entered his own room. He also looked round—& then—Sibylla turned in haste and fled towards the dressing-room . . . *completely* de-fabricated.[72]

Side by side with Vivien's romantic fantasy of being part of a "doctor-patient couple," expressive of her wish for a relationship which would supply the love lacking in her marriage, went her self-mocking admission that she was victim to those very "specialists" whose charm was merely professional, whose jokes were all part of the service. In this story, Vivien/Sibylla cannot afford her expensive treatments. This truth is brought home to her when she enters the dressing-room and is met by the strong whiff of scent and "opulence," signs which make her immediately suspect that "Lady Rotherbrooke" (Lady Rothermere) is a fellow patient. "You could not have convinced Sibylla," writes Vivien, "if you had proved it by algebra, that this opulence was *not* Lady Rotherbrooke." Sibylla enters the cubicle vacated by the absent lady, and begins to examine her discarded garments, although she does not touch them ("Sibylla had her 'lines' beyond which she did not go"). From her inventory of the fashionable clothes before her it is apparent that they do not resemble the "rosy gold and blue scintillations" of "Lady Beavermere" (another alias for the newspaper magnate's wife), who, remembers Sibylla, was "fantastically chic," sparkling like a Christmas tree angel, when last she saw her at luncheon.

Mortified, Sibylla leaves the cubicle and inspects herself in the long glass. "O monstrous." Her clothes are *démodés*. Nothing looks quite right. And because Sibylla is always six months behind with her outfits, in spite of much laborious planning and outlay, she is doomed to be in hiding from all but her boon companions for quite nine months of the year. The rest of her "sartorial time" is spent "in agony of mind and in infinity of buying and selling."

Emerging into the street (perhaps Welbeck Street, where Cyriax practised), her attention is caught by "an immense closed car standing waiting at the kerb." The chauffeur peers at Sibylla. "I expect he thinks I am an odd-looking party leaving this house." Nevertheless, she lingers for an instant, "the more fully to drink in every detail of this super car." Walking a few steps out of her way, she examines the bonnet: "Rolls Royce—ah." She glances up and down the street, reflecting upon the doctors who inhabit it: "Poor old Sir Roysten Robery on the right there—poor old Sir Evans Mason down on the left . . ." (perhaps an allusion to neurologist Sir Henry Head, whom Eliot had discussed with Leonard). But this ostentatious medical wealth reassures rather than alienates her, for Vivien considers herself someone who knows a good thing when she sees it and, as far as fashionable medicine is concerned, she is an epicure who can recognise "good doctoring" when she meets it as surely as she can recognise a good Paris hat. Are not high bills a guarantee of medical skill as they are of high fashion? She walks home "on little wings . . . She had found, at last, the treatment, the cure, the one perfect, certain ultimate treatment, and opening her hand, she grasped it as her own."[73]

Eliot never published "Médecine à la Mode" in the *Criterion,* probably because it was too revealing, but nevertheless it demonstrates Vivien's lively talent. In writing she found not only a therapeutic outlet, but a *métier* in which she could succeed, unlike dancing or acting, and which provided an outlet for her creativity and intelligence. Vivien's manuscripts also clarify the intricate links between her writing and Tom's, and make clear the literary partnership which existed between the Eliots in the early days of the *Criterion.* The first draft, in Vivien's hand, establishes her authorship, but the fair copy, which also begins in Vivien's handwriting, continues after several pages in Tom's. Eliot's firm, neat hand contrasts with her fluent, careless one, but his punctilious editing of her script is everywhere in evidence. In "Médecine à la Mode" "thin" is crossed out and "small" substituted, describing Sibylla's face. Tom changes Dr. Papadopoulos's "mouth smiling slightly" to "his slight smile." It was a husband-and-wife collaboration which extended to nearly all Vivien's writing, and much of Tom's in the early years of the marriage.[74] Abigail Eliot, Eliot's first cousin, remembered of Tom and Vivien: "In the beginning he lived through her. Her hand was all over his work," a judgement confirmed by Vivien's notebooks, as by the facsimile edition of *The Waste Land,* with its fifty lines of "Fresca" verse, some in Vivien's style; cut by Pound from "The Fire Sermon," some of these lines surfaced under Vivien's pen name ("F.M." for "Fanny Marlow") in the *Criterion* in April 1924, an indication of her authorship.[75] Nor can Vivien's artless remarks to Aldington that she told Tom what to write when he was "too tired" to think for himself, or Tom's praise of Vivien's ability to his assistant editor, fail to convince of the authenticity and extent of their literary union.

Tom's support was critical in the making of Vivien as a writer. "It is wonderful how keen her mind keeps with such pain," he had remarked admiringly to Ottoline at the end of 1922.[76] After the crisis with "German Jack" in May 1923, Eliot's approbation fostered Vivien's growing confidence and determination, as she worked quietly in the upstairs bedroom overlooking the sea at 2 Milestone Cottages. From this south-facing, peaceful room the couple put together the new journal. Perhaps a bargain was struck during this time of truce: Eliot would give Vivien her chance in return for her silence over his homosexual alliances, which were hidden from all but his closest confidants, Ezra, Mary, Ottoline and Vivien herself. At any event, in February 1924, the moment came when Eliot took the bold decision to publish his wife in his prestigious periodical.

It is possible that Eliot first encouraged Vivien's writing to assuage his own guilt. If he could not give her love, he could give her the benefit of his literary ability and editorial experience. Together they could make a quarterly, even if they could not make a child. And for Vivien her writing could become a substitute for the flesh and blood infant for which she longed. What began in part as therapy became a new career; Eliot learnt a genuine respect for Vivien's ability as she progressed from the role of shorthand-typist to that of indispensable contributor to the new review. When the editor was short of copy, who was on hand to fill the vacant columns? Vivien—quick and adept at writing sketches, poems, book reviews, whatever Tom needed to make up the paper when other writers handed in their pieces late or failed to meet his standards. And, as "Fanny Marlow's" success grew, so her health improved now that she had a job to do and was part of a team. Valued, busy, empowered, this new Vivien was sometimes simply too busy to be ill.

"We have both been working at top pitch for the last five weeks to get out the *Criterion*," Eliot told Sydney Schiff on 24 February 1924, explaining that the review was "all ready" and would be sent out on the 29th. The husband-and-wife team would at once set to work on the April number.[77] On the last day of March Vivien wrote importantly that although she longed to meet the Schiffs, "the next *Criterion* is blocking every moment until Saturday, when it MUST go to print. Until then—chaos!"[78]

17

Criterion Battles

From her first article, "Letters of the Moment," Vivien began to define herself as a writer who did not hesitate to shock as well as amuse. Her pieces were witty, provocative and often dangerously candid, despite their anonymity. Writing as "F.M." in "Letters of the Moment—I," published in February 1924, she attacked one of Bloomsbury's sacred cows, the theatrical Phoenix Society, founded in 1919, whose productions were a favourite of Tom and Virginia. Vivien scoffed at the "Mermaid Society's" "tawdry bawdry Caroline renovations" of Congreve's *The Way of the World,* and other plays which, she wrote scornfully, were performed on Sunday nights to "Whiggish patrons of the arts," and on Monday afternoons to an audience of resting actors, "unkempt sub-editors (of monthlies) goggling over the gallery rail, and ladies from Hampstead who have met there for a good talk and a cup of tea."[1]

Vivien's "fierce Welsh shriek," as she called her speaking voice, set a tone for the pieces to follow. In "Letters of the Moment—II" (April 1924), she continued her attack on "voguish" seventeenth-century revivals and the avant-garde fashion for watching

> what the cultivated call The Play ... When the poor dear Mermaid Society meritoriously started to dig out these dusty old plays and a sparse and earnest audience beaten up by the indignant Aquin half filled an unfrequented theatre, how little it suspected that it would turn a hitherto inconspicuous though tedious pose into a Movement.

She did not spare her husband, "Aquin" (a derivative of Thomas Aquinas), in her onslaught.[2]

Bloomsbury parties were another target of Vivien's criticism, but here her tone grew confessional. A quotation from Ronsard, neatly written out in French by Tom in her writing book, expressed her mood—and probably Tom's—of disillusionment that spring of 1924: "Le temps s'en va, le temps s'en va, madame: / Las! Le temps, non, mais nous nous en allons . . ." Time is fleeing, is Ronsard's message; Vivien's response is that she no longer wishes to join the party.[3] She had reached a turning-point. The severe mental and physical breakdown she had endured in 1923, as she was finally forced to acknowledge Tom's sexual preferences, had alienated her even further from pretentious, bickering, bisexual Bloomsbury, as she now viewed the writers and artists she had once felt privileged to know.

In 1924–25 Vivien used the *Criterion* as a vehicle for her anger and pain: "What happy meetings, what luminous conversations in twilight rooms filled with the scent of hyacinths, await me now?" she asks nostalgically in "Letters of the Moment—I": "The uncompromising voice of truth inside me answers, None at all. For I am not the same person who once played—as it seems to one—a leading part in those Spring fantasies."

> But, you say, what about the wonderful parties of your intellectual friends which you used to describe to me so gaily?
>
> I have not been to any.
>
> And why not? you say.
>
> Well, the enjoyment of parties belongs to the Spring that one has lost.

Only egoists enjoy "intellectual" parties, declared Vivien in another dig at the Bloomsbury Group: "All the odd minutes and odd hours and odd half-days which an egoist fills up so satisfyingly by toying with some aspect of himself are arid to a person without egoism." In fact, she argues, thinking about oneself corrodes the mind and, for the non-egoist, destroys his life purpose. Is an artist ever therefore an egoist, she asks. Never, comes the answer. And only an egoist can avoid boredom at a "party of the future," as Vivien designates an afternoon at the "Mermaid Society," where, she confided to Sydney Schiff, *King Lear* had nearly done her in.[4]

Looking back to her youth in "Letters of the Moment—II," Vivien recalled performing an act of "self-immolation," long ago, at a birthday dance at Hampstead. Then, "abashed and solitary," she had threaded her way up a staircase packed with "lusty maidenhead and manhood," only to find herself passed by her eager hostess into the expectant hands of a young gentleman with eyeglasses, in the belief that he and she would find many "high-souled things" in common, including a shared love of light opera. Behind the handsome Jacobean sideboard stood the butler, dispensing champagne cup and claret. The young gentleman turned his glasses on Vivien, and "without *gêne* or hesitation inquired whether I had yet secured my seats for the first night of *The Pirates of Penzance.* This was his test— having been misled into expecting to find me a superior person: it was in fact his Secret." Painfully aware that her answer would offend, Vivien replied bluntly that she found Gilbert and Sullivan a bore. The same expression convulsed her questioner's features as, at a certain moment in 1919, would have distorted those of an *aficionado* of the Ballets Russes, if one had said, "settling a pillow or throwing off a shawl: No, I do not care for the *Boutique* at all, not at all."[5]

Vivien was half-aware that she was performing a similar act of self-immolation now. It was a reckless move to exhibit such scorn of Bloomsbury tastes in the *Criterion,* despite the cloak of anonymity, but a continuing theme of Vivien's writing is her urge towards self-destruction. The impulsion towards social suicide at that Hampstead party, where she did not hesitate to shock a pretentious guest, and the "solitary" nature of her personality were characteristics set early in her life. And Vivien was defiant. She refused to compromise. Her writing became all-important to her and, unlike Mary Hutchinson, she was no longer prepared to fit it around the demands of society. Boldly she adopted the voice of Stravinsky, a "great classic master," whose Firebird she took as her own symbol of a woman aspiring to freedom:

A work does not have to be good or bad; it must be organic and identified with the artist. You must never present anything that isn't perfect. I have never given the public my experiments, my sketches. Each of my works represents something I tried to do the best I could, with all my strength. A piece is finished for me when I can go no further. I stop at the edge of the abyss.[6]

As Vivien developed her ideas in print, a particular target of her pen became the tendency she found in England "to turn everything involving personal tastes into a Secret." Once again her barbed attack was aimed at those who would understand it. Satire had long been the weapon of Bloomsbury and its hangers-on; it was an in-game whose satisfaction lay in writing for an élitist audience who would understand its thrusts, and the amusement of knowing that the majority of readers remained in ignorance of the victims' identity. Ottoline had been the victim singled out for caricature and ridicule by D. H. Lawrence, Aldous Huxley and Virginia Woolf. "Is the sunlight ever normal at Garsington?" demanded Virginia in 1924. "No, I think even the sky is done up in pale yellow silk, and certainly the cabbages are scented."[7] Now those who felt ill-treated were taking their revenge: Ottoline was recording her own impressions of her ungrateful guests in her journals, and in February Wyndham Lewis boldly satirised Lytton Strachey and the Sitwells in an article entitled "The Apes of God" in the *Criterion*.

Lewis's article caused a furore. "Everyone—that is Lytton, Osbert Sitwell, Mary Hutchinson, is claiming to be an Ape of God, and identifying the rest of the pack," Virginia informed Tom on 11 May 1924.[8] Eliot, however, defended his publication of Lewis's article, claiming unconvincingly that it had slipped through because of his careless editing. He had not had time to "read and expurgate" the article—there being only twenty-four hours in the day—he protested to Virginia; and if, as Sydney Schiff was threatening, a mass meeting of protesters met and dismembered him like a hero of Grecian tragedy (or even a "bungalow bride"—a murder victim, as featured recently in the tabloid newspapers) it was Virginia whom Tom would reproach and execrate with his last breath. "For you are my oracle and counsel in matters journalistic, and did you not advise me (with the supporting opinions too of Leonard and Clive as junior counsel) that it was 'in the best tradition of British journalism' to let one contributor say what he likes about another?"[9]

Privately Tom and Vivien joked about the article and composed their own verses on its scurrilous contents:

> . . . And what an awful thing to do
> To let upstarts who are Taboo

Write nasty article on Apes
Or speak of love in curious shapes.[10]

This verse, in Vivien's hand, is a reference to Lewis's Rabelaisian descriptions of Bloomsbury perversions (expanded in 1931 into a book, *The Apes of God),* in which he ridiculed "lesbian-apes" who lived in a "nest" of studios, "ape-flagellant" artists who kept a collection of whips in a cupboard, and other members of the "Apery," the "select and snobbish club" which Lewis alleged to be Bloomsbury, and in which he claimed the substitution of money for talent was a qualification for membership.[11]

Tom joined in the fun, copying out Vivien's verse into her writing book and adding his own blasphemous ending concerning "love in curious shapes": "The pal of God whose name is John/Is one safe bet to gamble on/Is glory hallelujah John."[12] This reference was to St. John, whom playwright Christopher Marlowe, according to his rival Thomas Kyd (author of *The Spanish Tragedie),* alleged was the homosexual lover of Jesus—an Elizabethan controversy of 1593 well known to Eliot, who was steeped in the "tragedy of blood," and had written an essay on Marlowe in 1919.[13] Vivien meanwhile pasted into her writing book a newspaper cutting which quoted Oscar Wilde's letter to Whistler describing his new bride: "Her name is Constance—and she is quite young, very grave and mystical with wonderful eyes—and dark brown coils of hair: quite perfect . . ." It was to Constance Wilde that Vivien now compared herself.[14]

Secrets related to parties, to money, to passions and to hatreds. Tom and Vivien shared such secrets with each other, and their liberated "friends." "This passion for Secrets appears in different classes and sections of society in very different manifestations," wrote Vivien. "But in every part of this viscous morass, this gently undulating bog of Anglo-Saxon democracy, Secrets of one kind or another are to be discovered . . ."[15] Sexual secrets amused Virginia, herself a lesbian whose interest was growing in Vita Sackville-West, "like a ripe grape in features, moustached, pouting . . . [who] strides on fine legs, in a well-cut skirt, & . . . has a manly good sense & simplicity about her . . ."[16]

As Vivien distanced herself from such an atmosphere, Virginia recorded Tom's presence at a "queer little party" earlier in May, after he had taken her to the Phoenix Society production of *King Lear,* at which they had both jeered, only for Virginia to find Tom praising the performance as "flawless" in the *Criterion,* and coming out with a "solemn & stately rebuke of those who jeer and despise." Such hypocrisy irritated Virginia, and the private thoughts she confided to her diary were less complimentary than the letters she wrote to the poet: "The sinister & pedagogic Tom cut a queer figure. I cannot wholly free myself from suspicions about him—at the worst they only amount to calling him an American schoolmaster: a very vain man . . . There's something hole & cornerish, biting in the back, suspicious, elaborate, uneasy, about him . . ." The party included Philip Ritchie, as well as Lytton Strachey, Duncan Grant and Vanessa Bell.[17] To Virginia the transvestite ballet *Don't Be Frightened,* designed by Duncan and performed at a party given by Maynard Keynes that July, was "enchanting, lyrical," only spoilt by finding Duncan's lover Bunny Garnett behaving like a "surly devil."[18] She did not record whether or not Vivien was present on that occasion, but a few weeks earlier, on 21 June 1924, Virginia made a hostile diary entry concerning her. She had seen, she wrote, "Mrs. Eliot—the last making me almost vomit, so scented, so powdered, so egotistic, so morbid, so weakly."[19]

Virginia's malicious portrait of Vivien can be attributed to the Woolfs' irritation with the Eliots that summer. Virginia and Leonard had been annoyed at the complaints which they believed Tom and Vivien were making about the Hogarth Press's failure to market *The Waste Land* efficiently. Gossip was going the rounds of Bloomsbury that Leonard and Virginia had only sold forty copies, and that Tom was furious about the poor sales. On 27 June 1924 Vivien wrote a dignified letter of apology to Leonard, protesting that the gossip was "complete fantasy": neither she nor Tom thought or imagined that Leonard or Virginia had ever written anything "insulting or unkind" about *The Waste Land.* She and Tom, she wrote, had merely indulged in a little "crude and meaningless badinage" which should not have given offence. Unconvincingly, Vivien professed to know nothing of the facts of private publishing: she would have no more idea of the success of the publication if she heard that forty copies had been sold by the Hogarth Press or four thousand, she declared, adding that the subject of the sales of the Hogarth Press had never once been discussed between Tom and herself:

We have never conceived it possible that Tom or any good poet could be popular in this country or any other country. We have never imagined that any money could be made out of good poetry. Therefore we have never considered poetry as a financial aset, and that is why Tom earns his living in other ways. We still cherish hopes of leisure and independence, bringing such command of conversation as will make it impossible for misunderstandings of this kind to occur.[20]

Once again Vivien's taste for gossip had got her into trouble, just as it had the previous year when she was blamed for starting a rumour that Maynard Keynes was going bankrupt. Vivien had been so upset on that occasion that on 11 June 1923 she had told Virginia that, as the "instigator of such a rumour," she felt too timid to return to London and "try my luck." Nor had she dared accompany Tom when he went to Oxford to lecture to the undergraduates, and then on to Garsington, although she would have loved to have gone with him.[21] As Ottoline knew to her cost, Bloomsbury could never be trusted. Professions of friendship could change overnight to cruel caricature and mocking laughter. Virginia might tell Tom that she was "subterraneously trying to get you and Vivien to come to London," and might write warmly "Give my love to Vivien and come and see us soon," but her diary knew a different reality.[22] And although Virginia is not a wholly reliable witness, her description indicates Vivien's struggle to disguise her misery and to mix in society she found essentially uncongenial; it also suggests her growing pride in her published writing which left her open to the very charge she repudiated: that of being an egoist.

Another "secret" was Vivien's part in the running battle in which Tom was engaged with John Middleton Murry, by now editor of the *Adelphi* and defender of Romanticism in opposition to Eliot's Classicism. Eliot's position was not a new one; although in 1928 he famously stated in the preface to *For Lancelot Andrewes* that he was "a classicist in literature, royalist in politics, and anglo-catholic in religion," this was no sudden turning from a previously revolutionary stance, as is sometimes supposed. Eliot has been viewed as a revolutionary who disappoints, failing to follow through the promise of modernism as he retreats from experimental verse into Anglo-Catholic orthodoxy, religious pageantry and derivative drama. But Eliot's profoundly pessimistic view of man was formed long before his formal conversion in 1927. He defined the Classicist point of view as essentially a belief in original sin, and his belief in this doctrine and man's need for "austere discipline" intensified, as he turned increasingly towards Catholicism. "There are only two things—Puritanism and Catholicism," he noted in Vivien's writing book. "You are one or the other. You either believe in the reality of *Sin* or you don't. *That* is the important moral distinction—not whether you are good or bad." Puritanism does not believe in "Sin," he continued, it merely believed that certain things must not be done.[23]

Vivien, although by instinct a Romantic rather than a Classicist—who identified with James's Rousseauesque heroine Daisy Miller—closely followed Tom's literary and political opinions in the 1920s. Now she was ready to lead a Celtic charge against Murry after he declared that the English writer (or the English divine) must listen to "the inner voice" rather than depend on outside authority. Eliot was the first to attack his rival: "The possessors of the inner voice ride ten in a compartment to a football match at Swansea, listening to the inner voice, which breathes the eternal message of vanity, fear and lust," he protested in the *Criterion* in October 1923, making a plea for order and discipline.[24] Vivien's idea was to write a spoof letter, something Eliot had used before to fill up blank pages of the *Egoist,* pretending to be a vicar, "the Rev. Mr. Grimble," or a schoolmaster, "J. A. D. Spence, Thridlington Grammar School," or even a Tory, "Charles Augustus Coneybeare, The Carlton Club, Liverpool"; it was a prank which belonged to the Eliot tradition of practical jokes, misleading footnotes, and the other tricks which E. M. Forster detected the poet was playing on his audience. Forster pointed out that in Eliot's book *Homage to John Dryden* he expressed the hope that his essays might "preserve in cryptogram certain notions which, if expressed directly, would be destined to immediate obloquy, followed by perpetual oblivion." What is he trying to put across here? demanded Forster. "Why, if he believes in it, can he not say it out straight and face the consequences?"[25] Again and again, complained Forster, the reader had the sense of being outwitted by Eliot. Whose fault was it, he asked. "The verse always sounds beautiful but often conveys nothing."

It amused Vivien to outwit an audience as much as it did Tom. Posing as two "young women earning our own living," aged twenty-six and thirty, one married with a baby to support (possibly herself and Pearl Fassett), Vivien puts a provocative question to Murry, who, said Virginia Woolf, had been beating his breast over his past sins like a "revivalist preacher," following the tragic early death of his wife, Katherine Mansfield, in January 1923: "What, Mr. John Middleton Murry, are your actual qualifications for the post of Junior Prophet, a general exponent of LIFE?" From a study of his editorials Vivien was forced to the conclusion that "your raison d'être is that your wife has died. To put the matter crudely, other men's wives have died. But few, we venture to suggest, have been able to extract such a plethora of copy—and other profit—from the supposedly lamentable event."[26] It was not an attack in the best of taste, and there is no record of the letter being published by Murry, who on 14 April 1924 married one of his contributors, Violet le Maistre. Perhaps Vivien never sent the letter, but her dislike of Murry was echoed by Eliot's own jeering remarks, hidden in Vivien's writing book and directed at Bloomsbury and Murry, whom he saw as an example of the harm that "autocratic" Bloomsbury could do in cramping a person for life "by having him put in a pot in youth" so that he begins to grow too late and becomes "pot bound." As time passes, says the poet, such "fonctionaires" shrivel, and "one sees them as a silly little collection of failures and little Japanese trees."[27]

Identical images often surface in Tom's and Vivien's writing, and illustrate their shared opinions. Although Vivien might write to Sydney Schiff that "the weekend was a strain (our weekends always are),"[28] in the work situation Vivien remained an indispensable partner. Eliot's notes on being "pot bound" are remarkably similar to the opening of Vivien's "Letters of the Moment—I," in which she writes: "My hyacinths are busting clumsily out of their pots, as they always do, coming into misshapen bloom before their time. And this is the essential spring—spring in winter, spring in London, grey and misty spring, grey twilights, piano organs, women at street crossings ..." before launching into her own attack on Bloomsbury.[29] To both the Eliots, Bloomsbury was autocratic, egotistical and self-regarding; it did not, Tom wrote accusingly, allow "growth," which fatigued and terrified it. Although Eliot appeared close to the Woolfs at a time when they were useful to him, Virginia was right in sensing that he was "uneasy" in her presence. It is doubtful whether Eliot ever felt genuine affection for Virginia.

The Eliots' hostility towards Murry, expressed in the columns of the *Criterion,* was, however, ungenerous, for the editor of the *Adelphi* was about to do Eliot a good turn. Despite their intellectual antagonism, Murry, Clark Lecturer at Cambridge for 1924–25, decided to nominate Eliot, the apologist for Classicism, to succeed him the following academic year. Excitedly Eliot would write on 20 February 1925, thanking Murry for the appointment and the £200 fee, which came like a ray of hope to him "just at the *blackest moment of my life,*" when Vivien was ill.[30]

Vivien may yet have sensed that her husband's star was in the ascendant, as she poked fun at the editor of the rival review. "Murry's star sank as Eliot's rose," writes Murry's biographer.[31] In any event, Vivien did not hesitate to satirise Murry; in "Letters of the Moment" (April 1924) Vivien describes the periodicals which lie on her drawing-room table: there are the monthlies, the weeklies, the quarterly reviews, "set out in rows like a parterre," the pink *Dial,* the golden *Mercury,* the austere *Nouvelle Revue Française,* the buff *Blackwood* and the lemon yellow *Adelphi.* Beneath all, "shamefully in sight the gaudy cover and uncouth dimensions of *Vogue.* One turns to *The Dial,* flip-flop go the pages. Very dull, very dull" until, reading the shocking Paris Letter, Vivien thinks of Mr. J. Middleton Murry. "Golly!" he says, revealing his "sensitiveness to the living soul of the language" and disclosing to his readers how much better a Professor of Poetry he would make than the insensitive present incumbent. "Crikey!" comments Vivien, "As one might say, what a go!"[32]

Emboldened by success, in the July 1924 *Criterion,* Vivien wrote a scathing review of Murry's novel *The Voyage* under the pseudonym "F.M." In the same issue she described David Garnett's *A Man in the Zoo* as "an enchanting book," but Murry's heroine is trite, and "humor is not Mr. Murry's strong suit." What is the novel all about, she demands. Who can tell? Has it style, form or rhythm? "In the words of Mr. Doherty, 'No-o, my child, no-o.' "[33] As she established herself as a reviewer in the "Books of the Quarter" section of the *Criterion,* Vivien began to deliver increasingly patronising judgements on some of Bloomsbury's greatest stars. Commenting in October on E. M. Forster's *A Passage to India* under the disguise of "I. P. Fassett," but in a style that is all her own, Vivien asks: "Why do we have to remind ourselves so incessantly that Mr. Forster's work is admirable?" before concluding that Forster's great novel lacks the missing ingredient which might lift it above the level of "Sound Contemporary Fiction where it must inevitably lie."[34] It was an equally rash and tactless move to criticise the Eliots' assistant editor, Richard Aldington, who was likely to discover that Vivien was contributing to the quarterly, but she had not forgiven Aldington for upsetting Tom earlier, and for criticising her choice of name for the review. Although Aldington's *Literary Studies and Reviews* had met with praise for their learning and erudition, Vivien wrote tartly, "a discriminating critic would have put [these] as the last of the book's qualities."[35] As for John Galsworthy's *The White Monkey,* "I am afraid he misses badly," was I. P. Fassett's damning comment.[36]

Soon Vivien was enjoying the gratifying experience of receiving payment for her work. On 18 September 1924 she banked her first pay cheque of £1.10.0d., made out to "Miss Fanny Marlow" by the printer J. Cobden Sanderson.[37] The Eliots' "Gunpowder Plot" to dominate literary London was coming to fruition, and Vivien was playing her part, contributing towards the family finances just as she and Tom had planned. Her income was yet another secret to hug to herself, to keep hidden from Mary and Ottoline and, as the months passed, she basked in her journalistic success. As "Fanny Marlow" Vivien had crossed the divide from private to public writing, and her new aliases began to fill more and more columns of the *Criterion,* completing her metamorphosis into an androgynous persona who took refuge behind a male *nom de plume* for her more daring pieces. In October 1924 it was difficult to miss Vivien's journalism: writing as "Feiron Morris" she published "Thé Dansant,"[38] as "Felix Morrison" she wrote "Mrs. Pilkington,"[39] and as "F.M." and "Irene Fassett" she reviewed several "Books of the Quarter." But it was "Fanny" who made the most money, spinning webs in which to catch the Eliots' supposed enemies: "There is no *end* to Fanny!" Vivien confided proudly to Sydney Schiff. "But Feiron will never make money. And he does not spin. He is a nasty fellow."[40]

By January 1925 Tom and Vivien were working so closely together that it was sometimes hard to tell who was the author of a piece: the

January issue of the *Criterion* carried "On the Eve: A Dialogue" by T. S. Eliot,[41] whose style is characteristically Vivien's, but as it was extensively edited by her husband was published under his name. It is probable that when Vivien was too ill to finish a prose sketch, Eliot polished it for publication; if Vivien sometimes had the keener ear for dialogue, Tom had the more precise and ironic eye. Certainly in January Vivien was busy on the first "Diary of the Rive Gauche," originally titled "Paris on £5 a Week," her reminiscences of Paris in the winter of 1921, written under her favourite pen name, "Fanny Marlow."[42]

The January *Criterion* also included a knowing review by Vivien writing as "Feiron Morris" of Virginia Woolf's essay on the novel "Mr. Bennett and Mrs. Brown," an expanded version of a lecture Woolf had given to the Society of Heretics at Cambridge in May 1924. It was extraordinary for Vivien to criticise Virginia, since Tom had previously begged Virginia to let him have the article for the July 1924 issue, offering her a special rate of £20 instead of £10 per 5,000 words, a rate he explained that he could only offer to Europe's four best contemporary writers.[43] "Five thousand words are no drawback, when the words are yours," he wrote flatteringly; "I wish for nothing better than to attract the sparkish wits of undergraduates . . . May I have [the article] at once, and set it up? I shall print it in the July number."[44] On 22 May 1924, after Virginia agreed, Tom wrote a gushing letter of thanks: "My dear Virginia, I must tell you how I appreciate your generosity in letting me have this article . . . If the Criterion should be extinguished, I want it to go out in full flame and with your paper and unpublished manuscripts of Marcel Proust and W. B. Yeats, the July number will be the most brilliant in its history . . . It will help me to feel that the Criterion has not been altogether without value or distinction."[45]

In Virginia's essay, which Tom published as "Character in Fiction," she praised her friend Tom's work, one of the habitual "puffs" which members of Bloomsbury gave each other; Clive Bell, for example, had previously drawn attention to the neglect of Virginia, Tom and Murry by critics. Tom modestly alluded to Virginia's praise, writing that her comments on him "do somewhat embarrass me as being excessive for what I know my own work to be . . . I feel myself that everything I have done consists simply of tentative sketches and rough experiments. Will the next generation profit by our labours?"[46]

It was as Tom's ally that Virginia had given him her article, which the Hogarth Press subsequently published at 2/6d. To have such contributors as Virginia Woolf added to the prestige of the *Criterion,* as Eliot acknowledged in his letter. Nevertheless, as editor, he allowed Vivien, posing as a male journalist, "Feiron Morris," to voice her naïve criticisms of Virginia in his quarterly in January 1925. At first Vivien praised Virginia for her "brilliant essay," but then proceeded to criticise her for citing Joyce and Eliot as examples of the creation of character from external observation.[47] "Did Mr. Eliot . . . deduce Sweeney from observations in a New York barroom?" asks Vivien, chastising Virginia for selecting the three "nightmare figures"—James Joyce, T. S. Eliot and Wyndham Lewis—as the only representatives of modern literature. "Such an idea is ludicrous," declares Vivien. "What about Proust, for example?" Condescendingly she concludes, using the editorial "we": "Mrs. Woolf has written a very able argument upon a thesis which we believe to be wrong. The argument is so clever that it is difficult to disprove the thesis: we can only wait in the hope that Mrs. Woolf will disprove it herself."[48]

It is possible that Eliot was too busy to "read and expurgate" Vivien's review; this was the excuse he had made previously to Virginia over the publication of Wyndham Lewis's notorious article on the Bloomsbury "Apes of God." But the evidence of Vivien's writing book shows unequivocally that Eliot shared her hostility to Bloomsbury. It is probable that Tom was as duplicitous and hypocritical as Vivien; both Eliots welcomed the Woolfs' friendship when it profited them, and disparaged them when Tom felt his rival Virginia's "superhuman cleverness" (in writing *Jacob's Room)* surpassed his own achievements.[49] Jokes and games held a constant appeal to both Eliots, and for Vivien to sneer at Virginia in the columns of the very paper in which Virginia had been published to widespread acclaim was the kind of private secret which held particular appeal for both Tom and Vivien.

By April 1925 Vivien had removed herself, "sore throat and all," to 38 Burleigh Mansions in search of "a room of her own" in which to work during the day. Although she and Tom still retained their flat at 9 Clarence

Gate Gardens, they had given up Milestone Cottages at Old Fishbourne. Despite the fact that she was "withering to death in this frightful winter in this intolerable country," Vivien's mood was buoyant. She was, she told Sydney, by now quite accustomed to reading a typed MS and having to form her opinions on it before she saw it in print; over the last year Cobden-Sanderson had been submitting proofs for her to pass for press "at her earliest convenience." Her pride grew at seeing her pseudonyms sandwiched between those stars of Bloomsbury—Huxley, Fry and Woolf— to whom she had for so long deferred, sharing space with Pound, Aldington and even distinguished continental writers such as André Gide, Dostoevsky and Proust. Proof-reader, editor, contributor, she felt herself to be any writer's equal. It was as such that she confided to Sydney in a letter dated only "Sunday" in the spring of 1925, that she believed she was trying the same experiment with form as he was in his new book: "But with this difference; I have not attempted to make each sketch from the *point of view* of a different person involved but rather the attempt is to make them all from the point of view of a very interested and *intimate* outsider . . ." This was of course a very important difference, wrote Vivien, and no doubt the only similarity was that both were a series of sketches which could appear separately, but which did, "when all is finished (not yet, alas with me!) make up a whole." Everything she told him, she wrote, was *"of course . . .* absolutely and irrevocably in confidence."[50]

Perhaps it was hubris which drove Vivien to risk disclosure. She now felt herself to be invincible, and could not resist the urge to express her secret feelings. In addition her illnesses provided an alibi. While Tom was complaining to Virginia on 4 February 1925, "the moment I try to use my mind at all, it's no use, and then up goes the temperature . . . Vivien is worse than I am by far,"[51] or writing on 19 April 1925, "Vivien can't move, with violent neuralgia and neuritis. It will be months before she can get right again," his correspondents had the impression from his exaggerated accounts that Vivien was far too incapacitated to even think of taking up a new career as a writer.[52]

In the *Criterion* of April 1925, therefore, Tom published Vivien's poem, "Necesse est Perstare" (originally entitled "Ennui"),[53] in which she vented her scorn for "intellectual" parties in economical and astringent *vers libre* which caused an instant stir:

A flurry of snow in the sky,
Cold blue English sky,
And then the lunch party broke up
And people said they must go
And there was an end (for a session)
   of the eternal Aldous Huxley—
Elizabeth Bibesco—Clive Bell—
   Unceasing clamour of inanities.
I looked at you and you had stretched
   Your arms up above your head
With such an air of weariness,
Like some very old monkey.
I looked at you and you looked at me.
I longed to speak to you,
   But I didn't. I longed
To come and stand beside you at the window and
   Look out at the fleering
   Cold English sunshine and say,
Is it necessary—
Is this necessary—
Tell me, is it necessary that we go through this?[54]

Princess Elizabeth Bibesco, daughter of H. H. Asquith, had had an affair with Middleton Murry in November 1920, and moved in the same circles as the Eliots. Vivien's ridicule of the socialite, as well as of Bell and Huxley, her description of Tom as "some very old monkey," became public when Ottoline at last guessed the identity of the author. "Yes, it is true that Vivien wrote that poem," replied Eliot on 1 May 1925. "In fact she has been writing for a long time—and I have always suspected that you knew it! And *I* think that she is a *very* clever and original writer, with a mathematical and abstract mind which ought to be trained—and I intend that it shall."[55] Soon plaudits were ringing in Vivien's ears. "I cannot believe that all the congratulations that Vivien receives on her writing is quite sincere," wrote Henry Eliot sourly to his mother on 10 May.[56]

It had always been part of the Eliot game-playing for Tom to allow the publication of Vivien's descriptions of him, revelations which he might have been expected to censor. Her pride in her own prolific output led her to contrast it with Eliot's own periodic writer's block in some cruel lines suggesting that he aspired to the conquest of too many literary peaks:

> "Isn't he wonderful?" whispered Felice. "He is the most marvellous poet in the *whole world.*"
>
> "He might be if he wrote anything," said Sibylla drily.
>
> "Yes, why *doesn't* he write more?"
>
> "Because he wants to be everything at once, I expect. Perhaps the devil took him up into a high mountain and showed him all the kingdoms of the world—unfortunately for him!"
>
> "And so, I suppose," asked Felice naggingly, "that he doesn't know which kingdom to choose?"
>
> "He's still up the mountain as far as I know . . ."[57]

Eliot nevertheless drew the line at publishing Vivien's most confessional writing, which drew a vivid picture of their personal incompatibility. "Ellison and Antony" is an account of a couple who live in "Mansions," a large, gloomy and somewhat sordid building with jangling lifts, staring lift-girls, wide dark staircases with stained carpets, and beetles and crickets in the kitchen of every flat. When "Antony" came home, wrote Vivien,

> Very quietly and carefully he hung up his hat and coat, put his stick in the corner, laid down the morning paper and the evening paper, both unfolded, and the book he had wanted to look at during the day. He hung for a moment in the hall, silent and undecided. There were many things he dreaded. That Ellison might have a headache, that she might be irritable and hate him, that she might be in despair or have with her her greatest friend who might have been quarrelling with her. If the flat was silent and dark with only the light from the glass over Jane's kitchen door, he was uneasy. Where was Ellison? . . . At last he would move, almost stealthily, towards his study, open the door, put just his head in, and there was Ellison, alone lying on the sofa. That was allright. And yet it was not allright. If only he could find his study empty, and Ellison in another room, occupied peacefully . . .

Antony stooped, kissed Ellison rather gingerly. Ellison's smile was strained . . . She said harshly and wearily, "Has anything happened?" . . . "No," said Antony. He smiled apologetically.[58]

Such a portrait was too private to be disclosed. Nevertheless, Vivien was skating on the thinnest of ice in criticising writers far greater than herself, as well as those who counted her among their friends. In "Fête Galante" by "Fanny Marlow," published in the *Criterion* in July 1925, Vivien delivered her final salvo against "intellectual" parties in a thinly disguised account of "Sibylla's" experiences at a glittering event hosted by Mary Hutchinson at River House. It followed hard on a sketch entitled "Night Club" written by "Feiron Morris,"[59] the second "Diary of the Rive Gauche" by "Fanny Marlow,"[60] and a stinging review of Rose Macaulay for whom "a delicate facetiousness stands for wit" by "I. P. Fassett" in the April issue;[61] even Stephen Hudson (Sydney Schiff) did not escape F.M.'s sharp criticism.[62] But none of these was as personally wounding, as malicious, and as clearly written by someone with a guest's inside knowledge, as "Fête Galante," with its savage portrait of Mary and St. John as the rich, superficial, social-climbing Becky and Rawdon Crawley from Thackeray's *Vanity Fair,* entertaining in their garden hung with Chinese lanterns like a scene from Whistler.

All High Bohemia are present: "Ethelberta Chaplin" (Edith Sitwell), stretching out a long white hand "on every finger of which was some blazing specimen of Florentine jewellery"; her brother, "Cedric Chaplin" (Osbert), "in his most aristocratic and blue-blooded mood," is also disapprovingly present:

> He stood very straight and tall, keeping his fair head rigid while his strained, prominent light blue eyes shifted incessantly from one person to another. Glancing obliquely down at the guests, he makes sarcastic comments in a low voice, although he remains protective of Sibylla ("Poor Sibylla," he thought, "But she is rather nice really.")

Sibylla, Cedric and Ethelberta attempt to escape "that awful woman . . . the Macaw" (Lady Diana Cooper) who, attended by her train, "had discovered champagne, iced punch, and a huge pile of bonbons," but, darting into the garden, Sibylla is accosted by "the great art critic, white locks gleaming in the moonlight, a loaded plate in each hand" (Roger Fry); he is too self-absorbed to listen to her. Disheartened, she leaves him eating "large mouthfuls of strawberries and cream" and wanders down the path, passing "Becky" (Mary) and "Steyne" (Clive Bell).

> Becky reached out a hand to her.
> "Do come and sit on the arm of my chair," she said seductively.
> "And be an audience for you and Steyne—no, thank you," Sibylla thought.

On the balcony "Sibylla" finds Rawdon, dispensing whisky and brandy-and-soda to a large group of men discussing Art. Among them is Eliot, "the American financier," leaning with exaggerated grace against the eighteenth-century marble fireplace. She is struck afresh by his strange appearance:

> the heavy, slumbering white face, thickly powdered; the long hooded eyes, unseeing, leaden-heavy; the huge, protuberant nose, and the somehow inadequate sullen mouth, the lips a little reddened. His head was exceptionally large, and not well shaped; the hair thin and plastered tightly down.

He is wearing a paper cap with streamers with which the Macaw has crowned him, and is haranguing his audience in a muffled, pedantic, and slightly drunken voice.

There is a sudden tumult among the crowds awaiting the arrival of the Ballets Russes. "The Ballet at last!" says someone. The Macaw leads her troupe into the room. "Rawdy, more drink, more drink!" she screeches. Sibylla runs across the deserted drawing-room to the balcony, and leans over the railing. Her eyes sweep the wide flat horizon.

> Beneath her, the sluggish river, flat-banked. Beyond it the vast unknown country of that London which lies on the other side. Over all lay a low, flat, smoky mist clinging to the ground and to

the river. Masts, spires, and tall buildings rose above the lake of mist. Down on the horizon lay the gibbous moon. The sky over-head was pearl-grey. The atmosphere had already the unearthly greenish-grey light of an English summer dawn.

"O Moon, I love you like that," said Sibylla. "I hate Shelley's old moon, like a wretched, dreary invalid escaped from an asy-lum. This is the moon for me, so fat, so comforting and solid. So *near*."

As she gazes at the hump-backed moon, Sibylla's friend Felice approaches, asking why the Ballet have not come. "Why should they come?" answers Sibylla lightly; "I shouldn't come if I was the Ballet." The two friends fetch their cloaks, make their farewells, and walk in a dream down the path to the gate. Becky shouts after them: "Have you liked my party?" "Loved it!" calls Sibylla.

Vivien's sketch was an act of *auto-da-fé*. St. John Hutchinson, stated Osbert Sitwell, was outraged by Vivien's "unflattering portrait" of his close friend Lady Diana Cooper, "comparing her, if I remember rightly, to a parrot." As Lady Diana's host, and as an old friend of Tom's, he decided to make a strong protest to Eliot. The real reason for Jack Hutchinson's protest was, of course, his outrage at the insulting portrait of himself and his wife, as well as of their friends.[63] But why, one may ask, did Eliot pub-lish "Fête Galante" when, with a few strokes of his editorial pencil, he could have cut the insulting description and dialogue which he must have known would cause offence? Did he intend to sacrifice Vivien, who must have been encouraged by his defence of Wyndham Lewis to think that he would stand by her in the event of criticism? It is possible that Eliot had grown jealous of Vivien's rising success, for it is hard to believe that he thought he and Vivien could continue to mock Bloomsbury with im-punity; it was only a matter of time before her cover was blown.

On the other hand, Tom may have allowed Vivien to express the anger and emotion both Eliots felt as they struggled to make a success of the *Criterion* in a viciously competitive literary environment. In April 1924 Eliot told Virginia how tired he was of "being supposed to edit the *Criterion* and being told by Oxford dons what a lucky young man he was at his age to have a review 'to do as I like with!' " "Do as I like!" he exploded. As if there were any satisfaction in editing a review "in the fragmentary evening hours given at the cost of sleep, society, recreation," in trying to bring out a paper of the same appearance as reviews with salaried editors and sub-editors and proper offices, in working "in one's sitting-room in the evenings, subject to a thousand interruptions; without staff, assistants or business manager; only since Christmas with a desk (the one Vivien shewed you: nine pounds ten saved up for) . . ."[64] His bitterness had deepened as he worried the paper might fold; in May he had written to Virginia that the *Criterion* "might be extinguished," but only one issue, Autumn 1925, failed to appear.[65] Jealousy of the wealthy and privileged members of High Bohemia rankled with both Eliots, but while Tom "Possum" hid his resentment, Vivien—passionate, impetuous and foolhardy—expressed the contempt they both shared for society's drones. She alone would pay the price.

18

On with the Dance

Tom yielded to Jack Hutchinson's complaints, making Vivien the scapegoat for his own ambivalent feelings towards Bloomsbury. At first he denied her authorship of "Fête Galante" in the July 1925 *Criterion,* but Virginia Woolf had recorded as early as 29 April her knowledge that Vivien has "done nothing but write since last June, because I told her to!"—a confession made by Tom on a visit to Rodmell. Two days later Tom had been forced to own up to the identity of "Fanny Marlow" when challenged by Ottoline. There was, therefore, no likelihood that the Hutchinsons would accept his denials.[1] In July, in Virginia's opinion, Tom treated Jack as "scurvily" as she felt he later treated her and Leonard by taking away *The Waste Land* and his other poems from the Hogarth Press and placing them behind her back with his new firm, Faber & Gwyer: "He treated Jack in the same way over Vivien's story in the *Criterion,*" wrote Virginia angrily. "The Underworld—the dodges & desires of the Underworld, its shifts and cabals are at the bottom of it. He intends to get on by the methods of that world; & my world is really not the underworld."[2]

Jack Hutchinson was not a man to take an insult lying down. A distinguished barrister, a King's Counsel and later a trustee of the Tate Gallery,[3] although mocked on occasions for being opinionated and sententious, he was nevertheless well liked in Bloomsbury[4]—and he was more than a match for Tom Eliot. Nor was Hutchinson alone in recognising his transparent portrait in "Fête Galante": Roger Fry had also held a garden party in June in which Chinese lanterns, referred to in the sketch, were much in evidence; Clive Bell, Lady Diana Cooper and the Sitwells, offended by Vivien's caricatures, also supported Jack and Mary. In the face of the Hutchinsons' outrage Tom agreed to their terms: he would never publish "Fanny Marlow" again. Vivien's star fell to the ground as fast as it had risen. The scandal precipitated a crisis: the autumn number of the *Criterion* failed to appear, and in the remodelled *New Criterion* of January 1926, only a short review under I. P. Fassett's name appeared in which Vivien probably had no hand.[5]

It is legitimate to ask whether Tom set Vivien up for her disgrace. Why did he allow her to drop the poison in the chalice? It seems inconceivable that Eliot as editor would allow a piece of hers to go through of whose contents he was ignorant. To the innocent eye the assumption must be that Eliot encouraged Vivien to risk her reputation by satirising their closest friends. Even if he were as supportive of her writing as he claimed and, despite his own insecurity, welcomed her unexpected fame, he may have had a darker motive: to eradicate her from the scene because he was negotiating a new contract with Lady Rothermere and Geoffrey Faber for a quarterly in which there would be no place for Vivien. In engineering Vivien's fall Tom cleared the decks for the future.

During 1925 Vivien tried to find another outlet for her writing, one which would relieve her dependence upon Tom and bring her work to a wider audience. Naturally, in view of her close friendship with Scofield Thayer, she turned to *The Dial,* submitting "The Paralysed Woman," the sketch so expressive of her own medical situation. But Thayer was in the process of bowing out of *The Dial* in 1925, handing over the editorship to the poet Marianne Moore, to whom he had awarded the *Dial Award* for 1924, hailing her as America's most distinguished poetess since Emily Dickinson. That spring Moore arrived at *The Dial* offices to take over from the previous managing editor, Alyse Gregory. Ellen Thayer, Scofield's cousin, agreed in March to work as her partner, and by July Scofield had finally relinquished *The Dial.*[6] The forty-one-year-old Ellen Thayer was the sister of Lucy Thayer, Vivien's oldest friend. By the time Vivien submitted her story in the late summer of 1925, it was too late for Scofield to do her any favours. Nevertheless Vivien still had hopes of publication: as she explained in a letter to Ezra Pound, in which Vivien adopted (as did Tom) Ezra's own idiosyncratic spelling.

After revealing to Pound that she had written nearly the whole of the last *Criterion* under different names all beginning with F.M., Vivien related how she was unfortunately misled into telling Scofield's cousin Lucy about her writing. Lucy Thayer had at first professed great admiration for Vivien's stories:

> She wrote to her sister Ellen . . . who Sco has left the Dial to, and her sister Ellen expressed much joy and sed my stories made her laugh & laugh & split her sides etc. etc. so I got ambitious and sent a long story to the Dial (O hell—blood why did I), thinking that Ellen Thayer was a just woman and knew her sister to be mad and bad and insane and shocking and murderous.
>
> Ellen Thayer *immediately* returned my story which is damn good *by means of a ghastly female* called Marriannnne Mooooore (or sum such name) a POETESS (Christ!) . . . Spouse had written letter concerning story to Ellen Thayer & at the same time enclosed my doctor's diagnosis of present disease, to explain why her sister is dangerous to me, but as the reply (curt and rude) came via Marianne Mooore, he rote and cursed her out. He cursed Ellen and Marrrriannnne and Lucy, and so ends the Dial for us.

Sending Vivien's doctor's diagnosis of her condition was not a move guaranteed to encourage publication, but this was not the reason for her rejection by *The Dial*'s new co-editor. Vivien and Lucy had quarrelled over an incident in which, according to Vivien, Lucy made unwelcome lesbian advances to her:

> Damn Sco's cousin. She has done me in . . . She came to my doctor's and told me her Pa was dead at larst and as she had already told me she ment to kill him it upsett me. Then she nelt down beside me and asked me if I loved her, & made love. I could not get anyone to help me & so nearly went mad. Helpless. Not dressed. Alone.[7]

Lucy, who shared with Vivien a history of "nerves," was unbalanced and, like Scofield, now under analysis with Sigmund Freud in Vienna, and indeed, like Vivien, would end her days as a psychiatric patient. The intensity of her relationship with Vivien is hinted at in the character of the confidante "Felise" in Vivien's fictional sketches, several of which seem to have been based on actual incidents in the lives of the two women. Lucy had returned to England after her mother's death from cancer, and she would have been in an emotional state when she arrived unexpectedly at Vivien's doctor's surgery to announce that her father also had died; Vivien, having listened to Lucy's past threats to kill her father, burst into tears which prompted Lucy's overtures.

Vivien may have misinterpreted Lucy's kisses, but Tom acted promptly to protect her. He "removed" Lucy, wrote Vivien: "He sent her a chit to say she should never see me again. She then left England, to poison France"—not, however, before taking her revenge: Ellen would never in future publish Vivien.

Vivien's rejection by *The Dial* was a devastating blow. All doors seemed closed to her. Her letter to Pound, written in late 1925, in which she said she was starving herself because she was "anxious to die," was a cry for help from a woman *in extremis*. "Am ill *(still* ill) not ill again (always ill)," she wrote. In September Vivien went down with shingles, her pain so acute—"all stuck up with bandages, ointments and loathsomeness"—that her parents looked after her.[8] To Pound she recalled her weakness earlier that year when she had nearly died just after Christmas and had taken to "swoons and trances." ("Am very *hypnotic, always was.* Could be first class MEDIUM.") Vivien told Pound that she enjoyed her trances and "went off" for two or three weeks at a time, and had some strange experiences on another dimension.[9] The drugs Vivien took are probably implicated in these trances, and in such altered states of mind, she said, she stopped eating. Fasting may also have presented its own attractions, making Vivien light-headed and distancing her from an unhappy reality: choosing not to eat offered her a measure of control over at least one aspect of a life which was, in so many ways, controlled by Tom. It is possible, too that fasting may have enhanced her creativity: Vivien found it impossible to moderate her writing, having never been trained in regular habits of work, Eliot told Leonard Woolf;[10] when she had an idea she wanted to work on it constantly.

The female doctor treating Vivien that February was baffled, confessing to Eliot that she had never seen such a case as Vivien's. Although her unlikely diagnosis was "rheumatism and neuralgia," Tom told Mary that on the 20th Vivien was again "practically at death's door" from continuous pain, which stopped her sleeping, and there were moments when he thought she would die simply from exhaustion.[11] His growing sense of entrapment was heightened by the effects of Dr. Marten's treatment which, recorded Virginia in April, "set V. off thinking of her childhood terror of loneliness, & now she cant let him, Tom, out of her sight. There he has sat mewed in her room these 3 months, poor pale creature, or if he has to go out, comes in to find her in a half fainting state." This exaggerated account was at odds with Virginia's other report that Vivien was writing constantly,[12] but it does suggest Vivien's terror of abandonment by Tom. He could only leave her for a few hours in the afternoon, he told Mary in April: Vivien was "in torture" again, so he was sorry to miss Mary at Viola Tree's.[13] Although, in an hysterical mimicry of organic illness, Vivien was able to use her sick body to get what she wanted—Tom's attention and presence—she could not stop his growing determination to break out from the circle of co-dependence, and to escape the "chaos and torment," as he expressed it to Ottoline, of his marriage.[14]

Some part of Tom's anger continued to be expended on Dr. Marten, whom he was threatening to sue in July, only being dissuaded from so doing by the necessity of travelling to Germany. It was in fact not until January 1926 that Marten was finally exposed as a charlatan, after Siegfried Sassoon arranged for an analysis of the liquid with which Ottoline, on Marten's instructions, was injecting herself. The liquid turned out to be nothing but milk.[15] Ottoline, whose organs were being X-rayed at Chirk Castle, North Wales, where she was undergoing a cure, "proved to be full of nothing but stale milk," marvelled Virginia to Lytton Strachey in January. "All her injections for the past five yrs at the hands of Dr. Martin of Freiburg were of nothing but that."[16]

In May 1925 an exasperated Eliot called in an Irish-American, Dr. West, who he remembered had helped Dorothy Pound, and who he hoped would undo the damage done by Marten, although by now both he and Vivien were convinced that "all ordinary medical men are *fools.*" Eliot questioned West about Vivien's trances, and the doctor replied that starvation induced trances in "mediumistics." West seems to have suspected that Vivien was anorexic. Although her skeletal appearance may have been partly due to Marten's fortnightly fruit and water diets, it is significant that

anorexia nervosa was once called "anorexia hysterica" and that eating disorders are a widely observed feature of hysteria, as are the "death-states"
or trances, which Vivien so readily entered, and the piercing pains with
which she, like Freud's Dora, suffered.[17] Perhaps for the first time, apart
from the "Scotch doctor" at Chichester, Vivien had found a doctor who
understood the hysterical roots of her symptoms.

After a thorough examination West told his patient that she was
"starved to death," related Vivien to Pound, and although she had "a
very very strong hart" and "no spine fuss" she had the most terrible and
shocking

"LIVER
I have ever
Seen or herd
Tell of in life or on any
Living or ded female. MUST
Go VICHY in the end."[18]

On 1 June Tom once again consulted the Woolfs on Vivien's health; he
was inclined to particularise the state of Vivien's bowels too closely for her
taste, recorded Virginia: "We both almost laughed; she has a queer rib, a
large liver, & so on."[19] That autumn Vivien dragged herself to West's
consulting rooms three times a week: the doctor was "always yelling"
about one thing or another, and Vivien became sickened by his robust
treatment.

It was during this time that Vivien told Ezra Pound that she was convinced she had experienced a nervous breakdown "owing to various
causes."[20] One of these was undoubtedly the collapse of her career as a
writer: she felt a pariah and, after her exposé, did not dare venture into the
society she had satirised. What had begun in part as a joke—an imitation
of other satirists—had led to her silencing. And yet writing was a necessity
for Vivien. It sprang, she wrote with painful prescience, from some "very
overgrown and hidden inner spirit":

When this begins to spurt, it is intolerable to choke it up, & will
lead to my going mad. It is agony either way, of course, but I

think at first, until one has got the spout of this long disused fountain clear, it is better to let the water burst out when it will & so
force away the accumulation of decayed vegetation, moss, slime &
dead fish which are thick upon & around it.[21]

Vivien disliked Dr. West, although at times she thought he was improving her health. She hated the noisy clinic and his *"very LOW Irish,"*
Californian ways; she was afraid of being bullied into going to the Vichy
clinic, suspecting that West earned a commission on patients who attended
it. But West continued to press her to go. "I say *no,"* wrote Vivien. "Spouse
all of a dither." She became increasingly suspicious and recalcitrant.
"Please relieve a tormented Celt (am ½ Welsh ½ Irish)," she begged
Ezra.

Years later, in November 1934, Vivien recalled how her disgrace at the
hands of Jack Hutchinson over "Fête Galante" had precipitated her fall
into a "fearful abyss." In this crisis Eliot turned to Jack for help:

Tom and Jack had complete control of everything, with Ellen
Kelland, when I lay for more than a year, a helpless unspeakable
wreck of drugs, fear, and semi-paralysis. When no-one even came
to the flat and the whole strange and very horrible affair was kept
in the hands of Tom and Jack.[22]

Tom's response to the crisis of 1925 was also an intense one. It marked a
turning-point in his life with Vivien, in which a cold antipathy increasingly overlaid his feelings of guilt and responsibility for her, and he began
to consider seriously the possibility of separation. His frustration was such
that, despite the coolness between them, he turned once again to his former
mentor and Vivien's old lover, Bertrand Russell, for advice. Russell, who
had in the meantime left Colette and married Dora Black, invited him to
stay at his home at Carn Voel, Porthcurno, Penzance, over Whitsun so that
Tom could explain more fully what was wrong. "Vivien has avoided me
for the last 7 or 8 years, and I suppose still wants to do so," Russell wrote;
"I shouldn't like her to imagine that there is any lack of friendliness on my
side." Russell assured Tom that he could count on him to help in any pos-

sible way.[23] But a visit to Penzance was out of the question. Tom replied despairingly that Vivien's health was a thousand times worse than before:

> Her only alternative would be to live quite alone—if she could. And the fact that living with me has done her so much damage does not help me to come to any decision. I need the help of someone who understands her—I find her still perpetually baffling and deceptive. She seems to me like a child of 6 with an immensely clever and precocious mind. She writes *extremely* well (stories etc.) and has great originality. And I can never escape from the spell of her persuasive (even coercive) gift of argument.
> Well, thank you very much, Bertie—I feel quite desperate.[24]

Tom's agonising over life with Vivien provoked the scorn of Virginia Woolf, who was herself ill after collapsing in a fainting fit at a Charleston party in August: "Poor Tom" was behaving "more like an infuriated hen, or an old maid who has been kissed by the butler, than ever," she confided to Roger Fry.[25] But Tom was less indecisive than he seemed. After another breakdown of his own that year, he had determined to make fundamental changes in his life. First he was no longer prepared to carry on bringing out the *Criterion* from the flat at Clarence Gate Gardens. Although publicly Tom defended Vivien, praising her to Ottoline for fighting "bravely and tenaciously" to recover her health, in reality the struggle had become unendurable to him, an expression of the "horror in the real world," captured by the dramatists Eliot had studied intensely, and with whose tormented and often vengeful protagonists he identified: Sophocles' Oedipus, Aeschylus' Orestes, Dante's Arnaut Daniel, Marlowe's Faustus and Shakespeare's Hamlet.[26]

In a letter of apology to Ottoline in February 1925 for the "silent estrangement" which had divided them after the fiasco with Dr. Marten, he described the horror of his life with Vivien, which was the trigger for the "sort of avocation," the "much more revolutionary style [crossed out] thing" he was experimenting with, and which would become *Sweeney Agonistes,*[27] Eliot's own hysterical narrative, in which he explored the theme of wife murder:[28] "We have been very ill," he wrote (bulletins of the Eliots' health were often collective). He was still confined to the house after six weeks of influenza; it would be several weeks more before he could take up any work; he was unable to read for more than a few minutes and could only write "necessary notes." Some part of his strength had left him "forever." The fact was that he had been very much more ill than he knew: "It was a real breakdown." Vivien, too, had collapsed a fortnight before that: she had simply got out of bed and fallen down with utter exhaustion of body and spirit. Even a few minutes conversation with him, said Tom in a revealing confession, sent her temperature up.[29] When he was not physically ill, imagined ailments such as the "suppressed influenza" Tom claimed to have had from July to November 1924, eroded his vitality.[30] It had got to the point when neither of them could stand it any more, he told Ottoline: "I *had* to make a change."

Eliot was resolved that he must either give up the *Criterion* or get a minimum salary from Lady Rothermere ("£300 a year is little enough, God knows") so that he and Vivien might "save what remains of our health." Playing on Ottoline's sympathy, he pleaded with her as early as February 1925 to help find him a group of backers who would take over the *Criterion* if Lady Rothermere backed out. Would Ottoline's half-brother, the Duke of Portland, allow his name to be put forward? "It is names (preferably titled) which will impress Lady R. not figures." If Lady Rothermere refused Tom a contract and a salary he planned to get a larger group of twenty or twenty-five people to subsidise the paper. Such a scheme would be more sympathetic than Bel Esprit, he argued, because he would be giving his services to a review instead of receiving charity.[31]

Ottoline, having had her fingers burnt over Bel Esprit, may have been less than enthusiastic. In the event her help was not needed. Lady Rothermere "didn't cut up anything but 'smooth,' " as a relieved Tom told Virginia. Suddenly he found himself facing the prospect of running two papers, the "Light" and the "Heavy," or "Criterion Junior" and "Senior," as Virginia described them. One was to be the continuing quarterly for Lady Rothermere and the other a new paper proposed by the publishing firm of Faber & Gwyer, for whom he finally, with enormous relief, left the bank in May 1925. It was the change in Eliot's fortunes for which he had longed. A Tory journalist, Charles Whibley, had introduced him to the publisher Geoffrey Faber, who had gone into partnership with a firm of scientific publishers, Gwyer, in 1923, and two years later launched a new general publishing house. Faber was impressed by Eliot who, remembered F. R. Leavis, had become "the important contemporary critic" with the publication of *Homage to John Dryden,*[32] as well as having proven experience as an editor and a reputation as a poet which would enable him to attract writers of renown;[33] he invited Eliot to join the Board of Directors. Suddenly, with one stroke of Faber's wand, the poet's economic troubles seemed at an end.

Virginia Woolf was critical of this development, which she suspected would adversely affect the Woolfs' Hogarth Press, and irritated at Tom's duplicity. Had he not begged and entreated her to let him have something of hers for his new review, while surreptitiously moving the publication of his poems to his new firm—a development that Virginia only discovered in the pages of the *Times Literary Supplement.* It was "a fact which he dared not confess, but sought to palliate by flattering me," she exploded to her diary on 14 September.[34] It certainly sounded irrational to run two reviews, agreed Tom smoothly, detecting "a note of disapproval" in Virginia's voice, but it was, he argued, less of a task to run two things as twins, with one proper office and full secretarial assistance, and his new firm to deal with the whole business part, than to run Lloyds Bank's "Extracts from the Foreign Press" in the City in the day and the *Criterion* from Clarence Gate Gardens at night.[35] His satisfaction at leaving banking for a more congenial form of business was immense: Lady Rothermere had offered to guarantee four-fifths of his present Lloyds salary if he ran the *Criterion* for another year, and it was soon decided that she and Faber & Gwyer would share the financial responsibility for a single revamped review, to be named the *New Criterion.* Hiding her displeasure, Virginia sent Tom her essay, "On Being Ill," for the *New Criterion.*[36] Even so, all through September she grumbled to her diary about Tom's behaviour, in particular his poaching of authors from the Hogarth Press (he was luring Herbert Read from the Woolfs, who had published his first book). "To-day we are on Tom's track, riddling & reviling him . . . There is the fascination of a breach; I mean, after feeling all this time conscious of something queer about him, it is more satisfactory to have it on the surface. Not that I want a breach: what I want is a revelation. But L. thinks the queer shifty creature will slip away now."[37]

It was hard to maintain the Eliot-Woolf friendship at the old level now that they had become publishing rivals, although Virginia continued to feel sorry for Vivien ("that little nervous self-conscious bundle"),[38] and sent her some earstoppers[39] and an inscribed copy of *The Common Reader,* which "she *will* read," Tom assured its author.[40] Tom was moving on to a new life, but Virginia and Richard Aldington were left to pick up the pieces of Bel Esprit: Tom had asked them to return the rest of the money to the subscribers, which involved Virginia in long letters of explanation to each donor and a rebuke from Leonard for her "vanity" in trying to help the afflicted.[41]

Vivien refused to go to Vichy in August. Instead, at the end of October, Tom sent her "to the country," a euphemism for a sanatorium near Watford, having called in "other (medical) opinions," according to which the country was absolutely necessary. On 5 November he told Ottoline he was leaving England for a short sea voyage the next day. A few days later he arrived jubilantly in the Alpes Maritimes, and stayed at the Savoy Hotel, La Turbie, near Lady Rothermere's villa and Monte Carlo, winter home of Diaghilev's Ballets Russes. The Côte d'Azur was "damned cold" but it could not dampen his delight at his new career. The pay was less than Bruce Richmond, editor of the *Times Literary Supplement,* had said an editor might get, he wrote to Richard Aldington, but there were additional perks from Faber & Gwyer, and now that they were combining with Lady Rothermere to own and manage the review, he had a cast-iron five-year contract. "So I am a Director of Faber & Gwyer and a humble publisher at your service!" Aldington, struggling in his Malthouse cottage, felt more than a flicker of jealousy, especially as the new editor asked him to write a book on Rémy de Gourmont for Faber for an advance of only £25.[42] "When one is a professional whore of letters it is not much fun to whore far under the skeduled [sic] price and be treated as if it were a favour," he complained to Pound.[43]

Although Eliot had seemed to Virginia in the spring of 1925 to be momentarily a little humbler and "more humane" to Vivien,[44] he nevertheless placed Vivien in the sanatorium against her will. On 14 December 1925

Vivien sent a desperate letter from the Stanboroughs, which advertised itself as "A Modern Hydrotherapeutic Health Institution," to Ezra in Rapallo, asking him to intercede on her behalf with her husband, now in Italy:

> Tell T. not to be a fool. He pretends to think I hate him, but its just a lie. . . . Speak to Tom. Ask him, dear Ezra, *make* him rescue me before Xmas. I am well now. At least I *shd* be well with/given one half grain of happiness, peace of mind, assurance, and time and opportunity to read and think. But O the starvation with all these things missing . . . I want a few books, my liberty, & peace. Is that too much? T. *is* unbalanced, and in the toils of . . . one Higgins. Pull him up O Ezra. S.O.S. V. H. Eliot.⁴⁵

In this letter Vivien stressed that she was more sane than Tom, whose actions she blamed on one of their doctors, Higgins. But Ezra's first loyalty lay with Tom, and he did nothing to help Vivien. Instead he kept Tom's secrets, while receiving Vivien's confidences. At some point he replied reassuringly to Vivien, for she sent him a gift, perhaps of money, with a note saying it was for "medical attendance," a "special long distance consultation," which came with her love and thanks.⁴⁶ Tom, meanwhile, was writing to Ezra, his "caro lapino," dear rabbit, from La Turbie, suggesting a meeting: but "don't give my address to *anyone,*" he instructed his compatriot.⁴⁷

Tom's ostensible reason for visiting the South of France was to find peace and quiet in which to begin writing the eight Clark lectures he was to deliver at Trinity College, Cambridge, the following Lent term. Middleton Murry's nomination had resulted in Eliot's being awarded the lectureship after the college's first choice, A. E. Housman, had turned it down in February 1925. Eliot had been delighted at the opportunity to take the seventeenth-century metaphysical poets and contrast them with Dante and his school, even though his stipend for eight lectures would be only £200, a sum unchanged for forty-two years. After a painful operation on his jaw, and the nail-biting *Criterion* negotiations, he needed isolation in which to write the first four lectures before returning to England.⁴⁸

But Tom made better progress than expected. By 8 December he was promising Ezra that "me and my lil old saxaphone" would be with him in Italy the following week. It was so cold in France that they had to break the ice in the horsetrough "to wash mah pants," and as soon as he had his new passport he wanted to come south.[49] After his passport had expired the previous week, Eliot had been forced to make a detour to Nice to get a new one, nearly missing his bus; "had to run my balls off across the Place Massena" to get a seat, he wrote, and sit with a bottle of wine in his lap and a parcel of medicines which he had bought for his chilblains, and for constipation, and some Eno's Fruit Salts, which he always took "on principle."[50]

Finally, Ezra's "Tarbaby," as Eliot signed himself, arrived at the older poet's home at 12, Via Marsala, Rapallo. There was no longer any need to wear the mask of conformity, to preserve the careful dress of the banking hall. "C'est à grands pas et en sueur/Que vous suivrez à peine ma piste,"* he had written in an earlier poem ("Mélange Adultère de Tout"), expressing his sense of multiple identities—as lecturer, teacher, journalist and bank clerk.[51] Now the twisted trail had led to the top of the mountain. Henceforth he would dominate English letters. Relaxing in the winter sunshine, Eliot could dress as he was accustomed to in Italy, in a "theatrical get-up with a little (not very clean) lace falling over his knuckles, in the role of *il decaduto,* the decadent, or dandy-aesthete.[52] Yet there was steel under the actor's costume, as Aldington noted: "Cibber . . . combined extreme caution and superiority with *un extérieur trés pimpant* and perfectly lovely manners . . . Oxbridge held the world's record for the lifted eyebrow, but Cibber raised his at least a semi-tone higher. His cool American wit . . . enabled him to score off even his most hirsute and erudite opponents, and soon made him a dreaded power."[53]

Vivien's demand for her liberty prompted Tom to return reluctantly to England after Christmas. He at once dismissed her complaints as "moonshine." She was physically fitter than he had ever seen her, he told Ezra on 27 December, but otherwise left "much to be desired," and he was not optimistic. He decided to send her to Brighton to a furnished flat with a nurse.[54]

In Tom's absence Vivien had consoled herself in the sanatorium with

* With large steps and much sweat/You will scarcely follow my tracks

Ezra Pound's poems, spending so much time reading them that the staff finally took them away from her.[55] She wrote to ask him to include her favourites—"In Tempore Senectutis," "Camaraderie" and "Vilanelle" [sic]—in any new collection, signing herself "Little Nell," Dickens's innocent but doomed child-heroine.[56] Brooding on her incarceration Vivien read and reread the poems which seemed relevant to her present state, such as "A Villonaud, Ballad of the Gibbet," with its image of the "lusty robbers twain," their tarred corpses swinging in the wind: "Black is the pitch of their wedding dress." Like the robbers, Vivien felt "the strain/Of love that loveth in hell's disdeign," sensing "the teeth thru the lips that press/Gainst our lips for the soul's distress."[57] Black sheets, black wedding dresses, were symbols of death on which she pondered in her writing book, as she contrasted Pound's paean to the contentment of old age ("In Tempore Senectutis") with her own uncertain future with Tom:

> For we are old
> And passion hath died for us a thousand times
>   But we grow never weary.

In Pound's verse the old couple or "twain" are never weary of each other's companionship, despite the flight of passion;[58] but Vivien knew her own case to be very different. She guessed why she was in the Stanboroughs. That autumn she had longed to go to Rapallo, telling Ada Leverson that she was lucky to be going there, for everyone they knew was at Rapallo at the moment.[59] Monte Carlo and Italy were magnets for artists and intellectuals, and Vivien suspected that Tom would be meeting his friends from the Ballets Russes and preferred not to have her company.

Diaghilev was touring Italy on "honeymoon" with his new favourite, Serge Lifar, before bringing his company to London for the new season at the Coliseum from 26 October, and then returning to Monte Carlo in December. Léonide Massine, divorced from Vera Savina in 1924, had returned to his old company as guest choreographer, having made up his quarrel with Diaghilev, who had been keeping a close eye on his former favourite's work for his rival impresario, the homosexual Comte Etienne de Beaumont, in ballets such as *Salade*. At a meeting engineered by the ballet maestro Cecchetti, at his studio in Shaftesbury Avenue in the summer of 1924, Diaghilev asked Massine to choreograph two new ballets for him. Massine accepted, arranging a *rendez-vous* in Monte Carlo at the end of that year, where he met the new stars of the ballet: Nikitina, Markova, Anton Dolin and Lifar, and at once began working on a new ballet, *Zéphire et Flore.*[60]

Tom, therefore, did not tell Vivien the truth about either his travels or his health, fobbing her off with promises of sun and sea-bathing the next year. It was difficult to keep up the fiction that his trip abroad had been entirely convalescent. There was an embarrassing moment when he found himself having to explain to his wife how he had heard "a bit of Antheil"—George Antheil, the "bad boy" American composer who was the toast of Paris and a protégé of Pound's.[61] Eliot pretended to Vivien that he and Antheil had not met, but that Pound had simply played his compositions on the bar-room piano. "Yew dropped a brick," Tom reproached Ezra on 27 December, for telling Vivien that he looked in excellent health: "It'll come out in the wash, but dr. [Dr. Higgins] was trying to impress her that I have been on the verge and was just pulling round with care and treatment." People in Vivien's state were always "inclined to vampire," warned Tom, implying that his wife was a blood-sucker upon his money and energy. "I shall thank God when the next six months is over, if still alive." He fretted that in his absence Vivien had been writing letters, spreading undesirable rumours about him. "If you shd at any time hear such, you'll be ready for them, & will have to say she has had a nervous breakdown." And you might let me know, said Tom: "I'm ready to wipe up after these rumours when necessary."[62]

It was a letter which suggested that Tom and Dr. Higgins were allies: Higgins would arrange for Vivien to enter a sanatorium to suit Tom's convenience, or exaggerate Tom's own mental distress to justify his absence abroad, so long as the doctor's bills were paid; likewise, Tom or Ezra would exaggerate Vivien's instability in order to discredit any stories she was spreading about Tom. Despite the fact that Tom claimed to Ezra, in a postscript, that he had found Vivien "very affectionate on the whole," he made plans to return to the Continent as soon as possible, asking his "dear Rabbit" if Possum could rent his flat.[63] Vivien, meanwhile, put a good face on the situation to "Dearest Ottoline," writing on 23 December that she was now nearly well.[64] In reply Ottoline, who had said she was doing no Christmas shopping that year, sent Vivien some "glorious scent." Vivien's response was light-hearted:

> Oh what a truly *Otto* trick
> Upon a friend to play
> To make her feel as green as grass
> Upon a Christmas Day![65]

Vivien begged Ottoline to come and visit her at Brighton, where she was going after a week at Clarence Gate Gardens, "to get really strong. Get your husband or a nice rich friend or relation to take you to Brighton for a long visit," she pleaded. *"Please do."*[66]

In the intervening months Mary Hutchinson had given up both River House in Hammersmith and Eleanor House in West Wittering, and had moved to 3 Albert Road, Regent's Park, where she commissioned Vanessa Bell and Duncan Grant to decorate her dining-room and study. Mary's status as an arbiter of taste and fashion had risen. *Vogue,* to which she contributed as "Polly Flinders," noted approvingly in 1926 that in the drawing-room at 3 Albert Road, "The book-filled alcoves on either side of the fireplace are surmounted by a lively design of fighting cocks and the purplish grey stippled overmantel is an ideal background for a fine Matisse *[Interior at Nice].*"[67] The panels by Bell and Grant, with a "delicate over-door decoration show a classical feeling befitting the period of the house."[68] Undeniably Mary had triumphed: she remained a leader of society. Invitations to her parties were eagerly sought, while Vivien, frozen out by Bloomsbury, could only write contritely to her old friend on 23 December that she would love to meet again after so long. "To do so," she wrote, "would seem like starting a new life."[69]

Vivien did not forgive Tom for incarcerating her in the Stanboroughs instead of taking her abroad with him. She and Tom had also moved house, leaving north London for Belgravia, where they had at last found the house with the garden they had been seeking, near Sloane Square, at 57 Chester Terrace (now Row), for a rent of only £58 a year. They had initially taken it in May 1925, when Virginia had piously hoped that the Eliots might be able to "start fresh."[70] But Vivien had found the move a shock: Mary's move from Hammersmith to Regent's Park had been a move "towards civilisation," wrote Vivien on 25 March 1926, but hers to Belgravia felt like a plunge into the outer suburbs. Indeed, after their initial move to Chester Terrace in 1925, intending to sub-let Clarence Gate Gardens furnished, Vivien had bolted back to "cower" in the flat when she had shingles, as she had difficulty in finding servants.[71]

They did not return to Chester Terrace until 1926. When Ottoline dined there with the Eliots on 3 March, she noticed that Tom was watching Vivien all the time. The couple seemed more cheerful than normal, and Vivien in particular appeared oddly elated, smoking and eating chocolates. Afterwards Ottoline heard from Bertie Russell that Vivien was threatening to sue her husband for putting her away, although Ottoline remembered indignantly that Vivien had herself told Ottoline earlier how happy she had been in the "home."[72]

There was a reason for Vivien's elation—and for Tom's careful watchfulness. Vivien had fallen in love. The resurgence in her vitality after she returned from Brighton—which at once struck Ottoline—was not only due to Dr. West's "regimen," but to the attention of the fast and thoughtless young men, the opposite of the intellectuals whom she professed to dislike, with whom she began to flirt at night clubs. According to Osbert Sitwell, in 1926 Vivien carried on "ostentatious flirtations," some with "squalid sub-fusc writers"; her aim was to make Tom jealous, to hold his attention now that she was excluded from writing for the *Criterion*.[73] Indeed, from the moment when the *New Criterion* began to be edited from the offices of Faber & Gwyer in Russell Square, Vivien's life lost much of its meaning. In her new house she was far from familiar north London, and the house was "terrible," full of workmen, Vivien told Mary, and Ellen, her maid, was leaving. None of this would have mattered to Vivien if she had still been at the heart of the *Criterion* coterie, but from 1926 she was redundant, in every sense of the word. Her stories were unacceptable, her secretarial skills displaced. The home which had once been their joint workplace, the heart of their literary partnership, had become a desert. With Ellen gone, Vivien was left with only "a mad ex-policeman aged seventy to help," the first reference to William Alfred Janes, the former detective, now handyman, who was to become an omnipresent and sinister figure in her life. The Eliots' old flat, which Vivien had left "as neat as a pin," was occupied by Tom's brother Henry and his new wife, Theresa Garrett Eliot, an artist, on an extended European honeymoon. Every time Vivien visited these cuckoos in her nest, she felt in a rage.[74] Confronted with such emptiness, she emulated her husband and turned outside the marriage for consolation.

Ottoline condemned Vivien's pursuit of frivolity, having previously considered her both intellectual and spiritual.[75] But in her search for sensation Vivien was in tune with the spirit of the age. *On with the Dance,* Charles B. Cochrane's new show with Noël Coward, expressed frenzied city life in "Crescendo," one of the "scenes" choreographed by Massine, who danced Bobo, the Spirit of the Age, to a swift and satirical score based on popular jazz melodies. *On with the Dance* had opened in April 1925, and the programme proclaimed that

> In an age when the romance of machinery is superseding the lilies and languor of Victorianism, Art must of necessity reflect the angular tendencies of the times . . . Man becomes a puppet and Beauty a slave to the new forms of the relentless progress of civilisation . . . Massine as the Spirit of the Age dominates the scene, and his puppets jig to the tune of cocktails and jazz, until, willy nilly, they are swept up to a frenzied climax of impressionistic movement.

The abstract backcloth featured the word "Café," the women wore flapper dresses, and sang the show's popular tune, "Pack Up Your Sins." The ballet was, remembered Massine, "a real period piece which, in its way, epitomised the whole of the early 1920s."[76] Ballet held up a mirror to contemporary life, borrowing from music-hall, jazz and vaudeville in productions such as *Parade.* It was "piquant, amusing, replete with accoutrements of modern living," writes Lynn Garafola, historian of the Ballets Russes. "Lifestyle modernism identified the new consumerist chic of the upper classes."[77] It was a brand of modernism which spoke to Vivien, flapper-slim, stylish, who painted her mouth with red lip-lotion in a perfect cupid's bow, wore a "surplice" as Maurice described her short, bustless, waistless dress, and was determined to dance her way out of unhappiness.

The flat at Burleigh Mansions now served a new purpose, not only as writing-room but a setting for nocturnal adventure for Vivien as well as for Tom. From the Eliots' eyrie behind the Coliseum, which they often used separately, Vivien addressed a poem to the illuminated Coliseum dome whose flickering light she loved to watch at night.

> Oh why, spangled globe must you darken so soon
> And leave me alone with the swift-marching moon?

But there was no need to be alone. Vivien was in the mood for sexual rebellion after the failure of her bid for literary recognition; indeed, extramarital affairs were but another aspect of Bloomsbury's resolve to *épater les bourgeois,* one already practised by Mary Hutchinson, Ottoline, and by Virginia and Vita Sackville-West. The search for novelty was the essence of modernism, and if one rebellion had been crushed Vivien would essay another kind of freedom, looking beyond Tom for personal satisfaction, as Mary had done in taking Clive as her lover.

> But my sparkling glittering swift-turning dome
> You're the first thing I look for when late I come home,
> And if you're still whirling and shining and gay
> Then something's come right at the end of the day.[78]

When the dome darkened, the moon shone over the lovers, high in the sky for it was late indeed when Vivien returned from the nightclub: "O moon dear/We spoon dear," she wrote, "When you guard the night."[79]

Ottoline judged both the Eliots to be self-absorbed. One day in 1926 Tom suddenly kissed her violently on the lips: he, too, was in love with somebody, she deduced. He had seemed detached the previous summer, hiding behind a smokescreen she could not penetrate, secretly meeting Mary Hutchinson to exchange confidences during her last summer at Eleanor.[80] Sometimes he apologised to Ottoline for being too busy to speak to her at the ballet but he had "Diaghilev etc. on my hands."[81] It was an admission of the importance that the Ballets Russes had come to have for him since their return to London. Was Eliot still in love with Massine, who was living close to Burleigh Mansions? No longer constrained by the short lunch hour of which he used to complain at Lloyds, Eliot could now keep the hours of a gentleman publisher; there was time to lunch with Léonide Massine, Serge Diaghilev, Kochno and the others at Gennaro's, and to join them backstage after performances at the Coliseum, before going on to the Savoy Grill.[82] In her unpublished memoir on T. S. Eliot, Mary Hutchinson wrote of Tom's "immense admiration of Massine," and her memories of Eliot at Diaghilev's ballets, often in a box, or walking the corridors of Covent Garden.[83] Significantly, one of Vivien's few surviving poems, "Perque Domos Ditis Vacuas," which translates as "Through the Empty Halls of Dis" (Dis was another name for Pluto, God of the Underworld), implied that in entering the gay world of Diaghilev, Eliot was entering the Underworld, a world of which she no longer wanted any part. Vivien took the title of her poem from a line in Virgil's *Aeneid,* Book VI, which relates Aeneas's voyage to the Underworld, and served as a model for Dante. On his way, Aeneas met the Sibyl of Cumae, with whom Vivien identified; the Sibyl's message to the hero was a stark one: "Facilis discencus Averni:/Noctes atque dies patet atri ianua Ditis . . ." ("Easy is the path that leads down to hell; grim Pluto's gate stands open night and day.") To re-trace one's steps and escape to the upper air is a hard task, says the Sibyl; nevertheless, she agrees to accompany Aeneas to the realms of Pluto. Vivien, who saw herself also as a prophetess, was delivering her own commentary on her husband's lifestyle. Despite Sibyl's—or Sibylla's—warnings, Eliot has entered the jaws of hell.

Vivien's poem expressed her own urgent need to escape from those "halls of Pluto," or corridors of death:

It was after the acrobats
And I left my box
And ran along the corridor
Fast
Because I wanted to get into the air
And in the suffused light of the empty corridor

In the stale air and soft suffused light of the corridor . . .
In the stifling scent of death and suffocation of the corridor
I met my own eyes
In another face.[84]

Perhaps it was after Anton Dolin's acrobatic feats in *Le Train Bleu,*
Cocteau's last ballet for Diaghilev, that Vivien ran from the "suffocating"
corridor. In the final years of the Ballets Russes, 1925–29, the atmosphere
at performances became more overtly "decadent" or homosexual, and Old
Bloomsbury began to withdraw from it. Young dandies such as Harold
Acton, Brian Howard and Cecil Beaton made Diaghilev their hero; the
promenoir at the back of the circle became a pick-up area for homosexuals,
and a newspaper suggested that the "young men in roll-top jumpers who
stroll about at the back of the circle and talk and talk and talk should be
thrown out."[85]

In the summer of 1926, Diaghilev and Lifar moved from the Savoy to
a flat in a house run as "bachelor chambers," at Albemarle Court, 27
Albemarle Street, off Piccadilly. It had, said Osbert Sitwell to his brother,
a "queer" reputation, and it may therefore have been he who recommended the chambers to Diaghilev. Nevertheless, Sacheverell emerged
from his visits there "unscathed."[86] He was collaborating on a new ballet,
The Triumph of Neptune, performed at the end of 1926; a few months later,
Serge Lifar appeared in his Neptune costume at the "Sailor party," organised by Howard and Edward Gathorne-Hardy in 1927 at the swimming-
baths in Buckingham Palace Road, attended by many Bright Young
Things, to celebrate the revival of *Les Matelots,* in which Massine danced
the French sailor for the first time.[87]

There was certainly talk in London that Eliot enjoyed the company of
sailors. On 22 January 1926 Vivien wrote to Mary, denying the rumour that
Tom had a studio in Marseilles. It was "false," she said, although it was
true that he was lecturing in Cambridge, and that he was giving a tea-party
on 31 January in honour of a gentleman from France, one connected with
the *Nouvelle Revue Française*—"and *very* handsome, so Tom says." She
wondered if Mary and Jack could come to tea.[88] In March Vivien wrote
an apologetic letter to Ottoline for not being able to come to stay at
Garsington, because Tom had "another marvellous Frenchman" coming

over that weekend.[89] This was the writer Henri Massis, editor of the *Revue,* who was lecturing in London, explained Tom to Ottoline.[90]

It was not love she was looking for, only oblivion, Vivien had written in "Night Club" *(Criterion,* April 1925), basing her story on the experiences outside marriage which "Sibylla" had sought as early as 1919, when she went off dancing with three airmen. To dance was to forget, to annihilate memory. In her reflection in the eyes of her young escorts Vivien had seen admiration instead of dislike, desire instead of rejection.

> "Love," said Sibylla at the night club—"You don't know what you are talking about. And I'm sure I don't know anyhow," she added carelessly, leaning her elbows on the table, and her chin on her hands. She stared about her.
>
> "But look here," her companion began to reply, in a tone full of emotion. His young face was beaded with perspiration . . .
>
> "Love," she said, "why there isn't such a thing nowadays that I know of. It's out of date. Nobody wants *love."* She flicked a crumb off the table. "Nobody gets it either for that matter. Don't you worry about love, my poor fellow, as you'll soon be in the soup or the cart or whatever it is you people like to be in at the moment."

Vivien's naïve and obtuse admirer is mystified, and protests.

> "Honestly," she continued. "You take it from me, no-one wants your love. I don't know what they do want, I'm sure and I don't care either—your money probably, or your brains, not that you've got any. But love, O hell . . ."
>
> She turned slightly round, and leaning now her head on one hand looked full into her admirer's face with brilliantly clear grey eyes holding an expression of the most virginal primeval innocence . . . that he or anyone in that large, hot and crowded room had ever seen. Her cynical, careless and unending chatter com-

bined with that gaze of blank purity finished him; and his mystification and agony of mind reached a climax.

"Look here, Sibylla," he said . . . "I don't pretend to understand
you God knows—"

"I don't know of anyone who does, as far as that goes," said
Sibylla. "Not that I care. Who wants to be understood? Not me
for one. I hate people who are always poking round understanding you. It bores me to tears to be understood. Besides there's
nothing to understand that I know of. Can't we dance this?"

"Oh Lord yes, come and dance." They walked out onto the
floor, and started to dance.

"You know you dance better than anyone in this infernal
room, you dance gloriously, you extraordinary little thing."

"Shut up now, don't talk. Surely you know I can't dance and
talk. No-one can dance and talk. What a horrible idea to talk
while you are dancing. Not another word for God's sake or I'll
kill you."[91]

In Vivien's sketch an elderly acquaintance and his wife discover
"Sibylla" with her admirer at the night club and, shocked at her behaviour,
remonstrate with her. "I am quite sure *you* don't want to leave yet," says
the "elderly being," "but all the same my dear girl, I must in honour bound
as an old friend say that I think, in fact *I have an absolute conviction,* in fact
I KNOW, that you would be a great deal better off in bed than staying on
in this pestiferous atmosphere."

> Sibylla stood up suddenly. She hardly dared to look at the devas-
> tation in her partner's face.
>
> "Don't fuss for the love of Mike," she muttered hastily.

Telling her escort on no account to telephone her, but to wait until she
rings him ("It isn't that I don't like you—"), Vivien allows herself to be
driven home. Secure in her flat, she muffles the telephone bell with a
woollen scarf, fills her hot water bottle, and turns on the reading lamp before climbing into her solitary bed.[92]

Despite the cynicism "Sibylla" affects, in reality she was hungry for love, and it is doubtful whether all Vivien's encounters ended so chastely. In a song she wrote, "Song in the Night," she pleads:

> Ah dream don't leave me
> Dream, don't fade away
> Dream, dream don't desert me
> To endure the day.

She cannot bear to exchange the "music, warmth, light of the night" for the "pain unendurable" of the day she must face.

> Need I wake ever?
> Ah let me dream, on
> Wings, flying ever
> Ah—fading—ah—gone.[93]

In her imagination Vivien remained Stravinsky's Firebird, symbol of good, fluttering her wings in her vain bid to escape the restraining arms of Ivan Tsarevich. "Did you ever see L'Oiseau de Feu?" she asked Pearl Fassett. "Do you remember in the first act, after the bird is captured, it tries to fly, over and over again, wings beating . . . Oh I am so sick, so physically sick—I could weep and fill the world with tears."[94] Vivien longed to rediscover the affection her father had given her during a childhood when she felt she was his "Princess," and in a nostalgic sketch imagined herself holding the hand of George Bernard Shaw as she recalled how once she lived in a "house of rosy glass through which one watched the envious world go by & how the glass house is broken and one wants to get back, inside, safe & beautiful & secure."[95]

But there was no way back inside the glass house. Instead, Vivien's search for lost love grew more dissipated. "You must be most frightfully tired," remarks her alter ego, Felise, severely: "I feel ninety in the shade," replies Sibylla. She guessed people were talking about her. On 13 March 1926 Ottoline dined with Bertrand Russell and his new wife Dora, and that evening the Eliots' "troubles" were the main topic of conversation; the Henry Eliots were also present and Theresa blamed Vivien for her possessiveness.[96] Vivien was vampire, Tom martyr, in this version of events, in which Henry, in his letters home to his mother, compared Tom to Job;[97] Vivien's "vampiring" drained "poor Tom" of his vitality, they all agreed, although Henry was pleased to see that his brother was taking a firmer line with Vivien. When she had objected to Tom playing their phonograph, he had insisted on carrying on.[98] Even so, Eliot still did not confide in his brother on the subject of Vivien, complained Henry to Charlotte on 15 March, although Henry suspected that it would be a "great mental relief" to him to do so.[99]

As Henry and Theresa left for Cambridge to listen to Tom lecture at Trinity, where he had given his first Clark lecture on 26 January, stories of Vivien's flirtations were circulating among the gossips of bohemian London. According to Osbert Sitwell, it was said that Vivien had now taken a lover. In her notebook she recorded a conversation in which "Sibylla" rings to tell the man in question that their secret is out:

"Hullo," said Sibylla. "Can you speak now or cant you?"

"Ye-es," said Mike . . . "Have you been to see Mrs.——?"

"Yes I have, and she was *all over me* . . . My dear—she *knew*—"

"She—she *knew*?"

"Yes. *She knew.*"

"But how could she possibly—have heard, have found out?"

"Ho, because she's a woman. She hadn't *heard,* you idiot. She just *knew*. Intuition."

"And what do you think she wants *now?*"

"If you please, she asked when André was going to Cambridge—you know André is going to Cambridge to lecture?"[100]

However, Vivien was not as light-hearted about her behaviour as she pretended. Nor, despite not having seen him for seven years, had she forgotten Bertrand Russell. In her notebook she carried on a dialogue with her conscience, personified by Bertie, the only man she felt had loved and understood her; although she claimed to bear no malice, and to reject any idea of revenge, it was in part Russell she blamed for her present predicament. In Vivien's sketch she pictures him paying an unexpected call just after she has given a party. "B.R. enters."

"I am afraid it is rather late to be paying a call," he said mincingly and dryly, "but I saw your light on as I was passing."

"Bertie, come in," said Sibylla, who hated to hear explanations as much as she hated to give them. "Fancy *him* turning up," she thought to herself. There had been a time when she had seen much of this aristocratic heretic, but he had revolutionized his way of life and for the past few years she had seen him scarcely at all. Missing him, she yet wasted no time on regrets—"It's no use having regrets; there simply *isn't time,"* she often said to Felise. It was the same with bearing malice, there *isn't time* for bearing malice in this world.[101]

Felise then arrives with Vivien's "young man of the moment," whom she has discovered on the doorstep.

"Well, how did you get on with your body-snatchers?" the young man asked. "You've had a sort of funeral party or something, haven't you?"

"It didn't seem funereal to me," said Sibylla coldly . . .

"Sibylla has always had a profound respect for body-snatchers," said the philosopher dryly.

"Perhaps that's why they come to her parties," said Felise.

"They are like white maggots," said the mathematician. "They feed like coffin-worms—they feed in the brains of artists."

"But I am not an artist," cried Sibylla.

This, despite her protestations, was not what Vivien believed; above all she longed to be an artist, to be the equal of Tom, of Ezra, of Virginia, at the very least of Mary. Into the mouth of another guest Vivien puts the words she believed described herself: "You have personality—you have vision—you have above all a distinctive point of view." You Sibylla, are "essentially an artist." "Besides, you're *Sybil,"* cried Felise ardently. "Isn't that enough. The old Sybil!" "You've said it, by God," exclaimed the young man, claiming that Sibylla could be in Parliament. While Felise and the other guests laugh, Vivien turns to Bertie. They share a different understanding:

"They're like barnacles on an old hulk."

"Or clinging to a piece of wreckage."

"Yes, they don't even know there's been a wreck," said Sibylla. And she added to herself, with her eyes fixed directly on the philosophical mathematician. "You are one of the people who have caused the wreck."

Vivien blamed Bertie in part for the post-war "waste land" of modern life ("It takes an aristocrat to overthrow tradition") but she was also referring to the detritus of their affair: "To be a nowadays person means you must not have any nasty little tentacles reaching back to behind the war," she wrote sadly. "You may have had such tentacles, but the war must have chopped them off." Try as she might to be a "nowadays person," Vivien was not a compulsive hedonist like Nancy Cunard; she remained under Bertie's influence and judged herself by his intellectual standards. She knew he would have condemned the "mountebanks" or coffin-worms of her sketch, who fed on the brains of artists; the coffin was a persistent image for her now, death the "wages of sin." In her sketch "Lonely Soldier," Vivien returned to the black-draped coffin, the "long box roughly wrapped with black cloth and corded," which she had watched being carried into the Paddington Street mortuary that morning.

The Eliots' life together continued to influence Tom's art, as did the interrelationship between his work and hers: "Sibylla" and "Felise" in Vivien's "Lonely Soldier" are as superstitious as Doris and Dusty in Eliot's *Sweeney Agonistes*. They cut the cards and tell each other's fortunes.

"Draw a card," said Felise, spreading out the other pack on her lap.

Sibylla drew one.

"Nine of diamonds," said Felise, "you're in luck."

"Let me see what does that mean?"

"Good luck, prosperity or business success," Felise replied promptly.

"Fancy, and I saw the new moon too."[102]

This card-playing dialogue of Vivien's is echoed in Tom's "Fragment of an Agon" (later incorporated into *Sweeney Agonistes*), first published in the

New Criterion in January 1927: "You've got to *think* when you read the cards,/It's not a thing anyone can do," Doris tells Dusty, in Eliot's words, which could also be Vivien's to Pearl Fassett or Lucy Thayer. Doris spreads out the cards, like Felise. "Here's the two of spades," Doris says. "The *two of spades!*" exclaims Dusty. "THAT'S THE COFFIN!! Oh good heavens what'll I do?" A page or two further on Doris begs Sweeney not to talk of murder, because she cut the cards before he came: "I drew the COFFIN very last card./I don't care for such conversation/A woman runs a terrible risk." Sweeney replies that he knew a man once who did a girl in. "Any man might do a girl in/Any man has to, needs to, wants to/Once in a life-time, do a girl in."[103]

There is a poignancy in Vivien's self-reproach, for she knew that she too was running "a terrible risk" in the lifestyle she was adopting. But she was in flight from *ennui,* from that "panic fear of boredom" which often assailed her:

> To be bored was perhaps the only fear that Sibylla ever really knew. In general she feared and detested a tête-à-tête. She would do anything to avoid it. She was more at ease with several people, feeling that the burden of their minds pressed on her less.

Vivien confesses that she has become adept at inventing little tricks and games by which to turn the conversation away from herself and back upon others. She is a performer, "constantly engaged in acting violent parts, or simulating various definite characteristics," inwardly rebelling against picking up cues offered by other performers, and prepared to "take the most fantastic courses to preserve herself from being thrust into such a position."[104] It is a revealing comment on Vivien's propensity to threaten people with knives, threats which her victims were never sure were entirely in jest. But role-playing was not enough to fill up the emptiness inside her; nor was alcohol. It is Felise who is pictured with a bottle of whisky and a siphon of soda beside her; "her friends had warned her so often against drinking in private (!) that she took every opportunity to drink in public," writes Vivien. Felise shares her whisky with "Horace" (Maurice), the "lonely soldier" of the title of her sketch, as they play "pseudo-bridge" together in Felise's "pseudo-studio," before putting on the gramophone and having "a little rously-tously," in Horace's words.[105] In these sketches Vivien never drinks, although she dances, goes to parties in Felise's studio, and plays bridge with the brother she despises. By her own account, cocktails did not "buck her up," although her escort in "Night Club" presses her to have one. "No thanks, I don't need bucking, and I can't drink," she replies. "I wish to God I could . . . I can't even smoke. Can't drink and can't smoke. What a horrible woman. Oh I am an awful woman—"[106] Vivien's prescription drugs were often alcohol-based, and therefore she could not drink socially, as Maurice recalled.

According to a signed statement made on 28 March 1970 by Theresa Eliot—to whom Vivien took an instant liking—during the Henry Eliots' stay to England in 1926, Vivien asked them to visit her doctor in order to discuss her health; he would tell them something that she could not tell them herself. The doctor informed Henry and Theresa that Vivien took drugs, and had started at the age of sixteen under doctor's orders. Charlotte Eliot Smith, Tom's sister, had already realised the "true" situation on an earlier visit to London with their mother in 1924; at that time Vivien, wary of her perceptive sister-in-law, had kept her distance, although she described one awkward afternoon visit to her in-laws: there was a bright fire burning in the sitting-room and "Charlotte and the old lady" were reading, making conversation, and obviously waiting for something to happen. At the same time there was an atmosphere of strain: "the repressed emotions of impending departure [were] in the air":

"Why, isn't this just lovely to see you again," exclaimed Charlotte, rising deliberately and extending her arms to Sibylla, who murmured vaguely, allowing herself to be kissed on both cheeks.

"Why Sibylla," the old lady said, "I did hope I'd see you again but I thought it would not be good for you to come to London to see me." She also embraced Sibylla, who submitted to her with a better grace than to Charlotte, and even lingered a little to allow the old lady to pat her shoulders and stroke her cheek, rather like some cool graceful cat which allows one to caress it for a moment before it bounds away.[107]

But Charlotte Smith was not deceived; she had communicated her suspicions to Henry, so Vivien's habit did not come altogether as a surprise to him in 1926.[108]

Apart from bromides and "Prince Chloral," did Vivien also experiment with cocaine? There is no doubt that narcotics were easily available in the set in which she mixed. Dope was a theme of Noël Coward's 1925 play *The Vortex*. In an article headed "The Cocaine Curse—Evil Habit Spread by Night Clubs" the *Evening News* reported that the drug habit was prevalent among "young women especially of the leisured class that regards itself as Bohemian." "Forty years later, when she was dining with pop stars in Cheyne Walk, Lady Diana Cooper announced, with a perceptible degree of ennui, that in her day, post-prandial cocaine was served in salt cellars," writes Philip Hoare.[109] Tom Eliot was certainly aware of the drug and its effects, as is evident from a note in his handwriting in Vivien's writing book. He poses a provocative question: "Ah yes, Fresca, but would you have the courage to stick a hypodermic cocaine needle into yourself— would you take the risk *once*—as [illegible] did every day?" If, as suggested, Fresca in the original version of *The Waste Land* was inspired by Nancy Cunard, a member of the "Corrupt Coterie" who knew both Tom and Vivien, this may have been a rhetorical reference to her lifestyle. But it begs other questions, for there are elements of Vivien, too, in Eliot's hostile portrait of "Fresca." Did he encourage Vivien in her addiction, and did he experiment with cocaine himself? It is unlikely that Vivien used narcotics, but it is not impossible: her hyperactivity and insomnia were longstanding, but the sexually stimulating and disinhibitory qualities of cocaine may have been a factor in the events which were to follow. What *is* certain, however, is Vivien's disgust at her drug dependence, and her selfknowledge: the theme of self-destruction is a continuing one in her writing: "The things Sibylla had *got* to do!" she writes in an undated scrap of dialogue. "They often included self-destruction." No one could stop her. "I *must*," she would say, "I am sorry, awfully sorry, but I've *got* to do it."[110]

For the first few weeks of his 1926 visit to England, Henry Eliot seems not to have sensed the bombshell which was about to fall, although he soon began to edit the version of events he sent to his mother Charlotte, whose long religious poem, "Savonarola," Eliot was dutifully publishing. Vivien came up to Cambridge on 9 March to hear the last of Tom's lectures, at which Theresa sketched Tom speaking on the nineteenth-century poets and comparing Donne to Laforgue and Corbière. Vivien looked, reported Henry, "well and cheerful," as did Tom.[111]

On another occasion, over tea at Garsington, where Henry was amazed by the insouciance of Oxonians such as Robert Gathorne-Hardy, who had a "fine shock of brown Byronic hair," Shelley-like features, and a monocle, he listened while Ottoline praised Eliot as the greatest poet of the period, but berated Vivien for being "hysterical over her health" and making Tom cancel engagements at the last minute. Ottoline's opinion was that Vivien was jealous of Tom's many friendships and recognition and was "altogether too touchy," recorded Henry. Tom nevertheless assured his brother that Vivien was now perfectly well, apart from occasional querulous moods, and said that her friendship with Theresa had had a "tonic effect" on her.[112] On their last day together in London, Henry and Theresa and Tom and Vivien went out to dinner at a hotel in Kensington and apparently had a very jolly time. The two couples danced together, and an exhilarated Vivien was in "fine humour and very nice."[113] Henry and Theresa then invited Tom and Vivien to join them in Paris and Rome on the next leg of their five-month honeymoon.

By 13 March Ottoline had learnt the identity of Vivien's supposed lover. She noted in her journal that Vivien was in love with a Mr. Haden Guest, or was using his "ardent attentions" to provoke Tom. Haden Guest was probably one of the young officers Ottoline had entertained at Garsington after the war, as the name of 2nd Lieutenant H. Guest MC, of the Queen's Own Royal West Kents, appears in her visiting book for July 1918.[114] The relationship between Vivien and Haden Guest no doubt ripened during the period of Tom's absence in Cambridge from 26 January 1926, for there is no reason to suppose that Vivien stayed long in Brighton, if indeed she ever consented to convalesce there. On the night of 13 April, however, Vivien and Tom joined Henry and Theresa on the 10:30 p.m. night express from Paris to Rome, Henry assuring his mother that the two weeks he was about to spend with his brother and Vivien in Rome would make it a regular picnic, since he would have extra time with Tom, and Vivien adored Theresa.[115] They expected to meet up with Maurice, who was also in Rome, a city well known to Charles and Rose Haigh-Wood, who often wintered there, but which Tom and Vivien had never visited.

Tom may have felt it was necessary to remove Vivien from London, hoping that a trip abroad would distract her from her admirer. At first his tactics seemed to work. In Rome, the fivesome stayed at the Pensione Fray, near the Borghese Gardens, after an expensive night at the Albergo Boston, chosen by Maurice for them because it was near the Victoria, where the Haigh-Wood parents had stayed. The *pensione* was good value at only eighty lire a day for a couple, including three meals, and the party apparently met up for merry lunches and dinners, attending a *thé dansant* in between sightseeing. They visited the English tennis club, where Suzanne Lenglen was playing, and bumped into Mary Hutchinson's brother, Jim Barnes.[116] It was during this visit to Rome that Theresa was astonished to see her brother-in-law fall on his knees before Michelangelo's *Pietà,* the first sign of his imminent conversion.[117] On 4 May Henry heard the news of the General Strike in England, and wrote that he was glad to be in Rome, although he was forced to tell Charlotte Eliot, who was missing her elder son and had been telegraphing impatiently to demand his return, that he had had to modify his plans. The holiday with Tom and Vivien had left them "behind schedule," he wrote discreetly; he and Theresa were unavoidably detained and would be two weeks late arriving in Cambridge, Mass.[118]

However, under the amicable surface, the joint holiday was not all it seemed. At some point in April, probably before Henry and Theresa moved north to Florence, Vivien decided to leave Tom—either for Haden Guest or a new lover. Richard Aldington fictionalised the episode in *Stepping Heavenward:* after the months in which

> many a time poor Adèle gazed into the mirror, clutching her hair distractedly, and whispering: "I'm going mad, I'm going mad, I'm going mad" . . . La Princesse Adèle ran away with a young man and plunged into a life of hectic dissipation in Berlin. As the sole reward for years of misery she begged Cibber to divorce her.[119]

Almost at once Vivien regretted her decision. From Rome she sent Ottoline an express letter on 16 April 1926, saying that she was "in great trouble," and did not know what to do. How she wished she could see Ottoline.[121] Vivien was then thirty-eight, and perhaps her young lover proved to be fickle. In "Mrs. Pilkington" Vivien had imagined a scene in which an older woman, a writer, is deserted by a younger man:

> A young man entered.
>
> "Hugh," cried Marion, "oh Hugh, I am so glad to see you. What are your plans for to-day? Can you take me to see the sights? It's poor fun going about without a man."
>
> "I'm very busy to-day," said Hugh dully, after a moment's hesitation . . . [He] looked at the writing-pad: "Are you writing now?" he asked, determined to stand his ground.
>
> "Writing? On a day like this? Good heavens, no; it would be a sin to stay in and write. Look at the sunshine."
>
> "I am going away," said Hugh, after a terrible silence.
>
> "Away?" she said, standing quite still, her voice dropping to its normal pitch.
>
> "Yes."
>
> "For a long time?"
>
> "Probably."
>
> "When did you decide?"
>
> He did not answer. He picked up his hat from the table where it had lain by the Russian novel and *The Mast*.
>
> "Goodbye," he said.[121]

In her distress Vivien also turned to the Sitwells. On the first or second day of the General Strike, wrote Osbert, he and Edith, in her flat in Moscow Road, Bayswater, both received

> long and incoherent letters from Vivienne, couched in almost identical terms. She wrote from Rome, where she had gone to stay, and declared that we should have inevitably have heard of the scandal to which she was referring, and in which she was involved. We should be aware, therefore, that if she returned to

Tom, it would inevitably bring disgrace upon him, of which he would never be able to rid himself. She appealed to us, in consequence, as old friends of his, to tell her what to do. Unless, she proceeded, she heard from us by cable or letter, advising her to go back to him, she would continue to remain abroad. We were on no account to let him find out that she had written to us.[122]

The Sitwells did nothing. Assuming that Tom—"the chief person to be considered"—might very probably not want her to go back to him, they decided not to answer Vivien's letters, especially as they had heard no rumours. In any event, wrote Osbert, owing to the General Strike, no letter or telegram from them could reach her. And, as far as he knew, as soon as it was possible to travel Vivien returned on her own initiative.[123] In fact Tom decided to hush the scandal up: he consigned Vivien to a sanatorium at Malmaison, outside Paris, and returned to England alone, writing to Ottoline on 24 June 1926 that he had seen the Woolfs that day and told them only that Vivien was in a sanatorium—that was therefore all Ottoline needed to know "officially." Tom would lunch the next day with Leonard, and would tell him more, as in the past he had found Leonard's experience and advice helpful; but, for various reasons (probably Virginia's tendency to gossip), it was not advisable that Virginia should know more than he had told her. He therefore asked Ottoline to keep his confidences secret. A few days later Tom returned to Paris, eventually bringing home a shamefaced and penitent Vivien.[124]

19

Mourning and "Madness"

Vivien's impetuous desertion gave Tom the opportunity for which it might seem he had been looking: a way out of torment. Certainly many men in his position might have left an adulterous wife at this juncture. Yet despite having a certain moral justification for separating from Vivien in the summer of 1926, Eliot chose to stay in the marriage. Guilt still kept him captive, and perhaps in addition marriage offered him a cloak of respectability he did not wish to lose. His protective instincts towards Vivien apparently came into play, as he turned on the Sitwells for failing to help his wife when she was in need: "Vivienne," wrote Osbert, "told Tom that when, finding herself in an agonising personal quandary she had appealed to us for counsel, neither of us had troubled to reply. As a result he was for some months angry with us, and the coolness made itself evident."[1]

Rather than leave Vivien, Eliot joined her in August 1926 at the Sanatorium de la Malmaison in Rueil, near Paris, for a joint cure: he apparently needed help for his own dependency problems. Aldous Huxley, who lunched with Eliot just before he entered the sanatorium, reported to Mary Hutchinson on 6 August: "Tom . . . looked terribly grey-green, drank no less than five gins with his meal, told me he was going to join Vivien in her Paris nursing home to break himself of his addictions to tobacco and alcohol . . ." Eliot was "eloquent about Parisian lunches with resoundingly titled duchesses," lunches which may have contributed to his need to dry out.[2] But neither Tom nor Vivien enjoyed successful rehabilitation at the hands of the French doctors, and they continued to travel Europe as medical tourists in the fashion of the time. The following summer found them in Switzerland together, subjecting themselves to a new form of treatment: *douche écossaise* (strong gushes of hot, alternating with icy cold water, played on the naked body), which apparently benefited Tom more than Vivien. They stayed at yet another centre offering treatment for nervous disorders, the Grand Hotel, Divonne-les-Bains, twelve miles from Geneva in the Jura mountains.

It was there in June 1927 that Robert Sencourt, who was a fellow patient, glimpsed Vivien's forlorn figure wandering ghost-like along a wooded trail; she was deeply depressed and suffering from extreme insomnia, wrote Sencourt. "Her black hair was dank, her white face blotched—owing, no doubt, to the excess of bromide she had been taking. Her dark dress hung loosely over her frail form; her expression was both vague and acutely sad." Sencourt, who shared Eliot's love of Dante and Donne, became an intimate friend and an influence in Eliot's imminent conversion to the Anglican faith, although not as significant a one as he claimed. Sencourt's own nerves were, he confessed, "like Vivienne's . . . often on a knife-edge," and he claimed to understand "her predicament and Tom's . . . The strain from which my new friends were suffering was that they no longer lived together in deepest unity."[3] Although Sencourt professed sympathy for Vivien, it was Tom whom he found the more congenial, taking the poet away on holiday to France for a fortnight. Alone with Sencourt, so the critic later told Frances Lindley, his editor at Harper & Row, Tom spoke openly of his sexuality and consequent incompatibility with Vivien: "the tragedy apparently resulting from Eliot's homosexuality and his entering into the marriage in the hope that he would become 'normal.' "[4] Immediately after returning from France, Eliot took a final and apparently paradoxical step, which made divorce from Vivien impossible: he formally converted to the Anglican Church on Wednesday, 29 June 1927. In November that year he also became a naturalised English citizen.

A more potent force in Eliot's conversion than Sencourt was fellow American, William Force Stead, Chaplain to Worcester College, Oxford, to whom Eliot was introduced by the printer of the *Criterion,* Richard Cobden-Sanderson, in 1923. Stead became Eliot's confidant and confessor, familiarising him with the sermons of Lancelot Andrewes, the seventeenth-century Bishop of Winchester, whose orderly, precise and yet deeply felt preaching appealed to the poet more than the sermons of Donne, with their dangerous indulgence in "sensibility" and romantic appeal to "personality." For Eliot, Andrewes represented the *via media* of the

English Church under Elizabeth I; he was "the first great preacher of the English Catholic Church."[5] Conversion to Anglicanism was nevertheless a greater step for Eliot than might appear, for, despite having been raised as a Unitarian, he told Stead that he felt that he had been brought up as an atheist; when Stead wrote of Eliot's "return" to the Church, the poet protested in the margin of his confessor's reminiscences: "Return? I was never there before."[6] Indeed, Eliot doubted whether his own baptism, not being in the name of the Trinity, qualified him for entry into the Anglican Church, although the position of his people in Boston Unitarianism was, he said, like that of the Borgias to the papacy. "I never communicated," he told Stead resentfully, although his parents did regularly. "They did not bother about me."[7] Kneeling was not a part of the Unitarian tradition, but it was part of an earlier rite. In the deepest recesses of Eliot's mind lay buried memories of attending Roman Catholic mass in St. Louis with his nurse Annie, whose photograph he kept on his office mantlepiece, and it was towards this dimly remembered ritual that he reached, within the framework of an Anglo-Catholic theology.

Andrewes drew Eliot's attention to the Incarnation, the subject of every Christmas Day sermon the bishop preached before King James I between 1605 and 1624. "It is only when we have saturated ourselves in his prose, following the movement of his thought, that we find the examination of his words terminating in the ecstasy of assent," wrote Eliot. It was an intellectual rather than emotional assent and, although it would be unfair to follow Richard Aldington in asserting that Eliot discovered God as a theorem not a faith, it was Andrewes's emphasis upon sin which spoke to the Puritan in Eliot: "Besides our skin and flesh a soul we have, and it is our better part by far, that also hath need of a Saviour . . . Indeed our chief thought and care would be . . . how to escape the wrath, how to be saved from the destruction to come, whither our sins will certainly bring us. Sin it is will destroy us all."[8] Andrewes's influence upon Eliot is underlined by the "flashing phrases" with which he supplied his disciple: the "cold coming" of "Journey of the Magi," "Christ the tiger" of "Gerontion," and the pious hope that he would not "turn again" of *Ash Wednesday.*[9]

Middleton Murry foretold Eliot's conversion the year before it took place, to the poet's annoyance. "It might conceivably be done, by an act of violence, by joining the Catholic Church," wrote Murry: "To be proved,"

was Eliot's terse comment on Murry's draft text.[10] But Eliot's conversion
had a long history: he had experienced visionary moments earlier in his
life, in particular at Marlow, while composing "Whispers of Immortality"
and again at Périgueux on holiday in August 1919 with Ezra Pound. "This
sense of dispossession by the dead I have known twice, at Marlow and
at Périgueux," he told Stead. Although he did not consider himself a
true Christian, a reading of Charlotte Eliot's "Savonarola," for which Eliot
was writing the introduction in 1926, demonstrates an emphasis on
bloody martyrdom which left its mark on her son. "Priests and prophets,
saints and sages/Martyred in successive ages," the subjects of Charlotte's
didactic and rejected poetry, began to assume a similar dominance in
Eliot's poetry and drama.[11]

Stead remembered the day in 1927 when he and Eliot had been taking tea in London: "When I was leaving he said, after a moment's hesitation: 'By the way, there is something you might do for me.' He paused with
a suggestion of shyness. After a few days he wrote to me saying he would
like to know how he could be 'confirmed into the Church of England.' "[12]
That February Eliot had begged Stead to keep his intentions secret, anticipating the outrage of Bloomsbury. He had written on 7 February that he
did not want any publicity or notoriety: "I *hate* spectacular conversions."[13]
Stead made secrecy a point of honour. For several months Eliot attended
communion, sometimes at Hickleton Church, where he worshipped with
Lord Halifax, to whom Sencourt had introduced him, "in a form which
only an expert could have detected was other than the Roman Catholic
mass, and where the building was exactly arranged with lights, lamps, pictures, images and the redolence of incense so as to have what one could
only call a Catholic atmosphere."[14] At last the moment came when Stead
summoned from Oxford Canon B. Streeter, Fellow of Queen's College,
and Vere Somerset, history tutor and Fellow of Worcester, to act as Eliot's
godfathers at Finstock Church, in the Cotswolds. "It seemed odd to have
such a large though infant Christian at the baptismal font," recalled Stead.
"So, to avoid embarrassment, we locked the front door of the little parish
church."[15] Stead himself baptised Eliot, and the next morning the poet was
confirmed privately at the Palace of Cuddesdon by the Bishop of Oxford.

Vivien had little sympathy for Tom's position; she resented the influence of Anglo-Catholic priests over her husband, rightly construing the

veiled misogyny of their counsel as inimical to her interests. Bloomsbury was as shocked as Tom had anticipated: "If only he had become a Dancing Dervish, an alchemist or an adept in Black Magic, he would have had his followers, and the cult looked upon as interesting—or amusing," wrote Stead. "But for the leaders of the 'Moderns' to become a Christian—that was beyond the pale. It was not amusing." Stead was accused of having "corrupted" Eliot.[16] Virginia Woolf's horrified reaction was typical: she had a "most shameful and distressing" interview with "poor dear Tom Eliot, who may be called dead to us all from this day forward," she confided to Vanessa Bell. "He has become an Anglo-Catholic, believes in God and immortality, and goes to church . . . A corpse would seem to me more credible than he is. I mean, there's something obscene in a living person sitting by the fire and believing in God."[17]

Eliot's conversion has been portrayed as the culmination of a long spiritual journey, whose ending might have come sooner had he not "turned aside" from his mission to marry Vivien. She, like Ezra Pound, is thus viewed as an aberration and interruption, an obstacle to his mystical quest: "Each distracted Eliot from his saint's dream," writes Lyndall Gordon,[18] who believes that Eliot's first "memory of bliss" can be traced to his unpublished poem "Silence," written in 1910.[19] At Harvard Eliot had made extensive notes on the saints and mystics, St. Thomas Aquinas, Dame Julian of Norwich, St. Bernard, and the sixteenth-century Spanish mystics, St. Ignatius, St. Theresa and St. John of the Cross; the latter was the subject of the long poem, tentatively entitled "Descent from the Cross," that Eliot began drafting in Marburg in 1914, in which he envisaged attending a masquerade in his underwear. It was to St. John that Murry now compared Eliot, a parallel the poet angrily rejected: "What St. John means by the 'dark night' and what Mr. Murry means by my 'dark night' are entirely different things."[20] Murry's implication was that Eliot shared the alleged homosexuality of St. John.[21] And, despite Eliot's denials, St. John *did* have a special meaning for him: as the blasphemous verse written in Eliot's handwriting in Vivien's notebook suggests with its reference to Bloomsbury perversions.[22]

In Gordon's hagiographic reading of *The Waste Land,* Pound is the culprit responsible for editing "the saint's dream" out of the poem, and Vivien the prima donna who distracted the "would-be saint" from his

Julian Morrell, Vivien and Mark Gertler at Garsington. On this occasion Vivien and Gertler annoyed Ottoline, who suspected them of gossiping about their hostess.

Vivien in the Eliots' Paddington flat. In the foreground is the Corona typewriter on which she took dictation from Tom and Bertie.

Mary Hutchinson, confidante of both Tom and Vivien, in a portrait by Vanessa Bell, 1915.

Tom and Vivien in Sussex in 1919. They rented cottages in Bosham and Old Fishbourne.

Vivien with Sydney Schiff, the novelist Stephen Hudson, at Eastbourne, 1919.

T. S. Eliot, his mother and favourite sister, Marian, on their visit to England in 1921, which precipitated his breakdown.

Eliot in Lausanne, 1922, where he received treatment from the psychiatrist Dr. Roger Vittoz.

Vivien, Tom, her sister-in-law Ahmé Hoagland Haigh-Wood and Maurice, Italy, 1930.

(*right*) No longer bank clerk but gentleman publisher at Faber & Gwyer; Tom's relief is evident in this photograph taken by his brother, Henry, in 1926.

(*below*) Her writing career in ruins, Vivienne's distress showed itself in anorexia and drug dependence. In the garden at 57 Chester Terrace, SW1, June 1928.

(*right*) September 1932. Vivienne, a wraith-like figure in white, on her last visit with Tom to Virginia Woolf at Monk's House, just before he left for America.

(*below left*) William Leonard Janes (1855–1939), ex-policeman and servant of the Eliots, at Chester Terrace, 1929.

(*below right*) Maurice Haigh-Wood and T. S. Eliot at the races. Both men were trustees of the Haigh-Wood estate.

Léonide Massine, principal dancer of the
Ballets Russes and intimate of Eliot.

Jekyll and Hyde: double-faced portrait of
T. S. Eliot by Patrick Heron, 1947, the year of
Vivienne's death.

T. S. Eliot and Sir Alec Guinness, who played
the psychiatrist, Sir Henry Harcourt-Reilly, in
The Cocktail Party.

Mary Trevelyan, Eliot's "guardian" for twenty
years until his second marriage in 1957.

The last photograph: Vivienne Eliot wearing a suit by Philips et Gaston for her presentation to the Prince of Wales at Londonderry House in October 1934.

search for faith in the years immediately afterwards.[23] Gordon argues that Eliot was circling "on the edge of conversion" in 1914, was already "bold convert, martyr or saint" and, but for his unwise marriage to Vivien, might have made a religious commitment at that point. But such an interpretation ignores Eliot's own powerful ambitions and inclinations: he was still under the influence of Henri Bergson, whose message was to abandon rational thought and plunge into the "flow of immediate experience" in order to arrive at the Absolute.[24] It was an injunction on which the shy intellectual had acted, first in the ecstatic union of souls he experienced with Jean Verdenal, and secondly in his ill-fated attempt to break out of the prison of self through marriage. It was a necessary road for Eliot to take in pursuit of both artistic and personal development, as he unconsciously realised when he chose to marry Vivien, a woman who worshipped him both as a man and as a poet, and was prepared to commit herself totally to furthering his career.

But by 1927 the thirty-nine-year-old poet no longer needed Vivien as a helpmate, as from September 1926 he was comfortably established at Faber & Gwyer. The fervent anguish of *The Waste Land* had given way to the paralysis of "The Hollow Men," as Eliot worked out, through many versions, how to transform the pain of separation and loss of a beloved object, who had crossed into "death's other Kingdom," into something meangingful and holy.[25] "Lost/Violent souls," like the poet himself, have become "the hollow men/The stuffed men," men of straw like a scarecrow or guy, husks empty of feeling, who exist in a dead "cactus land." "Eyes that last I saw in tears" have faded into memory ("There are no eyes here/In this valley of dying stars"), and he can only end with a prayer, "For Thine is the Kingdom."[26] Yet it was a difficult, and by no means inevitable path from the "broken jaw of our lost kingdoms" to belief; this was a point that Eliot made forcibly. His intention was, like his master Dante, to begin a new life. "INCIPIT VITA NUOVA," capitalised by Eliot in his 1929 essay in book form, signifies the importance of that acceptance which, he argued, precedes faith: "This *acceptance* is more important than anything that can be called belief. There is almost a definite moment of acceptance at which the New Life begins."[27]

Nor did Eliot's progress towards conversion appear to the poet himself to have been destined from adolescence. He acknowledged that the personal circumstances of his life were the trigger for that conversion. The primary catalyst was Vivien's affair with Russell, from which, argues Schuchard, Eliot created his own myth not only of double sexual betrayal, but also of psychological retribution and moral regeneration. Undoubtedly Eliot knew of Vivien's adultery, and was deeply hurt by it; it was the background to the tone of bitter disillusionment which runs through "Whispers of Immortality" (1918), in which Eliot wrote in a cancelled passage of the seduction of "wives of men." What angel hath cuckwoled thee?" enquired a curious Pound, after seeing the manuscript, adding his own jottings about "copulationion [sic] in carnal form/—et les anges."[28]

Russell became the greatest of Eliot's "lost illusions," as he acknowledged in a letter to Ottoline in 1933, remembering that he had at first admired Russell so much, until his tutor seduced Vivien: "He has done Evil, without being big enough or conscious enough to Be Evil," wrote Eliot, owning that the "spectacle of Bertie" had made a major contribution to his conversion. Grimly he listed the ways in which Russell had been a bad influence upon Vivien: he had excited her mentally, made her read pacifist books and become "a kind of pacifist"; he had flattered her in order to gain influence over her, although, claimed Eliot, "unfortunately" she found him unattractive.[29] Seven years after his conversion, in 1933, the name of Russell still aroused fury in Eliot, whom he blamed, perhaps more than Russell deserved, for the failure of the marriage; in his first Clark lecture on the poet John Donne, Eliot had praised the "fusion and identification of *souls* in sexual love," as expressed by Donne,[30] and the delights of the flesh captured by Sappho and Catullus, contrasting them bleakly with the horrors of a "happy marriage." Marriage is "one sort of bankruptcy," he told his audience, and if you seek the Absolute in marriage, adultery or debauchery, you are seeking it in the wrong place.[31] In an allusion to Vivien's relationship with Haden Guest, he remarked on Donne's preoccupation with "coffins, the day of judgement, sin, and even, perhaps, with jealous husbands!"[32]

The timing of Eliot's conversion also underlines the importance of Russell's influence. By 1927 Russell had become bitterly anti-Christian, a propagandist for atheism whose prominence infuriated Eliot. He seemed to flaunt his disregard for morals in Eliot's face, marrying his second wife

Dora when she was eight months pregnant. The reissue of *Principia Mathematica* in 1925 had consolidated the future earl's status as a mathematician and philosopher, and when his lecture "Why I Am Not a Christian," addressed to the National Secular Society at Battersea Town Hall, provoked outrage, Eliot was one of the first to attack its author and defend the Christian position: his review of August 1927 condemned Russell's text as a "pathetic document."[33] It was simply a "piece of childish folly," he wrote to Russell: "Why don't you stick to mathematics?" All the arguments Russell advanced had been familiar to him by the age of six, said Eliot, for he had been brought up an atheist, while Russell had evidently been brought up, and remained, an evangelical.[34] Unsurprisingly, when Eliot came to write *Murder in the Cathedral,* Russell was his chosen, diabolic model for First Tempter, the representative of atheism who attempts to turn St. Thomas from his martyrdom.[35]

Even though Eliot had been wounded by Vivien's infidelity, he was himself no solitary saint. The telling juxtaposition of epigraphs to his Clark lectures reveals his own struggle between spirituality and violent sensuality: on the one hand, the dedication to the Virgin, the Madonna who was "the end and aim of my love" ("Madonna, lo fine del mio amore fu già il saluto di questa donna, forse de cui voi intendete"), on the other a line from a music-hall song, "I want someone to treat me rough,/Give me a cabman."[36] Lines from Part II of "Ash Wednesday," his "conversion" poem, lines first published in 1927 as "Salutation," voice a prayer to the "Lady of silences" for release from his private hell: "Terminate torment/Of love unsatisfied/The greater torment/Of love satisfied."[37] He dedicated "Ash Wednesday" "To My Wife," for Vivien alone shared Tom's secrets. The poem is one of regret, even apology, for their joint past, of his need to escape a woman who had become "the devil of the stairs who wears/The deceitful face of hope and despair."

Nor did Eliot construct a simple myth of sexual betrayal by Vivien and Russell, as Schuchard argues; in his heart the poet knew, with a degree of self-loathing, why Vivien had run into Russell's arms. His own failure to consummate the marriage satisfactorily had created a situation in which he had colluded, in which Vivien had become the victim of her lover and her husband in an arrangement which profited both men at the expense of the woman. Sencourt has remarked on Eliot's fascination with *Bubu de Montparnasse,* the story of the pimp and the girl harlot. Why had Eliot continued for thirty-five years to be obsessed with "the miasma of sexual sin," he demanded of John Hayward after the poet's death.[38] The answer lay in Tom and Vivien's own story, for as the years passed Eliot became convinced that his wife was no better than a harlot, a polluting presence from whom he must turn away to be cleansed through faith.[39] At the heart of his hatred lay his own guilt and denial of the role he had consented to play (one as morally "unpleasant" as the adulterous Vivien's) in the three-handed drama of himself, Bertie and Vivien. For if Vivien had been "whore," who had been the pimp?

Eliot's powerful feeling that Vivien, female succuba or demon, deserved violent punishment, found an outlet in *Sweeney Agonistes,* first published in the 1926 *Criterion.* One of the epigraphs the playwright chose, St. John of the Cross's prayer for the soul to be divested "of the love of created beings" in order to achieve divine union, sits uneasily with Eliot's obsession with murder and retribution;[40] but he had long been interested in the "thriller" element in Elizabethan and Jacobean drama. His study of Kyd's *Spanish Tragedy* (forerunner of Shakespeare's *Hamlet)* had influenced the composition of *The Waste Land,* among whose last lines Eliot placed the sub-title of Kyd's play, "Hieronimo is mad againe." Kyd's hero, Hieronimo, has undergone a psychological change: he is mad with grief for his murdered son, and his passion for vengeance, which the audience may have felt was justified, shapes the play.[41] Eliot, too, felt he had undergone a psychological change through his marriage to Vivien. "Murder, help Hieronimo," cries a woman in a 1615 woodcut advertising the *Spanish Tragedy.* "Stop her mouth," is the stark response from the figure of Murder on the handbill, something Eliot longed to do to the wife who berated him for never speaking to her.

Just as Hieronimo's revenge quest was Kyd's central theme, so was it Eliot's in *Sweeney Agonistes.* Sweeney, like Hieronimo, can be viewed as a savage priest *(hieros* means holy or divine) presiding over an ancient fertility ritual, symbolising death and resurrection, a ritual similar to the virgin sacrifice in *The Rite of Spring,* another fertile source of inspiration to Eliot. In *Sweeney Agonistes* the hero also presides over a violent if farcical ritual,

in which he cooks eggs in a chafing dish and serves them to the two prostitutes, Doris and Dusty, who were based on Vivien and Lucy Thayer.
Doris's fate is to be killed and cooked by Sweeney in a "nice little, white little, missionary stew"; Mrs. Porter, the house's Madam, is shot and resurrected.[42]

Murder was an act which seems to have haunted Eliot's nightmares,
born of the fear that one day he might lose control and physically harm, or
even kill, Vivien. An early handwritten draft of *Sweeney Agonistes* shows
the play's gestation in the poet's "Terrors of the Night."[43] As an epigraph in
an early typescript he misquoted lines of Brutus the murderer from *Julius
Caesar:*

> Between the acting of a dreadful thing
> And the first motion, all the interim is
> Like a miasma, or hideous dream.[44]

It was "the *feeling* of a haunted conscience" which dominated the "strange
little piece" for Desmond MacCarthy, when he reviewed a production of
Sweeney by ex-Diaghilev dancer Rupert Doone's Group Theatre at 9
Newport Street in 1934. Eliot seemed to have assented to this interpretation by quoting, in the double epigraph, a passage by Orestes in which he
speaks of the Furies which are pursuing him: "You don't see them, you
don't—but *I* see them: they are hunting me down . . ." "In this case the
Furies of retribution are the police, as well as the lashes of remorse . . ."
wrote MacCarthy.[45] "And you wait for a knock and the turning of a
lock/For you know the hangman's waiting for you," wrote Eliot: "And
perhaps you're alive/And perhaps you're dead/Hoo ha ha/Hoo ha ha/Hoo
KNOCK KNOCK KNOCK."[46]

Later Eliot confessed his night terrors to Mary Trevelyan, when he
would wake, sweating, imagining that he had completed the wished-for
ritual of Vivien's extinction, and was about to meet his punishment. He
dreamt "that he was about to be hung and was standing in a grey holland
overall, with a rope round his neck." Auditory hallucinations also troubled
Eliot, who imagined that he heard voices, male and female, speaking to
him at night: "I sometimes wonder if I am schizophrenic," he told Mary in

1950.[47] Two years later, the "voices" were still keeping him awake, and he was trying to record a phrase or two to show her.

Sweeney Agonistes has a visceral intensity which puts it beyond any dream sequence and demonstrates that, as Eliot wrote of the Elizabethan dramatists, "actual life is always the material."[48] It was the horror of Eliot's life with Vivien which motivated him to write *Sweeney* and, as Vivien and Lucy, alias "Sibylla" and "Felise" or, in Tom's incarnation, Doris and Dusty, entertain their clients, including Canadian officers—Vivien had a weakness for officers—and cut the cards, they turn up the King of Spades; and the King of Spades is the murderer, is Sweeney, say the girls. In an early version of the play Sweeney, the only actor unmasked, sits drinking and arguing with Mrs. Porter. In the Group Theatre production he was dressed as a young clerk. Sullen and silent, Sweeney's mood becomes uglier as he drinks: the two girls become hysterical; he pulls out a gun, it gives a "dull roar"; the girls shriek. Mrs. Porter falls to the floor. She is dead. Or is she? "Life is death, death is life." In the second scene Sweeney addresses Doris, who has drawn the two of spades, the coffin. His speech is half sinister soliloquy, half confession, perhaps a threat to her:[49] "Any man might do a girl in/Any man has to, needs to, wants to/Once in a lifetime, do a girl in./Well he kept her there in a bath . . ." The verse is "popular," with its syncopated beat, its music-hall jollity, but the message is chilling. The black jazz drummers, "SWARTS AS TAMBO, SNOW AS BONES" join in: these fellows all get pinched in the end, avers Swarts. Snow disagrees. "What about them bones on Epsom Heath?" "A woman runs a terrible risk," murmurs Doris.[50]

The woman's refrain is brushed aside. "Let Mr. Sweeney continue his story," says Bones Snow. "This one didn't get pinched in the end," says Sweeney knowingly. He knew a murderer who'd done a girl in and got away with it. "This went on for a couple of months/Nobody came/And nobody went/But he took in the milk and paid the rent." "I'd give him a drink and cheer him up." "Cheer him up?" asks Doris. "Cheer him up?" repeats Dusty incredulously; the atmosphere of menace is compounded by the techniques of Greek and Roman drama: masks, a chorus and, from the music hall, the jazz drumming which heightens the incantatory rhythm of the dialogue as Doris's fear mounts. "He didn't know if he was alive/And the girl was dead/He didn't know if the girl was alive/And he was dead."

Behind Sweeney's threats lies the desperation of non-communication: "I gotta use words when I talk to you/But if you understand or if you don't/That's nothing to me and nothing to you." Eliot's most original piece of theatre is, for this reason, violently authentic in its *exposé* of marital disconnectedness. "Birth, and copulation, and death," says Sweeney. "I'd be bored," replies Doris. "You'd be bored," repeats Sweeney.[51]

Originally, Eliot intended a three-minute ballet to be performed between the two scenes. The drumbeat he planned to accompany it, like the dance itself, was modelled on Diaghilev's ballet and was typical of the 1920s: Lifar danced Icarus to an unaccompanied drum.[52] Massine was also much in Eliot's mind as he began working on *Sweeney,* soon after meeting the dancer on 22 June 1922. Memories of *Le Tricorne,* choreographed by Massine to Manuel de Falla's syncopated music, a ballet in which Massine danced the Miller "like one possessed" in his own version of the Spanish folk dance the *farucca,* was one of the strands which led the poet to try to create something as innovative in drama as that which Diaghilev had created in ballet by marrying music hall to classical dance. "What is needed in art is a simplification of current life into something rich and strange, wrote Eliot."[53] From 1923 onwards, as he struggled to match in his text Massine's ritualistic and impersonal control of popular contemporary forms, he compared with longing the grace and beauty of the Ballets Russes to the sordid daily world he inhabited with Vivien.

Yet another strand from daily life fed into *Sweeney.* Eliot, like a large section of the British public, had followed with fascination the fortunes of Dr. H. H. Crippen (who fell in love with his secretary, Ethel le Neve, poisoned his wife and dissected her body) and he made notes on the case when Crippen was hanged at Pentonville in 1910. Virginia Woolf sat next to Eliot at the Group Theatre's masked performance of *Sweeney Agonistes* in November 1934, and recorded in her diary: "Certainly he conveys an emotion, an atmosphere . . . something peculiar to himself; sordid, emotional intense—a kind of Crippen in a mask."[54] Perhaps the delight in police court horrors was something the Eliots shared, for Maurice recalled that at a fancy-dress party at the Schiffs, Eliot dressed as Crippen, Vivien as Ethel le Neve, disguised as a cabin boy as she was when the pair fled England on a transatlantic liner.[55] It was a disguise Eliot enjoyed: he was still wearing it in 1939, six months after Vivien was committed to Northumberland

House, when he attended Andrian Stephen's fancy-dress party in the costume of Crippen the poisoner.[56]

Vivien's failed romance in Rome in 1926 precipitated a serious depression and she had thoughts of suicide. A snatch of dialogue in her notebook, in which "Sibylla" pleads in vain with her lover not to give her up, hints at her misery:

> Sibylla went into Mike's little narrow bedroom, & shut the door after her.
>
> "Look here, Mike," she said, and made a dash at his dressing gown pocket to extract a handkerchief, but finding none, she looked round and saw it lying on the dressing table. Turning, she seized the handkerchief and blew her nose. "Look here," she said . . . hurriedly and furtively, "Will you ring me up at 3—at 3 o'clock. See? Will you? Because, I must tell you, I do still come over awfully—well awfully depressed—So—all the time."
>
> "Yes I know," said Mike.
>
> "It's my temperature; it's high—."
>
> "Yes," said Mike gloatingly, "I *knew* it was high to-night."
>
> "Damn you," thought Sibylla and she said, "Yes, yes, it's high all the time and it's a great strain to me to have people to dinner. I don't know—I might . . ."[57]

Sexual rebellion had brought Vivien no happiness, for none of her "admirers" could take Tom's place. Like Ibsen's Nora she had attempted to break out of her doll's house and forge a new role for herself; like Nora, she had impetuously left her husband, only to bitterly regret her decision and return, humiliated. To carve out an existence as a "modern" woman was no easy task. A woman might write, like the poet Hilda Doolittle, "I believe in women doing what they like. I believe in the modern woman." Living out the dream of freedom was a different reality; even H. D. was forced to acknowledge that "the modern woman" had no place on the map, and her quest for experience was "a very thin line to toe, a very, very frail wire to do a tight rope act on." In H. D.'s case only therapy with Freud restored her confidence in herself as a gifted woman, and taught her to exist in that borderline country in which old values have been discarded and new ones have yet to be learnt.[58] But for Vivien there was no Freud to heal her, only an estranged husband who imagined he had some skill as an analyst. And in March 1927 a further blow struck Vivien: she lost her most enduring male support—her father.

Charles Haigh-Wood was terminally ill with lung cancer in early 1927 and died on 25 March, aged seventy-two, at the Warrior House Hotel, St. Leonard's, Sussex, surrounded by his family: his wife Rose, sister-in-law Lillia Symes, Vivien, Tom, Maurice and Lucy Thayer, with whom Vivien was now reconciled, were all present. Vivien grieved deeply for her father, and her memories often drew her back to St. Leonard's.[59] Possibly her mourning became pathological in its intensity. Later, in 1932, she and Tom stayed at the Warrior House Hotel, and Vivien returned there once more in the autumn of 1934, the year after Eliot left her. On 15 September 1934 she drove out into the countryside in her Morris Minor with Polly, her Yorkshire terrier, on a blackberrying expedition. Afterwards she recalled how

> enjoying some of the richest of the English landscape . . . I longed that Father could have seen it with me, and I thought a great deal about him, and how he died here, in Sussex, and his dying eyes lingered on the sea & the sunset, sitting up in bed in room no. 9, poor, poor darling Father. I remember how he always begged me to stroke his head, and how I *wish* I had done that for him much more often and more patiently, and how I wish there was still *someone* who needs the touch of my hands, which are the best part of me. But there is only Polly.[60]

The following spring, on 24 March 1935, Vivien returned to her father's grave to plant two shamrock roots.[61] *"Full* of memories, Father & Tom, Tom & Father—those two of my heart," she wrote. *"The sea is so much in it all."*[62]

Bereft of her father, who had understood her as her mother never did, the final severance of the tie with Bertrand Russell hit Vivien hard. At the height of their affair, Russell had given Vivien some of the family jewels, as well as other small articles. "Russell gave Vivie dresses, then Russell family heirlooms," remembered Maurice: "Russell's family asked Vivie for a ring back," and so "Mummy made her give back the jewels."[63] Vivien herself remembered resentfully in her diary for April 1936 that her mother had never offered her "a stick of furniture," but Bertie Russell had given her one or two fenders,

> and of course all his jewellery which I returned but he made me keep one valuable pendant which has been stolen. I wish I could get back the pendant which BR made me keep. It was one large pearl in a dark blue enamel setting and a thick solid gold chain.[64]

In fact the truth was rather different, as Vivien had reluctantly confessed in a letter to Russell in 1926. Perhaps therapeutic sessions with her doctors abroad enabled her to confront her past and triggered the remorse which caused her to reopen correspondence with Russell on 6 December:

> I shall have to ask you to believe me that I became conscious, during the time I was in France, that I had stolen a part of this jewellery from you. Since getting back to England I have not had the courage to come to your house & give it to you, which is what I ought to do. So now I am asking Tom to hand you the packet, & as it is nothing to do with him, I hope you will not speak of it together, it wd be very painful to him. I am not showing this letter to him, or anyone. I shall not ask you to forgive me because you cannot.

Vivien had given one ring with turquoises in it to her maid, Ellen Kelland, she explained. The rest she returned, apart from the pearl pendant, which she may have kept back purposely or which Russell may have allowed her to keep.[65]

Vivien also raised the matter of the shares which Russell had transferred to Eliot during the war, and from which he was still drawing an income which he allowed Vivien to spend. Vivien was urging Tom, now well remunerated at Faber & Gwyer, to return them to Bertie, who had a wife and two young children to support: John Conrad, born in November 1921, and, two years later, Katharine Jane.[66] Russell had been forced to turn to popular journalism in order to fund the purchase of a house in Sydney Street, Chelsea, and was certainly in greater need of the income from the debentures than the Eliots, but, said Vivien, due to them "being in Tom's name, and our not yet having been able to agree about it, I must leave it till he sees it as I do. I shd have to get him to do the transferring." She added a final, sad sentence: "You see I have not had the courage to live alone."[67]

Eventually Eliot gave in to the promptings of Vivien's "entirely morbid conscience," as he described it.[68] On 16 May 1927, he wrote to tell Russell that he would shortly be transferring to him the debentures—£3,500 of Penty & Son Ltd. of Newbury. "There is no reason for you to demur." However, Eliot requested from Russell a letter exempting him from tax on the "gift" in the event of his death within three years, as he did not want his affairs "buggered up" if he should die suddenly.[69] A few weeks later Eliot wrote again to Russell, explaining that Vivien's father had died and she would shortly come into property which yielded income almost equal to that she was surrendering. He himself, he added, was influenced in his decision to return the debentures by the fact that Russell had heirs, and "I have, and shall have, none."[70]

This surprisingly personal remark, reminiscent of Eliot's almost filial relationship to Russell in the past, touched on a source of great pain to both Eliots—their childlessness. Much later, on 29 November 1939, Eliot confessed to his companion John Hayward that he had never loved a woman or enjoyed sexual intercourse with her: "I never lay with a woman I liked, loved, or even felt any strong physical attraction to." He no longer even regretted this lack of experience, he wrote, although for years he continued to "feel acutely the desire for progeny, which was very acute once."[71] Certainly the desire for children was a constant in Vivien and Tom's relationship at the time when Eliot was writing *The Waste Land*: "What you get married for if you don't want to have children?," a line added by Vivien to the manuscript was, according to Maurice, his own response to Rose Haigh-Wood's argument that Vivien should never have children, in case her "moral insanity" was hereditary.[72] The reproach implicit in "not marrying if you do not want to have children" is also that Eliot did not wish to make love to her, and may account for the continuing motif of lost or even murdered children in Eliot's work.[73] Sometimes children laughing in an apple tree, sometimes the "children at the gate/Who will not go away and cannot pray" of "Ash Wednesday," the anguished cry "O my daughter" of "Marina," or the theme of the madness of Hieronimo at the murder of his children, all point to the "acute desire" Eliot and Vivien had for a baby.[74] The emphasis on death and birth on the "cannibal isle" in *Sweeney Agonistes,* or in "Journey of the Magi," which took as its theme the birth of the Christ child, has been interpreted as an allusion to Eliot's spiritual rebirth. But it had its roots, too, in the longing of a childless couple for a baby of their own, which must have grown more powerful over the years and which was highlighted for Vivien by the presence of Russell, nearby in Chelsea, whose own wish for children was at last gratified. "Was Bertie there? Do you see Bertie much now?" she wrote wistfully to Ottoline in January 1928 from the Malmaison sanatorium.[75]

In the years when the Eliots lived at 57 Chester Terrace, Belgravia, Vivien turned for consolation to her pets, her garden and her servants. Her Yorkshire terriers, Peter and Polly Louise, became substitute children. The faded brown photograph album, inscribed "T. S. and V. H. Eliot 1924–1929," into which Vivien pasted her carefully captioned snaps, shows "Aunt Vivienne with Peter," the dog held tight in her arms, or "Uncle Tom" training Polly, although Eliot generally reserved his affections for Georgie the cat, shown on his lap in his study. The album demonstrates the new care with which Vivien began dating and signing the record of her life with Eliot, returning at this time to the original spelling of her name, "Vivienne." Her home became important to her as she withdrew into it, defeated: "Vivienne with household gods," she has titled a photograph of herself beside her well-polished sideboard on which stands gleaming silver, on the wall beside an oil painting of an ancestor.[76] In the morning room a meal is laid on a white linen tablecloth, a bottle of beer prominent on the table: Vivienne's meticulous account books from December 1927 to April 1932, which record how she ran the house on the £6 a week housekeeping money Tom gave her, often struggling to repay him the small sums he grudgingly loaned her when she overspent ("Lent by T.S.E. 1/9d"), contain several entries for beer, for instance: "V.H.E. for 2 b. beer." "Returned to T.S.E. 3s." writes a contrite Vivienne, for her husband did not approve of her regular spending on taxis, cigarettes, bridge debts, "chemises de Vaneck" (her favourite dress designer), grey silk stockings, impulsive purchases of flowers, lilies or violets for Edith Sitwell, or roses for her mother. Nor did the Vogue patterns she bought for dressmaking, plants for the window-boxes, doctors' and chemists' bills, and the continual expenditure on sanitary towels please him.[77] Vivienne tried to make amends, buying Tom orange writing paper and envelopes, sealing wax and blotting paper for his birthday in 1928; but Maurice, with whom Vivienne occasionally lunched, noted that: "Tom never spent money; Vivie lived in the shops, especially Vanecks."[78]

Behind the façade of domesticity, Vivienne and Tom now led separate lives. In July 1928, Theodora Eliot Smith, "Our neice" [sic], who stayed with the Eliots in Chester Terrace,[79] photographed the large bedroom with a writing table used by Tom, and the small bedroom with a narrow bed on which sat Vivienne, alone.[80] Omnipresent in the household was the handyman and ex-policeman W. L. Janes, a mysterious figure who was very close to Tom. Rose Haigh-Wood never liked Janes, remembered Maurice: he reminded her of a lavatory attendant. Later Tom told Mary Trevelyan that Janes had been a "great friend," who used to tell him stories of Disraeli; when Janes was ill in hospital Tom used to visit him and take him champagne. "If I ever write my reminiscences, which I shan't," he said, "Janes would have a great part in them."[81] Tom meanwhile continued to rent the flat at Burleigh Mansions, despite having an office at Faber, and Vivienne continued to arrange for it to be cleaned. The house in Chester Terrace was one of whispers and secrets, for all Vivienne's attempts to keep up appearances. Old friends began to avoid the Eliots. Surreal dinner parties, such as that given by the Eliots in the summer of 1927 to celebrate Vivienne's recovery after her course of treatment at the sanatorium, gave rise to rumour and gossip, as Osbert Sitwell recalled.

Shown into the drawing-room, Osbert found that he was not the first arrival: Geoffrey Faber, James Joyce and his wife Nora were already talking to their host:

> A few minutes later, Vivienne entered in a flustered manner, on her lips a rather twisted smile, which was opposed by the consternation and suspicion in her greenish eyes. Not quite certain what tone was suitable to adopt, I opened by remarking to her with heartiness, "It *is* splendid to see you again, Vivienne."

Looking me straight in the eye, she replied slowly, "I don't know about *splendid:* but it is strange, very *strange."*

Thereupon we went in to dinner. The table seemed set for a gala: for by each plate was set a bouquet or a large buttonhole, of sweet-peas, struggling through a white misty rash of gypsophila. The food was good, and accompanied by excellent hock . . .

As for our hostess, she was in high spirits, but not in a good mood. She showed an inclination to "pick on" Tom across the table, challenging his every statement, and at the same time insinuating that the argumentativeness was his; that he was trying to create a scene. All this he parried with his calm and caution, remaining patient and precise, with on his face an expression of wary good nature . . .

Her name was usually pronounced *Vivien:* but if he were irritated by her, we would notice that he would call her *Vivienne* . . . As dinner went on, things became a little better: and she began to leave him alone, and instead to talk to me about him. He was being very *difficult,* she averred; only one human being seemed now to interest him, an ex-policeman of about seventy years of age, who acted as odd-job man, and was a habitual drunkard . . .

After dinner, Tom was talking to Nora Joyce and Enid Faber in the drawing-room, but looking "as if he were keeping an eye open for a squall." Vivienne, who had been complaining that Tom would never give his guests enough to drink, found another bottle of hock for Osbert and her other guests, and left them at the table. "A door in the further wall of the passage suddenly swung back," wrote Osbert, "and out stepped the figure of an elderly man in a dark suit with white hair and moustache, blinking as if he had suddenly emerged from darkness into a strong light, and—rather singularly inside a house—crowned with a bowler hat."

My attention had been focused on him from the moment he appeared, as it were, out of his trap-door, since I had at once identified this rather tortoise-like individual as the ex-policeman of whom Vivienne had spoken. Silence now fell on the company.

The newcomer stopped in the doorway opposite us for a moment, and made to each of the three of us—Joyce, Faber and me—a sweeping bow with his hat, saying as he did so, "Goo' night, Mr. Eliot!" "Goo' night, Mr. Eliot!" "Goo' night, Mr. Eliot!," and then, while the last syllable was still on his lips, and without giving himself time to discover the failure of his ingenious method of insurance by address in triplicate against the possible charge of inebriation, he turned and went on his way humming to himself. The incident possessed atmosphere, and I was delighted by it, as was Vivienne when we returned to the drawing-room and told her about it. For once Tom refused to see the joke, looking rather as I imagine Dante would have looked had someone ventured to make a stupid pun in his presence.

Soon the moment came for the party to break up. Mrs. Faber rose . . . and observed, "It's been lovely, Vivienne."

Vivienne looked at her mournfully, and replied, "Well, it may have been lovely for you, but it's been dreadful for me."

Mrs. Faber, rather at a loss, rapped out at her, "Nonsense, Vivienne, you know it's been a triumph."

Vivienne repeated in desolate tones, "A triumph . . . Look at Tom's face!"[82]

Even Ottoline, most faithful of hostesses, who had asked Tom and Vivienne to Garsington after they returned from France in 1926, withdrew her invitation after a difficult visit to Vivienne at Chester Terrace. Nevertheless, both Vivienne and Tom depended on Ottoline, competing for her attention as they rehashed the problems of the marriage, both demanding her support for their version of events. Ottoline called regularly on Vivienne: on one occasion, in November 1926, Vivienne felt that "some sort of subconscious hope" that she had not known she still had, went out of her as Ottoline talked. She apologised for being "dull and unpleasant," for she did not want to hear what Ottoline had come to say: that the marriage was dead in all but name.[83] When Ottoline asked the Eliots to Garsington once more, Vivienne's confidence was too low to face the stares of other guests at the manor. Could Ottoline find them two rooms in the village, she asked: "I could then see you as much as you cared to see *me*, and shd not be in the way . . ." Vivienne said she was too "unendingly dull" and although Ottoline might bear with her out of "yr goodness of heart," she could not hope that other people would.[84] Perhaps Vivienne guessed that Tom was complaining, on his separate visits to see Ottoline, that Vivienne was always suspicious of his movements; and the growing feeling in Bloomsbury was that Tom was a martyr to his wife.

One May morning in 1927, when Vivienne, in a state of collapse after her father's death, was abroad, waiting for her husband to join her in the Swiss sanatorium, Eliot told Stead that he had had a letter from a girl in Boston whom he had not seen or heard from for years and years. This was Emily Hale, whom he had first met in 1912 when she was seventeen, and with whom he had acted in amateur theatricals at his cousin Eleanor Hinckley's.[85] Emily was then thirty-six: a disappointed, if well-bred woman, who had been brought up by her aunt and uncle, Unitarian minister, the Rev. and Mrs. John Carroll Perkins; they had prevented her from training as a professional actress as she had wished. Instead she had become a drama teacher in girls' colleges. It was on the pretext of needing help for a lecture on modern poetry that she wrote to Eliot, who responded by sending her his essay on "Shakespeare and the Stoicism of Seneca."[86]

Eliot's response revived Emily's dreams of romance with him. According to his account in the 1960s, Eliot had told her he was in love with her before he left for Europe in 1914, although he did not believe that she returned his feelings.[87] In the intervening years she had not married; perhaps no opportunities presented themselves as she ran the girls' dormitories at Milwaukee Downer College, Wisconsin, and played Juliet in a production of *Romeo and Juliet* which she put on as Assistant Professor of Vocal Expression.[88] She made several visits to England, studying at the Speech Institute in London, possibly in 1923. Certainly in September that year Eliot sent her a copy of *Ara Vos Prec,* his 1920 collection of poems and, according to her own résumé, she made five visits to England before 1930, taking a half year's leave of absence in 1927, when she stayed on in London until October.[89]

But Emily had mistaken her man. Even as she began to plan her resignation from the college and a long break from teaching, in order to spend time in 1930 with Eliot at Burford, near Oxford, Eliot was being drawn closer into the Anglo-Catholic community. In March 1928 he made his first confession, telling Stead that he felt that he had crossed "a very wide and deep river" from which there was no going back.[90] In the same month he took a vow of chastity. But his struggle between flesh and spirit did not abate, and in April he told Stead that he could not expect to make great progress. All he could do was "to keep my soul alive." Eliot's spiritual counselor was then Francis Underhill, warden of Liddon House, in London, an Anglican centre for the pastoral care of university students.[91] Eliot wrote to Stead "in confidence" that he felt he needed, "the most severe, as Underhill would say, the most Latin kind of discipline, Ignatian or other. It is a question of compensation. I feel that nothing could be too ascetic, too violent, for my own needs."[92]

The only role Eliot envisaged for Emily was that of spiritualised muse and soon she began to inspire his poetry, replacing Vivienne. Vivienne had become a virago but, in Eliot's imagination, Emily, despite being a drama teacher, was transmuted into the passive, mute "Lady of Silences" of "Ash Wednesday." Correspondence and meetings with her triggered thoughts of New England. Emily's influence stirred Eliot to write "Marina" (1930), a poem resonant with images of Maine,[93] of water lapping the bows of ships, of grey rocks and islands: memories of his youth flooded back to him, when he had gone out with the fishermen in their ships, "Bowsprit cracked with ice and paint cracked with heat . . . /The rigging weak and the canvas rotten."[94] In "Animula" (1929) he returned to his childhood in St. Louis, for Emily had roused the poet from another "dry spell" after his failure to finish *Sweeney Agonistes*. Eliot had been blocked, unable to recapture the revolutionary impulse with which he began his drama, and it was Geoffrey Faber who, concerned at the silence from the "sacred wood," had suggested to Tom that he write a poem for Faber's Ariel series. This led to "Journey of the Magi" in 1927. Emily provided another new stimulus in returning Eliot to his roots as a source of inspiration. Significantly, however, it is the poet's daughter whom he addresses in "Marina." The goodness and loveliness of his virginal Lady brings life to his dry bones in "Ash Wednesday"; and the image of lustrous brown hair ("Blown hair is sweet, brown hair over the mouth/Blown") suggests romantic attachment, but it was the devotion of a daughter Eliot sought, not a sexual tie. Emily, if she read "Marina" with care, would have heeded Eliot's message of damnation for copulating humans: "Those who suffer the ecstasy of animals, meaning/Death."

Before Emily returned to England in 1930, a flesh-and-blood figure hoping for a future with her former suitor who, said Boston gossip, had failed to marry her earlier because of fears that her mother's mental illness might be hereditary,[95] Eliot had decided that Emily was his Beatrice, the inspiration for his spiritual "New Life." When he and Stead discussed the way in which Dante's love for Beatrice led him to the "divine goal" of love of God, in the *Vita Nuova,* Eliot confided: "I have had that experience."[96]

Nevertheless Eliot encouraged Emily's hopes. Flirtatious and intimate letters, of the sort he wrote to married women such as Mary Hutchinson and Dorothy Pound, were easily misinterpreted by a single, inexperienced woman. Eliot blamed Vivienne for the fact that he, like Harry in *The Family Reunion,* felt "desexed" towards women. In 1938 he told E. Martin Browne, director of many of his plays, that for Harry, "the effect of his married life upon him was one of such horror as to leave him for the time at least in a state that may be called one of being psychologically partially desexed: or rather, it has given him a horror of women as of unclean creatures."[97] In Eliot's most autobiographical play, Harry meets Mary, a woman from his past, now aged thirty; he feels "repulsion for Mary as a woman," but attraction to her as a personality. In the end he leaves her for his "bright angels."

From the late 1920s, however, Eliot believed his new muse to be pure, undefiled—in contrast to Vivienne, fallen *femme fatale.* Unwilling to confront his own nature, he may have imagined that this "lady" from a Bostonian Brahmin background, the sort of wife his mother would always have wished for him, might stimulate him to some sort of heterosexual passion; certainly he allowed her to believe that he would marry her when freed to do so by Vivienne's death. Eliot's letters to Emily, still sequestered at Princeton University Library until 2019, number over a thousand, and testify to the depth of their friendship; and the fact that Eliot asked Peter du Sautoy, director at Faber, to burn her letters to him demonstrates his desire to destroy the evidence. Eliot's destruction of Emily's letters apparently followed her own decision to consign his letters to her to the safety of an archive in 1956.[98] Her intention must have been to put down a marker for the future and, like Vivienne, to claim her place in Eliot's life, allowing readers to judge whether he exploited her love and loyalty. Critics however have already traced a pattern of cruelty in Eliot's relations with women: Vivienne, Emily Hale, Mary Trevelyan, all in turn loved Eliot too much and suffered for it.[99]

Emily may have captured Eliot's imagination, and the Anglo-Catholic Church his heart, but it was the convivial *coterie* grouped around Geoffrey Faber, Frank Morley, and a new and devoted acolyte, John Davy Hayward, whom Vivienne perceived as her closest rivals in her struggle to retain her influence over Tom. Eliot had met John Hayward as early as October 1925, when Hayward, then an Exhibitioner at King's College, Cambridge, invited the poet to read a paper to the Heretics Society; Eliot declined because he was too busy with the Clark lectures, but the two kept in touch.[100] Hayward, the son of a Wimbledon surgeon, was already disabled by muscular dystrophy, but when he came down in 1927 Eliot asked him to tea at his office in Russell Square, and accepted Hayward's offer to review for the *Criterion*.[101] The two began lunching regularly; the malicious wit which earned Hayward the nickname "The Tarantula" appealed to Eliot as much as the younger critic's learning and sense of the macabre, which united both men in a shared fascination with seventeenth-century drama (Hayward had played the Fourth Madman in *The Duchess of Malfi*).[102] Once Hayward had settled at 22 Bina Gardens, in Earl's Court, his flat became the meeting place—or drinking-den—where Eliot (the Elephant), Geoffrey Faber (the Coot) and Frank Morley (the Whale) gathered to dance, drink gin, and declaim obscene verse together, which Hayward eventually had privately printed. A typical poem ("Vers pour la Foulque," "Verses for the Coot") ends: "Nous allons nous donner la peine/De chier sur le seuil. Sonnez! Laissons nos culs se ventiler . . ." ("We are going to crap on the doorstep. Ring the bell! Let our arses break wind . . .")[103] Through Hayward Eliot was drawn into the intellectual, and largely homosexual circle around John Sparrow, Warden of All Souls, Oxford, which included "our old friend Al," the historian A. L. Rowse. This led to a visit by Eliot in September 1929 to the Dragon School to watch the young boys perform *The Mikado,* followed by dinner at All

Souls, during which, as Eliot told Hayward, he urinated in the college grounds and so missed Faber's offer to share a few more drinks.[104]

The cumulative losses which Vivienne sustained from 1926 onwards triggered a mental deterioration which grew more marked in the early 1930s. Perhaps the turning-point was the realisation that Tom hated her: the savagery of his feelings led on occasions to bizarre behaviour. Conrad Aiken recalled how, in 1925, he wrote to compliment Eliot on a new volume of poetry. In reply the poet sent him a page torn out of the *Midwives' Gazette,* on which he had underlined various forms of vaginal discharge. The words *blood, mucus* and *shreds of mucus* were also underlined, as well as the phrase *purulent offensive discharge.* "I still shudder when I think of it," wrote Aiken.[105]

Like Doris before the unpredictable and drunken Sweeney, Vivienne was afraid of Tom. It was a fear she voiced to Ottoline on several occasions in early 1928, although she too was capable of violence. From the Malmaison sanatorium she wrote on 31 January, saying she was very miserable and "it is all quite useless." Ottoline would have gathered from Tom what a *"horrible* mess" all this was. "He simply hates the sight of me. And I *don't know what to do."*[106] Shortly afterwards Eliot reluctantly agreed to bring Vivienne home. In her diary Vivienne later recalled the day seven years before when she had returned to England from France: "My dear Tom brought me back with him, but he did not want to. He would have much preferred for me to remain in France." Vivienne had become overwrought as she struggled beforehand to arrange her return, taking the tram daily into Paris, getting her passport and papers in order and signed by the chaplain at the British Embassy. No one at the sanatorium would help as they were "furious" at her leaving. She, too, was frightened to leave, "so I was out of my mind, and so behaved badly to Tom and got very excited." When they arrived at Victoria, Vivienne and Tom were met by her mother and Maurice; their behaviour seemed to her "sinister and unkind." Rose and Maurice had hired a nurse to take care of Vivienne, which she resented, seeing it as a "futile effort" to justify their previous behaviour of putting her into the clinic.[107]

It was not the first time Vivienne had turned on Tom. In another 1920s story, "André and Sibylla" meet at Dickens and Jones to buy presents for his mother and sister who are staying. Sibylla, caught up by a fit of rage or passion, throws her parcels down the stairs, which are fortunately quite deserted:

> She hits André on the face with her umbrella. Having done it once she does it again. The whole world totters—it spins about her. She longs to destroy herself and looks wildly about but there is no window low enough from which to cast herself, no knife or weapon presents itself for her purpose.

"Sibylla" collapses on the stairs in a silent convulsion while André/Tom collects the parcels. "He then takes her arms tightly and gets her into the street, where she walks mechanically beside him sunk into utter blackness. Now and then a gust of violent rage returns like a glaring flash of lightning . . ."[108]

Eliot found the presence of so unpredictable a wife in the house unendurable, and Vivienne's fears that he would harm her increased. "I am very unhappy, and as you agreed with me—*quite* defenceless," wrote Vivienne to Ottoline on 28 February 1928. "If you hear of me being murdered, don't be surprised."[109] Ottoline was in a difficult position as a friend to both parties in the Eliots' marital disputes; she objected when Vivienne criticised Tom to her, and Vivienne hurried to apologise for talking at such length about Tom. He was, of course, a very old friend of Ottoline's, and a "great friend and no-one likes hearing their friends spoken against." Bravely Ottoline offered on 1 June 1928 to act a mediator, seeing both Eliots separately. This was "wonderful news," wrote Vivienne, full of gratitude.[110]

The long, tiring summer, with repairs to the house and a succession of American visitors—Irving Babbitt, Paul Elmer More and Tom's nieces—proved very fatiguing, and Ottoline's counselling had to wait, for she herself was seriously ill with necrosis of the jaw and had to submit to an operation to remove the diseased bone, which left her disfigured. Eventually, in early autumn, she was well enough to begin her Thursday tea-parties in her new house at 10 Gower Street, having given up

Garsington. But Tom's visits to Ottoline had aroused Vivienne's suspicions, although Ottoline had taken pains to visit Vivienne regularly for afternoon tea. On 7 June Virginia Woolf recorded that Tom and Vivienne "give parties, where she suddenly accuses him of being in love with Ottoline (and me, but this Ott. threw in as a sop) and Tom drinks, and Vivien suddenly says when talk dies down 'You're the bloodiest snob I ever knew'—so I have refused to dine there." Vivienne was, said Virginia, "as mad as a hare, but not confined."[111]

It was obviously ludicrous to suggest that Tom was in love with Ottoline, by then fifty-five and "an old volcanoe, all grey cinders," whose deafness caused her to depend on a black tin ear-trumpet to hear her guests' conversation. Only long-standing affection for Tom caused Ottoline to gather him up in a "long and cadaverous embrace," such as that which Virginia reported almost drew her under the following November.[112] Nervously Tom avoided Ottoline. He would like to see her soon, he wrote on 2 October 1928, but he would not like Vivienne to think that Ottoline wished to see him and not her. "V. is very much better everyone thinks." It would be unwise, he thought, to have any concealment from Vivienne or discrimination, so he would rather delay a bit.[113] In November he wrote again that he thought it would be better if Ottoline saw Vivienne first. "I hope you understand."[114] Ottoline was hurt, however, and accused Tom of "Neglect."

When Ottoline eventually called on Vivienne on 11 February 1929, the atmosphere was strained. Although at first Vivienne seemed more normal and "sane" to Ottoline, she became fractious and upset when Ottoline did not remember Pearl Fassett, Tom's secretary, who had died recently. Barely had Ottoline calmed her hostess down when Tom entered with Prince Mirsky, a White Russian writer whom Ottoline disliked intensely; her sympathies began to shift towards Vivienne and against Tom, whose contempt for other "uneducated" writers, such as Lawrence and Blake, annoyed her, as did Eliot's secret holding of Ottoline's hand, which she found patronising.[115] Tom considered himself as infallible as the Pope, decided Ottoline—a title also awarded him by Mary Trevelyan, who called her memoir of T. S. Eliot "The Pope of Russell Square." Vivienne, conscious of the awkward atmosphere, wrote the next day to apologise in a letter carefully composed on their new orange writing-paper. She was sorry that

Mirsky had been there; she had been afraid Ottoline would be bored if there was no one else. As for Tom, wrote Vivienne huffily, she was only too glad for him to have Ottoline's "intimate friendship." She understood now that Ottoline had not known that Miss Fassett was dead.[116] Two days later, on 13 February, Tom himself hurried to assure Ottoline that he had not "dropped" her, as she thought: "Neither of us wants to lose you, you may be sure." Apologising for Mirsky's presence, he invited Ottoline to dine with them both alone so that there would be no more misunderstandings.[117]

The truce did not last long. Vivienne, feverish with influenza, at home with a "very queer" Tom, who had toothache, brooded jealously over her husband's relationship with Ottoline. On 29 February she wrote a bread-and-butter note for Ottoline's tea-party, but defended herself vigorously against the accusation of speaking against her friend and advanced her own claims to Ottoline's friendship. "I never said anything against you," she wrote, "except on that one occasion under what I consider the *most extreme* provocation, and if T was ever worth knowing, I am worth knowing now."[118] And although she thanked Ottoline for her honesty in advising her last year to separate from Tom, she did not see what she could have done, for Vivienne was not prepared to agree to Ottoline's suggestion that she should live apart from Tom, perhaps in adjoining flats. Tom meanwhile continued to visit Ottoline in her garden at Gower Street, as her grandson Philip Goodman remembers, and wring his hands. What should he do about Vivienne, he asked. Should he leave her? Should he stay? Ottoline could only listen.[119]

But if one source of friendship was temporarily strained, another presented itself again. Vivienne turned back to Mary Hutchinson, who had once more swum into her orbit now that her long affair with Clive had ended in 1927, and she had detached herself from Aldous and Maria Huxley. Joyfully Vivienne welcomed Mary to Chester Terrace in June 1928; her guest had brought heliotropes for Vivienne to plant in her garden. Soon the old routine of tea and dinner-parties was re-established. Vivienne's gratitude to Mary for finding and keeping a little pearl necklace she had broken at Mary's dinner-party on 26 June, and which had been a Christmas present from Pearl Fassett, provoked a confession of unhappiness from Vivienne: "[Pearl's] death is the most *terrible loss,* and gap, in my life that you could possibly imagine . . . It leaves me *frightfully* lonely." Pearl had been constantly with her, wrote Vivienne, and no one could take her place; she had also been Tom's right hand at the *Criterion*. Vivienne had no idea how he got on without Pearl: "Of course, he is *so* reserved and peculiar, and one cannot get him to speak. That makes one much more lonely." Was Mary lonely too over there at Regent's Park, asked Vivienne. "I thought you seemed so." She herself could never get resigned to the loss of Clarence Gate and their life there. And she missed her servant Ellen, who could never be replaced, and was depressed by the glum, silent girl she had now. Complaints about the servants were followed by complaints about Tom's new friends, who took no interest in his "poetry side." He needed his old friends, wrote Vivienne. *"More* people of the *right* sort, (and less of the *wrong*.)"[120]

Vivienne's mental and physical deterioration became more pronounced over the next few months. In May 1929 she was bedridden, perhaps as a result of a fall when under the influence of drugs. Tom rang up Virginia, who found his story both tragic and sordid. "Vivien's legs." *"Legs,* did you say?" "Yes, both legs, but especially the left." . . . "My God, Tom, have you seen a doctor?" "We have already had ten doctors," and so on for an "hour or two." The long and the short of it all, gossiped Virginia to Clive, was that Vivienne was "recumbent for ever."[121] A month or two earlier Tom had asked Mary to call on Vivienne when she could, as "the commissariat is rather demoralised at present." It was difficult for Vivienne to get about to see people, explained Tom, as she was a bit unsteady since her accident, which Mary need not mention to her.[122]

Vivienne's "queer turns" and fainting fits continued, while Tom, by contrast, took up dancing to the gramophone again and began new driving lessons. Soon he was "a perfect master" of their Morris Minor. His relentless social life continued: autumn 1928 found him entertaining Ethel Sands in a box at the ballet, and at Edith Sitwell's party without Vivienne, who complained in November that she had no dress to wear and felt "ugly with rough hands."[123] Vivienne continued to stay at home while Eliot escorted the Princesse di Bassiano to tea at Virginia's or went to Mary's birthday party. Alone and "very miserable," so "terrible to look at" that she dared not go, for that was the sort of mortification one could not endure, Vivienne asked Mary to think of her while she was feasting. Send me something off the table, she begged, a cap, a mask, or a cracker. She would sit up late to hear Tom's account of the evening.[124]

Vivienne began to believe that if only she could return to north London, where she would be near Mary in Albert Road, she would be happy again. Too ill and lame to househunt herself, she left it to Tom to choose a flat. "Very stupid and unfair of me," she wrote regretfully to Mary from their new address at 98 Clarence Gate Gardens, to which they moved in June 1929. "Well, my dear, it is the most terrible flat." The flat was barrack-like, very expensive, and they were surrounded by builders. "Hammer, hammer, hammer. Cranes, drills, etc."[125] Wistfully she asked Mary, who had taken Salt Mill House at Fishbourne for the summer, if there was a small, vacant, workman's cottage nearby: *"Is there?* This is serious." Eliot added his own chorus of complaints to Vivienne's. She was at the end of her strength, he said. The flat had turned out much more frightful than anticipated. Finally, in a postscript, Vivienne claimed to be "homesick" for their old home.[126] But there was no escape from London for the Eliots. They renewed their old cycle of restless flat-moving, one which reflected their own desperation, moving again in October to 177 Clarence Gate Gardens. Virginia recorded in May 1930 that Tom had written to say he was just moving to a house from a flat—"the 5th move in 6 months; which means I suppose that the worm in Vivien turns and turns, and not a nice worm at that."[127]

On 10 September 1929, Eliot received a cable to say that his mother had died. "I fear for Tom, at this time," wrote Vivienne to Mary.[128] In her later diary she remembered it as an agonising time for Tom, who had not had a chance to see Charlotte again since abandoning both his Unitarian faith and his American nationality. Tom was guiltily aware of the pain he had caused her, despite the propitiatory gesture of publishing her "Savonarola"; nevertheless, he had made the decision to sever the bonds with Charlotte long ago. Vivienne was, perhaps, the more shocked when she received the news of her brother Maurice's sudden marriage in Italy in March 1930 to a twenty-five-year-old American, Ahmé Hoagland, one of the dancing Hoagland sisters, who had performed in Monte Carlo—"All done without our knowledge." Vivienne and her mother were both annoyed that Maurice, having brought his new wife to London to introduce her to his sister and mother, returned almost instantly to Italy.

Over the next few months Vivienne continued to try to find another "little house as nice as 57 Chester Terrace."[129] At last they moved again "without much hope" to 43 Chester Terrace. It proved a brief flirtation. January 1931 found them back in Clarence Gate Gardens, at number 68. Vivienne had had, she told Mary, "a sort of breakdown."[130]

From 1930, stories of Vivienne's bizarre behaviour were legion in literary London, many centering around her abuse of ether, then used as an anaesthetic, which could be inhaled or rubbed on the body. To apply ether as a local anaesthetic would have numbed the pain of neuralgia; in fact, according to his relatives, Dr. Miller, Vivienne's doctor who practised at 110 Harley Street, prescribed paraldehyde for her as a massaging gel, which smelt strongly of ether.[131] Eventually paraldehyde "was given up because of its smell, and because patients became dependent on it, as it was a potent sedative moving towards a tranquilliser."[132] Miller was acting responsibly within the limits of the medical knowledge of the time. Nevertheless, Vivienne's use of the paraldehyde he prescribed for her led some observers to believe that she was an ether-drinker who entered that state, described by Eliot in "East Coker," "when under ether, the mind is conscious, but conscious/of nothing."[133]

Aldous Huxley noted that Vivienne's face was "mottled, like ecchymmotic spots, and the house smelled like a hospital."[134] Ottoline was another such witness. Visiting Vivienne on 15 November 1930, she walked into marital war. Vivienne was restless, constantly leaving the room and returning smelling more and more strongly of ether. She spoke to Tom as if he were a dog; he "grim . . . fat . . . horrid" remained formally polite to her until Vivienne went to sit sulking in a corner of the sofa where she was ignored by Ottoline and Desmond MacCarthy. After ten minutes' absence she made a dramatic re-entrance, demanding that someone come to talk to her. Ottoline spent a moment or two alone with Vivienne in her room, and then fled, vowing never to return. Vivienne's breath had, she recorded in her journal, filled the air with ether and she was "half-crazed." Ottoline felt an almost equal measure of repulsion for Tom, who tried as usual to hold her hand. She sensed in him an hypocrisy and humbug, which demonstrated itself in his poetry, and which Ottoline now found a meaningless form without faith, and also in his attitude towards Vivienne, towards whom he still claimed to feel affection.[135] Ottoline did not believe him.

Yet Ottoline was too generous-spirited to abide by her decision not to see either Eliot again. July 1931 found Vivienne sitting next to Ottoline at a Gower Street tea-party with Virginia Woolf, David Cecil, Elizabeth Bowen, Alida Monroe, Leslie Hartley, Juliette Huxley and Dorothy and Simon Bussy among others. Diplomatically, Ottoline decided to look after Vivienne, whom she feared might make a scene, and left Virginia and Elizabeth Bowen to talk to each other, while L. P. Hartley discussed with Vivienne a detective story she was planning to write. It was, decided an exhausted Ottoline afterwards, rather like conducting an orchestra, trying to induce harmony among her disparate guests.[136] But Vivienne did not forget Ottoline's kindness: in her 1934 diary she recalled how, "ill, late, flustered," she used to motor to fetch Tom to take him to 10 Gower Street. "Inconspicuous (and) as inoffensive as possible," she would sit in the shadows in the garden: "Ottoline used to keep me by her which was kind of her," while the literary ladies and gentlemen talked.[137]

Behind the scenes Tom's priests pressed him to end his marriage. He was now worshipping daily at St. Cyprian's, near the flat at 68 Clarence Gate Gardens. The service was Anglo-Catholic, the vicar Father Mayhew, who added his voice to that of others, urging Eliot to separate from Vivienne. Robert Sencourt, who stayed with the Eliots in 1930, noted disapprovingly that Vivienne refused to join in Eliot's religious life, which she mockingly called "monastic," a reference perhaps to Kelham Theological College in Nottinghamshire, to which he was introduced by his spiritual adviser, Father Underhill, and where he began to join the brethren in retreats. Vivienne followed Bloomsbury in its mockery of Eliot's conversion, needling him as Stephen Spender watched the Woolfs do: " 'Tom, do you really go to church?' 'Yes.' 'Do you hand round the collection?' 'Yes.' 'Oh, really! What are your feelings when you pray?' They waited rather tensely for his answer to this question. Eliot leaned forward, bowing his head in that attitude which was itself one of prayer, and described the attempt to concentrate, to forget self, to attain union with God."[138] Vivienne refused to accompany him on weekend visits to Bishop Bell of Chichester, with whom Eliot stayed in December 1930. At that point, recalled Sencourt unctuously, "his spiritual counsellors became decisive: he had a duty to his career and his spiritual life. He must not wreck the work he was doing for the Church."[139] That month Eliot wrote to Stead: "I want to talk to you about your suggestion, my dear." The suggestion that he should leave Vivienne, said Eliot, had already been put *strongly* to him by Vivienne's Roman Catholic doctor, by Underhill, and by others less qualified, but it was to Stead he wished to speak because he alone knew how difficult it would be. "I will say that I have now a certain happiness which makes celibacy easy for me for the first time. I think you will know what I am speaking of."[140]

The battle of wills continued. As Tom wavered, an answer came to his prayers for deliverance. An invitation arrived from Harvard University to deliver the Charles Eliot Norton poetry lectures in the academic year 1932–33. It would mean leaving England in the autumn of 1932. Eliot barely hesitated before accepting.

20

Ghosts and Shadows

By 1932 Vivienne resembled the "restless shivering painted shadow" of Eliot's most painfully confessional play, *The Family Reunion*. When Conrad Aiken came to dinner with the Eliots in the autumn of 1930 he had painted an almost identical portrait of his "shivering, shuddering" hostess.[1] Vivienne herself wrote to the poet Ralph Hodgson in May 1932 that she lived in "a world of ghosts and shadows and unrealities."[2] She was to be pushed "beyond the confines of sanity," believed Sencourt, by Eliot's decision to go to America without her.[3]

The question of his guilt for Vivienne's condition was to torment Eliot for years to come. In *The Family Reunion* the protagonist, Harry, Lord Monchensey, recalls the death of his wife, who had apparently been swept off the deck of a liner in the middle of a storm. But Harry remembers, "That cloudless night in the mid-Atlantic/When I pushed her over." "Pushed her?" asks Violet, his aunt. "You would never believe that anyone could sink so quickly," replies Harry. He had supposed that whatever he did, his wife was "unkillable." He expected to find her when he went down to the cabin. Later, he became excited. The purser was sympathetic, the doctor very attentive. That night he slept heavily, alone.[4]

Did Tom push Vivienne over the edge—into insanity, and even death?[5] It was a question which would become his purgatory. You mustn't indulge such dangerous fancies, Harry is told in *The Family Reunion,* and Eliot leaves it unclear whether Harry's wife fell, jumped "in a fit of temper," or was pushed over; yet Harry's cool reaction to the disclosure that his father, too, once wanted to murder his mother ("In what way did he wish to murder her?") suggests similar premeditation.[6] *You* have no reason to reproach yourself, your conscience is clear, says Charles, uncle to Harry/Eliot. It goes a good deal deeper than what people call their conscience, protests Harry. You must believe that I suffer from delusions. I am afraid of sleep—and also waking. *She* is nearer than ever: "The contamination has reached the marrow/And they are always near."[7] The delusions to which Eliot refers may have had some basis in the voices which, as he would confess to Mary Trevelyan, he heard at night: "quite indeterminate voices, neither male nor female—I hear what they say—but it's never anything notable . . ."[8] "They are very distinct—the individual voices I mean," he repeated to Mary on 21 October 1952. "They are never the *same* voices I have heard on other nights . . ." These voices, perhaps, spoke the words of reproach which tortured Eliot, and lent authenticity to his portrait of the Eumenides.

Eliot's torment is well-documented: "We were married for seventeen years—I mean, we lived in the same houses," he told Mary Trevelyan. "Happy? NO, I was never happy—but I don't think I have ever been happy."[9] Yet Vivienne's torment was greater. Her end was not, in the final years of the marriage, as the murder victim she sometimes feared she would become, but in psychic death, a lapse into non-being for which Eliot was to feel as responsible—as if, for one second, his icy control had snapped and he had hit or shot or drowned the shadow of a woman who had haunted him. It was an end he had foreseen, quoting in 1929 Dante's description of the lost lovers, Paolo and Francesca, whose fate was metamorphosis into shades: "So I saw the wailing shadows come, wailing, carried on the striving wind."[10]

Vivienne slipped into non-being the longer she lived with Eliot. In the last photograph of her with Tom and Virginia Woolf she stands apart from the other two, a wraith-like woman in white, preparing to vanish. It was the final act of the drama. Trapped in the strange, claustrophobic world they had created, Vivienne was weaker than Tom in the battle of wills which ensued. The kitten had met a cat, Great Tom, Old Possum, whose claws were sharper than hers.

Jean-Paul Sartre writes, "I exist my body: this is its first dimension of being. More importantly, I exist as a body known by the Other." In any human relationship, the Other's look defines us for ourselves, and we see ourselves through the Other's eyes.[11] Vivienne, through Tom's eyes, saw herself as worthless. Her psychic pain translated into physical pain or disease, as the "lived pain" became "the suffered illness," a process illuminated by Sartre's ideas on hate, domination and submission. He argues that every relationship is a circle, in which each tries to assimilate and make an object of the Other. Conflict ensues, as each struggles to regain his or her freedom. "While I seek to enslave the Other, the Other seeks to enslave me . . . the Other holds a secret—the secret of what I am. He makes me be and thereby he possesses me . . . He has stolen my being from me."[12] Even love, says Sartre, is destructive: Vivienne's love for Eliot, which existed at the beginning of the relationship, ultimately proved destructive for them both as he came to resent the alienation of his freedom, the drying up of his creative spring in the trap of marriage—after "Ash Wednesday" he found himself unable to complete the two poems later published as "Coriolan"[13]—and the reproach of ill-matched sexuality. "The more I am loved the more I lose my being," writes Sartre. "The more I lose my being, the more I am thrown back on my own responsibilities." In the end such conflict provokes total despair.[14]

For Vivienne and Tom, love turned to indifference, then to hatred and sadism. Both felt the burden of having failed themselves and the Other. Vivienne punished herself through starvation and drugs because she accepted Tom's definition of her as a burden, as an inadequate, useless wife, while he grew to hate her as she cuckolded him and attempted to usurp his role as writer, encroaching on his own territory and taking on aspects of his dominating mother.[15] But at the core of the revulsion Eliot felt for Vivienne was her very femininity, which reminded him of the shameful, feared feminine part of himself. It became impossible for her to preserve self-esteem in the face of this instinctual, primitive hatred. Forced once more to submit to his control, as he asserted male literary hegemony and ended her writing career, she was left the object of Bloomsbury's scorn and ridicule, as well as Tom's. In the end Vivienne saw no justification for existing, and simply ceased to be.

In so doing she was fulfilling Tom's wishes. "When I hate," says Sartre, "I hate the whole psychic totality of the Other. I wish to rediscover a freedom without limits . . ." This is equivalent to projecting the realisation of a world in which the Other does not exist. In his poetic drama Eliot did indeed continually rehearse Vivienne's removal from his life. Yet hate is in turn a kind of failure because even if one being brings about the abolition of the Other, "it could not bring it about that the Other had not been," writes Sartre. "What I was for the Other is fixed by the Other's death."[16] Hate at the moment of realisation by the Other's death is transformed into failure. Hate does not free us from the circle. Leaving Vivienne did not bring Eliot release from the furies of conscience which were to pursue him; thus, even after separation, the imago of Vivienne acted as Eliot's prime creative stimulus. As Virginia Woolf admitted in 1936 to Clive Bell, Vivienne was "the true inspiration of Tom . . . He was one of those poets who live by scratching, and his wife was his itch."[17]

Vivienne's devastation was evident to Robert Sencourt, an insidious presence in the Eliots' flat. When he stayed with them in 1930, Vivienne seemed on the edge of "the abyss of despair," quoting to her guest Hardy's poem "In Tenebris":

> Black is night's cope
> But death will not appal
> One who, past doubtings all,
> Waits in unhope.

Sencourt watched as Vivienne made valiant efforts to hold together a fast fragmenting social life. One evening she asked some literary friends to meet the poet Ralph Hodgson, an old friend of Tom's. Hodgson was born in County Durham, the son of a coal merchant, and perhaps his "homely accent," as Sencourt described it, reminded Vivienne of her own northern background; certainly she felt at ease with Hodgson, who had the same passion for his bull terrier Pickwick as she had for her Yorkie Polly. She also liked his companion, Aurelia Bollinger, a former student at Missionary College, whom Hodgson had seduced, and grew close to them both in the last two years of her life with Eliot.[18] On the evening in question a group of younger writers read their work aloud, but the centre of attention was Ottoline to whom, wrote Sencourt, "Vivienne deferred as if to royalty"; Tom read "Difficulties of a Statesman" ending with the shout: RESIGN, RESIGN.[19] It was an awkward gathering: Ottoline balefully observed Vivienne flirting excitedly with Hodgson who was, apparently, a patient listener; but his hostess, grotesque in flowered chiffon, her little face with its grey-green make-up reminding Ottoline of an overdressed monkey, presented a bizarre yet pitiful spectacle. Nor was the Eliots' tea-party for James and Nora Joyce in July 1931 any more successful. Tom and Vivienne greeted Joyce like a king as well, and this time it was Ottoline who felt left out as the two writers fell into deep conversation and she was ignored. The company listened to a gramophone recording of Joyce reading "Anna Livia Plurabella," followed by Tom reading "Ash Wednesday"; it was, thought Ottoline, greatly inferior to Joyce's work.[20]

There were mysterious comings and goings at the Clarence Gate Gardens flat. Sencourt remembered Maurice, as well as Montgomery Belgion, one of Eliot's many right-wing, French contacts, and the "Bolshevised" Mirsky, who was a frequent visitor; unknown to his hosts, the wrinkled, watchful aristocrat, with his crooked, yellow teeth, while flirting with Vivienne was also gathering material for a Marxist analysis of Bloomsbury, which would ridicule its members after his return to Russia.[21] Vivienne did not, however, know all her husband's male guests as well as she did Mirsky. Sometimes there were secret visitors. On 27 January 1931, she asked Mary if she knew of the man Tom had staying, whom she only saw for a few minutes late at night after all the servants and nurses had departed. "He sometimes stays with us. Tom can bear him. Perhaps you could find out why."[22]

Old friends became captive but embarrassed witnesses to the Eliots' escalating marital warfare. On 1 June 1931 Mary and Jack yielded to Vivienne's repeated invitations to visit her new "strange" flat at number 68, and came to dinner with Mary's brother Jim Barnes. An explosive scene ensued, in which Tom lost his temper. "Something seemed to upset Tom very much indeed yesterday," wrote Vivienne. She was dreadfully sorry and shocked at what happened the previous night. "We are now quite 'calm' and so *please* can you telephone tomorrow morning and suggest any meal for you and Jim . . ."[23] Predictably, Jim Barnes proved unavailable when Vivienne rang him three times to make another date.

The evening from which the Hutchinsons fled in horror was probably similar to that endured by Conrad Aiken a few months earlier. A battle had broken out almost as soon as he had arrived. Vivienne looked like a scarecrow, and both Eliots directed streams of hatred at each other throughout the meal. There was no such thing as pure intellect, declared Eliot. Vivienne interrupted angrily: "Why, what do you mean? You know perfectly well that *every* night you tell me that there *is* such a thing: and what's more that *you* have it, and that nobody *else* has it." "You don't know what you're saying," retorted Eliot, but it seemed to Aiken that the arrow had struck home. Vitriolic, sarcastic, maybe, but Vivienne did not appear mad to Aiken.[24]

Christmas Day 1931 found the Eliots alone together. Vivienne was glad that Ottoline's Christmas had been "nice and calm." "Ours," she wrote, "was rather terrible."[25] It followed hard on another "fearful" evening when Vivienne had four people to dinner, who did not seem to have "at all a good effect, anyhow not in *combination*" on Tom, who had erupted in a drunken rage. Vivienne was horrified, she confided to Ottoline, for it was so long since anything like that had happened. Don't speak of it to anyone, she instructed her friend. *"I know you won't."* She was thankful for the presence of Sencourt, who had been staying again in December and managed to calm Tom down. However, Sencourt's soothing words could not mask the fundamental problem of Tom's alcoholism, which often made Ottoline, who was a teetotaler, feel apprehensive before dining with the Eliots.[26] Would Tom be sober or drunk, that was the question; or if sober, hungover and surly, his eyes bloodshot.[27] Tom sometimes took the opportunity to defend his consumption of gin and wine; alcohol kept one young, he told Ottoline, citing de Quincey and Coleridge as examples of this generalisation, a remark which Vivienne found in bad taste, and it required all Ottoline's tact to avoid yet another argument.[28] But however well-preserved his looks, Eliot's drinking was widely known from the late 1920s. Anthony Powell recorded in his memoirs: "Someone remarked, 'They say Eliot is always drunk these days . . .' "[29]

Nor was Tom's temper helped by Vivienne's jealousy of his fame, which provoked further outbursts. One young man called at the flat and Vivienne opened the door; on hearing that he wanted to see Eliot, she complained bitterly: "Why, oh why, do they all want to see my husband?"[30] The poet was angry, too, at the knowledge that he was the subject of mocking laughter among the *literati* since the publication of Richard Aldington's satirical story *Stepping Heavenward* in 1931, with its caricature of Eliot as the sanctimonious but ruthless "Blessed Jeremy Cibber," a genius with whom it is "quite awful" to live. Aldington also sneered at Eliot's "death-worshipping" in "The Hollow Men." Those who had fought in the war like himself, he said, were "healthy-minded" individuals, struggling to escape the "perpetual suicidal mania," in which only those who had not fought, like Eliot—cowards by implication—yearned to wallow.[31] It was a criticism which struck a raw nerve with Eliot, who was concerned about perceptions of his own effeminacy. He preserved among his papers a cutting by the American critic Louis Untermeyer:

> The charge that the poet is, by nature, effeminate is still prevalent. And it is patently absurd . . . The essential manliness of the arts—and particularly the art of finding words for our deepest emotions—may be proved by examining the biographies of the great poets of all nations.

Under this cutting Eliot scrawled in enormous, angry letters his own initials: "TSE."

Eliot's sensitivity over being the subject of rumour, whether financial, such as the Bel Esprit leaks, or concerning his private life, had already led him to threaten legal action, as in the case against the *Liverpool Post*. It was further exacerbated by Vivienne's predilection for outspoken public attacks on him. Stephen Spender, who first met Eliot in 1928, was struck by Vivienne's ability to expose him to humiliation before strangers.[32] Eliot grew nervous of blackmail; such was his reputation that the writer E. W. F. Tomlin felt it necessary to state that his friendship with the poet was "devoid of sexual feeling . . ." despite the "persistent insinuations that Eliot, owing to his friendship with Jean Verdenal and perhaps with others, was either homosexual or, as one fellow-poet remarked, suppressed homosexuality."[33]

In this climate of fear, Aldington's malicious satire, the product of jealousy of his old friend's dominance of English letters, seemed the last straw. It had been tactless, perhaps, of Eliot to have recommended "a good broker" to the struggling writer, or to have invited the country mouse to a "London soirée" in November 1927.[34] "Certainly the party was a silly one," Eliot had replied breezily, justifying his own attendance on the grounds of a liking for "drinking beer in company." He had never intimated that London parties were superior to provincial ones, he protested.[35] But after visiting Eliot's spacious office at Faber, furnished in red Chinese Chippendale, with its fine view over the church spire and square,[36]

Aldington had determined on revenge. Eliot's reaction to *Stepping Heavenward* was swift. Geoffrey Faber wrote at once to the novelist's publisher, Chatto's, requesting that the book be withdrawn because it would offend Eliot and Vivienne; his letter also contained "what looked like the threat of a libel action." Aldington told Sydney Schiff that if Eliot were to send him a straightforward request, that is, one that was not too "Christian-slimy," he might feel obliged to cancel publication but, since none was forthcoming, and the story had already been previously published twice, he went ahead.[37]

Many accounts exist of Tom and Vivienne's marriage in the years 1930–32, but it is the hostile pen of Virginia Woolf which has been responsible for the most "violently" vivid descriptions of Vivienne's "insanity." Woolf's accounts of her last sightings of Tom and Vivienne together have, as her biographer Hermione Lee writes, "powerfully affected all the versions of the Eliot story."[38] Woolf's disdain for Eliot's religiosity certainly influenced her against him; she observed him in November 1930, "all suspicion, hesitation & reserve. His face has grown heavier fatter & whiter. There is a leaden sinister look about him." But it was Vivienne from whom she was determined to distance herself, from a "madness" which seemed contagious and threatening to someone who was herself, in all probability, manic-depressive.

> But oh—Vivienne! Was there ever such torture since life began!—to bear her on ones shoulders, biting, wriggling, raving, scratching, unwholesome, powdered, insane, yet sane to the point of insanity, reading his letters, thrusting herself on us, coming in wavering trembling—"Does your dog do that to frighten me? Have you visitors? Yes we have moved again. Tell me, Mrs. Woolf, why do we move so often? Is it accident?" That's what I want to know (all this suspiciously, cryptically, taking hidden meanings.) Have some honey, made by our bees, I say. Have you any bees? (& as I say it I know I am awakening suspicion.)[39]

"Have you any bees?" It was a question which must have seemed ridiculous to a woman living in a north London flat, and Vivienne answered with ironic mockery: "Not bees. Hornets. But where? Under the bed." After half an hour in which Vivienne pitted her own sharp and mordant wit against Virginia's, her hostess was relieved to bid farewell to her unwelcome guest, damning Vivienne for posterity with her final verdict which has been so often quoted: "This bag of ferrets is what Tom wears round his neck."[40]

As Hermione Lee points out, Virginia understood "suspicion" very well. She too suffered from paranoia. The passage describing Vivienne echoes a remark Virginia made about herself in 1921: "A wife like I am should have a label to her cage: She bites!" Vivienne's alarming presence, like a *doppelgänger* of Woolf, must have provoked the novelist's anxiety and paranoia and threatened her own fragile equilibrium.

Virginia's ambivalence towards Vivienne was profound. On another occasion she could be impulsively kind, hunting up and down Oxford Street on Boxing Day 1928 for a 3/6d present for Vivienne. She was looking for a "green smooth knife" like the one Ottoline had given her for Christmas.[41] Perhaps it was this exchange of knives which gave rise to Virginia's stories that Vivienne was trying to stab her and Ottoline in the street, as she believed them to be Tom's mistresses, and skin them with a carving knife. Tom and Vivienne both, according to Maurice, bought joke knives from the same shop where Tom bought the whoopee cushions for his office at Faber, and the "giant" fire crackers he exploded in the coal scuttle on Independence Day.[42] As Eliot related to John Hayward, there were often "high jinks" at the Faber book committee meetings, with stinkbombs, gin and vermouth, and a sharing of his collected "Psuedoxia Contemporanea": previous items in the collection included the fact that "a fart, strained through bath water, loses both odour and inflammability," the information that to rub the fingers between the toes and sniff them was "sovereign against costiveness," and the discovery that cigarette ash, stirred into black coffee, was "most urgently aphrodisiac."[43] It was, therefore, not unusual for Vivienne, at Christmas 1931, to give Ottoline "a funny little Christmas token," which Ottoline felt was a wand, but, wrote Vivienne enigmatically, she did not take or give it as such: "To me it is a Sword, and one has to be careful to whom one gives swords." The sword, she wrote, was mightier than the pen. This "sword," like Ottoline's gifts to Vivienne, had some strange connection in Vivienne's mind, as her propensity to read significance into "signs" grew. Such paranoia was certainly a feature of bromism, and led Vivienne, who was frustrated in her desire to communicate privately with Ottoline by her friend's deafness, to feel she had to choose between writing, which was always a "risk," or communicating "by *signs*" which she thought *"low and brutal and degrading."*[44]

Such a letter suggests that Vivienne was becoming temporarily deranged yet her correspondence with Ralph Hodgson and Aurelia Bollinger gives a very different impression of her state of mind. Her writing changes to a more upright, determined hand, although it is sometimes shaky as a result of drugs, and the content is rational, the letters carefully dated and signed. On 12 May 1932 Vivienne wrote a sensitive letter of condolence to Hodgson, who had just lost his brother, offering the sympathy of "a real friend if you will allow me to think of myself as being your friend." Hodgson had brought so much into her life, she wrote, and done so much for her, clearing up things which she never understood. "You have seemed to me like some very solid tower of strength and reality in a world of ghosts and shadows and unrealities." She would never cease to be grateful to him, although "nothing is finished yet, or quite clear." She was with him in his grief, in which she had seen his courage, wonderful patience, kindness and tact. Please let us see you over Whitsun, she begged, although Tom had announced that he was taking to his bed for the next three days.[45]

Battling with ghosts took every ounce of Vivienne's strength in the months which followed. Like Mrs. Aveling, through whom, in *Ghosts,* Ibsen develops the character of Nora, Vivienne began to think "we are all ghosts . . . every one of us," weighed down by the burden of the past, of parents, old beliefs and old lovers. "I've only to pick up a newspaper and I seem to see ghosts gliding between the lines," says Mrs. Aveling. "Over the whole country there must be ghosts, as numerous as the sands of the sea. And here we are, all of us, abysmally afraid of the light."[46] Much of the time Vivienne too stayed in the shadows, within the walls of her flat, only venturing out with the support of trusted friends. If only she could be induced to go out of doors with you, complained Tom to Mary, it might build up her self-confidence. "She can't *drive* without me or a driver—" and she needed persuading that people she liked wanted to see *her*.[47] But despite Vivienne's eccentricity and the paranoia which caused her to open Tom's letters behind his back, some friends stayed remarkably loyal without his prompting. They not only responded dutifully to Vivienne's often articulated need, but also to the warmth which she had not entirely lost. Aurelia Bollinger became "one of the family," spending evenings with the Eliots while Vivienne wrote nineteen letters and Tom read and grumbled. There were outings to Hindhead with Ralph and Aurelia to see Rose Haigh-Wood and her sister, Lillia,[48] trips to the theatre and, despite Vivienne's confusing letters cancelling appointments, days in the country. On 27 May 1932 Vivienne thanked Aurelia effusively for their *"perfect"* day out, when they had visited Arundel, and arranged for Aurelia to come to stay for a week with Ralph's bull terrier Picky while Hodgson was visiting Siegfried Sassoon.[49]

Vivienne knew Aurelia well enough to complain to her about Tom. "Mr. Eliot is playing the Wireless and driving me *MAD*," she had confided to her friend on 19 May, while arranging a day at the Derby in the Eliots' car.[50] Tom, meanwhile, as spring turned to summer, laid silent plans for his escape to America. Lunching with Eliot and Jim Barnes that March to plan a "fascist" book on modern politics, Harold Nicolson found the poet "very yellow and glum . . . dyspeptic, ascetic . . . Inhibitions."[51] The lines Eliot wrote about himself and sent to Ralph Hodgson reveal a sardonic awareness of the impression he made on others: "How unpleasant to meet Mr. Eliot!/With his Coat of Clerical Cut," wrote the poet; "And his Face so Grim/And his Mouth so Prim . . ."[52] The pen and ink sketch of himself with which Eliot decorated the poem bears a striking resemblance to the self-righteous Unitarian ministers he had satirised in his youth: his exuberant sketch of Hodgson and his dog, by contrast, suggests a certain envy of the portly, good-natured friend of whom he wrote, "How Delightful to Know Mr. Hodgson!/(Everyone Wants to Know *Him*)."[53]

In the last months of the Eliots' marriage, Vivienne's character assassination at the hands of Bloomsbury proceeded apace. Edith Sitwell described the "very exciting" afternoon in 1932 when Vivienne came to visit her, to Osbert's lover, David Horner:

A certain lady (Osbert will tell you who I mean) came to tea without her husband. As she entered, a strange smell as though four bottles of methylated spirits had been upset, entered also . . . Nellie, (the maid) who was once what is known as an Attendant, enquired if she might speak to me on the telephone, and, as soon as she got me outside, said (looking very frightened): "If she starts anything, Miss, get her by the wrists, sit on her face, and don't let her bite you. Don't let her get near a looking-glass or a window." I said, "What *do* you *mean?*" and she replied that what I thought was an accident with the M.S. was really the strongest drug given by attendants when nothing ordinary has any effect!! She concluded gloomily: "Often it takes six of us to hold one down."— You can imagine my feelings, and when I got back into the room, I found that Mrs. Doble [mother of Georgia Sitwell, Sachie's wife] had offered the lady a cigarette, and had been told the lady *never* accepted anything from strangers. It was too dangerous.

Poor Mrs. D was terrified as she thought the Patient was going to spring at her throat . . .[54]

In fact Mrs. Doble was in no danger. Vivienne was never violent but, if Edith is to be believed, she had begun to experience delusions as a result of her addiction. In the summer of 1932 Edith met Vivienne walking down Oxford Street.

"Hullo, Vivienne!" she called to her.

Vivienne looked at her suspiciously and sadly, and replied, "Who do you think you're addressing? I don't know you."

"Don't be so silly, Vivienne: you know quite well who I am."

Vivienne regarded her with profound melancholy for a moment, and then said, "No, no: you don't know me. You have mistaken me *again* for that *terrible* woman who is so like me . . . She is always getting me into trouble."[55]

As the date of Eliot's departure grew closer, Vivienne manifested some of the symptoms of *grande hystérie*. She found it difficult to function normally, to eat, sleep or even walk. At the Derby, on 1 June, she was carried fainting from the Epsom race course, and she never forgot that day when she had tried to cross the course with Tom and Ralph Hodgson and Aurelia Bollinger and had collapsed—the intense heat, the fearful crowds, Tom and a policeman carrying her out of the crowd. The police were always kind to Tom and to her, she remembered.[56]

It is probable that Vivienne's collapse was caused by her panic at the thought of losing Tom. It is also possible, although very unlikely, that she was suffering from "etheromania" or ether drunkenness, a form of intoxication produced by drinking ether,[57] similar to that produced by alcohol, but which came on more rapidly and was more transitory. Ether was commonly used as a narcotic and antispasmodic in the treatment of hysteria or asthma.[58] It is more probable that anxiety, and increased dependence on the drugs already prescribed by Dr. Miller, accounted for Vivienne's bizarre behaviour in the final months of her marriage. Chloral and bromide—prescribed for Vivienne's hypertension—and purgatives such as croton-oil acted as a chemical cosh on the patient.[59] Virginia, who was taking a variety of medication, found that taking "somnifène" left her "quite drugged" in January 1929.[60] She could hardly walk, reported Leonard, and was in "a drugged state. She says she has only taken twenty drops. She has been in bed ever since."[61] As Virginia's mental and physical collapse continued, her doctors gave her "stiff doses of bromide," she told Vita Sackville-West. "Its rather nice. Ones head feels grown to the pillow. One floats like a log."[62] Virginia enjoyed her days under the influence of bromide, when she felt like a fish at the bottom of the sea. It was from her underwater vantage point perhaps that she dispassionately recorded Vivienne's "madness" when Tom and Vivienne made a final visit to Rodmell on 2 September 1932:

> She as wild as Ophelia—alas no Hamlet would love her, with her powdered spots—in white satin, L said; Tom, poor man, all battened down as usual, prim, grey . . . Then her chops & changes. Where is my bag? Where—where—then a sudden amorous embrace for me—& so on: trailing about the garden—never settling—seizing the wheel of their car—suddenly telling Tom to drive—all of which he bears with great patience: feeling perhaps that his 7 months of freedom draw near . . .[63]

Vivienne also recalled the same occasion with Virginia when "We had tea, & as I was *very nearly insane* already with the Cruel Pain of losing Tom . . . I paid very little attention to the conversation . . . We got back to the Lansdowne [Hotel, Eastbourne], I felt *very ill & was in a fever.* Tom also *seemed very strange.*"[64]

Hope Mirrlees's recollection in 1971 of Vivienne echoes Virginia's:

Fear, that's it. Because she gave the impression, you see, of absolute terror. Of a person who'd seen a hideous ghost; a goblin ghost, and was always seeing a goblin in front of her. Her face was all drawn and white; and wild, frightened, angry eyes, and an over-intensity over nothing, you see; over some little thing you'd say. Suppose you were to say to her: "Will you have some more cake?"; and she'd say (in a wild voice): "What's that, what's that, what d'you mean, what did you say that for?" She was terrifying. At the end of an hour, when she used to come and see me, I was absolutely exhausted, sucked dry; and I felt to myself, poor Tom this is enough. But—she was his Muse all the same.[65]

In August, Frank Morley invited the Eliots to Pikes Farm, near Crowhurst, Surrey, for the christening of his daughter Susannah, to whom Eliot was to be godfather. Since the reorganisation of Faber & Gwyer as Faber & Faber under the chairmanship of Geoffrey Faber in April 1929, the Fabers, Eliots and Morley had become close friends. Vivienne remembered later that "my poor Tom had great difficulty in getting me up and dressed and ready to start," on the drive to Oxted, where they were to meet Morley in his car. Eliot only succeeded by reminding Vivienne that she was keeping two old people waiting: Morley's parents, who came from Baltimore.[66] At last they made their *rendez-vous:* Tom driving Vivienne in their tiny Morris Minor, following Morley's car, a second-hand American Ford V-8, which blazed the trail, at 20 mph, for the Morris Minor to follow through the twisting lanes. Morley came to a hill, which the Ford breasted with ease. Tom "missed his gear-change, pressed everything pulled everything, stalled, began to roll back—I draw a veil," remembered Morley. "Another thing I had forgotten was that in the back of the Morris there would be the heaviest of suitcases—Tom never journeyed without the *heaviest* of suitcases. Another thing I remembered was that Tom would intensely dislike any notice taken, any assistance. I went on waiting . . . At a third attempt and with unexampled gallantry Tom with the heart of a lion did charge to the top of the mountain. Vivien's nerves withstood the strain better than mine."[67]

Nevertheless, it turned out a "happy, memorable day," and Morley made no comment on Vivienne's eccentricities; indeed, he remembered that

> When I knew her it was quite obvious that she had been a person of immense charm and vivacity, and quickness of uptake. And I'm quite sure of one thing: that she, rather like Ezra, was an immense help to Eliot—to Eliot as a poet—and her contribution, and indeed, her courage, in encouraging the publication of *The Waste Land,* which many wives would have blanched from, is something that is worthy of a tribute, and memory. I doubt if he'd have ever written *The Waste Land* if it hadn't been for Vivien.[68]

Ottoline, too, bravely continued to entertain Vivienne, who clung to her friend for support, feeling that the part of her life which was around Ottoline was "the only part I can endure to contemplate." She regularly attended Ottoline's "glorious" summer tea-parties, writing to her on 4 July 1932: "You *know* that it is entirely due to you that I have been able to keep up."[69] Ottoline could not have entertained Vivienne weekly if she had been as insane as Virginia Woolf suggested, and there were times when the mistress of Gower Street recorded that Vivienne was cordial, lively and quite normal, in contrast to Eliot, whose cruelty hurt Ottoline deeply when he contemptuously dismissed her religious faith.[70] Tom appeared duly grateful to Ottoline for her care of Vivienne, who was, he wrote, so much "a creature of environment" that it was a vital matter what company she frequented; not only had Ottoline exerted her own influence but she had helped Vivienne to add a number of "desirable people" to her acquaintance. "I am especially glad of this because I shall be so long absent."[71]

But it was Mary, not Ottoline, who came to Vivienne's rescue as Tom's absence drew nearer. The courage with which Vivienne had at first greeted the news that Tom would be away from September till May, writing to Mary, "It is all of our duties to keep things going for him *here,*" was fast evaporating.[72] She needed Mary's help so much, begged Vivienne on 8 June 1932, adding that she hardly dared telephone her friend for fear of disappointment. "You don't suppose *I* don't need a change *too*—do you?" How could she be expected to stay alone at Clarence Gate Gardens for eight months? She would hate it.[73] Within four days Mary had come up with an ingenious solution. She suggested that Vivienne and Tom should take rooms in the Strachey family home at 51 Gordon Square, as the top-floor flat was vacant following the death of Lytton in January 1932. Vivienne would be next door to Adrian and Karin Stephen at number 50, near the Keyneses at number 46, and not far from the Woolfs at 52 Tavistock Square. At first Vivienne responded enthusiastically to Mary's proposal, and on 12 June she and Tom were shown around Lytton's two rooms by his sister, Pippa Strachey, who was, said Vivienne, "sweet . . . and so *kind* to us both." The rooms were more beautiful and desirable than she ever dreamed, wrote Vivienne: "Tom very *much* likes the rooms and knows that he would be happy there." She began to fantasise about the coming winter; how she would decorate and furnish the flat "beautifully," live there quietly and "cultivate my mind." Could she not found a Society or Fund to keep Lytton's rooms "always perfect" in his memory? Tom could use them for writing, reading and thinking, and Mary could be the "Curator."[74]

Nothing came of these plans. Perhaps Vivienne began to think twice about doing without the "*economy* and convenience of constant hot water," which was not available in Lytton's flat as it was in Clarence Gate Gardens. Although on 18 July she was writing to Mary, saying she wished to move to 51 Gordon Square because she could not endure her present servants a moment longer, Vivienne's mind was now pursuing another suggestion of Mary's: that she should take a job. You are more practical than most of my friends, Vivienne told Mary gratefully, after another "lovely tea," where they talked over Vivienne's problems alone together: "It is *kind* of you to *interest* yourself in what I shall do this next year. I do appreciate that!!!"[75] She hurried to ask her doctor's advice about doing some work. He replied that it would be "very very *nice* and a *very good thing,*" Vivienne confided excitedly to Mary.[76]

Three weeks before he left, Tom took Vivienne away for a short holiday. She had no inkling that it was to be their last. He gave no hint of his intentions, as she talked nervously of their imminent separation. Huge moons and "boiling days" marked that August. In September the weather became chilly and disagreeable. Vivienne decided to give Tom a farewell party which took place on Thursday, 15 September, two days before he sailed from Southampton. "He is really going—next Saturday," she wrote wonderingly to Ottoline,[77] who tried to decline the invitation, having experienced Vivienne's last fiasco of a party that January, at which Alida Monro, widow of Harold, read Tom's poems aloud to a hand-picked audience.[78] "Yes I do know you hate parties," countered Vivienne sternly, but this one was to be "a kind of *gathering* together of people which Tom would *like to remember,*" people who genuinely desired his "ultimate good" in every possible way, above all spiritually. They would be *very* sorry indeed if she was not with them, even if only for a very short time. Ottoline finally yielded, also acceding to Vivienne's wish that she would have a final farewell meeting alone with Tom on Friday 16th, after which he was only to see Vivienne's mother Rose.[79] But Ottoline made the decision that, after Tom's departure, she would never again meet Vivienne.

In order to allay Vivienne's fears that he would stay in America and never return to her, Tom had written "my dear Vivienne" a letter dated 4 March 1932, stating the terms on which he had been appointed Charles Eliot Norton Professor of Poetry at Harvard University. The post was only for the academic year 1932–33, for a fee of $10,000. Eliot undertook to return to England the following May. He wished to make it clear, he wrote, that the appointment was not renewable, signing off, "affectionately yours, your husband."[80] With this paper reassurance Vivienne had to be content, and yet she did not trust him. Even as the Eliots left their flat in a cab, weighed down with his ample luggage, and followed by Maurice and his wife Ahmé in another cab, Tom discovered that Vivienne had locked some of his important papers in the bathroom. He asked a friend to go back and a pageboy from a nearby hotel had to be pushed through the bathroom window. The papers were retrieved and handed to Tom at the station a few minutes before the boat-train left for Southampton.[81]

On board, Tom and Vivienne walked the deck together, while Maurice and Ahmé waited on the quayside. At last it was time for Vivienne to leave. With a sense of deep foreboding she joined her brother and sister-in-law as they waved goodbye to Tom, and the liner steamed out to sea, bearing his receding figure across the Atlantic to Montreal and thence to the homeland he had not seen since 1915. Vivienne could barely guess at the scale of the welcome which awaited Eliot in the United States, the country he had left as an unknown graduate student and to which he now returned, seventeen years later, as a conquering hero, creator of a modernist canon which had changed the face of literary history.

From the moment Tom left, Vivienne's social life imploded. Her network of friendships vaporised. It took many months for her to understand the cruel fact that she had only been tolerated as the poet's wife; and, as that title was taken from her, doors closed in her face. Many Bloomsbury "friends" did not return her calls; even her dearest friend, Ottoline, was suddenly not "at home" to her. It was a savage blow which Vivienne found bewildering, for she alone had no share in the secret to which Ottoline and Virginia were privy, and which was soon the subject of gleeful gossip at Bloomsbury parties: that Tom Eliot had no intention of ever seeing his wife again. "I have felt frightful being quite cut off from you all these terrible months," wrote Vivienne plaintively to Ottoline the following year. "I do not see why it is necessary." She begged for an opportunity to speak to Ottoline, or "a message even," signing her letter, "Vivienne Haigh-*Eliot,*" the Eliot underlined three times.[82] But Ottoline remained obdurate.

From Cambridge, Massachusetts, Eliot wrote early in February 1933 to Ottoline, saying he understood her decision not to see Vivienne but wished to have trustworthy reports of his wife's mental and physical condition. If Ottoline were to see Vivienne, he would be glad of "a line of description."[83] It was a detached letter. Eliot reserved his warmth for references to his family, his three sisters and brother, who surrounded him with affection, and the mass of "secondary" relatives, who gave him the sense of belonging to a clan, and an important clan to boot. Outside of Boston, he wrote, he was simply T. S. Eliot, "but *here I am an Eliot.*"[84] After his prolonged tour of New York, California ("a nightmare"), Missouri, Minnesota, Chicago, Buffalo and Baltimore, he was relieved to be back in Harvard Yard, which felt like home, at B-11 Eliot House, lecturing to undergraduates on English literature.[85] This break in his life, he told Ottoline cautiously, would be "very significant" and would alter his life.[86]

Eliot forbore to mention either to Ottoline or Virginia one interlude in California which may have helped him come to his final decision over Vivienne: his visit to Scripps College, Claremont, to see Emily Hale, who now held the post of Assistant Professor of Oral English at this recently founded college for women. Emily's career had flourished in California: she played an imposing Lady Bracknell in a production of *The Importance of Being Earnest,*[87] bringing the same authority to her performance as that which caused Ottoline to dismiss her as a "sergeant-major" with a hand-bag when she and Eliot came to tea in October 1935.[88] But despite Emily's apparent bossiness, Eliot responded happily to the fuss she made of him when he visited Scripps College. Their contact continued during the Easter holidays, which Emily spent in Boston, where her uncle had be-come minister of King's Chapel, the historic heart of Unitarianism. After an Eliot family holiday, in which Emily was included, at Mountain View House, Randolph, New Hampshire,[89] Eliot wrote a nostalgically autobio-graphical poem, "New Hampshire." "Twenty years and the spring is over." The motif of children—regrets for those unborn—returned; their voices echo in the orchard, and they "swing up into the appletree."[90] It is a poem of hope, reflecting the illusion to which Eliot clung, that the happiness he felt in Emily's company could "normalise" him, as once he had hoped Vivienne's might. When Eliot even included her in a visit to his old school, Milton Academy, where he gave the Prize Day Oration—proudly telling Virginia Woolf by letter that he had "done the Old Boy properly"[91]— Emily could be forgiven for thinking that Eliot was serious about her and, if he were free, would wish to marry.

But part of the exhilaration Eliot felt was simply due to being back in America. A letter he wrote to Virginia in March 1933 bubbles with excite-ment at the mixture of familiarity and novelty which he encountered as he crossed the continent. After a time in America, nothing could surprise you, he told her. He had learnt how to pronounce Los Angeles and Albuquerque, but Terre Haute was beyond him. In Los Angeles, "They have a sky-scraper and it is bright green"; and in a restaurant called the Brown Derby, built of concrete to look like a brown bowler hat, he ate "Buckwheat Cakes and Maple Syrup and Coffee at Midnight, and it seems just as normal as an ABC . . ." In Providence, Rhode Island, a plump, somewhat tipsy lady from the "best society of the place" made eyes at him for three hours, responding to his every remark with "My! What a line you've got." Cocktails and champagne smoothed his way; a "nincompoop" of a congressman named Henry Cabot Lodge pressed three kinds of liqueurs on him, and beer and whisky. At Yale he lectured on English writers and met Thornton Wilder, at Baltimore he just missed Einstein, and at Vassar the young ladies performed *Sweeney Agonistes.* Eliot was learning what it meant to be a celebrity; it was a gratifying experience, despite his protests to Virginia that he would be happier to be back in England, consuming a dozen Whitstable oysters and a pint of Guinness.[92]

His mood was not always so buoyant. In Virginia, where in April to May 1933 he gave the three Page-Barbour lectures at the university, which were published as *After Strange Gods: A Primer of Modern Heresy* in 1934, he knew "iron thoughts," attacking D. H. Lawrence for being "spiritually sick" and, in some of his stories, even an instrument of "the daemonic powers."[93] The anti-Semitism which Eliot expressed, arguing that in "the society that we desire . . . reasons of race and religion combine to make any number of free-thinking Jews undesirable," has been excused on the grounds that "he merely reflected the pejorative feeling of his class and religion about Jews; that they are partly comic, partly sinister . . ."[94] However, the intimate letters between Pound and Eliot of the early 1930s reveal a shared anti-Semitism directed at the critic F. R. Leavis ("Leavis louse"), who, wrote Pound, dumped his "anglo-yittisch and other diseased putrid secretions/notably a mess . . . spewing his Whitechapel spittle upon Sitwell," his "Leavis jew ooze," etc.[95] Eliot also continued his habit of using the lower case "j," attacking a "jew politician" called Julius Bender,[96] and had returned to his Jewish protagonist Bleistein in a Dirge which Pound had had the good sense to cut from *The Waste Land:* "Full fathom five your Bleistein lies/Under the flatfish and the squids," wrote Eliot. "Graves" Disease in a dead jew's eyes!/Where the crabs have eat the lids."[97] Now Bleistein lay "lower than the wharf rats"; slowly Eliot's verse dissected his body: the "lace that was his nose," the lips unfolding from the teeth, "gold in gold," while the lobsters kept watch. "Hark! Now I hear them scratch scratch scratch."

Over twenty years later, in 1955, Eliot stayed in Cape Town with Mr.

Justice Millin and his wife, Sarah Gertrude Millin, a novelist published by Faber & Faber. "That night before going to bed," wrote Tom Matthews, "Mrs. Millin was brushing up her acquaintance with Eliot's verse . . . when her eye fell on 'Burbank with a Baedeker: Bleistein with a Cigar,' and particularly these lines:

> The rats are underneath the piles.
> The jew is underneath the lot.

Mrs. Millin was a Jew. She went and rapped on Eliot's door, asked whether he acknowledged these lines (he did) and then asked him to leave her house next morning."[98] Eliot never recanted or changed these lines, although, according to William Empson, he later justified his lectures on the grounds that he was "very sick in soul" when he wrote them.[99]

As the months of Tom's absence passed, Vivienne waited expectantly for his return. She was not to know that Ottoline had advised him in March 1933 that she thought Vivienne would "flourish better" alone. It was exactly what Eliot wanted to hear, reinforcing a decision he had already made. In February 1933 he wrote to his solicitor, instructing him to draw up a Deed of Separation and enclosing a letter which the solicitor was to take personally to Vivienne, breaking the news. Eliot related that as he dropped the letter into the postbox he quoted the lines of Brutus from *Julius Caesar,* that he had once chosen as the epigraph to *Sweeney Agonistes:*

> Between the acting of a dreadful thing
> And the first motion, all the interim is
> Like a phantasma, or a hideous dream.[100]

Father Underhill and Ottoline had both argued it would be in both Tom's and Vivienne's interests to separate. Their promptings offered a salve to Eliot's conscience, and his attitude towards Vivienne had hardened. To Ottoline he wrote that he would prefer never to see Vivienne again, arguing that it could do no good to a woman to live with a man to whom she was "morally unpleasant," as well as physically repugnant. The heavily scored underlinings and crossings-out in this letter from Eliot, normally the neatest of correspondents, bears witness to the strength of his feelings. In his Calvinist eyes Vivienne's flesh was corrupt as the result of her carnal sins, and he judged her harshly. Judge/witch, doctor/patient, husband/wife, were patriarchal oppositions in which male/female power was ill-matched, whether the woman's "sin" was her supposed league with the devil, her wilful womb, or her adultery. As Eliot split off his idealisation of the Virgin, or an asexual "woman in white"—a role into which Emily Hale was forced to fit—from Vivienne—viewed as whore, temptress and Eve—her fate was sealed. Like the women of Canterbury in *Murder in the Cathedral* (1935) who invite rape, Vivienne had in his eyes consented to "the horror of the ape," and was "violated." Like these women, all women, the "living worms" of original sin lay coiled in her guts.[101]

While Eliot in New England brooded on the state of Vivienne's soul, his thoughts turned again to the witches of nearby Salem, who were said to have had carnal knowledge of the devil at their sabbaths. His ancestors had judged the witches; on his mother's side he was descended from Isaac Stearns, who had migrated from England to Salem in 1630. He felt himself to be a witchfinder still: "As for me, I can't help it," he had told Pound. "My great-grandfather was on the same witch jury as Nat Hawthorne's great-grandfather; and I just naturally smell out witches etc."[102] Was this not God's mission for him? In his bible he marked God's call to Isaiah:[103] "Thou *art* mine . . . The voice said, Cry. And he said, What shall I cry? All flesh is grass . . ."[104] But he kept his thoughts to himself: "Tell no-one what I have said," he instructed Ottoline: not Vivienne, nor anyone else.[105]

Vivienne, meanwhile, waited at home, ignorant of her husband's decision. To her great regret Ralph Hodgson and Aurelia Bollinger had returned to Japan, where Ralph had been invited to lecture. They left a final present of a "beautiful Kimono and scarf . . . which," wrote Vivienne, "I shall always treasure." It was almost too much pleasure for her to have them, she said sadly, feeling unworthy of such gifts.[106] She tried to fill the vacuum by turning to Alida Monro, who she felt understood Tom because he was so like Alida's late husband, Harold.[107] Alida, described by Virginia Woolf as "a handsome swarthy Russian looking woman in a black astrachan cap,"[108] was, declared Ottoline, extremely kind to Vivienne while Tom was away.[109] But Bloomsbury whispers led to stories that Alida was saying "disagreeable things" about Vivienne. Tom confided to Ottoline that Alida shared the same instinctive "antipathy" towards Vivienne as he did, one which she (and by implication he) had tried in vain to overcome.[110] Shocked by his misplaced criticism of Alida, Ottoline sent robust messages through Sencourt, Eliot's go-between, and forced him to apologise.[111]

At first Vivienne was not alone in her flat after Tom's departure. Robert Sencourt had introduced her to Tim and Mabel Nelson, two friends of his from New Zealand, and Mabel moved in with Vivienne. She was then replaced by Vivienne's old friend Lucy Thayer, who stayed with her at the request of the Haigh-Woods. On 29 November 1932 Vivienne sent a cheerful, meticulously typed letter to Mary Hutchinson, who had of-fered her the post of secretary.[112] "This is a sample of my typewriting," she wrote, wanting to tell Mary how happy the news made her. "I may really consider myself your Secretary from now on, may I not?" She asked Mary if she would dictate the articles she wrote for *Vogue* on fashion and home decoration, so that Mary would have no need to write them in longhand. "I can take them straight down for you on the typewriter, as I have done for Tom." They could work either at Mary's house or at Vivienne's flat, wrote Vivienne, saying that she was so happy about the whole thing that she was writing immediately to Tom. "Do hurry up with your notes, I am impatient to begin."[113]

The winter passed uneventfully. Vivienne had several tea-parties and gave a dinner-party on 14 December for the poet Walter de la Mare and his wife, to which she also asked Mary and Jack. She repeatedly asked if Mary was getting on with her article, as she was so impatient to start work.[114] Then in December a crisis occurred: Lucy Thayer, perhaps unable to stand the strain of Vivienne's demanding and volatile friendship, fled se-cretly to America. She was "vanished, flown." Vivienne had rung up her hotel to find that she had sailed on the *Europa,* and was distraught, not only because she had been planning to spend Christmas with Lucy, but because she was afraid that her friend would meet Tom in her flat in New York and betray Vivienne's confidences about him. Aware that she had spoken indiscreetly to Lucy, Vivienne complained guiltily to Mary that it was "vile" of her friend to do this.[115] Her first reaction was to follow Lucy, and she wrote to Tom, offering to come to America. When he read her letter, Eliot told Sencourt, he felt as if he had received an electric shock.[116]

Mary showered Vivienne with Christmas presents, calling on Christmas Eve when Vivienne was entertaining her family to dinner. She promised to call again to admire Vivienne's Christmas tree. This concern was not as spontaneous as it seemed. Mary, like Ottoline and Virginia, corresponded frequently with Eliot in America and, to some extent, acted as his agents in carrying out his instructions. Indeed, the Bloomsbury triumvirate of Virginia, Ottoline and Mary were in competition as to which one was most intimate with Eliot; he, in turn, played one off against the other, sharing confidences parsimoniously amongst his eager acolytes. Immediately after arriving in Boston in September 1932, Eliot had asked Mary to visit Vivienne from time to time: "It would be a kindness to me too."[117] Mary, unlike Ottoline, obeyed; perhaps she was fonder than Ottoline was of Vivienne, and had forgiven Vivienne for having compared her to Becky Crawley. Mary's own sexual adventurousness had foundered with age, but she would never judge Vivienne's amours as harshly as Eliot did; and, after the comparative failure of Mary's book *Fugitive Pieces,* which the Hogarth Press had published in 1927, she may have felt a certain sympathy for Vivienne's own abortive attempts to carve out a literary career. The depression Mary also suffered in 1928, as she came to realise that the pose of decadent coolness and detachment she had adopted under the influence of Aldous Huxley—he sent her his translation of Baudelaire's *Femmes Damnées*—left her simply confused and weary, lent her a measure of understanding of Vivienne's mental problems.

In March 1933 Vivienne appealed again to Ottoline to see her. Ottoline's only response was to suggest that Vivienne enter the sanatorium at Malmaison. Vivienne was horrified. How miserable to go to a nursing home without Tom to visit her. "No, I still have Liberty." She would stay at the flat, she protested, although she was "aneaimic" [sic] and looked awful. "I have had only 2 or 3 baths since Tom went away." The self-neglect Vivienne describes, only washing her hair twice, hair grey, hands red and rough, teeth "all broken . . . Children in the street do not look as dreadful," cannot be taken too literally: it was no doubt an exaggeration designed to provoke a meeting with Ottoline, and as such, it failed.[118] Maurice, by contrast, reported that Vivienne had redecorated the flat, and had given a small party at which Tom's health was drunk. Vivienne herself recalled the sunny day in early June 1933 when she asked her friend Isobel Lockyear to lunch at 68 Clarence Gate Gardens, where they discussed which bed Eliot would prefer to sleep in, and Isobel admired the new decorations and Harold Monro's old wardrobe which Vivienne had bought from Alida for Tom.[119]

On 26 June Eliot reluctantly caught the *Tuscania* to Greenock, Scotland. Vivienne, who had been waiting expectantly for his return since May, received a cable to say he had sailed for England, but by early July she had no news of her husband. She feared he had drowned. To Ottoline, Vivienne wrote on 7 July of her great anxiety about Tom, and belief that he was "in *danger.*" She had been "nearly insane" with anxiety for two weeks: "I do not know *where he is* and *no-one* knows where he is."[120] All day long she was receiving enquiries for Tom and was in "absolute terror." By Monday, 10 July, Bloomsbury was ringing with the news that "Tom has finally deserted Vivienne." Jack Hutchinson told Virginia that Vivienne "has by today worked herself into a frenzy—in bed, with a nurse." Jack then telephoned to Faber, at Leonard Woolf's suggestion:

> They say mysteriously that they cannot discuss the matter on the telephone, but if V will pull herself together she will realise that there is no reason for anxiety. This we interpret to mean that Tom is back; he has told Faber that he is parting from her; but it is kept secret, until he gives leave—which he may do today.

Jack told Virginia that he had read one of Tom's last letters, which he described as "a very cold and brutal document." Eliot had provided for Vivienne, said Virginia, and made Leonard her executor, but Vivienne had shut the letters in her cupboard with sealed string.[121]

Vivienne's concern was wholly understandable if she had not received the explanatory letter from Eliot's solicitors. It is possible that, as Virginia suggested, she did not read the post and shut the letters unopened in a cupboard. But she remained unaware that she was the victim of a conspiracy: that, while she waited in despair at Clarence Gate Gardens, Eliot was secretly travelling down to Surrey, to be hidden by Frank Morley. "I can neither conceal nor evade the fact that when Tom returned from Harvard . . .

he did not return to Vivien but came to Pikes Farm," wrote Morley. Eliot
had given him "carte blanche to commit me to anything" on 3 May, and
confirmed the arrangement to stay with him on 2 June. It seemed better to
Tom to accept that Vivienne's relations and Enid Faber would do what
they could for Vivienne in London, while he sheltered with the Morleys at
the farm, wrote Frank in extenuation of his friend's plans. As instructed by
Eliot's telegram from the *Tuscania,* Morley met him from the boat-train
and took his heavy luggage to the country; after a night at his London club
Eliot took the branch line to Surrey. Morley met him at the local station
with the dog-cart, a touch which reminded Eliot of Sherlock Holmes and
pleased him very much.[122] The poet was taken to the battered seventeenth-
century brick farmhouse; there were no cows, of which he was "scary."[123]
Soon Eliot had settled into "Uncle Tom's Cabin," where he had a bed and
working-room, and was taking his meals at the house of Mrs. Eames, wife
of the foreman of the adjacent brickworks.

Mary Hutchinson, left to face a hysterical Vivienne in London, complained indignantly to Tom that it was unfair of him to leave her and Jack
to deal with the situation. "I am very sorry that you and Jack have had such
a bad time—I did not anticipate this, and I do not know how else I could
have managed," wrote an unrepentant Tom. His overriding desire from
now on would be to avoid Vivienne at all costs, to conduct all negotiations
through solicitors, and to sever completely all connection with his former
life. The letter he sent, he wrote, must have made clear his reasons for concealing his movements, although he feared it might take some time to
make Vivienne realise that his decision was irrevocable—"She is tenacious." He would, therefore, have to remain "in obscurity" for some little
time.[124]

By 20 July Virginia had satisfied herself that her statement of events
was quite correct. Gleefully she reported that Tom had left Vivienne "irrevocably": "& she sits meanwhile in a flat decorated with pictures of him,
& altars, & flowers." She and Leonard were to dine with the Hutchinsons
that night, "& shall I expect found some sort of Vivienne fund" (a reference to the ill-starred fund for Eliot).[125] Virginia's attitude towards
Vivienne continued to oscillate. Her cold novelist's eye prompted the remark: "It was a most interesting process, to one who loves the smell of the
rubbish heap as I do, to watch."[126] And yet, when she heard the next day

that Vivienne had finally met Tom she wrote with some sympathy: "Vivi E said of the scene with Tom at the solicitors: he sat near me & I held his hand, but he never looked at me."[127]

Vivienne refused to accept Tom's desertion. Her only thought was to win her husband back. She would pay a large sum, and put everything into Tom's hands, if he would honestly come back to her, she told her solicitor. "But I will NOT sign any blackmailing paper relinquishing all rights to him for anybody."[128] The more she thought about the situation, the more Vivienne became convinced that Tom had not left her of his own free will, but at the instigation of their "enemies." "Because I *showed* I *enjoyed* our brief period of *Prosperity,* and because I *made* the *most* of it, *Jealousy* and *Envy* and *Hate* surrounded us both, and finally *tricked* Tom into going to *America,* and worse, to deserting *me,*" she wrote in her diary on 28 January 1934.[129]

Denial is a typical immediate reaction to loss, but it was one which left Tom intensely frustrated. "It would seem that Vivienne adopts the attitude that I have simply and unaccountably chosen to absent myself, leaving her in suspense and very much in the dark," he wrote in annoyance to Mary in September. On the contrary, it was *Vivienne* who was holding matters up. *He* had made it clear that he insisted upon a permanent separation, although he had thought it "fruitless and unnecessary" to give Vivienne any reasons for his decision, beyond saying that he was convinced that it would be the best thing for them both in the long run.[130]

It was natural for Vivienne to feel that she must see Tom, and hear from his own lips his reasons for leaving her. Without such a meeting, how could she accept that their marriage was over? "To induce her to regard the separation as final is quite impossible," wrote Vivienne's solicitors. "She asks that her husband shall return to her and manage her affairs and is ready to accept any conditions he may impose. If only Mrs. Eliot could be given some hope, however faint, of occasional visits by her husband and of eventual re-union it would help enormously."[131]

By September 1933 Eliot had become tired of Pikes Farm and the Surrey countryside, being anxious, said Morley "to get into theatre." He was again experiencing a poetic block after completing the "Five-Finger Exercise," which included the two poems on Ralph Hodgson and himself, and had given up the attempt to complete *Sweeney Agonistes.* "I seemed to myself to have exhausted my meagre poetic gifts, and to have nothing more to say," he wrote.[132] From this dry spell he was rescued by E. Martin Browne, a former actor who had been appointed by Bishop Bell to the post of Director of Religious Drama for Chichester. Browne asked Eliot to write the verse chorus for a pageant to raise money for forty-five churches in London, an offer which he welcomed after the drudgery of writing his American lectures. The pageant, to be named *The Rock,* was to be performed at Sadler's Wells Theatre, which its manager, Lilian Bayliss, had offered to the poet. Eliot now needed urgently to return to the capital. But, on the other hand, as he wrote petulantly to Mary, he could not think of returning to his marriage, a situation "to which I have already given the best years of my life." He railed at Vivienne's "obstruction and cajolery" at refusing to accept the separation. What steps could he take to make her see sense? He could not afford to blow his cover. Eliot became obsessional about preserving his secrecy, concealing his address, and the date of his visit, when he saw Virginia on 9 September at Rodmell. "The mystery I imagine flatters him," wrote Virginia sarcastically.[133]

When he arrived, Eliot seemed changed. "He is 10 years younger: hard, spry, a glorified boy scout in shorts and yellow shirt. He is enjoying himself very much. He is tight & shiny as a wood louse." At forty-six, he wanted "to live, to love." Over breakfast Tom and Virginia discussed Vivienne, with Tom showing "some asperity." He refused to admit the "excuse of insanity for her." Vivienne was not insane, said Tom, but "put it on." He was resentful of the past waste of his life. Virginia, sympathetic to suffering genius—as she believed Tom to be—promised to find him lodgings in Sussex.[134]

Ezra Pound proposed a meeting to "The Rt. Rev. Wunkus T. Possum." "You must come incognito, as I shall be the same," replied Eliot, offering to meet "Rabbit" in some "predetermined sequestered spot," such as Cliftonville or Reigate.[135] Pound suggested he should come to Rapallo, but Eliot demurred: "I must live cheap until I get things settled." His hair had started falling out on one side during 1932, he said, and he didn't know if there was a good wigmaker in Rapallo. Write to me at 24 Russell Square, he asked Pound, and mark the envelope "PERSONAL"; in a postscript he added a discovery made by most newly separated men: "Solicitors *are* expensive."[136]

Tom's refusal to divulge his address irritated Ottoline, as did his intimacy with Robert Sencourt. Robert had no greater facility to communicate with him than anyone else, protested Eliot: all his letters were forwarded from Faber at Russell Square because he did not wish to inconvenience any friends by entrusting them with an address which they would be expected to conceal.[137] A fortnight later, Ottoline complained she was still receiving messages through Sencourt rather than directly from Tom. "Robert is very sweet and good," replied Tom; his only fault was that he was something of a chatterbox, and liked to give people news of each other. Eliot promised Ottoline to come out of hiding soon.[138] However, the truth was that he enjoyed the mystery: the actor in him revelled in the role of Sherlock Holmes. He referred to Morley as "Inspector Morley," an assistant who, like the patient Watson, did his bidding in plodding but loyal fashion.[139] Of his oldest sister Ada, the only other intellectual in his immediate family, Tom often said that she was the Mycroft to his Sherlock Holmes.[140] Morley himself entered into the spirit of the saga, writing of his subsequent career, which took him away from Eliot: "I have often missed my Sherlock Holmes."[141]

Eliot's ducking and diving continued. He enlisted the help of Vivienne's doctor, Dr. Reginald Miller, who agreed to write her "an explicit letter," explaining that Tom's decision was irrevocable.[142] In November 1933 he was still waiting to hear whether Vivienne was prepared to sign the agreement,[143] but by the new year he was no further forward. Vivienne's only response was to write Tom letters, begging him to return to her to "be protected."[144] In his mind she became the pursuer; but in hers he was simply an errant husband, who must be coaxed back to the marital home. "The only thing I *yearn* for and *bleed* for is the day when Tom *calmly turns the keys* in the front door, walks *leisurely* in . . . and then has a good look round, *smiles* with quiet satisfaction, draws a *long breath,* and goes *quietly* to his *dear* books and to his bed," she wrote. "And if he *can* *then* say, God bless my little Welsh wife Vivienne. Surely he *wld* say that . . ."[145]

Eliot continued to house-hunt, and to obfuscate. On 31 October he had told Virginia that he intended to look for a room in Kensington, a district which he disliked, on his next visit to town, and take it temporarily while he looked about elsewhere. The room he was considering was three guineas a week for one room with breakfast and dinner, but he thought he could find two rooms for that price in a cheaper part of London, such as Clerkenwell, Blackheath or Greenwich.[146] Four days later, on 3 November, he was apologising to Mary for not receiving her invitation to dinner, because "my Miss Gilbert" at the office had made a muddle and failed to forward the card. "I wish I had given you my address," he wrote, not altogether convincingly; "it is only that I have not been able to give it to anyone lest it might be an inconvenience to them to know it . . ." He was, he wrote, hoping to find "a temporary abode" in London within the next fortnight, from which to conduct a search. He was going to Inverness, and then Paris for a day or two, and then wanted to settle in London while he waited to hear whether Vivienne would accept his terms.[147] Nevertheless, by December he was still lying low, declining Mary's invitation to her daughter Barbara's wedding: "In the present circumstances I don't go to parties." He was, however, prepared to go to *Measure for Measure* with the Hutchinsons and Woolfs at Sadler's Wells.[148] Eliot could get a house with grounds on the banks of Loch Lomond for £10 per annum, he joked to Pound in December. "But I don't like the climate." Even Wiltshire was "really too exposed."[149] In the end it was Sencourt who rescued Eliot from his country exile. He found him a room in a gaunt Victorian lodging-house in which he had himself formerly stayed, at 33 Courtfield Road, South Kensington.[150]

The lodging-house at Courtfield Road was devoid of women, apart from the housekeeper, Freda Bevan, who cooked for the residents. It was run by an "Old Catholic" eccentric, a once dubiously ordained bishop, William Edward Scott-Hall, and was something of an Anglo-Catholic enclave. Next door lived a prominent Anglo-Catholic, Miss Muriel Forwood, and nearby was the leading Anglo-Catholic layman Athelstan Riley, as well as Axel Munthe, author of *The Story of San Michele*.[151] Eliot played with Miss Bevan's cat, Bubbles, a tabby who became an inspiration for his cat verses, as did a majestic Persian named Xerxes; but a more important consideration than cats was Anglo-Catholicism, and fortunately Courtfield Road was only a few minutes' walk from St. Stephen's Church, Gloucester Road, where the priest, Father Eric Cheetham, held services which Eliot attended regularly.

It is unclear whether Eliot stayed for more than a few weeks at Courtfield Road. He continued "tramping Clerkenwell" in the search of better value accommodation, asking Virginia on 7 December to look out for anything "well recommended (furnished bed and sitting room)" with a bathroom geyser that worked, in "East Bloomsbury," between Southampton Row and Grays Inn Road.[152] Eventually it was Virginia who indirectly solved Eliot's accommodation problem—by reintroducing him to a fellow Hogarth Press author, the homosexual novelist C. H. B. Kitchen, who took pity on the poet and offered him "sanctuary" in his flat in Great Ormond Street. At the end of the year Eliot moved in with Clifford, and his two gay flatmates.[153]

21

Separation

Eliot experienced his time in Great Ormond Street as liberation. It was an all-male establishment: the poet's flatmates were his old friend, novelist Clifford Kitchin, Richard Jennings, a gay book collector, and Ken Ritchie, later Chairman of the Stock Exchange, who had a policeman lover. It was, recalls the novelist Francis King, "a gay household," in which Eliot felt free to venture out in the evenings, wearing "a bit of slap." "Clifford told me how Eliot went out rouged and lipsticked, with eye shadow," says King. "Clifford was absolutely convinced he was carrying on a gay life then." All three men liked to bring back "trade" to the flat; and why, asked Clifford, would Eliot choose to lodge in such a house were he not gay?[1] However, it was still a period in which discretion was all-important for a man like Eliot, who depended on his income from his work, and could not afford the aristocratic disdain shown by Osbert Sitwell, who was living openly with David Horner. Eliot kept his own counsel, and did not discuss his nightly jaunts with Kitchin.[2] But Stephen Spender, who had met Eliot in 1928 and had been published by Faber, was aware that Eliot wore cosmetics; in May 1996 Spender's widow Natasha confirmed the truth of the Sitwells' stories of Eliot's use of "pale green powder" to Alec Guinness, who played the psychiatrist Sir Henry Harcourt-Reilly in *The Cocktail Party*.[3]

Eliot was experimenting with a new lifestyle free of Vivienne and free, too, from the constraints of family life with Frank Morley. Sometimes he went out with Kitchin, whose new novel, *Crime at Christmas,* was published in October 1934 by the Hogarth Press. On 19 November he and Clifford dined with the Woolfs in Tavistock Square, Virginia finding Kitchin something of a misfit, "a little fat & white and cunning & not up to the mark. A rather conceited touchy man, I guess . . ."[4] And Eliot had the courage to support Djuna Barnes in her struggle to have her novel *Nightwood* (1936) published, after it had been turned down by her previous publisher, Boni & Liveright, as being "nothing more than a welter of homosexuality."[5] In Eliot's preface for the novel, which was published by Faber, he praised Barnes's characterisation of the cross-dressing doctor, Dr. Matthew O'Connor, whose original was her friend Dan Mahoney; once Barnes found Mahoney in bed dressed for a scene from *Nightwood,* "all bathed and perfumed and made up like a hussy, the clock was ticking, the radio going, the kitchen kettle steaming, and he was eating peppermints!"[6]

Yet Eliot was still living a falsehood. The closet remained a prison within which his isolation grew. In 1932 he had confessed in the foreword to Harold Monro's posthumous *Collected Poems* that "the compensations for being a poet are grossly exaggerated; and they dwindle as one becomes older, and the shadows lengthen and the solitude becomes harder to endure."[7] In *Sweeney Agonistes* Eliot had written of the loneliness within an unhappy marriage with startling innovation, anticipating the plays of Pinter; now he experienced a different solitariness, one relieved only by casual encounters, guarded friendships and office routine: Eliot's Hell was not "other people," as Sartre famously stated, but the condition he now experienced. "Hell is oneself,/Hell is alone, the other figures in it/Merely projections," says Edward in *The Cocktail Party*.[8] As Eliot told Princeton theologian Paul Elmer More in 1928, he looked into the void, that "void that I find in the middle of all human happiness and all human relations . . . I am one whom this sense of void tends to drive towards asceticism or sensuality, and only Christianity helps to reconcile me to life, which is otherwise disgusting."[9] He walked in a "daily terror of eternity," for religion had brought him, not happiness, but something "more terrifying than ordinary pain and misery."[10] Eliot was "really shocked" that More did not believe God had made hell; his own fear of damnation lived with him daily, as he relived the horrors of his marriage, which he described as a Dostoevsky novel written by Middleton Murry,[11] and brooded over the nature of good and evil and his private sins. Introspection brought little comfort, for by the standards of his own harsh Puritan morality, same-sex orientation and love was an abomination before the Lord. And yet it was the only form of relationship to which Eliot was attracted at that time.

Ottoline concluded that Eliot was either very sick or "rather crazy" when he viciously denounced D. H. Lawrence to her as "Evil" in April 1934, and recoiled in horror when she showed him some books of fourth-century Greek statues, saying they repelled him and were not far removed from serpent worship. What a strange relic of his Calvinist ancestry the poet was, thought Ottoline, as he talked obsessively of evil spirits, demonology and original sin, arguing that those who did not partake of Christian sacraments were possessed by devils. His censure of Lawrence and Vivienne, as of himself, revealed a dark and punitive seam within American Puritanism. Intuitively Ottoline understood that Tom saw evil spirits where no one else saw them because he felt them in himself, and that was why he had fled into the arms of the church, where priests could ward them off.[12] Only ritual and routine sustained him as he fought with the demons of his conscience. "What people call their conscience," wrote Eliot, is "just the cancer/That eats away the self."[13]

Eliot drew closer to Father Eric Cheetham, who in 1934 appointed him Vicar's Warden at St. Stephen's. At some point in late 1934 Eliot moved in with his vicar, whose rectory at 9 Grenville Place, Cromwell Road, shared with a number of curates, offered him a more congenial and discreet sanctuary than Clifford's flat. He had considered sharing a flat with A. L. Rowse, whose *Politics and the Younger Generation* he had nursed into print in 1931. In a letter dated 12 October 1934, Eliot set out his marital and legal difficulties, and the idea fell through.[14] This was probably due to Eliot's unwillingness to commit himself to any arrangement from which he could not immediately "decamp," as he put it later to Dorothy Pound. It is uncertain whether Eliot was still in Great Ormond Street or living with Eric Cheetham when in November Virginia Woolf asked where she might find him. Tom was so fearful that she might spy out his hiding-place that he replied, "You shall have my address only if and when you will come to see me, because it is Secret."[15]

Vivienne, meanwhile, was still in shock from Eliot's desertion. On Tuesday, 30 January 1934 she had had a meeting with her solicitor, Moxon Broad, and discussed the burning question of Tom's whereabouts. She instructed Broad "to *find out* his *domicile secretly* and *at once*. With *no view* to my attempting to *upset* him,"[16] for all she wanted, as she had told Ottoline on 31 December 1933, "is my *own* husband, and to be able to look after him and take *care* of him again," saying that she could not be persuaded into "what I think is wrong, or converted to cruelty"—a reference to the deed of separation.[17] Five months later, she and Broad had made no progress in tracing Tom: "I have no idea where my husband Tom is, and whether he is alive or dead," she wrote on 4 June 1934, one year after she had expected Eliot to walk through the doorway of their flat at 68 Clarence Gate Gardens.[18] Blotting out her brief meeting with him at his solicitor's office, she told Mr. Hope, her bank manager, the following summer, she had no proof that her husband had ever returned from America, although, as time passed, "it is easy . . . to say that he is living in England and to scare me, by every kind of bogey, from seeing him."[19] From Vivienne's point of view, the mystery deepened. Eliot had vanished as surely as Macavity, the mystery cat. No answer came to her requests, via her solicitor, for a meeting in which Eliot would give her the explanation he owed her. Vivienne therefore remained in denial, unable to accept the reality of his desertion. Maurice Haigh-Wood, who may have known Eliot's address, asked his brother-in-law if there were any other, less cruel way, than of writing through solicitors, but Eliot replied: "What other way *can* I find?"[20]

Eliot's pusillanimity was linked to his paranoid fear of Vivienne, a fear which had at its core the belief that further contact with her could drive him insane. As he had confessed to John Hayward in February 1931, he had had "considerable mental agony" at one time or another, and "once or twice felt on the verge of insanity or imbecility," feeling, until his conversion, that everything was "just waste and muddle,"[21] a phrase which echoes the last lines of the first of the *Four Quartets,* "Burnt Norton": "Ridiculous the waste sad time/Stretching before and after." Although, Eliot told Hayward, after his conversion "a pattern emerged," he never found the courage to face Vivienne honestly. As a result she remained baffled and frustrated, imagining that he was held prisoner and prevented from returning to her. She continued to refuse to sign the Deed of Separation.

On Boxing Day 1933 Vivienne had made a final appeal to Ottoline for a meeting: "I had such a terrible shock in the summer, and since then an increasing nightmare." Her strength, she wrote, could not last much longer. What appalled and amazed and completely bewildered her was that she was expected to *"agree and acquiesce* in a *wicked plot. And still am—! Bombarded. Threatened."* Her days had been spent mostly in bed over the last three months, she wrote, and she could only dress for a few hours. "I had no little presents from anyone this year." It was a self-pitying letter and Ottoline ignored it.[22]

To Ottoline, as to so many other judges of Vivienne, such talk of a "plot" seemed either evidence of paranoia and "madness" or wilful exaggeration, but in fact Vivienne's "paranoia" was justified. She *was* the victim of Eliot's determination, aided by her unscrupulous brother Maurice, to eradicate her from his life. His decision, the legacy of so many tempestuous years of marriage, was to lead—by a path of humiliation and subterfuge—to the first attempt to commit Vivienne to an asylum, while she, for her part, remained equally resolute in her own aim, to win Tom back by whatever weapons at her disposal. It was to be a bitter, but unequal war, one with a financial twist, in which Vivienne had at first no inkling that Tom was supported by her own mother and brother. The odds were stacked against her in a way she only slowly came to realise. It was a war she could not win.

The opening shots had already been fired by 1934, a year in which Vivienne felt embattled. "This is the sternest fight one delicate nerve-wrecked Englishwoman of 46 ever had to fight," she wrote on 14 June. "It is just relentless *warfare,* me and Polly, and a few crippled mercenaries, v the world."[23] She was at first an innocent in the struggle, a woman who had no experience of solicitors and had relied on her husband and brother to see to financial affairs. It was only her friends and neighbours, Charles and Ella de Saxe, who warned her *"not* to put my signature to any paper or document connected with Tom," by which she might have signed away her rights to her property and papers.[24] The de Saxes supported Vivienne, seeing her almost every day for six "terrible" months and keeping her head "clear," until they left for South Africa at the end of 1934. With their support Vivienne remained firm and refused to sign any "dirty paper" presented to her by James & James, the Haigh-Wood family solicitors. But after the de Saxes went abroad, Vivienne was vulnerable to pressure from James & James, who took advice from Maurice, and to demands from her husband's solicitors, Bird & Bird. Maurice, now a stockbroker at

Northcotes in the City, managed the Haigh-Wood estate which he, Vivienne, and their mother Rose, had inherited from Charles Haigh-Wood on his death. At first Vivienne trusted her brother to look after her interests, until Charles de Saxe suggested that Maurice had "bungled" the purchase of some de Havilland shares. Feeling that the truth of her financial situation was being kept from her, Vivienne became concerned to discover the full extent of her legacy from her father, and instructed her own solicitor, Moxon Broad. In the four-year struggle over the family money, which ensued until Vivienne's final committal, Broad was her ally.

Vivienne's domestic situation was also one to justify fears of persecution, for she was kept under surveillance by the Eliots' servant, William Leonard Janes, who was in Tom's pay, but whom Vivienne mistakenly regarded as a friend ("not a servant"), and whom she innocently but unwisely took into her confidence. Janes regularly monitored her behaviour and reported to Eliot, who may at first have been motivated by concern for her condition without him. "I have not seen or herd [sic] from Mrs. Eliot since she came last Saturday week when she came to take away the Tin Base . . ." wrote Janes.[25] "Janes stayed on at 68 Clarence Gate Gardens just to watch over Vivie," said Maurice.[26] The ex-detective's reports furnished evidence for the first, unsuccessful attempt to commit Vivienne to a private mental home.[27] Yet on 1 August 1934 Vivienne recorded gratefully in her diary that W. L. Janes and Jan Culpin (possibly the mother of Eliot's Oxford friend Karl Culpin),[28] were the only two people who cared for her: "These two are both *old* people, who can *expect nothing from me, gain nothing by my death*—and there is *no* way in which I can reward them, *nor do they look for reward,*" she wrote, comparing "these 2 *old* people with *my* mother, *my brother, my aunts, and My Husband* . . . These questions did not come to my mind during my Father's lifetime."[29]

It is ironic that Vivienne, who fervently desired to preserve her papers in order that posterity might judge her fairly, trusted Janes, who passed information to his master, which made possible the removal by force of some of those records from 68 Clarence Gate Gardens. Although Vivienne prized her liberty so highly that she refused Ottoline's suggestion that she enter the Malmaison sanatorium in 1932, she allowed Janes to know the details of her health, including her almost daily visits to collect her drugs from her chemist Allen & Hanbury at 7 Vere Street, as well as her unwavering determination to pursue Tom. Had she not confided so freely in Janes, she might have preserved both her liberty and her possessions with more success.

Yet at times Vivienne was frightened of Janes. In January, he "banged and bawled" at her cook, Mrs. Forminger, and made such a *"hideous* row" in the kitchen that she was driven to speak to him: "he then became most abusive, railed against Mrs. Forminger whom he really seems to hate, and finally banged out, leaving me quite sick and faint; saying he would never come back any more . . ."[30] When she kept him waiting he reminded her of his high blood pressure and said "he wished me to understand that he is close to 80 years old and *my* troubles are no affair of his."[31] Nevertheless, Vivienne often called on Janes and his wife at 101 Lumley Buildings, their flat in Pimlico, joining them for Mrs. Janes's birthday tea on 7 October 1934; when Mrs. Janes was ill on October 29, Vivienne hurried out to buy her a bottle of whisky, and when Vivienne herself collapsed on 11 November, Janes handed her "a *very* hot water bottle" and told her: "If you can stay in bed all day, it is the best place for you and I advise you to do so." Such daily intimacy lulled Vivienne into a false sense of security.

As Vivienne painfully came to realise that her life with Eliot was over, it became her priority to find a place of safety for the records which charted that life. On 31 December 1933 she had told Ottoline: "The truth will all come out, if not in *our* life—*then after it."*[32] In her diary of 1 August 1934 she addressed future researchers: "You who in later years *will read these very words of mine* and will be able to trace a true history of this epoch, by my Diaries and Papers."[33] Anticipating the blame which would be heaped upon her for the failure of the marriage, and already suspicious of Maurice and her mother, she considered to which institution she should leave her archive of diaries, drafts of fiction and poetry, photograph albums, account books and letters. Oxford had happy associations with Tom's courtship, of punting on the river with Scofield and Lucy Thayer, and she therefore chose the Bodleian Library. Within a year of Tom's desertion Vivienne decided to write her decision into her will, having her first meeting with her solicitor, Moxon Broad, on 30 January 1934, and writing in her diary: "N.B. Change Wills . . . Instruct to keep J & J [James & James] off me entirely, & to procure a moderate *rent* for a new home." Soon Moxon Broad had nineteen letters between Vivienne and James & James in his file, as

Vivienne began the long process of attempting to gain control over her share of her father's legacy. Interestingly, one of Vivienne's early impulses was to make a will "leaving to Theodora," Eliot's niece, some of her estate.[34]

On 24 June 1934, the anniversary of the day, one year ago, on which "T. S. Eliot, my *husband,* was to have *sailed from Boston . . .*" Vivienne reflected on a year in which "there has been more serious damage and *evil* and abomination in my life than I should have believed *possible* in *England* in 1934 to go *unpunished.* This is a black document." Two days later, 26 June, was an even more unhappy day for Vivienne, marking as it did the nineteenth anniversary of "the Wedding Day of Thomas Stearns and Vivienne Haigh Eliot." Nevertheless, conscious that the seventeen years she had shared with Eliot would prove of enormous interest to future readers, she wrote with pride in her diary that day: "What an example to hand down from generation to generation, and what an *invaluable* gift I have made to the *Bodleian* Library, Oxford." Her hope was that her papers, manuscripts and diaries would be published "without *alterations.*"[35] On 22 July 1934, Vivienne signed a new will at 1 Great Winchester Street, EC1, the office of Moxon Broad, in which she bequeathed her papers to the Bodleian in order to avoid their falling into the hands of either T. S. Eliot or Maurice Haigh-Wood.[36] Vivienne Haigh Eliot signed her final will, witnessed by Moxon Broad and his stenographer, on 1 March 1936, in which she gave to the Bodleian Library "absolutely and free of duty all my papers manuscripts diaries journals photographs albums and sketches"; advised by Broad, she supposed that in making this bequest she was also leaving copyright in her unpublished manuscripts to the library, as the Copyright Act 1911 had apparently created a rule of presumption that the legatee was the owner of the copyright. To Eliot she left first choice of her family portraits, and her "personal chattels," as well as her Yorkshire terrier Polly and cat Whiskers.[37]

Vivienne was afraid that Tom, who was in possession of the keys to 68 Clarence Gate Gardens, which he had taken with him when he left for America on 17 September 1932, might return without her knowledge to the flat when she was absent and remove documents such as her diaries. On Monday 23 July, she decided to ask the Hutchinsons if they knew where these keys were now, because Mary had taken such a "keen interest" in her keys during the time Tom was in America.[38] She gave instructions to her maid, Ivy, that the door was not to be opened to anyone. "I am *not* at home," said Vivienne, forbidding Ivy to open the door even to her mother when she rang the bell.[39] But Vivienne now found another ruse by which she hoped to outwit Tom: she had, according to Maurice, asked the management of the blocks for another little flat "for a servant," and they had offered her number 177, on the second floor, a tiny flat but one which served her purpose of storage. "One flat—number 68—was in Tom's name still," said Maurice. "And Vivien was paying *somehow* for 177. She moved all she could upstairs."[40]

Vivienne's longing to see Tom grew during the anguished hours she spent puzzling over his disappearance. Between 1934 and 1938 she and Eliot played out a game of cat and mouse, in which she was at first the pursuer, he the quarry. Her first impulse was to "collar" him at the theatre. In April 1934 Vivienne attended a party on the stage at Sadler's Wells, a few weeks before the opening of *The Rock,* the pageant play Eliot had written at the invitation of Martin Browne. The invitation from Lilian Bayliss, the manager of the theatre, was perhaps addressed to both Eliots, as a large volume of post, as well as many telephone calls for Eliot, continued to be directed to the flat. Vivienne was nervous about attending, but a new friend, artist Margaret Smith, "incited" her to go. Ella de Saxe, too, continued to encourage Vivienne in her struggle to survive her mysterious abandonment by Eliot, *"urging* me to *courage* and *endurance* by *reminding* me I *must* fight on and not funk anything . . ."[41] It was in this spirit that Vivienne slowly dressed in her blue velvet dress on 16 April and took a taxi at 10:30 p.m. to Sadler's Wells. It was terrible at first, she recorded, but Miss Bayliss was very kind and came up and greeted her. Vivienne sat close to the door, keeping her eyes "fixed for Tom." At first she saw no one she knew, but at last in came Mary and Virginia, together. Both greeted her, and were "very nice." Jack Hutchinson and Leonard then entered, and Mary reintroduced her to her son, Jeremy.[42] Food and drink were handed round; Vivienne waited in hope, but of Eliot there was no sign. Holmes had given her the slip.

On 28 May, Vivienne's birthday, *The Rock* opened at Sadler's Wells. "He did it for my birthday, I know," she comforted herself. That evening, sitting in cheap seats with Margaret Smith and munching her sandwiches, Vivienne looked down on the stalls where St. John Hutchinson sat smoking a big cigar. The Fabers, in evening dress, were chatting to the great and the good. Nothing could have underlined more clearly the change in her lifestyle. She and Margaret waited until the very end, and saw everyone leave: "We walked all round and hung about but no sign of TS Eliot at all," wrote a frustrated Vivienne.[43] Four days later she renewed her quest, returning to Sadler's Wells for another performance of the pageant. The theatre was full but, once again, there was no sign of Tom: bewildered, she left in the interval.[44] Was Tom alive or was he dead, she demanded of her diary.[45] On 7 June she took two buses to the theatre, and stood in the gods, jostled by the crowds, craning her neck for a glimpse of the playwright. After the curtain came down, "I hung about a long time," she wrote sadly: "No sign of Tom."

On 9 June Vivienne attended *The Rock*'s final performance, a small figure among the audience of 1,500. That night the pageant made a powerful impression upon her: she found it both moving and terrible as the masked chorus declaimed Eliot's words, castigating society for its materialism and holding up to ridicule the lives of commuters, those "decent godless people" whose only monument was "a thousand lost golf balls."[46] The evening was an emotional experience "in the heat and the *horror*." She found it hard to believe that Tom had written it and she felt the author was "certainly a very wicked man to so play (and prey) on the *emotions*." As she, like Tom, turned over the past in her mind, she came to the conclusion that Eliot was immoral; although the pageant was "*very* beautiful," with its exhortations to the audience not to neglect God, "It is the man who wrote it, *if that is TSE,* whose soul must be saved . . ."[47]

That summer was a time of despair for Vivienne. A day or two after seeing *The Rock,* an experience which brought her old life with Tom vividly back to her, she recorded that "a very queer *stunned, lost, dazed* feeling is creeping over me. It is the strangest episode—like a vast preparation for a *death*. Crépescule [sic] des Dieux." A foray into Camden Town to see her cleaner, Margaret Clee, whom she had sacked, left Vivienne frightened and nervous, and she began at last to take note of Jan Culpin's warning not to trust the servants: "Now I do see what Jan means and that no doubt it is a plant and a crib, and all my servants are tampered with and paid agents . . ." Hurriedly she threw 30 shillings on to the camp-bed, once Tom's bed, which Clee had stolen, and fled in a taxi.[48]

Day after day Vivienne walked with her dog Polly to Allen & Hanbury at 7 Vere Street to collect her medicine, which included the sleeping-pill Soneril, and saw her pharmacist friend Louie (Louise) Purdon, with whom she sometimes lunched at the ABC café. Vivienne rose late and ate out, often visiting Selfridges for waffles and coffee or shopping in Marshall & Snelgrove; sometimes she visited her favourite doctor, physiotherapist Dr. Anna Cyriax, who practised with her husband, Dr. James Cyriax, and father-in-law, Dr. Edgar Cyriax, at 41 Welbeck Street, for a "treatment," but although she and Polly roamed the streets of London, between Marylebone, Kensington and Pimlico, remarkably Vivienne never caught a glimpse of Eliot. It was a "blisteringly hot" summer that year. 12 June 1934 was one of the most perfect June days Vivienne had ever seen:

> A pure blue sky, a still, hot, yet fresh air. No dust or mist, but almost like Italy. The high white buildings here look most beautiful against the sky and now that Clarence Gate Gardens is painted outside it holds its own with the newer buildings. It must be *exquisite* in the *country* to-day, or on the river. The *height* of the *Season,* and here I am, *lost* in London. Was there ever a more *strange* life than mine?[49]

By the end of July Vivienne felt that her nerve had completely gone. "I look like the *ghost* of a street child," she wrote. "My face is yellow like parchment, no colour, dead eyes, am as thin as a rat." She was too restless to rest, too tired to think constructively.[50] The black and white head and shoulders portrait of her, drawn by Margaret Smith that summer, showed "the bland expression of one who has learnt to keep out of the way. Out of anyone's way. A hard school," and was it a wise one, asked Vivienne, who was beginning to question her own docility. "Isn't it better to throw one's weight about?"[51] But she remained nervous. Frightened of sleeping alone in the flat, from which she had had the telephone removed, she preferred to spend the night at a hotel at 20 Roland Gardens, Kensington, staying in room number seven, Jan Culpin's room, during her absence in Germany.

During the day Vivienne returned to 68 Clarence Gate Gardens. She maintained the flat meticulously, often cleaning it herself with Mrs. Forminger. Although Vivienne had packed up the silver in March, depositing it in the District Bank, and had arranged the auction of the surplus furniture, she had no intention of leaving the flat, renewing the lease in June for a further five years. Instead, Vivienne kept their former home as a "Shrine to Tom," similar to the shrine to Oswald Mosley, leader of the British Union of Fascists, which she much admired at the BUF Christmas Bazaar held in Chelsea on 8 December. Vivienne was impressed by Lady Cynthia Mosley, whom she saw at the bazaar, and congratulated herself on having joined the movement at the Women's Fascist Headquarters at 12 Lower Grosvenor Place three days earlier. Vivienne felt "glad and relieved" to join the Fascists, believing the movement would bring a return to the "happy, organised public service" she remembered from the war.[52] She had shared Eliot's right-wing beliefs: the year 1934 was the one in which his lectures at the University of Virginia were published as *After Strange Gods: A Primer of Modern Heresy,* lectures for which Isaiah Berlin was to take him to task in 1951, pointedly referring to the fact that, in the year after Hitler came to power, "You thought it a pity that large groups of 'free-thinking Jews' should complicate the lives of otherwise fairly homogeneous Anglo-Saxon Christian communities? And that it were better otherwise? . . . And that it would be better for such communities if their Jewish neighbours . . . were put 'beyond the borders of the city'?" Berlin quoted Eliot's words back to him: "reasons of race and religion make any large number of free-thinking Jews undesirable." How could he insist that "race" had nothing to do with the "Jewish problem"? Although Eliot apologised to Berlin for the offensive sentence, writing, "the sentence of which you complain would of course never have appeared at all at that time, if I had been aware of what was going to happen, indeed had already begun in Germany . . . ," he did not, even then, abandon the idea of "race" altogether, writes Michael Ignatieff.[53] Nevertheless Eliot was no supporter of Mosley,[54] but Vivienne felt her husband would be pleased as she hung a large portrait of him by Sir William Rothenstein in the drawing-room, highlighted just as the portrait of Lady Cynthia's husband had been high-lighted at the bazaar. Her "altar" to Tom was flanked on each side by two Venetian mirrors given to her by Charles and Ella de Saxe. On another wall she hung a sketch of Eliot by Wyndham Lewis. She also displayed three oil paintings by her father, and two of his watercolours.

Over the summer months of 1934 Vivienne fought a running battle with cockroaches in the kitchen, but finally the local vermin officer brought the problem under control. By October the flat was *"Quite* per-fect," and it accorded the perfect setting, too, for Vivienne to indulge an-other passion: her fervent royalism. With pride she displayed on the drawing-room mantelpiece her invitation to a reception given by the English Speaking Union at Londonderry House to meet HRH The Prince of Wales, and arranged white roses in the room in honour of "Elizabeth, Princess [sic] of York."[55] She had seals made with the crests of the Earls of Carnarvon and St. Germans, to whom Eliot claimed connection, and used them to seal her private papers. And on 30 October 1934 she and W. L. Janes walked to Londonderry House, Vivienne in her blue dress and cloak from Barkers, her hair newly waved, for her presentation to the Prince of Wales. She felt so faint as she waited in the immense crowd that two American ladies brought her some sherry; until at last her turn came to walk up the wide staircase and stand beside the two ushers. Vivienne was momentarily annoyed that they did not call out her name: but then, "in front of me stood his royal highness, the Prince of Wales, first gentleman of Europe. He looked so young, and is about my height and build. His head is on the small side, his shoulders very square and a very fine car-riage . . ." When the prince held her hand in his own "very strong grip" she almost fainted with joy; and she remained, fixed to the ground, until at last the usher said, walk straight on.

Despite these high points in an otherwise humdrum life, Vivienne sometimes felt that she was on the verge of "nervous collapse," but her new help, Mrs. Read, had "a true mother's heart," and shopped and cooked for Vivienne daily. Meanwhile her fascination with the royal family contin-ued: in November she sent a copy of Eliot's poem "Marina" to Prince George, Duke of Kent, and Princess Marina as a wedding present, signing it "from VHE and TSE, with sincere wishes for their happiness,"[56] just as she sent out Christmas cards from "Mr. and Mrs. T. S. Eliot" in 1935.[57] For the Silver Jubilee of George V in 1935, Vivienne decorated her balcony with large Irish and French flags, the Union Jack, Stars and Stripes, and "two small royal standards," plus an electric light from Woolworth's with red, white and blue lamps: "I meant to make my balcony a success no matter what it cost for their royal highnesses Queen Mary and King George," she wrote in her diary. She volunteered to sell flowers on 3 June, collecting her tray of red, white and blue flowers, and walking the streets all afternoon, gratified to find that she sold far more than she expected.[58]

The English Speaking Union continued to be the centre of Vivienne's social life, giving her an excuse to indulge her interest in fashion, as well as an outlet for the snobbery of which she had often accused Eliot. Early December 1934 found Vivienne once again at Barkers, having her hair dressed in Empire style, with five hanging curls, and her nails manicured in preparation for a reception for Mr. and Mrs. Bingham, the American ambassador and his wife. Lovingly Vivienne selected the cream chiffon and black lace Agnes Decolt model dress she had bought for Tom's return; and, although her maid Gretel dressed her in a red and black velvet dress which she had altered, her mistress immediately changed her mind. In the cream chiffon with a blue sash, gold shoes and stockings, long cream suede gloves and pearls, Vivienne and her friend, Mrs. Winden, took a taxi to Berkeley Square. This time her name was loudly and clearly announced, but otherwise the evening did not live up to expectations. Vivienne had hoped to make some new, American friends, writing in her diary: "I only came for Americans, Royalty, French cultured people." Perhaps she dreamt of finding a successor to Eliot; if so, she was disappointed.[59]

As time passed, Vivienne grew increasingly apprehensive at the prospect of suddenly coming face to face with Tom in public. She fretted over whether or not to attend a meeting of the Sadler's Wells Theatre at Lord Howard de Walden's in Belgrave Square on 28 June. The only reason she had for hesitating, she wrote, was the reason she had for hesitating to attend *any* function: "The determination I have formed *NOT* to meet my husband *anywhere* but *in his* (and my) own home. Alternatively at the Sanatorium de la Malmaison in the presence of *witnesses* of my own *choosing* . . . Never having seen him in his own home *since September 17th 1932* I have formed this *determination* for my own *protection* and it is very necessary."[60] But in reality Vivienne was no closer to finding Tom's "domicile" than she had been since he returned to England in July 1933. Dinner with Geoffrey and Enid Faber in March 1934 had yielded no clues, even though Faber and Eliot worked together daily. Vivienne was happy that evening: Enid looked "charming," and the Fabers' new house at Oak Hill Park was "nice and homelike." But "Tom's name was not mentioned, *that* we had agreed beforehand."[61] Although Vivienne dared asked no questions of Faber, without doubt he reported to Eliot on Vivienne's condition, as did the "eccentric impulsive odd ecstatic" writer Hope Mirrlees, who brought her black dachshund to have tea with Vivienne and "Polly Eliot" the same month.[62] Vivienne wrote to Violet Schiff and Virginia Woolf, as well as Ottoline, but the wall of silence which protected Eliot was impenetrable. Nevertheless, by March, Vivienne was, she recorded, "feeling saner," an impression also gained by Virginia, who had told Ottoline two months earlier that she had received a "remarkable letter" from Vivienne Haigh-Eliot.

> Happily she doesn't ask me to do anything. She merely says that Tom refuses to come back to her, and that it is a great tragedy— so I suppose I can agree and say no more. She has made Leonard her executor, but writes sensibly—rather severely, and with some dignity poor woman, believing, she says, that I respect marriage.[63]

Once Vivienne's initial panic subsided, she began to consider more logically the best means by which to locate Tom. It is strange that it did not at first occur to her that her mother and brother were in touch with Eliot. Maurice had become closer still to Tom after returning from Lagos, where, as Colonel Haigh-Wood, he had been Chief of Police; not only had he and Ahmé shared continental holidays with Tom and Vivienne as recently as 1930, Maurice and Tom went to the races together, and no doubt Maurice, as a stockbroker and joint trustee of the Haigh-Wood estate, also discussed market movements and the rise and fall of the Haigh-Wood and Eliot portfolios with his brother-in-law. For by the terms of Charles Haigh-Wood's will of 3 January 1920, Rose, Maurice and Tom had all been appointed trustees of the Haigh-Wood estate, but Vivienne was excluded and was simply paid an allowance through the District Bank. Vivienne resented this dependence, especially when Alfred E. James, solicitor for the

Haigh-Wood estate, wrote her a "Fatherly but threatening" letter in March when he "spied out" that she had not collected her income from the bank and sent her the Selfridges account to settle. She was annoyed: "It is the old game," she wrote, "and it is vile, *caddish,* and it *won't do.*"[64] She was being treated like a child, and she knew it. Now that she no longer lived with Eliot, in whose management of the family money she had implicitly trusted, she became concerned to discover the value of her third of the estate, for by the terms of Charles Haigh-Wood's will and codicil of 18 May 1927, she was entitled to equal shares in the trust funds with her brother Maurice, subject to her mother Rose's life interest.[65]

Vivienne then began an arduous campaign. Her first step was to try to obtain a copy of her father's will in the early months of 1934, as well as his death certificate. Maurice tried to distract her, aware that if Vivienne remained in ignorance of the true extent of her wealth, he and Tom, also a trustee, could get away with paying her an allowance below her real entitlement. In February Maurice brought Vivienne a bunch of violets and snowdrops and took her for a walk in Regent's Park. On 10 April he took his sister out to lunch at Trinity House in the Strand: "He gave me a *very good* meal," reported Vivienne with delight. "We had an amusing conversation which I shall record and try to get published in a short collection called 'Conversations Embittered.' "[66] Even in July, when she dropped in on her mother at 3 Compayne Gardens, and found "Maurice lunching with Mother and both of them *very* well and complacent," Vivienne still felt her brother's motives were altruistic. She had walked past Maurice's house in London every day, she told him pathetically, for she longed to see him. Maurice, who had resolved never to receive his sister, coolly informed her that he and Ahmé had been living in the country since June.

As the months passed, Vivienne struggled to penetrate the mystery of the Haigh-Wood finances. April found her at the Inland Revenue Office, enquiring about a tax rebate on the Irish rents she received, and at Somerset House, where on the 18th she finally obtained her father's will. However, it was explained to her that she needed permission from one of the trustees to obtain an affidavit to enquire into the disposition of the Estate. At last Vivienne discovered her father had left nearly £40,000 in one trust, but she could find no record of the 1927 codicil regarding the Irish estate and the properties in Kingstown. Grudgingly Maurice gave her a letter entitling her to obtain a Power to Search, although, as a trustee, he already knew the contents of the codicil and could have saved her this trouble. For Vivienne, it was like wading through treacle. In July she visited the Warrior House Hotel at St. Leonards in the hope that an inspection of the ledgers for March 1927 would reveal the signatories to the Irish codicil which her father had made on his death-bed, but her visit was to no avail: the manageress refused to let her see the register.[67] Maurice continued to obstruct her efforts to find out what the Irish estate was worth and therefore whether she was receiving a fair share of income from the trust funds set up by their father.[68] Shortly before his death in 1980—at the age of eighty—Maurice finally confessed his greed in a remorseful interview with Michael Hastings: "We did not want Vivie to have her share [although] she always said a third was hers."[69]

Thus, Vivienne had little hope of discovering the truth. By 1 January 1935 she suspected she was being deceived:[70] "A whole mistake they all made was to try to keep me in ignorance of how much money I really had and would have," she wrote, having come upon some figures jotted down by Tom. "It appears that it is a much larger income than I had ever been told."[71] But Maurice told her that her income was only £400 a year, Eliot carried her cheque book in his briefcase, and Vivienne's spending was controlled by the men of the family who were determined to override Charles Haigh-Wood's intentions to make just and generous provision for his beloved daughter.

Once Vivienne gained sight of her father's codicil, she demonstrated her loyalty towards her estranged husband by an initial, generous impulse to leave him half of the share of the Irish estate which she would inherit on her mother's death. On 7 April 1935 she drafted a new will: "To Tom, all the rest of my estate, unconditionally and absolutely, our house in Ireland—Eglington House—or rent of the same."[72] As trustees she appointed Tom, Maurice, St. John Hutchinson, Geoffrey Faber, and Philip Morrell—a naïve choice, perhaps, but who else did Vivienne have to trust? At this point, in early 1935, Vivienne felt sure that Tom had made a will, leaving "everything without exception" to her—apart from his ring and his stick to Henry—and that she and Geoffrey Faber were joint trustees of his literary estate and would inherit Eliot's copyrights.[73] In this she was deeply mistaken: by 18 February 1938 Eliot was pressing John Hayward to act as his literary executor, pleading that he knew no one except John whom he could altogether trust in that capacity, and stressing his "mania for posthumous privacy." Your job, Eliot wrote to Hayward, would be "to suppress everything suppressable, however F & F might be tempted."[74]

However, Vivienne soon changed her mind about Maurice. By June 1935 she was complaining that her acquisitive brother was a "DIRTY DEVIL," who had "wiped up" all their mother's dining-room furniture. "Poor old lady, how dare he?" she demanded of her diary. Maurice and Ahmé were "proper gangsters," she wrote, who had stolen from Rose.[75] In November she wrote to Maurice at his office at Gresham House, Old Broad Street, protesting at his threatening letters warning her to keep away from mother, which Vivienne began burning, unread. "Kindly cease interfering with me," she ordered her brother.[76] It is puzzling, therefore, ten months later, to find Vivienne signing a new will, making over her entire share in the Irish estate to Maurice. Why did she change her mind? It is possible that at this time Eliot offered to give up any share in the Irish rents willed to him by Vivienne, after his financial position had improved with his director's salary and the royalties due from his *Collected Poems* in 1935, in return for Maurice's promise to silence Vivienne. Alternatively, Eliot may not have wished, on moral grounds, to benefit from the estate of the wife from whom he was separated. Without doubt, though, as joint trustees Tom and Maurice would have discussed the wills which Vivienne was making in 1934–36, and which Maurice, from the evidence of Vivienne's diary, was "helping" her draft.

Unaware of her mother's true feelings towards her, Vivienne frequently visited Rose, and her aunts Lillia and Jackie, dining and sometimes staying at Compayne Gardens; in March 1934 Rose celebrated her seventy-fourth birthday and Vivienne sewed "a tea-cosy for mother."[77] "If only my husband had had the gentleness not to give her this last blow," she lamented. "So late in her poor life. It is cruel and shameful—and a black scar. She *did* admire him and has been so hurt."[78] But Rose and Vivienne had a volatile relationship, as proved by Rose's will of 1936, in which she cut Vivienne out altogether, leaving all her personal chattels to Maurice, and the capital and income of the trust fund to her grandson Charles, as well as legacies to her sisters Lillia Symes and Ada Woolff, and niece Edna Zeistell. Even the maid received a legacy, but of Rose's only daughter

Vivienne there is no mention, indicating that the family had come to the joint conclusion that she was unfit to inherit.[79]

Rose and Maurice remained in touch with Eliot and his family, but kept Vivienne in the dark. For instance, Rose knew in July 1934 that Eliot's niece Theodora Eliot Smith, of whom Vivienne was very fond, was staying in London at the Constance Hotel. She refrained from telling Vivienne, who, left in ignorance, went on holiday to the Warrior House Hotel in Eastbourne. But in September another of Tom's relatives, Elizabeth Wentworth, arrived in London, writing in advance to tell Vivienne of her visit. Delighted to receive an Eliot at 68 Clarence Gate Gardens, where she had had a new carpet laid in the drawing-room, Vivienne entertained Miss Wentworth to tea, and showed her around the flat with its portraits and photographs of Tom and other Eliot relatives. The next day Vivienne and Elizabeth Wentworth lunched together at the English Speaking Union, and Vivienne arranged to have two handkerchiefs embroidered with the name "Marian Eliot," for Elizabeth to take home to Tom's sister Marian, who lived in the same block of flats in Cambridge, Massachusetts.[80] "Point counter point," she wrote triumphantly in her diary.

In September 1934 Vivienne stepped up her efforts to contact her husband. On the 13th she tried to place an advertisement in the personal column of *The Times:* "Will T. S. Eliot please return to his home 68 Clarence Gate Gardens, which he abandoned September 17, 1932." The newspaper did not publish her message, but a few days later, on 22 September, W. L. Janes told Vivienne that he had seen Eliot in the street, and had handed him a letter in a sealed envelope which Vivienne had given to Janes to keep until her death. The news made Vivienne's head reel. She drafted a hasty statement: "There is no reason why Mr. T. S. Eliot should not come to 68 Clarence Gate Gardens NW1 at *any time* and *no* reason why he should *not live* at Clarence Gate Gardens NW1 and there is *nothing* to prevent his doing so, as 68 Clarence Gate Gardens NW1 is his *home.* Anyone making any *statement to the contrary is lying.* Signed V. H. Eliot." This note she handed to Janes.[81] Then she had another flash of inspiration: "I *saw* at *last* just what I needed to do." Tom's birthday was in a few days' time, on 26 September, when he would be forty-six. Vivienne took two spare keys to the flat and labelled them, "26th September 1934. Keys of 68 Clarence Gate Gardens for T. S. Eliot wishing him *many* happy returns." She ordered Janes to take the labelled keys at once to the Faber office at 24 Russell Square, to demand to see Tom, and to hand him the keys.[82] Surely now Tom would return.

22

Cat and Mouse

Eliot was unlikely to have responded to any of Vivienne's distraught messages. In September 1934 he was in the Cotswolds, holidaying with Emily Hale. Emily had sailed from Boston in July and was staying with her aunt and uncle, Dr. and Mrs. Carroll Perkins, who had rented Stamford House at Chipping Campden; they gave their niece the adjoining Stanley Cottage, where Eliot was a frequent visitor.[1] Edith Perkins, Eliot and Emily toured nearby gardens, including Hidcote Manor, and Eliot took Emily on long walks around the Gloucestershire countryside. It seems that Eliot felt almost as nervous of Emily as he did of the cows they tried to evade on these walks, writing in an unpublished poem, "The Country Walk," addressed to "Miss E—— H——," and later dedicated "For J. H." (John Hayward), of the alarm he felt "when walking/With country dames in brogues and tweeds/Who will persist in hearty talking."[2] Emily, however, remained unaware of the malicious joke about her that Eliot shared with his confidant, John.

Eliot's decision to leave his sick wife had encouraged Emily to hope for a shared future with him; perhaps she anticipated that he would ask her to stay on in England when she wrote euphemistically to her employer Dr. Jaqua, President of Scripps College, Claremont, California, that she was "optimistic" about "the final decision" from the "doctor" under whose care she was.[3] In late August or early September Eliot and Emily paid a visit to the rose garden at Burnt Norton, seat of the Earls of Harrowby, outside Chipping Campden. In 1934 the house was unoccupied, the garden all but deserted, as the couple wandered past the box hedges and empty pools in the sunshine. It was the romantic moment for which Emily had been waiting, an opportunity for a declaration of love. Eliot would have held her hand as they walked, as he used to hold Ottoline's and later Mary

Trevelyan's. And it seems from a fragment of verse (the "Bellegarde" fragment), which he sent his brother in 1935, that Eliot did experience momentary physical arousal: he wrote of the "leaping pleasure" he felt, which reached a "matchless moment," before desire died in detumescence, "impaired by impotence." In naming these few lines "Bellegarde," Eliot had in mind an early Henry James work, *The American,* in which an American in Europe, Christopher Newman, falls in love with a mature woman of good family, a family who abort the romance just as it appears likely to succeed. "In James," writes Lyndall Gordon, "the pure woman retreats into a convent . . . in Eliot's 'Bellegarde' . . . it is the writer—stricter than the Bellegardes themselves—who shuts off the woman."[4] "Footfalls echo in the memory," wrote Eliot in "Burnt Norton," "Down the passage which we did not take/Towards the door we never opened/Into the rose-garden."[5]

Their love, if love it was, would remain unconsummated; Eliot would not try again. In the years leading up to the Second World War he would continue to see Emily, to bring her, usually unsuccessfully, to meet his literary friends. She was dismissed as that "dull, impeccable Bostonian lady" by Virginia Woolf when they met in November 1935. Nevertheless Eliot enjoyed Emily's respectful worship of his genius, and her "hearty" company. Domineering she may have been, as Ottoline noted when Emily insisted that she and Eliot go in a bus together into Oxford instead of by car,[6] but Eliot was used to dominating women and liked to have his life organised by them. Emily represented a mother figure to him. Even more importantly, she served as a useful smokescreen, a counter to the whispers of homosexuality which gathered about him, and a deterrent to other females, who imagined the poet was already spoken for. But there was never a chance, as Peter Ackroyd asserts, that Eliot would have married Emily if Vivienne had not been alive.[7]

Eliot kept Emily dangling for many years, and behaved towards her with an indecision, indeed deviousness, which does him no credit, but which followed a pattern he had already established with Vivienne. Emily lingered long in England, hoping for Eliot to make a move, perhaps towards a formal engagement which, however long it lasted, would have offered her the promise of an eventual union after Vivienne's death, and would also have provided her with a certain status. As the Deanery of

Chichester Visitors' Book records, Miss Emily Hale, T. S. Eliot and the Perkinses visited on 30 November 1934.[8] As a result of her delayed return Emily was unable to give Dr. Jaqua an answer in the autumn of 1934, and so lost her job. And she was still in England in the summer of 1935, returning in 1937 and 1938; in 1936 Eliot visited her in America. The outward signs of affection Eliot gave her as he was to give Mary Trevelyan from 1938—the regular letters, the shared meals and excursions, the confidences and comic verses—kept hope warm in the breasts of these two middle-aged spinsters; but it was a hope based on the shakiest of foundations.

The intimate relationships Eliot knew in the years immediately after leaving Vivienne were in fact within the Anglo-Catholic community. By March 1935 he had settled in with Eric Cheetham at the Kensington Rectory in Grenville Place. When Virginia Woolf finally visited him for tea there one Sunday at the end of the month, she was depressed by the "decorous ugliness" of Tom's surroundings as he pressed her to eat bread rolls, nestling in frills of paper, while they sat together in a small angular room. Conversation was heavy going. Virginia poured tea from Tom's "respectable" teapot, while the great poet perched on a hard chair before a spluttering gas fire and made literary small talk to her and his other visitor, Alida Monro. Virginia was relieved when Alida left. Tom showed her his bedroom, which was directly over the District line which ran towards Gloucester Road tube station. "I forgot to ask you to drink sherry," he said to Virginia, pointing to the bottle and glasses on the bedroom window sill, and joking that he had to share a bathroom with the curates. "The hot water runs very slowly," he twinkled at her; sometimes he took the bath prepared for the curates. "I discover a certain asperity in him towards the woman—a priestly attitude," recorded Virginia.[9] Earlier she had noted that Tom was "petrifying into a priest"; he reminded her of a "great toad with jewelled eyes." When she had pressed him in April 1934 to define his belief in God, he refused.[10]

The repressed violence and the contradictions within the poet struck Virginia again when she entertained Eliot and his friend Clifford Kitchin to dinner that November in 1934, ten days after seeing *Sweeney Agonistes* and noticing Tom's resemblance to a masked Crippen; "Such a conflict; so many forces have smashed against him: the wild eye still; but all rocky, yellow, riven, & constricted . . . self-confident, didactic."[11] To the poet John Lehmann, Virginia's assistant at the Hogarth Press, she also stressed the violence in Tom which she felt accounted for his success as a poet compared with younger, coming men such as Wystan Auden (who had joined the Faber list in 1930), Stephen Spender, and C. Day Lewis: "Tom is much more violent; and I think by being violent, limits himself so much that he only attacks a minute province of the imagination."[12] Virginia had detected, as few others did, that it was Tom's secrets which shaped his poetry.

Tom and Eric Cheetham lived together for six years. In 1937 they left the clergy-house and set up home together in a nearby flat at 11 Emperor's Gate, South Kensington. The vicar, who was not apparently "altogether masculine," was an eloquent preacher who spent his spare time dressmaking. His impetuous appointment of Eliot as Vicar's Warden proved to be "highly irregular," as the poet was not formally elected, a fact Eliot discovered on Father Cheetham's death; Eliot at once appealed to the archdeacon for an act of indemnity, and was forgiven, staying on as churchwarden until 1959. Cheetham, recalled Eliot, "was very lovable and was also, at times, extremely irritating, and one loved him the more for the irritation he caused." It was only the Blitz in 1940 which caused Eliot, reluctantly, to leave Cheetham and retire to lodge with the Mirrlees family in Shamley Green, near Guildford; the vicar moved into the basement of the Albert Hall.[13]

Soon after joining Cheetham, Eliot had gone into retreat at St. Simon's, Kentish Town, where he met two priests who became his spiritual counsellors: Father Frank Hillier, who was the same age as Tom, and Father Bacon, who became Eliot's "ghostly father." Every two months Eliot escaped to Kentish Town to make his confession to the priests,[14] as well as going into frequent retreat at the Anglican religious community at Kelham, Nottinghamshire, where, from 1931, he enjoyed the company of theological students at the headquarters of the Society of the Sacred Mission. He formed a lasting relationship with Brother George Every, himself an aspiring poet and playwright, who became a close personal friend and remained in touch with Eliot during the war and after. An episode at Kelham wove itself into "Burnt Norton": George Every related to Dame Helen Gardner how on a hot day in the summer of 1935, when Eliot was staying there, he saw a kingfisher on a stream running into the river Trent by Averham church, a short walk over the fields from Kelham. Eliot was apparently much excited by the sight of the bird. In the church-yard stood a yew, and clematis bloomed abundantly in the rectory garden next door.[15] "Will the clematis/Stray down, bend to us?" asks Eliot in "Burnt Norton." "Fingers of yew be curled/Down on us? After the king-fisher's wing/Has answered light to light . . . At the still point of the turn-ing world."[16] When, in the autumn of 1935, Eliot began writing "Burnt Norton," it was his memory of that Kelham kingfisher, associated with Every, which was as fresh in his mind as the rose garden traditionally as-sociated with Emily. At Burnt Norton itself there would have been no kingfisher on the dried pool.

In the spring of 1936 George Every sought Eliot's advice concerning a verse play he had written, "Stalemate—The King at Little Gidding." Every's unpublished play took as its subject King Charles I's flight to Little Gidding after his defeat at the battle of Naseby in June 1645.[17] Little Gidding, near Huntingdon, Cambridgeshire, was already a place of pil-grimage for Anglicans after the seventeenth-century mystic, the Rev. Nicholas Ferrar, set up a religious community there in 1625, and Eliot, too, made his own pilgrimage on "a really lovely day," as he told Mrs. Perkins, in May 1936 to the chapel which had inspired Every. The young priest gave Eliot both the subject of his fourth *Quartet* and the impetus to com-plete the series which the poet eventually decided, after finishing "East Coker," should be based upon the four seasons and the four elements.[18]

The sea poetry of the third *Quartet,* "The Dry Salvages," which cele-brates the courage of the Gloucester fishermen to whose tales of cod-fishing on the Grand Banks Eliot had listened in his boyhood, had come easily to the poet. It sprang from his own experience of sailing out of Gloucester harbour in his nineteen-foot catboat; on one occasion, Eliot and his friend Harold Peters sailed up to Maine, taking shelter in a gale in Somesville, a "hurricane hole" in Penobscot Bay. Eliot knew how to lay a course avoiding the Salvages, bare granite rocks off Cape Ann which, just protruding from the water, could wreck the unwary sailor. In 1631, relates an early New England chronicle, a "Mr. William Eliot" was among the party of one Thatcher and his friends who were wrecked off Cape Ann.[19] Eliot understood "the menace and caress of wave that breaks on water," the dangers of navigation through the swift-descending fog of a coast where "the salt is on the briar rose,/The fog is in the fir trees." As a youth he would have visited the Gloucester church of Our Lady of Good Voyage, which stands high on a hill, its twin towers a beacon to returning fishermen; in her arms the Virgin holds, not the infant Jesus, but a model of a schooner. For the fishermen and their wives Eliot felt deep sympathy, urging his reader to repeat a prayer to the Queen of Heaven on behalf of "Women who have seen their sons or husbands/Setting forth and not returning."[20] At sea, during the dawn watch, he felt a sense of time eternal as his boat was carried forward by the sea's rhythm: "And the ground swell, that is and was from the beginning,/Clangs/The bell." The bell buoys rang, it seemed to him, a perpetual Angelus for the drowned mariners who had ended their lives "in the sea's lips/Or in the dark throat which will not reject them."[21]

"The Dry Salvages" was a reworking of earlier lines from *The Waste Land,* describing a schooner's voyage from the Cape to the eastern banks ("We laid our course/From the Dry Salvages"). Never had the codfish run so well; the men laughed, and thought of "home, and dollars . . . and the girls and gin;" but the narrator "laughed not."[22] He had had a premonition of disaster. A gale sprang up, two dories were lost and then the trysail. One night on watch the poet saw in the cross-trees three women, their white hair streaming behind, who sang songs of enchantment to him; they were water witches, who "release omens/By sortilege" as in the "Dry Salvages." This earlier "Death by Water" passage ends when the ship collides with an iceberg, in contrast to the quieter ending of the third *Quartet,* in which Eliot ponders the way in which meaning must be wrung from experience, and thinks of Krishna: "Time the destroyer is time the preserver." Debating the nature of grief, he is sure of one thing only, that time is no healer.[23]

To complete his series, Eliot needed a fourth poem, whose theme would be fire, as "the spirit unappeased and peregrine" traced its final journey. Every provided the source he required. Eliot had already read J. H. Shorthouse's popular novel *John Inglesant* (1880), which described the way of life at Little Gidding, but it was his close study between February and October 1936 of several drafts of Every's play, in which John Ferrar, the head of the community, debates what should be done after the defeat of the King's cause at Naseby, which gave the poet a text from which to work. In Every's manuscript, Ferrar responds to another member of the community, who declares they must leave behind "the conflagration of forest fire" which rages in England, to demand "Would you walk away or walk through the fire?" Suffering must be endured "to find the meaning which God intends in it . . . for God has meaning in defeat," writes Every, an argument dear to Eliot's heart. In Every's manuscript, King Charles arrives that night with his chaplain, to ask for refuge before travelling north to give himself up to the Scots.[24] Interestingly, there are references to Richard III's death at the battle of Bosworth, and Eliot also alluded to "the crown hanging in a thornbush," in almost identical words to those of Every in his own early drafts.[25] Working with Every on his manuscript and criticising the young priest's "uneven" verse—by October there was "a great improvement"—gave Eliot not only the fire metaphor, developed as either purgatorial or pentecostal fire, but the symbol of the rose, which can be understood both as the Yorkist rose (according to Hope Mirrlees, Eliot always wore a white rose on the anniversary of Bosworth, in memory of "the last English king") and the "sensuous" ghost of a rose in which the poet commemorated Nijinsky's famous leap in *Le Spectre de la Rose.*[26]

Every acted as a male muse for Eliot, a more powerful one than Emily Hale, whose influence waned after "Burnt Norton"—the young man's urgent enthusiams proving a spur to the disillusioned middle-aged poet. As well as bringing the suffering of the "broken king" to Eliot's mind, and the stoic devotion of Ferrar, Every may have led Eliot to Ferrar's more famous follower, the poet George Herbert, of whom Eliot became an ardent admirer. Eliot wove into "Little Gidding" the ideals of Ferrar and Herbert which he associated with St. John of the Cross's detachment from earthly desire, arguing for "love beyond desire," and borrowing, too, the words of Julian of Norwich, one of the fourteenth-century mystics who followed the *via negativa:* "Sin is Behovely, but/All shall be well, and/All manner of things shall be well."[27]

But was the pull of sensuality banished as completely as Eliot was pretending? It seems not. The period immediately after his separation from Vivienne was a time in which homosexuality seems to have been at the forefront of his mind. Eliot's correspondence with Ezra Pound in 1934 is full of obscene jokes about bestiality, elephants in chastity belts, and Pound's plan to send him an elephant's vagina under the "snotty nose" of the postal authorities;[28] it was a time in which Tom was open about his sexual prowess to Ezra. "About COARSENESS I don't want to boast," he wrote on 3 January 1934, so he wouldn't tell Ezra what one sea-captain had said about Eliot to another: that apart from old Ike Carver of Mosquito Cove—and "He was the man who fucked the whole of Marshall's Island in one night, at the age of 70," so it was only fair to except a man like that— Tom was unbeatable in bed. The obscene verse he included in this letter dwells, with violent and tedious repetition, upon the pleasures of buggery: "Grasp hard the bastards by the short hair./Not once, or twice, shalt thou bugger 'em, in our/rough island story,/But again and again and again and again, leaving/their arseholes all glory." Compulsively he continues: "And when I say, again and again, I mean repeatedly, I/mean continually, I mean in fact many times." The orgiastic hero of Eliot's verse, "Lord of a hundred battles," is proud of his "1000 hard won scars."[29]

Even Pound was shocked by his correspondent's language: "Dearest Possum you pertinacious old whoreHound," he wrote. "I ain't nebber heeerd sech langwitch not even from de deacons in the methikerkiskpiple church . . . Jess try to normalfy your vices."[30] But Eliot felt he could afford to let the mask slip in letters to his old friend, to whom he opened his heart just as he did to John Hayward, whose proud boast to American writer John Brinnin (Director of the New York Poetry Center) in 1950 was that, in Eliot's bedroom "confessional" at 19 Carlyle Mansions, Cheyne Walk, Chelsea, where the two men lived together after the war, "He tells me *ev*erything."[31] Pound, too, probably knew "everything." "Dearest Possum," wrote Ezra on 3 February 1935, when an over-worked Eliot was busy helping to edit the *New English Weekly,* whose editor A. R. Orage had died in late 1934, "Where is your blushing Ganymede? Why don't he co/lab?? [orate]." In all probability this was an allusion to George Every. How was Eliot's "pimp and pansy series" (his poetry list at Faber, which included Auden, Isherwood and Spender), asked Pound: "I commend you for putting all the flowers in one box."[32]

In Eliot's letter of 25 June 1934 to John Hayward, he made very plain the nature of the attraction priests had for him. His suggestive pen and ink sketches of a row of headless male torsos in various stages of undress, the first wearing plus fours, the second shorts, the third underpants, and the fourth nude but for a single fig leaf, are labelled figures one, two, three and four, and described accordingly: "cold, cool, hot, torrid"; the nude torso is decorated with exuberant radial lines which, according to Eliot's "key," indicate the "peculiar emanation or rather effulgence which usually accompanied with the odour of violets is accustomed to envelop the limbs and torso of very Holy persons."[33] The erotic charge which priests held for the poet is indisputable.

Love "without desire" therefore remained an ideal only, for in reality Eliot was living, as he admitted in Fable XIV "The Whale, the Elephant, the Coot and the Spider," in *Noctes Binanianae,* a Jekyll and Hyde life. Churchwarden and publisher by day, at night Eliot became Tom "tusker," who enjoyed the "red light time" with his bisexual friend Geoffrey Faber.[34] In his vestry, jokes Tom, "pious Jekyll purloins letter-paper," that "Hyde may cut a rogue elephant's caper," trusting to "an ecclesiastical alibi." And although, like the Chairman at Faber & Faber, the Elephant is "always in temptation," and "must do what nature bids him do," being sometimes "by nature speedy/In Après-midi," it is at night that their most spectacular transformations take place. The nightly revels ("Late at Night-time/Is the Red-light time") are accompanied by a chorus of "Nigger Minstrels" singing "Who dat Man? See Them Roll...See Them Ro-hole," as Possum transforms his elegant shape into that of Tom Elephant, "a tusker at that, the biggest extant." Together, the Elephant and Coot visit a palace, not the palace of peace at the Hague, or the "Palace of Sorts" at Geneva, or even Alexandra Palace, but a House in the Euston Road, "where Friend meets Friend," though what a friend would say if a friend were a whale (Morley) remains an "unimaginable tale." In another "Ode to a Roman Coot," Eliot recalled shared memories of the "festal drunks" at All Souls' Hall, of the Coot at dawn on Hampstead Heath, "forever panting and in cotton pants," of charming the "loud roisterers" in the Common Room, and amazing "th' attendants in the Turkish Bath." In the final chorus, the Elephant, Coot and black minstrels cry "Berry Berry: Let the grave close over the nights that were."[35]

Safe at least, within the bosom of the church, at the office Tom remained vulnerable to Vivienne. On 26 March 1934, six days after dining with Geoffrey and Enid Faber, Vivienne telephoned Faber & Faber, and was amazed to discover that "Tom *had* been there and does go every day, a great relief to me. Poor, silly boy. His poor, hot, stuborn [sic] head."[36] Two days later she rang again at 3:30 p.m., to be told he was in a committee meeting. At five she rang again: he had just left. At six she spoke to Miss Swan, the receptionist. They were all very nice to her, recorded Vivienne in her diary: "So I shall go on!"[37] She continued to call, "a slight, pathetic, worried figure, badly dressed and very unhappy," who screwed up her handkerchief as she wept, recalled Bridget O'Donovan, Eliot's secretary from 1934 until 1936. O'Donovan, who was in love with Eliot herself, knew her duties. She went downstairs to the foyer, where Vivienne sat weeping in the corner, and explained that it was not possible for her to see her husband, but that he was quite well. Eliot, meanwhile, was slipping down the backstairs out of the building; sometimes he hid in the lavatory. The rest of the day he would be on edge, speaking slowly and hesitantly.[38]

At first Vivienne believed Swan and O'Donovan. In early 1935 she was still wondering if Tom was a "prisoner," or if he was "FREE" and receiving the letters she continued to send him: "My heart urges me to make every endeavour to get Tom to accept the absolute possession of 2 rooms in this flat," she wrote on 1 January. She clung to the fantasy that he would use the Yale keys she had sent him, and treat the flat as "his most private offices," coming and going, unmolested by herself; on 7 February she sent him a chit informing him that she left the front door open every night from 10:30 until 11 p.m. "for TS Eliot. Here is your home and here is your protection. Which you need."[39] On 27 February she delivered another letter, telling Tom that she worked night and day on his behalf: "Every thought I have is for you and all my strength . . . I take note of all things so that it will be known, in time."[40] In March, an alarming letter from Maurice about Tom made her tremble with fear for her husband's health: "I felt all of a sudden that I must go at once to Tom." She would have gone then, in the night, she wrote, had she known where to go. The next day, 8 March, Vivienne's courage came to her. She walked "fast and straight" to Russell Square: "To think I have allowed myself to be frightened and intimidated into a state of mind in which I have never dared to go openly and honestly to Faber & Faber and demand to see Tom. What a history for the English nation to read and marvel at in years to come when these records of mine have been released . . ." At Faber, Vivienne was met by "dear Miss Swan" and Bridget O'Donovan ("a very nice timid girl"), who once again put her off with excuses. "We did not see Tom," reported

Vivienne. "They said he was not there and that he is very erratic." Her suspicions were at last aroused. "Tom was never erratic. He was the most regular of men," she noted. ". . . A most sweet and homely man. It is not right
of Tom to refuse to come home." Bridget succeeded in calming Vivienne a
little, and Miss Swan promised to come and have tea with her.[41]

Protecting the boss continued to be part of Miss O'Donovan's duties.
On 13 March 1935 Vivienne marched again to Faber, determined to talk to
Eliot face to face. At first Miss Swan said he was in; her heart leaped. She
sat in reception, promising herself that she would be "very quiet and gentle" with Tom. Then Miss Swan "bethought her," wrote Vivienne sarcastically, that she had not after all seen Tom come back after lunch. "Swannie"
called O'Donovan, who came down, looking "rather sick." Was not Mr.
Eliot always in for the board meetings, demanded Vivienne. There was no
answer. "Of course you know I shall have to keep on coming here," said
Vivienne. "Of course it is for you to decide," replied O'Donovan. "It is too
absurd, I have been frightened away too long," declared Vivienne. "I am
his wife."[42] But her protests changed nothing. Although the secretaries felt
sympathy for her plight (ground to powder by the "Mills of God"), they
could only listen as Vivienne protested her loyalty to Tom, poor Tom
("poor headstrong and noble Tom"), her belief in his innocence ("The sin
is not my husband's") and her longing for "the great happiness of taking
care of him again." That night Vivienne returned to her flat, and dreamed
that Tom was in danger. "I wish I could see Bertie again," she wrote wistfully, recalling that she had not seen Russell for ten or eleven years.[43] Two
days later Vivienne returned to Faber & Faber and pushed a piece of
chocolate through the letter box for Tom.[44]

From Janes, meanwhile, Vivienne had learnt tantalising news of Eliot:
"He reported to me that he had *seen* him, for a very hurried few moments,"
she recorded incredulously.[45] How could Eliot, so available to Janes, elude
her still? Why did he act "in this queer way," she wondered. Still unaware
of Janes's duplicity, Vivienne clung to the belief that Tom, "the poor fellow," had been under a delusion for two years, which made him fail to understand that "we here are his friends and true champions and loyal to the
death and that we still wait for him with open arms."[46] Two days before
Christmas 1935 Vivienne made her final visit to Faber & Faber that year;

she spoke to O'Donovan and bought five books. "I told her everything." The following year, O'Donovan, a female Oxford graduate who realised there was no chance of promotion at Faber & Faber, left the firm. Perhaps she was tired of the subterfuge; "Swannie," her successor, continued to shield Eliot from Vivienne.

It became even more difficult for Vivienne to cling to notions of Eliot's innocence, or the illusion that he might ever return, when the bailiffs came knocking on her door. Vivienne was still asleep at 68 Clarence Gate Gardens when the first raid took place early on 11 December 1934. She was awoken by loud banging, and still in her nightdress and dressing-gown, she went to the door. "A man put his foot in and pushed me violently, forced the door open, and five or six men pushed their way in." Vivienne screamed for Louie Purdon, who was staying the night, "and she came very quickly," she recorded. The flat was wrecked; the shelves were wrenched from the walls and not only were all Eliot's books taken, but many of Vivienne's, including all her copies of the *Criterion*. Janes came quickly to the flat by taxi; he seemed dazed, but Vivienne suspected he knew in advance about the raid,[47] which was the result of a court order obtained by Eliot's lawyers, Bird & Bird, after Vivienne had failed to respond to his demands for the return of his possessions.[48] Maurice recalled that "Tom got Fabers to enter 68, but Vivie held on to all the things in 177."[49] Vivienne no longer knew whom to trust, and was conscious only that she was the victim of "incessant persecuting, . . . devilish cruelty, open treachery and conspiracy." On Christmas Day 1934, she prayed: "God grant that I am dead."

Vivienne cared "excessively" about the theft of her copies of the *Criterion* because they contained all her writing under her various pen-names.[50] When they were not returned, she wrote a polite letter to Geoffrey Faber in March 1935, pleading with him to intervene on her behalf:

> Dear Geoffrey, I should be so grateful if you would have my books and my *Criterions* returned to me . . . It is not a question of their monetary value but a question of the names and signatures which are inscribed on the front pages and the personal notes and markings which they all contain . . .[51]

Evidently the message reached Eliot and Vivienne's *Criterion*s were returned. Geoffrey Faber was in an awkward position as go-between, having to reassure Vivienne that he did, in fact, pass on her letters to Eliot as requested, and the fault was not his if they were returned to her unopened, as happened when Vivienne sent Eliot a cheque for £1 for his birthday, 26 September 1935: "Dear boy," she wrote. "I wish you everything in this life and for all eternity. Can't you let me have another address, except 24 Russell Square. With love, your wife, VH Eliot. Buy yourself some socks at Marshall & Snelgrove."[52] On this occasion she was upset enough to take her "private letter," marked "Private and Confidential," which was returned, to Marylebone police station. Telling her that there was no evidence that 24 Russell Square was not Eliot's correct address, the police turned her away.[53]

After the first "smash and grab raid," Tom became even more determined to repossess his family silver and photographs. The bailiffs had been foiled in their search for the silver during the first raid, because Vivienne had already crated it up and deposited it in the District Bank vaults. A long list of cutlery, itemising every fish knife and teaspoon, was sent to Moxon Broad by Bird & Bird. Broad attempted to mediate in the dispute. On 22 December 1934 he wrote to tell Vivienne that he had persuaded Bird & Bird that it would be more desirable in the interests of everybody that they should not exercise their rights until they had given her the opportunity to set aside the silver and plate. He knew that she would be "quite willing to hand over to Mr. Eliot what properly belongs to him," and offered to accompany her to the bank. But Vivienne was implacable. Her mind remained firmly fixed on her goal—Tom's return. She had asked Broad to raise this matter with Tom's solicitor, and this he assured her he had done. Although he hoped that her wishes would be passed on to Mr. Eliot, wrote Broad, he could hold out no hopes whatsoever that anything would result from it: "I am very sorry indeed, but I think it would only be giving yourself greater pain to entertain hopes which I feel certain would be disappointed."[54]

The fighting over the family silver escalated. Vivienne demanded to be hidden somewhere, perhaps in a wardrobe, in the flat at Clarence Gate Gardens, so that she could spy on Tom and ensure that it was indeed he who was calling to claim his property.[55] Bird & Bird refused her request.

Vivienne in turn refused to return the crested Eliot cutlery. Eliot's relentless, but unseen, pressure on her continued: on 7 June 1935 Vivienne was informed by the bank clerks at the District Bank that Tom was thinking of stopping her allowance of £5 a week for fifteen weeks "as a punishment for something."[56] In response she promptly opened a new account at Eliot's branch of Lloyds, getting a cheque book "just like Tom's" from the friendly bank manager (though her account was later declined). But Vivienne was also alarmed by her husband's threats, as her diary references to being kidnapped, arrested, "done in or murdered" demonstrate. Now the roles were reversed: it was she who needed "protection." But who would protect her? Vivienne had no faith in her family or her servants. She felt as nervous as she had in 1918, when Osbert Sitwell used to say, "The spies are out, Vivienne," as they went into the Café Royal to meet their friends.

One day in June 1935, as Vivienne hid in her "shrine to Tom," a taxi came to the door. Out stepped Dr. Cyriax and Dr. Reginald Miller; the latter had trained at the Royal Psychological Association and practised as a specialist in nervous troubles, later becoming senior physician at Great Ormond Street Hospital. It was, recalled Maurice, "William Leonard Janes who got the doctors round in a taxi," because "Janes did everything Tom said," and Tom and Maurice had decided that Vivienne should be certified. But Vivienne appeared too rational on this occasion to meet the criteria of the Involuntary Reception Order; she answered the doctors' questions calmly and sensibly. That day Miller and Cyriax declined to sign the order. Vivienne remained, for the moment, free.[57]

Terrified that next time she would not be so lucky, Vivienne decided to flee to France. "She went to Paris to get away," remembered Maurice.[58] On 18 June Vivienne visited the British Fascist HQ to buy a uniform, which she saw as some kind of protection, only to be disappointed to learn that Fascists were not permitted to wear uniforms abroad. The next day she spent alone in the flat, in dread of being "arrested." But nobody came to take her away, and the day passed uneventfully. On 21 June, which was to be her last day in England, Vivienne went to Vere Street for "two light doses" and to say goodbye to Louie Purdon. Before leaving, she took every possible precaution to safeguard her papers, packing them with her jewellery and depositing them in a safe at Selfridges' safe deposit department. In the flat she left only "certain trinkets" in her blue and silver jewel box, which she locked in her tin deed box, in which she usually kept her papers, sealing it in the green room cupboard. She wore the key of her deed box around her neck. Finally, armed with the address of the Paris Fascist HQ, on 22 June Vivienne set off, having booked a room by telegram at the Hotel Cécile, rue St. Didier, under the name of Thayer.

Even the use of a false name barely seemed sufficient protection, and Vivienne walked the streets in fear of unknown assailants. "If the assassination of Edith Cavell is a crime which shook the world, I say the assassination of Vivienne Haigh Eliot is a crime which will shake the world with far more consequence," she wrote defiantly on 23 June 1935. "I sit, alone, in France."[59] She could not rest. She hardly knew where she found the strength to do all she achieved, she wrote. "But of course it all came from God." The previous year, on 22 August, Vivienne had written to Dr. Prevost at the Sanatorium at Malmaison, saying she was coming to see him, an arrangement she cancelled in September as she felt too weak to make the journey. This time, as she recalled better days when the Princess de Bassiano had visited Tom and herself at the Hotel Cécile and entertained them at her house at Versailles, Vivienne wrote again to Dr. Prevost, saying she had been a week in Paris, was sorry to miss him, but she would meet him, not at Malmaison, but at her hotel.[60] On 7 July, Prevost replied, expressing his regret at missing her. Vivienne's refusal to see the doctor at his sanatorium was a direct result of her fear of being detained against her will. When at last, anxious about the security of her flat, Vivienne returned to London, she wrote of her French visit: "Chaque jour et chaque soir j'ai marché dans les rues, exactement comme nous marchons ici à Londres, pour montrer comme nous sommes, maintenant, en Angleterre, si bien et si libres."*[61] Vivienne had become not cat, but mouse in the game of hide and seek she and Tom were playing out.

By 12 July Vivienne thought she had turned the tables on Tom. She wrote triumphantly: "It looks as though I have cornered him." Vivienne had sent Eliot a registered letter with a cheque for 11s. for three of his books, which she had bought from Faber, reasoning that since he would have to endorse her cheque and pass it through her bank, he could not fail

---

*Each day and each evening I walked the streets, exactly as we do here in London, to show how here in England now we are so well and so free.

to open her letter, in which, "for the thousandth time," she begged him to face up to his "enemies and blackmailers" by coming to Clarence Gate Gardens, where there was nothing but security and safety for him. Chiding him for his cowardice in the face of the blackmail to which Vivienne apparently believed he was subject, on grounds of homosexuality, she wrote:

> It almost makes one doubt your sanity, the way you are hiding yourself up as if you are committing a crime. The shame and slight on your family, the name of Eliot, is more than one could believe an Eliot could do. Have you lost all shame? And have you forgotten Christianity and become a heathen or are you STILL terrorised and blackmailed . . . ?

No one need put up with blackmail, she told him, if they had the courage of a dog. She would make it hot for anyone who wasn't kind to Tom, threatened Vivienne. "You know that I have always said that if a hair of your head is harmed, I will make the whole world pay."[62] Vivienne's continuing misplaced loyalty led her to plan to follow Eliot to Paris, where she thought he was about to travel. "It is worth anything to me to get him back," she confessed to her diary. She *would* go to Paris. "My belief is that *he* wants to get back to me, and is in *chains*."[63] Once again, her letter was returned unopened.

Tom's response was not what Vivienne had hoped for. On 15 July there was "the usual foot in the door," and once again two large men forced themselves into her flat. Vivienne was better prepared for this second raid; she at once rang Dr. Miller, who came within twenty minutes and spoke to the intruders. After the doctor had left, Vivienne slipped out of the door and locked all the men in with her patent key. When she returned triumphant at 7:30 p.m. they had escaped out of the kitchen window with a ladder, leaving behind most of the "booty," which Vivienne and Ivy, her maid, packed up and hid, probably in number 177.[64] The following month Janes brought back the mandolin which had been snatched from the flat, and which Vivienne had given to Eliot when they had gone to Margate together in October 1921.

For Vivienne, the raids were a violation. Her flat was no longer a home but a place where she felt like "hell," and from which she now fled. From 23 July 1935 she made the Constance Hotel in Lancaster Gate her refuge, where she had "a dear little room" and friends among the residents. The hotel was already familiar to her because Lucy Thayer had stayed there, as had another friend, Violet Jones, and "poor darling Theodora" and Marian Eliot: "So they have the names Thayer, Jones and Eliot on their ledgers."[65] Regular meals and the "warm welcome" she received lifted Vivienne's spirits, and when Eliot's dentist, Dr. Henry Moore, informed her that her husband lived "somewhere in Kensington," and that he had seen him on 5 July when he pulled one of Eliot's teeth at his rooms in Portland Place, she was able to record simply: "I am so relieved."[66] Vivienne made nostalgic trips to Oxford, touring Trinity College, and Merton, "the best, the oldest college." On 28 July she looked up at the "very window of the room poor little loyal Tom had, and where I saw him sitting, quietly reading his books in 1915." She also visited the Bodleian Library, purchasing a catalogue and recording her expenses in her account book, although she did not contact the Keeper of Western Manuscripts at the library to discuss the bequest of her papers.

Staying at the Constance Hotel for five weeks had one important consequence for Vivienne. No longer terrified of sudden intrusion, she began to sleep much better and was thus able to cut down her drug use. On 22 August, Allen & Hanbury confirmed that they would in future deliver two Adalin tablets and two Phenacetin tablets (an analgesic) to her every morning, together with "one draught." This, noted Vivienne, represented a great reduction in her sleeping draughts since staying at the Constance. Another influence, which brought comfort and increased stability into her life, was religion. In 1935 she began attending services at St. Cyprian's Church, Marylebone, where the priest, Father Mayhew, encouraged her to come to Mass. She began the practise of visiting St. Cyprian's whenever she felt in distress, going to pray in the church, for example, during the second raid on her flat. On 29 September, when Father Mayhew left St. Cyprian's, Vivienne was heartbroken. She attended two services on that Sunday, listening attentively to Father Mayhew's sermons and, after she shook hands to say goodbye, lit four candles in his memory.[67]

Perhaps it was the choral evensongs which Vivienne attended, as well as the reduction in her medication, that enabled her to discover her greatest consolation during the years of separation from Eliot—music. In September 1935 Vivienne began singing lessons at the Marylebone Studios, and was excited to be told by her teacher, Miss Gale, that she had a natural soprano voice. "She let me sing up to F but she will be able to take my voice up higher later on," she wrote. Her middle register was weak, and Miss Gale warned her against harming her voice by singing to herself, or humming and crooning in the flat. She felt so strong after her lesson, Vivienne wrote, that it was like a new life beginning. "To think that after all these years of longing to sing, and being laughed at and ignored, I have got a real voice. A gift," she recorded incredulously.[68] Vivienne also began practising her piano-playing and singing for an hour and a half a day at her flat, and on 26 September sat the entrance examination in pianoforte at the Royal Academy of Music, York Gate, Marylebone. She passed, and was accepted to study piano as her first subject and piano accompaniment as her second, with classes also in aural training and elements of music. Full of joy, she wrote, "I can attend all the concerts. A most wonderful thing in my life. And I thank God."[69]

Music gave Vivienne a new identity and a new purpose. When Harriet Weaver asked her to tea in 1936, she declined on the grounds of being a full-time music student, adding that as she was no longer a member of "Lady Ottoline Morrell's little court" she could not undertake to interest Ottoline in Miss Weaver's forthcoming edition of Chaucer's "Hymn to the Virgin," illustrated by the daughter of James Joyce.[70] Vivienne exulted in her "huge" voice. Her piano-playing improved at the hands of her "nice and gentle" teacher, Mr. Webbe: "I want to please him," she wrote: "Went home, lit my fire with logs and played the Peer Gynt suite."[71] With great pride she recorded her attendance at the Queen's Hall, on 6 December 1935, as "the very greatest event in my life after my marriage to Thomas Stearns Eliot on June 26 1916. This was to sit on the platform among the students as a student of the Royal Academy. Dressed all in white with the great scarlet ribbon across my chest . . ." Vivienne, stylish in her new white corduroy suit from Vanecks, faced Sir Henry Wood, who was conducting the concert, her heart swelling with pride.[72] Earlier she had written: "I shall make a great singer. I shall win a fortune for my producers."[73] At last her artistic and narcissistic personality had found an outlet, and music had begun to fill the gap left in her life by Tom's desertion.

It was unfortunate, therefore, that just at the point when her pursuit of Eliot was no longer all-consuming, Vivienne at last succeeded in tracking down her quarry. As she wrote earlier, Eliot wanted her to disappear. As an abandoned wife who knew his secrets she was both a reproach and an embarrassment, and her appearance in public at his plays resurrected the horrific moments of their marriage, which he longed to forget, and which filled him with guilty terror at the prospect of meeting her. But Vivienne refused to vanish: her musical success bolstered her confidence. On 2 October 1935, in what may be seen as a dress rehearsal for her actual meeting with Tom, she attended a performance of *Sweeney Agonistes* at the Westminster Theatre, with her friend Louie. Membership of the Fascists, who had asked her to write for their magazine, *Blackshirt,* had also stirred up Vivienne's fighting spirit, as had her admiration for Lenin, whose thrilling and poignant revolutionary songs reduced her to tears at the film society to which she belonged. She had therefore chosen to wear her Fascist uniform as she and Louie entered the theatre. The audience hissed "Mrs. Eliot," recalled Louie, as the two women marched down the aisle to their seats in the front stalls. She and Vivienne found this funny. As for the play itself, Louie, "a somewhat earnest spinster," who was dedicated to her work for the National Society for Lunacy Law Reform in North Harrow, understood little. "It was all about birth, copulation and death," she told her cousin. "My only consolation is that at the time I did not know what copulation was."[74]

However, Vivienne recognised the play's roots in her life with Tom. "How I contrived not to faint I do not know," she wrote, startled at "the absolute horror of the thing." Fascinated, she returned to the Westminster Theatre at least twice more to watch *Sweeney Agonistes.* Her lasting emotion was pride in Tom and gratitude for the years they had shared: "He made me a woman among thousands, a sort of superbeing," she wrote, "He is a prophet."[75] "Dear Tom, how proud of him I am," she recorded on Boxing Day 1935, remembering how Ottoline used to admire Tom. Now she felt no more malice towards Ottoline ("however much she regrets me now") than she did towards Tom.[76]

Yet Vivienne's instinct for the limelight made it impossible to ignore her. She dressed carefully for her entrances. When she visited the

American Women's Club in Grosvenor Gardens in September 1935 it was the result of five days of intense preparation, which included two expensive visits to Francis, her hairdresser. She had ordered a car. At last she started out, "dressed in my thin, fine black suit and black felt hat with red feather, black shoes and gloves, sunburn stockings and cerise macintosh cape," only to be disappointed by being told that she was not eligible to join as Eliot was a naturalised British citizen. To join the club was "the ambition of a lifetime," declared Vivienne. The three American ladies were sorry. As Vivienne was British born, there was nothing American about her or Tom at all. If only Vivienne had come before Tom got naturalised. "I said yes, but I never wanted him to get naturalised. . . . They were very nice and said you cannot make husbands do what you think they ought to."[77]

Meanwhile Vivienne continued to act as a private eye, stalking Eliot outside the office. On 4 November 1935 she waited in her car outside 2 Whitehall Court from 8:30 until 9:15 p.m., because a friend had tipped her off that he would attend a meeting at that address. "Did not see Tom—a great many large men in grey suits who *might* have been him," she reported. Her neatly typed list of over thirty car numbers which she noted in the vicinity of Whitehall Court indicates how obsessive she had become in her pursuit of her husband.[78]

The next time Vivienne was not to be thwarted. The public confrontation which Eliot had sought for so long to avoid at last occurred on 18 November, at the *Sunday Times* Book Fair at Dorland House, Lower Regent Street. Apart from their brief meeting at the solicitors' office, it was the first time since September 1932 that they had come face to face. Once again Vivienne had dressed for the starring role. She chose to wear her Fascist uniform, a black beret, with the penguin pin which Tom had given her when she was at the Malmaison sanatorium, and a large black macintosh cape, the outfit she had worn in the streets when distributing Fascist leaflets during the 1935 General Election.[79] A small, fierce, dramatic figure, she strode in, clutching three of Eliot's latest books and holding her dog Polly in her arms; she fought her way to the front of the lecture room, passing Bridget O'Donovan. Directly she was in the midst of the crush, she heard steps behind and, turning around, found Tom just behind her.

I turned a face to him of such joy that no-one in that great crowd could have had one moment's doubt. I just said, Oh *Tom,* & he seized my hand, & said how do you *do,* in quite a loud voice. He walked straight to the platform then & gave a most remarkably *clever,* well-thought out lecture . . . I stood the whole time, holding Polly *up* high in my arms. Polly was very excited & wild. I kept my eyes on Tom's face the whole time, & I kept nodding my head at him, & making encouraging signs. He looked a *little* older, more mature & smart, much *thinner & not* well or robust or rumbustious at *all.* No sign of a woman's *care* about him. No cosy evenings with dogs and gramophones I should say.

As Eliot finished his talk to great applause, Vivienne pushed her way up to the platform, and let the dog off the lead. The terrier ran to Eliot, scampering around his feet and jumping up at him. Vivienne, too, mounted the platform, and stood beside Eliot, her hands on the table on which were piled the poet's books. "I said quietly, Will you come back with me?" "I cannot talk to you now," replied Eliot, hurriedly signing the books Vivienne had brought. He then left with a young writer, Richard Church, who had been chairing the evening.[80]

Vivienne wasted no time in writing to James & James on 25 November to inform them that she had met her husband and that, "Everything was perfectly all right between us . . . In short he turned up and I turned up and I took my dog, and my dog pursued him." There were, she said, many witnesses to their meeting.[81] But Vivienne also drew the solicitors' attention to the "slight young man" called Richard Church, who introduced Tom to the audience, and whom she had never seen before. It struck her as "extremely odd," she wrote, that her husband should have with him in what *"seemed* rather a familiar relation, a young man, no relation, no particular bond in common . . ." This young man, said Vivienne, walked after Tom and was behind him when she spoke to her husband. Vivienne requested Messrs. James & James to lay her chronicle of the event before Dr. Prevost and the other distinguished mental specialists who would be competent to judge it, declaring that in the streets of London there was now "a disgusting and filthy parade of *Sex,*" and England was just a dung heap, crawling with "maddened worms and filthy maggots."[82] The importance Vivienne attached to her "chronicle" is shown by the fact that she took down shorthand notes, which she preserved. Her letter indicates also the type of sexual stories she was likely to spread, to Eliot's alarm. He remembered in 1954: "I was afraid of the dreadfully untrue things she said of me and afraid that my friends believed her. I couldn't say anything—a kind of loyalty perhaps and partly a terror that they would show me that they believed her and not me . . ."[83] If Vivienne was suggesting to James & James her husband was homosexual, she was no doubt also writing in similar vein to others, and Eliot must have shuddered at the thought of her accusations dropping onto his friends' doormats.

A few days later, on 30 November, Vivienne visited the Mercury Theatre to watch *Murder in the Cathedral,* which had transferred from Canterbury to Ashley Dukes' studio theatre. Once again she was a conspicuous figure, sitting in the stalls beside Aldous and Maria Huxley and Sybille Bedford. It was an encounter which Sybille Bedford remembers as "terrifying." Gaunt and swaying, still smelling of ether, her make-up misapplied, half recognising people and half not, Vivienne made such an intense impression on Sybille that she was forced to leave the room and have a brandy.[84] Like "wrong'd Aspatia," Vivienne refused to stay locked in her charnel vault, but issued from the shadows to haunt Tom. She watched the play at least nine times. "Tom," she forecast, "will be a big noise as a playwright. He has got everything. Historic sense, music in his very blood, rhythm and sound and time sense to an extent which is almost incredible."[85] By 26 December *Murder in the Cathedral,* with Robert Speaight in the role of Becket, was a sell-out. And, as Tom's fame grew, so did Vivienne's longing to share his celebrity status. She *would* be noticed. She was his wife, as she repeated over and over again. She was shunned because she was "mad"—Tom's Ophelia, as Virginia wrote—and so she would be mad, acting out her label in ever more bizarre and embarrassing public appearances which, four years after leaving her, still forced Eliot to hide from public life.

It was Tom's "callous cruelty" which made her "act in a queer and abnormal way," wrote Vivienne in justification of her behaviour.[86] She was taking her revenge. Had Eliot confronted her just once, and spoken to her honestly, he might have given her the sense of closure she needed. Instead, his cowardice prolonged her agony—and his.

Vivienne knew she was courting danger. It was time to become "Daisy Miller."

23

Into the Dark

In June 1936 Vivienne began her double life. It was the final act in the melodrama she and Tom played out for five years between 1933 and 1938. Her frustration at her situation had grown. Nothing had changed since she had cornered Eliot at the *Sunday Times* Book Fair, as she was forced to confess to Louie Purdon over lunch in December 1935. "Do you know where he lives?" asked Louie, when Vivienne told her that she had at last seen Tom. "I said no, and I am not going to torture myself unnecessarily—I said, I *trust* the man. He has some very strong reasons . . ."[1] For Eliot himself, Vivienne's love remained undiminished; it was his "enemies" she blamed for her predicament. No closer to penetrating the impregnable fortress that was Faber & Faber, she began to suspect Geoffrey Faber. "I am innocent," protested the publisher when, on 13 March 1936, Vivienne again accused him of not forwarding her invitation to "T. S. E. . . . I handed it to him myself. What happened to it after that is not my responsibility."[2] "Either you see that Tom receives it, or else you will give me an explanation," retorted Vivienne.[3] Although at first Vivienne believed that "my husband has now found me . . . When I say found, I mean he claimed me in public," in reality the meeting had proved an anti-climax. She was still "a woman alone," as she expressed it to Moxon Broad—a single middle-aged woman alone in north London, nursing her dream of reconciliation.[4]

The trail had gone cold, and yet Vivienne's terror intensified. She felt increasingly hounded by unseen pursuers. Following Tom and Maurice's first bid in June 1935 to certify her, she did not dare enter the Malmaison sanatorium as a voluntary patient, as she wished. Aware that she was in need of the help which her old friend Dr. Prevost was offering, Vivienne had again booked a room, for December 1935: "Vous savez que vous serez toujours ici la bienvenue, et que nous vous reçevrons comme une amie,"* the kindly doctor had written on 15 November; but Vivienne was still too afraid to take up her place at the clinic and receive the psychiatric support from which she could have benefited. Had she done so, her life might have ended differently.[5] Instead, in London, faceless "Kidnappers" seemed to wait on every street corner for her; and yet only out of doors, among the familiar London landmarks she had known since childhood, was her anxiety bearable. In her own flat, a "black prison" since the bailiff's raids, where she kept a single bed in the corridor, she was unable to sleep or rest. How she wished that after her piano lesson she could come home to a meal and settle down to practise, she wrote. Instead, "I am always driven out, to tramp the streets—this way and that until I get such a horror of the streets that the streets only understand."[6]

There were, felt Vivienne, demons at her heels, and at Tom's: "The only way to get rid of Tom and Vivienne is to wear them out—hurry the pace . . . Make them work till they drop—crack the whip. Then hustle them into an untimely grave," she wrote on 11 November 1935. As she remembered her last conversation with Eliot, she imagined that he was warning her of kidnap or murder: "This may be done in various manners—unlimited are the ways." She shivered as she remembered Tom's words: "The poor gentleman said to me, 'Do not go to sleep anywhere where nobody knows where you are, will you?' I said, 'Why shouldn't I? You do.' He said, 'It is very easy to remove one.' "[7] So great were Vivienne's fears that in her will of 1 March 1936 she requested that her coffin should not be closed until the expiration of at least four days after her death, and not until death had been certified by Dr. Miller and another doctor.[8]

Wandering the streets by night as well as by day that November, Vivienne recorded walking from Westminster, through Horseguards, and up the side steps leading to Waterloo Place. "I love it so. It's often fine and cold, and then it's beautiful. I shall walk back from there to-morrow night." It was a reassuring route, for Vivienne was retracing the steps she had taken when her father first fell seriously ill, and she, Ottoline and Tom had paced the streets around Crawford Mansions. It was to this area, which she associated with the early years of her marriage, that she re-

---

* You know you will always be welcome here, and we will receive you as a friend.

turned with nostalgia, to her "young days ... when Tom and I were first married [and] we used to walk about London at night. I loved it so. We even had the honour of spitting into Monty Sherman's letter-box in the Adelphi! So many mad mad nights."[9] On Vivienne's "Route marches," as she called them, she often dressed in her Fascist uniform as she inspected the streets, deciding that it was the Fascists who had tidied up Sloane Square and, "IF they can make a world where every man, woman and child, can go about their business in peace, unmolested and unhindered, ... then the fascists will deserve this new world."[10] On one occasion she rescued a tramp, bringing him back to her flat for bread-and-butter and giving him 7/6d to find a bed; on another, she found a starving black dog which she took to Battersea Dogs Home, but such incidents were mere crumbs in her search for solace.

The influence of the *fascismo* upon someone as impressionable, lonely and vulnerable as Vivienne was a harmful one. On 22 March 1936 she fulfilled a long-felt ambition to see Sir Oswald Mosley in the flesh, when she attended a Mass Rally at the Royal Albert Hall. The police were out in *"immense* force" for an area of at least two miles around the Albert Hall, mounted and unmounted, as hundreds and thousands of people gathered to hear their leader, whom Vivienne excitedly compared to Prince André in *War and Peace,* another "man of action." As she stood amidst the hysterical crowd, applauding Mosley as he ranted that England's civilisation was rotten, its morals decayed, Vivienne drank in his propaganda, which she reproduced in agitated diary entries. London's children were "degenerate imbeciles in clattering perambulators," she wrote, and in the streets she was followed by "low class men," who "propagated their own loathesomeness."

On Easter Sunday 1936, alone in her flat and lame with a poisoned foot, Vivienne brooded over several mysteries: Richard Church, the "very handsome, elegant and properly behaved young man," who at the Dorland Hall the previous November had introduced the speaker by saying, "Mr. T. S. Eliot is a man who cannot endure the slightest pain." What was Church's connection with Tom? Tom himself looked no older, and *"just as handsome."* And the bewildering "disgusting persecution" to which she was subjected in her flat, which was no home but a place where she had been *"incessantly molested* and my nervous system shaken and ruined":[11] who was behind it? Her thoughts, she wrote, were not clear, for Vivienne could not bear to listen to the warnings of Moxon Broad, her solicitor and ally, against Eliot. "There is more in this than you know of," Broad had maintained after the second raid, but Vivienne had shut her mind to suspicion of her husband. "He is a queer man and his idea of Tom is so mad and so away from the truth that I often wonder if he was Tom's solicitor all those years," she wrote after a long interview with Broad at his City office the previous October, at which he had tried to tell her that Eliot was the culprit.[12] Humankind, as Eliot knew, cannot bear very much reality.[13]

Inevitably, considering the amount of time Vivienne spent walking around central London, the day at last came, in the summer of 1936, when she bumped into Tom. It was an event which triggered an extreme reaction in him: "I am rather shaky at the moment, because I ran into my late wife in Wigmore Street an hour ago, and had to take to my heels," he wrote to Dorothy Pound on 28 July. "Only people who have been 'wanted' know the sort of life I lead." If he could afford to live anywhere but London, he would, Eliot told Dorothy, only he had to have an address from which he could "decamp" quickly.[14]

Vivienne's distress, which had greater foundation than Eliot's, now led her to adopt a different identity—to see whether she could disappear as completely as he had done, and outwit her unknown pursuers. She also hoped to discover a new peace of mind in which to prepare for her music exams in July. As so often, Vivienne's actions imitated Tom's: she would continue to be his shadow, as he was hers; she, too, would lead a double life, her disguise enabling her not only to preserve her freedom, but to track him down, as she confided to her bank manager, Thomas Hope. "You may not know it, but I make it the first interest in my life to follow his movements, and it is the perpetual anxiety of my life."[15] In June 1936 Vivienne informed Moxon Broad:

> I have chosen the incognita of Miller to allow it to be supposed by as many as possible that I have gone to America . . . —for two reasons, one to give me more time for work at the Royal Academy of Music . . . but also to try if possible this experiment to reduce the strain on my brain, and at the same time to see if I could succeed in disappearing as completely and baffling all attempts to trace me as my husband has. And at the same time I have in mind

such undying resentment against all those who had any part in this business that I want them to know what it is like to suffer in this same way.

Tiresias.

At this point I have become Daisy Miller.[16]

On 20 July Vivienne, writing as "Daisy Miller," informed her daily woman, Mrs. Flint, that Mrs. Eliot had left the day before for America, and had let the flat to her as she was a fellow student at the Royal Academy of Music. Mrs. Eliot's address in America, wrote "Daisy," would be 83 Brattle Street, Cambridge, the apartment block in which both Marian Eliot lived and another Eliot relative, Elizabeth Wentworth, with whom Vivienne remained on friendly terms.[17]

Like Tiresias, Vivienne had experienced a mythical transformation. Like Tiresias, she would see all things, spying them out as Eliot's spies had done. The incognita she chose, Daisy Miller, symbolised in Vivienne's eyes her innocence of any crime, and would have been immediately understood by those who read her words. Vivienne knew that, just as Daisy had compromised her reputation by her outing with Winterbourne in a boat on Lake Leman at eleven o'clock at night without a chaperone, so had Vivienne, in Eliot's eyes, compromised her own by her outing with him in a punt on the River Cherwell. It was said of Vivienne, as of Daisy: "She is very crazy."[18] Daisy's ruin was assured when she went out at night with Giovanelli, an Italian fortune-hunter, and caught malaria; she had paid the price for breaking the rules of polite society: ostracism, isolation and early death. In choosing the name "Daisy Miller" Vivienne made it clear that she believed that she would also have to die; and that the verdict of history upon her should be the same as that of James upon Daisy, underlined by Giovanelli's final words to Winterbourne:

> "She was the most beautiful young lady I ever saw, and the most amiable." And then he added in a moment, "And she was the most innocent."
>
> Winterbourne looked at him, and presently repeated his words, "And the most innocent?"
>
> "And the most innocent!"[19]

Vivienne's message was that Eliot, like Winterbourne in his relationship with Daisy, contributes to her death through rigidity, snobbery and lack of compassion. Choosing to be "Daisy" was a powerful and defiant indictment of her husband; but it also suggests that Vivienne was sinking into depression as she turned her anger inwards. Like the Cumaean Sibyl, she wanted to die. *"Very* depressed," she recorded in her diary in 1934. "There will be plenty of time for fighting after I am dead," she remarked prophetically to Moxon Broad on 10 August 1936. "And I have had quite enough of it."[20] Over time, her sense that she had lost the battle against Eliot grew, as her defiant protests at the way in which "everything is liable to be twisted and perverted and coercion and the foulest methods are used to direct or misdirect opinion and action" against her were replaced by a mood of hopelessness and, at times, suicidal thoughts.

Her bizarre behaviour continued to attract comment. Stephen Spender related that a friend of his who shared a hairdresser with Vivienne used to find herself sitting side by side with her under the dryers. On one occasion, Vivienne complained bitterly that when she was in the street people in the road persistently stared at her. "My friend found this as unaccountable as Mrs. Eliot did, until leaving the hairdressers, Mrs. Eliot put on her hat," wrote Spender. "This had stitched on it the rather garish purple and green wrapper of Eliot's play, with the letter print MURDER IN THE CATHEDRAL very prominent around the rim."[21]

Vivienne's frequent presence at the tiny Mercury theatre in Notting Hill Gate continued to be a potential source of embarrassment to Eliot, to his friend, producer Rupert Doone, and Doone's lover, designer Robert Medley; she had joined the Group Theatre Society and Film Club, and managed to discover Doone's address. As Vivienne was liable to wait outside the houses of those she suspected of sheltering Eliot, recording car numbers and spying on any man in a grey suit who she thought might be Tom, this was, yet again, a limitation upon his freedom of movement. And Vivienne was closer upon his heels than he realised: in January 1935 Eliot had commissioned W. H. Auden to write "Dogskin" *(The Dog Beneath the Skin)* with Christopher Isherwood, which was subsequently staged by Doone, and watched by Vivienne, who kept her programme. Between 24 January and 28 February 1936 alone, Vivienne attended performances of *Murder in the Cathedral* at least nine times, carefully hoarding the tickets among her papers. She even followed the play on tour, being given complimentary tickets in the front stalls at the Cambridge Arts Theatre and Oxford Playhouse. It is no wonder that to Eliot she appeared a malevolent presence, haunting his life, a phantom who "fed upon me while I fled."[22]

Vivienne, meanwhile, continued to act as if she and Eliot were a couple—as indeed they were in law. On Armistice Day 1935 she had bought two yellow roses which she left at the Cenotaph with cards signed from Tom and herself. All she wished for, she wrote, was to have her old life back. On 13 April 1936 she longed to catch, "If only a glimpse of my husband, the only man now living for whom I have the slightest respect. Many men have passed my line of vision since the autumn of 1932, but never one for whom I would trouble to turn my head . . ."[23] Vivienne's photograph, taken on the day on which she was presented to the Prince of Wales in 1934, shows a slim, dark-haired woman with bobbed hair, her complexion unblemished, her eyes large and arresting; she looks young for her age, forty-seven, and might have made new male friends, had she not remained mired in grief over Eliot's desertion. For Vivienne never adjusted to the loss of her husband. One of her last acts was to buy some sheet music at Selfridges: "Can't Help Loving that Man of Mine," from *Showboat*.[24]

Although Vivienne repeatedly visited the theatres where Eliot's plays were performed, she was determined to hide her private address from him, as he had hidden his from her. From June 1936, when Vivienne became "Daisy Miller," she seemed to have given W. L. Janes—who she believed was implicated in the raids on the flat—the slip. She began using the Three Arts Club, 19a Marylebone Road, opposite Madame Tussaud's, as her poste restante address, writing to the English Speaking Union, her bank, and even Moxon Broad, as "Daisy Miller." That summer she advertised on the Three Arts Club notice-board for "an educated shorthand typist *(expert,* and accustomed to a Remington portable machine)" to manage "Daisy Miller's" correspondence.[25] And she continued to search for a house rather than a flat in which to live, nearly renting 53 Chester Terrace, and then 8 Edge Street, Church Street, Kensington, in March 1936; she was tempted by a "charming" summer cottage at Meads End, Eastbourne, which she and Tom had rented before from Sir William Collins. He showed her around again, but when she decided to take the cottage for the summer of 1936, the estate agent told her that the owner was withdrawing the property from the market. A furious Vivienne threatened to sue for wasted expenses, suspecting that the real reason was that she had unwisely given as her reference the British Union of Fascists.[26]

Loneliness ("ghastly morbid solitary confinement") and rows with other tenants contributed to Vivienne's desire to leave 68 Clarence Gate Gardens for good.[27] At her mother's "definite request," in early summer 1936 Vivienne finally left the flat she had shared with Eliot: "It is impossible to live at 68 Clarence Gate Gardens, for a woman alone, as I told you," she explained to Broad.[28] Unable to find a house to rent, she lived "a nomad life," as she described it, moving from hotel to hotel. On occasions she enjoyed the company of other guests, as at the Constance Hotel the previous Christmas, when Vivienne took Polly for

> a most lovely walk in Regent's Park, where the ice was thick on the lake and pond, and where the fine mist, the red sun and the delicate bare trees against the pale misty sky and the flocks of birds standing about in the ice and flying slowly, made one of the most beautiful pictures I have *ever* seen. Everything is so much finer, cleaner and quieter in a *freezing* cold winter, than in the summer. I love it. At dinner I found all my old friends and had a nice evening . . .[29]

But her restless movement from one hotel to another made friendship an increasingly rare commodity. Her favourite venue was the Three Arts Club. But even the Club, "a very very nice club," was reluctant to allow Vivienne to be a long-term resident, probably because of her unconventional behaviour. "Unhappily it has been for a long time too full up with country members to take me in," she wrote to Harriet Weaver, former editor of *The Egoist,* on 12 June 1936, "so that I live about from one Hotel to another."[30] From the Three Arts Club Vivienne moved to Durrants' Hotel, Manchester Square, to the Cliftonville Hotel in Dorset Square, and thence to the Welbeck. Polly was boarded out in Hampstead. Increasingly, public occasions became a substitute for intimacy: "Mrs. Eliot . . . has had very great friends, and she prefers to mourn their losses rather than to fill the gaps they leave," she informed her lawyer.[31]

Church offered a certain solace. The new priest at St. Cyprian's invited Vivienne to attend his services again, and she began going to High Mass. Otherwise, in whichever direction she turned, Vivienne found herself courteously, but very firmly, rebuffed. She had approached Jack Hutchinson. Why did she want to meet, he asked. "For no reason at all except that it is more normal to see one's friends than not to," replied Vivienne with dignity.[32] In September 1936 she wrote to Faber, suggesting that if they were considering a new edition of Eliot's poem "Marina," which was out of print, she would like to offer an illustration she had made for the front page.[33] Faber & Faber replied that it was "most unlikely" that a new edition of the poem would be printed, as it had already been included in Eliot's *Collected Poems 1925–1935,* published last spring. Otherwise they would, of course, have been very glad to consider Mrs. Eliot's "kind suggestion."[34] In February, Vivienne offered to help the English Speaking Union entertain American visitors: the Reception Secretary wrote encouragingly to enquire how Mrs. Eliot could help: "As you know, our members from America and the Dominions appreciate nothing so much as friendly and informal contact with British members and the opportunity of visiting British homes, or of sightseeing under the guidance of local people . . ."[35] But nothing came of Vivienne's suggestion. Her application in February to St. James's Palace for a seat at the coronation of Edward VIII met with the inevitable refusal from the Earl Marshall, who explained that invitations to the Ceremony of the Coronation in Westminster Abbey would be issued only to those included in Government lists approved by His Majesty.[36] Once again Vivienne had set herself up for rejection. The pathos of these letters, in which she makes vain attempts to cling to the fringes of that society at whose centre she had once glittered, is powerful. A pitiful, doomed figure, she stood at the Dorland Hall listening to Bertrand Russell lecture, but did not speak to him. She attended Arthur Bryant's "thrilling lecture" at London University on Two American Poets, and dreamed of her husband.[37] Her need for human contact made it impossible for her to maintain the charade that "Mrs. Eliot" was in America, and Eliot and Geoffrey Faber were aware that Vivienne alias "Daisy" remained somewhere in London. They did not, however, know her address, for by July 1936 Vivienne had signed a six-year lease on 8 Edge Street, at a rent of £160 per annum, in addition to the £215 p.a. she was still paying for Clarence Gate Gardens.[38]

Vivienne's battle now was to maintain her mental equilibrium. "You know how terribly nervous and timid she is, and how she is apt to lose her wits and go all to pieces," wrote "Daisy Miller" of her friend Mrs. Eliot to Moxon Broad on 5 August 1936, after Vivienne had created one of her most confused "muddles" over the new Ibach grand piano she was buying on hire purchase from Selfridges, who were storing the old upright for which she had exchanged it. Vivienne, with her usual delusions of grandeur, believed that "the progress I am making in my piano studies does justify my having a really first class instrument to work on,"[39] and when she found she could buy a Bechstein grand from the Wigmore Hall, through the Royal Academy of Music, where she was still a student, nothing would stand in her way. "I wish you could get Selfridges to fetch this piano away," complained Daisy Miller of the Ibach grand, as it was "not a very satisfactory instrument." Mr. Broad replied that he would endeavour to straighten the matter out. "Yes, I have been very much upset and shaken by what I told you about Mr. T.S. Eliot," explained Daisy, who was "lingering in London trying to get things cleared up for my friend." "It would un-nerve Mrs. Eliot so much if she knew I am only thankful she is out of the country."[40] The problem was, explained the patient Broad, that Mrs. Eliot had signed HP (Hire Purchase) agreements for two grands.[41]

Yet it was music which continued to give Vivienne's life focus: "One whole hour of Bach. I loved it," she confided to her diary after one of her piano and singing lessons. Although she longed for the sunshine, Vivienne had turned down Ella de Saxe's invitation to stay with her in Monte Carlo in January, because she wanted to "stick to the music" and make up, during the vacation, what she had not understood during the term.[42] In the spring term Vivienne, despite a minor operation on her infected foot, had struggled on, failing only her Elements of Music examination, and by the summer was well enough to write to her piano teacher that, "If it would not be considered unreasonable, I would also like to learn the violin, as an extra study."[43] July 2 found her "working up to the last" for her exams the next day.

Vivienne's new identity as a full-time music student led to a truce with her mother. Rose Haigh-Wood was both surprised and proud to be invited by Vivienne to the Music Students' Concert at the Queen's Hall in April, at which Vivienne, once again dressed all in white, sat with the students. Rose wrote to congratulate "My dearest little Vivy" on the "splendid concert,"[44] and she served as a more stabilising influence in her daughter's life at this time than hitherto, as the following letter shows:

> My dearest Vivy—for you are my dear little Vivy—and I think you are very brave and persevering in taking up serious study now—so I am very proud of you dear—So go on with your work dear . . . It is a *real* pleasure to study. So I do hope you will continue—You are welcome to tea or supper at *any* time—Of course I only have simple meals—but you *are* welcome as you know. The little walk backwards and forwards is pleasant for you. So—let us all be happy together—Granny used to sing it to us.
>
> Fondest love from yr *devoted* Mother.[45]

Rose's loving encouragement in 1936 presented a contrast to Maurice's continued avoidance of his sister. In May Vivienne decided to be assertive: "As I have not seen you for so long, or your wife and child, and have never even seen the inside of your home, I propose calling on you Sunday afternoon, if you will be at home."[46] Maurice replied that no one would be in: "No-one ever is in chez moi. I invariably spend the whole weekend playing golf, or at any rate out of London . . . Vive le sport!" Grudgingly he agreed to meet her at the Three Arts Club "at cocktail time," but he and Ahmé kept Vivienne at arm's length. Eliot was godfather to Maurice and Ahmé's son Raggie, of whom Vivienne was very fond; she now took over this duty, sending Raggie gifts of lead soldiers and having him to tea with his nanny, but seeing little of Ahmé. Later, Maurice recalled the relationship between his sister and his thirty-one-year-old wife from South Carolina:[47]

> Ahmé tried to like Vivien, but Vivien fought her off. [As for] Ahmé and Tom . . . Ahmé playfully pulled his leg about his Englishness. Tom never thought that funny. Tom wanted her to take his side against Vivien. Ahmé never would.

Of his own disloyalty, Maurice recalled in 1980, shortly before he died: "Tom appealed to me—and I always took his side. Never Vivy's. I was a fool for doing so. Later I realised. Not then."[48] In old age Maurice blamed Tom for his behaviour to his sister; Tom, at least, blamed only himself.

The year 1936 witnessed a late, brief artistic flowering for Vivienne. Her self-confidence had increased as she developed a new life at the Royal Academy of Music. She began to draw and paint again at the Three Arts Club, which held a spring exhibition. Vivienne offered the club "an extraordinary clever and witty Cartoon" by Eliot for the exhibition; this the committee turned down on the grounds that it was not the work of a club member. They did, however, select two of Vivienne's own sketches for exhibition, to her great joy. She at once sent invitations to Tom, Maurice, Geoffrey and Enid Faber to come to the private view, which was to be opened by Mark Gertler. Enid promised to come although Geoffrey pleaded a business engagement after his ticking-off by Vivienne for not delivering Tom's invitation. Typically, Vivienne priced her sketches too highly for them to be put into the Club lottery, but her success prompted her to have one drawing photographed and printed as her Christmas card for 1936. It also prompted her to challenge Faber & Faber in a provocative fashion: if the publishers refused to use her sketch to illustrate "Marina" themselves, wrote Vivienne on 5 September, she proposed to have Eliot's poem privately printed with her own illustration "in a similar way to Miss Lucia Joyce's *Hymn to the Virgin* by Geoffrey Chaucer."[49] The prospect of Vivienne setting herself up as a rival publisher of T. S. Eliot's poems, with illustrations by his deserted wife, must have been an alarming one to the directors of Faber & Faber.

And in 1936, attracted by the name, Vivienne joined Eliot's Club in the Charing Cross Road, a club which advertised itself as being near twenty-five West End theatres, with supper and dancing every night till 2 a.m.: "Indian Curry every Thursday, cabaret with unique turns, evening dress always optional." Vivienne's bohemian nature was reasserting itself, and she planned to attend the dancing on Sunday night "to dispel the gloom of Sunday night in London."[50]

But on 9 November a tragedy befell the Haigh-Wood family: Rose had a stroke. Her illness precipitated a violent row between Maurice and Vivienne, who was horrified to find that 3 Compayne Gardens which, two years ago, was "fully furnished with good old furniture collected by my Father, her proper right," had become an "empty barn, practically everything having been snatched away before her eyes" by her brother, including her parents' double bed. Impetuously Vivienne ordered a new double bed for Rose. It was useless to expostulate with Maurice, Vivienne told Moxon Broad:

> But when it comes to her lying in her last illness on a little old brass single bed, not good enough for a modern servant girl, and two so-called nurses sleeping on the same bed, I am not going to stand by and look on. Such things are not tolerated nowadays, and unless altered she would be better in The London Clinic . . .[51]

Maurice was furious with Vivienne when one of the nurses told him that his sister expected him to pay for the bed and other items she had ordered for their mother. "I may as well make it clear that I am naturally *not* going to pay for such things either out of Mother's money or my own,"[52] he wrote to Vivienne on 20 November. Mother might have a long illness, and her money was "extremely limited. God knows what the doctors' and nurses' bills will be." As Vivienne knew, he repeated angrily, the whole of the Haigh-Wood capital was in trust and could not be realised. "Most of the things you have sent here have been really useless." A new bed made no difference to Mother, declared Maurice: "her mind is dreadfully confused, poor darling."

On the contrary, declared Vivienne two days later, Mother was perfectly rational. "When I saw [her] on Thursday morning she was very sweet and perfectly herself." The crisis aroused in Vivienne's mind memories of her own recent crisis with Tom: "You never offered me a word of sympathy or understanding in my most desperate need, my most incredible shock," she accused Maurice.[53] Concerned that her mother was emaciated, Vivienne asked Dr. Reginald Miller to call. But Miller and Vivienne had crossed swords before. In October 1935 Vivienne had refused to pay Miller his fee of nine guineas as a protest against his action in refusing to allow her to see Eliot, who was also his patient.[54] Now Miller demanded payment in advance, before contacting Rose's own doctor. "There is urgent need for action," replied Vivienne impatiently. "You can say that I am your patient and it is necessary for my mental health that you see my Mother."[55] But not until Miller had received his two guineas in advance, on 13 November, did he consent to call on Rose.[56] Using her "mental health" as a weapon was a dangerous tactic with doctors, and one which could backfire on Vivienne. Dr. Miller, like Maurice, was no friend to Vivienne, and both took their orders from Eliot.

Rose remained seriously ill, and Vivienne was very much "lowered" by her mother's illness. She suffered with a recurrence of severe back pain from her permanent spinal injury, and had to have physiotherapy with Dr. Cyriax four mornings a week, and was no longer able to attend her music lectures before midday.[57] In this crisis Vivienne turned in despair to Mary Hutchinson. On 11 November 1936 she sent Mary a typed letter from Durrant's Hotel, explaining that her mother was very seriously ill. "If you could see me I should be so glad . . . If you send me a postcard, I will meet you anywhere you say. *Please.*" Vivienne enclosed a stamped addressed postcard for Mary's reply. Mary ignored her appeal.[58]

Vivienne's records are missing from 1937, but according to Maurice, the sixty-year lease on 3 Compayne Gardens expired in 1939. The Haigh-Wood estate then bought Rose a house in Pinner, Middlesex, at 97 Marsh Road, where she was nursed until her death in April 1941.[59] Although Vivienne still used her old home in Compayne Gardens as a refuge until 1938, she no longer had her mother to accompany her to concerts, but only Aunts Jackie and Lillia, whom Vivienne by now disliked and whom she felt disliked her. Rose's affection had been a significant factor in mitigating Vivienne's loneliness and sense of insecurity, and without it she was "distraught."

On 10 December another event occurred which Vivienne, as an ardent royalist, found profoundly shocking: the abdication of Edward VIII. Vivienne had worshipped the Prince of Wales, "the young and handsome king emperor, who with his blue eyes, his elegant if diminutive form, and his golden locks [is] the idol, the joy, the one and only ray of light and colour on which all eyes in this land should focus."[60] "I quite agree about the King. The whole thing is appalling," wrote Maurice on 17 December, in a letter thanking Vivienne for her Christmas present for Raggie. "However, it's no earthly use allowing it to upset us. Life is difficult enough already."[61]

But life was certainly less difficult for Maurice than it was for Vivienne. Determined that "I must get all clear before I die," in 1936 she asked Moxon Broad to add a codicil to her will, appointing her brother-in-law Henry Eliot as another trustee in addition to Tom, Maurice, and the others, writing that this had been her original intention, "but, as you know, I was obstructed in carrying the matter out in the way I believed to be right then, and still do."[62] She requested that if Tom Eliot predeceased his brother, Henry Eliot would become beneficiary and trustee on the same terms as her husband. Vivienne's letter is neatly and accurately typed, and makes perfect sense, as does all her business correspondence (of which she kept carbon copies) to Broad, and to her bank manager, Thomas Hope. By 1 March 1936 Vivienne had signed her new will, of which Maurice was the main beneficiary and, on his death, his son Charles ("Raggie") Warren Haigh-Wood. Tom was now left only the "residue" of her property, but to her brother Vivienne bequeathed her title and interest in the Haigh estate in the Irish Free State, comprising 1, 3, 4 and 5 Haigh Terrace, 1–10 Eglington Park, and Eglington House leased from the ground landlords, the Lords Vescy and Longford.[63] Signing this will was her downfall. Now only Vivienne's freedom stood in Maurice's way.

Maurice and Ahmé lived extravagantly; nor did he meet with great success as a stockbroker, later losing £200,000 in Slater Walker.[64] Vivienne was also by nature extravagant. She found it impossible to live on her allowance from the Haigh-Wood estate, and had no hesitation about eating into capital. "Simply choose a security to sell and send it to me for my signature," she blithely instructed Hope when he complained that her overdraft was too high.[65] Maurice watched with growing alarm as Vivienne bought Bechsteins and beds and a new Ford four-seater car (she sold her Morris Minor for £45), rented flats at whim, as well as ordering white and scarlet dresses, claret-coloured silk model suits, a fashionably short shingle wig, and having her leopard skin coat remodelled for receptions at the French Embassy, the English Speaking Union to meet Dame Margaret Lloyd George, and a luncheon with the Archbishop of York. By 1936 the Haigh-Wood estate was funding Vivienne's leases on 68 Clarence Gate Gardens, 8 Edge Street, her numerous hotel bills, music lessons and doctors' bills. Although Vivienne kept careful notes on her Irish property, calculating that she was entitled to £569.3.4d in rent between 1927 and 1933, her insouciant attitude towards money was an increasing drain upon the estate.[66] For Maurice and Tom, the only trustees of the estate now that Rose was too ill to have any say, the idea of putting Vivienne away was increasingly tempting. Not only would it remove her embarrassing presence from their lives, it would enable them to stop her reckless spending, and allow Tom at last to retrieve the Eliot family treasures still hoarded by Vivienne.

However, Eliot had different, though equally pressing, motives for locking his wife up: gagging Vivienne would put a stop to her innuendos about his private life and prevent her attendance at his plays. By the summer of 1938 Eliot had finished the second draft of *The Family Reunion,* whose theme was the death of an unwanted wife, possibly at the hands of her husband Harry, Lord Monchensey, possibly by accident. Its autobiographical nature was at once evident to Virginia Woolf, who considered the characters to be "as stiff as pokers. And the chief poker is Tom . . . A cold upright poker."[67] Even Emily Hale had a role as a faded spinster to whom Harry was close in his youth, while Charlotte Eliot is immortalised as Amy, the matriarch who detests her daughter-in-law. What could be worse than the resurrection of Lady Monchensey in the stalls, a shrieking reproach to the author? It was inevitable that Vivienne, who had attended productions of *Sweeney Agonistes* and *Murder in the Cathedral* repeatedly, would appear, probably in Fascist uniform, probably very often, at the Westminster Theatre, where *The Family Reunion* was due to open in March 1939. Martin Browne, the producer, and Eliot had originally planned a production for autumn 1938. The playwright, wrote Browne, was "already troubled by the looming clouds of war and anxious to get the play finished and on the stage before they broke."[68]

Undoubtedly Maurice and Tom discussed what was to be done about Vivienne in the years before her committal. Cassius knew Brutus's wishes, even if Brutus himself did not wish to be the instrument of his victim's removal. But as Vivienne, fearful of a second attempt to certify her, fled from hotel to hotel and studied regularly at the Royal Academy of Music, no opportunity or pretext for certification presented itself. Nevertheless, it was easy enough to trace her. Vivienne's attempts at secrecy after becoming "Daisy Miller" were half-hearted: on 6 July she sent her sister-in-law Theresa a poignant but prickly letter in which she reproached Theresa for not keeping in touch with her ("Good manners requires me to write to you from time to time, and requires you to write to me"), and confessed that she had not, as she allowed it to be supposed, gone to America but was at the Three Arts Club where any of the Eliot family could find her. "I should enjoy a good talk with you and Henry," she wrote wistfully.[69] At the same time Vivienne was aware she was no longer acceptable to her in-laws: it was Eliot whom Theresa would entertain at her apartment in Cambridge, Massachusetts, and would continue to do so after Henry's death in April 1947.[70] Theresa knew, as she had known her so long, wrote Vivienne, that she never sought friends. "And if people seek me, I have come to the point of wondering what they 'want.' "

Vivienne's neat entries in her 1936 account book detail her movements. In September she spent 2s on a visit to Dr. Moore, the dentist; on the 13th she sent a registered letter to "T. S. Eliot" and, a few days later, spent 1/6d on tips to the porter and chambermaid at the Constance Hotel, where she spent the night. On the 16th Vivienne bought an 8s ticket to Oxford, where she purchased postcards of the Bodleian Library and a catalogue, and had tea with a former servant, Annie. And in December she paid the bill for the coming term at the Royal Academy of Music, which she now intended to attend full time as her health had improved. There were periods of virtual normality in Vivien's eccentric life, but it was only a matter of time before a crisis broke. She was "not waving, but drowning." And Maurice was waiting.

In June 1937 Vivienne bought tickets for the fifteenth exhibition of the Art Union of the Three Arts Club. After that date, she vanishes. Did she tumble, once again, into the "abyss" of drugs she had experienced in 1925, drugs which caused delusion? Her tone on 10 December, the day of Edward VIII's abdication, is agitated and confused. She wrote to Geoffrey Faber:

> Dear Geoffrey
> I am obliged to complain of a fact of which I am quite sure you are unaware, that on the very rare occasions when I go to 24 Russell Square, where I find an extremely agreeable and courteous atmosphere—I am *OSTENTATIOUSLY FOLLOWED* by persons who have no claim on me, & whose acquaintance I deny. I write, merely to make you acquainted with a state of affairs which I am sure you will agree with me is in detestably bad taste, hoping that I may rely on your wisdom in not extending a welcome to such persons who follow in my train to your affairs, and

who are the enemies of my husband and myself, and the parasites
and no friends to your household. I write on this day of disaster
and defeat for England. The last weeks, which have included the
serious illness of my mother, preceded by a stroke, have been the
severest strain which my existence has ever had to support.[71]

Faber replied that he had no idea who the persons of whom Vivienne complained might be. "But I need hardly assure you that if I *did*, I should share
your objections of the kind you describe."

The belief that one is being followed is a symptom of anxiety and
paranoia, although in Vivienne's case her paranoia was entirely justified, as
events were to prove. Overwhelmed by panic and loss, she became irrational and mentally disturbed. But there is no evidence that Vivienne was
schizophrenic. She never manifested the social withdrawal of the schizophrenic, nor does her dedication to music, reaching the high standards of
the Royal Academy of Music, or her correspondence or diaries, indicate a
psychosis; rather, her behaviour continued to suggest a tendency to manic-
depression shared by numerous artists and writers. In Vivienne's case, her
symptoms became more florid under stress, for example her extravagance,
a symptom of mania. She knew her pursuit of the truth was a provocative,
dangerous policy, but principle mattered too much for her to abandon her
efforts to collect and preserve her records: "As you know I am always morbidly anxious to have the truth . . . which makes me such an unpleasant
person to have about," she wrote to Moxon Broad in August 1936, pressing him to obtain copies of all the cables sent to 68 Clarence Gate Gardens
from the Western Union Cable Company in July 1933. Vivienne had stuck
the original cables onto cartridge paper and put them into a sealed cupboard, only to find the contents now missing. She was certain they had
been "thieved" from the cupboard by one of those who had reasons for
wishing to make things appear otherwise than they actually were.[72] "The
average mind concerns itself so much more with articles of jewellery or silver that mere Scraps of Paper are of no account whatever," she wrote.
"That is not my view."[73]

It seems that Vivienne had a premonition that she would be "removed" before long. In the autumn of 1936 she had watched Rupert

Doone's production at the Group Theatre of the *Agamemnon* of Aeschylus, in which Robert Speaight, whom she had admired as Becket, took the part of Agamemnon. She would have read the note by its translator Louis MacNeice that in the world of Aeschylus there is such a thing as sin, and that not only are their fathers' sins visited upon the children, the children themselves have to sin in their turn and to some extent are responsible agents: "The worst sins are those against one's family, which are punished by the . . . Furies that belong to that family," wrote MacNeice.[74] Perhaps Vivienne saw herself as Cassandra in her own Greek tragedy—the part was taken by a Vivienne Bennett—as she kept her programme, along with a postcard of the Ritz Hotel in Paris from Mary Hutchinson, in her album, inscribing her own delphic captions:

"COMING EVENTS CAST THEIR SHADOWS BEFORE. HEAVIER THE INTERVAL THAN THE CONSUMMA-TION" (T. S. Eliot).[75]

Beside Mary's postcard, Vivienne also wrote: "ALIBI?" Did she believe that Tom was hiding in Paris, while she waited, full of dread, for the second arrival of the doctors?

Vivienne's "consummation" or committal took place in July 1938. Maurice's letter of 14 July 1938 to Tom, who was on holiday with Emily Hale in Gloucestershire, appears to exonerate him and Eliot from any responsibility.

> Dear Tom
>
> I am very sorry to write to you on your holiday but I'm afraid I must.
>
> V. was found wandering in the streets at 5 o'clock this morning and was taken into Marylebone police station . . . The inspector of the police station told me she had talked in a very confused and unintelligible manner and appeared to have various illusions, and if it had not been possible to get hold of me or someone to take charge of her, he would have felt obliged to place her under mental observation.

As soon as I got to the city I rang up Dr. Miller . . . He got a reply from Allen & Hanbury's this morning in which they said that V. called every day for her medicine, that she appeared to be in a deplorable condition and that they had no idea of her address. Dr. Miller was therefore on the point of writing to me because he feels that something must be done without much more delay . . . (He) feels that V. must go either to Malmaison or to some home, and I am also inclined to think that, because there is no telling what will happen next.

V. had apparently been wandering about for two nights, afraid to go anywhere. She is full of the most fantastic suspicions and ideas. She asked me if it was true that you had been beheaded. She says she has been in hiding from various mysterious people, and so on.

I have made a provisional appointment with Dr. Miller for 3.15 tomorrow (this was before I discovered you were away).

I really don't know whether to suggest your running up to town tomorrow and returning to Gloucestershire in the evening, or not. You will be able to decide that for yourself, but I would be grateful if you would send me a telegram in the morning to say what you decide.[76]

Yours ever
Maurice.

Mrs. Valerie Eliot, the poet's second wife, in interview with the writer Blake Morrison, produced from her handbag a photostat of the above letter, and a second letter from Maurice to Tom, dated 14 August 1938, one month later. This describes Vivienne's certification by two doctors, Dr. Hart and Dr. Mapother, and subsequent committal to Northumberland House, a private mental asylum in Green Lanes, Finsbury Park.

Both doctors felt strongly that she should be put into a home. They handed me their certificates. I then had to go before a magistrate to obtain his order. I got hold of one in Hampstead.

I then went to Northumberland House, saw the doctor there, and arranged for a car to go with nurses to Compayne Gardens that evening. The car went at about 10 pm. Vivienne went very quietly with them after a good deal of discussion.

I spoke to the doctor yesterday evening, and was told that Vivienne had been fairly cheerful, had slept well and eaten well, and sat out in the garden and read a certain amount . . .

I gather . . . that Vivienne was in the habit often of saving up her drugs and then taking an enormous dose all at once, which I suppose accounts for the periodical crises.

As soon as you get back I should very much like to see you . . .
Yrs. Ever
Maurice.

"Tom would *not* sign the committal order," remembered a resentful Maurice. Eliot was not prepared to take responsibility for Vivienne's final committal. According to Maurice, it was Jack Hutchinson, who had met Vivienne in 1936, who signed the order.[77] Enid Faber confirmed to Michael Hastings, in a letter of 26 August 1983, that she did not sign an involuntary reception order on behalf of Vivienne Eliot—"And I do not think my husband Geoffrey did." Enid remembered that "some member of the family did."[78] Maurice later said: "I don't think I did. If I did I can't remember," but guilt clouded his memory. It was he who orchestrated Vivienne's committal. Of his sister he said shortly before his death: "She was never a lunatic. I'm as sure as the day I was born."[79]

The doors of the "home" closed behind Vivienne:

O dark dark dark. They all go into the dark . . .[80]

"Our only health is the disease," wrote Eliot in "East Coker." We must obey the nurse, "whose constant care is not to please," but to remind us of Adam's curse, "And that, to be restored, our sickness must grow worse."[81] Vivienne did not take kindly to institutionalisation, and her sickness did "grow worse." She refused to obey the nurses, or the rules of the home, which was not, alleged Valerie Eliot, a mental hospital but "a glorified nursing home in which degrees of restraint were necessary . . ." (although Eliot referred to it as an "asylum" to Mary Trevelyan). At first

Vivienne was in the nicest part, the Villas, where the patients who needed least watching lived. They only moved her when she began stealing from and worrying other patients. She stirred up a lot of havoc in the place, apparently.[82]

Vivienne was unhappy enough to try to escape. She appealed to Louie Purdon, then increasingly active in the Harrow Lunacy Law Reform Society, which was composed of volunteers aiming to befriend and help those who had been certified and confined. Basil Saunders, son of Louie's cousin and close friend, Marjorie Saunders, recalled that its members believed that "many people had relatives certified because they were tiresome and, quite often, to get hold of their money, when they may have been no more than eccentric."[83] England had a long tradition of husbands imprisoning unwanted wives in private madhouses. Such asylums, writes the historian Lawrence Stone, were "squalid private prisons which, as long as the fees were paid, would accept anyone and keep them behind bars, regardless of their mental condition or the motives of the person who ordered their confinement." In 1774 Parliament had passed a law to put a stop to these abuses but, although madhouse-keepers had thenceforth to be licensed and to keep records, and were forbidden to accept patients without a doctor's order, such regulations could be evaded.[84] In the 1930s, writes Saunders,

> The law provided that if anyone certified could "escape" and evade "capture" for six weeks . . . they automatically became de-certified and had a chance to resist re-certification. This was the main style of help of the lunacy law reformers: sheltering individuals during these six weeks . . .

Marjorie Saunders, a Christian Scientist, provided a refuge for escaped psychiatric patients at her pebble-dashed semi-detached house in Parkside Way, Harrow; it was to this liberal household she intended to bring Vivienne.[85] Basil Saunders takes up the story.

> One evening my mother went up to a café near Allen & Hanbury's off Oxford Street. There she was to receive Vivien and

take her home to stay. Instead she was told "Mrs. Eliot" would not be coming and that the arrangement was off. I believe Vivien had been apprehended before she got to Louie.

Thereafter Louie was not able to communicate with Vivien. The "home" she was in would not pass on telephone messages. Louie's letters were returned.[86]

Eliot never visited Vivienne in Northumberland House. Why not? Blake Morrison asked Valerie Eliot.

Because the doctors had told him he mustn't . . . But he did get regular reports, through his solicitors, on how she was doing. And because she'd been made a Ward in Chancery, there was this outside person looking after her interests. I'm quite sure that if a doctor had said, "She can come out," Tom or Maurice would have done something about it . . . I talked to Maurice for many hours . . . I'd pour whisky down him and he'd talk and talk—but he never expressed regret to me. He must have realised it was for her own good.[87]

By contrast, Eliot visited W. L. Janes regularly on Thursday afternoons in St. Stephen's Hospital, Fulham, smuggling champagne in for his servant during the winters of 1937 and 1938, and telling John Hayward how he "dashed down to Fulham" the day after buying Sir John Gielgud and Browne oysters, Guinness and tournedos for dinner at the Reform Club, during which Gielgud failed to persuade his host to allow him to direct and act the leading part in *The Family Reunion*.[88] Dinner, recalled Eliot, made "quite a hole" in a pound note.[89] It may have been Gielgud's extravagant habits, rather than the fact, as Sybil Thorndike told him, that he had no faith, that prevented Eliot from letting Gielgud have the play. Gielgud's indiscreet homosexuality, which was well known in the theatrical world before his conviction in 1953 for importuning, may also have alarmed Eliot as the post-war moral climate became increasingly homophobic.

During Janes's final illness Eliot visited twice a week.[90] Oddly personal details on which Eliot remarked to Hayward, such as the "fact" that, although all policemen have big feet, Janes turned out to have smaller feet than Eliot, indicate the closeness of their relationship.[91] Even Ottoline noticed Eliot's desire to befriend "sixth-rate writers and detectives," whom he could dominate.[92]

Vivienne's committal opened the way for Maurice to take sole control of the Haigh-Wood estate. When Rose died in 1941, Eliot relinquished his trusteeship. Maurice was Vivienne's heir by her will of 1936. But although her death would benefit him, it also brought him anguish, as he confessed to Michael Hastings:

> It was only when I saw Vivie in the asylum for the last time I realized I had done something very wrong. She was as sane as I was. She said, "God knows that may not amount to much, Maurice, but I'm as sane as you are," and I did what I hadn't done for years. I sat in front of Vivie and actually burst into tears ... What Tom and I did was wrong. And Mother. I did everything Tom told me to. Not ashamed to say so. But when it came to our family, I think he bit off more than he could chew. He didn't understand the rules, actually. You see—you have to be kind to Vivie.[93]

Yet Vivienne never lost her faith in Tom. "The sin is not my husband's" remained her mantra.[94] She spent the Second World War in the asylum,

> Locked away in Northumberland House, listening to German bombs dropping on London, waiting in vain for her husband to take her home.
>
> Hearing his poems in her head. Alone, forced to reconsider everything.

> *What is that sound high in the air.*
> *London Bridge is falling down falling down falling down.*[95]

In London Eliot watched for fires from the roof of Faber & Faber. As he waited for the drone of the bombers and the gentle rain of grey ash upon his clothes, he felt reproached by the circumstances of Vivienne's committal. He knew that Miller could have referred Vivienne, as the doctor suggested, to Malmaison as a voluntary patient, to stay until she was stabilised and well enough to be discharged. Her income was more than adequate to pay for her to live at 8 Edge Street with a nurse and a maid. Permanent confinement had not been necessary. It had only been arranged in response to his wishes and Maurice's. The second letter Maurice wrote, in which he described how Vivienne "went quietly," after a good deal of discussion, to Northumberland House, and was certified, not by Miller or Cyriax, but by doctors unfamiliar to her and possibly connected with the asylum, could have been composed after he and Eliot had conferred on the telephone, in order, as Vivienne put it, "to make things appear otherwise to what they actually were." Certainly it reads like a deliberately worded statement of justification.

Eliot repressed these inconvenient thoughts. "Where does one go from a world of insanity?" he asks in *The Family Reunion*. "Somewhere on the other side of despair." As soon as Vivienne was safely behind bars, the play was performed in 1939. In it Eliot takes his revenge upon Vivienne, and upon his mother.[96] His play was as much a sponge in prussic acid as the revenge drama Djuna Barnes wrote after seeing *The Family Reunion—The Antiphon.*[97] Eliot's unforgettable portrait of an unbalanced wife who, "a restless shivering painted shadow/In life," is "less than a shadow in death," fixed Vivienne's character in history like a fly in aspic. Instantly recognised as the author's wife, the play seemed to justify the murder of such a crazed, demonic creature. And although the author, "Harry," a modern Orestes, is supposedly cursed because he has sinned against the family just as surely as Orestes did in killing his mother Clytemnestra, the audience's sympathies are supplicated for the suffering protagonist, in his quest for "bright angels," rather than his unnamed, disappeared wife, the portrait of whom is irredeemably hostile.

In reality, Vivienne, although technically still living, had vanished as suddenly as Lady Monchensey, and also without leaving a body. In *The Family Reunion* Eliot imagined her life: "Up and down, through the stone passages/Of an immense and empty hospital/Pervaded by a smell of disinfectant." She would look straight ahead as she walked, "passing barred windows./Up and down. Until the chain breaks."[98]

From the evidence of the Hayward letters, it seems Eliot's life was less penitential in the years after Vivienne's committal than has been claimed. During raids he sheltered in the "fashionable" Russell Square coal cellar, number four, which he shared with Geoffrey Faber and the senior secretaries. As in the First World War, he ordered a new winter coat before the price of wool went up; this time he also bought a portable wireless and a pair of pince nez.[99] In his office he made fashion sketches for John Hayward of gentlemen in gas masks, with wing collars and spotted ties, decorated with "Old Possum's" dictum: "Gas Masks to be worn under, not over the Necktie," and joked that at 6:30 he had had "an unmistakable attack of emerods," and fifteen minutes later an air-raid warning came, which "goes to show that emerods cause air raid warnings and not vice versa." At the weekends he continued to enjoy excellent meals with the Tandys in Dorset, the Kauffers in the Chilterns, and at Rodmell with the "Woolves ... where food is easy to get." One November Sunday in 1939 Eliot lunched with Clive, Vanessa, Duncan and Angelica on a "most noble" sirloin of beef, washed down by brown ale, and enjoyed some hilarious small talk. Heavy drinking with Geoffrey Faber continued over dinner at All Souls; that was the evening when the poet was forced to urinate in the college garden, and A. L. Rowse, with whom Eliot nearly shared a flat in 1934, proved "endearing";[100] Eliot rejoiced in the fact that he was still in demand for weekend house-parties: even the Bishop of Bath and Wells had to go on his waiting list. Otherwise his time was spent with Robert Sencourt, and "poor Stephen" (Spender), whom he was consoling because his wife Inez had left him.[101] Against the view that Eliot's post-1938 life was one of grim despair must be set his remark to John Hayward on 29 November 1939 that "the last six years have been the only happy years of my life."[102] Once he had used his marriage as the source and subject of his work in *The Family Reunion,* as he had done in *The Waste Land* and *Sweeney Agonistes,* Eliot banished thoughts of Vivienne, and allowed himself to enjoy certain "menus plaisirs de la vie—quant au grands, said Gourmont, ils n'existent guère"*—such as French tobacco, shirts, socks, and a good snooze in a club armchair, preferably at the Garrick.[103]

After the Second World War Eliot moved in with Hayward, the "sapient Tarantula." It was an interesting choice. John Hayward, confined

---

*Small pleasures in life—as for the large ones, said Gourmont, they scarcely exist.

to a wheelchair, was as needy as Vivienne had been in 1915. For the second time Eliot entered into a co-dependent relationship with someone weaker than himself. It was an arrangement which Hayward had proposed as early as 1935, but Eliot's fear of an address that could be discovered by Vivienne prevented him from accepting. All through the 1930s, Hayward had remained at the heart of the Faber coterie around Eliot, publishing in 1937 *Noctes Binanianae,* the "Satyrical Compliments and Verses" exchanged between the Coot (Faber), the Elephant (Eliot), the Whale (Morley) and Hayward, the Vesperal Spider, verses which bear witness to the nature of the parties at his flat in Bina Gardens, as well as Eliot's and Geoffrey Faber's nights out on the town.[104] In March 1946, after leaving the Mirrlees family in Shamley Green and returning to London, the Elephant joined the Spider, "who spinneth his web above all," in his new flat in 19 Carlyle Mansions, Cheyne Walk, once the home of Henry James. There Hayward, progressively more disabled, lived in some disorder in the large room overlooking the river, and Eliot existed in a small bedroom as monastic as that which he had had in Father Cheetham's Rectory.

The poet John Malcolm Brinnin, director of the New York Poetry Center, was given an introduction to Hayward, through whom he hoped to persuade Eliot to speak at the Center. One winter Sunday he called on Hayward.

"How d'je do," said a Quasimodo figure in a wheelchair. Grotesquely bent, he had a big head, thick lips the colour of raw liver.

"You'll have to get used to me," he said, "just like everybody else."

The hand he offered hung like a broken wing.

"Make yourself a drink." He pointed to a table on wheels. "And one for me, some whisky and a little water. You can have ice, if you insist."

The flat "echoed with the absence of its other tenant." A salver full of six-pences for the buses to Russell Square indicated Eliot's occupancy. "Let me show you round," said Hayward. He made a ninety-degree turn and pointed his wheelchair in the direction of a closed door.

"His," said Hayward, indicating the room we had entered. Its walls looked as if they'd been uniformly stained with nicotine. There was one bare bulb on a chain, an ebony crucifix over the single bed. The wardrobe closet was open: crow-black silk ties on a rail, a scarlet water-silk sash, three glen plaid suits, others in shades of gray and black . . . "The confessional," said Hayward. "Here we have our bedtime chats."[105]

Hayward's protection of Eliot's privacy—he took all the phone calls at the flat—his skills as literary critic, offering advice which Eliot prized highly on the *Four Quartets,* and his malicious and ribald wit, ensured that their companionship lasted for eleven years. Nevertheless, they retained different sets of friends, and contemporaries speculated as to why Eliot, and his cat Pettipaws, whose expensive tastes were the despair of their French housekeeper, Madame Amory, chose to share his life with Hayward. There was gossip about the two which, wrote his friend, the writer E. W. F. Tomlin, "disgusted me."[106] Some speculated, erroneously, that it was a gay partnership, others that living with someone so physically incapacitated gave Eliot the control he desired. It was Eliot on whom Hayward depended for weekend walks to watch the football in Royal Hospital Gardens, although one or two devoted women took the bibliophile to parties. And Hayward's role as confidant, the recipient of Eliot's secrets, meant that he understood when Eliot explained, in December 1939, that he felt obliged to present the prizes to the "infant damned" of Raynes Park, where among 320 undersized, weedy, gangly pale boys at the grammar school, the future broadcaster Robert Robinson was a pupil.[107]

Robinson realised that his headmaster, John Garrett, was "as queer as a coot," but had distinguished friends. W. H. Auden had written the school song. Other poets helped out. "You simply couldn't say no," remembered Stephen Spender. Nor could Eliot. Robinson was amazed when the illustrious poet descended upon the suburban "waste land" from which he longed to escape. "Why do I do this?" Eliot asked Hayward, answering his own question. Because the headmaster was John Garrett, one of the dimmer *Criterion* contributors, one of the "young men," a friend of Auden, Rupert Doone, et al., who therefore seemed to have a claim upon him.[108] So

Eliot made his first, and probably last, visit to Raynes Park, SW20, as a token of his solidarity with "Les Boys," as he described MacNeice, Auden, Spender and David Gascoyne ("one of the nicest of les jeunes, but not so far a good poet").[109] It was an example of his membership of what Wystan Auden dubbed "the homintern," the international fraternity of gay men in literature and the arts between the wars, who befriended each other, collaborated and commissioned work from each other.[110]

In July 1938, the month in which Vivienne was committed, Eliot gave a poetry reading at the Student Christian Movement Conference at Swanwick, Derbyshire. There he met a gifted and energetic forty-one-year-old woman, Mary Trevelyan, Warden of Student Movement House in Gower Street, London. Mary was the daughter of the Rev. Philip Trevelyan, and a descendant of the Victorian historian Thomas Babington Macaulay; her brother Humphrey was already carving out a distinguished career in the diplomatic service. A talented musician, Mary, unlike Vivienne, came from a clerical family that could claim equal distinction with Eliot's, and he felt he had found a sympathetic ear as he confided to Mary that in American society there were "Eliots, non-Eliots, and foreigners." Mary later recalled that when she first met him, "T.S.E. was all the rage in the student world. Young men in corduroy trousers, floppy ties and long hair, carried his poetry about and looked intense." She was flattered when the poet agreed to read his work to her students. When she was appointed the only woman member of the Anvil, a BBC religious brains trust programme, it was to Eliot she turned for advice on the weekly questions sent round to the team.

Religion drew the two together. Mary and Eliot both worshipped at St. Stephen's, Kensington, where they sometimes met to pray in the darkened church for the service of Tenebrae. Mary had a gift for breaking through Eliot's reserve. They shared Sunday suppers of bacon and eggs, and drives into the country, with Mary doing the driving. She was introduced to his favourite sister Marian. And Mary, like Emily, fell in love with Eliot. During the war she served as YMCA Programme Director with the British Liberation Army in Belgium and France, and became Head of the Field Survey Bureau in Paris, organising post-war reconstruction work, service which prompted Eliot to write from the Mirrlees' house that "the Shambly family is consumed with admiration for you . . . as a Man of Action."[111] After the war Mary returned to London and she and Eliot renewed their friendship.[112]

In 1942, Mary apparently learnt from Eliot's friend George Every that the poet was married, but that his wife had "gone out of her mind." Eliot still had no contact with Vivienne, although Enid Faber visited her all through the war, and Mary Hutchinson also did so, according to Maurice. Otherwise both her visitors and her mail were censored. Her pleading letters to Faber & Faber continued to be returned unopened. She was silenced and immobilised, a prisoner in all but name. Over dinners with Mary Trevelyan at the Etoile in Charlotte Street, Eliot spoke distractedly of his marriage, explaining that it was at his instigation that his wife had been made a Ward of Chancery. In June 1944, aware how frightened Vivienne would be of the doodle bug bombs, one of which had exploded in Russell Square, blasting the Faber office and flat while Eliot was in the country, he wrote to his solicitors suggesting she be moved. The Official Solicitor's reply was that Maurice must give permission. Maurice was out of touch in Sicily and Italy, and therefore Vivienne remained in Northumberland House. Her own wishes were never considered.[113]

On 22 January 1947 Vivienne died. She was only fifty-eight. The cause of her death was given as a heart attack (syncope and cardiovascular degeneration) on the death certificate. But there is no reason to suppose that this was any more accurate than it had been in the case of Ottoline, who had died in April 1938 after being given a dose of a powerful antibiotic called Prontosil. The cause of her death was also given as heart failure. The doctor who prescribed the drug was threatened with medical investigation following the deaths of other patients, and committed suicide.[114] Medical negligence might have caused Vivienne's death, but it is more probable that Vivienne saved up her drugs, as Maurice said was her habit, and overdosed. Her depression can only be guessed at, as her efforts to escape were foiled, her contact with the outside world cut off, and her misery grew too great to bear. Suicide may have seemed her only option. Like Dora Carrington, who found life without Lytton Strachey intolerable, Vivienne saw no meaning in a life without Tom.

"Life is like a hurried walk in the dark: a blind stumble," Vivienne once wrote. "Death must be like the opening of a door into a lighted house, and saying breathlessly, 'Well, I've got here, but I don't know how I did it.' "[115] In dying by her own hand, if indeed she did so, she took her last gamble: to move from the darkness into the light.

The announcement of her death in *The Times* was curt, the shortest in the Deaths column: "On Jan. 22 1947, Vivienne Haigh Eliot, in London. Funeral Private." Tom was annoyed that Maurice had not included his name in the notice. Vivienne's death, he confided to Mary Trevelyan, was "quite sudden and unexpected. She was supposed to be in quite good physical health . . . It was therefore a particular shock and left me more disintegrated than I could have imagined. Curiously enough, I believe it is much more unsettling to me now, after all these years, than it would have been fifteen years ago."[116]

Snow was falling as Eliot, Maurice and the Fabers travelled to Pinner on a bleak winter's day for Vivienne's funeral. She was buried in Pinner Cemetery, her grave close to her mother's, although her wish had been to be buried beside her father in Eastbourne.[117] The headstone, ordered by Maurice, reads: "In Loving Memory of Vivien Haigh Eliot, Died 29th January 1947." The stone-mason carved the wrong date. No one troubled to correct it.[118]

Epilogue

When Maurice telephoned to say that Vivien had died suddenly, John Hayward took the call, and broke the news to his flat-mate.

"Oh God! Oh God," Eliot said, and buried his face in his hands.[1] His shock at Vivienne's early death was greater than anyone expected. Mary Trevelyan noted that "he talked much of his wife and did, indeed, seem to be very much upset at her death."[2] The thought had at once leapt into Eliot's mind that Vivienne might have committed suicide. It was a threat she had made many times before, he never knew how seriously. "Downing, do you think it might have been suicide,/And that his Lordship knew it?" Harry's Uncle Charles in *The Family Reunion* asks of Harry's servant and chauffeur (a character who was in all probability based on W. L. Janes, who had similarly been with his master for "over ten years . . .") as they discuss Lady Monchensey's death. "I don't think she had the courage," replies Downing. Charles asks whether Harry's wife ever talked of suicide. Oh yes, replies Downing, but she only did it to frighten people. Was she in good spirits? She was always up and down, says Downing. "Down in the morning, and up in the evening,/And *then* she used to get rather excited." She was irresponsible, and wouldn't let the master out of her sight. Up and down, down and up. It was an accurate description of the manic-depressive personality. When Eliot learnt of Vivienne's sudden and unexpected death, he must have suspected that she had, at last, found the courage. The chain had broken.

An inherited predisposition to manic-depression or bipolar affective disorder may, indeed, have existed in the Haigh-Wood family: Vivienne's nephew, Raggie, committed suicide in 1976, six years after his mother Ahmé's death from cancer.[3]

Vivienne's death gave Eliot his freedom, while reviving and intensifying his remorse. The way now lay open for him to remarry. There were two contenders for the title of the second Mrs. Eliot: Emily Hale and Mary Trevelyan. Emily had the prior claim, having been waiting in the wings for as long as Eliot could remember, but her expectations had become a burden to him. Theresa Eliot confirmed to E. W. F. Tomlin, who spent many hours in her company in Cambridge in 1959, that at one point Eliot did give Emily to understand that, if Vivienne were to die, he would marry her. "Consequently, she began to go about as if she were his fiancée presumptive, and she would dutifully kiss the members of the Eliot family—at a time when the bestowal of kisses was by no means so free as it is now—almost as if she were already an in-law." Emily was so insistent that she was to all intents and purposes the next Mrs. T. S. Eliot, that Henry wrote to Tom to enquire whether there was any basis for her behaviour. To his surprise he received a letter confirming that there was. Henry tore up the letter in a rage, exclaiming: "Tom has made one mistake, and if he marries Emily he will make another."[4]

On 15 April 1947 Eliot told Mary that he was dreading his forthcoming visit to America, and it would be a relief to get started, as then he would have his return to look forward to. He did not tell Mary that Emily was waiting, this time for official confirmation of their unofficial understanding. However, soon after Eliot's arrival in Boston on 5 May, Henry Eliot died of leukaemia. Eliot, shaken by this second death, knelt by his brother's body, saying prayers, and kissing him goodbye.[5] He returned to his sister Margaret's house at 41 Kirland Street, Cambridge. Not long afterwards, Henry's well-meaning widow, Theresa, invited Eliot to her apartment to meet Emily, who was producing *Richard II* in nearby Concord. Theresa intended to facilitate Tom's wedding plans: instead he turned on her with a white fury which she never forgot to the end of her life.[6] Refusing to accompany her to the cemetery to scatter Henry's ashes, Eliot stumped out, announcing, "I've got to get something over with." When he returned, he told Theresa that he had completed his mission to tell Emily that all thought of marriage between them must be forgotten.[7]

For Emily, Tom's subsequent visit to Concord Academy (where she was now teaching) was a "nightmare." They had another private conversation: "He loves me—I believe that wholly," she wrote to her friend

Lorraine Havens, "but apparently not in the way usual to men less gifted ie with complete love thro' a married relationship."[8] She hoped that Eliot would recover his feelings for her after the shock of two deaths, his wife's and his brother's, had faded, but by 1948 he had made it clear to her that his decision was final.[9] Later, Eliot explained to Mary Trevelyan that for many years he had believed himself to be in love with "someone": "Then, when finally I was free, I realised quite suddenly that I was deluding myself with emotions I had felt in the past, that I had changed more, and in ways unsuspected, than I had thought. I found that I actually could not bear the thought of it . . ." The relationship, when it reached the possibility of completion, was found no longer to exist, he said. And now, "I prefer not to see her, feel embarrassed and unhappy when I do, seem to have very little in common now. There is also of course the feeling, which only a man can understand, that a man, in all these situations, is somehow in the wrong . . ."[10]

Had Eliot learnt the lesson, as he claimed, that reticence, and the desire not to inflict pain, "can often approach very near to cowardice"? It seemed not, for he allowed a near identical situation to develop with Mary. By 1949 Mary was established in a flat in Brunswick Square and working for the University of London, her flat and office both only a few minutes walk from Eliot's office at Russell Square. Eliot was taking her out so often that she began to feel he owed it to her to clarify their relationship. He gave many indications that he reciprocated her feelings, sending her a stream of presents, and holding her hand for "an embarrassingly long time" so that, as she wrote in her memoir, "I really didn't know where I was at all." In addition Mary, who was conductor of the Chelsea Madrigal Society and the Kensington Choral Society, put her musical skills at Eliot's disposal for *The Cocktail Party,* scoring the tune of "One Eyed Riley" as Eliot sang it to her in his thin tenor.[11]

On 18 April 1949 Mary proposed to Eliot. "Oh dear, oh dear," he responded. "As for yourself and me, I didn't think it was anything like that." He was, he said, "burnt out": his years of agony with Vivienne had crippled and exhausted him. Even to think of sharing his life with someone had become a "nightmare." Mary accepted that the "psychological change of life," which Eliot told her he had undergone, made it impossible for him to love again. But as she listened to his repetitive complaints—"I feel so lonely going to Receptions alone" and "What shall I do if I get ill?" and "I can't plan a holiday" because he had no one to holiday with, Hayward being too handicapped to travel—an obvious solution presented itself again to Mary. "Why should we both be lonely?" she asked on 29 May 1950. Again she met with a rebuff. This time Eliot explained that it was because of the catastrophe over Emily Hale that he could not contemplate except "with horror, the thought of marrying anyone else, or of any relationship except that of friendship."[12] "His conscience about Emily, and the way he 'jilted' her must be very bad," commented Mary drily, when Eliot went to meet a train on which she was arriving in August 1953. "He hardly ever meets trains!"

Mary accepted with fortitude Eliot's rejection of her third proposal. She told him that he could enjoy, without embarrassment, the knowledge that there was one person who loved him and that he had better accept her as one of the family. "Tom, with a beaming smile, said, 'Yes, indeed—and I'll give you a toast—TO THE GUARDIANS.'" Unlike Emily, Mary saw Eliot almost weekly and gained a realistic insight into the limitations of his character. She played her allotted role with dignity, remaining a loyal and devoted "guardian" for twenty years from 1938 until 1957. Henceforth, she and John Hayward functioned as a surrogate family to Eliot, sometimes conferring when they felt the poet was in danger of becoming too self-important. By the 1950s Eliot had become "the Pope of Russell Square," possessor of an authority which was semi-divine within the Vatican-like confines of Faber & Faber, and even beyond; it was after he made Mary a present of a good "practical" rosary, one of two which he had been given by the Pope in Rome, that Mary gave Eliot this mocking, but wholly fitting title. In 1948 he received the Order of Merit and the Nobel Prize, and honorary doctorates by the handful—from Yale, Princeton and even, finally, from Harvard. The shell which guarded his personality grew more rigid; he imposed strict "Trade Union" rules upon Mary in order to ration their meetings.[13] "He is a man in prison, a prison largely of his own making," she surmised in 1950. "I had to spend all these years loving him and being hurt often—and now, perhaps, the prison door has opened just a chink." But Eliot's door barely opened before it slammed shut again. "I have noticed of late his *immense* indignation with anyone who disagrees with *him*—and that is a bad state to get into," wrote Mary to John

Hayward on 21 April 1955. "So I consider it's practically your mission to tell him what you really think ... It is indeed a terrible strain on any human being to feel he is a Classic in his lifetime, & Tom needs, more than he will ever know, honesty from his closest friends."[14]

In the 1950s Eliot took to "snapping" at John and Mary, who often found themselves the victims of his moods. In August 1954 he was "in one of his most towering rages—white with anger, and practically non-speaking" during a visit from Marian and Theodora.[15] The year before, Eliot had met Mary at the Armistice Day Requiem on 8 November; he was tired after dining with the King of Sweden, who was on a state visit, and "very wheezy" during the long service. Mary drove him home to Cheyne Walk and said that she was looking forward to dining with him on Thursday as arranged. "He replied petulantly that he'd no idea what he was doing this week and the thought of dining with *anyone* filled him with horror ... and departed. Oh La! La!" recorded an exasperated Mary. Generally, however, she waited patiently for Eliot to thaw; a few days after an argument might find the poet with a gin in Mary's kitchen, mixing the salad, cooking the bacon, getting in the way and enjoying himself very much.[16] "You spoil him," said Marian, who wanted Mary for a sister-in-law. "She thinks that I ought, for my own sake, to leave him," wrote Mary. "I didn't say so to her, but I fear it is too late."

Eliot's letters to Hayward reveal why he rationed his intimacy with Mary. Damningly he confided to his friend in November 1939, after giving his first poetry reading at Student Mission House, that "Miss Mary Trevelyan, the hearty Warden" of the settlement, whisked him upstairs for a couple of glasses of bad sherry afterwards. "Hearty," the same epithet he had used for Emily on their country walks, spelt death to any woman's hopes of marriage to the poet. Nevertheless both Mary and Emily were immortalised in Eliot's drama: in *The Cocktail Party,* originally entitled "One-Eyed Reilly," Emily features as the martyred Celia, and Mary as Julia, who hopes to fill the gap in Riley's life left by his vanished wife Lavinia.

Despite the popular and financial success of his first drawing-room comedy, Eliot's unhappiness seemed to deepen after Vivienne's death. It seemed that he faced his own Eumenides, and only by the practise of Christian ritual could guilt be expiated, or redemption glimpsed. It has been suggested that Eliot deliberately undertook a ten-year penance from

1947, one in which he condemned himself to walk across "a whole Thibet of broken stones" in atonement. This is judgement by hindsight, and it should not be supposed that Eliot deliberately set a term on his remorse, after which he felt he warranted absolution. But undeniably he experienced the "terrifying guilt," as Josef Chiari has described it, of knowing he had "loathed one woman to the point of wishing, or perhaps even causing her death."[17] His ill-controlled anger was a sign of the strain under which he laboured, and others besides Mary and John were subjected to his wrath.[18]

Eliot's producer, E. Martin Browne, concluded at the end of his long collaboration with the playwright that Eliot's plays after *The Family Reunion* represented a failure of nerve. Neither *The Confidential Clerk* (1953) nor *The Elder Statesman* (1958) was as successful, dramatically or financially, as *The Cocktail Party,* which, *Time* magazine estimated, grossed a million dollars during its run of 325 performances in New York, of which Eliot's own share was £29,000. "I feel that, by adopting this pattern of ironic social comedy, Eliot placed upon his genius a regrettable limitation," writes Browne. "He tied himself to social, and still more theatrical, conventions which were already outworn when the plays were written . . ."[19] Without his Muse—Vivienne—Eliot the revolutionary had become a reactionary. As early as 1939 Eliot wrote to Hayward that he had no family, no career, and nothing particular to look forward to in this world. "I doubt the permanent value of everything I have written." These doubts grew as, during the 1950s, his energies diminished, and he traded innovation for West End success. Fame and financial security, craved for so long, did not assuage loneliness. Eliot remained in the bleak bedroom in Carlyle Mansions, Cheyne Walk. Increasingly he clung to worldly honours, signifiers of worth, slipping out of the flat to peek at the photograph of himself on the front of *Time* in 1950, and even accepting the Hanseatic Goethe Award in Hamburg despite his dislike of Goethe. Ronald Duncan asked Eliot: "Isn't it a bit of a grind for you to write about Goethe?" To which Eliot replied: "It is. I can't stand his stuff."[20] And the friendship of younger poets and writers such as E. W. F. Tomlin, Josef Chiari, Djuna Barnes and the American priest William Turner Levy, whom he often published at financial and editorial cost to himself, provided confirmation of his position.[21] Such people deferred to Eliot's almost legendary status as a literary icon, and never challenged him as Hayward and Mary were liable, brusquely, to do. The memory of his marriage to Vivienne might have faded had not the threat of future biographies begun to haunt him.

Worries about his health and his reputation began to weigh on Eliot. By 1956, despite the solicitude of friends such as Tomlin and Levy, his tachycardia (abnormally rapid heartbeat) and bronchitis were giving serious cause for concern. Often he asked Mary Trevelyan to feel his pulse. He was, by this period, seriously addicted to the tranquilliser Nembutal, prescribed for anxiety and phobias connected with lifts and large animals.[22] On 12 June 1956 he returned from a trip to America on the *Queen Mary:* "Exhausted T. S. Eliot rushed to hospital. Taken Off Liner, American Trip Wearies Poet" screamed the headline. The United Press added, "The 67-year old Nobel Prize Winner was stricken two days outside New York on the voyage back from his trip to America . . . When the ship reached Southampton, he was taken ashore, pale but smiling, by wheelchair and put into an ambulance."[23] His doctors, Eliot told Tomlin, said that although he had obeyed their orders to give up smoking, his chances of surviving were only fifty-fifty.[24]

Rumours continued to grow that Eliot was homosexual. On 11 November 1952 he met Mary in her flat, bringing "a nasty little article from an American magazine, practically accusing him of homosexuality and mentioning John." He also told her of Canadian academic John Peter's "more serious" article in *Essays in Criticism,* "hinting the same so transparently that he is consulting his solicitor about a possible libel action."[25] On Sunday 30 November Eliot mentioned to Mary that Helen Gardner was very angry about the latter article, and had written a strong protest about it. Tom was not "one of the fraternity," he assured Mary, although the following January, when she remarked that the Chelsea "pansies" were said to have a club in the block of flats to which she had moved, he burst out that homosexuals lived "a life of fear and ostracism—like souls in hell. I believe in hell, yes I do," with a vehemence that astonished her. "I live in constant fear of it myself."[26]

Eliot expressed his outrage at Peter's article to Tomlin and took legal advice. When he wrote to the "young man" with the veiled threat of legal action, John Peter replied, wrote Tomlin, "with a touchingly contrite letter."[27] All copies of *Essays in Criticism* containing the article were pulped, in response to a formal letter from Eliot's solicitor. This did not prevent Peter republishing his allegations in 1969, after Eliot's death. Tomlin has recalled how Eliot's threats of legal action were interpreted as a desire to suppress the truth: "Eliot has been credited with more than one *sub rosa* liaison, and with the extremes of hypocrisy in trying to pretend to be what he was not." At Cambridge, too, F. W. Bateson cited the "King Bolo" poems in a lecture as evidence that Eliot had written a quantity of obscene poetry. In a decade in which homosexual writers and artists were acutely aware of a legal situation which could destroy careers—as it nearly did for John Gielgud, who was unable to work in the United States for four years in the mid-1950s after his conviction for cottaging—the fear of scandal was very real. Gielgud's sentence triggered a debate on homosexuality which led to the Wolfenden Report in 1957, but not until 1967, two years after Eliot's death, was homosexuality decriminalised.

In February 1938 Eliot had pressed John Hayward to become his literary executor. There was, he wrote, no one else whom he could altogether trust in that capacity. Hayward's function would be chiefly negative: to say no to republication of the "junk" he had written for periodicals in the past, and which ought never to be reprinted. "And I don't want any biography written," he stipulated, or any intimate letters published. "So again your job would be to discourage any attempts to make books of me or about me, and to suppress everything suppressible." He would, he wrote, leave instructions in his will to this effect.[28]

By 1956, however, Eliot had begun to wonder whether Hayward's health would enable him to carry out the task of literary executor for long. There was no guarantee that the younger man would outlive him for many years; and yet Eliot was seriously concerned about his own failing health. His thoughts turned to his own death. In 1948 he requested that Father Cheetham should preside over a Requiem Mass, followed by burial in Brookwood Cemetery, Woking. Later, in June 1956, he decided that he would prefer to be buried in the old graveyard, near the church of East Coker, Somerset, from which his ancestor Andrew Eliot had journeyed to the New World. His second choice, were he to die in the United States, was the Bellefontaine Cemetery, St. Louis, near his parents and grandparents. He had, he wrote, very strong objections to being buried in any cathedral or abbey church, such as Westminster Abbey or St. Paul's.[29]

Hayward had hinted in May 1956 to the poet John Brinnin that the situation was becoming critical:

> "Tom's now developed something called emphysema. It's rapidly becoming apparent that he needs a nurse more than I do. And I have an informed suspicion that the ever-adoring Miss Fletcher is ready to assume the role. You know her?"
>
> "The young woman in his office?"
>
> "There's somewhat more to that flower of the Yorkshire marshes than meets the eye," he said. "The perfect secretary has begun to see herself as the lady with the lamp."[30]

Valerie Fletcher had become T. S. Eliot's secretary in 1949. Growing up in Leeds, where playwright Alan Bennett, son of the local butcher, used to deliver her mother's orders of meat on his bicycle, she heard John Gielgud's recording of "The Journey of the Magi" at the age of fourteen.[31] It was her first introduction to Eliot's poetry, and she was captivated. "My obsession became a family joke," she recalled. She took a secretarial course and travelled to London, where she worked for the writer Charles Morgan before Eliot engaged her as his secretary.[32]

By 1956 Valerie Fletcher had become indispensable to Eliot, as indispensable a secretary as Vivienne had once been. Margaret Behrens, the "Field Marshall," as Eliot nicknamed her when he knew her at Shamley Green, owned a house in the south of France to which she invited Miss Fletcher. Prompted by Mrs. Behrens, Eliot came to stay at a nearby hotel. The barriers of formality began to break down, but not until Eliot had slipped his written proposal into the letters his secretary was typing for him, and she had accepted, did he suddenly say, "Do you know my Christian name?" Even so, the couple kept their engagement secret at the office, where Valerie wore a finger stall over her engagement ring.

T. S. Eliot and Valerie Fletcher were married on 10 January 1957, ten years after Vivienne's death, at St. Barnabas's Church, Kensington, the church in which Jules Laforgue had married. The "curiously furtive" ceremony took place at 6 a.m. with only Valerie's parents and a friend present. She was thirty, he sixty-eight. Eliot had married a woman young enough to be his daughter; he had at last found the laughing, loving child which featured so often in his poetry. It was a father/daughter relationship which inspired the newfound tenderness between Lord Claverton and Monica in *The Elder Statesman* (which Eliot began shortly before his second marriage), a play based on Sophocles' *Oedipus at Colonus*. The drama, as Kenneth Tynan acutely observed, tells "the old story of the great man whose past catches up with him, the hero who has Lived a Lie."[33]

Eliot abandoned Hayward with the same abruptness and moral cowardice with which he left Vivienne; Hayward had no foreknowledge of the wedding. According to one version, he was simply left a letter of explanation by Eliot on the morning when he slipped out to be married, as secretly as he had gone to his baptism thirty years earlier. Geoffrey Faber and Mary Trevelyan, to whom Eliot gave a false address in France, received similar letters on the same day.[34] However, Hayward told another version: that Eliot came into his room very early on 10 January and handed him the letter, asking him to read it at once. Hayward did so. He assured Eliot he was not angry. "Then Eliot leaned forward, put his arm around him, and kissed him, saying, 'Oh, I knew I could always rely on you.' Hayward said later, with a resigned grin, 'Since I am the most un-homosexual man in London, I found this a most offensive gesture.' "[35] Thenceforth Hayward referred to himself as "the widow," a different species of spider.

Mary thought Tom had gone out of his mind, having being thrown off the scent by his remarks to her that Miss Fletcher was "such a tiresome girl, she will keep on working late. I do wish she wasn't so devoted." Attributing Tom's second marriage to his hypochondria and panic over death, and to his increasing inability to accept criticism or contradiction, Mary felt that he needed someone who "would always tell him he was right and everyone else was wrong." The two letters of good wishes she sent Tom prompted "a very angry reply" from the poet, accusing her of "gross impertinence." She had no further contact with him. Soon she found herself struck off the Eliots' Christmas card list, and sorrowfully concluded that Tom was no longer the person she had known: "But have I known the real person? Have John and I known and loved the real man?" Now there was "no to-morrow—but I have had my years and I wouldn't have missed them." Tom had left, wrote Mary, "so great a sadness in the hearts of his old friends"; nevertheless, she continued to say a nightly prayer for him, in words of his own, in which he asked God for protection from "the Voices [and] the Visions."[36] Emily Hale, on hearing Eliot's news, had a breakdown and was admitted to Massachusetts General Hospital in Boston. She never recovered completely.

Eliot's second marriage brought him the happiness that the first had denied him. No longer was he jostled by ghosts. But in old age, during the seven years of his second marriage, he wrote neither poetry nor plays of distinction, in contrast to the outpouring from the "sacred wood" which had marked his seventeen years with Vivienne. He died at the age of seventy-six, on 4 January 1965, comforted by the impregnability of his reputation; Vivienne, meanwhile, lay forgotten in the Pinner cemetery.

Acknowledgments

The suggestion to write about Vivienne Eliot came from novelist Pauline Neville, to whom I am grateful for the germ of an idea, which grew, with the encouragement of Peter Day, then Editorial Director of Allison & Busby, into a book proposal. When, sadly, Peter's ill-health prevented him taking the book on, I was extraordinarily fortunate to find in Carol O'Brien, Editorial Director of Constable & Robinson, someone who believed in this book almost as passionately as I did. For sharing my vision, and contributing her own determination, unwavering encouragement, negotiating and editorial skills over the last four years, particularly in our struggle to quote from Vivienne Eliot's Bodleian Papers, I owe her a particular debt of gratitude. I am also indebted to Nick Robinson, Managing Director of Constable & Robinson, for his conviction that the book merited a legal defence by Queen's Counsel. Nick's support has played an essential part in making this book a reality. I am very grateful to Kim Witherspoon, my agent in New York, and Nan Talese, Editorial Director of Doubleday, for their guidance, and for Nan's perceptive editorial advice.

I wish to thank John Stallworthy for his critical reading of several chapters, in particular those concerning *The Waste Land,* and for his support; Andrew Motion for his generous assistance, and Matthew Evans and John Bodley of Faber & Faber for a close reading of the typescript, and their subsequent decision, on behalf of Mrs. Valerie Eliot, to give permission for quotations from Vivienne Eliot's Papers.

Valuable encouragement in the early stages of my research came from Michael Hastings. I am immensely grateful to him for making available to me his notes of a series of interviews with Maurice Haigh-Wood, other research notes, correspondence, Haigh-Wood family photographs, and for introductions to Vivienne's descendants.

I am greatly indebted to Humphrey Carpenter and Kate Trevelyan, literary executors for Mary Trevelyan, for permission to read and quote from Mary's important unpublished memoir of T. S. Eliot, which spans twenty years; to Adrian and Philip Goodman for making available extracts from the unpublished journals of Lady Ottoline Morrell; to Pamela Matthews, widow of T. S. Matthews, for giving me unrestricted access to her late husband's archive; and to Paul Delany for permission to quote from his unpublished research on the Eliots' finances.

I am most grateful to the Harry Ransom Humanities Research Center at the University of Texas at Austin for their award of the Paul Mellon Visiting Fellowship 1999–2000. This enabled me to return for a second visit to the Center in autumn 1999 to work on important sources for Vivienne's life: the Richard Aldington Papers, Mary Hutchinson Papers, Ottoline Morrell Papers, Léonide Massine Papers, Sitwell Papers and others. Although there is no collection bearing Vivienne Eliot's name at Texas, her intimate correspondence with more famous figures provided a rich source of information. The knowledge and efficiency of so many members of staff speeded my task, and I wish to thank all those who helped me, especially Thomas F. Staley,

Director, and Cathy Henderson for her advice on copyright issues. The enthusiasm of academics, archivists and librarians for my quest and their belief in freedom of information heartened me on many occasions. I also wish to thank Pat Fox for shared outings; Brian Bremen, for making available correspondence from the Edmund Wilson Papers; Margaret Ratliff, for permission to quote from her thesis on the Correspondence of Mary Hutchinson; Brian Parker, for discussions on T. S. Eliot and Members of the British Studies Group, including Charlotte Rhodes, whose hospitality I appreciated over Thanksgiving.

At the Bertrand Russell Archive, Mills Memorial Library, McMaster University, Hamilton, Ontario, I was greatly helped by Carl Spadoni, Director, whose extensive knowledge of the Russell Papers aided my research immeasurably. I am most grateful to Carl, to Kenneth Blackwell, Editor of the journal *Russell,* and to Nicholas Griffin, Editor of Russell's letters, for their interest and encouragement, and to all the staff; I am indebted to the university for its generous decision to waive permissions fees. I also wish to thank Phyllis Urch, literary executor of Lady Constance Malleson (Colette O'Niel), for permission to quote from the unpublished letters between Malleson and Russell, and from Mrs. Urch's unpublished typescript.

I would like to thank the following librarians, archivists and institutions for their help: Mary Clapinson at the Bodleian Library (Vivienne Eliot Papers); Richard Burns, Curator, at Bury Art Gallery; Alan Bell at the London Library; Elizabeth Inglis, former Head of Special Collections at Sussex University Library (Monk's House and Charleston Collections); Ros Moad at King's College Library, Cambridge (John Davy Hayward Bequest); the Librarians at the British Library Manuscript Dept. (Schiff Papers), and at the New British Library; the Librarian at the Wellcome Library; the Librarian at the New York Public Library (The Henry W. and Albert A. Berg Collection); William Stoneman and Elizabeth Falsey at the Houghton Library, Harvard University; the Librarian at the Beinecke Rare Book and Manuscript Library, Yale University (Scofield Thayer/*Dial* Papers, Ezra Pound Papers, W. F. Stead Papers, Osborn Collection, and John Quinn Papers); the Librarian at the Lilly Library, Indiana University (Eliot letters to Ezra and Dorothy Pound); and the Librarian at Princeton University Library (the Paul Elmer Moore Papers).

I am indebted to many wise and generous people over the last four years for interviews, answers to my queries, advice, inspiration and hospitality: Sybille Bedford, Moris Farhi, Lyndall Gordon, Rosalind Ingrams at Garsington, Francis King and Frances Partridge; Peter Ackroyd, Rachel Billington, Ray Bown, David Bradshaw, Anthony and Sarah Cassidy, Cherry and Robert Clarke, Ania Corless, Ken Craven, David Davidson, Dawn and Philip Firth, Jonathan Fryer, John Gielgud, Victoria Glendinning, Pat Grayburn, Lord Hutchinson, Christopher Hutchings, Dr. Frank Keane, Hermione Lee, Mark Le Fanu, Jane Mays, Blake Morrison, Jenny MacKilligan, Lucy Popescu, Diana Pullein-Thompson and Dennis Farr, Elizabeth Parker, Peter Parker, Jocelyn and Christopher Rowe, Bill Saunders, Ann and Richard Salter, Reresby Sitwell, Miranda Seymour, Michael Silverleaf, QC, Christopher Sinclair-Stevenson, Sue and Christopher Singer, Ann R. Jones and Peter Stallybrass, Bill Stallybrass, Gunnvor Stallybrass, Kate Tait (daughter of Bertrand Russell), Dr. Tom Stuttaford, Dr. Graham Tyrell, and Moira Williams.

I would like to thank Jane Robertson for her patience and industry in copy-editing the typescript; Lorna Owen for extra editorial work; Gary Chapman, Andrew Hayward and all the Constable team for their commitment to this book; my father, Tony Seymour-Jones, FRCS, for assistance with medical research; my children, Emma and son-in-law Andrew, Edward and Lucy, for their ever-present support; and especially my partner, Geoffrey Parkinson, for reading and discussing the manuscript over many hours, for his illuminating suggestions, for his understanding during my absences abroad, and for his sense of humour.

I am grateful to the following for permission to quote material in copyright: the executors of the Virginia Woolf Estate and The Random House Group *(The Diaries and Letters of Virginia Woolf* published by The Hogarth Press); Faber & Faber on behalf of Mrs. Valerie Eliot (for unpublished and published letters and texts by T. S. Eliot, Vivienne Eliot and Ezra Pound); Adrian and Philip Goodman (Lady Ottoline Morrell); Bruce Hunter (Osbert Sitwell). For illustrative material I wish to thank: the Bury Art Gallery; Jane and Anne Haigh-Wood; the Houghton Library, Harvard University; the Beinecke Library, Yale; McMaster University, Hamilton, Ontario; Mrs. Phyllis Urch; the Tate Gallery; King's College, Cambridge; A. C. Cooper; the Harry Ransom Humanities Research Center; University of Texas at Austin; Musée de l'Opéra; Bibliothèque Nationale and Kate Trevelyan.

Notes

Abbreviations Used in the Notes

Beinecke	Beinecke Rare Book and Manuscript Library, Yale: Ezra Pound Papers, Scofield Thayer/*Dial* Collection, W. F. Stead Papers
Berg	Berg Collection, Manuscript Division of New York Public Library
Bodleian	Bodleian Library, Oxford
BR	Bertrand Russell
C. C. Eliot	Charlotte Champe Eliot (TSE's mother)
CM	Colette O'Niel, stage name of Lady Constance Malleson
CP	T. S. Eliot, *Collected Poems 1909–1962* (London: Faber & Faber, 1974)
EP	Ezra Pound
Houghton	Houghton Library, Harvard: Eliot Collection
IMH	Christopher Ricks (ed.), *Inventions of the March Hare, T. S. Eliot: Poems 1909–1917* (New York: Harcourt Brace Jovanovich, 1996)
JH	John Hayward
JHB	John Hayward Bequest, King's College, Cambridge
JQ	John Quinn
Letters I	Valerie Eliot (ed.), *The Letters of T. S. Eliot, Volume 1, 1898–1922* (New York: Harcourt Brace Jovanovich, 1988)
Lilly	Lilly Library, Indiana: Ezra Pound Papers, including correspondence of T. S. Eliot to Dorothy Pound
McMaster	Bertrand Russell Archives, McMaster University, Hamilton, Ontario
MH	Mary Hutchinson, wife of St. John (Jack) Hutchinson
OM	Lady Ottoline Morrell
RA	Richard Aldington
Schiff	British Library: Schiff Papers
Sussex	The Manuscript Section of the University of Sussex Library: Leonard and Virginia Woolf Collection
ST	Scofield Thayer
Texas	Harry Ransom Humanities Research Center, University of Texas at Austin, Texas: Mary Hutchinson Collection and Ottoline Morrell Collection
TSE	Thomas Stearns Eliot
VE	Vivien(ne) Eliot. Maiden name on birth certificate, Vivienne Haigh-Wood. By 1915 Vivienne spelt her name "Vivien," and continued to do so for the greater part of her marriage. In Chapter 1 she is "Vivienne," and returns to this spelling in Chapter 19, in 1928.

VW   Virginia Woolf
WL Facs   Valerie Eliot (ed.), T. S. Eliot, *The Waste Land: A Facsimile and Transcript of the Original Drafts including the Annotations of Ezra Pound* (New York: Harcourt Brace Jovanovich, 1971)

Preface

1. Herbert Read, "T.S.E.—A Memoir," in Allen Tate (ed.), *T. S. Eliot, the Man and His Work* (London: Chatto & Windus, 1967).

2. Anne Oliver Bell (ed.), *The Diary of Virginia Woolf,* vol. 4, 1931–35 (London: Penguin, 1983), p. 123, 2 September 1932.

3. Bell (ed.), *Diary of Virginia Woolf,* op. cit., vol. 3, p. 331, 3 November 1930.

4. Donald E. Stanford, "The First Mrs. Eliot," *Library Chronicle of the University of Texas at Austin,* new series, p. 40.

5. T. S. Matthews, *Great Tom: Notes Towards the Definition of T. S. Eliot* (London: Weidenfeld & Nicolson, 1974), p. 40.

6. Peter Ackroyd, *T. S. Eliot* (London: Penguin, 1993), p. 63.

7. Mary Clapinson, Keeper of Special Collections and Western Manuscripts, Bodleian Library, to the author, 24 March 2000.

8. TSE to John Hayward, February 1938, John Hayward Bequest, King's College, Cambridge.

9. Valerie Eliot (ed.), *The Waste Land: A Facsimile and Transcript of the Original Drafts including the Annotations of Ezra Pound* (New York: Harcourt Brace Jovanovich, 1971).

10. Will of Vivienne Haigh Eliot, 1 March 1936.

11. VE to Ottoline Morrell, 31 December 1933, Texas.

1. A Bohemian from Bury

1. T. S. Eliot to Eleanor Hinkley, 27 November 1914, Valerie Eliot (ed.), *The Letters of T. S. Eliot, Vol. 1, 1898–1922* (New York: Harcourt Brace Jovanovich, 1988), p. 70.

2. T. S. Eliot to J. H. Woods, 5 October 1914, *Letters I,* p. 60.

3. T. S. Eliot to Conrad Aiken, 31 December 1914, *Letters I,* 74.

4. Osbert Sitwell, unpublished memoir on T. S. Eliot and his marriage, 19 February 1950, Texas.

5. T. S. Matthews, *Great Tom: Notes Towards the Definition of T. S. Eliot,* (London: Weidenfeld & Nicolson, 1974) p. 41.

6. Vivienne Eliot Diary, 1 September 1934, Bodleian.

7. Richard Lewis, "Tom & Viv: The Bury Connection," *Bury Times,* 15 April 1994.

8. Vivienne Haigh-Wood's birth certificate gives the residence of the father, C. Haigh-Wood, as Knowsley Street.

9. Vivien Eliot to Henry Eliot, 11 October 1916, MS Houghton, *Letters I,* p. 154.

10. The 1841 Census records Charles Wood, carver and gilder, living in Union Square. By 1851 he had moved to 22 Fleet St. (now the Rock) and had five children aged between nine and one living with him, including Charles.

11. There is a discrepancy in the difference between the ages of Charles and Mary on the different censuses, but it appears to have been between seven (1881) and ten years (1871).

12. Census, April 1861, shows eight people living at 22 Fleet Street: Charles and Mary Wood and their five children, and Kate Lee servant.

13. The Census of April 1871 shows Charles Wood, aged sixty, Master Carver and Gilder, still living at 22 Fleet Street, Bury.

14. Michael Karwowski, "The Bride from Bury," *Lancashire Life,* March 1984.

15. Charles Haigh-Wood Collection, Bury Art Gallery and Museum, Lancashire. I am indebted to the present Curator, Richard Burns, for showing me the collection now in store.

16. Ibid.

17. Information from Electoral Rolls and Directories gathered by Penney Farrell, Assistant Reference and Information Services Librarian, Bury Central Library.

18. Maurice Haigh-Wood, interview with Michael Hastings, 12 March 1980.

19. "Mr. C. H. Wood and His Work," *Bury Times,* July 1899.

20. Charles Haigh-Wood Collection, Bury Art Gallery and Museum.

21. Quoted by C. Billingham, Senior Curator, Bury Art Gallery and Museum, in his letter to Norman Wood, 4 May 1990.

22. VE Diary, 23 July 1935, Bodleian.

23. Catalogue no. 37, Charles Haigh-Wood, 1910 Bury Art Gallery exhibition details, from a transcription by the artist's great-granddaughter, Anne Haigh-Wood, with additional notes by Ken Craven.

24. Charles Haigh-Wood Collection, Bury Art Gallery and Museum. This painting is still reproduced as a greetings card with the caption, "I'll Be Sorry . . . If You'll Be Sorry," and is entitled *Boy with Apple and Girl.*

25. Osbert Sitwell, unpublished memoir on T. S. Eliot and his marriage, op. cit.

26. Brigit Patmore, *My Friends when Young* (London: Heinemann, 1968), p. 85.

27. "The Night Club," a short story, May 1924, Vivien Eliot Papers, Bodleian.

28. Notes for a short story, May 1924, Vivien Eliot Papers, Bodleian.

29. Conversations with Dr. Thomas Stuttaford, October 1998, and Dr. Graham Tyrell, November 1998.

30. Maurice Haigh-Wood, interview with Michael Hastings, 21 January 1980.

31. "Rosa Buckle" sketch, ?1924, MSS Eng. Misc. c. 624, loose-leaf paste-up book, Vivien Eliot Papers, Bodleian.

32. Anthony Clare, *Psychiatry in Dissent: Controversial Issues in Thought and Practice* (London: Routledge, 1989), pp. 186, 187.

33. Adam Phillips, *Winnicott* (London: Fontana, 1988), p. 48.

34. VE Diary, 24 August 1935, Bodleian.

35. Patmore, op. cit., pp. 84, 85.

36. Stephen Trombley, *All That Summer She Was Mad* (London: Junction Books, 1981), p. 115.

37. Henry Maudsley, "Moral Insanity versus Will," in Vieda Skultans, *Madness and Morals: Ideas on Insanity in the Nineteenth Century* (London: Routledge and Kegan Paul, 1975), p. 194.

38. VE Diary, 18 March 1935, Bodleian.

2. The River Girl

1. Loose-leaf book, MSS Eng. Misc. c. 624, Vivien Eliot Papers, Bodleian.

2. Stephen Spender, *T. S. Eliot* (London: Fontana, 1975), p. 49.

3. Osbert Sitwell, "T. S. Eliot," an unpublished memoir, Sitwell Papers, Harry Ransom Humanities Research Center, University of Texas at Austin.

4. Loose-leaf book, Vivien Eliot Papers, Bodleian.

5. Statement by Theresa Eliot, Houghton Library.

6. VE Diary, 12 February 1914, Bodleian.

7. Maurice Haigh-Wood, interview with Michael Hastings, 21 January 1980.

8. Nicholas Joost, *Scofield Thayer and* The Dial, *An Illustrated History* (Southern Illinois University Press, 1964), p. 8. In 1918 Thayer bought *The Dial,* a Chicago review founded by Francis F. Browne in 1880.

9. President's Secretary, Magdalen College, Oxford, to T. S. Matthews, 26 September 1972, citing entry on Scofield Thayer from J. Brett Langstaff, *Oxford 1914* (New York: Vantage Press, 1965).

10. VE Diary, 23 February 1914, Bodleian.

11. VE Diary, 26 February 1914, Bodleian.

12. Maurice Haigh-Wood, interview with Michael Hastings, 28 January 1980.

13. "Rosa Buckle" sketch, loose-leaf book, Vivien Eliot Papers, Bodleian.

14. Maurice Haigh-Wood, interview with Michael Hastings, 4 March 1980.

15. VE Diary, 3 March 1914, Bodleian.

16. VE Diary, 5 March 1914, Bodleian.

17. VE Diary, 8 March 1914, Bodleian.

18. VE Diary, 11 March 1914, Bodleian.

19. VE Diary, 12 March 1914, Bodleian.

20. VE Diary, 14 March 1914, Bodleian.

21. Maurice Haigh-Wood, interview with Michael Hastings, 28 January 1980.

22. VE Diary, 16 March 1914, Bodleian.

23. VE Diary, 17 March 1914, Bodleian.

24. VE Diary, 19 March 1914, Bodleian.

25. VE Diary, 20 March 1914, Bodleian.

26. VE Diary, 22 March 1914, Bodleian.

27. VE Diary, 25 March 1914, Bodleian.

28. VE Diary, 29 March 1914, Bodleian.

29. VE Diary, 2 April 1914, Bodleian.

30. VE Diary, 12 April 1914, Bodleian.

31. VE Diary, 16 April 1914, Bodleian.

32. VE Diary, 17 April 1914, Bodleian.

33. VE Diary, 21–25 April 1914, Bodleian.

34. VE Diary, 30 April 1914, Bodleian.

35. VE Diary, 6 August 1914, Bodleian.

36. VE Diary, 22 August 1914, Bodleian.

37. VE Diary, 24 August 1914, Bodleian.

38. Horace, *Odes,* III.ii.13.

39. VE Diary, 28 August 1914, Bodleian.
40. VE to Scofield Thayer, 22 February 1915, Beinecke.
41. VE to Scofield Thayer, 3 March 1915, Beinecke.
42. Ibid.

3. An Alien in America

1. Henry Ware Eliot Sr. to Thomas Lamb Eliot, 26 September 1888, Houghton.
2. Charlotte Champe Eliot to Richard Cobb, end September 1905, *Letters, I,* p. 11.
3. Eleanor Hinkley, quoted in "The Mysterious Mr. Eliot," BBC1 TV Programme, 3 January 1971.
4. Mary Trevelyan, "The Pope of Russell Square," unpublished memoir of T. S. Eliot, 1957.
5. T. S. Eliot, *To Criticize the Critic and Other Writings* (London: Faber & Faber, 1963), pp. 43–60.
6. Family genealogies, Houghton. Charlotte Blood (1818–93) was descended from General Thomas Blood. She married Thomas Stearns (1811–96). Her daughter Charlotte was born in Baltimore, Maryland, on 22 October 1843.
7. TSE to Ezra Pound, 10 December 1933, Beinecke.
8. Prufrock-Littau, furniture wholesalers, advertised in St. Louis in the early twentieth century. Hugh Kenner, *The Invisible Poet: T. S. Eliot* (London: Methuen, 1960), p. 3.
9. Charlotte C. Eliot to R. Cobb, 4 April 1905, *Letters, I,* p. 7.
10. T. S. Eliot, Preface to Edgar Ansel Mower, *This American World* (London: Faber & Gwyer, 1928), quoted in Helen Gardner, *The Composition of the Four Quartets* (London: Faber & Faber, 1978), p. 48.
11. TSE to John Hayward, 27 December 1939, John Hayward Bequest, King's College, Cambridge.
12. T. S. Eliot, "The Dry Salvages," from *Four Quartets, Collected Poems 1900–1962* (London: Faber & Faber, 1963), p. 209.
13. Smith Academy Record, February 1905.
14. Quoted in Lyndall Gordon, *Eliot's Early Years* (Oxford: Oxford University Press, 1977), p. 4.
15. Henry Ware Eliot Sr., "Reflections of a Simpleton," unpublished memoir, 1911, Houghton.
16. Clara H. Scudder, The Wednesday Club, "Charlotte C. Eliot, In Memoriam," 1929. Charlotte died on 10 September 1929, and these notes were collected by Henry Ware Eliot Jr.
17. Herbert Howarth, *Notes on Some Figures Behind T. S. Eliot* (London: Chatto & Windus, 1965), p. 28.
18. Poems of Charlotte C. Eliot, and typescript of *Savonarola,* with corrections by T. S. Eliot, Houghton.
19. William Turner Levy and Victor Scherle, *Affectionately, T. S. Eliot: The Story of a Friendship* (London: J. M. Dent & Sons, 1968), pp. 53–54.
20. Henry Ware Eliot to Thomas Lamb Eliot, 7 March 1914, quoted in John Seldo, "The Tempering of T. S. Eliot, 1888–1915," unpublished Harvard dissertation, 1972.
21. T. S. Eliot, "East Coker," *Four Quartets, CP,* p. 197.
22. TSE Address to the Mary Institute, 1 November 1959, published as *From Mary to You* (St. Louis, 1959), p. 135.
23. TSE to John Hayward, 27 December 1939, John Hayward Bequest, King's College, Cambridge.

24. T. S. Eliot, *Selected Essays, 1917–1932* (London: Faber & Faber, 1932), p. 273.

25. Translation by A. David Moody, *Thomas Stearns Eliot, Poet* (Cambridge: Cambridge University Press, 1979), pp. 77–78.

The original (*CP*, p. 101.) reads:

J'avais sept ans, elle était plus petite,

Elle était tout mouillée, je lui ai donné des primevères . . .

"Je la chatouillais, pour la faire rire.

J'éprouvais un instant de puissance et de délire."

26. Undated typescript, "Dans le Restaurant," Pound's corrections, Ezra Pound Papers, Beinecke, Yale.

27. TSE to John Hayward, 27 December 1939, John Hayward Bequest, King's College, Cambridge.

28. Lyndall Gordon, *Eliot's Early Years* (Oxford: Oxford University Press, 1977), p. 4.

29. T. S. Eliot, "Animula," 1929, *CP*, p. 113.

30. Alessandra Lemma-Wright, *Invitation to Psychodynamic Psychology* (London: Whurr Publishers Ltd., 1995), pp. 32, 149. See the case study of "Mark," and his "very strong, yet highly ambivalent attachment to his mother . . . Mark's difficulty in settling down with another woman, and his recurring problem with impotence, were understood as being in some way connected to his very close relationship with his mother and the rivalry she felt towards any woman Mark introduced her to. In order to appease his mother Mark reached the only compromise which he felt was open to him: he would see other women but he was frequently unable to fully consummate the relationship sexually . . . thereby never establishing any relationship that would seriously threaten his mother. In many respects he remained his mother's 'little boy.' "

31. Sigmund Freud, *Inhibitions, Symptoms and Anxiety* (London: Penguin Freud Library, vol. 10, 1979), pp. 230–38.

32. Randall Jarrell, unpublished notes for an article on T. S. Eliot, n.d., Berg Collection.

33. Address to the Mary Institute, Locust Street, St. Louis, Missouri, op. cit.

34. Quoted in Bernard Bergonzi, *T. S. Eliot* (London: Macmillan, 1972), p. 6.

35. T. S. Eliot, "The Love Song of J. Alfred Prufrock," *CP*, p. 14.

36. Helen Gardner, *The Composition of the Four Quartets* (London: Penguin, 1993).

37. TSE to William Force Stead, 30 June 1930, W. F. Stead Papers, Beinecke.

38. Herbert Read, "T.S.E.—A Memoir," in Allen Tate (ed.), *T. S. Eliot: The Man and His Work* (London: Chatto & Windus, 1967), p. 15.

39. Hugh Kenner, *The Invisible Poet: T. S. Eliot* (London: Methuen, 1960), p. 17.

40. T. S. Eliot, *Poems Written in Early Youth* (London: Faber & Faber, 1967), p. 26.

41. Quoted in Bernard Bergonzi, *T. S. Eliot* (London: Macmillan, 1972), p. 9.

42. Arthur Symons, *The Symbolist Movement in Literature* (London: William Heinemann, 1899), p. 113.

43. Robert Sencourt, *T. S. Eliot: A Memoir,* edited by Donald Adamson and L. P. Addison (London: Garnstone Press, 1971), pp. 33–34.

44. Charlotte C. Eliot to TSE, 3 April 1910, *Letters, I*, p. 13.

45. *CP*, p. 57.

46. T. S. Eliot, "Circe's Palace," *Poems Written in Early Youth*, p. 26. The poem was first published in the *Harvard Advocate*, lxxxvi, 5, 25 November 1908.

47. According to Melanie Klein, splitting is the first mechanism of defence of the infant ego. Identifying with the ideal object or Madonna figure keeps at bay the persecutors, whores

and prostitutes who represent the bad object. For a child such as Eliot, omnipotent denial would have been used against the fear of persecution, as he would have needed to maintain excessive idealisation of his mother in order to defend against paranoid feelings about her. His early paranoid fears of annihilation of the ego by his mother, identified not only as the good but also as the bad object—the withholding breast which failed to give him love—threatened to burst out. He was left with a "schizoid fear of loving," as Hanna Segal terms it, which led him to cut himself off from close relationships. See Hanna Segal, *Klein* (London: Harvester, Karnac, 1989), pp. 80, 114. English paediatrician Donald Winnicott developed Klein's view of the manic defence further to argue that the infant develops a "false self" in order to comply with the demands of the mother who is not "good enough." It is "the good, compliant child in the family who can become the bad child in adolescence—ending up as the mad child ... However Laing shows how the phase of being good is often experienced as one of existential death or nothingness by the patient." See Emmy van Deurzen-Smith, *Everyday Mysteries: Existential Dimensions of Psychotherapy* (London: Routledge, 1997), pp. 165–66. The mask behind which Eliot appeared to many observers to hide may be interpreted as the "false self."

48. *CP*, p. 26.
49. George Whiteside, "T. S. Eliot: The Psychobiographical Approach," *Southern Review* (Adelaide) 6, no. 1 (March 1973), p. 23.
50. T. S. Eliot, "Circe's Palace," op. cit.
51. John T. Mayer, *T. S. Eliot's Silent Voices* (Oxford: OUP, 1989), p. 33.
52. Gordon, op. cit., p. 8.
53. Unpublished Bolo and Colombo verses, Ezra Pound Papers, Beinecke, and published, *Noctes Binanianae,* Houghton.
54. T. S. Eliot, "First Caprice in North Cambridge," "Second Caprice in North Cambridge" in Christopher Ricks (ed.), *Inventions of the March Hare, T. S. Eliot Poems 1909–1917* (New York: Harcourt Brace Jovanovich, 1996), pp. 13, 15.
55. T. S. Eliot, Preface to Charles-Louis Philippe, *Bubu de Montparnasse* (Paris, 1890).
56. Charles-Louis Philippe, *Bubu de Montparnasse* (Paris, 1890).
57. Ibid., Chapter vii.
58. T. S. Eliot, "Rhapsody on a Windy Night," Berg Collection, New York Public Library; published in *IMH*, p. 338.
59. T. S. Eliot, "Bacchus and Ariadne," "2nd Debate Between Body and Soul," Ricks (ed.), *IMH*, p. 68.
60. See the *Mandarin* series of poems, August 1910, written the summer before TSE left for Paris, Ricks (ed.), *IMH*, pp. 19–22.
61. Interview, 15 October 1998, Cambridge, Mass., with Mary Eliot, granddaughter of Edward Cranch Eliot, son of William Greenleaf Eliot and therefore cousin to T. S. Eliot, whom she met frequently at the home of Theresa Garrett Eliot (Mrs. Henry Ware Eliot Jr.) in Cambridge, and on occasions with Mrs. Valerie Eliot in London. Miss Eliot spoke of being teased for speaking like a Bostonian on return to St. Louis as an occasion for mirth rather than embarrassment. Eliot's concern over this was due, she believed, to his "extreme sensitivity."
62. T. S. Eliot, "Prufrock's Pervigilium," cancelled lines originally part of "The Love Song of J. Alfred Prufrock," Ricks (ed.), *IMH*, p. 43.
63. Donald Gallup, "The Lost Manuscripts of T. S. Eliot," reprinted from *Times Literary Supplement,* 7 Nov. 1968, Yale University Library.

64. T. S. Eliot, "While You Were Absent in the Lavatory," Ricks (ed.), *IMH,* p. 60 and pp. 6, 7. The text in manuscript at the Beinecke Library, Yale, has "around the corner" instead of "hopped beneath the table." The former is closer to the original White Rabbit "as it turned a corner."

65. Leaves excised from "The Inventions of the March Hare Notebook," Ezra Pound Papers, Beinecke. These poems are written in a much smaller, spikier hand than Eliot's letters; they are frequently corrected and many are in pencil. There is more than one version of many of the poems, but certain characters and themes constantly recur: Colombo and his black bodyguard of "Jersey Lilies," "Orlando" the cabin boy, Bolo and his big black Kween, and the Ship's Chaplain.

66. Rémy de Gourmont, *Physique de l'amour: essai sur l'instinct sexuel* (1904), ch. xv, quoted by Ricks (ed.), *IMH,* op. cit., p. 7.

67. Leaves excised from the Notebook, Ezra Pound Papers, Beinecke, and *IMH,* Appendix A, p. 314.

68. Leaves excised from the Notebook, Ezra Pound Papers, Beinecke. A number of Colombo poems featuring the Chaplain remain unpublished.

69. Leaves excised from the Notebook, Ezra Pound Papers, Beinecke. See also Ricks (ed.), *IMH,* pp. 315–19.

70. The earliest recorded instance of the use of the word "bullshit" is in a letter from Wyndham Lewis, before July 1915 ("Eliot has sent me Bullshit"), Ricks (ed.), *IMH,* p. 308.

71. Fragments, leaves excised from the Notebook, Pound Papers, Beinecke.

72. "The Triumph of Bullshit," Pound Papers, Beinecke, Ricks (ed.), *IMH,* p. 307.

73. Leaves excised from the Notebook, Pound Papers, Beinecke, and Ricks (ed.), *IMH,* p. 315.

74. Ricks (ed.), *IMH,* p. 314.

75. Ezra Pound to TSE, n.d., Pound Papers, Beinecke.

76. T. S. Eliot, "The Whale, the Elephant, the Coot and the Spider," *Noctes Binanianae,* Houghton Library, Harvard. Privately "printed without castration" in 1939. The Whale represented Frank Morley, The Elephant, T. S. Eliot, the Coot, Geoffrey Faber (directors of Faber & Faber) and the Spider, John Hayward. In this poem Eliot refers to himself as "pious Jekyll" (he was then a Churchwarden) who "purloins letter paper/That Hyde may cut a Rogue Elephant's caper."

77. Osbert Sitwell gives an account of a visit to "Captain Eliot" in "T. S. Eliot," an unpublished memoir on the marriage of Tom and Vivienne Eliot, in the Sitwell Papers, Harry Ransom Humanities Center, Austin, Texas. See also a postcard from TSE inviting Mary Hutchinson to visit him and ask for "Captain Eliot," Hutchinson Papers, Texas.

78. Quoted by Eliot in "What Dante Means to Me" in *To Criticize the Critic* (London: Faber & Faber, 1965).

79. Martin Turnell, *Baudelaire: A Study of His Poetry* (New York: New Directions, 1972), p. 101.

80. Ibid., pp. 41–58.

81. Moody, op. cit., p. 289.

82. *CP,* p. 36.

83. *IMH,* p. 57.

84. André Gide, *Préludes* (Paris, 1895) quoted by Jean Verdenal, Letter to TSE, 5 February 1912, Houghton, *Letters I,* p. 30.

85. Jean Verdenal to TSE, 22 April 1912, Houghton, *Letters I,* p. 32.

86. "As I remember, there are no copies of my husband's letters to him." Letter from Mrs.

Valerie Eliot to Prof. James E. Miller, of the University of Chicago, refusing him permission to see the letters of Jean Verdenal, 23 July 1974, Houghton.

87. Jean Verdenal to TSE, "Dimanche" (?mid-July 1911), Houghton, and *Letters I*, p. 20.

88. Houghton, and *Letters I*, p. 21n.

89. Alain-Fournier to TSE, 25 July 1911, Houghton, and *Letters I*, p. 25.

90. Jean Verdenal to TSE, 5 February 1912, Houghton, and *Letters I*, p. 28.

91. *CP*, p. 64.

92. Jean Verdenal was reading *Le Mystère de la Charité de Jeanne d'Arc* by Charles Péguy (Paris 1909), particularly liking the account of the Passion of Christ. Jean Verdenal to TSE, mid-July 1911, Houghton, and *Letters I*, p. 23.

93. Eliot's notes on the Bergson lectures, which he attended in January and February 1911, are in the Houghton Library.

94. Jean Verdenal to TSE, 5 February 1912, Houghton.

95. Jean Verdenal to TSE, 22 April 1912, Houghton.

96. Memorandum by Charlotte Champe Eliot in respect of a request by her son, Henry Ware Eliot Jr., who was preparing in 1921 a family record of the descendants of William Greenleaf and Abigail A. Eliot, Houghton.

97. Jean Verdenal to TSE, 26 August 1912, Houghton.

98. Jean Verdenal to TSE, 26 December 1912, Houghton.

99. *Criterion,* April 1934, quoted by John T. Mayer, *T. S. Eliot's Silent Voices* (Oxford: OUP, 1989), p. 200.

100. This Temple Classics translation (reprinted 1909) is the one which Eliot knew; his copy is in the Houghton Library. It is probable that TSE wrote out this epigraph in the Notebook when he sold it to John Quinn in 1922. The epigraph first appeared in *Ara Vos Prec* (1920) but with no dedication; the dedication and epigraph, with slightly different wording from that in the Notebook, first appeared together in *Poems 1909–1925* (1925). See *IMH*, pp. 3, 4.

101. Memorandum by Charlotte Champe Eliot prepared for her son, Henry Ware Eliot Jr., Houghton.

102. Conrad Aiken, *Ushant* (London: W. H. Allen, 1963), p. 168 and *passim*.

103. Conrad Aiken, "King Bolo and Others" in Richard March and Tambimuttu, *T. S. Eliot: A Symposium* (London: P.L. Editions, 1948), p. 21.

104. Anne Olivier Bell (ed.), *The Diary of Virginia Woolf,* vol. 2, 1920–1924 (New York: Harcourt Brace Jovanovich, 1981), p. 68.

105. Valerie Eliot, Introduction to *Letters I*, p. xvii.

106. "Do I know what I feel?" *IMH*, p. 80. This undated and untitled poem from the Notebook was probably written after Eliot's return to Harvard but before he went to England in 1914.

107. TSE to Conrad Aiken, 25 July 1914, Huntingdon Library, *Letters I*, p. 44.

108. "After the turning," "I am the Resurrection," "So through the evening," the two "Saint" poems, and "the Burnt Dancer," all written in 1914, see Gordon, *Eliot's Early Years* (Oxford: OUP, 1977), p. 58. For a chronology of the poems 1905–1920 see *IMH*, pp. xxxvii–xlii.

109. Diary of Virginia Woolf, September 1920, Berg Collection.

110. T. S. Eliot broadcast talk to Germany, "The Unity of European Culture," 1948, quoted in Gardner, op. cit., p. 55; T. S. Eliot dissertation, *Knowledge and Experience in the Philosophy of F. H. Bradley*, p. 55, quoted by Gordon, *Eliot's Early Years,* op. cit., p. 53.

111. TSE to Conrad Aiken, 19 July 1914, Huntingdon Library, *Letters I*, p. 41.

112. TSE to Conrad Aiken, 25 July 1914, Huntingdon Library, *Letters I*, p. 44.

113. Henri Dorra, *Symbolist Art Theories: A Critical Anthology I* (California, Berkeley: University of California Press, 1994), p. 7.

114. Ibid., p. 27.

115. Ibid., p. 46. See also Joris-Karl Huysmans, *Certains* (Paris, 1889), on Gustave Moreau.

116. Mayer, op. cit., p. 132.

117. Donald Gallup, "The Lost Manuscripts of T. S. Eliot," *Times Literary Supplement,* 7 November 1968.

118. Valerie Eliot (ed.), second draft, "The Death of St. Narcissus," *The Waste Land: A Facsimile and Transcript of the Original Drafts including the Anotations of Ezra Pound* (New York: Harcourt Brace & Co., 1971), p. 97.

119. First draft, "The Death of St. Narcissus," ibid., p. 93.

120. Dante Alighieri, *The Divine Comedy, Inferno,* translated by Allen Mandelbaum (New York: Bantam, 1982), p. 133.

121. *Bhagavad-Gita,* chapter 11.

4. A Clandestine Marriage

1. VE Diary, 13 December 1934, Bodleian.

2. Osbert Sitwell, *Laughter in the Next Room, vol. 4, Left Hand, Right Hand!* (London: Macmillan, 1949), p. 43.

3. TSE to Charlotte Champe Eliot, 23 August 1914, *Letters I,* p. 52.

4. Conrad Aiken, *Ushant* (London: W. H. Allen, 1963), pp. 200–201.

5. TSE to Henry Eliot, 8 September 1914, *Letters I,* p. 56.

6. TSE to Eleanor Hinkley, 8 September 1914, *Letters I,* p. 57. Eleanor Hinkley was the second daughter of Susan Heywood Stearns, his mother's sister, who married Holmes Hinkley.

7. "Morning at the Window" (1914), *CP,* p. 29.

8. T. S. Eliot's speech replying to the toast of "The Guests," Christ Church, Oxford, 23 June 1948.

9. T. S. Eliot to Conrad Aiken, 25 February 1915, *Letters I,* p. 88. Eliot's thesis was published under the title *Knowledge and Experience in the Philosophy of F. H. Bradley* (1963).

10. Bertrand Russell, *Autobiography, Vol. 1, 1872–1914* (London: George Allen & Unwin, 1967), p. 212.

11. Robert Gathorne-Hardy (ed.), *Ottoline: The Early Memoirs of Lady Ottoline Morrell* (London: Faber & Faber, 1964), p. 257.

12. Frances Partridge interview with author, 27 November 2000. Frances Marshall became part of the Bloomsbury group in 1921 after leaving Cambridge, and later married Ralph Partridge.

13. "Mr. Apollinax," published in *Poetry* (Sept. 1916), and in *Prufrock and Other Observations* (1917). Christopher Ricks (ed.), discusses changes in the text in *Inventions of the March Hare, Poems 1909–1917* (New York, Harcourt Brace Jovanovich, 1996), p. 345; *CP,* p. 33.

14. TSE to Eleanor Hinkley, 10 October 1914, *Letters I,* p. 64.

15. Aiken, op. cit., p. 205. A joke based on Browning's monologue of the same title, which had

occurred to Pound years earlier, see Humphrey Carpenter, *A Serious Character: The Life of Ezra Pound* (London: Faber & Faber, 1988), p. 257.

16. Carpenter, op. cit., p. 23.

17. Peter Ackroyd, *Ezra Pound and His World* (London: Thames & Hudson, 1981), p. 25.

18. Despite a verse repeated in literary circles: "Ezra Pound/And Augustus John/Bless the bed/That I lie on," Richard Aldington believed Pound to be sexually naïve, although he posed as a roué. Carpenter, op. cit., pp. 136, 241, also cites Pound's poem, "Mr. Styrax": "Mr. Hetacomb Styrax . . . has married at the age of 28,/He being at that age a virgin" from *Moeurs Contemporaines.*

19. Ackroyd, op. cit., p. 14.

20. Quoted in Carpenter, op. cit., p. 100.

21. Richard Aldington, *Life for Life's Sake* (London: Viking, 1941), p. 105.

22. Ford Madox Ford, *Return to Yesterday* (London: Victor Gollancz, 1931).

23. Carpenter, op. cit., p. 113.

24. Richard Aldington to Amy Lowell, 20 November 1917, in Norman T. Gates (ed.), *Richard Aldington: An Autobiography in Letters* (Philadelphia: University of Pennsylvania Press, 1992), p. 28. Hugh Kenner, *The Pound Era* (London: Faber & Faber, 1976), p. 277, reads Pound's comment as ironic. Charles Doyle, *Richard Aldington: A Biography* (London: Macmillan, 1989), points out that Aldington's *vers libre* was inspired by the chorus of Euripides' *Hippolytus.*

25. Hilda Doolittle, *End to Torment* (New York: New Directions Publishing, 1979), p. 18.

26. Aldington, op. cit., p. 135.

27. Aldington, op. cit., p. 127.

28. Carpenter, op. cit., p. 209.

29. Ezra Pound to Amy Lowell, 19 October 1914, in D. D. Paige (ed.), *The Letters of Ezra Pound 1907–1941* (London: Faber & Faber, 1951), pp. 84–85.

30. P. Wyndham Lewis, *Blasting and Bombardiering* (London: Calder & Boyars, 1967), p. 280.

31. Ibid., pp. 254, 255.

32. EP to Harriet Monroe, 30 September 1914, *Letters of Ezra Pound,* op. cit., p. 80.

33. EP to Harriet Monroe, 9 November 1914, *Letters of Ezra Pound,* op. cit., p. 85. He also sent "Portrait of a Lady" to *Smart Set,* another American periodical.

34. EP to Harriet Monroe, 31 January 1915, *Letters of Ezra Pound,* op. cit., p. 92.

35. EP to Harriet Monroe, 10 April 1915, ibid., p. 101.

36. EP to Harriet Monroe, (August) 1915, ibid., p. 107.

37. TSE to Conrad Aiken, 30 September 1914, ibid., p. 59.

38. Doyle, op. cit., p. 18.

39. Wyndham Lewis, *Blasting,* op. cit., pp. 283–85.

40. Richard Aldington married Hilda Doolittle (known as "H.D.") in October 1913, with Pound and the Doolittle parents as witnesses. The same month Dora Marsden offered Aldington the job of sub-editor of *The New Freewoman,* following the resignation of Rebecca West. Doyle (in op. cit., p. 24) rejects the idea that the Aldington/Doolittle marriage was simply one of convenience after Pound rejected Hilda Doolittle. Doolittle's novel, *Bid Me Live,* suggests she reciprocated Aldington's love while retaining a strong emotional bond with Pound.

41. TSE to Conrad Aiken, 31 December 1914, *Letters I,* p. 73.

42. TSE to Conrad Aiken, 21 November 1914, *Letters I,* p. 69.

43. TSE to Conrad Aiken, 30 September 1914, *Letters I*, p. 59.

44. Wyndham Lewis to EP,? January 1915, *The Letters of Wyndham Lewis*, op. cit., p. 67. None of the Bolo/Colombo verses were published in *Blast*.

45. Wyndham Lewis, *Blasting*, op. cit., p. 284.

46. TSE to E. Hinkley, 21 March 1915, *Letters I*, pp. 91, 92.

47. TSE to E. Hinkley, 24 April 1915, *Letters I*, p. 97.

48. Vivien(ne) Haigh-Wood to Scofield Thayer, 22 February 1915, Scofield Thayer/*Dial* Papers, Beinecke.

49. V. Haigh-Wood to Scofield Thayer, "Thursday," ?March 1915, from Thyme Cottage, Upper Bourne End, Bucks. This letter follows a previous letter dated 3 March 1915, Beinecke.

50. V. Haigh-Wood to Scofield Thayer, 22 Feb. 1915, Beinecke.

51. Signed statement by Theresa Eliot, Vivien's sister-in-law, 28 March 1970.

52. V. Haigh-Wood to Scofield Thayer, 3 March 1915, Beinecke.

53. The Army Lists show that a Charles Buckle was commissioned 2nd Lieutenant on 19 Sept. 1914 in the Royal Garrison Artillery, Territorial Force, based in Kent. A "galloper" would have ridden one of the horses pulling the guns. Maurice Haigh-Wood thought that Buckle was killed during the war, but the lieutenant listed above did survive. According to the Commonwealth War Graves Commission records, none of the three officers killed in the First World War named C. Buckle had a London connection, and none of the soldiers killed seemed a likely candidate.

54. T. S. Eliot, *Poems Written in Early Youth* (London: Faber & Faber, 1950), p. 33. *Harvard Advocate*, lxxxix, 8, 24 June 1910.

55. V. Haigh-Wood to Scofield Thayer, 3 March 1915, Beinecke.

56. V. Haigh-Wood to Scofield Thayer, 2 August 1915, Beinecke.

57. M. Haigh-Wood, interview with Michael Hastings, 21 January 1980. Pound also surmised that Vivien was going out with Scofield: see letter to John Quinn, 24 March 1920, in Lyndall Gordon, *Eliot's Early Years* (Oxford: OUP, 1972), p. 72n.

58. Bertrand Russell, *Autobiography, vol. 2* (London: George Allen & Unwin, 1968), p. 54.

59. Journal of Lady Ottoline Morrell, August 1921, Goodman Papers.

60. Michael King (ed.), *Ezra Pound, Collected Poems* (London: Faber & Faber, 1977), p. 186.

61. Charles Norman, *Ezra Pound, I* (London: MacDonald, 1969), p. 81.

62. V. Haigh-Wood to Scofield Thayer, 3 March 1915, Beinecke.

63. Aldous Huxley to Ottoline Morrell, 21 June 1917, Robert Gathorne-Hardy (ed.), *Ottoline at Garsington: Memoirs of Lady Ottoline Morrell 1915–1918* (London: Faber & Faber, 1974).

64. VE Diary, 26 December 1935, Bodleian.

65. Gaudier-Brzeska's last testament from the trenches. He was killed on 5 June 1915.

66. Valerie Eliot (ed.), Introduction, *The Waste Land: A Facsimile and Transcript of the Original Drafts including the annotations of Ezra Pound* (New York: Harcourt Brace Jovanovich, 1971), p. ix.

67. Valerie Eliot (ed.), Introduction, *Letters I*, p. xviii.

68. Ibid., p. 20, note 1.

69. Robert Sencourt, *T. S. Eliot: A Memoir*, edited by Donald Adamson and L. P. Addison (Garnstone Press, 1971), pp. 47, 48.

70. Karl Culpin was born on 10 September 1893. He died of wounds received in action near Fresnais, 15 May 1917.

71. Sencourt, op. cit., p. 53.

72. T. S. Matthews, *Great Tom: Notes Towards the Definitions of T. S. Eliot* (London: Weidenfeld & Nicolson, 1974), pp. 43–44.

73. TSE to Scofield Thayer, 7 May 1916, *Letters I,* p. 137.

74. Stephen Spender, *World Within World: The Autobiography of Stephen Spender* (New York: St. Martin's Press, 1951), p. 185.

5. The Poet's Bride

1. *Blast,* no. 2, July 1915.

2. Robert Sencourt, *T. S. Eliot: A Memoir,* edited by Donald Adamson and L. P. Addison (London: Garnstone Press, 1971), p. 50.

3. Michael Hastings, "The Haigh-Woods: The Story of a Family," introduction to the programme of *Tom and Viv,* first performance 3 February 1984 at the Royal Court Theatre, London. The introduction is based on Hastings's series of interviews with Maurice over five months in 1980, which came to an end with Maurice's death that year.

4. Codicil to the will of Charles Haigh-Wood, 18 May 1927.

5. Maurice Haigh-Wood, interview with Michael Hastings, 21 January 1980.

6. Rose Haigh-Wood to VE, "Friday," n.d. ?June 1916. Quoted in "The Haigh-Woods: The Story of a Family," programme of *Tom and Viv* by Michael Hastings.

7. Army List 1915–21, information supplied by the National Army Museum, 18 January 1999.

8. TSE to Charlotte C. Eliot, 18 May 1915, *Letters I,* p. 120.

9. Interview with Michael Hastings, 19 March 1980.

10. Pound was proposing that a writer could live in London on $1,000 a year (£200), of which Eliot's father was being asked to provide half. This seemed a reasonable request, since Henry Ware was apparently wealthy. Probate of his will suggests that he owned about 4,000 preferred shares, of 52,000 outstanding, in the Hydraulic Press-Brick Co. of St. Louis. The dividend, stopped in 1913, was resumed in 1918. Paul Delany, "T. S. Eliot's Personal Finances, 1915–1929," chapter in *Literature, Money and the Market from Trollope to Amis* (Basingstoke: Palgrave, 2001). Eliot's first job as a schoolmaster at High Wycombe paid less than £3 a week. At the other extreme, Lytton Strachey was able to earn between £2,000 and £3,000 per annum after the publication of *Eminent Victorians* in 1918, see Michael Holroyd, *Lytton Strachey* (London: Vintage, 1995), p. 430.

11. Ezra Pound to Henry Ware Eliot, postmark 28 June 1915, *Letters I,* p. 99.

12. Bertrand Russell to Charlotte C. Eliot, 3 October 1915, *Letters I,* p. 118.

13. Charlotte C. Eliot to Bertrand Russell, 18 January 1916, *Letters I,* p. 130.

14. *St. Louis Globe Democrat,* 16 July 1915, Houghton.

15. Statement signed by Theresa Garrett Eliot, 28 March 1970, Houghton.

16. TSE to Henry Eliot, 2 July 1915, *Letters I,* p. 104.

17. TSE to Mrs. Jack Gardner (Isabella), ?10 July 1915, *Letters I,* p. 107.

18. Bertrand Russell, *Autobiography, vol. 2, 1914–1944* (London: George Allen & Unwin, 1968), p. 54.

19. VE to Scofield Thayer, 2 August 1915, Beinecke.

20. Bertrand Russell to Ottoline Morrell, July 1915, *Autobiography, vol. 2,* op. cit., p. 54.

21. VE to Scofield Thayer, 2 August 1915, Beinecke.

22. VE Diary, 1936, Bodleian.

23. VE to Scofield Thayer, 3 March 1915, Beinecke.

24. TSE to Henry Ware Eliot, 23 July 1915, *Letters I,* p. 110. This unposted letter was found among Vivien's papers.

25. VE to Scofield Thayer, 2 August 1915, Beinecke.

26. TSE to Conrad Aiken, 5 August 1915, *Letters I,* p. 111.

27. P. Wyndham Lewis, *Blasting and Bombardiering,* 2nd ed. (London: Calder & Boyars, 1967).

28. C. C. Eliot to Bertrand Russell, 18 January 1916, *Letters I,* p. 131.

29. Quoted in Ray Monk, *Bertrand Russell: The Spirit of Solitude* (London: Vintage, 1997), p. 359.

30. Russell, *Autobiography, vol. 1, 1872–1914* (London: George Allen & Unwin, 1967), p. 204.

31. Ibid., p. 151.

32. Robert Gathorne-Hardy (ed.), *Ottoline at Garsington: Memoirs of Lady Ottoline Morrell 1915–1918* (London: Faber & Faber, 1974), p. 276.

33. Ibid., p. 272.

34. Russell, *Autobiography, vol. 1,* op. cit., p. 213.

35. Bertrand Russell to Ottoline Morrell, 1 June 1914, McMaster.

36. Bertrand Russell to Ottoline Morrell, 23 June 1914, McMaster.

37. Bertrand Russell to Ottoline Morrell, 2 August 1914, McMaster.

38. Quoted in Miranda Seymour, *Ottoline Morrell: Life on the Grand Scale* (London: Hodder and Stoughton, 1992), p. 201.

39. Bertrand Russell to Ottoline Morrell, 19 January 1915, McMaster.

40. Gathorne-Hardy (ed.), *Ottoline at Garsington,* op. cit., p. 43.

41. Ibid., p. 56.

42. Seymour, op. cit., p. 290.

43. Quoted in Monk, op. cit., p. 408.

44. Bertrand Russell to Ottoline Morrell, 8 July 1915, McMaster.

45. Gathorne-Hardy, op. cit., p. 57.

46. Russell, *Autobiography, vol. 2,* op. cit., pp. 22–23.

47. Monk, op. cit., p. 430.

48. Russell, *Autobiography, vol. 2,* op. cit., p. 23.

49. Gathorne-Hardy, op. cit., p. 286.

50. Frances Partridge, interview with author, 27 November 2000.

51. VE to Scofield Thayer, 24 October 1915, Beinecke.

52. Monk, op. cit., p. 440.

53. Irene Cooper-Willis wrote a novel, *The Green-Eyed Monster,* published under the pen-name "Althea Brook," in which Russell appears as "Tom Wolfe." See Monk, op. cit., p. 394.

54. T. S. Eliot, *Collected Poems,* p. 33. "Mr. Apollinax" was published in *Poetry* in September 1916. During Russell's visit to Harvard he was invited to stay a weekend with Benjamin Apthorp Fuller, a historian of philosophy and friend of George Santayana. Fuller and his mother were the inspiration for "Professor Channing-Cheetah" and the "dowager Mrs. Phlaccus."

55. TSE to Prof. J. Woods, 16 August 1915, *Letters I,* p. 113.

56. TSE to Scofield Thayer, 9 August 1915, Beinecke, and *Letters I,* p. 112.

57. VE to Scofield Thayer, "Thursday"? March 1915, Beinecke.

58. TSE to Scofield Thayer, 4 September 1915, Beinecke, and *Letters I,* p. 113.

59. Typescript of *The Family Reunion,* edited by Emily Hale, Houghton.

60. Charlotte Champe Eliot, typescript of "Savonarola" (London: Cobden-Sanderson, 1926), Foreword by T. S. Eliot, Houghton.

61. C. C. Eliot to Bertrand Russell, 18 January 1916, *Letters I,* p. 131.

6. Triple Ménage: Bertie, Vivien and Tom

1. Bertrand Russell, *Autobiography, vol. 2, 1914–1944* (London: George Allen & Unwin, 1968), p. 25.

2. Only three letters remain from Vivien to Russell at the Bertrand Russell Archive, McMaster.

3. Nicholas Griffin, editor of Russell's *Selected Letters, vols. 1 and 2,* is of the opinion that Russell and Eliot made a pact not to reveal their secrets, and Russell destroyed the majority of Vivien's letters to him. None of his to her have been preserved either. Conversation with Nick Griffin, June 1999.

4. Michael Davie (ed.), *The Diaries of Evelyn Waugh* (London: Weidenfeld and Nicolson, 1976), p. 73.

5. The suggestion that Vivien was the inspiration for Mrs. Ellerker was originally made in "Bertrand Russell and T. S. Eliot: Their Dialogue," by Gladys Garner Leithauser and Nadine Cowan Dyer, *Russell 2 (1),* summer 1982, pp. 7–28. Leithauser and Dyer also consider the relationship between Appleplex (Russell) and Eeldrop (Eliot) described in T. S. Eliot's "Eeldrop and Appleplex," published in *The Little Review,* May and September 1917, see Ray Monk, *Bertrand Russell: The Spirit of Solitude* (London: Vintage, 1997), p. 650.

6. Monk, op. cit., p. 12.

7. Bertrand Russell, *Satan in the Suburbs and Other Stories* (London: Bodley Head, 1953), p. 29.

8. Ibid., pp. 44–45.

9. Ibid., p. 48.

10. TSE to Henry Ware Eliot, 10 September 1915, *Letters I,* p. 115.

11. TSE to Bertrand Russell, 11 September 1915, *Letters I,* p. 115.

12. Caroline Moorehead, *Bertrand Russell* (London: Sinclair-Stevenson, 1993), p. 219.

13. Ronald W. Clark, *The Life of Bertrand Russell* (London: Jonathan Cape and Weidenfeld and Nicolson, 1975), p. 311.

14. Peter Ackroyd, *T. S. Eliot* (London: Hamish Hamilton, 1984), p. 84.

15. Bertrand Russell to Constance Malleson, 21 October 1916, McMaster.

16. See Chapter 9, "Priapus in the Shrubbery," for an account of the circumstances leading up to this night.

17. Michael Hastings to the author, 22 April 1999.

18. Constance Malleson to Bertrand Russell, 30 October 1917, quoted in Monk, op. cit., pp. 510–11, including footnote p. 511, quoting Colette's letter to Kenneth Blackwell, dated 12 February 1972. Peter Ackroyd in *T. S. Eliot* writes (p. 84) that Russell "made love to Vivien," but the experience was "hellish and loathsome." "He did not explain why it was quite so 'loathsome,' although no doubt Vivien's own physical problems had something to do with it. It was the pointless and messy end of what had been an intense but 'platonic' relationship." Ackroyd cites not Colette's letter but a paraphrase of it given in "Bertrand Russell and the Eliots" by Robert H. Bell, *The American Scholar,* summer 1983, pp. 309–25, in which the phrase "hellish and loathsome" is used, and this paraphrased description is

also used by Caroline Moorehead in *Bertrand Russell,* op. cit. Russell's letter to Colette in fact explains that love-making with Vivien was only "loathsome" because it was not with Colette. Vivien's letters to Scofield in the autumn of 1915 are those of a contented mistress, and there is no evidence that her relationship with Russell was "platonic" as Ackroyd says, apart from Russell's remarks to Ottoline, which cannot be taken at face value.

19. BR to Lucy Donnelly, 26 March 1914 quoted *Letters I,* p. 115n.

20. Quoted in Clark, op. cit., p. 311. Draft letter of Russell's to Ottoline, dated "1916," but apparently September 1915, private source. There is a copy of this letter at McMaster, dated 9 September.

21. Clark, ibid., p. 312. BR to Ottoline Morrell, 10 September 1915, McMaster.

22. Maurice Haigh-Wood, interview with Michael Hastings, 21 January 1980.

23. T. S. Eliot, "Ode," in Christopher Ricks (ed.), *Inventions of the March Hare, T. S. Eliot: Poems 1909–1917* (New York: Harcourt Brace, 1996), p. 383.

24. "Ara vos prec, per aquella valor,
    que vos guida al som de l'escalina,
    sovegna vos a temps de ma dolor"
    Poi s'ascose nel foco che gli affina. (XXVI, 145–48).
    ("I pray you, by that virtue
    that guides you to the summit of the stair,
    be mindful in your time of my pain."
    Then he dived back into the fire that refines them.)
    Quoted in James E. Miller Jr., *T. S. Eliot's Personal Waste Land: Exorcism of the Demons* (Philadelphia: University of Pennsylvania Press, 1977), p. 47. For a discussion of the significance of "Ode" see Chapter 5, "A Suppressed Ode," pp. 47–58.

25. "And this, O this shall henceforth be the token of comrades, this calamus-root shall,/ Interchange it youths with each other! Let none render it back." Walt Whitman, from *Leaves of Grass.*

26. Dr. Harry Trosman, "T. S. Eliot and *The Waste Land:* Psychopathological Antecedents and Transformations," *Psychoanalytic Studies of Biography,* George Moraitis and George H. Pollock (eds.), (International Universities Press Inc., 1987), p. 202.

27. Sigmund Freud, "Some Neurotic Mechanisms in Jealousy, Paranoia and Homosexuality" (1922), *On Psychopathology: Inhibitions, Symptoms and Anxiety* (London: The Penguin Freud Library, vol. 10, 1979), pp. 205–206.

28. T. S. Eliot, *Poems Written in Early Youth* (London: Faber & Faber, 1967), p. 26.

29. The reference to Perseus, son of Zeus and Danaë, who killed the Gorgon Medusa and used her head to turn to stone those who gazed upon it, is more difficult to decode. The story is told in Ovid's *Metamorphoses,* a favourite source of lines and allusion for Eliot. For a discussion, see Miller, op. cit., pp. 55–56. He argues that there may be an allusion to the trickery by which Perseus won Andromeda, or to the death of Athis and Lycabus which followed:

    Perseus turned, and swung
    The scimitar that once had slain the Gorgon
    And now slew Lycabus, who, in the darkness
    That swam before his eyes, looked once around
    For Athis, and once more lay down beside him
    And took this comfort to the world of shadows
    That in their death the two were not divided.

30. Lyndall Gordon, *Eliot's Early Years* (Oxford: OUP, 1977), p. 75.
31. Miller, op. cit., pp. 55–58.
32. Maurice Haigh-Wood, interview with Michael Hastings, 4 March 1980.
33. BR to Ottoline Morrell, n.d., McMaster.
34. Robert Gathorne-Hardy (ed.), *Ottoline at Garsington: Memoirs of Lady Ottoline Morrell 1915–1918* (London: Faber & Faber, 1974) p. 279.
35. BR to Ottoline Morrell, 23 June 1914, McMaster.
36. Gilbert Murray was Professor of Greek at Oxford, a classical scholar and historian. Bertrand Russell's reply, "The Policy of the Entente, 1904–1914: A Reply to Professor Gilbert Murray," was published in December 1915. See Monk, op. cit., pp. 438–39.
37. TSE to Henry Ware Eliot Sr., 27 September 1915, *Letters I,* p. 117.
38. Paul Delany, "T. S. Eliot's Personal Finances, 1915–1929," chapter in *Literature, Money and the Market from Trollope to Amis* (Basingstoke: Palgrave, 2001).
39. BR to Ottoline Morrell, n.d., Texas, quoted in Clark, op. cit., p. 312.
40. BR to Ottoline Morrell, 24 November 1915, McMaster.
41. Gathorne-Hardy, op. cit., p. 120.
42. VE to Scofield Thayer, Sunday, 24 October 1915, Beinecke.
43. Ronald Clark, *Bertrand Russell and His World* (London: Thames and Hudson, 1981), p. 80.
44. Monk, op. cit., pp. 140–41.
45. Maurice Haigh-Wood, interview with Michael Hastings, 21 January 1980.
46. Delany, op. cit.
47. *Letters I,* p. 132.
48. Trosman, op. cit., p. 712.
49. TSE to BR, 11 October 1915, McMaster, *Letters I,* p. 119.
50. BR to Charlotte C. Eliot, 3 October 1915, McMaster, *Letters I,* p. 118.
51. Monk, op. cit., p. 442.
52. VE to Scofield Thayer, 8 May 1916, Beinecke.
53. Constance Malleson to Kenneth Blackwell, 12 February 1972, McMaster.
54. Russell, *Autobiography,* pp. 55–56.
55. BR to Charlotte C. Eliot, 3 December 1915, McMaster, *Letters I,* p. 123.
56. BR to Ottoline Morrell, 8 December 1915, McMaster.

7. A Child in Pain

1. Bertrand Russell to Ottoline Morrell, 3 December 1915, McMaster.
2. BR to OM, 1 January 1916, McMaster.
3. Bertrand Russell, *Autobiography, vol. 2, 1914–1944* (London: George Allen & Unwin, 1968), p. 24.
4. Richard Shone, *Bloomsbury Portraits* (London: Phaidon, 1976), p. 153.
5. BR to OM, 3 January 1916, McMaster.
6. OM to BR, ?21 January 1916, McMaster.
7. BR to OM, 7 January 1916, McMaster.
8. Ibid.
9. OM to BR, "Monday," January 1916, McMaster.
10. BR to OM, 15 December 1915, McMaster.
11. OM to BR, 13 January 1916, McMaster.

12. Russell, op. cit., p. 58.
13. BR to OM, 12 January 1916, McMaster.
14. TSE to BR, 11 January 1916, McMaster, *Letters I,* p. 127.
15. BR to OM, "Wednesday mg.," n.d., 1916, McMaster.
16. Caroline Behr, *T. S. Eliot: A Chronology of his Life and Works* (London: Macmillan, 1983), p. 10. The *Catholic Anthology* was published in November 1915.
17. TSE to Conrad Aiken, 10 January 1916, *Letters I,* p. 126.
18. TSE to Henry Ware Eliot Sr., 14 January 1916, *Letters I,* p. 127.
19. TSE to BR, 14 January 1916, McMaster, *Letters I,* p. 127.
20. TSE to BR, 17 January 1916, McMaster, *Letters I,* p. 130.
21. Russell, op. cit., p. 18.
22. Shone, op. cit., pp. 143–44.
23. Maynard was granted a certificate of exemption by the Permanent Secretary to the Treasury on the grounds that he was doing work in the national interest. According to Clive Bell he objected to "being made to fight." Maynard sent £50 to the National Council for Civil Liberties. See Shone, op. cit., p. 148.
24. The lectures were published as *Principles of Social Reconstruction,* and in America as *Why Men Fight.*
25. Quoted in Michael Holroyd, *Lytton Strachey* (London: Vintage, 1995), p. 344.
26. BR to OM, 30 January 1916, McMaster.
27. OM to BR, 16 February 1916, McMaster.
28. OM to BR, 1 January 1916, McMaster.
29. OM to BR, n.d. March 1916, McMaster.
30. OM to BR, 3 March 1916, McMaster.
31. Robert Gathorne-Hardy (ed.), *Ottoline at Garsington: Memoirs of Lady Ottoline Morrell 1915–1918* (London: Faber & Faber, 1974), p. 96.
32. D. H. Lawrence, *Women in Love* (first published 1921; London: Heinemann, 1960), with an introduction by Richard Aldington, p. 83. "Hermione strange like a long Cassandra . . . Like a priestess she looked unconscious, sunk in a heavy half-trance." In the novel, Birkin represents Lawrence, Ursula, Frieda Lawrence, Gudrun, Katherine Mansfield and Gerald, Middleton Murry.
33. Charlotte C. Eliot to BR, 23 May 1916, *Letters I,* p. 138.
34. BR to Henry Ware Eliot, 7 April 1916, *Letters I,* p. 136.
35. BR to OM, 29 March 1916, McMaster.
36. Published in 1964 as *Knowledge and Experience in the Philosophy of F.H. Bradley* (Oxford: OUP, 1969).
37. TSE to J. H. Woods, 3 May 1916, *Letters I,* p. 136.
38. OM to BR, 28 March 1916, McMaster.
39. OM to BR, 29 March 1916, McMaster.
40. OM to BR, 11 April 1916, McMaster.
41. OM to BR, 19 May 1916, McMaster.
42. Russell, op. cit., p. 19.
43. Holroyd, op. cit., p. 343.
44. Gathorne-Hardy (ed.), *Ottoline at Garsington,* op. cit., pp. 101–2.
45. Helen Gardner, *The Composition of the Four Quartets* (London: Faber & Faber, 1978), p. 48n.
46. Gathorne-Hardy (ed.), op. cit., pp. 101–2.

47. VE to Henry Eliot, 1 June 1916, *Letters I*, p. 139.

48. VE to Scofield Thayer, 8 May 1916, Beinecke.

49. TSE to Scofield Thayer, 7 May 1916, *Letters I*, p. 138.

50. This description of Thayer by Alyse Gregory, managing editor of *The Dial*, is quoted in Nicholas Joost, *Scofield Thayer and* The Dial: *An Illustrated History* (Carbondale and Edwardsville: Southern Illinois University Press, 1964), p. 78.

51. The Thayers divorced in 1921. Notes to *The Dial* Collection, Beinecke.

52. The correct version is: "Quis desiderio sit pudor aut modus/Tam cari capitis?" *The Oxford Book of Latin Verse,* chosen by H. W. Garrod (Oxford: OUP, 1912), p. 141. Translation by C. S. Calverley, p. 485.

53. Translation by C. S. Calverley, ibid., p. 485.

54. Statement by Theresa Eliot, wife of Henry Ware Eliot Jr., 28 March 1970, Houghton.

55. VE to Henry Ware Eliot Jr., 1 June 1916, *Letters I*, p. 139.

56. VE to Henry Ware Eliot Jr., 11 October 1916, *Letters I*, p. 154.

57. VE to Charlotte C. Eliot, 8 March 1917, Houghton, *Letters I*, p. 161.

58. BR to OM, 26 January 1916, McMaster.

59. VE to Henry Ware Eliot Jr., 11 October 1916, *Letters I*, p. 155.

60. Statement of Theresa G. Eliot, 28 March 1970, Houghton.

61. TSE to Conrad Aiken, 21 August 1916, *Letters I*, p. 143.

62. TSE to Bertrand Russell, Monday (6 March? 1916), McMaster.

63. VE to Henry Ware Eliot Jr., 11 October 1916, *Letters I*, p. 154.

64. BR to OM, 21 May 1916, McMaster.

65. Quoted by Robert H. Bell, "Bertrand Russell and the Eliots," *The American Scholar,* Summer 1983, pp. 309–75.

66. BR to J. H. Woods, 4 March 1916, *Letters I*, p. 132.

67. TSE, "Eeldrop and Appleplex," *The Little Review,* Part I in May 1917; Part II is September 1917.

68. Gathorne-Hardy (ed.), *Ottoline at Garsington,* op. cit., pp. 120–21.

69. BR to OM, 6 June 1916, McMaster.

70. BR to OM, in Ray Monk, *Bertrand Russell: The Spirit of Solitude* (London: Vintage, 1997), p. 469.

71. TSE to Wyndham Lewis (November? 1915), *Letters I*, p. 122.

72. Brigit Patmore, *My Friends When Young* (London: Heinemann, 1968), pp. 84–86.

73. Ibid.

74. TSE to Conrad Aiken, 21 August 1916, *Letters I*, p. 143.

75. BR to OM, 20 August 1916, McMaster.

76. Anne Olivier Bell (ed.), *The Diary of Virginia Woolf,* Vol. 1 (London: Penguin, 1977), 29 July 1918, p. 175.

77. BR to OM, undated, ? August 1916, McMaster.

78. BR to OM, 20 August 1916, McMaster.

79. BR to OM, 16 August 1916, McMaster.

80. BR to OM, 20 June 1916, McMaster.

81. BR to OM, 1 September 1916, McMaster.

82. BR to OM, 28 August 1916, McMaster.

83. Constance Malleson ("Colette O'Niel"), *After Ten Years* (London: Jonathan Cape, 1929), p. 104.

84. Ibid., p. 107.

85. Russell, *Autobiography,* Vol. 2, op. cit., p. 26.

8. Wartime Waifs

1. Earl Russell married Elizabeth, Countess of Arnim, in February 1916.

2. TSE to Eleanor Hinkley, 5 September 1916, *Letters I*, p. 146.

3. VE to Henry Ware Eliot Jr., 1 June 1916, *Letters I*, p. 140.

4. Michael Ball, National Army Museum to the author, 18 January 1999.

5. Virginia Woolf had noticed the farmhouse just below Firle Beacon on the South Downs on one of her walks near Firle village, and thought it might be rented by her sister. It was arranged that Duncan and Bunny would work for a nearby farmer, and Charleston Farmhouse was rented from Lord Gage. Richard Shone, *Bloomsbury Portraits* (London: Phaidon, 1976), p. 155.

6. VE to Charlotte Champe Eliot, 28 June 1917, *Letters I*, p. 186.

7. "Hysteria," *Collected Poems 1909–62* (London: Faber & Faber, 1974), p. 34.

8. "Tradition and the Individual Talent," *Selected Essays* (op. cit., 1932), p. 18. The full quotation is "The mind of the poet . . . may partly or exclusively operate upon the experience of the man himself; but, the more perfect the artist, the more completely separate in him will be the man who suffers and the mind which creates; the more perfectly will the mind digest and transmute the passions which are its material."

9. Ibid., p. 17.

10. "Shakespeare and the Stoicism of Seneca," *Selected Essays* (Faber & Faber, 1932), p. 137.

11. A. David Moody, *Thomas Stearns Eliot, Poet* (Cambridge: CUP, 1979), pp. xvii–xviii.

12. "Tradition and the Individual Talent," *Selected Essays,* op. cit., p. 21.

13. Moody, op. cit., p. 11.

14. "Shakespeare and the Stoicism of Seneca," *Selected Essays,* op. cit., p. 137.

15. H. W. H. Powel Jr., in an unpublished MA thesis, "Notes on the Life of T.S. Eliot" (Brown University, 1954). Powell demonstrates that Adeleine Moffat, who entertained Eliot to tea in Boston when he was a student at Harvard, was the inspiration for "Portrait of a Lady."

16. "Hysteria," published in *The Catholic Anthology,* November 1915, *Collected Poems 1909–1962* (London: Faber & Faber, 1974), p. 34.

17. R. D. Laing, *The Divided Self* (London: Pelican, 1965), pp. 39–45. Laing makes a distinction between the ontologically secure individual who "may experience his own being as real, alive, whole; as differentiated from the rest of the world in ordinary circumstances so clearly that his identity and autonomy are never in question"; and the ontologically insecure, who "may feel more unreal than real; in a literal sense more dead than alive; precariously differentiated from the rest of the world, so that his identity and autonomy are always in question . . . He may feel more insubstantial than substantial, and unable to assume that the stuff he is made of is genuine, good, valuable. And he may feel his self is partially divorced from his body" (pp. 41–42). Laing distinguishes between the "sane schizoid way of being-in-the-world" and the psychotic.

18. George Whiteside, "Eliot: The Psychobiographical Approach," *Southern Review* (Adelaide), vol. V, 1972, p. 12.

19. TSE to Henry Eliot, 6 September 1916, *Letters I,* p. 151.

20. VE to Henry Eliot, 11 October 1916, *Letters I,* p. 155.

21. C. C. Eliot to Bertrand Russell, 18 January 1916, McMaster.

22. TSE to J. H. Woods, 23 March 1917, *Letters I,* p. 171.

23. *Harvard College Class of 1910, Seventh Report* (June 1935), p. 219.

24. VE to Henry Eliot, 11 October 1916, *Letters I*, p. 154.

25. Ronald Schuchard, *Eliot's Dark Angel: Intersections of Life and Art* (Oxford: OUP, 1999), gives Eliot's syllabuses in full, pp. 25–51.

26. TSE to Eleanor Hinkley, 23 March 1917, *Letters I*, p. 168.

27. *CP*, op. cit., p. 49.

28. TSE to C. C. Eliot, 6 September 1916, *Letters I*, p. 149.

29. Cyril Connolly, *Previous Convictions* (London: Hamish Hamilton, 1963), p. 241.

30. OM to BR, February 1916, McMaster.

31. *CP*, p. 17.

32. A. David Moody, "Tracing T. S. Eliot's Spirit," in *"The Waste Land" in Different Voices* (London: Edward Arnold, 1974), p. 42.

33. His article "Reflections on Vers Libre" appeared in the *New Statesman* in March 1917: "The division between Conservative Verse and *vers libre* does not exist, for there is only good verse, bad verse and chaos."

34. TSE to John Quinn, 25 January 1920, *Letters I*, p. 357.

35. Ezra Pound to Margaret C. Anderson, ?January 1917, D. D. Paige (ed.), *The Letters of Ezra Pound 1907–1941* (New York: Harcourt Brace, 1950), p. 161.

36. Margaret Anderson, editorial in the *Little Review*, March 1918.

37. Schuchard, op. cit., p. 39.

38. VE to C. C. Eliot, 28 June 1917, *Letters I*, p. 186.

39. TSE to C. C. Eliot, 1 July 1917, *Letters I*, p. 187.

40. "La sueur aestivale, et une forte odeur de chienne . . ." From "Lune de Miel," *CP*, op. cit., p. 50.

41. T. S. Eliot, "The Death of the Duchess," Valerie Eliot (ed.), *The Waste Land: A Facsimile* (New York: Harcourt Brace, 1971), p. 105.

42. TSE to C. C. Eliot, 3 October 1917, *Letters I*, p. 198.

43. TSE to BR, 13 March 1917, McMaster.

44. TSE to BR, "Thursday," 1917, McMaster.

45. VE to C. C. Eliot, 8 March 1917, Houghton, *Letters I*, p. 161.

46. TSE to Henry Ware Eliot, 1 March 1917, *Letters I*, p. 160.

47. OM to BR, 2 March 1916, McMaster.

48. *CP*, op. cit., p. 142–43.

49. Constance Malleson, *After Ten Years* (London: Jonathan Cape, 1931), p. 35.

50. Ibid., p. 109.

51. Constance Malleson to BR, September 1916, "Letters to Bertrand Russell from Constance Malleson, 1916–1969, Edited with a Preface by P.M. Urch," unpublished typescript, 1973, p. 5, McMaster.

52. BR to OM, 31 August 1916, Texas.

53. CM to BR, 2 October 1916, McMaster.

54. CM to BR, "afternoon," October 1916, Mrs. Urch (ed.), unpublished typescript, 1973, p. 14, McMaster.

55. BR to CM, 20 October 1915, in the train to Manchester, McMaster.

56. CM to BR, 25 October 1916, Urch, op. cit., pp. 30–31, McMaster.

57. Katharine Tait, *My Father Bertrand Russell* (New York: Harcourt Brace Jovanovich, 1975), p. 101. This description by Russell's daughter, Katharine, is of the "new morality" practised by Russell and her mother, his second wife, Dora Black.

58. BR to CM, 29 October 1916, midnight, McMaster.

59. BR to CM, 4 November 1916, McMaster.

60. CM to BR, 5 November 1916, Urch, op. cit., p. 38, McMaster.

61. BR to CM, 26 October 1916, McMaster.

62. Bertrand Russell, *Autobiography, vol. 2, 1914–1944* (London: George Allen & Unwin, 1968), p. 27.

63. CM to BR, December 1916, Urch, op. cit., p. 50, McMaster.

64. Russell, op. cit., p. 27.

65. BR to OM, n.d., Texas (archived letter no. 1439).

66. Katherine Mansfield to BR, December 1916, in Ronald Clark, *The Life of Bertrand Russell* (London: Jonathan Cape and Weidenfeld & Nicolson, 1975), p. 309.

67. CM to BR, 7 September 1916, McMaster.

68. BR to OM, n.d., Sunday, Texas (archived letter no. 1436).

69. BR to OM, "June 1917," McMaster.

70. BR to OM, n.d., 1917.

71. Constance Malleson, *The Coming Back* (London: Jonathan Cape, 1933), p. 307, quoted by John G. Slater, "Lady Constance Malleson, 'Colette O'Niel,'" *Russell,* Journal of the Bertrand Russell Archive, p. 11.

72. OM to BR, 2 January 1917 postmark, Texas.

73. OM to BR, 6 January 1917 postmark, Texas.

74. OM to BR, 19 March 1917, Texas.

75. OM to BR, 31 August 1917 postmark, Texas.

76. BR to CM, 28 November 1916, McMaster.

77. BR to CM, 3 December 1916, McMaster.

78. BR to CM, 5 January 1917, McMaster.

79. The letter was presented to the American Neutral Conference Committee on 22 January.

80. BR to CM, March 1917, McMaster.

81. BR to CM, 27 March 1917, McMaster.

82. CM to BR, 6 January 1917, McMaster.

83. CM to K. Blackwell, 12 February 1972, McMaster.

84. VE to C. C. Eliot, 8 April 1917, *Letters I,* p. 173.

85. TSE to C. C. Eliot, 11 April 1917, *Letters I,* p. 174.

86. VE to C. C. Eliot, 30 April 1917, *Letters I,* p. 178.

87. T. S. Eliot, "Mélange Adultère de Tout," in *Collected Poems,* p. 49.

88. Malleson, *After Ten Years,* op. cit., p. 111.

89. CM to BR, 2 May 1917, Urch, op. cit., p. 94, McMaster.

90. BR to CM, 2 April 1917, McMaster.

9. Priapus in the Shrubbery

1. The official date of the U.S. declaration of war was 6 April 1917.

2. Charlotte (1874–1926) married George Lawrence Smith in September 1903, and was an artist. Her daughter Theodora, born 25 July 1904, became a favourite niece of Vivien's.

3. VE to Charlotte Eliot Smith (Mrs. George Lawrence Smith), 4 April 1917, Houghton.

4. VE to Charlotte C. Eliot, 8 April 1917, Houghton, and *Letters I,* p. 173.

5. Karl Henry Culpin (1893–1917), Anglo-German, Exhibitioner at Merton College, First in

Modern History 1915; his call-up was delayed owing to poor eyesight, but he became a 2nd Lieutenant in the Gloucestershire Regiment.

6. TSE to C. C. Eliot, 11 April 1917, *Letters I*, p. 174.

7. John Quinn to Ezra Pound, 2 June 1917, Ezra Pound Papers, Beinecke.

8. TSE to Eleanor Hinkley, 23 July 1917, *Letters I*, p. 189.

9. TSE to C. C. Eliot, 15 November 1917, *Letters I*, p. 207.

10. Constance Malleson to Bertrand Russell, 25 December 1916, McMaster.

11. BR to CM, 21 September 1917, McMaster.

12. OM to BR, 30 July 1917 (wrongly dated 17 July by BR), Texas.

13. VE to C. C. Eliot, 28 June 1917, *Letters I*, p. 185.

14. Ibid.

15. Pound put £5 towards the cost of printing by the Egoist Press. The little book cost one shilling, and the print run was 500 copies. *Letters I*, p. 179.

16. TSE to Mary Hutchinson, 2 July 1917, *Letters I*, p. 188.

17. Alfred A. Knopf to John Quinn, 17 August 1917, Beinecke.

18. John Quinn to Ezra Pound, 29 April 1917, Beinecke.

19. Clive Bell, "How Pleasant to know Mr. Eliot," R. Marsh and Tambimuttu, *T. S. Eliot: A Symposium* (London: P.L. Editions, p. 17. Clive's memory must have been at fault, as *Prufrock and other Observations* was not published until June 1917, see *Letters I*, p. 179, note 4).

20. VE to C. C. Eliot, 22 October 1917, *Letters I*, p. 200.

21. TSE to C. C. Eliot, 3 October 1917, *Letters I*, p. 198.

22. VE to C. C. Eliot, 22 October 1917, *Letters I*, p. 200.

23. TSE to Henry Ware Eliot, 22 November 1917, *Letters I*, p. 208.

24. CM to BR, 19 August 1917, McMaster, Urch typescript, p. 126.

25. CM to BR, 23 August 1917, McMaster, Urch typescript, pp. 131–32.

26. BR to CM, 17 August 1917, McMaster.

27. Constance Malleson, *After Ten Years* (London: Jonathan Cape, 1931), p. 123.

28. BR to CM, 23 September 1917, Bertrand Russell, *Autobiography,* vol. 2, 1914–1944 (London: George Allen & Unwin, 1968), p. 179.

29. BR to CM, "What She Is and What She Might Become," 25 September 1917, McMaster.

30. CM to BR, 28 September 1917, McMaster, Urch typescript, vol. 2, p. 161.

31. BR to CM, 6 September 1917, McMaster. Russell visited Garsington in between his two meetings with Katherine Mansfield. Phyllis Urch writes: "To judge from the only unpublished evidence available—a letter from Katherine Mansfield to Russell, postmarked January 25, 1917—one would not care to pronounce on the exact nature of her relations with Russell. His statements, in letters to Colette, can hardly be taken as evidence; for, although they no doubt contain a part of the truth, it might be rash to assume they contain the whole of it." See Mrs. P. Urch, unpublished thesis, 1973, p. 112.

32. BR to CM, 26 June 1917, Urch, op. cit., vol. 2, p. 112.

33. CM to BR, 11 October 1917, Urch, op. cit., vol. 2, pp. 167–68.

34. BR to CM, 16 October 1917, McMaster.

35. TSE to C. C. Eliot, 24 October 1917, *Letters I*, p. 203.

36. VE to C. C. Eliot, 22 October 1917, Houghton, *Letters I*, p. 200. From the original letter it seems that the farm mentioned is possibly Tanhurst Farm, which is within two miles of Leith Hill, as described in Eliot's letter of 24 October to his mother, rather than "Senhurst," as given in the published version of Vivien's letter. There is no farm of the

name of Senhurst in the area around Leith Hill, according to Matthew Alexander, curator of Guildford Museum. A study of the 1916 6" ordnance survey map gives two possible
farms in the area described, Tanhurst or Hartshurst. Conversation with Matthew
Alexander, 21 July 1999.

37. As Peter Ackroyd surmises in his biography, *T. S. Eliot* (London: Penguin, 1993) p. 84, because she was menstruating, which there is no reason to think was the case. Since she was
at the farm for three weeks, Vivien was unlikely to have invited Russell at such a time.
Ackroyd's interpretation is based on a paraphrase of Russell's letter of 30 October 1917 in
"Bertrand Russell and the Eliots" by Robert H. Bell (*The American Scholar,* summer 1983,
pp. 309–25).

38. BR to CM, 25 October 1917, McMaster.

39. BR to CM, 30 October 1917, McMaster.

40. CM to BR, 31 October 1917, McMaster.

41. BR to CM, n.d., Gordon Square, November 1917, McMaster.

42. Ronald Clark, *The Life of Bertrand Russell* (London: Jonathan Cape and Weidenfeld and
Nicolson, 1975), pp. 334–35.

43. BR to CM, 7 November 1917, McMaster.

44. BR to CM, 13 November 1917, McMaster.

45. BR to CM, 14 November 1917, McMaster.

46. BR to CM, ibid.

47. BR to CM, "Thursday," 22 November 1917, McMaster.

48. CM to BR, 29 November 1917, Urch, op. cit., vol. 2, p. 186.

49. BR to CM, 6 December 1917, McMaster.

50. VE to Mary Hutchinson, n.d., ?November 1917, Texas.

51. VE to C. C. Eliot, 22 November 1917, *Letters I,* p. 210.

52. *Roads to Freedom: Socialism, Anarchism and Syndicalism,* "undertaken for an American
publisher, 'solely for the sake of filthy lucre,' " Clark, op. cit., p. 333.

53. BR to CM, 13 December 1917, McMaster.

54. Lady Constance Malleson to Kenneth Blackwell, 1 February 1975, in reply to his query
whether Russell paid for her abortion. I differ from Ray Monk in dating Colette's pregnancy by Elvey and subsequent abortion as December 1917 (as Colette does), following her
stay with him in Blackpool during filming, rather than December 1918, when Russell suspected her of having an affair with the American Colonel Mitchell while he was in
Brixton. Colette denies that Russell paid for the abortion, as stated by Monk, op. cit.,
p. 542. It is of course possible that Colette's stay in the nursing home in 1918 was for another abortion, as she said she had had "a number of abortions" in her youth.

55. BR to CM, 14 December 1917, McMaster.

56. BR to CM, 1 January 1918, McMaster.

57. CM to BR, Urch, op. cit., vol. 2, pp. 198–204.

58. BR to CM, 6 January 1918, McMaster.

59. BR to CM, 9 January 1918, McMaster.

60. BR to CM, 10 January 1918, McMaster.

61. Monk, op. cit., p. 524.

62. BR to OM, 4 February 1918, McMaster.

63. "Mr. Apollinax" in Christopher Ricks (ed.), *Inventions of the March Hare, T. S. Eliot: Poems
1909–1917* (New York: Harcourt Brace, 1971), p. 344. First published in *Poetry,* September
1916.

64. Russell appropriated this personalisation of himself as "Satan" in his short story, "Satan in the Suburbs."

65. Andrew Laing, *R.D. Laing: A Biography* (New York: Thunder's Mouth Press, 1994), p. 232.

66. Alessandra Lemma-Wright, Chapter 14, "I'm Homosexual," *Invitation to Psychodynamic Psychology* (Whurr Publishers, 1995), pp. 148–56.

67. TSE to Ezra Pound, 23 September 1917, *Letters I*, p. 198.

68. Part I of "Eeldrop and Appleplex" was published in May and Part II in September 1917 in the *Little Review*.

69. Joan Acocella, "Dancing with Demons," *Independent on Sunday*, 8 August 1999, writes that Nijinsky "ushered ballet into modernism" with his productions of *L'Après-midi d'un Faune, Jeux,* and *The Rite of Spring*. See also Lynn Garafola, *Diaghilev's Ballets Russes* (New York: Da Capo Press, 1998), p. 50.

70. Lyndall Gordon, *T. S. Eliot: An Imperfect Life* (London: Vintage, 1998), p. 106, makes this suggestion.

71. Virginia Woolf confessed, "I was jealous of her writing—the only writing I have ever been jealous of," quoted on the cover of Katherine Mansfield, *Bliss and Other Stories* (London: Penguin, 1962).

72. TSE to Henry Ware Eliot Sr., 31 October 1917, *Letters I*, p. 204.

10. Bloomsbury Beginnings

1. Ray Monk, *Bertrand Russell: The Spirit of Solitude* (London: Vintage, 1997), pp. 520, 521.

2. T. S. Matthews, *Great Tom: Notes Towards the Definition of T. S. Eliot* (London: Weidenfeld & Nicolson, 1974), p. 45. Matthews argues that Eliot has taken an acknowledgement of guilt and made it read as a curse. See also C. Ricks (ed.), *Inventions of the March Hare, T. S. Eliot: Poems 1909–1917* (New York: Harcourt Brace Jovanovich, 1996), p. 183. The quotation from *Coriolanus,* IV.v, reads:

> My name is Caius Marcius, who hath done
>
> To thee particularly, and to all the Volsces,
>
> Great hurt and mischief.

Undoubtedly Eliot identified with the banished Coriolanus, and compared his mother Charlotte to the courageous Volumnia, mother of Coriolanus, who boasted that she had the courage to perform the labours of Hercules. "Ode" was included in *Ara Vos Prec,* published by John Rodker (1919). Part of this edition bore the title *Ara Vus Prec,* which Eliot later blamed on his ignorance of Provençal.

3. Frances Partridge, interview with author, 27 November 2000.

4. Ibid.

5. Michael Holroyd, *Lytton Strachey* (London: Vintage, 1995), p. 59.

6. David Bradshaw, "These Extraordinary Parakeets," Part I in *Charleston Magazine,* 16, Autumn/Winter 1997; Part II in *Charleston Magazine* 17, Spring/Summer 1998.

7. James Strachey Barnes, *Half a Life* (London: Eyre & Spottiswoode, 1933), pp. 87–93.

8. The character of Jinny, a socialite, is based on Mary, that of Louis very probably on Eliot, although Angelica Garnett suggests Leonard Woolf in her introduction to *The Waves,* in which Jinny and Louis play hiding and kissing games together. Virginia Woolf, *The Waves* (London: Vintage, 1992), p. 5. See Hermione Lee, *Virginia Woolf* (London: Vintage, 1997), p. 383.

9. Jane Dunn, *A Very Close Conspiracy* (London: Jonathan Cape, 1990), p. 243.

10. Ibid., p. 103.

11. Ibid., p. 105.

12. Vanessa Bell to Maynard Keynes, Regina Marler (ed.), *The Selected Letters of Vanessa Bell* (New York: Pantheon, 1993), p. 163.

13. Bradshaw, op. cit., p. 1.

14. Richard Shone, *Bloomsbury Portraits* (London: Phaidon, 1976), p. 169.

15. VE to Mary Hutchinson, 11 November 1936, Texas.

16. Osbert Sitwell, *Laughter in the Next Room* (London: Macmillan, 1949), p. 17.

17. River House was previously the home of bookbinder and printer T. J. Cobden-Sanderson, and was next door to Kelmscott House, which formerly belonged to William Morris. See Bradshaw, op. cit., p. 22.

18. "Polly Flinders," "Fireworks," *Vogue*, 67 (early January, 1926), p. 49. Reprinted in Mary Hutchinson, *Fugitive Pieces* (London: Hogarth Press, 1927). Quoted by Bradshaw, op. cit., p. 23.

19. Vincent O'Sullivan and Margaret Scott (eds.), *Collected Letters of Katherine Mansfield*, vol. 1 (Oxford: Clarendon Press, 1984), p. 312. Quoted by Bradshaw, op. cit., p. 24.

20. VE to Mary Hutchinson, "Southview," n.d., 1917, Texas.

21. VE to MH, "18 Crawford Mans.," n.d., 1917, Texas.

22. VE to MH, n.d., ?1917, Texas.

23. VE to MH, n.d., ?1917, Texas.

24. TSE to Ezra Pound, 31 October 1917, Beinecke, and *Letters I*, p. 206.

25. Sitwell, op. cit., pp. 32–33.

26. VE to MH, n.d., ?1918, Texas.

27. Clive Bell, "How Pleasant to know Mr. Eliot," Richard March and Tambimuttu, *T. S. Eliot: A Symposium* (London: P. L. Editions Poetry, 1948), p. 15.

28. Robert Gathorne-Hardy (ed.), *Ottoline at Garsington: Memoirs of Lady Ottoline Morrell 1915–1918* (London: Faber & Faber, 1974), p. 52.

29. Michael Holyroyd, *Lytton Strachey* (London: Vintage, 1995), p. 59.

30. TSE to C. C. Eliot, 17 January, 6 February 1918, *Letters I*, pp. 218–19.

31. TSE to MH, 6 September 1916, *Letters I*, p. 151.

32. Clive Bell to MH, 16 January 1917, Hutchinson Papers, Texas.

33. MH to Lytton Strachey, 17 January 1917, Texas.

34. Shone, op. cit., pp. 119–20.

35. MH to Lytton Strachey, 14 June 1918, Texas.

36. Clive Bell to MH, 8 April 1917, Hutchinson Papers, Texas.

37. Clive Bell to MH, 20 September 1917, Texas.

38. Clive Bell to MH, 23 September 1917, Texas.

39. O'Sullivan and Scott (eds.), *Collected Letters of Katherine Mansfield*, vol. 1, op. cit., p. 312.

40. Maurice Haigh-Wood, interview with Michael Hastings, 21 January 1980.

41. TSE to MH, 19 September 1917, *Letters I*, p. 197.

42. VE to MH, 13 March 1918, Texas, *Letters I*, p. 224.

43. MH to Lytton Strachey, 19 May 1919, Texas.

44. VE to MH, n.d., 1921, Texas.

45. VE to MH, 6 September 1929, Texas.

46. VE to MH, 10 July 1931, Texas.

47. TSE to C. C. Eliot, 24 March 1918, *Letters I*, p. 225.

48. VE to MH, 31 March 1918, Texas, *Letters I,* p. 224.

49. Ibid.

50. L. M. Findlay (ed.), *Algernon Charles Swinburne, Selected Poems* (Manchester: Fyfield Books, 1982), p. 84.

51. Ronald Clark, *The Life of Bertrand Russell* (London: Jonathan Cape and Weidenfeld & Nicolson, 1975), p. 345.

52. Bertrand Russell to Constance Malleson, n.d. (?May), archive letter no. 200305, McMaster.

53. The day after Helen sailed Russell confessed his affair with her to Colette. Clark, op. cit., p. 352.

54. BR to CM, n.d., McMaster.

55. I am indebted to Dr. Carl Spadoni, Director, Bertrand Russell Archive, for this suggestion.

56. BR to CM, April 1918, McMaster.

57. "Sweeney among the Nightingales," "Whispers of Immortality," "Dans le Restaurant," "Mr. Eliot's Sunday Morning Service." Published as "Four Poems" in the *Little Review,* v, 5 (September 1918), pp. 10–14. Valerie Eliot (ed.), Introduction to *The Waste Land: A Facsimile,* xiv, note.

58. Ricks (ed.), *IMH,* p. 384. In *Ara Vos Prec,* "Ode on Independence Day, July 4 1918" followed "Mélange Adultère de Tout" and preceded "The Love Song of J. Alfred Prufrock." It is the only poem published by TSE not in a subsequent collection.

59. Quoted in Keith Thomas, *Religion and the Decline of Magic* (London: Penguin, 1973), p. 679.

60. Quoted in Ackroyd, *T. S. Eliot* (London: Penguin, 1993), p. 86.

61. Brigit Patmore, *My Friends When Young* (London: Heinemann, 1968).

62. Brigit Patmore, op. cit., pp. 88–89.

63. T. S. Eliot, "Whispers of Immortality," *CP,* p. 55; Ricks (ed.), *IMH,* p. 365.

64. *International Journal of Ethics,* January 1917, quoted in George Whiteside, "T. S. Eliot: The Psychobiographic Approach," *Southern Review* (Adelaide) 6, no. 1 (March 1973), p. 22.

65. Whiteside, ibid., p. 23. "Whispers of Immortality" can be compared to "Circe's Palace" (1908), whose Freudian imagery is similar, and betrays the twenty-year-old Eliot's dawning self-knowledge of his homosexuality.

66. T. S. Eliot, "Portrait of a Lady," in Ricks (ed.), *IMH,* p. 327. The original epigraph for this poem was from Webster's *The White Devil.*

67. Ricks (ed.), *IMH,* p. 363; *CP,* op. cit., p. 53.

68. BR to CM, n.d. (?July), archive letter no. 200325, McMaster.

69. BR to CM, Urch, op. cit., p. 73.

70. Constance Malleson, *After Ten Years* (London: Jonathan Cape, 1931), pp. 123–24.

71. VE to Mary Hutchinson, 30 August 1918, Texas.

72. TSE to Henry Ware Eliot Jr., 25 August 1918, Houghton, *Letters I,* p. 241.

73. TSE to John Quinn, *Letters I,* p. 244.

74. VE to MH, n.d., ?August 1918, Texas.

75. Ibid.

76. John Quinn to Major Turner, August 1918, Houghton.

77. TSE to Charlotte C. Eliot, 28 July 1918, Houghton, *Letters I,* p. 239.

78. TSE to Mary Hutchinson, 25 August 1918, Texas.

79. Ibid.

80. Ibid.

81. BR to CM, 24 August 1918, McMaster.

82. Urch, op. cit., p. 266.

83. Ibid., p. 285.

84. Malleson, op. cit., p. 127.

85. TSE to John Quinn, 13 November 1918, *Letters I,* p. 254.

86. TSE to Mrs. Jack Gardner, 7 November 1918, *Letters I,* p. 251.

87. TSE to Henry Eliot Jr., ibid., p. 250.

88. Sitwell, op. cit., p. 5.

89. VE to Henry Eliot Jr., 21 November 1918, *Letters I,* p. 258.

90. TSE to C. C. Eliot, 8 December 1918, *Letters I,* p. 259.

91. VE to C. C. Eliot, 15 December 1918, *Letters I,* p. 261.

92. VE to C. C. Eliot, 30 December 1918, *Letters I,* p. 264.

93. VE to Richard Aldington, in pencil, n.d., ?spring 1922, Texas.

94. VE to Henry Eliot Jr., 27 October 1918, *Letters I,* p. 245.

95. TSE to Eleanor Hinkley, 31 December 1917, *Letters I,* p. 216.

96. Henry James, *Daisy Miller,* with an Introduction by Geoffrey Moore (London: Penguin Classics, 1986), p. 62.

97. CM to BR, 7 September 1918, McMaster.

98. BR to OM, 20 November 1918, Texas.

99. Clark, op. cit., p. 353.

100. Urch, op. cit., p. 292.

101. BR to CM, 26 September 1918, McMaster.

102. BR to CM, 23 October 1918, McMaster.

103. BR to CM, 26 November 1918, McMaster.

104. BR to CM, 27 November 1918, McMaster.

105. Urch, op. cit., p. 309.

106. Ibid.

107. Ibid., p. 317.

108. CM to BR, 7 February 1919, Urch, op. cit., p. 318.

109. Ibid., p. 319.

110. TSE to BR, 3 February 1919, McMaster and *Letters I,* p. 270.

111. BR to TSE, 27 February 1919, McMaster.

112. Urch, op. cit., p. 309.

113. TSE to BR, 14 February 1919, McMaster, *Letters I,* p. 271.

114. BR to TSE, 19 March 1919, McMaster.

115. TSE to John Quinn, 6 January 1919, *Letters I,* p. 166.

116. TSE to John Quinn, 16 January 1919, *Letters I,* p. 169.

117. VE to Mary Hutchinson (postmark) 28 February 1919, Texas.

118. TSE to Henry Ware Eliot Jr., 27 February 1919, *Letters I,* p. 272.

119. TSE to BR, 26 March 1919, McMaster.

120. VE to BR, 13 April 1919, McMaster.

121. TSE to C. C. Eliot, 12 March 1919, *Letters I,* p. 276.

122. Katherine Tait, *My Father Bertrand Russell* (New York: Harcourt Brace Jovanovich, 1975), p. 101.

123. TSE to Mary Hutchinson, 4 March 1919, *Letters I,* p. 275.

11. Possum's Revenge

1. Donald Stanford, quoted in Margaret Clare Ratliff, "The Correspondence of Mary Hutchinson: A New Look at Bloomsbury, Eliot and Huxley," thesis, University of Texas at Austin, 1991, ch. 4, "Mary Hutchinson and the Eliots," p. 143.

2. VE Diary, 1919, Bodleian.

3. Osbert Sitwell, "T. S. Eliot:" unpublished memoir on T. S. Eliot and his marriage, 19 February 1950, Texas.

4. Richard Aldington, *Stepping Heavenward: A Record* (London: 1931), pp. 28–53.

5. Sitwell, memoir, op. cit., pp. 3–5.

6. Ibid., p. 12.

7. "Burbank with a Baedeker: Bleistein with a Cigar," *Collected Poems,* pp. 42–43.

8. Anthony Julius, *T. S. Eliot, Anti-Semitism, and Literary Form* (Cambridge: Cambridge University Press, 1995), p. 2.

9. Ibid., pp. 19–20. These poems dominate *Ara Vos Prec* (London: The Ovid Press, 1920).

10. *Criterion,* April 1925, iii, p. 330.

11. Basil Saunders to Lyndall Gordon, 18 August 1993.

12. T. S. Eliot, *Ara Vos Prec,* op. cit.

13. Anne Olivier Bell (ed.), *The Diary of Virginia Woolf, vol. 1, 1915–1919* (London: Penguin, 1979), p. 257.

14. Lewis had his first novel *Tarr* published by The Egoist Ltd. in July 1918.

15. *Diary of Virginia Woolf,* vol. 1, op. cit., p. 140, entry for 18 April 1918. Eliot suggested to Harriet Weaver that the Woolfs might print *Ulysses* on their private press, which Weaver's printers were refusing to do because of printers' liability for prosecution under the laws of obscene libel. The Woolfs declined to do so.

16. Leonard Woolf, *Beginning Again: An Autobiography of the Years 1911 to 1918* (London: Hogarth Press, 1964).

17. TSE to C. C. Eliot, 29 March 1919, *Letters I,* p. 279.

18. Sitwell, op. cit., p. 6.

19. Aldington, op. cit., p. 46.

20. TSE to Richard Aldington, 30 June 1922, Texas, *Letters I,* p. 535.

21. VE Diary, 17–22 November 1919, Bodleian.

22. TSE to Henry Eliot, 27 February 1919, *Letters I,* p. 272.

23. TSE to C. C. Eliot, 27 February 1919, *Letters I,* p. 274.

24. VE Diary, 2 March 1919, Bodleian.

25. VE Diary, 1–10 November 1919, Bodleian.

26. TSE to C. C. Eliot, 26 June 1919, *Letters I,* p. 309.

27. VE Diary, 9 July 1919, Bodleian.

28. VE Diary, 6 July 1919, Bodleian.

29. *Diary of Virginia Woolf,* op. cit., note 262.

30. Wyndham Lewis, in R. March and Tambimuttu, *T. S. Eliot: A Symposium* (London: P. L. Editions Poetry, 1948), p. 31.

31. TSE to C. C. Eliot, 29 March 1919, *Letters I,* p. 280.

32. TSE to Henry Eliot, 6 April 1919, *Letters I,* p. 283.

33. TSE to J. H. Woods, 21 April 1919, *Letters I,* p. 285.

34. Stephen Spender, *Eliot* (London: Fontana, 1975), p. 93.

35. Paul Delany, "T. S. Eliot's Personal Finances, 1915–1929," in *Literature, Money and the Market from Trollope to Amis* (Basingstoke: Palgrave, 2001).

36. Delany, op. cit., p. 261.

37. Signed statement by Theresa Eliot, 28 March 1970, Cambridge, Mass., Houghton.

38. Delany, op. cit., p. 261.

39. The Woolfs did not acquire their first treadle machine until after moving the Hogarth Press to 52 Tavistock Square, Bloomsbury, in 1924. Even then conditions were primitive, as their assistant, John Lehmann, recalled.

40. VE to MH, 1 May? 1919, Texas, and *Letters I*, p. 288.

41. V. Woolf to Vanessa Bell, 4 April 1919, in Nigel Nicolson and Joanne Trautmann (eds.), *The Letters of Virginia Woolf*, vol. II. (London: Hogarth Press, 1976), p. 344.

42. TSE to Eleanor Hinkley, 17 June 1919, *Letters I*, p. 304.

43. *Diary of Virginia Woolf*, op. cit., p. 209.

44. British Library, 13 October 1918, quoted in Ratliff, op. cit., p. 116.

45. V. Woolf to Duncan Grant, 17 April 1919, Nicolson and Trautmann (eds.), *Letters*, vol. II, op. cit., p. 350.

46. TSE to Eleanor Hinkley, 17 June 1919, *Letters I*, p. 304.

47. VE to MH, 10 May 1919, *Letters I*, p. 292.

48. *Diary of Virginia Woolf*, 10 April 1919, op. cit., p. 262.

49. V. Woolf to Duncan Grant, 17 April 1919, Nicolson and Trautmann (eds.), *Letters, vol. II*, op. cit., p. 350.

50. VE to MH, 10 May 1919, *Letters I*, p. 292.

51. Clive Bell, *Old Friends, Personal Recollections* (London: Chatto and Windus, 1956), p. 170.

52. Stephen Spender, "Remembering Eliot," in Allen Tate (ed.), *T. S. Eliot: The Man and His Work* (London: Chatto & Windus, 1967), p. 58.

53. Vivien Eliot, "Thé Dansant," *Criterion,* 3 October 1924.

54. VE Diary, 2 March 1919, Bodleian.

55. TSE to MH, 4 June 1917, Texas.

56. Vivien did not visit Bosham in 1919 until 14 June when she was "delighted to see it again," VE Diary, Bodleian.

57. TSE to MH, 16 May 1919, Texas.

58. VE to MH, n.d. ?May 1919, Texas.

59. Mary Hutchinson, "T. S. Eliot," unpublished biographical sketch, n.d., Texas.

60. "The Fire Sermon," *The Waste Land, CP,* p. 73.

61. T. Sharpe, *T. S. Eliot* (London: Macmillan, 1991), p. 63.

62. *CP,* p. 39.

63. TSE to MH, "Sunday," ?15 June 1919, Texas, *Letters I,* p. 302.

64. *Diary of Virginia Woolf,* op. cit., 16 May 1919, p. 272.

65. VE to MH, n.d., ?June 1919, Texas.

66. VE to MH, n.d., ?June 1919, Texas.

67. VE Diary, 14 June 1919, Bodleian.

68. VE to OM, ?25 June 1919, Texas, *Letters I,* p. 307.

69. VE to OM, ?4 June 1919, Texas, *Letters I,* p. 301.

70. VE to MH, "Thursday," ?26 June 1919, Texas.

71. VE to MH, "Wed.," ?early July 1919, Texas.

72. Ibid.

73. VE to MH, 16 July 1919, Texas, *Letters I,* p. 320.

74. VE to MH, ?late July 1919, Texas.

75. TSE to Henry Ware Eliot Jr., 2 July 1919, *Letters I,* p. 310.

76. TSE to MH, ?11 July 1919, Texas, *Letters I,* p. 317.

77. In 1927 Mary spent at least one night with Vita Sackville-West, see V. Glendinning, *Vita: The Life of Vita Sackville-West* (London: Penguin, 1984), p. 178. Dr. David Bradshaw states that it is clear from their letters to her in the Mary Hutchinson Collection, Texas, that "overlapping with her affair with Clive, Mary had also had relationships with both Aldous Huxley and his wife Maria," "Those Extraordinary Parakeets," *Charleston Magazine,* Part I, Autumn/Winter 1997, issue 16; Part II, Spring/Summer 1998, Issue 17.

78. Clive Bell to MH, 19 April 1918, quoted in Margaret Ratliff, "A Bloomsbury Friendship: The Correspondence of Mary Hutchinson and Lytton Strachey," *The Library Chronicle of the University of Texas at Austin,* no. 48 (1989), p. 199.

79. Hermione Lee cites a letter from Clive Bell to MH, 20 October 1922, Texas; Hermione Lee, *Virginia Woolf* (London: Vintage, 1997), note 383.

80. VE to MH, 1 September 1919, Texas.

81. MH to Lytton Strachey, 31 July 1927, Texas.

82. MH to Maria Huxley, 1 August 1925, Hutchinson Papers, Texas.

83. Mary Hutchinson, unpublished memoir of Aldous Huxley, Texas.

84. Ratliff, op. cit., ch. 5, p. 224.

85. VE to MH, n.d., ?September 1919, Texas.

86. VE Diary, 31 August 1919, Bodleian.

87. VE to MH, 3 October 1919, Texas, *Letters I,* p. 338.

88. VE to MH, 8 May 1919, Texas.

89. VE to MH, 20 March 1919, Texas.

90. VE to MH, 26 September 1919, Texas, *Letters I,* p. 334.

91. Ronald Schuchard, *Eliot's Dark Angel: Intersection of Life and Art* (Oxford: OUP, 1999), p. 50.

92. VE to MH, 29 October 1919, Texas, *Letters I,* p. 342.

93. Tate Gallery Archives, quoted in Bradshaw, op. cit., p. 29.

94. Bell, *The Diary of Virginia Woolf,* op. cit., vol. 4, p. 230.

95. VE to MH, n.d., ?November 1919, Texas.

12. Breakdown

1. TSE to C. C. Eliot, 15 February 1920, *Letters I,* p. 365.

2. Charlotte C. Eliot settled at 27 Concord Avenue, Cambridge, Massachusetts.

3. Anne Olivier Bell (ed.), *The Diary of Virginia Woolf, vol. 2, 1920–1924* (London: Penguin, 1981), p. 67, 19 September 1920; see also Hermione Lee, *Virginia Woolf* (London: Vintage, 1997), pp. 439–40.

4. TSE to Henry Eliot, 15 February 1920, *Letters I,* p. 363.

5. *CP,* p. 44.

6. T. S. Matthews, *Great Tom: Notes Towards the Definition of T. S. Eliot* (London: Weidenfeld & Nicolson, 1974), p. 62.

7. Charles Doyle, *Richard Aldington: A Biography* (London: Macmillan, 1989), p. 71.

8. TSE to C. C. Eliot, 27 July 1920, *Letters I,* p. 393.

9. When Scofield Thayer sent Aiken's *House of Dust* to Eliot from *The Dial* for review he

wrote that "the workmen called in to build the house were Swinburne and myself, the Dust being provided by Conrad." He pointed to a quotation on p. 83 which appeared to be derived from *Prufrock,* and declined to review the book as it would "strain his friendship" with Aiken. TSE to Scofield Thayer, 17 October 1920, *Letters I,* p. 413.

10. Eliot wrote to John Quinn on 22 January 1920 that he did not want Knopf to publish Osbert Sitwell's poems at the same time as his, as "some of them are rather clever imitations of myself and other people." *Letters I,* p. 358.

11. TSE to Wyndham Lewis, ?16 April 1921, *Letters I,* p. 446.

12. Philip Ziegler, *Osbert Sitwell* (London: Chatto & Windus, 1998), pp. 68–69.

13. Peter Ackroyd, *Ezra Pound and His World* (London: Thames and Hudson, 1980), p. 57.

14. Donald Gallup, "The Lost Manuscripts of T. S. Eliot," *Times Literary Supplement,* 7 November 1968; quoted in Trosman, "T. S. Eliot and the Waste Land: Psychopathological Antecedents and Transformations," *Emotions and Behavior Monographs, 4* (University of Chicago, 1987), p. 208.

15. Caroline Behr, *T. S. Eliot: A Chronology of His Life and Works* (London: Macmillan, 1983), p. 21.

16. Matthews, op. cit., p. 65.

17. TSE to C. C. Eliot, 26 January 1920, *Letters I,* p. 359.

18. Ezra Pound to Hugh Walpole, 30 June 1920, in D. D. Paige (ed.), *The Letters of Ezra Pound 1907–1941* (London: Faber & Faber, 1951), p. 218.

19. TSE to Maxwell Bodenheim, 2 January 1921, *Letters I,* p. 431.

20. Henry Eliot to C. C. Eliot, 30 October 1921, Houghton, quoted in Lyndall Gordon, *T. S. Eliot: An Imperfect Life* (London: Vintage, 1998), p. 171.

21. Charles W. Eliot to TSE, 25 July 1919, Houghton, *Letters I,* p. 322.

22. Richard Aldington, *Life for Life's Sake* (New York: Viking Press, 1941), quoted in Behr, op. cit., p. 20.

23. Journal of Lady Ottoline Morrell, 7 December 1919, Goodman Papers.

24. Lee, op. cit., p. 439.

25. *Diary of Virginia Woolf,* op. cit., vol. 1, 18 September 1928, p. 197.

26. David Bradshaw, "Those Extraordinary Parakeets," *Charleston Magazine,* Part I, Autumn/Winter 1997, issue 16; Part II, Spring/Summer 1998, issue 17.

27. Herbert Read, "T.S.E.—A Memoir," in Allen Tate, *T. S. Eliot: The Man and His Work* (London: Chatto & Windus, 1967), p. 23.

28. VE to OM, n.d. (?December 1919), Texas.

29. Bell, *The Diary of Virginia Woolf,* op. cit., vol. 1, 16 May 1919, p. 272.

30. Bell, *The Diary of Virginia Woolf,* op. cit., vol. 2, 1920–24, p. 87.

31. VE Diary, 22 July 1919, Bodleian.

32. Clive Bell to M. Hutchinson, 23 September 1917, Texas.

33. Journal of Lady Ottoline Morrell, 16 March 1920, Goodman Papers.

34. Matthews, op. cit., p. 55.

35. TSE to C. C. Eliot, 22 February 1920, *Letters I,* p. 368.

36. Bell, *The Diary of Virginia Woolf,* op. cit., vol. 2, p. 281.

37. Richard Aldington to TSE, 18 July 1919, Houghton, *Letters I,* p. 321.

38. Middleton Murry's book, *The Critic in Judgment,* had attracted even more severe reviews than Eliot's *Poems.* Virginia Woolf's story, *Kew Gardens,* published like the other two by The Hogarth Press on 12 May 1919, had been received more favourably.

39. Bell, *The Diary of Virginia Woolf,* op. cit., vol. 2, p. 15.

40. *Letters I,* pp. 168–69.
41. TSE to Professor Woods, *Letters I,* p. 171.
42. Virginia Woolf to VE, 20 July 1920, Nigel Nicolson and Joanne Trautmann (eds.), *The Letters of Virginia Woolf, vol. II* (London: Hogarth Press, 1976), p. 436.
43. Virginia Woolf to TSE, 28 July 1920, in ibid., p. 437.
44. Virginia Woolf to Vanessa Bell, 15? September, in ibid., p. 444.
45. Virginia Woolf to TSE, 15 September 1920, in ibid., p. 443.
46. Bernard Bergonzi, *T. S. Eliot* (London: Macmillan, 1972), p. 70.
47. Ibid., p. 71.
48. VE to OM, n.d. (?December 1919), Texas.
49. TSE to OM, 10 April 1920, *Letters I,* p. 379.
50. Read, op. cit., p. 32.
51. TSE to MH, "Wed." 1920, Texas.
52. TSE to MH, "Wed." 1920, Texas.
53. TSE to MH, "Sunday" 1920, Texas.
54. TSE to MH, "Monday" 1920, Texas.
55. TSE to MH, "Thursday" 1920, Texas.
56. Behr, op. cit., p. 19.
57. TSE to Ezra Pound, ?June 1920, *Letters I,* p. 385.
58. TSE to C. C. Eliot, 27 July 1920, Houghton, *Letters I,* p. 393.
59. TSE to C. C. Eliot, 9 August 1920, *Letters I,* p. 399.
60. P. Wyndham Lewis, *Blasting and Bombardiering* (London: Calder & Boyars, 1967), pp. 270–75.
61. Wyndham Lewis, "Early London Environment," R. March and Tambimuttu, *T. S. Eliot: A Symposium* (London: P. L. Editions, 1948), p. 30.
62. TSE to C. C. Eliot, 20 September 1920, *Letters I,* p. 408.
63. There was an awkward encounter in May 1921 at the Private View of the Picasso Exhibition in Paris, witnessed by Vanessa Bell, when Juana and her aunt arrived, only to come face to face with Jack, Mary and Clive.
64. Clive Bell to Mary Hutchinson, quoted in Margaret Ratliff, "The Correspondence of Mary Hutchinson: A New Look at Bloomsbury, Eliot and Huxley," thesis (University of Texas at Austin, 1991), p. 204.
65. Vanessa Bell to Roger Fry, 25 May 1921, Regina Marler (ed.), *Selected Letters of Vanessa Bell* (New York: Pantheon Books, 1993), pp. 249, 250.
66. TSE to MH, 22 September 1920, Texas, *Letters I,* p. 409.
67. TSE to MH, 28 September 1920, Texas, *Letters I,* p. 410.
68. "Fanny Marlow," "Fête Galante," *Criterion iii* (July 1925), pp. 557–63.
69. TSE to MH, "June," n.d., Texas.
70. Journal of Lady Ottoline Morrell, 16 March 1920, Goodman Papers.
71. VE to MH, 28? September 1920, Texas, *Letters I,* p. 411.
72. Letter from Abigail Eliot, 12 June 1965, quoted in programme of *Tom and Viv.*
73. VE to MH, 25 October 1920, Texas.
74. VE to MH, "11 o'clock," Texas.
75. TSE to C. C. Eliot, 31 October 1920, *Letters I,* p. 418.
76. VE to MH, n.d., ?December 1920, Texas.
77. VE to MH, 22 November 1920, Texas.
78. Charles Dickens, *Our Mutual Friend,* chapter xvi: "Sloppy is a beautiful reader of a news-

paper. He do the Police in different voices." Valerie Eliot (ed.), *The Waste Land: A Facsimile and Transcript of the Original Drafts including the Annotations of Ezra Pound* (New York: Harcourt Brace Jovanovich, 1971), note 125.

79. TSE to John Quinn, 5 November 1919, *Letters I*, p. 343.

80. Behr, op. cit., p. 20.

81. TSE to C. C. Eliot, 22 January 1921, *Letters I*, p. 432.

82. TSE to MH, 3 February 1921, *Letters I*, p. 435.

83. TSE to Brigit Patmore, 17 March 1921, *Letters I*, p. 441.

84. Richard Aldington, *Stepping Heavenward. A Record* (Florence: 1931), pp. 47, 48.

85. Conrad Aiken, who was lunching regularly in the City with Eliot in 1920, noted that he always carried his pocket Dante with him. Conrad Aiken, "An Anatomy of Melancholy," in Allen Tate op. cit., p. 194.

86. T. S. Eliot as Gus Krutsch, "Song to the Opherian," *Tyro,* May 1920. Eliot's choice of pseudonym seems significant. In the *Swanee Review* (vol. Lxxiv, No. 1, Special issue, Winter 1966), Francis Noel traces the influence of Petronius's *Satyricon* on *The Waste Land,* noting that "Gus Krutzsch" is "remarkably reminiscent of the English of 'Encolpius,' namely the Crutch or Crotch." "Encolpius" in the *Satyricon* may be translated as "Mr. Encrotch, an appropriate choice for the protagonist of a predominantly sexual story." See Valerie Eliot (ed.), *WL Facs,* op. cit., p. 125, note 8. Seven of the thirteen lines of "Song for the Opherian" appeared later, slightly revised, in Eliot's poem "The wind sprang up at four o'clock."

87. Joseph Conrad, *Heart of Darkness* (London: Wordsworth, 1995), pp. 84–87, 97.

88. T. S. Eliot, *The Sacred Wood,* (New York: Dover Publications Inc., 1998), pp. 30–32.

89. Eliot wrote on *The Duchess of Malfi* for *Art and Letters,* Winter 1919/20.

90. TSE to C. C. Eliot, 6 March 1921, *Letters I*, p. 438.

91. TSE to C. C. Eliot, 31 October 1920, *Letters I*, p. 417.

92. Maurice Haigh-Wood, interview with Michael Hastings, 25 January 1980.

93. VE Diary, 13 December 1935, Bodleian.

94. Bell, *The Diary of Virginia Woolf,* op. cit., vol. 2, p. 77.

95. Visitors' Books of Lady Ottoline Morrell, Garsington Manor, 1921.

96. Journal of Lady Ottoline Morrell, August 1921, Goodman Papers.

97. Osbert Sitwell, unpublished memoir, 19 February 1950, Texas.

98. Quoted in Lyndall Gordon, *T. S. Eliot,* op. cit., p. 171.

99. Michael Hastings, "The Haigh-Woods: The Story of a Family," Introduction in programme for *Tom and Viv,* 3 February 1984.

100. C. C. Eliot to H. Eliot, 8 April 1922, Houghton, quoted by Paul Delany, "T. S. Eliot's Personal Finances, 1915–1929," in *Literature, Money and the Market from Trollope to Amis* (Basingstoke: Palgrave, 2001), p. 260.

101. T. S. Eliot, *The Family Reunion* (London: Faber & Faber, 1939), pp. 20, 21.

102. Giles Evans draws attention to these lines in *Wishwood Revisited: A New Interpretation of T. S. Eliot's "The Family Reunion"* (Lewes: The Book Guild, 1991), p. 32.

103. C. C. Eliot, Memorandum on T. S. Eliot, 1921, prepared for family record of the descendants of William G. and Abigail A. Eliot, Houghton.

104. Mary Lilian Share married Harold Sidney Harmsworth, first Viscount Rothermere (1868–1940) in 1893. He was the younger brother of Alfred Harmsworth, Viscount Northcliffe, who founded the *Daily Mail* (1896) and the *Daily Mirror* (1903). Rothermere took over the *Mirror* in 1914 and was made a viscount in 1919.

105. TSE to OM, 14 July 1921, Texas, *Letters I*, p. 461.

106. VE to Scofield Thayer, 20 July 1921, Beinecke, *Letters I,* p. 462.

107. VE to H. Eliot, 23 August 1921, Texas, *Letters I,* pp. 465–66.

108. H. Eliot to C. C. Eliot, 30 October 1921, Houghton, quoted in Gordon, *T. S. Eliot,* op. cit., p. 171.

109. VE to MH, n.d., Texas.

110. TSE to MH, 1 September 1921, Texas, *Letters I,* p. 467.

111. TSE to MH, postcard, n.d., ?Mid-September 1921, Texas.

112. Quoted in Doyle, op. cit., p. 76. Aldington had left his wife "H.D.," after she had a daughter by another man, for "Arabella" (Dorothy Yorke).

113. TSE to Richard Aldington, 16 September 1921, Texas, *Letters I,* p. 469.

114. In the September 1921 issue of *To-day* Aldington reviewed *The Sacred Wood,* which was published by Methuen with a dedication to H.W.E. (Henry Ware Eliot, TSE's father). Aldington described it as "the most original contribution to our critical literature during the last decade." Other reviews were more disappointing.

115. TSE to Henry Eliot, 3 October 1921, Houghton, *Letters I,* p. 471.

116. VE to MH, n.d., ?December 1921, Texas.

117. TSE to Richard Aldington, 13 October 1921, Texas, *Letters I,* p. 476.

118. VE to Scofield Thayer, 13 October 1921, Beinecke, *Letters I,* p. 478.

119. VE to Violet Schiff, 26 October 1921, British Library, *Letters I,* p. 479.

120. Ibid.

121. Miranda Seymour, *Ottoline Morrell: Life on the Grand Scale* (London: Hodder & Stoughton, 1992), p. 415.

122. TSE to Sydney Schiff, Friday night (?4 November 1921), *Letters I,* p. 484.

123. VE to Bertrand Russell, 1 November 1921, *Letters I,* pp. 482–83.

124. VE to OM, "Monday," n.d., from 39 Inverness Terrace, W2, Texas.

13. The Waste Land

1. VE to MH, "Tuesday," ?November 1921, Texas.

2. VE to MH, 16 November 1921, Texas.

3. Charles Norman, *Ezra Pound* (London: MacDonald, 1969), pp. 243–49.

4. Scofield Thayer to VE, 27 July 1921, Beinecke.

5. ST to VE, 20 October 1921, Beinecke.

6. Humphrey Carpenter, *A Serious Character: The Life of Ezra Pound* (London: Faber & Faber, 1988), p. 415.

7. VE to Henry Eliot, 22 October 1918, *Letters I,* p. 245.

8. TSE to OM, 1 May ?1925. Vivien's poem "Necesse est Perstare" was published in the *Criterion,* April 1925.

9. OM to Dorothy Brett, n.d., 1916, Texas.

10. TSE to Richard Aldington, 4 July 1922, Texas.

11. Vivien Eliot, "A Diary of the Rive Gauche," *Criterion,* vol. III, no. 10 (December), January 1925, pp. 290–94.

12. TSE to OM, 14 March 1933, Texas.

13. TSE to Richard Aldington, 6 November 1921, Texas, *Letters I,* p. 486.

14. Bertrand Russell to OM, n.d., quoted in Donald E. Stanford, "The First Mrs. Eliot," *The Library Chronicle of the University of Texas at Austin,* New Series 40, 1987, p. 89.

15. VE to St. John Hutchinson, 8 December 1935, Texas.

16. TSE to Julian Huxley, 26 October 1921, in Valerie Eliot (ed.), Introduction to *WL Facs* (Harcourt Brace, 1971), p. xxii.

17. Mary Trevelyan, "The Pope of Russell Square 1938–1958," unpublished memoir, 1954. See Chapter 22 for a discussion of Eliot's "voices."

18. Harry Trosman, MD, "T. S. Eliot and the Waste Land: Psychopathological Antecedents and Transformations," *Emotions and Behavior Monographs,* 1987, no. 4 pp. 191–218.

19. T. S. Eliot, 1933, quoted in Trosman, ibid., p. 214.

20. Robert Gathorne-Hardy (ed.), *Ottoline: The Early Memoirs of Lady Ottoline Morrell* (London: Faber & Faber, 1964), p. 237.

21. Huxley remained sceptical about the claim that Vittoz could feel his brain vibrations, although he did feel that he "got a little more control over my depression." Trosman, op. cit., p. 205.

22. TSE to OM, 30 November 1921, Texas.

23. TSE to Henry Eliot, 13 December 1921, Lausanne, *Letters I,* p. 493.

24. Edmund Wilson, "The Poetry of Drouth," *The Dial,* vol. 73, December 1922, pp. 611–14.

25. Edmund Wilson, "Philoctetes: The Wound and the Bow," in *The Wound and the Bow, Seven Studies in Literature* (Athens: Ohio University Press, 1997 [first pub. 1929]), with an introduction by Janet Groth, p. 223. See also Grover Smith Jr., *T. S. Eliot's Poetry and Plays* (University of Chicago Press, 1956).

26. Eliot had read Jessie L. Weston's *From Ritual to Romance.* She linked the Fisher King to an ancient fertility god, identified with Nature itself, arguing that the lance and the grail were sexual symbols, and the adventure in Chapel Perilous an initiation rite. According to Jessie Weston, the worship of the Fisher King was part of the popular Persian cult of Mithraism brought north to Gaul and Britain by Roman legionnaires; when Christianity prevailed, the cult went underground.

27. Virginia Woolf to David Garnett, 20 October 1922, Nigel Nicholson and Joanne Trautmann (eds.), *The Letters of Virginia Woolf, vol. 2, 1912–1922* (New York: Harcourt Brace Jovanovich, 1976), p. 572.

28. From the *Satyricon* of Petronius. The new epigraph replaced Eliot's original choice from Joseph Conrad's *Heart of Darkness.* Valerie Eliot (ed.), *WL Facs,* op. cit., p. 126.

29. Wilson cites the Vedic hymns, Buddha, the Psalms, Ezekiel, Ecclesiastes, Luke, Sappho, Virgil, Ovid, Petronius, the Pervigilium Veneris, St. Augustine, Dante, the Grail Legends, early English poetry, Kyd, Spenser, Shakespeare, John Day, Webster, Middleton, Milton, Goldsmith, Gérard de Nerval, Froude, Baudelaire, Verlaine, Swinburne, Wagner, *The Golden Bough,* Miss Weston's book, various popular ballads, and TSE's earlier poems.

30. Hugh Kenner, *The Invisible Poet: T. S. Eliot* (London: W. H. Allen, 1960), p. 125.

31. "I regret having sent so many readers off on a wild goose chase after Tarot cards and the Holy Grail." T. S. Eliot, *The Frontiers of Criticism* (Minneapolis: University of Minnesota Press, 1956), quoted in James E. Miller, *T. S. Eliot's Personal Waste Land: Exorcism of the Demons* (Philadelphia: University of Pennsylvania Press, 1977), p. 93.

32. A. David Moody, *Thomas Stearns Eliot, Poet* (Cambridge: 1979), p. 79.

33. John T. Mayer, *T. S. Eliot's Silent Voices* (Oxford: OUP, 1989), p. 241.

34. Valerie Eliot (ed.), *WL Facs,* op. cit., p. 1.

35. "Did he live his life again in every detail of desire, temptation, and surrender during that supreme moment of complete knowledge? He cried in a whisper at some image, at some vision—he cried out twice, a cry that was no more than a breath—'The horror! the hor-

ror!.' " Joseph Conrad, *Heart of Darkness,* quoted by Valerie Eliot (ed.), *WL Facs,* op. cit., p. 3.

36. T. S. Eliot, *On Poetry and Poets,* (London: Faber & Faber, 1957), pp. 107–8, quoted in Miller, op. cit., p. 43.

37. Norman, op. cit., p. 351, argues that the foreign phrases were not the portents of the collapse of Western civilisation as some critics afterwards said, but the talk of patients.

38. Robert Sencourt, *T. S. Eliot: A Memoir,* edited by Donald Adamson and L. P. Addison (London: Garnstone Press, 1971), pp. 40, 41.

39. Valerie Eliot (ed.), *WL Facs,* op. cit., note, p. 126.

40. John Peter, "A New Interpretation of *The Waste Land,*" *Essays in Criticism,* 2 (July 1952), p. 245.

41. Miller, op. cit., p. 2.

42. John Peter, "Postscript," *Essays in Criticism,* 19, (April 1969), pp. 165–66.

43. T. S. Eliot editorial, "A Commentary," *The Criterion,* April 1934.

44. Similar lines occur in French in an earlier poem, "Dans le Restaurant": "Phlebas the Phoenician, suspended 15 days drowned,/Forgot the cries of sea gulls and the surge of Cornwall . . . Nevertheless, he was once a handsome man, and tall," quoted in Miller, op. cit., p. 111. See Grover Smith, "Observations on Eliot's 'Death by Water,' *Accent 6* (Summer 1946), pp. 257–63, for speculations on the sexual connotations of the section, including the origin of the name Phlebas, which Smith believed to be derived from the Greek "phlép: phlebós," a vein. "But even more remarkable," writes Smith, "is the fact that the Greek word has another meaning, which is the same as that of 'phallos' . . . it confirms my theory that the Phoenician Sailor represents the commerce of lust."

45. Miller, op. cit., pp. 68, 69, Valerie Eliot (ed.), *WL Facs,* p. 93.

46. Richard Wagner, *Tristan und Isolde,* Scene 2, lines 1–4.

47. The character of Mr. Scogan, who impersonates Sesostris the Sorceress in *Chrome Yellow,* is based on Bertrand Russell. Informed readers of *The Waste Land* would have recognised Russell as Madame Sosostris, who in the first draft was a "clairvoyant," later changed to "clairvoyante."

48. John Peter, "A New Interpretation . . .," op. cit., pp. 247–48.

49. Valerie Eliot (ed.), *WL Facs,* op. cit., "He Do The Police in Different Voices," Part 1, "The Burial of the Dead," pp. 6–9. Eliot said he associated "the man with three staves" from the Tarot pack, "quite arbitrarily, with the Fisher King himself." Notes to *The Waste Land,* p. 147.

50. Helen Gardner, *The Art of T. S. Eliot* (London: Faber & Faber, 1949), p. 172. "As in the *Waste Land,* it is by 'the awful daring of a moment's surrender' that we exist, by praying . . . The meaningless monotony and pointless waste of living finds its purpose in the Virgin's words: 'Be it unto me according to thy word.' "

51. Valerie Eliot (ed.), *WL Facs,* p. 77.

52. There are several versions of the line: "My friend, my blood, shaking within my heart," is another. Ibid.

53. Ibid., "Dirge," p. 123.

54. The first of "Doris's Dream Songs" was republished as "Eyes that last I saw in tears," *CP,* p. 147; and the other two became incorporated in "The Hollow Men," p. 87.

55. T. S. Eliot, "Doris's Dream Songs," I, II, III, *The Chapbook, A Miscellany* (No. 39), November 1924.

56. Valerie Eliot points out that there is no such word as "Opherian," and it is possible that

Eliot meant "Orpharion," a musical instrument known as the "poor man's lute" (*WL Facs,* p. 130). In an interesting discussion, Mayer (op. cit.) speculates that "the Opherion is a split-self symbol . . . of Eliot himself, who, as Gus Krutzsch, bleeds between two worlds, that of the *August* Spirit and the real *crotch,* combining lover and uncertain artist, person and . . . ineffective instrument . . ." The mythical Orpheus entered the world of shades to rescue his wife Eurydice, which he was allowed to do on condition that he did not look back; to do so condemned her to remain in hell—as Vivien is condemned because Eliot looks back to Verdenal. The poem focuses on the love that is looked back upon. Similarly the allusion to Arion emphasises the backward glance to a beloved friend from the past; Arion was a musician and favourite of Periander, King of Corinth, whom he left to travel overseas, despite Periander's pleas. Arion is abandoned at sea to die, but his song casts a spell on a dolphin, which saves him and reunites him with Periander. It is another myth which for Eliot would have had parallels with his relationship with Verdenal, both men being separated unwillingly by journeys over water. See Mayer, op. cit., pp. 257–58.

57. Valerie Eliot (ed.), *WL Facs,* p. 99, published in *The Tyro* (April 1921) by "Gus Krutsch." This poem contains Eliot's line, comparing the river to "a face that sweats with tears," which Pound cut from *The Waste Land.*

58. Miller, op. cit., pp. 17, 18.

59. Mayer, op. cit., p. 206.

60. Alan Ansen, *The Table Talk of W. H. Auden* (London: Faber & Faber, 1991), p. 54.

61. "The Death of the Duchess," Valerie Eliot (ed.), *WL Facs,* pp. 105–7.

62. Vivien Eliot, "The Paralysed Woman," unpublished short story, 1922, Bodleian.

63. Elizabeth M. Brennan (ed.), John Webster, *The Duchess of Malfi* (London and Tonbridge: Ernest Ben), p. 45, III, ii, lines 69–70.
    You have cause to love me, I entered you into my heart
    Before you would vouchsafe to call for the keys.

64. TSE to Henny Ware Eliot Senior, 23 July 1915, *Letters I,* p. 110.

65. E. W. F. Tomlin, *T. S. Eliot: A Friendship* (London: Routledge, 1988), p. 230. Valerie Eliot confirms that Eliot restored the line from memory in 1960, *WL Facs,* p. 126.

66. Valerie Eliot (ed.), *WL Facs,* op. cit., p. 107.

67. Eliot suggested his inspiration came from the game of chess in Thomas Middleton's *Women, Beware Women* (c. 1623).

68. VE as "F. M.," "Letters of the Moment—1," *Criterion,* vol. 2, no. vi (February 1924), pp. 220–22.

69. VE n.d., writing book, Bodleian.

70. Vivien portrays herself as "Sybilla" or "Sibylla" in unpublished stories, "The Paralysed Woman" (1922) and "Médecine à la Mode," n.d., and in "Thé Dansant" (1924), and "Fête Galante," (1925) in *Criterion.*

71. Valerie Eliot (ed.), *WL Facs,* op. cit., p. 11.

72. Valerie Eliot (ed.), *WL Facs,* op. cit., p. 11; see also Mayer, op. cit., p. 264.

73. *WL Facs,* op. cit., p. 13: This is another reference to the doomed Paolo and Francesca, to whom Eliot compared himself and Vivien. They are in the second circle of Hell, among the souls of the lustful: ". . . the two that go together and seem so light upon the wind." Dante, *Inferno,* v, lines 73–75. See Valerie Eliot's note, *WL Facs,* p. 126.

74. VE to MH, 27 September 1928, Texas.

75. Mary Trevelyan, "The Pope of Russell Square 1938–1954," November 1942.

76. Mayer points out that in *Metamorphoses* Ovid relates that Apollo vows to keep Hyacinth

with him in memory and in his poetry: " 'You will be/With me forever, and my songs and music/Will tell of you, and you will be reborn/As a new flower.' Eliot mentions both the flower (lowercase hyacinth) and the myth (uppercase Hyacinth)." Mayer op. cit., p. 255.

77. Valerie Eliot (ed.), *WL Facs*, p. 148.

78. Viola Tree, "Mayfair and Bohemia," *Criterion*, vol. 3, no. 10, January 1925.

79. Aldous Huxley, untitled poem, 14 February 1927, quoted in Margaret Ratliff, "The Correspondence of Mary Hutchinson: A New Look at Bloomsbury, Eliot and Huxley," thesis (University of Texas at Austin, 1991), ch. 5, "Mary Hutchinson and the Huxleys," p. 221.

80. Mary Hutchinson to Lytton Strachey, 3 August 1917, Texas.

81. Osbert Sitwell, unpublished memoir on TSE and his marriage, 19 February 1950, Texas.

82. Valerie Eliot (ed.), *WL Facs*, op. cit., p. 15.

83. VE to MH, n.d., ?1922, Texas.

84. Miller, op. cit., p. 87.

85. Valerie Eliot (ed.), *WL Facs*, op. cit., p. 23.

86. Ibid.

87. Valerie Eliot (ed.), *WL Facs*, op. cit., pp. 23, 27.

88. T. S. Eliot, *Selected Essays* (London: Faber & Faber, 1932), pp. 234–35. Quoted by John Peter, "Postscript" to his "A New Interpretation of *The Waste Land*," *Essays in Criticism*, 19 (April 1969).

89. Miller argues that the "effect of the original passage is to lend emphasis to the Eugenides encounter, with the frantic singing of the nightingale in a fragmentary context, coming immediately after it, highly suggestive as to some obscure and sordid consummation, some kind of hasty and covert fulfillment of the poet's momentary need." Miller, op. cit., p. 97. See Valerie Eliot (ed.), *WL Facs*, op. cit., p. 31: "London, the swarming life you kill and breed,/Huddled between the concrete and the sky;/Responsive to the momentary need . . ." follows the sudden interjection, "Twit twit twit/Jug jug jug jug jug jug/Tereu" of the "rudely forc'd" Philomel.

90. John Peale Bishop to Edmund Wilson, November 1922, 28 rue de la Rochefoucauld, Paris, Edmund Wilson Papers, Yale. I am indebted to Brian Breman at University of Texas for drawing my attention to this letter.

91. "The Fire Sermon" in Valerie Eliot (ed.), *WL Facs*, op. cit., p. 53. T. S. Eliot's note is on p. 148.

92. Peter, "A New Interpretation . . . ," op. cit., pp. 259–60.

93. Eliot, *Selected Essays*, op. cit., pp. 374–75.

94. Valerie Eliot (ed.), *WL Facs*, op. cit., p. 85. Eliot recalled, in his notes to *The Waste Land*, that during one of Shackleton's Antarctic expeditions the explorers, at the extremity of their strength, had the constant delusion that there was one more member than could be actually counted. See *WL Facs*, p. 148.

95. Ibid., p. 79.

96. Jessie Weston writes of the initiation ritual in the Chapel: "the Mystery ritual comprised a double initiation, the Lower, into the mysteries of generation, i.e. of physical Life; the higher, into the Spiritual Divine Life, where man is made one with God." See Mayer, op. cit., p. 284.

97. See Peter, "A New Interpretation . . . ," op. cit., p. 265. See also Miller, op. cit., pp. 39, 131.

98. T. S. Eliot, *The Use of Poetry and the Use of Criticism* (Harvard: Harvard University Press, 1986), p. 119.

99. Valerie Eliot (ed.), *WL Facs,* op. cit., p. 117.

100. Thomas Kyd, *The Spanish Tragedy* (London: Penguin, 1998). Hieronymo, an antecedent of Shakespeare's "Hamlet," is driven nearly mad with grief after his son is murdered. His life became an "endless Tragedie," as Eliot felt his own to be.

14. A Wild Heart in a Cage

1.   Ezra Pound to TSE, 24 Saturnus An 1 (24 December 1921), *Letters I,* p. 497.

2.   TSE to EP, ?24 January 1922, *Letters I,* p. 504.

3.   EP to TSE, ?27 January 1922, *Letters I,* p. 505. Pound addressed Eliot as "Filio dilecto mihi, my beloved son."

4.   "Eliot's *Waste Land* is I think the justification of the 'movement' of our modern experiment since 1900." EP to Felix Scheling, *Letters I,* pp. 180–81. Pound cut three poems: "Exequy," with its confessional lines "SOVEGNA VOS AL TEMPS DE MON DOLOR/Consiros vei la pasada folor (Be mindful in due time of my pain/In thought I see my past madness," from Eliot's favourite Canto XXVI of Dante's *Purgatorio,* the canto of "the lustful," (facs 130); "Elegy"; and "Dirge."

5.   Ezra Pound, "Sage Homme": a humorous poem sent by Pound to Eliot on 24 December 1922, in which he described himself as the midwife of *The Waste Land.*

6.   VE to Mary Hutchinson, 12 January 1922, Hotel du Bon Lafontaine, Paris, Texas.

7.   TSE to EP, ?24 January 1922, *Letters I,* p. 504.

8.   EP to TSE, ?27 January 1922, *Letters I,* p. 505.

9.   Philip Hoare, *Oscar Wilde's Last Stand* (New York: Arcade Publishing Inc., 1977), p. 109.

10. MH to Lytton Strachey, 9 September 1927, Texas.

11. Michel Foucault, *The History of Sexuality: An Introduction* (Harmondsworth: Penguin, 1984), p. 43.

12. Lytton Strachey to Dora Carrington, 3 June 1923, Michael Holroyd, *Lytton Strachey* (London: Vintage, 1995), p. 856.

13. Hoare, op. cit., p. 90.

14. Joan Smith, *Moralities: Sex, Money and Power in the Twenty-first Century* (London: Penguin Press, 2001), p. 110.

15. Hoare, op. cit., p. 126.

16. Hoare, op. cit., p. 188.

17. Foucault, op. cit., p. 101.

18. Louis Stanley, *Public Masks & Private Faces* (London: Quartet Books, 1986), p. 59.

19. TSE to John Quinn, 15 June 1922 and 19 July 1922, in B. L. Reid, *The Man from New York: John Quinn and His Friends* (New York: Oxford University Press, 1968), pp. 534–35.

20. John Quinn to TSE, 28 July 1922, in Reid, op. cit.

21. TSE to Scofield Thayer, 20 January 1922, Pound Papers, Beinecke.

22. ST to TSE, 14 July 1921, Beinecke.

23. ST to TSE, 18 December 1921, Beinecke.

24. ST to TSE, 29 January 1922, Beinecke.

25. ST to TSE, 12 March 1922, Beinecke.

26. TSE to ST, 16 March 1922, Beinecke.

27. TSE to Sydney Schiff, 20 April 1922, British Library, *Letters I,* p. 522.

28. T. S. Eliot, "London Letter," May 1922, *The Dial,* vol. LXXII, Jan.–June 1922.

29. VE to MH, n.d., Texas.

30. TSE to OM, n.d., Texas.

31. TSE to Richard Aldington, 13 July 1922, *Letters I,* p. 541.

32. TSE to OM, n.d., ?early summer 1922, Texas.

33. EP to John Quinn, postmark 21 February 1922, Timothy Materer (ed.), *The Selected Letters of Ezra Pound to John Quinn 1915–1924* (Durham and London: Duke University Press, 1991), p. 206.

34. *Letters I,* p. xxvi.

35. EP to William Carlos Williams, 18 March 1922, D. D. Paige (ed.), *The Letters of Ezra Pound 1907–1941* (London: Faber & Faber, 1951), p. 238.

36. Bel Esprit circular, ibid., pp. 238–39.

37. Arsenic and bismuth compounds were the standard treatment for syphilis before the discovery of penicillin.

38. EP to JQ, 4–5 July 1922, Materer (ed.), *Selected Letters of Pound to Quinn,* op. cit., pp. 209–11.

39. TSE to OM, 26 April 1922, Texas.

40. Richard Aldington to Amy Lowell, 5 May 1922, Norman T. Gates (ed.), *Richard Aldington: An Autobiography in Letters* (Philadelphia: University of Pennsylvania Press, 1992), p. 67.

41. This letter has not been traced.

42. VE to Richard Aldington, n.d., ?Spring 1922, Texas, *Letters I,* pp. 543–44.

43. Thomas S. Szasz, MD, *The Myth of Mental Illness: Foundations of a Theory of Personal Conduct* (New York: Harper and Row, 1974) revised edition, pp. 111–21.

44. Bertrand Russell, *Autobiography, vol. 1* (London: George Allen & Unwin, 1968), p. 10.

45. John T. Mayer, *T. S. Eliot's Silent Voices* (Oxford: 1989), p. 185.

46. Szasz, op. cit., pp. 121–24. See also S. Freud, *On Psychopathology: Inhibitions, Symptoms and Anxiety and Other Works* (London: Penguin Freud Library, vol. 10, 1979), p. 99.

47. TSE to OM, "Castle Hotel, Tunbridge," n.d., ?April 1922, Texas.

48. TSE to OM, postcard of Lugano, 27 May 1922, Texas.

49. EP to JQ, 4 and 5 July 1922, Materer (ed.), *Selected Letters of Pound to Quinn,* op. cit., p. 210.

50. VE to EP, 27 June 1922, *Letters I,* pp. 532–33.

51. VE to Violet Schiff, 26 October 1921, British Library.

52. TSE to OM, 15 June 1922, Texas.

53. VE to EP, 27 June 1922, *Letters I,* p. 532.

54. TSE to OM, 15 June 1922, Texas.

55. TSE to Richard Aldington, 7 April 1921, Texas.

56. TSE to OM, 18 July 1922, Texas.

57. VE to MH, 16 November 1921, Texas.

58. VE to MH, 19 July 1922, Texas.

59. "Disorders of the digestive system due to psychological factors are common and they may mimic organic disease. Stress may be associated with a symptom such as dyspepsia ('indigestion'), abdominal discomfort or diarrhoea . . . Gastrointestinal functions . . . can alter with change in emotion. Patients with anxiety states may develop a wide range of alimentary symptoms such as dryness of the mouth, a feeling of a lump in the throat . . . anorexia, nausea, vomiting . . . abdominal pain, diarrhoea or constipation. Patients with a depressive illness may have similar complaints . . ." John Macleod (ed.), *Davidson's Principles and Practices of Medicine* (London: Churchill Livingstone, 1977), p. 418.

60. VE to OM, "2 Creed Cottages," n.d., ?summer 1922, Texas.

61. TSE to EP, 19 July 1922, *Letters I,* p. 549.

62. Evelyn Waugh, *The Ordeal of Gilbert Penfold* (first published London: Chapman & Hall, 1957; Penguin, 1962), pp. 23, 63, 138, 156. Waugh encouraged Muriel Spark, whose first novel *The Comforters* (1957) treated a similar theme of a Catholic novelist hearing voices and confessed to her that, as most of his friends knew, his novel was based on his own experience of auditory hallucinations. See Muriel Spark, *Curriculum Vitae* (London: Penguin, 1993), pp. 207–8.

63. VE to Sydney Schiff, "Sunday," ?April 1924, from 38 Burleigh Mansions, St. Martin's Lane, London WC2.

64. Virginia Woolf, "On Being Ill," *The Moment and Other Essays* (New York: Harcourt Brace & Co., 1947), pp. 11, 12.

65. Lyndall Gordon suggests (*T.S. Eliot: An Imperfect Life,* p. 216) that "Felice" may be based on Mary Hutchinson, but I feel Mary was too sophisticated to have been the model for "Felice," who does the chores in her overall. Vivien seems to have had a help/companion named Felise (*sic*) to whom she refers in a letter to Ottoline Morrell, n.d., saying she has "settled" with Felise, whom she can afford to keep if she gives up Ellen.

66. Vivien Eliot, "The Paralysed Woman," 1922, Bodleian.

67. Ibid.

68. Elaine Showalter, *Hystories: Hysterical Epidemics and Modern Culture* (London: Picador, 1997), p. 103. In a 1991 production of *Hedda Gabler,* influenced by feminist interpretations of hysteria, Deborah Warner and Fiona Shaw presented Hedda as a woman having a nervous breakdown.

69. VE to MH, 19 April 1923, Texas.

70. Vivien Eliot, "The Paralysed Woman," 1922, Bodleian.

71. Showalter, op. cit., p. 101.

72. VE to MH, "Thursday," August 1922, Texas.

73. The Hogarth Press published *The Waste Land* in September 1923. See introduction to Jan.–March 1923, Nigel Nicolson and Joanne Trautmann (eds.), *The Letters of Virginia Woolf, vol. III, 1923–28* (London: Hogarth Press, 1977), p. 1, and Anne Olivier Bell (ed.), *The Diary of Virginia Woolf,* vol. 2 (London: Hogarth Press, 1978), 23 June 1922, p. 178.

74. Virginia found *Ulysses* "an illiterate, underbred book," which seemed to her "the book of a self-taught working man, & we all know how distressing they are, how egotistic, raw, striking, & ultimately nauseating." Bell (ed.), *Diary of Virginia Woolf,* vol. 2, op. cit., p. 189.

75. "Great Tom," Bell (ed.), *The Diary of Virginia Woolf,* vol. 2, op. cit., p. 189. "If it were not for his wife's . . ." VW to Maynard Keynes, 12 Feb. 1923, Nicolson and Trautmann (eds.), *Letters of Virginia Woolf,* vol. 3, op. cit., pp. 11–12.

76. TSE to EP, 28 July 1922, *Letters I,* p. 553.

77. TSE to Richard Aldington, "Friday," ?1922, Texas.

78. TSE to RA, 30 June 1922, *Letters I,* p. 537.

79. TSE to RA, "Friday," ?end 1922, Texas.

80. Bell (ed.), *The Diary of Virginia Woolf,* vol. 2, op. cit., 3 August 1922, p. 187.

81. Ibid., 12 March 1922, p. 170.

82. Ibid., 27 September 1922, p. 204.

83. Ibid., 6 and 17 March 1923, pp. 238–39.

84. Osbert Sitwell, *Laughter in the Next Room* (London: Macmillan, 1949), pp. 15, 16.

85. Léonide Massine to OM, n.d., 38 Bloomsbury Street. Massine Papers, Texas.

86. Léonide Massine, *My Life in Ballet* (London: Macmillan, 1968), p. 137.

87. Sitwell, op. cit., p. 14.

88. TSE to MH, 28 April 1922, Texas, *Letters I,* p. 523.

89. TSE to MH, "Friday," postmark 24 June 1922, Texas, *Letters I,* p. 529.

15. "Fanny Marlow"

1. VE to OM, 15 September 1922, Texas, *Letters I,* p. 570.

2. VE to MH, postcard of Eglise St. Germain, 23 September 1922, Texas.

3. VE to MH, postcard of Lyon, 20 October 1922, Texas.

4. VE to MH, 21 October 1922, Texas.

5. TSE to MH, 7 October 1922, Texas.

6. TSE to MH, 18 June 1921, Texas.

7. TSE to MH, "Tuesday," n.d., ?late 1922, Texas.

8. Anne Chisholm, *Nancy Cunard* (London: Sidgwick & Jackson, 1979), p. 331.

9. Ibid., p. 163.

10. T. S. Eliot, "London Letter," *The Dial,* August 1921, p. 214, quoted in Lynn Garafola, *Diaghilev's Ballets Russes* (New York: Da Capo Press, 1998), pp. 338–39. Garafola remarks that allusions to the Russian ballet appear in many of TSE's writings.

11. T. S. Eliot, "Dramatis Personae," *Criterion,* April 1923, pp. 305–6.

12. Garafola, op. cit., p. 339.

13. Eliot, "Dramatis Personae," op. cit., p. 306.

14. Edward J. Dent, "Covent Garden: 'Pulcinella,' " *Athenaeum,* 18 June 1920, quoted in Garafola, op. cit., p. 341.

15. Garafola, op. cit., p. 242.

16. T. S. Matthews, *Great Tom: Notes Towards the Definition of T. S. Eliot* (London: Weidenfeld and Nicolson, 1974), p. 78.

17. "Personally I should not have cut out some of the parts that Pound advised you to cut out." Quinn to TSE, 26 February 1923, in B. L. Reid, *The Man from New York: John Quinn and His Friends* (New York: Oxford University Press, 1968), p. 580. Quinn immediately realised that the real value of the *Waste Land* manuscript lay in the fact that it was the only evidence of the difference which Pound's criticism made to the poem (p. 540). Eliot also gave Quinn the leather-bound notebook containing the Bolo and Colombo verses dating back to 1909, which, he told Quinn, "have never been printed and which I am sure you will agree ought never to be printed, and, in putting them in your hands, I beg you fervently to keep them to yourself and see that they are never printed" (21 September 1922).

18. Humphrey Carpenter, *A Serious Character: The Life of Ezra Pound* (London: Faber & Faber, 1988), p. 415. Pound was finally awarded the *Dial* prize in 1927.

19. Peter du Sautoy, "T. S. Eliot: Personal Reminiscences," in James Olney (ed.), *T. S. Eliot: Essays from The Southern Review* (Oxford: Clarendon Press, 1988), from *The Southern Review,* vol. 21, no. 4 (Autumn 1985), pp. 947–56.

20. Manuscript leaves from the 1909 notebook, Colombo and Bolo poems in ink and pencil, Pound Collection, Beinecke.

21. VE to Sydney Schiff, 16 October 1922, *Letters I,* p. 584.

22. Reid, op. cit., p. 538.

23. EP to John Quinn, 4–5 July 1922, Timothy Materer (ed.), *The Selected Letters of Ezra Pound to John Quinn 1915–1929* (Durham and London: Duke University Press, 1991), p. 209.

24. Quoted in John Pearson, *Façades: Edith, Osbert and Sacheverell Sitwell* (London: 1978), p. 176.

25. VE to EP, 2 November 1922, Lilly, *Letters I,* p. 588.

26. TSE to EP, 3 November 1922, Lilly, *Letters I,* p. 589.

27. VE to EP, 2 November 1922, *Letters I,* p. 588.

28. EP to TSE, 4 November 1922, *Letters I,* p. 589.

29. TSE to EP, 7 November 1922, *Letters I,* p. 592.

30. *Criterion,* April 1923, p. 307.

31. "Felix Morrison," "Mrs. Pilkington," in *Criterion,* October 1924, pp. 103–6; "Fanny Marlow," "Diary of the Rive Gauche," in *Criterion,* January 1925, pp. 291–97; "Fanny Marlow," "Diary of the Rive Gauche II," in *Criterion,* April 1925, pp. 425–29. Compare Katherine Mansfield, "Je Ne Parle Pas Français," *Bliss and Other Stories* (first pub. London: Constable, 1920; Penguin, 1962), p. 62. See also Lyndall Gordon, *T. S. Eliot: An Imperfect Life* (London: Vintage, 1998), p. 217.

32. EP to TSE, 4 November 1922, *Letters I,* p. 589.

33. VE to MH, n.d., 1919, Texas.

34. VE to MH, "November," ?1919, Texas.

35. Gordon, *T. S. Eliot,* op. cit., p. 193.

36. TSE to EP, 28 July 1922, *Letters I,* p. 553.

37. TSE to EP, n.d., 1927, Beinecke.

38. Carpenter, op. cit., p. 413.

39. VE to EP, n.d., ?1924, Beinecke.

40. TSE to Richard Aldington, 8 April 1924, Texas.

41. EP to John Quinn, 5 July 1922, Materer (ed.), *Selected Letters of Ezra Pound to John Quinn,* p. 209.

42. VE to OM, 15 September 1922, Texas, *Letters I,* p. 570.

43. Richard Aldington to Amy Lowell, 7 July 1922, Norman Gates (ed.), *Richard Aldington: An Autobiography in Letters* (Philadelphia: University of Pennsylvania Press, 1992), p. 69.

44. This receipt, June 1923, signed by TSE over two George V penny stamps, is in the Pound Collection, Beinecke.

45. *Liverpool Post,* 16 November 1922, cutting enclosed by TSE in a letter to RA, 18 November 1922, Texas.

46. TSE to RA, 18 November 1922, Texas.

47. Quoted in Hermione Lee, *Virginia Woolf* (London: Vintage, 1997), p. 442, from Anne Olivier Bell (ed.), *The Diary of Virginia Woolf,* vol. 2 (London: Hogarth Press, 1978), 22 March 1921, pp. 103–4.

48. Virginia Woolf to RA, 21 January 1923, Nigel Nicolson and Joanne Trautmann (eds.), *The Letters of Virginia Woolf,* vol. 3 (London: Hogarth Press, 1977), p. 7.

49. VW to OM, 21? January 1923, Nicolson and Trautmann (eds.), *The Letters of Virginia Woolf,* vol. 3, op. cit., p. 8.

50. VW to RA, 26 January 1923, in ibid., p. 9.

51. VE to MH, ?late 1922, Texas, *Letters I,* p. 587.

52. VW to Clive Bell, early February 1923, in Nicolson and Trautmann (eds.), *The Letters of Virginia Woolf,* vol. 3, op. cit., p. 11.

53. VW to Maynard Keynes, 12 February 1923, in ibid., p. 12.

54. VW to Lytton Strachey, 23 February 1923, in ibid., p. 14.

55. Anne Olivier Bell (ed.), *The Diary of Virginia Woolf,* vol. 2, op. cit., 19 February 1923, p. 236.

56. Ibid., 17 March 1923, p. 239.

57. VW to Vanessa Bell, ?12 March 1923, Nicolson and Trautmann (eds.), *Letters,* vol. 3, op. cit., p. 21.

58. VW to Maynard Keynes, 13 March 1923, in ibid., p. 20.

59. Bell (ed.), *The Diary of Virginia Woolf,* vol. 2, op. cit., 17 March 1923, p. 239.

60. Ibid., 23 March 1923, p. 240.

61. Gordon, *T. S. Eliot,* op. cit., pp. 197, 199.

62. Ibid., p. 198.

63. TSE to EP, 15 November 1922, *Letters I,* pp. 597–98.

64. TSE to Henry Eliot, 11 October 1922, *Letters I,* p. 579.

65. TSE to Richard Aldington, ?April, 1924, Texas.

66. T. S. Eliot, "On the Eve," in *Criterion,* January 1925. The style of this piece is typical of Vivien, and from the manuscript it seems unlikely that TSE did more than tinker with it.

67. TSE to EP, 7 November 1922, *Letters I,* p. 593.

68. VE to MH, 5 December 1922, Texas.

69. TSE to OM, 12 December 1922, Texas, *Letters I,* p. 611.

70. TSE to RA, 8 November 1922, *Letters I,* p. 594.

71. TSE to Henry Ware Eliot Jr., 31 December 1922, *Letters I,* p. 627.

72. TSE to OM, 5 January 1923, Texas.

73. John Pearson quotes Osbert Sitwell's unpublished memoir of Eliot, Texas, in *Façades,* op. cit., p. 239.

74. Sitwell memoir, op. cit., p. 14.

75. Pearson, op. cit., p. 239.

76. TSE to MH, postmark 1923, Texas.

77. RA to Harold Monro, 24 October 1920, Norman Gates (ed.), *Richard Aldington,* op. cit., p. 63.

78. TSE to VW, 2 April 1923, Berg.

79. TSE to MH, 23 March 1923, Texas.

80. TSE to OM, 2 March 1923, Texas.

81. VE to MH, 5 March 1923, Texas.

82. VE to MH, 5 March 1923, Texas.

83. TSE to OM, n.d., ?early April 1923, address "2 Milestone Cottages, Nr. Chi, Sussex," Texas.

84. Ibid.

85. TSE to MH, 3 April 1923, Texas.

86. TSE to MH, 26 and 30 April 1923, Texas.

87. TSE to OM, n.d., ?May 1923, Texas.

88. See Keith Thomas, *Religion and the Decline of Magic* (London: Penguin, 1973), pp. 209–51, for an explanation of the magical tradition.

89. Michel Foucault, *Madness and Civilization: A History of Insanity in the Age of Reason,* trans. Richard Howard (New York: Random House, 1965), pp. 274–75.

90. TSE to OM, n.d., "2 Milestone Cottages, Old Fishbourne," ?April 1923, Texas.

91. VE to OM, 28 May 1923, Texas.

92. VE to MH, 19 April 1923, Texas. In her entry for 13 June 1923, Virginia says she should

be writing to Vivien, and will do so "directly, on the instant." TSE mentions in a letter to Ottoline (n.d.) ?May 1923 that Vivien has received a "curious" letter from Virginia. He chides Ottoline for not writing to Vivien, who "hopes for a line."

93. VW to Roger Fry, 18 May 1923, Nicolson and Trautmann (eds.), *The Letters of Virginia Woolf,* vol. 3, op. cit., p. 38.

94. VE to MH, n.d., "2 Milestone Cottages, Old Fishbourne," ?May 1923, Texas.

95. TSE to MH, 9 August 1923, Texas.

96. TSE to MH, telegram, 10 August 1923, Texas.

97. Bell (ed.), *The Diary of Virginia Woolf,* vol. 2, op. cit., 17 July 1923, pp. 256–57.

98. VE to MH, pencil note, n.d., ?May 1923, Texas.

99. TSE to OM, p.m. 18 June 1923, Texas.

100. VW to TSE, 4 June 1923, Nicolson and Trautmann (eds.), *The Letters of Virginia Woolf,* vol. 3, p. 45. This was Virginia's first meeting with Edward Sackville-West, who was already a friend of TSE's.

101. VW to Jacques Raverat, 24 January 1925, in ibid., p. 155.

102. Bell (ed.), *The Diary of Virginia Woolf,* vol. 2, op. cit., 4 June 1923, pp. 243–44. Virginia visited Garsington on 2 June, Eliot a fortnight later.

103. Ibid., 19 February 1923. Philip Morrell had a son by his secretary, Alice Jones, in 1917, and another child by one of the Garsington maids in 1923.

104. TSE to OM, n.d., "The Criterion," paper, 9 Clarence Gate Gardens, ?May 1923, Texas.

105. VE to OM, pencil, n.d., ?June 1923, Texas.

106. TSE to OM, 10 July 1923, Texas.

16. Deceits and Desires

1. VE to MH, n.d., ?1923, Texas.

2. VE to OM, n.d., ?1923, Texas.

3. TSE to Dorothy Pound, 27 Oct.? 1923, Lilly.

4. TSE to VW, 22 May 1924, Monk's House Papers, Sussex.

5. TSE to OM, September 1923, Texas.

6. Untitled verse about Jack's "row" with Tom at 2 Milestone Cottages, Old Fishbourne, n.d.,?December 1923, loose-leaf book (MSS. Eng. Misc. c. 624), VE Papers, Bodleian.

7. Maurice Haigh-Wood, quoted in Michael Hastings, *Tom and Viv* (London: Penguin, 1985), p. 51.

8. Untitled verses about Jack, ?December 1923, MSS Eng. Misc. c. 624, loose-leaf book, VE Papers, Bodleian.

9. VE to VW, "Sunday 5th" 1923, Monk's House Papers, Sussex.

10. Michael Holroyd, *Lytton Strachey* (London: Vintage, 1995), p. 777 fn.

11. Journal of Lady Ottoline Morrell, 26 March 1934, Goodman Papers.

12. Anne Olivier Bell (ed.), *The Diary of Virginia Woolf,* vol. 2, 1920–1924 (London: Penguin, 1978), p. 278. Bell notes that the Woolfs had been dining with Clive and Vanessa Bell and Mary Hutchinson at the Commercio before going on to Eliot's party.

13. Michael Hastings, interview with the author, April 2000.

14. Hastings, Introduction to *Tom and Viv,* op. cit., p. 18.

15. VE Personal Account Book, Dec. 1927–April 1932, MSS Eng. Misc. c. 621, VE Papers, Bodleian.

16. VE Diary, 1 January 1935, Bodleian.

17. Mary Trevelyan, unpublished memoir, "The Pope of Russell Square, 1938–1958 (Twenty Years 'and no to-morrow')," 28 February 1952, p. 91.

18. Ibid., 16 August 1954, p. 119.

19. Ibid., p. 121. There are many references to Eliot's "Trade Union rules" with regard to not seeing people, which Mary found "frightening" (p. 94 and passim). The "Rules" governed his life minutely, for example, he did not allow himself to play Patience before breakfast during Lent. One Rule to which Mary objected was that he would not see the same person two days running.

20. Ibid., Preface, and p. 68.

21. T. S. Eliot, *The Cocktail Party* (London: Faber & Faber, 1958), p. 123; Sir Henry Harcourt-Reilly, the psychiatrist, tells Edward: ". . . You realised, what your wife has justly remarked,/That you had never been in love with anybody;/Which made you suspect that you were incapable/Of loving. To men of a certain type/The suspicion that they are incapable of loving/Is as disturbing to their self-esteem/As, in cruder men, the fear of impotence." (Act II, sc. 1.)

22. Quoted in Humphrey Carpenter, *A Serious Character: The Life of Ezra Pound* (London: Faber & Faber, 1988), p. 415.

23. Journal of Lady Ottoline Morrell, 19 June 1923, Goodman Papers.

24. Mary Trevelyan, "Pope of Russell Square," op. cit., 20 August 1950, p. 75, and 28 August 1954, p. 122.

25. T. S. Eliot, "Sweeney Erect," published in *Art and Letters* (Summer 1919) and *Poems* (1920) and in Christopher Ricks (ed.), *Inventions of the March Hare. T. S. Eliot: Poems 1909–1917* (New York: Harcourt Brace, 1996).

26. Ronald Schuchard, *Eliot's Dark Angel: Intersections of Life and Art* (Oxford: Oxford University Press, 1999), p. 92.

27. "Sweeney Erect," *CP,* p. 92.

28. T. S. Eliot, "Elegy," in Valerie Eliot (ed.), *WL Facs,* p. 117.

29. Schuchard, op. cit., p. 124.

30. TSE to EP, 3 January 1934, Beinecke.

31. "The Hollow Men," *CP,* op. cit., p. 87.

32. "East Coker" from *Four Quartets* (1940), *CP,* op. cit., p. 200.

33. TSE to VW, 12 June ?1924, Monk's House Papers, Sussex.

34. TSE to VW, 27 August 1924, Monk's House Papers, Sussex.

35. TSE to MH, 27 August 1924, Texas.

36. Trevelyan, "Pope of Russell Square," op. cit., August 1958.

37. Henry Eliot Jr. to C. C. Eliot, 15 March 1925, Houghton.

38. Henry Eliot Jr. to C. C. Eliot, 9 January 1924, Houghton.

39. Henry Eliot Jr. to C. C. Eliot, 17 February 1925, Houghton.

40. Henry Eliot Jr. to C. C. Eliot, 21 November 1923, Houghton.

41. Henry Eliot Jr. to C. C. Eliot, 16 March 1924, Houghton.

42. Paul Delany, "Appendix: T. S. Eliot's Personal Finances, 1915–1929," in *Literature, Money and the Market from Trollope to Amis* (Basingstoke: Palgrave, 2001), pp. 264, 265.

43. A complicated formula was discussed by which Tom would be compensated for any loss of profit.

44. Henry Eliot Jr. to C. C. Eliot, 3 March 1924, Houghton.

45. TSE to MH, 2 January 1924, Texas.

46. VE to Sydney Schiff, 26 December 1923, British Library.

47. VE to MH, December 1923, Texas.

48. VE to VW, "Sunday 5th" 1923, Monk's House Papers, Sussex.

49. TSE to Sydney Schiff, 24 February 1924, British Library.

50. VE to MH, 29 December 1923, Texas.

51. VE to Sydney Schiff, 31 March 1924, British Library.

52. This speech, delivered to the Heretics at Cambridge on 18 May 1924, developed from a *Nation* article (December 1923), became "Mr. Bennett and Mrs. Brown." Virginia offered it to Eliot for the *Criterion* on 5 May 1924. Virginia described it as "elementary and loquacious," being designed for undergraduates, but Eliot accepted the 5,000-word article with alacrity and offered Virginia a special rate of £20 per 5,000 words, reserved only for her and James Joyce. TSE to VW, 7 ? May 1924. Monk's House Papers, Sussex.

53. MH to Lytton Strachey, 23 April 1924, Texas.

54. VW to TSE, "Sunday," 1924, Monk's House Papers.

55. TSE to VW, 3 March 1923, Monk's House Papers.

56. TSE to VW, 1 May 1924, Monk's House Papers.

57. VW to TSE, n.d., ? 1924, Monk's House Papers.

58. Journals of Lady Ottoline Morrell, 19 June 1923, Goodman Papers.

59. VE to VW, 13 June 1924, Monk's House Papers.

60. TSE to VW, 4 February 1925, Monk's House Papers.

61. VE to VW, "Sunday 5th" 1923, Monk's House Papers.

62. TSE to VW, 19 April 1925, Monk's House Papers.

63. TSE to OM, 19 April ? 1925, Texas.

64. TSE to OM, 1 May ? 1925, Texas.

65. Henry Eliot Jr. to C. C. Eliot, 10 May 1925, Houghton.

66. Leonard Woolf to TSE, 30 April 1925, Frederic Spotts (ed.), *Letters of Leonard Woolf* (New York: Harcourt Brace Jovanovich, 1989), pp. 227–28.

67. Sir Henry Head, neurologist, was recommended by Roger Fry to the Woolfs; Head's rejection of "label" and understanding of hysteria in which "the symptoms of the disorder may be seen as the direct result of living in an untenable situation" (Stephen Trombley, *"All That Summer She Was Mad," Virginia Woolf and Her Doctors* [London: Junction Press, 1981], p. 176) might have made him a better choice of doctor than Marten or Cyriax for Vivien. He believed that a sexless marriage could contribute to neurosis: "Marriage without physical affection is an impossible human relation; one of the simplest methods of escaping from such difficulties is the development of physical illness" (Henry Head, "The Diagnosis of Hysteria," *British Medical Journal,* 1, 1922, pp. 827–29).

68. TSE to OM, Pencil note, "Sunday? 1925, Texas."

69. Trombley, op. cit., pp. 140–43. Savage was the author of the popular textbook, *Insanity and Allied Neuroses* (1884).

70. Trombley, op. cit., p. 142, quotes Anne Olivier Bell (ed.), *The Diary of Virginia Woolf,* vol. 3 (London: Penguin, 1982), p. 315. Leonard Woolf also noted that Virginia had a very bitter taste in the roof of the mouth, p. 143. Trombley suggests that it was Craig who prescribed a sleeping draught, probably containing hyoscyamine.

71. Henry Eliot Jr. to C. C. Eliot, 30 October 1921, Houghton.

72. Notebook 2, VE Papers, MSS Eng. Misc. c. 936, pp. 1–4, 1–36. Notebook 1, representing Vivien's earliest writing, is missing from the collection, having disappeared from the Duke

Humphrey room in June 1990, but Notebook 2 can be dated 1923–24 from an untitled sketch on p. 8, dated May 1924.

73. Ibid.

74. Very occasionally there is a third hand, probably that of Irene Pearl Fassett, but invariably Vivien writes a piece which Eliot edits, often interspersing a few lines of his own with her text.

75. VE as "F.M.," "Letters of the Moment—II," *Criterion,* April 1924.

76. TSE to OM, 29 December 1922, Texas.

77. TSE to Sydney Schiff, 24 February 1924, British Library.

78. VE to Sydney Schiff, 31 March 1924, British Library.

17. Criterion *Battles*

1. "Letters of the Moment—I," *Criterion,* February 1924.

2. "Letters of the Moment—II," *Criterion,* April 1924. Vivien's lists of dramatis personae for her sketches confirm that Tom is "Aquin," VE Collection, Bodleian.

3. Ronsard, "On sent le printemps," in TSE's hand in Vivien's loose-leaf book, MSS. Eng. Misc. c. 624.

4. "Letters of the Moment—I," op. cit.

5. "Letters of the Moment—II," *Criterion,* April 1924, pp. 360–64.

6. "Letters of the Moment—II," op. cit.

7. VW to Barbara Bagenal, 24 June 1924, quoted in Clive Bell, *Old Friends* (London: Chatto & Windus, 1956), p. 103.

8. VW to TSE, 11 May 1924, Nigel Nicolson and Joanne Trautmann (eds.), *The Letters of Virginia Woolf,* vol. 3, 1923–28 (London: Hogarth Press, 1977), p. 108. Lewis published *The Apes of God* in book form in 1930.

9. TSE to VW, 7 April 1924, Berg.

10. Untitled verse, n.d., VE loose-leaf book, Bodleian.

11. Wyndham Lewis, *The Apes of God* (London: Nash & Grayson, 1930), p. 123. Richard Aldington, who had his own grievances against Bloomsbury, described *The Apes of God* (which was an expanded version of the original article) as "one of the cruelest, [and] one of the most tremendous farces ever conceived in the mind of man," which could be compared to Rabelais.

12. VE loose-leaf book, Bodleian.

13. John Pitcher (ed.), *Thomas Kyd, The Spanish Tragedie* (London: Penguin, 1998), p. iii. When in prison in 1593 and accused of atheism, Kyd "squealed" on Marlowe, arguing that the atheistical materials found belonged to his former companion. Eliot's essay on Marlowe was published in 1919. "Four Elizabethan Dramatists" followed in 1924, in *Selected Essays 1917–1932* (London: Faber & Faber, 1932), pp. 109, 118.

14. VE loose-leaf book, Bodleian.

15. "Letters of the Moment—II," op. cit.

16. Anne Olivier Bell (ed.), *The Diary of Virginia Woolf,* vol. 2 (London: Penguin, 1981), 15 September 1924, p. 313.

17. Ibid., 5 May 1924, p. 302; see Bell's footnote.

18. VW to Marjorie Joad, 20? July 1924, Nicolson and Trautmann (eds.), *The Letters of Virginia Woolf,* vol. 3, op. cit., p. 120.

19. Bell (ed.), *The Diary of Virginia Woolf*, vol. 2, op. cit., 14 June 1924, p. 404.

20. VE to Leonard Woolf, 27 June 1924, Monk's House Papers.

21. VE to VW, 11 June 1923, Monk's House Papers.

22. VW to TSE, 5 May 1924, Nicolson and Trautmann (eds.), *The Letters of Virginia Woolf*, vol. 3, op. cit., p. 107.

23. Vivien's loose-leaf book, Bodleian.

24. "The Function of Criticism," *Criterion*, October 1923.

25. E. M. Forster, "T.S. Eliot," *Abinger Harvest* (London: Penguin, 1936), p. 105.

26. VE loose-leaf book, Bodleian, p. 101.

27. TSE's notes on being "Pot Bound," n.d., VE loose-leaf book, p. 105, Bodleian.

28. VE to Sydney Schiff, 31 March 1924, British Library.

29. "Letters of the Moment—I," op. cit.

30. Ronald Schuchard (ed.), Introduction, T. S. Eliot, *The Varieties of Metaphysical Poetry: the Clark Lectures at Trinity College Cambridge 1926 and The Turnbull Lectures at Johns Hopkins University 1933* (New York: Harcourt Brace Jovanovich, 1993), p. 6.

31. F. A. Lea, *The Life of John Middleton Murry* (London: Methuen, 1959), p. 130.

32. "Letters of the Moment—II," *Criterion*, April 1924, p. 362.

33. "F.M.," "Books of the Quarter," *Criterion*, July 1924, pp. 483–86.

34. "I. P. Fassett," "Books of the Quarter," *Criterion*, October 1924, pp. 136–39.

35. Ibid., p. 139.

36. "I. P. Fassett," review of *The White Monkey* by John Galsworthy, *Criterion*, January 1925.

37. VE loose-leaf book, Bodleian.

38. "Feiron Morris," "Thé Dansant," *Criterion*, October 1924, pp. 73–78.

39. "Felix Morrison," "Mrs. Pilkington," *Criterion*, October 1924, pp. 103–6.

40. VE to Sydney Schiff, n.d., British Library.

41. T. S. Eliot, "On the Eve: A Dialogue," *Criterion*, January 1925, pp. 278–81.

42. "Fanny Marlow," "Diary of the Rive Gauche," *Criterion*, January 1925, pp. 291–97.

43. TSE to VW, 1 May 1924, Monk's House Papers.

44. TSE to VW, 7 May 1924, Monk's House Papers.

45. TSE to VW, 22 May 1924, Monk's House Papers.

46. Ibid.

47. Virginia Woolf's "Mr. Bennett and Mrs. Brown" was published in the *Criterion* (July 1924); see Nicolson and Trautmann (eds.), *The Letters of Virginia Woolf*, vol. 3, op. cit., p. 106n.

48. "Feiron Morris," review of "Mr. Bennett and Mrs. Brown" by Virginia Woolf (The Hogarth Press, 2/6d.) in "Books of the Quarter," *Criterion*, January 1925.

49. TSE to VW, 1 May 1924, Monk's House Papers.

50. VE to Sydney Schiff, "Sunday," ?end March/early April 1925, British Library.

51. TSE to VW, 4 February 1925, Monk's House Papers.

52. TSE to VW, 19 April 1925, Monk's House Papers.

53. Early drafts of the poem give the alternative titles of "Ennui," "Exhaustion" and "Fatigue."

54. VE ("F.M."), "Necesse est Perstare," *Criterion*, April 1925.

55. TSE to OM, 1 May ?1925, Texas.

56. Henry Eliot Jr. to C. C. Eliot, 10 May 1925, Houghton.

57. "Fête Galante," *Criterion*, July 1925, pp. 557–63.

58. "Ellison and Antony," MSS Eng. Misc. c. 624, VE Papers, Bodleian.

59. "Feiron Morris," "Night Club," *Criterion*, April 1924, pp. 401–4.

60. "Fanny Marlow," "Diary of the Rive Gauche—II," *Criterion,* April 1925, pp. 425–29.

61. "I. P. Fassett," review of *Orphan Island,* by Rose Macaulay, *Criterion,* April 1925.

62. "F.M.," review of *Myrtle* by Stephen Hudson, *Criterion,* April 1925.

63. Osbert Sitwell, "unpublished memoir of T. S. Eliot," 19 February 1950, p. 22, Texas.

64. TSE to VW, 7 April 1924, Berg.

65. Nicolson and Trautmann (eds.), *The Letters of Virginia Woolf,* vol. 3, op. cit., p. 110n. "Is there any danger that the Criterion is dying?" asked Virginia. "I hope not." VW to TSE, 23 May 1924.

18. On with the Dance

1. Anne Olivier Bell (ed.), *The Diary of Virginia Woolf,* vol. 3 (London: Penguin, 1982), 29 April 1925, p. 14.

2. Ibid., 14 September 1925, p. 41. Virginia objected to a letter from Tom which "fawns & flatters," but hid the fact that his new firm, Faber & Gwyer, would be publishing his poetry—"a fact which he dared not confess, but sought to palliate by flattering me." "Tom has treated us scurvily, much in the manner that he has treated the Hutchinsons," wrote Virginia. Editor Anne Olivier Bell writes (note 5): "The parallel with Jack Hutchinson and Mrs. Eliot has defied explanation." The furore over "Fête Galante" explains Virginia's comparison.

3. Alan and Veronica Palmer, *Who's Who in Bloomsbury* (Brighton: The Harvester Press, 1987), p. 80.

4. Bell (ed.), *The Diary of Virginia Woolf,* vol. 3, op. cit., 27 June 1925, p. 33.

5. "I. P. Fassett," review of *Daimon* by E. L. Grant Watson (London: Jonathan Cape, 1926), "Books of the Quarter," *Criterion,* January 1926.

6. Nicholas Joost, *Scofield Thayer and* The Dial: *An Illustrated History* (Southern Illinois University Press, 1964) pp. 84–87.

7. VE to EP, n.d., Beinecke.

8. VE to OM, pencil, n.d., "temporarily" 9 Clarence Gate Gardens, Texas.

9. VE to EP, n.d., Beinecke.

10. TSE to Leonard Woolf, n.d., Berg.

11. TSE to MH, 20 February 1925, Texas.

12. Bell (ed.), *The Diary of Virginia Woolf,* vol. 3, op. cit., 29 April 1925, pp. 14, 15.

13. TSE to MH, 3 April 1925, Texas.

14. TSE to OM, 30 November 1924, Texas.

15. Miranda Seymour, *Ottoline Morrell: Life on the Grand Scale* (London: Hodder & Stoughton, 1992), pp. 448–49. Ottoline faithfully followed Dr. Marten's starvation diets of fruit and water until she was "so weak she could scarcely sit up." She did not leave Marten until 1932.

16. VW to Lytton Strachey, 26 January 1926, Nigel Nicolson and Joanne Trautmann (eds.), *The Letters of Virginia Woolf,* vol. 3 (London: Hogarth Press, 1977), p. 234.

17. Juliet Mitchell, *Mad Men and Medusas* (London: Penguin Press, 2000), p. 25.

18. VE to EP, n.d., Beinecke.

19. Bell (ed.), *The Diary of Virginia Woolf,* vol. 3, op. cit., 1 June 1925, p. 26.

20. VE to EP, n.d., Beinecke.

21. Draft of a letter pasted into Vivien's writing book in the Bodleian, quoted by Lyndall Gordon, *T. S. Eliot: An Imperfect Life* (London: Vintage, 1998), p. 200.

22. VE Diary, 14 November 1934, Bodleian.

23. Bertrand Russell to TSE, 23 April 1925, McMaster.

24. Bertrand Russell, *Autobiography,* vol. 2 (London: Allen & Unwin, 1968), p. 174.

25. VW to Roger Fry, 16 September 1925, Nicolson and Trautmann (eds.), *The Letters of Virginia Woolf,* vol. 3, op. cit., p. 209.

26. *After Strange Gods* (London: Faber & Faber, 1934), quoted in Ronald Schuchard, *Eliot's Dark Angel* (Oxford: OUP, 1999), p. 128.

27. TSE to OM, 30 November 1924, Texas. Eliot describes his experiments with *Sweeney Agonistes.*

28. Mitchell, op. cit., pp. 41, 42.

29. TSE to OM, 20 February 1925, Texas.

30. TSE to OM, 30 November 1924, Texas.

31. TSE to OM, 4 March ? 1925, Texas.

32. *"The Sacred Wood*... had very little influence or attention before the Hogarth Press brought out *Homage to John Dryden*... It was with the publication in this form of those essays that Eliot became the important contemporary critic. It was the impact of this slender new collection that sent one back to *The Sacred Wood* and confirmed with decisive practical effect one's sense of the stimulus to be got from that rare thing, a fine intelligence in literary criticism." F. R. Leavis, *Anna Karenina and Other Essays* (London: Chatto & Windus, 1967), pp. 177–78, quoted in Ronald Schuchard (ed.), *T. S. Eliot: The Varieties of Metaphysical Poetry, The Clark Lectures at Trinity College, Cambridge, 1926 and The Turnbull Lectures at the Johns Hopkins University, 1933* (New York and London: Harcourt Brace Jovanovich, 1993), p. 5.

33. Peter Ackroyd, *T. S. Eliot* (London: Penguin, 1993), p. 151.

34. Bell (ed.), *The Diary of Virginia Woolf,* vol. 3, op. cit., 14 September 1925, p. 41.

35. TSE to VW, 5 September 1925, Monk's House Papers.

36. It was published in the *New Criterion* in January 1926.

37. Bell (ed.), *The Diary of Virginia Woolf,* vol. 3, op. cit., 30 September 1925, p. 45.

38. Ibid., 29 April 1925, p. 15.

39. TSE to VW, n.d., ?1925, Monk's House Papers. Tom said the earstoppers were "a blessing." He could testify that Vivien was sleeping better since she had them than for about four years.

40. TSE to VW, "Sunday," ? May 1925, Monk's House Papers.

41. VW to Richard Aldington, early November, mid-November, 1924, Nicolson and Trautmann (eds.), *The Letters of Virginia Woolf,* vol. 3, pp. 139, 142.

42. TSE to RA, 26 November ?1925, Texas.

43. RA to EP, 5 October 1925, in Charles Doyle, *Richard Aldington: A Biography* (London: Macmillan, 1989), p. 89. Aldington was annoyed that Eliot, as he thought, was paying him low rates for reviewing in the *Criterion,* and that his poem "A Fool i' the Forest" was seen as a second-rate *Waste Land.* He began to suspect Eliot of condescension towards him (pp. 101–3). The rift with Eliot grew wider after Routledge asked Aldington to collaborate in a series of critical biographies to be edited by William Rose and with Aldington as possible co-editor; it was to be called "The Republic of Letters." Aldington invited Herbert Read and Eliot to contribute, and was upset when both refused. Eliot, as director of Faber & Gwyer, then initiated a similar scheme, "The Poets on the Poets," under the joint imprint of the two publishing houses and the joint editorship of himself and Rose.

Aldington was distraught over losing the editorship, calling it his biggest "setback . . . since the war [which] loses me the fruit of years of work." He felt betrayed by Eliot in his efforts to lift himself "out of the mire of journalism and poverty." See Norman Gates, *Richard Aldington: An Autobiography in Letters* (Philadelphia: Penn State University Press, 1992), p. 76. His jealousy of Eliot increased subsequently.

44. Bell (ed.), *The Diary of Virginia Woolf,* vol. 3, op. cit., 29 April 1925, p. 14.

45. VE to EP, 14 December ?1925, Beinecke.

46. VE to EP, n.d., Beinecke.

47. TSE to EP, postcard, 24 November 1925, Beinecke.

48. Introduction by Schuchard (ed.), *T. S. Eliot: The Varieties of Metaphysical Poetry,* op. cit., pp. 8–11.

49. TSE to EP, second postcard, 8 December 1925, Beinecke.

50. TSE to EP, 11 December 1925, Beinecke.

51. "En Amérique, professeur;/En Angleterre, journaliste;/C'est à grands pas et en sueur/Que vous suivrez à peine ma piste./En Yorkshire, conférencier;/A Londres, un peu banquier," from "Melange Adultère de Tout," *Collected Poems,* p. 49. Eliot gave Extension Lectures at Ilkley, Yorkshire, in the autumn of 1916.

52. Gordon, op. cit., p. 210.

53. Richard Aldington, *Stepping Heavenward* (London, 1931), p. 55.

54. TSE to EP, 27 December 1925, Beinecke.

55. Ibid.

56. Charles Dickens, *The Old Curiosity Shop.*

57. "A Villonaud, Ballad of the Gibbet," Michael John King (ed.), *Collected Early Poems of Ezra Pound* (London: Faber & Faber, 1977); p. 16; "Camaraderie," p. 30.

58. Ibid., p. 27.

59. VE to Ada Leverson, n.d., Berg. From the content it is clear that this letter was written shortly after the marriage of Sacheverell Sitwell to Georgia Doble, which took place on 12 October 1925 in Paris.

60. Léonide Massine, *My Life in Ballet* (London: Macmillan, 1968), pp. 162, 163.

61. Lynn Garafola, *Diaghilev's Ballets Russes* (New York: Da Capo Press, 1998), p. 353.

62. TSE to EP, 27 December 1925, Beinecke.

63. TSE to EP, 12 February 1926, Beinecke.

64. VE to OM, 23 December 1925, Texas.

65. VE, "Poem to Ottoline," 26 December 1925, Texas.

66. VE to OM, 30 December 1925, Texas.

67. Now in the St. Louis Art Museum. David Bradshaw, "Those Extraordinary Parakeets," *Charleston Magazine,* 16, Autumn/Winter 1997; 17, Spring/Summer 1998.

68. "The Work of Some Modern Decorative Artists," *Vogue,* 68 (late August 1926), pp. 27–33, quoted by Bradshaw, op. cit.

69. VE to MH, 23 December 1925, Texas.

70. Bell (ed.), *The Diary of Virginia Woolf,* vol. 3, op. cit., 29 April 1925, p. 14.

71. VE to OM, pencil, n.d. (temporarily 9 Clarence Gate Gardens), ?late 1925, Texas.

72. Journal of Lady Ottoline Morrell, 3 March 1926, Goodman Papers.

73. Osbert Sitwell, unpublished memoir of T. S. Eliot, Goodman Papers. 19 February 1950, Texas.

74. VE to MH, 25 March 1926, Texas.

75. Ottoline varied in her opinions of Vivien, finding her sometimes dedicated to frivolity and passing pleasure, at other times intellectual and spiritual. Journal of Lady Ottoline Morrell, 1921–26.

76. Massine, op. cit., pp. 164, 165.

77. Garafola, op. cit., pp. 114–15.

78. VE, "The Coliseum Dome," 17 October 1925, MSS Eng. Misc. c. 624, loose leaves pasted into a book, Bodleian.

79. VE, "Verse," ibid.

80. MH to Lytton Strachey, 6 August 1925, Mary Hutchinson Collection, Texas. Mary wrote that she was amused and enchanted by "Mr. E" at Eleanor.

81. TSE to OM, 30 November 1924, Texas.

82. Massine, op. cit., pp. 166, 167. Massine's letters to Ottoline (Texas) show that he rented different rooms in Bloomsbury St.

83. "T. S. Eliot, A Biographical Sketch," n.d. Significantly Mary makes no mention of Vivien in this sketch of Tom's character. She demonstrated her own admiration of the poet by sending him tamarisk and sea lavender to be woven into laurels and roses with which his head would be crowned. Texas.

84. "F.M." "Perque Domos Ditis Vacuas" ("Through the empty halls of Dis"), n.d., Bodleian; the title is taken from Virgil, The Aeneid, Book VI, line 269. I am indebted to Patricia Grayburn, Governor, and the Head of Classics, Sherborne School for Girls, for identifying and translating this quotation. Translation of other lines is by James Brodie Ltd. Ezra Pound's choice of Latin titles for many of his poems may have influenced Vivien to do the same, although it was probably Eliot, with his love of Dante and classical scholarship, who introduced her to Virgil.

85. Richard Buckle, Diaghilev (London: Weidenfeld & Nicolson, 1993), p. 453, from an unidentified press cutting Dolin's album. The paragraph is headed "Ballet of Degenerates."

86. Ibid., p. 470.

87. Garafola, op. cit., p. 365.

88. VE to MH, 22 January 1926, Texas.

89. VE to OM, "Cambridge," 10 March ?1926, Texas.

90. TSE to OM, Trinity College, Cambridge, 10 March 1926.

91. VE draft of "Night Club," Notebook 3, 10, Bodleian.

92. "Feiron Morris," "Night Club," Criterion, April 1925, pp. 401–4.

93. "Feiron Morris," "Song in the Night," Vivien's loose-leaf book, Bodleian.

94. VE to Pearl Fassett, n.d., letter in loose-leaf book, Bodleian.

95. VE draft of "Letter of the Moment," ibid.

96. Journal of Lady Ottoline Morrell, 13 March 1926, Goodman Papers.

97. Henry Eliot to C. C. Eliot, 25 February 1925, Houghton.

98. Henry Eliot to C. C. Eliot, 2 March 1926, Houghton.

99. Henry Eliot to C. C. Eliot, 15 March 1925, Houghton.

100. VE, "Telephone Conversation," Notebook 2, Bodleian.

101. VE, draft of Bertrand Russell story, loose-leaf book, Bodleian.

102. VE notes for "Lonely Soldier," loose-leaf book, Bodleian.

103. "Fragment of a Prologue," CP, pp. 125, 126. "Fragment of an Agon," Sweeney Agonistes, CP, p. 134. Eliot first published "Fragment of an Agon" in the New Criterion (January 1927).

104. Ibid.

105. VE drafts for "The Lonely Soldier" and "Pseudo-Bridge," partly in TSE's handwriting. Vivien lists the characters as: "Sibylla, Horace, Felice, a dago, a German, an American (André) Mary, Dorothea, St. John, a Cambridge undergraduate" (p. 91). An earlier list identifies Maurice as Horace, the Hutchinsons as the Rawdon Crawleys, "T" as Aquinas, "W.L." (Wyndham Lewis) as Lieut. Bonaparte, Osbert as "Mr. Botch," and The Phoenix as the Mermaid; loose-leaf book, Bodleian.

106. "Night Club," *Criterion,* April 1925, p. 402.

107. VE, Notebook 3, 1924, Bodleian.

108. Theresa Eliot, signed statement, 28 March 1970, 84 Prescott St., Cambridge, Massachusetts. Houghton.

109. Philip Hoare, *Oscar Wilde's Last Stand* (New York: Arcade Publishing, Inc., 1998), pp. 36–38.

110. VE loose-leaf book, Bodleian.

111. Henry Eliot to C. C. Eliot, 9 March 1926, Houghton. In a letter of 21 March, Henry wrote that twelve copies of "Savonarola" were shipped to Charlotte Eliot last week, and Tom said that they had already sold fifty copies.

112. Henry Eliot to C. C. Eliot, postmark 31 March 1926, Houghton.

113. Henry Eliot to C. C. Eliot, 6 April 1926, Houghton.

114. I am indebted to Mr. Adrian M. Goodman for this information.

115. Henry Eliot to C. C. Eliot, postcard, 13 April, letter 16 April 1926, Houghton.

116. VE to Mary Hutchinson, postcard, 12 May ?1926, Texas.

117. Theresa Garrett Eliot, interview in BBC production, *The Mysterious Mr. Eliot,* televised 3 January 1971.

118. Henry Eliot to C. C. Eliot, 4 May 1926, Houghton.

119. Aldington, *Stepping Heavenward,* op. cit., pp. 57, 60.

120. VE to OM, express letter, 16 April 1926, Texas.

121. "Felix Morrison," "Mrs. Pilkington," *Criterion,* October 1924, pp. 103–6.

122. Sitwell, unpublished memoir, op. cit., Texas.

123. Ibid.

124. TSE to OM, 24 June 1926, Texas.

19. Mourning and "Madness"

1. Osbert Sitwell, unpublished Memoir on T. S. Eliot," 19 February 1950, p. 16, Texas.

2. Aldous Huxley to Mary Hutchinson, 6 August 1926, Texas.

3. Robert Sencourt, *T. S. Eliot: A Memoir,* edited by Donald Adamson and L. P. Addison (London: Garnstone Press, 1971), pp. 102, 103.

4. Frances Lindley, editor, Harper and Row Publishers, New York, to T. S. Matthews, 3 September 1971. Lindley was T. S. Matthews's editor, who was in touch with Dodd, Mead, the publishers of Sencourt's memoir, over their authors' joint difficulties with the Eliot estate. Sencourt hoped that his memoir would assist Tom Matthews in writing *Great Tom.*

5. T. S. Eliot, "Lancelot Andrewes" (1926), *Selected Essays 1917–1932* (London: Faber & Faber, 1932), p. 344.

6. W. Force Stead, "Some Personal Reminiscences of T. S. Eliot," Alumni Journal of Trinity College, Washington, vol. XXXVIII, Winter 1965, no. 2.

7. TSE to W. F. Stead, 7 February 1927, Osborn Papers, Beinecke.

8. Ibid., p. 349.

9. Hugh Kenner, *The Invisible Poet: T. S. Eliot* (London: W. H. Allen, 1960), p. 209; "Lancelot Andrewes," in *Selected Essays,* op. cit., p. 350.

10. Lyndall Gordon, *T. S. Eliot: An Imperfect Life* (London: Vintage, 1998), p. 222, quotes David W. S. Goldie's Oxford thesis, "John Middleton Murry and T. S. Eliot: Tradition versus the Individual in English Literary Criticism, 1919–1928" (1991). Murry's attack, "The Classical Revival," *Adelphi* (Feb.–March, 1926). Goldie discovered a draft of the attack annotated by Eliot.

11. Charlotte Eliot's handwritten draft of "Savonarola" is at the Houghton Library.

12. Stead, op. cit.

13. TSE to W. F. Stead, 7 February 1927, Beinecke.

14. Sencourt, op. cit., p. 104.

15. Stead, op. cit.

16. Ibid.

17. VW to Vanessa Bell, 11 February 1928, Nigel Nicolson and Joanne Trautmann (eds.), *The Letters of Virginia Woolf,* vol. 3, 1923–28 (London: Hogarth Press, 1977), pp. 457–58.

18. Lyndall Gordon, *Eliot's Early Years* (Oxford: OUP, 1977), p. 66.

19. Ibid., p. 15.

20. T. S. Eliot draft of Clark Lecture III, Houghton. Schuchard writes: "In the 'Classical Revival' Murry had compared the nihilistic voice of *The Waste Land* to the voice of St. John of the Cross: 'Once its armour of incomprehensibility is penetrated the poem is found to be a cry of grinding and empty desolation . . . This is a voice from the Dark Night of the Soul of a St. John of the Cross—the barren and dry land where no water is.' " Ronald Schuchard (ed.), *The Varieties of Metaphysical Poetry, the Clark Lectures at Trinity College, Cambridge, 1926 and the Turnbull Lectures at Johns Hopkins University, 1933* (New York: Harcourt Brace, 1993), p. 52, note 104.

21. John Pitcher (ed.), *Thomas Kyd, The Spanish Tragedie* (London: Penguin, 1998), p. xiii.

22. VE loose-leaf book, Bodleian.

23. Gordon, *T. S. Eliot: An Imperfect Life,* op. cit., pp. 192, 199, 189.

24. T. S. Eliot draft of Clark Lecture III, Houghton. Schuchard, op. cit., p. 99.

25. A. David Moody, *Thomas Stearns Eliot, Poet* (Cambridge: CUP, 1994), pp. 117–21. The evolution of "The Hollow Men" can be traced from "Song to the Opherian" (1921) through "Doris's Dream Songs" (1924), "Three Poems" by Thomas Eliot (*Criterion,* January 1925) to "The Hollow Men" (*Dial,* March 1925) and the final "The Hollow Men" in *Poems 1909–1925.*

26. Ibid., p. 122.

27. Quoted by Moody, op. cit., p. 125.

28. Christopher Ricks (ed.), *IMH,* p. 369 and see Ronald Schuchard, *Eliot's Dark Angel: Intersections of Life and Art* (Oxford: 1999), p. 91.

29. TSE to OM, n.d., 1933, from "B-11 Eliot House, Cambridge," Mass. Texas.

30. T. S. Eliot, draft of Lecture 1, Houghton. Schuchard, *Varieties of Metaphysical Poetry,* op. cit., p. 54.

31. Ibid., Sappho's "Ode to Anactoria" is an example of the description of a "love trance" praised by Eliot.

32. Ibid., p. 149.

33. *Monthly Criterion,* vol. 6 (August 1927) quoted by Ronald Clark, *The Life of Bertrand Russell* (London: Jonathan Cape and Weidenfeld & Nicolson, 1975), p. 413.

34. TSE to BR, 22 June 1927, McMaster.

35. Lyndall Gordon, *Eliot's New Life* (Oxford: OUP, 1988), p. 30.

36. Misquoted from section XVIII of Dante's *La Vita Nuova,* "Madonne, lo fine del mio amore fu gia il saluto di questa donna, di cui voi forse intendete . . .": "Ladies, the end and aim of my Love was but the salutation of that lady of whom I conceive that ye are speaking." Translation, Dante Gabriel Rossetti, *Early Italian Poets* (London: George Newnes, 1904).

37. *Ash Wednesday* (London: Faber & Faber, 1930), dedicated "To My Wife," p. 12. Grover Smith, *T. S. Eliot's Poetry and Plays: A Study in Sources and Meaning* (The University of Chicago Press, 1956), p. 135. The dedication to Vivien was removed from later editions of the poem.

38. Robert Sencourt to John Hayward, 15 July 1965, John Hayward Bequest, King's College, Cambridge.

39. TSE to OM, 14 March 1933.

40. "Hence the soul cannot be possessed of the divine union, until it has divested itself of the love of created beings." The epigraph is from St. John of the Cross, *Ascent of Mount Carmel,* (book 1, ch. 4).

41. Introduction by Emma Smith (ed.), *Thomas Kyd: The Spanish Tragedie* (London: Penguin, 1998), pp. xiv–xxii.

42. *Sweeney Agonistes, CP,* p. 123.

43. Draft of *Sweeney Agonistes,* John Hayward Bequest, King's College, Cambridge.

44. The title of this typescript is "The Superior Landlord," and the cancelled title: "Pereira" or "The Marriage of Life and Death—A Dream." King's College, Cambridge.

45. Desmond MacCarthy, *"Sweeney Agonistes," Listener,* 9 January 1935.

46. Draft of *Sweeney Agonistes,* John Hayward Bequest, King's College, Cambridge. In this early draft Eliot wrote that there should be eighteen knocks, like the Angelus.

47. Mary Trevelyan, "The Pope of Russell Square" memoir, 25 July 1950, 10 February 1952.

48. T. S. Eliot, "Four Elizabethan Dramatists," *Selected Essays,* op. cit., p. 111.

49. MacCarthy, op. cit.

50. Draft of *Sweeney Agonistes,* op. cit.

51. Robin Grove, "Eliot's theater," A. David Moody (ed.), *The Cambridge Companion to T.S. Eliot* (Cambridge: CUP, 1994), p. 173.

52. Ibid.

53. *Dial,* 71 (August 1921), p. 214. See Schuchard, op. cit., pp. 110–13.

54. Anne Olivier Bell (ed.), *The Diary of Virginia Woolf,* vol. 4, 12 November 1934.

55. Maurice Haigh-Wood, interview with Michael Hastings, 1980.

56. VW to Elisabeth Bowen, 29 January 1939, Nicolson and Trautmann (eds.), *The Letters of Virginia Woolf,* op. cit., vol. 6, p. 313.

57. VE Notebook 2, p. 68, Bodleian.

58. Louis Martz, Introduction to *H.D. Collected Poems, 1912–1944* (New York: New Direction Books, 1925).

59. VE Diary, 18 April 1936, Bodleian.

60. VE Diary, 15 September 1934, Bodleian. Charles Haigh-Wood's death certificate cites "cancer of the mediastinum" as the cause of death. Lillia Symes, sister-in-law, of 37 Stratford Road, London W8, informed the registrar of the death, at which she was present.

61. VE Diary, 24 March 1935, Bodleian.

62. VE Diary, 1 September 1934, Bodleian.

63. Maurice Haigh-Wood, interview with Michael Hastings, 28 January 1980.

64. VE Diary, 20 April 193, Bodleian.

65. VE to BR, 6 December 1926, McMaster.

66. According to Russell's daughter, Mrs. Katharine Tait, the family jewellery did not pass down to his children, but "was probably all given to his various wives at different times." Katharine Tait to the author, 21 September 2000.

67. VE to BR, 6 December ?1926, McMaster.

68. TSE to BR, 22 June 1927, McMaster.

69. TSE to BR, 16 May 1927, McMaster.

70. TSE to BR, 22 June 1927, McMaster.

71. TSE to John Hayward, 29 November 1939, "St. Andrews Eve," John Hayward Bequest, King's College, Cambridge.

72. According to Maurice, at some point Vivien had an abortion, but this fact is uncorroborated.

73. Eliot used as an epigraph for "Marina" (1930) lines from Seneca's *Hercules Furens,* Hercules' words when he wakes to discover he has murdered his own children. Grover Smith, op. cit., p. 131.

74. Bernard Sharratt traces the motif of lost or murdered children in Eliot's work in "Eliot: Modernism, Postmodernism, and after," in Moody (ed.), *The Cambridge Companion to T. S. Eliot,* op. cit., pp. 225, 226. Eliot singled out "Yeats's lines about having reached forty-nine with only a book, not a child, to show for it."

75. VE to OM, 31 January 1928, Texas.

76. Vivien's photograph album 1924–29 is at King's College, Cambridge.

77. VE's Account Books, December 1927–April 1932, Bodleian.

78. Maurice Haigh-Wood, interview with Michael Hastings, 28 January 1980.

79. Daughter of Eliot's sister Charlotte, who had married Lawrence Smith.

80. Theodora's photographs and sketch plan of 57 Chester Terrace are at the Houghton Library, Harvard. She stayed at least twice with Tom and Vivien in 1928 and 1929.

81. Mary Trevelyan, "The Pope of Russell Square" memoir, 2 April 1951.

82. Osbert Sitwell, unpublished memoir on T. S. Eliot, Texas; also quoted in John Pearson, *Façades: Edith, Osbert and Sacheverell Sitwell* (London, 1978), pp. 240–42.

83. VE to OM, postmark 25 November 1926, Texas.

84. VE to OM, 27 March ?1927, Texas.

85. Lyndall Gordon, *Eliot's New Life* (Oxford: OUP, 1988), p. 8.

86. T. S. Eliot, "Shakespeare and the Stoicism of Seneca" (1927), *Selected Essays,* op. cit., p. 126.

87. Valerie Eliot, Introduction, *Letters I,* p. xvii.

88. Gordon, *T. S. Eliot,* op. cit., pp. 234–45.

89. Ibid., p. 205.

90. TSE to W. F. Stead, 15 March 1928, Beinecke.

91. Sencourt introduced Eliot to Underhill, who became Dean of Rochester in 1932. Sencourt, op. cit., pp. 112, 114.

92. TSE to W. F. Stead, 10 April 1928, Beinecke.

93. The poem describes Casco Bay, Maine.

94. "Marina" (1930), *Collected Poems,* p. 115.

95. Gordon, *Eliot's New Life,* op. cit., p. 10.

96. Ibid., p. 12.

97. TSE to E. Martin Browne, 19 March 1938, *The Making of T. S. Eliot's Plays* (Cambridge: CUP, 1969), p. 107.

98. Valerie Eliot, Introduction, *Letters I,* p. xvi.

99. A. David Moody, "Being in Fear of Women," in *"The Waste Land" in Different Voices* (London: Edward Arnold, 1974), pp. 184–91, writes: "It becomes difficult not to identify Eliot also with Harry in *The Family Reunion,"* p. 190.

100. TSE to JH, October 1925, John Hayward Bequest, King's College, Cambridge.

101. TSE to JH, 27 September 1927, loc. cit.

102. Gordon, *T. S. Eliot,* op. cit., p. 257.

103. JH to Frank Morley, 15 November 1937, list of poems for *Noctes Binanianae,* John Hayward Bequest.

104. TSE to JH, 14 November 1939, Kings College, Cambridge.

105. Quoted in Peter Ackroyd, *T. S. Eliot* (London: Penguin, 1993), pp. 150–51.

106. VE to OM, 31 January 1928, Texas.

107. VE Diary, 16 February 1935, Bodleian.

108. "Story 3," VE Notebook 3, Bodleian.

109. VE to OM, 28 February ?1928, Texas.

110. VE to OM, 1 June 1928, Texas.

111. VW to Vanessa Bell, 7 June 1928, Nicolson and Trautmann (eds.), *The Letters of Virginia Woolf,* vol. 3, p. 508.

112. VW to Vita Sackville-West, 13 November 1929, in ibid., vol. 4, p. 108.

113. TSE to OM, 2 October 1928, Texas.

114. TSE to OM, 1 November 1928, Texas.

115. Journal of Lady Ottoline Morrell, 14 February 1929, Goodman Papers.

116. VE to OM, Monday, 11 February 1929, Texas.

117. TSE to OM, 13 February 1929, Texas.

118. VE to OM, 29 February 1929, Texas.

119. Conversation with Philip Goodman, 1999.

120. VE to MH, 29 September 1928, Texas.

121. VW to Clive Bell, 2 May 1929, Nicolson and Trautmann (eds.), *The Letters of Virginia Woolf,* vol. 4, pp. 49, 50.

122. TSE to MH, 20 November 1928, Texas.

123. VE to MH, 9 November 1928, Texas.

124. VE to MH, n.d., Texas.

125. VE to MH, 6 September 1929, Texas.

126. TSE to MH, 23 June 1929, Texas.

127. VW to Clive Bell, 6 February 1930, Nicolson and Trautmann (eds.), *The Letters of Virginia Woolf,* vol. 4, p. 133.

128. VE to MH, 10 September 1929, Texas.

129. VE to MH, 25 March 1930, Texas.

130. VE to MH, 3 January 1931, Texas.

131. Michael Hastings, in conversation with relatives of Dr. Miller, 1981.

132. Professor Derek Russell Davis to Michael Hastings, October 1981, Hastings Papers.

133. "East Coker," *CP,* p. 200.

134. Ackroyd, op. cit., p. 158.

135. Journal of Lady Ottoline Morrell, 15 November 1930, Goodman Papers.

136. Ibid., 16 July 1931.

137. VE Diary, 12 November 1934, Bodleian.

138. Stephen Spender, *Eliot* (London: Fontana, 1975). p. 130. Pound was equally scornful, writing the following couplet:
"In any case let us lament the psychosis
Of all those who abandon the Muses for Moses."
Ackroyd, op. cit., p. 172.

139. Sencourt, op. cit., p. 121.

140. TSE to W. F. Stead, 2 December 1930, Beinecke.

20. *Ghosts and Shadows*

1. Conrad Aiken to Theodore Spencer, 31 October 1930, Joseph Killorin (ed.), *Selected Letters of Conrad Aiken* (New Haven, Conn., 1978).

2. VE to Ralph Hodgson, 12 May 1932, Beinecke.

3. Robert Sencourt, *T.S. Eliot: A Memoir* edited by Donald Adamson and L. P. Addison (London: Garnstone Press, 1971), p. 121.

4. T.S. Eliot, *The Family Reunion* (London: Faber & Faber, 1939), p. 30.

5. A. David Moody, *"The Waste Land" in Different Voices* (London: Edward Arnold, 1974), p. 190.

6. John Peter, "An Artistic Failure" (1949) in Arnold P. Hinchliffe (ed.), *T. S. Eliot Plays, A Casebook* (London: Macmillan, 1985), p. 127.

7. *The Family Reunion,* op. cit.

8. Mary Trevelyan, "The Pope of Russell Square . . . ," unpublished memoir, 10 February 1952.

9. Ibid., 28 October 1954.

10. T. S. Eliot. "Dante," *Selected Essays 1917–1932* (London: Faber & Faber, 1932), p. 245.

11. Jean-Paul Sartre, *Being and Nothingness* (1943), (London: Routledge edition 1989), pp. 354–57.

12. Ibid., "First Attitude Toward Others: Love, Language, Masochism," p. 365.

13. *CP,* p. 139. "Triumphal March" and "Difficulties of a Statesman" on which Eliot worked in the final years of his marriage, were never completed, and were finally published as "Coriolan" in his *Collected Poems.* Nor was he able to finish *Sweeney Agonistes.* Eliot published his translation of St. John Perse's *Anabase* in 1930. His frustration over this inability to complete work, which was only partly due to Vivien, is revealed in his sub-title to "Four Elizabethan Dramatists," *Selected Essays:* "Preface to an unwritten book." Only four essays of the proposed work were completed.

14. See Emmy van Deurzen-Smith, "Jean-Paul Sartre" in *Existential Dimensions of Psychotherapy* (London: Routledge, 1997), pp. 45–57.

15. Diane Long Hoeveler, *Romantic Androgyny: The Women Within* (Philadelphia: University of Pennsylvania Press, 1990), p. 7. Hoeveler traces the process by which the "Eternal Feminine" became for the Romantic poets "the encroaching feminine, an usurping and castrating power that needed to be suppressed rather than simply exalted."

16. Sartre, op. cit., "Second Attitude Toward Others: Indifference, Desire, Hate, Sadism," p. 412.

17. Clive Bell to Mary Hutchinson, September 1936, Texas. Quoted in Hermione Lee, *Virginia Woolf* (London: Vintage, 1997), p. 828 n.

18. Journal of Lady Ottoline Morrell, 12 April 1932, Goodman Papers.

19. Sencourt, op. cit., pp. 118–20.

20. Journal of Lady Ottoline Morrell, 23 July 1931, 17 November 1931, Goodman Papers.

21. Mirsky wrote a Marxist critique of Bloomsbury in his book *The Intelligentsia of Great Britain,* which was published in an English translation in 1935; it upset Bloomsberries much as Lewis's *Apes of God* had done. Mirsky was, said Lydia Lopokova, "a dirty little cad." Anne Olivier Bell (ed.), *The Diary of Virginia Woolf,* vol. 4 (London: Penguin, 1983), pp. 112, 288, 292.

22. VE to MH, 27 January 1931, Texas.

23. VE to MH, 2 June 1931, Texas.

24. Conrad Aiken to Theodore Spencer, October 1930, Killorin (ed.), *Selected Letters of Aiken,* op. cit.

25. VE to OM, 28 December 1931, Texas.

26. VE to OM, 11 December 1931, Texas.

27. Journal of Lady Ottoline Morrell, 17 November 1931, Goodman Papers.

28. Ibid., ?November 1931.

29. Quoted in Peter Ackroyd, *T. S. Eliot* (London: Penguin, 1993), p. 168.

30. Ibid., p. 184.

31. Charles Doyle, *Richard Aldington: A Biography* (London: Macmillan, 1989), p. 149.

32. Stephen Spender, *T. S. Eliot* (London: Fontana, 1975), p. 130.

33. E. W. F. Tomlin, *T. S. Eliot: A Friendship* (London: Routledge, 1988), p. 48.

34. TSE to RA, ?April 1924, Texas.

35. TSE to RA, 1 November 1927, Texas.

36. Henry Eliot to C. C. Eliot, 21 March 1926, Houghton.

37. Doyle, op. cit., p. 148.

38. Lee, op. cit., p. 449.

39. Bell (ed.), *The Diary of Virginia Woolf,* op. cit., vol. 3, 8 November 1930, p. 331.

40. Ibid.

41. VW to OM, 26 December 1928, Nigel Nicolson and Joanne Trautmann (eds.), *The Letters of Virginia Woolf,* vol. 3, p. 565.

42. Morley notes some of Eliot's practical jokes at the office: "OK Sauce (for Faber) which was very far from OK, the coffee which foamed over, the cigarettes which produced snow-storms . . . Something noisy" was always rigged up on the Wednesday nearest to the Fourth of July. Frank Morley in Richard March and Tambimuttu (eds.), *T.S. Eliot: A Symposium* (London: P.L. Editions, 1948), p. 69.

43. TSE to John Hayward, Notes on Practical Jokes, n.d. 1938, John Hayward Bequest, King's College, Cambridge.

44. VE to OM, 28 December 1931, Texas.

45. VE to Ralph Hodgson, 12 May 1932, Beinecke.

46. Henrik Ibsen, *Ghosts,* Act II.

47. TSE to MH, 28 October 1931, Texas.

48. VE to Aurelia Bollinger, 12 May 1932, Beinecke.

49. VE to Aurelia Bollinger, 27 May 1932, Beinecke.

50. VE to Aurelia Bollinger, 19 May 1932, Beinecke.

51. Harold Nicolson, 2 March 1932, Nigel Nicolson (ed.), *Diaries and Letters 1930–39* (New York and London: Harcourt Brace, 1977), p. 111.

52. TSE to Ralph Hodgson, Two typescripts with sketches, 16 August 1932, Beinecke. Published as "Lines for Cuscuscaraway and Mirza Murad Ali Beg," *CP,* p. 151.

53. "Lines to Ralph Hodgson Esqre," *CP,* p. 150.

54. The visit took place in March 1932. Edith Sitwell quoted in John Pearson, *Façades: Edith, Osbert and Sacheverell* (London: 1978), p. 277.

55. Ibid., p. 278.

56. VE Diary, 14 September 1934, Bodleian.

57. Henry W. Cattell, MD, *Lippincott's New Medical Dictionary* (London: Lippincott Co., 1910) p. 325. Wellcome.

58. Robert Hooper, MD, *Lexicon Medicum* (London: Longman, 1839), p. 46. Wellcome.

59. "The belief that madness was caused by the build-up of bodily toxins led to the often punitive use of laxatives such as croton-oil, which could result in griping, sickness, colitis, fainting and even total collapse in a weak patient. Dr. Montagu Lomax, "The Experiences of an Asylum Doctor with Suggestions for Asylum and Lunacy Law Reform" (1921) in Roy Porter (ed.), *The Faber Book of Madness* (London: Faber & Faber, 1991), pp. 314–16.

60. VW to Vita Sackville-West, 27 January 1929, Nicolson and Trautmann (eds.), *Letters of Virginia Woolf,* vol. 4, op. cit., p. 8.

61. Leonard Woolf to Vanessa Bell, in ibid., p. 9.

62. VW to V. Sackville-West, 1 February 1929, Nicolson & Trautmann (eds.), *Letters of Virginia Woolf,* vol. 4, op. cit., p. 12.

63. Bell (ed.), *The Diary of Virginia Woolf,* vol. 4, op. cit., p. 123.

64. VE Diary, 1 April 1935, Bodleian.

65. Hope Mirrlees, "The Mysterious Mr. Eliot," BBC television programme, 3 January 1971.

66. VE Diary, 5 September 1934, Bodleian.

67. Morley, in March and Tambimuttu (eds.), *T. S. Eliot: A Symposium,* op. cit., p. 104.

68. Morley in Mirrlees, "The Mysterious Mr. Eliot," op. cit.

69. VE to OM, 4 July 1932, Texas.

70. Journal of Lady Ottoline Morrell, 12 April 1932, Goodman Papers.

71. TSE to OM, 11 July 1932, Texas.

72. VE to MH, 21 April 1932, Texas.

73. VE to MH, 8 June 1932, Texas.

74. VE to MH, 12 June 1932, Texas.

75. VE to MH, 18 July 1932, Texas.

76. VE to MH, 28 July 1932, Texas.

77. VE to OM, 11 September 1932, Texas.

78. Journal of Lady Ottoline Morrell, 12 January 1932, Goodman Papers.

79. VE to OM, 13 September 1932, Texas.

80. TSE to VE, 4 March 1932, Bodleian.

81. Sencourt, op. cit., p. 121.

82. VE to OM, 26 December 1933, Texas.

83. TSE to OM, 9 February 1933, Texas.

84. TSE to OM, 14 March 1933, Texas.

85. Eliot's Charles Eliot Norton Professor of Poetry lectures were published in 1933 as *The Use of Poetry and the Use of Criticism* (Harvard: Harvard University Press, 1933).

86. TSE to OM, 9 February 1933, Texas.

87. Lyndall Gordon, *Eliot's New Life* (Oxford: OUP, 1988), p. 18.

88. Journal of Lady Ottoline Morrell, 22 October 1935, Goodman Papers.

89. Gordon, op. cit., pp. 20, 21.

90. *CP,* p. 152.

91. TSE to VW, 25 April 1933, Berg.

92. TSE to VW, 5 March 1933, Berg.

93. "Virginia," *CP,* p. 153.

94. T. S. Matthews, *Great Tom: Notes Towards the Definition of T. S. Eliot* (London: Weidenfeld & Nicolson, 1974), p. 113.

95. EP to TSE, ? January 1934, Beinecke.

96. TSE to EP, n.d., 1927, Beinecke. "Julius or Joe" Bender had written a book on Propertius.

97. "Dirge," Valerie Eliot (ed.), *WL Facs* p. 119 and Stephen Spender, *T. S. Eliot* (London: Fontana, 1975), p. 54.

98. Matthews, op. cit., p. 163.

99. Spender, *Eliot,* op. cit., p. 131.

100. Sencourt, op. cit., p. 122. In the earlier misquotation Eliot wrote "miasma" for "phantasma," thinking of the "miasma of sexual sin" of which he often spoke to Sencourt.

101. T. S. Eliot, *Murder in the Cathedral,* part II (London: Faber & Faber, 1935). See also Robin Grove, "Pereira and After: The Cures of Eliot's Theater," A. David Moody (ed.), *The Cambridge Companion to T. S. Eliot* (Cambridge: CUP, 1994), p. 169.

102. TSE to EP, 8/10 December 1933, Beinecke.

103. Eliot lifted the words of Isaiah 40:6–8: "The voice said, Cry, And he said, What shall I cry? All flesh is grass, and all the goodliness thereof is as the flower of the field" to use as the first lines of "Difficulties of a Statesman": "Cry what shall I cry?/All flesh is grass . . ." It was yet one more example of his remark, "Immature poets imitate, mature poets steal" *(Selected Essays,* op. cit., p. 182). One acerbic reviewer wrote of *The Waste Land:* "The borrowed jewels he has set in its head does not make Mr. Eliot's toad the more prepossessing." For a discussion of Eliot's practice of "stealing," see James Longenbach, " 'Mature poets steal'": "Eliot's allusive practice," in Moody, *Cambridge Companion to T. S. Eliot,* op. cit., p. 176.

104. Isaiah 40:6–8. On 1 December 1932, Eliot quoted from Psalm 130 in King's Chapel, Boston: "I wait for the Lord, my soul doth wait . . ." Gordon, *Eliot's New Life,* op. cit., p. 39.

105. TSE to OM, 14 March 1933, Texas.

106. VE to Aurelia Bollinger, 28 July 1932, Beinecke.

107. Journal of Lady Ottoline Morrell, 12 April 1932, Goodman Papers.

108. Bell (ed.), *The Diary of Virginia Woolf,* vol. 4, op. cit., 31 March 1935.

109. Journal of Lady Ottoline Morrell, 20 August 1933, Goodman Papers.

110. TSE to OM, 9 August 1933, Texas.

111. Journal of Lady Ottoline Morrell, 20 August 1933, Goodman Papers.

112. Mary Hutchinson wrote for a variety of journals, including *The London Mercury, Vogue,* and *The London Magazine.*

113. VE to MH, 29 November 1932, Texas.

114. VE to MH, 30 November 1932, Texas.

115. VE to MH, 18 December 1932, Texas.

116. Sencourt, op. cit.

117. TSE to MH, 29 September 1932, Texas.

118. VE to OM, 31 March 1933, Texas.

119. VE Diary, 4 June 1934, Bodleian.

120. VE to OM, 7 July 1933, Texas.

121. Bell (ed.), *The Diary of Virginia Woolf,* vol. 4, op. cit., p. 167.

122. Frank Morley, in Allen Tate (ed.), *T. S. Eliot: The Man and His Work* (London: Chatto & Windus, 1967), pp. 104–5.

123. Eliot's poem, "The Country Walk," with the dedication "For J.H." (John Hayward), expresses not only his fear of cows but also of women: "when walking/With country dames in brogues and tweeds/Who will persist in hearty talking . . . ," John Hayward Bequest, King's College, Cambridge. There is another copy of this unpublished poem which Eliot gave to Emily Hale, at Princeton.

124. TSE to MH, 13 July 1933, Texas.

125. Bell (ed.), *The Diary of Virginia Woolf,* vol. 4, op. cit., 20 July 1933, p. 168.

126. VW to Francis Birrell, 3 September 1933, in Nicolson and Trautmann (eds.), *The Letters of Virginia Woolf,* vol. 5, p. 222.

127. Bell (ed.), *The Diary of Virginia Woolf,* vol. 4, op. cit., 21 July 1933, p. 169.

128. VE Diary, 20 January 1934, Bodleian.

129. VE Diary, 28 January 1934, Bodleian.

130. TSE to MH, 20 September 1933, Texas.

131. Ibid.

132. "The Three Voices of Poetry," reprinted in *On Poetry and Poets* (London: Faber & Faber 1957), quoted in Peter Ackroyd, *T. S. Eliot* (London: Penguin, 1993).

133. Bell (ed.), *The Diary of V. Woolf,* vol. 4, 2 September 1933, p. 177.

134. Ibid., 10 September 1933, p. 178.

135. TSE to EP, "Vigil of Ascension Day 1933," Beinecke.

136. TSE to EP, 21 September 1933, Beinecke.

137. TSE to OM, 9 August 1933, Texas.

138. TSE to OM, 21 August 1933, Texas.

139. EP to TSE, ?1934, Beinecke.

140. Frank Morley, in Tate (ed.), *T. S. Eliot,* op. cit., p. 109.

141. Frank Morley, "T. S. Eliot as a Publisher," March and Tambimuttu (eds.), *T. S. Eliot: A Symposium,* op. cit., p. 70.

142. TSE to MH, 26 September 1933, Texas.

143. TSE to MH, 3 November 1933, Texas.

144. TSE to MH, 1 January 1934, Texas.

145. VE Diary, 1 November 1934, Bodleian.

146. TSE to VW, 31 October 1933, Berg.

147. TSE to MH, 3 November 1933, Texas.

148. TSE to MH, 5 December 1933, Texas.

149. TSE to EP, 8/10 December 1933, Beinecke.

150. Sencourt, op. cit., p. 129.

151. Ibid.

152. TSE to VW, 7 December 1933, Berg.

153. Francis King, *Yesterday Came Suddenly* (London: Constable, 1993), p. 197.

21. Separation

1. Francis King, *Yesterday Came Suddenly* (London: Constable, 1993), p. 197.
2. Francis King in conversation with the author, 4 April 2000.
3. Alec Guinness, *My Name Escapes Me* (London: Hamish Hamilton, 1996), p. 185.
4. Anne Olivier Bell (ed.), *The Diary of Virginia Woolf,* vol. 4, 21 November 1934 (London: Penguin, 1983), pp. 262–63.
5. Phillip Herring, *Djuna: The Life and Work of Djuna Barnes* (London: Penguin, 1995), p. 222.
6. Ibid., p. 231.
7. Quoted in Tony Sharpe, *T. S. Eliot: A Literary Life* (London: Macmillan, 1991), p. 128.
8. T. S. Eliot, *The Cocktail Party* (London: Faber & Faber, 1958), p. 99.
9. TSE to Paul Elmer More, "Shrove Tuesday" (20 February) 1928, in Ronald Schuchard, *Eliot's Dark Angel: Intersections of Life and Art* (Oxford: OUP, 1999), p. 152.
10. TSE to Paul Elmer More, 29 June 1930, Schuchard, op. cit., p. 129.
11. Valerie Eliot in interview with Timothy Wilson, "T. S. Eliot and I," *Observer,* 20 February 1972.
12. Journal of Lady Ottoline Morrell, 7 April 1934, Goodman Papers.
13. T. S. Eliot, *The Family Reunion* (London: Faber & Faber, 1939).
14. Phillip Herring, *A Man of Contradictions: A Life of A. L. Rowse* (London: Penguin, 1999).
15. TSE to VW, 3 November 1934, Berg.
16. VE Diary, 30 January 1934, Bodleian.
17. VE to OM, 31 December 1933, Texas.
18. VE Diary, 4 June 1934, Bodleian.
19. VE to Hope Esq., 8 January 1935, Bodleian.
20. Peter Ackroyd, *T. S. Eliot* (London: Penguin, 1993), p. 206.
21. TSE to JH, 1 February 1931, John Hayward Bequest, King's College, Cambridge.
22. VE to OM, 26 December 1933, Texas.
23. VE Diary, 14 June 1934, Bodleian.
24. VE Diary, 2 August 1935, Bodleian.
25. T. S. Matthews, *Great Tom: Notes Towards the Definition of T. S. Eliot* (London: Weidenfeld & Nicolson, 1974), p. 118.
26. Maurice Haigh-Wood, interview with Michael Hastings, 4 March 1980.
27. Maurice Haigh-Wood, interview with Michael Hastings, 19 March 1980.
28. Tom and Vivienne had remained in touch with Karl Culpin's sister, Mary, who had helped them move into 18 Crawford Mansions. Donald Adamson and L. P. Addison (eds.), Robert Sencourt, *T. S. Eliot: A Memoir* (London: Garnstone Press, 1971), p. 52.
29. VE Diary, 1 August 1934, Bodleian.
30. Ibid., 29 January 1934.
31. Ibid., 6 July 1934.
32. VE to OM, 31 December 1933, Texas.
33. VE Diary, 1 August 1934, Bodleian.
34. Ibid., 30 January 1934, Bodleian.
35. Ibid., 26 June 1934.
36. Ibid., 22 July 1934.

37. Will of Vivienne Haigh Eliot, 1 March 1936. Section 17 (2) of the Copyright Act 1911 created a rule of procedural law that there shall be a rebuttable presumption that a legatee of an unpublished manuscript is the owner of the copyright. This presumption can be rebutted by evidence to the contrary.

38. VE Diary, 23 July 1934, Bodleian.

39. Ibid., 8 July 1934.

40. Maurice Haigh-Wood, interview with Michael Hastings, 4 March 1980.

41. VE Diary, 21 March 1934, Bodleian.

42. Ibid., 16 April 1934.

43. Ibid., 28 May 1934.

44. Ibid., 1 June 1934.

45. Ibid., 4 June 1934.

46. E. Martin Browne, *The Making of T. S. Eliot's Plays* (Cambridge: CUP, 1969), p. 30.

47. VE Diary, 11 June 1934, Bodleian.

48. Ibid., 3 June 1934.

49. Ibid., 12 June 1934.

50. Ibid., 25 July 1934.

51. Ibid., 10 May 1934.

52. Ibid., 5 September.

53. Michael Ignatieff, *Isaiah Berlin, A Life* (London: Chatto & Windus, 1998), pp. 186–87.

54. Eliot warned Pound, who had become pro-Fascist, against Mosley on 12 March 1934. Lyndall Gordon, *Eliot's New Life* (Oxford: OUP, 1988), p. 22.

55. VE Diary, 24 October 1934, Bodleian.

56. Ibid., 28 November 1934.

57. The final item in Ottoline Morrell's file of correspondence with Vivienne is the Christmas card Vivienne sent her from herself and Tom for Christmas 1935, Texas.

58. VE Diary, 3 June 1935, Bodleian.

59. Ibid., 4 December 1934.

60. Ibid., 28 June 1934.

61. Ibid., 20 March 1934.

62. Anne Olivier Bell (ed.), *The Diary of Virginia Woolf,* vol. 4 (London: Penguin, 1983), 12 November 1934. Despite Hope's critical description of Vivienne, she met her regularly and Vivienne praised Hope's "wonderful personality." According to Virginia, Hope's dachshund had a "snappy screech" (p. 162) and was a distracting dog. Hope met Eliot at Virginia's after dinner on 12 November 1934.

63. VW to OM, 31 December 1933, Nigel Nicolson and Joanne Trautmann (eds.), *The Letters of Virginia Woolf,* vol. 5 (New York: 1980), p. 207.

64. VE Diary, 13 March 1934, Bodleian.

65. Last Will and Testament of Charles Haigh-Wood, 3 January 1920, and codicil of 18 May 1927.

66. VE Diary, 10 April 1934, Bodleian.

67. Ibid., 26 July 1934.

68. In her will of 1936, Vivienne stated that, subject to her mother's life interest, "I and my said Brother Maurice are . . . respectively entitled to equal shares" in Charles Haigh-Wood's estate.

69. Maurice Haigh-Wood, interview with Michael Hastings, 12 March 1980.

70. Will of Charles Haigh-Wood, 18 May 1927.

71. VE Diary, 1 January 1935, Bodleian.

72. Ibid., 7 April 1935.

73. Ibid., 1 January 1935.

74. TSE to JH, 18 February 1938, John Hayward Bequest, King's College, Cambridge. Eliot wrote that he always counted on making a new will every five years, so Hayward's commitment need only be for that period.

75. VE Diary, 10 June 1935, Bodleian.

76. Ibid., 13 November 1935.

77. VE Diary, 14 March 1934, Bodleian.

78. Ibid., 26 April 1934.

79. Will of Rose Esther Haigh-Wood, 20 February 1936.

80. VE Diary, 18, 20, 21 September 1934, Bodleian.

81. Ibid., 23 September 1934.

82. Ibid., 26 September 1934.

22. Cat and Mouse

1. Lyndall Gordon, *Eliot's New Life* (Oxford: OUP, 1988), p. 43.

2. John Hayward Bequest, King's College, Cambridge.

3. Gordon, *Eliot's New Life,* op. cit., p. 44.

4. Ibid., p. 47. The "Bellegarde" fragment is in the Houghton Library, with the Notes for *Murder in the Cathedral* made by Eliot between December 1934 and May 1935, and collected by Henry Ware Eliot Jr. The rose garden sequence in "Burnt Norton" was also the genesis for the similar scene in *The Family Reunion* between Mary and Harry. Early drafts of *The Family Reunion* date from 1934–35. See Gordon, *Eliot's New Life,* Appendix 1, pp. 274–76. I do not, however, agree with Lyndall Gordon that Emily was the inspiration for Eliot's "memory and desire" when he looked into "the heart of light, the silence" in *The Waste Land* (p. 48), which, I submit, was inspired by Jean Verdenal.

5. T. S. Eliot, "Burnt Norton," *Four Quartets, CP,* p. 189.

6. Journal of Lady Ottoline Morrell, 22 October 1935, Goodman Papers.

7. Peter Ackroyd, *T. S. Eliot* (London: Penguin, 1993), p. 230.

8. Helen Gardner, *The Composition of the Four Quartets* (London: Faber & Faber, 1978), p. 35.

9. Anne Olivier Bell (ed.), *The Diary of Virginia Woolf,* vol. 4 (London: Penguin, 1983), 31 March 1935, p. 294.

10. Ibid., 19 April 1934, p. 208.

11. Ibid., 21 November 1934, pp. 262–63.

12. VW to John Lehmann, 1932, John Lehmann, *Thrown to the Woolfs* (New York: Holt, Rinehart and Winston, 1979), p. 31. V. Woolf's *A Letter to a Young Poet* was published in 1932.

13. T. S. Matthews, *Great Tom: Notes Towards the Definition of T. S. Eliot* (London: Weidenfeld & Nicolson, 1974), p. 117.

14. Donald Adamson and L. P. Addison (eds.), Robert Sencourt, *T. S. Eliot: A Memoir* (London: Garnstone Press, 1971), p. 133.

15. Gardner, op. cit., p. 38.

16. Eliot, "Burnt Norton," op. cit., p. 194.

17. Ronald Schuchard, *Eliot's Dark Angel: Intersections of Life and Art* (Oxford: OUP, 1999), p. 181.

18. Eliot gave Hayward five typed drafts of "Little Gidding," beginning with "First Complete Draft 7 July 1941": on a page torn from his scribbling pad are notes showing that he had come to see the four seasons and four elements as the organising principle behind the sequence of poems. Gardner, op. cit., p. 157.

19. Herbert Howarth, *Notes on Some Figures Behind T. S. Eliot* (London: Chatto & Windus, 1965), p. 118.

20. "The Dry Salvages" (1941) *Four Quartets, CP,* pp. 205–13.

21. Ibid.

22. "Death by Water," Section IV, Valerie Eliot (ed.), *WL Facs,* p. 59.

23. "The Dry Salvages," *Four Quartets, CP,* pp. 209–10. Gardner thought the poem had a "lame close," which did not lead forward to the theme of the next poem. Gardner, op. cit., p. 149.

24. A window in Little Gidding church commemorates the visit of the king and displays his arms with the inscription: "Insignia Caroli Regis qui latitabat apud Ferrarios 2do Maii A.S. 1646." Helen Gardner writes of Eliot: "Having read the first draft of [Every's play], it seems to me that when, four or five years later, he planned to write a fourth poem on 'Fire,' it was Mr. Every's play that linked fire with Little Gidding in his mind and that his memory of it coloured the discussion of victory and defeat in Part III." Gardner, op. cit., pp. 62–63.

25. Every wrote: "King dead, the crown/One day was plucked by a crafty hand from a thornbush." Gardner, op. cit., p. 209.

26. Gardner, op. cit., p. 202.

27. "Little Gidding" (1942) in *CP,* p. 214. Whereas "The Dry Salvages" demonstrates Eliot's debt to Indic philosophy, in "Little Gidding" he returned to Dante, Yeats, and Julian of Norwich's *Revelations of Divine Love* (Cressy, 1670), as well as Evelyn Underhill's edition of *The Cloud of Unbeknowing,* from which he also quoted ("With the drawing of this love and the voice of this calling"). Evelyn Underhill reviewed for the *Criterion,* and her death in June 1941, when Eliot was writing "Little Gidding," may have prompted his return to the English mystics, whom she had popularised. Eliot read Underhill's *Mysticism* (1911) when he was at Harvard. Gardner, op. cit., pp. 69–71.

28. EP to TSE, ?1934, Beinecke. In July, Eliot replied that he was "right proud" to have that elephant and thanked Pound from the bottom of his heart.

29. TSE to EP, 3 January 1934, Beinecke.

30. EP to TSE, n.d., ?January 1934, Beinecke.

31. John Malcolm Brinnin, *Sextet: T. S. Eliot & Truman Capote & Others* (London: André Deutsch Ltd., 1982), p. 253.

32. EP to TSE, 3 February ?1935, Beinecke.

33. TSE to JH, 25 June 1934, John Hayward Bequest, King's College, Cambridge.

34. Francis King in conversation with the author, 4 April 2000.

35. Fable XIV, "The Whale, the Elephant, the Coot and the Spider," "Ode to a Roman Coot," "Nobody Knows How I Feel About You" (from Geoffrey Faber to Eliot), *Noctes Binanianae* (1939), no. 10 of 25 copies printed, Houghton.

36. VE Diary, 26 March 1934, Bodleian.

37. Ibid., 28 March 1934.

38. Bridget O'Donovan, "The Love Song of Eliot's Secretary," *Confrontation,* 11, Martin Tucker (ed.), Fall/Winter 1975.

39. VE Diary, 7 February 1935, Bodleian.

40. Ibid., 27 February 1935.
41. Ibid., 8 March 1935.
42. Ibid., 13 March 1935.
43. Ibid., 14 March 1935.
44. Ibid., 16 March 1935.
45. VE Diary, 10 October 1934.
46. Ibid., 11 October 1934.
47. Ibid., 11 December 1934.
48. Bird & Bird obtained a Court Order to enter 68 Clarence Gate Gardens, with which Vivienne refused to comply (Bird & Bird to VE, 30 October 1934). James & James refused to put forward Vivienne's claim for compensation because "had our advice been taken the necessity for breaking into your flat would not have arisen" (James & James to VE, 19 August 1935). Vivienne replied that if she had succumbed to James & James's pressure she would have signed "an offensive and damaging paper" in 1933 (signing away her rights to her property and papers to Eliot), and only Ella de Saxe's advice prevented her (VE to James & James, 20 August 1935, Bodleian).
49. Maurice Haigh-Wood, interview with Michael Hastings, 4 March 1980.
50. James & James to VE, 25 July 1935, Bodleian.
51. VE to Geoffrey Faber, copy, 29 March 1935, Bodleian.
52. VE to TSE, 25 September 1935, Bodleian.
53. VE Diary, 28 September 1935, Bodleian.
54. Moxon Broad to VE, 22 December 1934, Bodleian.
55. VE to T. Hope, District Bank, 8 January 1935, Bodleian.
56. VE Diary, 7 June 1935, Bodleian.
57. Maurice Haigh-Wood, interview with Michael Hastings, 19 March 1980.
58. Ibid.
59. VE Diary, 23 June 1935, Bodleian.
60. VE to Dr. Prevost, 28 June 1935, Bodleian.
61. VE Diary, 27 June 1935, Bodleian.
62. VE to TSE, 12 July 1935, Bodleian.
63. VE Diary, 12 July 1935, Bodleian.
64. Ibid., 15 July 1935.
65. Ibid., 23 July 1935.
66. Ibid., 12 August 1935.
67. Ibid., 29 September 1935.
68. Ibid., 10 September 1935.
69. Ibid., 26 September 1935.
70. VE to Harriet Weaver, 12 June 1936, Bodleian. Vivien wrote that her only free day was Saturday.
71. VE Diary, 15 October 1935, Bodleian.
72. Ibid., 6 December 1935.
73. Ibid., 25 October 1935.
74. Basil Saunders to Lyndall Gordon, 18 August 1993. I am indebted to Lyndall Gordon for making this correspondence available to me, and to Basil Saunders, for further information about Louie and Vivien's friendship.
75. VE Diary, 2 October 1935, Bodleian.
76. Ibid., 26 December 1935.

77. Ibid., 20 September 1935.
78. Ibid., 4 November 1935.
79. Ibid., 13 April 1936.
80. Ibid., 18 November 1935.
81. VE to James & James, 28 November 1935, Bodleian.
82. VE to James & James, 25 November 1935.
83. Gordon, *Eliot's New Life,* op. cit., p. 65.
84. Sybille Bedford, interview with author, 1 August 2000.
85. VE Diary, 30 November 1935, Bodleian.
86. Ibid., 11 October 1934.

23. Into the Dark

1. VE Diary, 11 December 1935, Bodleian.
2. Geoffrey Faber to VE, 13 March 1936, VE Paste-up book, MSS. Eng. Lett c. 383, Bodleian.
3. VE to Geoffrey Faber, 17 March 1936, Bodleian.
4. VE to Moxon Broad, 22 November 1935, Bodleian.
5. Dr. Prevost to VE, 15 November 1935, Bodleian.
6. VE Diary, 1 November 1935, Bodleian.
7. Ibid., 11 November 1935.
8. Will of Vivienne Haigh Eliot, 1 March 1936, Probate Registry, York. If she died in France Dr. Prevost and Prof. Claude were to certify death.
9. VE Diary, 18 March 1935, Bodleian.
10. Ibid., 1 November 1935, Bodleian.
11. Ibid., Easter Sunday 1936, Bodleian.
12. Ibid., 15 October 1935, Bodleian. Vivien had an interview with Broad in his City office in which he voiced his opinion of Eliot.
13. "Burnt Norton," *Four Quartets, CP,* p. 190.
14. TSE to Dorothy Pound, 28 July 1936, Lilly.
15. VE to T. Hope, District Bank Manager, 7 November 1935, Bodleian.
16. VE Notes to Moxon Broad, n.d., Bodleian.
17. VE to Mrs. Flint, 20 July 1936, Bodleian.
18. Henry James, *Daisy Miller* (1878; Penguin, 1986).
19. Ibid., p. 115. Mrs. Costello, Winterbourne's aunt, a member of New York society, declares of Daisy and her mother: "They are very common. They are the sort of Americans that one does one's duty by not—not accepting." Mrs. Costello, in whom Vivien would have seen a parallel to Charlotte Eliot, puts pressure on Winterbourne to drop the "vulgar" Daisy. James refers (p. 79) to Cherbuliez's novel *Paule Méré* (1865), in which the innocent but unconventional heroine has her reputation blackened by malicious gossip, which destroys her relationship with the hero. A character remarks: "What is this weakness which makes us listen to a society which we despise?" (p. 123, note 42). Reference to this novel by James emphasises his message of Daisy's innocence to the reader.
20. VE to Moxon Broad, 10 August 1936, Bodleian.
21. Stephen Spender, *T. S. Eliot* (London: Fontana, 1975), p. 130.
22. *The Family Reunion* (London: Faber & Faber, 1939), p. 113.
23. VE Loose-leaf book 1936, entry 13 April 1936, Bodleian.
24. VE Diary, 12 July 1936, Bodleian.

25. Advertisement for secretary, VE Loose-leaf book 1936, Bodleian.

26. VE to Edgar Horn, Estate Agent, 14 June 1936, Bodleian.

27. VE Diary, 24 December 1935, Bodleian.

28. VE to J. Moxon Broad, 22 November 1935, Bodleian.

29. VE Diary, 22 December 1935, Bodleian.

30. VE to Harriet Weaver, 12 June 1936, Bodleian. T. S. Eliot dedicated his *Selected Essays* in 1932 "To Harriet Shaw Weaver in gratitude, and in recognition of her services to English Letters."

31. VE, "Notes for Moxon Broad," n.d., Loose-leaf book, 1936, Bodleian.

32. VE to St. J. Hutchinson, 8 November 1935, Bodleian.

33. VE to Literary Manager, Faber & Faber, 2 September 1936, Bodleian.

34. Bridget O'Donovan to VE, 4 September 1936, Bodleian.

35. Joan Skelton, Reception Secretary, English-Speaking Union, to VE, 21 February 1936, Bodleian.

36. Earl Marshall to VE, 24 February 1936, Loose-leaf book, Bodleian.

37. VE Diary, 13 December 1935, Bodleian.

38. On 17 July, J. Moxon Broad wrote to Vivien, c/o Miss Daisy Miller, to say that he had insured 8 Edge Street for £1,500 during the repairs she was having done. The rent was £160 p.a., Bodleian.

39. VE to T. Hope, District Bank, 19 July 1936, Bodleian.

40. "Daisy Miller," The Three Arts Club, to Moxon Broad, 5 August 1936, Bodleian.

41. Moxon Broad to "Daisy Miller," 6 August 1936, Bodleian.

42. VE to Ella de Saxe, 30 December 1935, Bodleian.

43. VE to Miss Hutchins, Piano Teacher, Royal Academy of Music, 24 July 1936, Bodleian.

44. Rose Haigh-Wood to VE, 5 April 1936, Bodleian.

45. Rose Haigh-Wood to VE, n.d., Bodleian.

46. VE to Maurice Haigh-Wood, 13 May 1936, Bodleian.

47. Ahmé was born in Charleston, South Carolina, in 1905.

48. Maurice Haigh-Wood, interview with Michael Hastings, 23 March 1980.

49. VE to Literary Manager, Faber & Faber, 5 September 1936, Bodleian.

50. Eliot's Club Brochure, March 1936.

51. VE to Moxon Broad, 15 November 1936, Bodleian.

52. Maurice Haigh-Wood to VE, 20 November 1936, Bodleian.

53. VE to Maurice Haigh-Wood, 22 November 1936, Bodleian.

54. VE to T. Hope, District Bank, 27 October 1935, Bodleian.

55. VE to Dr. Reginald Miller, 11 November 1936, Bodleian.

56. Dr. Miller to VE, 13 November. Miller thanked Vivien for payment of his fee and agreed to call that day, Bodleian.

57. VE to Royal Academy of Music, 27 November 1936, Bodleian.

58. VE to Mary Hutchinson, 11 November 1936, Texas.

59. Maurice Haigh-Wood, interview with Michael Hastings, 12 March 1980.

60. VE Diary, 13 April 1936, Bodleian.

61. Maurice Haigh-Wood to VE, 17 December 1936, Bodleian.

62. VE to Moxon Broad, 11 February 1936, Probate Registry, York.

63. Last Will and Testament of Vivienne Haigh Eliot, 1 March 1936.

64. Maurice Haigh-Wood, interview with Michael Hastings, 23 March 1980. Maurice said that in 1965 he lost £200,000 in Slater Walker, and by 1980 was "down to £250,000."

65. VE to T. Hope, 27 October 1935, Bodleian.

66. Vivienne noted that the total rents for the Irish property at Haigh Terrace, 16 Tivoli Road, and 1–10 Eglinton Park, and Eglinton House for six years, 1927–33, was £1144.15.0d, of which she was entitled to one third. 1 February 1935, VE Diary.

67. Anne Olivier Bell (ed.), *The Diary of Virginia Woolf,* vol. 5, 1936–41 (London: Penguin, 1985), 22 March 1939, p. 210.

68. E. Martin Browne, *The Making of T. S. Eliot's Plays* (Cambridge: CUP, 1969), p. 144.

69. VE to Theresa Eliot, 6 July 1936, Bodleian. Henry and Theresa Eliot were then living at 315 East 68th Street, New York City.

70. Lyndall Gordon, *Eliot's New Life* (Oxford: OUP, 1988), p. 169.

71. VE to G. Faber, 10 December 1936, Bodleian.

72. VE to Moxon Broad, 23 August 1936, Bodleian. The Cable Company replied that all copies of the cables were destroyed a year after sending.

73. Vivienne emphasised to her bank, too, that she was "morbidly careful" about papers, and never burnt or destroyed one without consideration. Her account books and lists of rents on her Irish property demonstrate this.

74. Louis MacNeice, translator's note, programme for *Agamemnon,* music by Benjamin Britten, masks by Robert Medley, choreography and production by Rupert Doone, 1 November 1936, Bodleian.

75. MH to VE, postcard, n.d., 1936, Texas.

76. Blake Morrison, "The Two Mrs. Eliots," *Too True* (London: Granta Books, 1998), pp. 139–40, first published in *Independent on Sunday,* 24 April 1994.

77. VE to St. J. Hutchinson, 29 November 1935, Bodleian. Vivienne wrote to tell Jack that she had seen Tom, and was now living at the Constance Hotel.

78. Enid Faber to Michael Hastings, 26 August 1983, MH Papers.

79. Maurice Haigh-Wood, interview with Michael Hastings, 19 March 1980.

80. "East Coker," *CP,* p. 199.

81. Ibid., pp. 201–2.

82. Blake Morrison, op. cit., p. 141.

83. Basil Saunders to Dr. Lyndall Gordon, 18 August 1993.

84. Lawrence Stone, *Road to Divorce, England 1530–1987* (Oxford: OUP, 1992), pp. 167, 168.

85. Bill Saunders, grandson of Marjorie Saunders *(née* Purdon), e-mail to author, 14 September 1999.

86. Basil Saunders to Lyndall Gordon, 18 August 1993.

87. Blake Morrison, op. cit.

88. John Gielgud, *An Actor's Life* (London: Penguin, 1981), p. 133. Gielgud also recalled the oysters, as well as the formality of the occasion. He thought he had created quite a good impression on Eliot, until a few days later Sibyl Thorndike told him that Eliot was not going to let him have the play, fearing he was going to turn it into "a fashionable Shaftesbury Avenue comedy." Years later, meeting in Marrakesh, Gielgud told Eliot that he had played Harry in *The Family Reunion* on the radio, and made a recording of his "Journey of the Magi." The poet asked Gielgud to send him a copy. Although Gielgud never met Vivienne, he well remembered Derek Patmore and Edith and Osbert Sitwell, and made an unsuccessful attempt to make a film in which he would play Sir George Sitwell. Sir John Gielgud to the author, 22 May 1998.

89. TSE to John Hayward, 19 November 1937, 20 October 1938, John Hayward Bequest, King's College, Cambridge.

90. TSE to Mrs. Webster, 28 October 1938, King's College, Cambridge.

91. TSE to JH, 4 May 1938, King's College, Cambridge.

92. Journal of Lady Ottoline Morrell, 26 March 1934, Goodman Papers.

93. Michael Hastings, Introduction, *Tom and Viv* (London: Penguin, 1984).

94. VE Diary, 24 August 1934, Bodleian.

95. Martha Cooley, *The Archivist* (London: Little, Brown & Company, 1998), p. 3.

96. Having seen *The Family Reunion,* Djuna Barnes wrote *The Antiphon* (1939), her own revenge drama. Phillip Herring, *Djuna: The Life and Work of Djuna Barnes* (London: Viking, 1995), p. 262.

97. In his review (1958) of *The Antiphon,* Eugenio Montale described Barnes as a sponge of prussic acid. Herring, op. cit., p. 259.

98. *The Family Reunion,* op. cit., p. 113.

99. TSE to JH, 6 September 1939, King's College, Cambridge.

100. Richard Ollard, *A Man of Contradictions: A Life of A. L. Rowse* (London: Penguin, 1999) serialised in the *Daily Telegraph,* 22 September 1999, cites a letter dated 12 October 1934 from TSE to Rowse, in which he sets out the marital and financial difficulties he faced, and the idea lapsed.

101. TSE to JH, 8 November 1939, King's College, Cambridge.

102. TSE to JH, 29 November 1939, King's College, Cambridge.

103. Ibid.

104. TSE to JH, 19 November 1937, King's College, Cambridge. Eliot's letter comments on the design of the title page of *Noctes Binanianae.*

105. John Malcolm Brinnin, *Sextet: T. S. Eliot & Truman Capote & Others* (London: André Deutsch, 1982), pp. 252–53.

106. E. W. F. Tomlin, *T. S. Eliot: A Friendship* (London: Routledge, 1988), p. 149.

107. TSE to JH, 13 December 1939, King's College, Cambridge.

108. Robert Robinson, *Skip All That: Memoirs* (London: Century, 1996), p. 22.

109. TSE to JH, 2 June 1940, King's College, Cambridge.

110. Jonathan Fryer, *Eye of the Camera: A Life of Christopher Isherwood* (London: Allison & Busby, 1993), p. 106. In 1935 Auden and Isherwood were writing *The Dog Beneath the Skin,* which was commissioned by Eliot at Faber & Faber, staged by Rupert Doone et al., and watched by Vivienne, who preserved her programme.

111. It was while Eliot was staying at the "Cat Farm," as he called the Mirrlees house, that Robert Sencourt took him over to meet the Duchess of Northumberland, whose guest he was at Albury Park. While Sencourt was pointing out the Turners to Eliot, the Duchess came in, and Sencourt explained to her that he had brought his friend over to give her the opportunity of meeting him. "I detected, however, that she knew nothing of Tom's work and it was therefore with diffidence that I introduced them. Tom noticed this at once and said with his usual good humour, 'Are you getting to be ashamed of me, Robert?' " Robert Sencourt, *T. S. Eliot: A Memoir,* edited by Donald Adamson and L. P. Addison (London: Garnstone Press, 1971), p. 141. Mary also visited Eliot in Shamley Green, bravely walking the five miles from Peaslake as instructed by Eliot.

112. Mary Trevelyan, "The Pope of Russell Square 1938–1958: Twenty Years 'and no-tomorrow,' " unpublished memoir.

113. Ibid., p. 19.

114. Sandra Jobson Darroch, *Ottoline: The Life of Lady Ottoline Morrell* (London, 1976), p. 288.

115. VE Quotation on death, ?mid-1920s. Loose-leaf book, MSS Eng. Misc. c. 624, Bodleian.

116. Trevelyan, op. cit., p. 35.
117. Will of Vivienne Haigh Eliot, 1 March 1936.
118. Vivienne is buried in plot G6–78 and Rose nearby in G6–92 in Pinner Cemetery, Middlesex. Maurice was responsible for the upkeep of the grave according to the Cemetery Superintendent. Ray Bown to the author, 26 April 2000.

Epilogue

1. Lyndall Gordon, *Eliot's New Life* (Oxford: OUP, 1988), p. 147.
2. Mary Trevelyan, "The Pope of Russell Square 1938–1958," unpublished memoir, p. 35.
3. Maurice Haigh-Wood, interview with Michael Hastings, 12 March 1980.
4. E. W. F. Tomlin, *T. S. Eliot: A Friendship* (London: Routledge, 1988), p. 218.
5. Trevelyan, op. cit., p. 37.
6. Gordon, *Eliot's New Life,* op. cit., p. 169.
7. Tomlin, op. cit., p. 219.
8. Ibid., p. 171.
9. Emily gave Eliot's letters to her to Princeton after hearing the devastating news of his second marriage to his secretary in 1957. She retired from her post, and after treatment for a nervous breakdown in Massachusetts General Hospital in Boston, returned to Chipping Campden, where she appeared disturbed. She died in 1968. For a fuller account of the relationship between Eliot and Emily Hale, see Gordon, *Eliot's New Life.*
10. Trevelyan, op. cit., 2 June 1950, p. 72.
11. In Mary Trevelyan's copy of *The Cocktail Party,* Eliot inscribed with characteristic formality: "To Miss Mary Trevelyan, with the author's compliments" and, in addition, "See Appendix and with thanks for her contribution to the character of Julia, eg p. 151." The Appendix consists of "The tune of One Eyed Riley, as scored from the author's dictation by Miss Mary Trevelyan." Page 151 includes lines in which Julia interrupts Riley. Tom, Mary recalled, used to derive great pleasure from interrupting her longer "and more fascinating" stories so that she lost the thread entirely.
12. Trevelyan, op. cit., 2 June 1950, p. 72.
13. One of Eliot's rules was never to see *anyone* two days in succession. She was hurt when he made John and Madame Amory, the French housekeeper, his excuse for vetoing his Sunday night suppers with Mary; the routine was changed from Wednesdays and Sundays to Tuesdays and Thursdays in 1952.
14. Mary Trevelyan to John Hayward, 21 April 1955. King's College, Cambridge.
15. Trevelyan, op. cit., p. 119.
16. Ibid., 26 August 1954, p. 120.
17. Josef Chiari, *T. S. Eliot: a Memoir* (London: Vision Press, 1972), p. 129.
18. T. S. Eliot exploded to Hayward over an article by his former protégé novelist Richard Church, who had published an article in *Books* which Eliot interpreted as an attack upon himself. Eliot threatened to resign as Vice-President of the National Book League, and it took all Geoffrey Faber's diplomatic skill to persuade him to stay on. TSE to JH, 9 May 1950, King's College, Cambridge.
19. E. Martin Browne, *The Making of T. S. Eliot's Plays* (Cambridge: CUP, 1969), p. 342.
20. Ronald Duncan, *How to Make Enemies* (London: Rupert Hart-Davis, 1968), p. 384.
21. Eliot underwrote a loss of £1,500 on Duncan's play *Stratton,* see Peter Ackroyd, *T. S. Eliot*

(London: Penguin, 1993), p. 301. He took enormous trouble with Djuna Barnes' *Nightwood,* cutting it extensively and writing a 1,500 word preface. Faber published it in 1937. Phillip Herring, *Djuna: The Life and Work of Djuna Barnes* (London: Viking, 1995), p. 230.

22. Ackroyd, *Eliot,* op. cit., pp. 304, 305.

23. William Turner Levy and Victor Scherle, *Affectionately, T. S. Eliot: The Story of a Friendship: 1947–1965* (London: Dent & Sons, 1969), p. 88.

24. Tomlin, op. cit., p. 195.

25. Trevelyan, op. cit., p. 95.

26. Ibid., pp. 96, 98.

27. Tomlin, op. cit., p. 184.

28. TSE to JH, 18 February 1938, King's College, Cambridge.

29. Eliot's instructions to his executors, 29 June 1956. Originally Eliot had purchased plot no. 2150 at Brookwood Cemetery, Woking, for his burial.

30. John Malcolm Brinnin, *Sextet: T. S. Eliot & Truman Capote & Others* (London: André Deutsch, 1982), p. 274.

31. Alan Bennett, *Writing Home* (London: Faber & Faber, 1994), p. ix.

32. Timothy Wilson, "T. S. Eliot and I," interview with Valerie Eliot, 20 February 1972, *Observer.*

33. Browne, op. cit., pp. 340–41.

34. Trevelyan, op. cit., p. 167. Although Mary was struck off his Christmas card list, her mother received a Faber card. As for John, apart from two visits to collect his possessions from the flat, Eliot had no contact with him for six months, until John was invited to lunch with Robert Frost and Rosamund Lehmann.

35. T. S. Matthews, *Great Tom: Notes Towards the Definition of T. S. Eliot* (London: Weidenfeld & Nicolson, 1974), p. 160.

36. Postscript to Trevelyan, op. cit., Chelsea, August 1958. The prayer Mary said every night for Tom ran as follows:

> Protector of travellers
> Bless the road.
> Watch over him in the desert.
> Watch over him in the mountain.
> Watch over him in the labyrinth.
> Watch over him by the quicksand.
> Protect him from the Voices
> Protect him from the Visions
> Protect him from the tumult
> Protect him in the silence.

Bibliography

A Note on Sources

The conspiracy of silence which has grown up around the life of Vivienne and T. S. Eliot over the years created difficulties when I began my search and it is clear that some sources for Vivienne's life still remain closed to me. Many letters, perhaps, remain in the possession of Mrs. Valerie Eliot, as we await the publication of further volumes of T. S. Eliot's own correspondence, and significant collections remain under the control of the Eliot estate. John Hayward's letters to Eliot at King's College, Cambridge, may only be read by permission of Mrs. Valerie Eliot. At the Houghton Library, Harvard, Eliot's letters to Emily Hale remain restricted, as does a larger collection at Princeton. As well as collections which are closed to researchers, others may be read but quotation is prohibited, as was the case with Vivienne's own papers in the Bodleian Library, Oxford, when I began my research.

In addition, correspondents tended to throw away their letters from Vivienne—as the mere wife of a great man—while retaining those from her husband. As her reputation became blackened by scandal and the label of insanity, others, such as Bertrand Russell, destroyed them deliberately in an attempt to distance himself from her. Maurice Haigh-Wood delivered Vivienne's papers to the Bodleian Library in 1947, but when he did so much was missing. Vivienne's diaries are incomplete, covering only the years 1914, 1919, and the period of her separation from T. S. Eliot, ending in 1936. Unfortunately, one of the black notebooks in which she wrote drafts of her stories, often edited in T. S. Eliot's hand, went missing from the library in 1990, but three remain, as well as her day-books, which include drafts of fiction and poetry, some published in the *Criterion;* there is also Vivienne's correspondence relating to the period before her committal, as well as postcards, theatre tickets to see Eliot's plays, press cuttings, photographs and her account books. Together they provide a window into the Eliots' life together. The many other sources for Vivienne's life remain buried within the collections of more famous figures.

In the United States, at the Beinecke Rare Book and Manuscript Library at Yale, are Vivienne's letters to Scofield Thayer, an early confidant. The Ezra Pound Papers, also at the Beinecke Library, include Vivienne's surviving letters to Pound, whom she, like Tom, regarded as a mentor and friend. Vivienne's pitiful letters here can be laid side by side with Eliot's to Pound of the same period, revealing how Tom and Ezra delighted in deceiving her. Eliot's letters to Pound's wife, Dorothy, demonstrate that she, too, was a supporter of the poet against Vivienne, and refer to the fact that some of the Pound/Eliot correspondence was censored by Eliot at some point. The library also holds Eliot's letters to W. F. Stead, his confessor.

Within the Pound Papers are the manuscript "Colombo" and "Bolo" poems on pages which Eliot had excised from the notebook of early poems begun in 1910, which he sold to John Quinn in 1922 for £29 24s. 10d. ($140). Before sending Quinn the notebook, Eliot cut out those leaves containing parts of the Bolo series. He seems to have given them, along with scraps of other versions, to Pound, who put the obscene verses in an envelope labelled: "T.S.E. Chançons ithyphallique."

The Harry Ransom Humanities Research Center at the University of Texas at Austin holds a number of significant collections: the Ottoline Morrell Papers and Mary Hutchinson Papers, which contain the intimate letters to her two closest female friends, recording the long process of deterioration of her marriage and health, as well as Eliot's duplicity; the Aldington Papers, which reveal the extent of the Eliots' literary partnership during the *Criterion* period; and the Sitwell Papers which furnished further depth and detail for Vivienne's story.

The monumental Eliot collection at the Houghton Library at Harvard holds the letters from Vivienne to her formidable mother-in-law, Charlotte Champe Eliot, although, to my regret, these were not catalogued and proved difficult to access. There were also the original letters from Jean Verdenal, the French medical student who shared an intimate friendship with Eliot. The Houghton Library has a rich cache of photographs, as well as the writings and poems of Charlotte Eliot, the correspondence between Eliot's elder brother Henry and his mother, which betrays the Eliots' hostility to Vivienne, and drafts of Eliot's drama, including *The Family Reunion,* with Emily Hale's annotations, and *Sweeney Agonistes.* There is also a copy of *Noctes Binanianae,* the bawdy poems by Eliot and Geoffrey Faber, which were privately printed by John Hayward, and of Eliot's drafts of the Clark Lectures.

The Berg Collection in the New York Public Library houses some of Eliot's correspondence to Virginia and Leonard Woolf relating to Vivienne's health. There are also early manuscripts of T. S. Eliot's poems, among them the manuscript of *The Waste Land* which Eliot gave to John Quinn in 1922.

The many letters between Tom and Vivienne Eliot and Lady Ottoline Morrell at the Harry Ransom Center revealed the length and significance of Vivienne's affair with Bertrand Russell, and led me to the Bertrand Russell archive at McMaster University, Hamilton, Ontario. It holds Vivienne's few remaining letters to Bertie, together with the extensive correspondence between Bertie and Ottoline, his "senior" mistress, and Bertie and Colette, the mistress who supplanted Vivienne, as well as the typescript by Phyllis Urch, literary executor of Colette (Lady Constance Malleson), which includes many of Colette's letters to Russell.

In England, meanwhile, access to a number of private collections made it possible to add pieces to the jigsaw: Mary Trevelyan's detailed and objective memoir of her twenty-year friendship with Eliot; Lady Ottoline Morrell's unexpurgated journals, which filled in many gaps in her published two-volume memoirs; the notes which Michael Hastings made of his interviews with Col. Maurice Haigh-Wood just before Maurice's death in 1980.

In public collections in the UK, besides the Bodleian Library, there are the John Hayward Bequest at King's College, Cambridge, which includes correspondence between Hayward and Eliot, and the Schiff Papers in the British Library.

Vivienne Eliot's Writings

Unpublished drafts of the following sketches are in the Bodleian Library, MSS. Eng. misc. d. 936/1–4.

Notebook 1   noted to be missing on 15 June 1990
Notebook 2   "Médecine à la Mode," edited by T. S. Eliot

	"The Lonely Soldier"
	"Parties"
	"Sibylla and Mike"
	"Dream Song"
Notebook 3	"Letter of the Moment"
	"The Ginger Kitten"
	"The Night Club"
	Bertrand Russell sketch for "Parties"
	Sketch: "André and Sibylla Go Shopping"
Notebook 4	4 November 1924. "A Paris Diary" or "A Diary of the Rive Gauche," or "Paris on £5 a Week," edited by T. S. Eliot

MSS Eng. Misc. c. 624. Loose-leaf book, includes drafts of sketches, poems, letters to Vivienne (some in T. S. Eliot's hand also)

"Ellison and Antony"

Poems: "Necesse est Perstare" (alternative titles "Ennui," "Exhaustion," "Fatigue"); "Perque Domos Ditis Vacuas"; Poem about Jack at Fishbourne; "The Coliseum Dome," 17 October 1925

Drafts of "Letters of the Moment, I and II"

"Song in the Night" by "Feiron Morris"

Verses in both Eliot's and Vivienne's handwriting on "Love in Curious Shapes"

"Rosa Buckle" sketch

"The Paralysed Woman" by "Feiron Morris"

"Dancing" in Eliot's hand

"Pseudo-Bridge"

Notes on "Self-Destruction." The book ends with the death certificate of Charles Haigh-Wood, d. 25 March 1927

Vivienne's account books are dated December 1927–April 1932.

Vivienne's work was published in the *Criterion* under different pen names:

"F.M.," "Letters of the Moment I," *Criterion,* vol. 2, no. 6, February 1924

"F.M.," "Letters of the Moment II," *Criterion,* vol. 2, no. 7, April 1924

"F.M.," "Books of the Quarter" reviews, *Criterion,* July 1924

"Felix Morrison," "Mrs. Pilkington," *Criterion,* vol. 3, October 1924

"Feiron Morris," "Thé Dansant," *Criterion,* vol. 3, October 1924

T. S. Eliot, "On the Eve: A Dialogue," *Criterion,* January 1925

   (This dialogue is written in Vivienne's style, although Eliot probably edited it.)

"Fanny Marlow," "Diary of the Rive Gauche," *Criterion,* January 1925

"F.M.," "Books of the Quarter," reviews of Virginia Woolf, G. Stern

"F.M.," Poem: "Necesse est Perstare," *Criterion,* April 1925

"Feiron Morris," "Night Club," *Criterion,* April 1925

"Fanny Marlow," "Diary of the Rive Gauche II," *Criterion,* April 1925

"I. P. Fassett" and "F.M.," "Books of the Quarter," reviews of Rose Macaulay and others, *Criterion,* April 1925

"Fanny Marlow," "Fête Galante," *Criterion,* July 1925

"I. P. Fassett," "Books of the Quarter," *The New Criterion,* vol. 4, January 1926

A Note on The Waste Land

Quotations from *The Waste Land* are taken from the original 1,000-line manuscript which, on his return from Dr. Vittoz's Lausanne clinic, T. S. Eliot gave to Ezra Pound in Paris in early January 1922. Pound, as editor, reduced the size of the text and sacrificed much of the personal element of the poem. Sections and additional poems such as "The Death of the Duchess," "Death by Water," "The Fire Sermon," "The Death of St. Narcissus," "Exequy," "Elegy," and "Dirge" were either dramatically cut or omitted altogether. The title of the poem was changed from "He Do the Police in Different Voices" (a quotation from Dickens's *Our Mutual Friend*) to *The Waste Land.* On 23 October, Eliot sent the manuscripts of *The Waste Land,* consisting of fifty-four leaves, to John Quinn, the New York attorney who acted as his agent. On 28 July 1924 Quinn died, and the manuscripts were subsequently lost; in the 1950s they were rediscovered by his niece, Mrs. Thomas F. Conroy, who, on 4 April 1958, sold them privately to the Berg Collection of the New York Public Library for $18,000. Neither Eliot nor Pound knew of this transaction; in the summer of 1968, three years after Eliot's death, his widow Mrs. Valerie Eliot was informed of the acquisition by Mr. James W. Henderson, Chief of the Research Libraries of the New York Public Library. She subsequently edited and wrote an Introduction for *The Waste Land: A Facsimile and Transcript of the Original Drafts including the Annotations of Ezra Pound* (Harcourt Brace and Co., 1971); the facsimile edition of *The Waste Land* also included the editorial comments and additions made by Vivien Eliot who wrote two, possibly three lines of *The Waste Land,* writing on page fifteen, for example: "Make any of these alterations—or *none* if you prefer. Send me back this copy & let me have it." I am indebted to Valerie Eliot for her scholarship.

Published Sources of T. S. Eliot's Works and Letters

Donald Gallup's bibliography, *T. S. Eliot: A Bibliography* (1969), lists T. S. Eliot's major works. I cite only those which have been most relevant to the writing of this book.

Prufrock and Other Observations (London: Egoist Ltd., 1917)
Poems (London: Hogarth Press, 1919)
Ara Vos Prec (London: The Ovid Press, 1920)
The Sacred Wood (London: Methuen & Co., 1920)
The Waste Land (London: Hogarth Press, 1923)
Homage to John Dryden (London: Hogarth Press, 1924)
Poems, 1909–1925 (London: Faber & Gwyer, 1925)
Journey of the Magi (London: Faber & Gwyer, 1927)
For Lancelot Andrewes (London: Faber & Gwyer, 1928)
Ash Wednesday, with the dedication "To My Wife" (London: Faber & Faber, 1930)
The Use of Poetry and the Use of Criticism: The Charles Eliot Norton Lectures for 1932–33
      (Cambridge, Mass.: Harvard University Press, 1961)
Selected Essays 1917–1932 (London: Faber & Faber, 1932)
The Varieties of Metaphysical Poetry: The Clark Lectures at Trinity College, Cambridge, 1926 and

The Turnbull Lectures at The Johns Hopkins University 1933, edited by Ronald Schuchard (New York: Harcourt Brace Jovanovich, 1993)

Sweeney Agonistes (London: Faber & Faber, 1932)

After Strange Gods (London: Faber & Faber, 1934)

The Rock (London: Faber & Faber, 1934)

Murder in the Cathedral (London: Faber & Faber, 1935)

Old Possum's Book of Practical Cats (London: Faber & Faber, 1939)

The Family Reunion (London: Faber & Faber, 1939)

Four Quartets (London: Faber & Faber, 1944)

The Cocktail Party (London: Faber & Faber, 1949)

Poems Written in Early Youth (London: Faber & Faber, 1950)

The Confidential Clerk (London: Faber & Faber, 1954)

On Poetry and Poets (London: Faber & Faber, 1957)

The Elder Statesman (London: Faber & Faber, 1959)

To Criticize the Critic (London: Faber & Faber, 1965)

Valerie Eliot (ed.), T. S. Eliot, *The Waste Land: A Facsimile and Transcript of the Original Drafts including the Annotations of Ezra Pound* (New York: Harcourt Brace Javanovich, 1971)

Collected Poems 1909–1962 (London: Faber & Faber, 1974)

Valerie Eliot (ed.), *The Letters of T. S. Eliot, Volume I, 1898–1922* (New York: Harcourt Brace Jovanovich, 1988)

Christopher Ricks (ed.), *Inventions of the March Hare, T. S. Eliot: Poems 1909–1917* (New York: Harcourt Brace Jovanovich, 1996)

Select Bibliography

This does not pretend to be an exhaustive bibliography, but merely lists some of the books, collections, essays and articles I found most helpful.

Ackroyd, Peter, *Ezra Pound* (London: Thames and Hudson, 1980)

Ackroyd, Peter, *T. S. Eliot* (London: Penguin, 1993)

Aiken, Conrad, *Selected Letters of Conrad Aiken,* Joseph Killorin (ed.) (New Haven, Conn., 1978)

Aiken, Conrad, *Ushant* (London: W. H. Allen, 1963)

Aldington, Richard, *Stepping Heavenward, A Record* (London, 1931)

Aldington, Richard, *Richard Aldington: An Autobiography in Letters,* Norman Gates (ed.) (Philadelphia, Penn.: University of Pennsylvania Press, 1992)

Aldington, Richard, *Life for Life's Sake* (New York: Viking Press, 1941)

Behr, Caroline, *T. S. Eliot: A Chronology of His Life and Works* (London: Macmillan, 1983)

Bell, Clive, *Old Friends: Personal Recollections* (London: Chatto & Windus, 1956)

Bell, Quentin, *Bloomsbury* (London: Weidenfeld & Nicolson, 1968)

Bell, Vanessa, *Selected Letters,* Regina Marler (ed.) (New York: Pantheon Books, 1993)

Bergonzi, Bernard, *T. S. Eliot* (London: Macmillan, 1972)

Bradshaw, David, "Those Extraordinary Parakeets," *The Charleston Magazine,* Part I, Autumn/Winter 1997, 16; Part II, Spring/Summer 1998, 17

Brinnin, John Malcolm, *Sextet: T. S. Eliot & Truman Capote & Others* (London: André Deutsch, 1987)

Browne, E. Martin, *The Making of T. S. Eliot's Plays* (Cambridge: Cambridge University Press, 1969)

Buckle, Richard, *Diaghilev* (London: Weidenfeld & Nicolson, 1993)

Carpenter, Humphrey, *A Serious Character: The Life of Ezra Pound* (London: Faber & Faber, 1988)

Chiari, Joseph, *T. S. Eliot: A Memoir* (London, 1982)

Clare, Anthony, *Psychiatry in Dissent: Controversial Issues in Thought and Practice* (London: Routledge, 1980)

Clark, Ronald W., *The Life of Bertrand Russell* (London: Jonathan Cape and Weidenfeld & Nicolson, 1975)

Cooley, Martha, *The Archivist* (London: Little, Brown, 1998)

Darroch, Sandra, *Ottoline: The Life of Lady Ottoline Morrell* (London, 1976)

Delany, Paul, "T. S. Eliot's Personal Finances 1915–29," chapter in *Literature, Money and the Market from Trollope to Amis* (Basingstoke: Palgrave, 2001)

Doyle, Charles, *Richard Aldington, A Biography* (London: Macmillan, 1989)

Duncan, Ronald, *How to Make Enemies* (London: Rupert Hart-Davis, 1968)

Gallup, Donald, "The Lost Manuscripts of T. S. Eliot," *Times Literary Supplement,* 7 November 1968

Garafola, Lynn, *Diaghilev's Ballets Russes* (New York: Da Capo Press, 1998)

Gardner, Helen, *The Art of T. S. Eliot* (London, 1949)

Gardner, Helen, *The Composition of the Four Quartets* (London: Faber & Faber, 1978)

Garnett, Angelica, *Deceived with Kindness: A Bloomsbury Childhood* (Oxford: Oxford University Press, 1984)

Glendinning, Victoria, *Edith Sitwell: A Unicorn Among Lions* (London: Phoenix, 1993)

Gordon, Lyndall, *Eliot's Early Years* (Oxford: Oxford University Press, 1977)

Gordon, Lyndall, *Eliot's New Life* (Oxford: Oxford University Press, 1988)

Gordon, Lyndall, *Virginia Woolf: A Writer's Life* (Oxford: Oxford University Press, 1991)

Gordon, Lyndall, *T. S. Eliot: An Imperfect Life* (London: Vintage, 1998)

Grover, Smith, Jr., *T. S. Eliot's Poetry and Plays* (Chicago: University of Chicago Press, 1956)

Hastings, Michael, *Tom and Viv,* with introduction by Michael Hastings (London: Penguin, 1984)

Hoare, Philip, *Oscar Wilde's Last Stand, Decadence, Conspiracy, and the Most Outrageous Trial of the Century* (New York: Arcade Publishing Inc., 1998)

Hoeveler, Diana Long, *Romantic Androgyny: The Women Within* (Philadelphia, Penn.: University of Pennsylvania Press, 1990)

Holroyd, Michael, *Lytton Strachey: A Critical Biography* (London: Vintage, 1995)

Howarth, Herbert, *Notes on Some Figures Behind T. S. Eliot* (London: Chatto & Windus, 1965)

James, Henry, *Daisy Miller* (London: Penguin, 1984)

Joost, Nicholas, *Scofield Thayer and* The Dial: *An Illustrated History* (Southern Illinois University Press, 1964)

Julius, Anthony, *T. S. Eliot, Anti-Semitism, and Literary Form* (Cambridge: Cambridge University Press, 1995)

Kenner, Hugh, *The Invisible Poet: T. S. Eliot* (London: W. H. Allen, 1960)

Lee, Hermione, *Virginia Woolf* (London: Vintage, 1997)

Lehmann, John, *Thrown to the Woolfs, Leonard and Virginia Woolf and the Hogarth Press* (New York: Holt, Rinehart & Winston, 1979)

Levy, William Turner and V. A. Scherle, *Affectionately, T. S. Eliot* (London, 1969)

Lewis, Wyndham, *Blasting and Bombardiering* (London: Calder & Boyars, 1967)

Lewis, Wyndham, *The Apes of God* (London, 1931)

Lewis, Wyndham, *The Letters of Wyndham Lewis,* W. K. Rose (ed.) (London, 1963)

Litz, A. Walton (ed.), *Eliot in His Time: Essays on the Occasion of the Fiftieth Anniversary of The Waste Land* (Princeton: Princeton University Press, 1973)

Malleson, Constance, *After Ten Years* (London: Jonathan Cape, 1929)

Mansfield, Katherine, *Bliss and Other Stories* (London: Constable, 1920)

March, Richard and Tambimuttu (eds.), *T. S. Eliot: A Symposium* (London: P.L. Editions, 1948)

Massine, Léonide, *My Life in Ballet* (London: Macmillan, 1968)

Matthews, T. S., *Great Tom: Notes Towards the Definition of T. S. Eliot* (London: Weidenfeld & Nicolson, 1974)

Mayer, John T., *T. S. Eliot's Silent Voices* (Oxford: Oxford University Press, 1989)

Miller, James E. Jr., *T. S. Eliot's Personal Waste Land* (Philadelphia, Penn.: University of Pennsylvania Press, 1977)

Mirrlees, Hope, BBC 1 television programme, "The Mysterious Mr. Eliot," 3 January 1971

Mitchell, Juliet, *Mad Men and Medusas: Reclaiming Hysteria and the Effects of Sibling Relations on the Human Condition* (London: Allen Lane, The Penguin Press, 2000)

Monk, Ray, *Bertrand Russell: The Spirit of Solitude* (London: Vintage, 1997)

Moody, A. David, *Thomas Stearns Eliot, Poet* (Cambridge: Cambridge University Press, 1979)

Moody, A. David (ed.), *The Cambridge Companion to T. S. Eliot* (Cambridge: Cambridge University Press, 1994)

Moody, A. David (ed.), *"The Waste Land" in Different Voices* (London: Edward Arnold, 1974)

Morrell, Ottoline, *Ottoline at Garsington: Memoirs of Lady Ottoline Morrell 1915–1918,* Robert Gathorne-Hardy (ed.) (London: Faber & Faber, 1974)

Morrison, Blake, "The Two Mrs. Eliots," *Independent on Sunday,* 24 April 1994

Nicolson, Harold, *Diaries and Letters 1930–39,* Nigel Nicolson (ed.) (New York and London: Harcourt Brace Jovanovich, 1977)

Norman, Charles, *Ezra Pound* (London: Macmillan, 1960)

Olney, James (ed.), *T. S. Eliot: Essays from the* Southern Review (Oxford: Clarendon Press, 1988)

Patmore, Brigit, *My Friends When Young: the Memoirs of Brigit Patmore,* Derek Patmore (ed.) (London: William Heinemann, 1968)

Pearson, John, *Façades: Edith, Osbert and Sacheverell Sitwell* (London, 1978)

Peter, John, "A New Interpretation of *The Waste Land*" (1952) with postscript (1969), *Essays in Criticism,* vol. 19, 1969

Pound, Ezra, *Collected Early Poems,* Michael John King (ed.) (London: Faber & Faber, 1977)

Pound, Ezra, *The Letters of Ezra Pound 1907–1941,* D. D. Paige (ed.) (New York: Harcourt Brace Jovanovich, 1950)

Ratliff, Margaret, "A Bloomsbury Friendship: The Correspondence of Mary Hutchinson and Lytton Strachey," Ph.D. thesis, Harry Ransom Humanities Research Center, University of Texas at Austin, Texas, 1989

Russell, Bertrand, *Satan in the Suburbs and Other Stories* (London: The Bodley Head, 1953)

Sartre, Jean-Paul, *Being and Nothingness* (1943, Routledge translation, 1969)

Sartre, Jean-Paul, *Nausea* (1938, Penguin translation, 1965)

Sax, Joseph L., *Playing Darts with a Rembrandt: Public and Private Rights in Cultural Treasures* (Ann Arbor: University of Michigan Press, 1999)

Schuchard, Ronald, *Eliot's Dark Angel: Intersections of Life and Art* (Oxford: Oxford University Press, 1999)

Segal, Hanna, *Klein* (Karnac Books, 1989)

Sencourt, Robert, *T. S. Eliot: A Memoir,* Donald Adamson and L. P. Addison (eds.) (London: Garnstone Press, 1971)

Seymour, Miranda, *Ottoline Morrell: Life on the Grand Scale* (London: Hodder & Stoughton, 1992)

Shone, Richard, *Bloomsbury Portraits* (Oxford: Phaidon Press, 1976)

Sitwell, Osbert, *Left Hand, Right Hand: An Autobiography,* vol. 4, *Laughter in the Next Room* (London, 1949)

Spalding, Frances, *Vanessa Bell* (London: Weidenfeld & Nicolson, 1983)

Spender, Stephen, *World Within World* (London: Hamish Hamilton, 1951)

Spender, Stephen, *T. S. Eliot* (London: Fontana, 1975)

Symons, Arthur, *The Symbolist Movement in Literature* (London: Heinemann, 1899)

Szasz, Thomas S., *The Myth of Mental Illness: Foundations of a Theory of Personal Conduct* (New York: Harper and Row, 1974)

Tate, Allen (ed.), *T. S. Eliot: The Man and His Work* (London: Chatto & Windus, 1967)

Tomlin, E. W. F., *T. S. Eliot: A Friendship* (London, 1987)

Trombley, Stephen, *"All That Summer She Was Mad," Virginia Woolf and Her Doctors* (London: Junction Press, 1981)

Turnell, Martin, *Baudelaire: A Study of His Poetry* (New York, 1972)

Watson, George, "Quest for a Frenchman," *The Swanee Review,* vol. 84, 1976

Wilson, Edmund, *The Wound and the Bow: Seven Studies in Literature,* with an introduction by Janet Groth (Ohio University Press, 1997)

Wilson, Timothy, "T. S. Eliot and I," *Observer,* 20 February 1972

Woolf, Leonard, *Letters of Leonard Woolf,* Frederic Spotts (ed.) (New York: Harcourt Brace Jovanovich, 1989)

Woolf, Leonard, *Beginning Again: An Autobiography of the Years 1911–1918* (London: Hogarth Press, 1964)

Woolf, Leonard, *Downhill All the Way: An Autobiography of the Years 1919–1939* (London: Hogarth Press, 1967)

Woolf, Virginia, *The Diary of Virginia Woolf,* Anne Olivier Bell (ed.), vols. 1–5 (London: Penguin, 1979, 1981, 1982, 1983, 1985)

Woolf, Virginia, *The Letters of Virginia Woolf,* Nigel Nicolson and Joanne Trautmann (eds.), vols. 2, 3, 5 (New York: Harcourt Brace Jovanovich, 1976, 1977, 1980); vol. 4 (London: Hogarth Press, 1994)

Ziegler, Philip, *Osbert Sitwell* (London: Chatto & Windus, 1998)

Index

T. S. Eliot and Vivienne Eliot referred to as TSE and VHE throughout index.

THE UNABRIDGED JOURNALS OF SYLVIA PLATH

edited by Karen V. Kukil

Sylvia Plath's journals were originally published in 1982 in a heavily abridged version authorized by Plath's husband, Ted Hughes. This new edition offers these haunting, vibrant diaries in their complete and uncensored form. Sixty percent of the book is material that has never before been made public, more fully revealing the intensity of the poet's struggles, and providing fresh insight into both her frequent desperation and the bravery with which she faced down her demons. *The Unabridged Journals of Sylvia Plath* is essential reading for all who have been moved and fascinated by Plath's life and work.

Autobiography/0-385-72025-4

ANNE MORROW LINDBERGH

by Susan Hertog

Anne Morrow was a shy teenager yearning for adventure when she wrote, "I want to marry a hero." At 23, she married the dashing aviator Charles Lindbergh and was instantly swept up in the tides of history. She went on to become a pioneering aviator in her own right and an acclaimed author of many books, included the bestselling *Gift from the Sea.* Drawing on five years of exclusive interviews with Anne Morrow Lindbergh as well as countless documents, Susan Hertog gives us the woman whose triumphs, struggles and elegant perseverance riveted the public for much of the twentieth century.

Biography/0-385-72007-6

THE SCARLET PROFESSOR

by Barry Werth

During his tenure at Smith College, Newton Arvin published studies of Hawthorne, Whitman, Melville, and Longfellow that stand today as models of scholarship and psychological acuity. A social radical and closeted homosexual, Arvin cultivated friendships with the likes of Lillian Hellman and Truman Capote. But in September 1960, his apartment was raided, and his cache of beefcake erotica was confiscated, provoking his panicked betrayal of several friends. *The Scarlet Professor* deftly captures the essence of a conflicted man and offers a provocative and unsettling look at American moral fanaticism.

Biography/Gay Studies/0-385-49469-6

EUDORA

by Ann Waldron

Eudora Welty was a beloved institution of Southern fiction and American literature, whose closely guarded privacy has prevented a full-scale study of her life and work—until now. A significant contribution to the world of letters, *Eudora* chronicles the history and achievements of one of our greatest authors, from a Mississippi childhood to the sale of her first short story, from her literary friendships with Katherine Anne Porter and Elizabeth Bowen to her rivalry with Carson McCullers. Elegant and authoritative, this is the first biography to chart the life of this national treasure.

Biography/0-385-47648-5

A LIKELY STORY

by Rosemary Mahoney

In 1978, Rosemary Mahoney, an aspiring young writer of seventeen, wrote her personal idol Lillian Hellman inquiring whether she might need domestic help for the summer. When Hellman responded affirmatively, Mahoney imagined an idyll of mentoring and friendship. But in reality Mahoney's summer unfolded into a grueling exercise in humiliation at the hands of the acerbic Hellman and her retinue of celebrated acquaintances. By turns heartbreaking and uproariously funny, *A Likely Story* portrays the coming-of-age of a brilliant and troubled young woman—a universal tale of illusions shattered and an object lesson in the often misdirected search for heroes.

Memoir/0-385-47931-X

ANCHOR BOOKS
Available at your local bookstore, or call toll-free to order:
1-800-793-2665 (credit cards only).